The School in the

American Social Order

The

Second Edition

School in the

American Social Order

Newton Edwards • Herman G. Richey

THE UNIVERSITY OF CHICAGO

Houghton Mifflin Company • Boston

Contents

v

Teachers · The New England College in the Eighteenth
Century · Ventures in Adjusting Education to Social Needs
— the Rise of Private Schools

PART TWO

The School and the Emergence of
the Democratic National State, 1776–1860

PART THREE

The School in Modern Society — The Past Century

Preface

THE PURPOSE OF THIS BOOK is to give those who read it an understanding of the development of American education as an integral part of our evolving civilization and to help equip them for intelligent decision-making in the area of education and, to some extent at least, in the broader area of public policy.

The central concept that has governed the selection and organization of materials is that education derives its purpose, form, and content from the particular social environment in which it develops. Of this environment, an important dimension is the past. Education can never be fully understood unless it is viewed historically, and the history of education, to be fully understood, must be viewed as a part of the total history of a people. Since education, however much it may be influenced by custom and tradition, is a product of the civilization of which it is a part, consideration must be given to such matters as the worth and dignity accorded the individual, religious ideals, the sources of political power, the class structure, the nature and operation of the economy, and the thought pattern of the age because all are woven, at any given time and place, into the purpose and form of the educational enterprise. It is not too much to say that, in the long run, these and other social forces that impinge upon the school determine the main tenets of its philosophy, the amount and kind of educational opportunities afforded the various social classes, the content and organization of the curriculum, the preparation and status of teachers, the source of financial support, the agencies of administration, and the structural form of the educational system.

The purpose of educational institutions is to prepare the learner to participate intelligently and helpfully in the social order of which he is a part. But society is rarely static for any long period of time. New social classes emerge and seek to shape events in their own interest; the prevailing ideology is modified or supplanted by one essentially new; political power passes from one dominant element in society to another; the role of government is modified; the whole pattern of economic life may be greatly changed by technological progress; and the whole society may be transformed from one that is essentially religious or ecclesiastical to one that is essentially lay or secular. When changes such as these occur in the social order, the old educational institutions may function

xi

so inadequately that they prepare youth to take their place in a society that no longer exists. There is always a tendency for educational policy and practice to lag behind contemporary social change. Thus, youth who will never become entirely literate in the vernacular may be required to study Latin. The authors have noted throughout the book that when such a lag becomes too great, educational reformers and statesmen have been able to make their voices heard and have made serious and often successful attempts to fit education more closely to contemporary needs. At times, this has involved fundamental changes in the goals of education, modifications of curriculums and methods, and other important adjustments. It is the view of the authors, however, that the dynamics of educational change is to be found, not primarily in the work or influence of educational philosophers and reformers but in the social forces operating in the society.

The authors have attempted to organize their presentation in accordance with their view concerning the close relation between educational history and broad social history. In each social order studied, attention is directed first to the essential features of the social order itself, to the dominant ideology, to the social structure, to the range of economic interests, to the sources of political power and the form of political institutions, to the prevailing political, economic, and social arrangements. This broad general treatment of the social order is followed by detailed study of the educational policies and practices under examination. Part One deals with the transplanting of European ideals and institutions to America, the effect of the frontier environment on these inherited ideals and institutions, and the establishment of educational arrangements to meet the changing needs of Colonial life. In Part Two, an analysis is made of the social forces that were responsible for the emergence of the democratic national state and the educational adjustments required to meet the needs of a democratic social order. Part Three deals with the sociological and technological revolutions that have, during the past century, transformed the United States into a vast industrial civilization. It also analyzes and interprets at considerable length the educational adjustments and adaptations that have been made as America moved from an essentially rural to a complex industrial social order. The book closes with a discussion of the problems that must be solved if we are to preserve our priceless heritage and move forward toward an enduring all-inclusive democracy.

Much more space is devoted to the treatment of recent than of earlier periods. The emphasis on the recent and the contemporary is deliberate. It is based upon the belief that teachers and others working in the field of education need to cultivate a comprehensive and realistic view of the society into which they are helping to induct youth. Also, it seemed desirable to enlarge the discussion of social forces as the treatment moved from the long past, in which there is much agreement among scholars, to the recent period, which is not so clearly understood and on which there is less agreement.

The first chapters of the book, those dealing with the period before 1860, have undergone some revision. Research since the publication of the first edition has made necessary some rewriting but it has not necessitated an extensive reinterpretation of the history of education of the period. The part of the book dealing with the period since 1860 has undergone extensive revision. Although a considerable volume of new material has been added, the number of chapters dealing with the changing conditions of American life during the past century have been reduced. The chapter on the educational problems of a changing population has been omitted, but more attention has been given to these problems in other chapters, particularly in the chapter on the expansion of the educational enterprise. The chapter was omitted, not because the authors have come to consider these problems less important but because what they once considered to be a great need is presently being met by numerous studies of scholars and publications of educational organizations and agencies.

Experience has shown that the use of the materials presented in this book can lead to the development of understandings which the authors believe all teachers, supervisors, administrators, and other educational personnel should possess. The treatment of the materials reflects the authors' conviction, also based on long experience, that students who have selected education as a career and who have been admitted to teacher-education or other professional programs have the intellectual capacity and motivation needed to acquire those understandings. It is hoped that the second edition will prove no less helpful than the first as a text for courses in the history of education and for the introductory courses of teacher-education programs such as "Social Foundations of Education," "American Public Education," and "Introduction to Education" and as a companion text in such courses as the history and philosophy of education, the economics of education, educational sociology, and in other courses designed to relate education to significant forces in modern American life.

The authors are indebted to the many persons whose acceptance of the first edition made the second one appear worthwhile.

NEWTON EDWARDS
HERMAN G. RICHEY

The School in the
American Social Order

PART ONE

The School in Colonial Society:
Preview

The American colonies should be viewed, not as isolated settlements fringing the shores of a great continent, but as integral parts of an expanding European civilization. They were, in fact, Europe's western frontier, and they were bound in a thousand ways by the traditions and customs of the Old World, by its ideology and by its religious, social, economic, and political institutions. The history of colonial life, therefore, is in no small degree the history of the transplanting of European culture to American soil. But that is by no means the whole story. First, all aspects of the culture were not equally represented in the transplanting, which was, for several reasons and to some extent, a selective process. The colonists did not represent a cross section of the population of the lands from which they came, and their attitudes, beliefs, values, and aspirations influenced both the selection of the cultural elements that they sought to reproduce in the New World and those that they were content to leave behind them. For example, those Englishmen who came to New England in order to establish what they considered a more perfect society than they had known before sought to transplant a number of ideals, values, and practices that were acceptable to relatively few Englishmen; and they were as interested in sealing the society of which they were the architects against some of the elements of the dominant English culture as they were in perpetuating others. Furthermore, the colonists did not hesitate, as they struggled to subdue a raw continent, to modify inherited ideas, values, and institutions to meet their needs. Two phases, then, of colonial history bulk large: (1) the persistence of European culture, and (2) the selection and development of patterns of institutional arrangements to meet the peculiar aspirations of the colonists and the needs imposed by the circumstances of life in the New World.

In Part One, education in the American colonies is viewed in its relation to its European origins and as the product of many forces. Chapter 1 is devoted to a treatment of those aspects and elements of the European inheritance that had the most profound effect upon education in the colonies. Chapter 2 deals with the experiment to establish Puritan commonwealths in New England and with the role that education played in Puritan social policy. Chapter 3 traces the transfer of power — political, economic, and social — from the Puritan theocracy to the merchant-capitalists and the rising yeomanry and mechanics, and appraises the changes in educational policy and practice which that transfer brought about. Chapter 4 traces the transfer of English ideas and institutions to the South, the rise of a planter aristocracy, and the arrangements that aristocracy worked out for the education of youth. Chapter 5 shows how education in the Middle Colonies was affected by the mingling of many diverse population elements from Europe and by the retarded development of a common culture.

Old Institutions in a New Setting:
The European Background of Education
in Colonial America

The colonies established along the Atlantic seaboard during the early decades of the seventeenth century were essentially a new frontier of the expanding European civilization. The mere crossing of the Atlantic did not transform Europeans into Americans. The ideals, values, sentiments, superstitions, and prejudices which they had held in the Old World were transported to the New. The Englishmen who dominated the early colonial ventures remained essentially English in temper and outlook. Their attitudes toward religion, government, the economy, the arrangement of social classes, and the education of youth were the attitudes entertained by one group or another of the Englishmen who made up seventeenth-century England. And the early colonists did what colonists generally do in similar circumstances; they established social institutions that resembled, as closely as their peculiar needs permitted, the ones with which they had been familiar in the homeland. It is not strange that most of the institutional arrangements of the early colonists reflected, in the main, the values and sentiments that lay at the base of the English way of life. Englishmen, however, were not the only ones who participated in the colonization enterprise; in the building of colonial America people were drawn from many lands. In greater or lesser numbers, the Dutch came to New Netherlands, Swedes to settlements along the Delaware, Scotch-Irish and Germans to Pennsylvania, Swiss to North Carolina, and French-Huguenots to South Carolina. All of these groups contributed elements of the Old World culture to the swelling stream of American life.

Among the early colonists, both the outlook on life and the institutional

arrangements were transplanted from the Old World. But as each succeeding generation pushed deeper into the wilderness and pitted its
strength against that of a raw continent, Europe receded in distance and
thought, centuries-old traditions lost their binding force, and a new society
began to emerge, with purposes and social institutions more distinctly its
own.

The new social order that took form in the settlements extending from
Maine to Georgia came to be characterized by a striking diversity of cultural patterns and institutional arrangements. Life in a New England
town differed sharply from life on a southern plantation. By the end of
the seventeenth century, as one moved southward from New England from
colony to colony and from region to region, one could have discerned fundamental differences in political organization, in economic structure, in
the arrangement of the social classes, in religious ideals and practices, and
in the provisions made for the education of youth.

These differences were caused, in part, by all the factors in the local
environment that made for variation, such as climate, fertility of soil, and
the configuration of the country. In the process whereby men subdued
the environment to their needs, men themselves underwent a marked
change. In fact, it is difficult to determine which had the greater influence
on the other, men on the environment or the environment on men. Be
that as it may, it is certain that as men adjusted to a variety of environ-
ments, they came to reflect differences in outlook and to establish different
patterns of social organization. These regional differences were also attributable, in part, to Old World inheritances. From the beginning, the
ideology of the New England Puritans was different from that of the
Englishmen who settled in the Middle Colonies and the South. Diverse
elements in the population of England and the Continent were drawn to
the different American colonies in disproportionate numbers, and each
element transplanted to American soil some portion of its Old World inheritance.[1] Puritans in New England, Dutch and English in New York,
Quakers and Germans in Pennsylvania, Catholics in Maryland, and Anglicans in the South exhibited a variety of attitudes toward the problems of
social organization. Landed gentry and merchant, yeomen and tenants,
wage earner and indentured servant — all were drawn to migrate to
America, and all contributed to the diversity of the colonial social order.

Clearly, then, colonial society was a product of many factors, the result
of varied and converging streams of influence. Viewed in a broad perspective, it appears to have been European in its essential elements; but only
a few decades had passed from the time of the original settlements before
American life began to take on a color and spirit distinctly different from
that of the Old World. Although it retained the hallmarks of its origin,

---

[1] Thomas A. Bailey, *The American Pageant: A History of the Republic,* Second
Edition (Boston: D. C. Heath & Company, 1961), pp. 13–43.

it exhibited a progressive tendency to become more distinctly American, and manifested striking variations that were to produce social orders as different as those of New England and the planter South.

Church and State in Relation to Education

One of the most significant Old World influences on colonial education was the view that men entertained with respect to the relative responsibility of state and church for the maintenance of a system of education. The Puritans in New England and the Dutch Calvinists in New Netherland regarded the state as the proper instrument for the establishment of schools, and to some extent they made practical use of civil government for that purpose. To be sure, the state was acting principally in the interest of the church, but, nevertheless, education was regarded as a proper function of government. This attitude toward the state's responsibility to promote education set the pattern of education in colonial New England. Englishmen other than Puritans who came to America held tenaciously to the view that education was no business of the state. The Protestant Reformation in England had in no way seriously disturbed the church's relation to education.

Anglicans everywhere, in the Old World and the New, were firmly convinced that education was the responsibility of the church, of the home, and of charity and philanthropy. And the other colonists outside New England generally entertained the same conviction. This attitude that education was the proper responsibility of the church, of the home, and of philanthropy kept the state inactive in education in most of the colonies during the whole colonial period. It was an attitude that was exceedingly difficult to change. As we shall see later, it persisted well into the national period and was modified only by the rise of the democratic state as a form of political organization during the early decades of the nineteenth century.

The Long Shadow of the Renaissance

The Renaissance, with its emphasis on ancient languages and literature, cast a long shadow over education in both western Europe and America. The early Renaissance movement before its infiltration by religious forces represented a repudiation of medievalism in all its forms — its subordination of the individual to the universal order of things, its otherworldliness, its emphasis on the primacy of faith over reason, its system of education. For these values the Renaissance substituted freedom of individual action and expression, reason and scientific method, emphasis on life in this world, and the ideal of a liberal education as entertained by the ancient Greeks. To realize the ideal of a liberal education, it was necessary to find a new content of learning and to develop a new type of school. The new content of learning was found in the newly recovered literature of classical antiquity. A knowledge of Greek and Latin would enable one to appropriate the thought and culture of two great civilizations. If one was interested in poetry, drama, history, science, philosophy, medicine, or agriculture, he could find in the writings of the Greeks and the Romans the best thought that man had yet achieved. Moreover, since Latin was the language of respectable written discourse — in law, diplomacy, and scholarship — men of affairs in all areas of life were obliged to write and speak it. It is little wonder then that Latin and Greek came to dominate the content of learning. And the Protestant Reformation, although it produced a narrowing of the concept of a liberal education of the early Renaissance, gave new value to a knowledge of the ancient languages. Latin, Greek, and Hebrew (the last made important by the Reformation) were the languages of the Old and New Testaments and of the early Church Fathers. To hold one's own in the religious controversies of the day, one needed to be able to go to the Scriptures, early Church History, and the writings of the Fathers and to study them in the original or, at least, in the languages in which they had been written or preserved.

The Renaissance developed new schools which became the carriers of the humanistic tradition. In Italy the new type of school was known as the court school and later in France as the *lycée,* in German lands as the *Gymnasium,* and in England as the Latin grammar school. The Latin grammar school, brought to America during the early years of colonization, dominated secondary education during the entire colonial period.

Among the ideas transplanted to America, few were more firmly fixed than the belief that study of the classics, and of Latin in particular, should constitute the chief activity carried on in the secondary schools, as well as a major part of the work of the colleges. The content of the curriculum above the vernacular elementary school was pretty well dominated by the classical tradition throughout the whole colonial period, and, indeed, with somewhat less force, for many years thereafter. As we shall see later, at least nine-tenths of the time spent in the Latin grammar school was devoted to the study of Latin, and in colonial colleges much attention was devoted to the study of ancient languages. A knowledge of Latin and, to a lesser extent, of Greek was the badge of an educated man. The scholar alone could turn to the highly regarded authorities of classical antiquity and buttress his argument by an apt quotation from Cicero, Horace, or another ancient. Latin served all the recognized fields of learning. New subjects — mathematics, science, history, economics, agriculture, and even modern languages — found their way into the curriculum slowly, so complete was its domination by the classical heritage of earlier days.

Clearly, the influence of the Renaissance established a classical tradition in American education which was to endure for many generations, and of which certain manifestations are still to be observed.

Religious Domination of the Intellectual Life

The Renaissance did much to move western Europe in the direction of a lay, secular civilization. Currents of thought and feeling had swept away from the deeply religious outlook on life so characteristic of the Middle Ages toward the secular view of life and the world held by the ancient Greeks. But the Protestant Reformation checked and even reversed this secular trend. It aroused men's deepest emotions, touched off religious controversies and strife, and established religion once again as the dominant intellectual interest of the age. Education was called back to the service of the church, and for centuries to come one of the chief ends of education — if not *the* chief end — was to serve the interests of institutionalized religion. As we shall see, America was not to escape the dominance of religion over the intellectual life. Nor was education to escape the influence of the religious tradition. Its major goals were religious, the content of the curriculum was predominantly religious, and the control over education was largely in the hands of the church.

The Influence of the Protestant Reformation on the Colonization of America

By the time the peoples of Europe began to establish colonies in America, the Protestant Reformation had been in progress for nearly a century. Large elements of the population of northern and western Europe had rallied around the banner of one or another of the Protestant reformers. It was from these Protestant groups that all the colonies except Maryland drew the great majority of their early inhabitants. Educational policy and practice in these colonies were profoundly influenced by Protestant ideas with respect to religion, government, social organization, and education.

Colonial America was peopled by representatives of practically every Protestant sect of any numerical or historical importance. From Germany, Lutherans and German Reformed (Calvinists) were drawn in large numbers. Out of Germany came also adherents of the more radical religious sects — Anabaptists, Mennonites, Dunkers, Amish, New Born, Moravians, and many others. French Huguenots, fleeing persecution of the most violent kind, took refuge in South Carolina, and, to some extent, in the cities of other colonies; members of the Dutch Reformed Church settled in New Amsterdam; Swedish Lutherans established a colony on the Delaware River; and Scotch-Irish Presbyterians in large numbers settled in the back-country South. The early colonization of America, however, was an enterprise carried forward in the main by English Protestants — by Anglicans, Separatists, Puritans, and Quakers.

The English Reformation and the Clash of Religious and Class Interests

The Reformation in England, unlike in most other countries, was directed largely by the crown. Beginning with Henry VIII (1509–47), each succeeding ruler down to Queen Elizabeth (1558–1603) gave the Reformation a different direction. The settlement finally arrived at failed to satisfy large elements of the English people and deep religious conflict developed. This conflict, by no means confined to religious differences, developed into a struggle to modify and control the national state itself, and it came to represent a fundamental clash of class interests. It is to the nature and outcome of this conflict that some of the American colonies owe their origin.

When Henry VIII failed to obtain papal sanction of his divorce from Catherine of Aragon he broke with the Roman Church. In 1534, by the Act of Supremacy, he announced himself as the head of the new church in England. Henry's main purpose, no doubt, was to nationalize the church, to erase "Pope" and write "King." Although he did nationalize the church, he remained Catholic in spirit and permitted little change in ritual or doctrine. By confiscating the property of the monasteries and dividing their lands among his favorites, he was able to create a new landed aristocracy, loyal both to him and to the nationalized church. From the beginning, the new church in England had a semifeudal basis, retained a symbolism in its ritual that appealed to the aristocracy, and permitted relatively little popular participation in its government.

Under Henry's son, Edward VI, England officially became more radically Protestant, only to become more definitely Catholic again under Edward's half sister, Queen Mary. When Elizabeth ascended the throne in 1558, she was confronted with grave problems in both state and church. Being the daughter of Henry VIII and Anne Boleyn, whose marriage had never been sanctioned by the Roman Church, she was regarded as illegitimate by the Papacy and her right to govern was challenged, but in England neither Council nor Parliament was ever willing to deprive her of her statutory place in the order of succession. Although at the close of Mary's reign England had reverted to being Catholic in form and in the main Catholic in sentiment, Elizabeth's succession was welcomed, in spite of the opposition of some bishops, by widespread rejoicing. Elizabeth, like her father, was little disposed to brook the opposition of bishops or any other supporters of the Roman cause, and she met the situation with the Act of Supremacy of 1559 and the Act of Uniformity (also 1559). Interested little in theological disputes and subtleties, and concerned chiefly with laying the foundation of a great commercial empire, Elizabeth was ready to turn to the Protestants for support, although at heart she was probably more Catholic than Protestant.

The religious settlement at which Elizabeth arrived was characterized by two important elements: (1) supremacy of the state over the church, and (2) a compromise in religious doctrine, church organization, and ritual. By asserting the right of the crown to rule the consciences of men, Elizabeth paved the way for religious dissent and persecution which was to drive thousands to America, where they hoped they could worship God as they pleased. Three main dissenting religious groups now appeared on the scene: Anglicans, Puritans, and Separatists.

The Church of England which Elizabeth had set on its course was buttressed by the landed nobility and by men of means and high social position. Its membership embraced the hereditary rulers of England. Anglicans generally accepted the principle of absolutism in church and state and they were disposed to regard both bishop and king as God's anointed, responsible only to him.

The Puritans, the second most powerful religious party to emerge, were unwilling to accept the principle of absolutism in either church or state. They were composed, in the main, of a new middle class in the towns and the smaller landed gentry. At first they directed their attack on the ceremonials of the church and, as many intensely religious groups before them, upon the laxness of morals, for which they held the established religion largely responsible. In the area of church ritual they took offense at such practices as the wearing of surplices by the clergy, kneeling at Communion, the sign of the cross at baptism, and use of organ music. All of these were reminders of Catholicism, evidence that the Established Church was far removed from the simplicity of Christianity in apostolic days. It was not long before the Puritans leveled their attack on the government of the church as well.[2] For the absolutism of bishop and king they would substitute the presbyterian system of government, an arrangement which placed ecclesiastical power largely in the hands of the minister and elders of the local congregations within a district. Representatives of the presbyteries of a larger area made up the synod, and above the synods stood the assembly. Clearly, the presbyterian system of church government was a challenge to the authority of church and state, and one can well understand what James I had in mind when he said, "No bishop, no king."

But the deeper meaning of Puritanism is not to be found in its attack

[2] W. E. Lunt, *History of England,* Fourth Edition (New York: Harper & Brothers, 1956), pp. 384–425.

on the ceremonials of the church, in its strict moral code, or in its system of church governance. Puritanism represented a middle-class revolt, a revolt of the burgesses and the smaller landed gentry against king and landed aristocracy. The battle for religious freedom could not be separated from the battle for political and economic freedom. The trade interests of the London burgesses and of others who joined them in the Puritan cause required a freedom from political and economic restraint quite as impelling as the urge for freedom of conscience. Puritanism was an expression of individualism in intellect, in religion, in government, and in economics. It contributed to the emergence of a capitalistic class and it promoted the development of parliamentary government. Those of our own day can well understand the association of capitalism and constitutionalism, the desire of men of means to be free of restraint, whether in the area of government or of economics.

Major movements against the established order are almost sure to be accompanied by lesser movements of a more radical type, and such was the case with respect to Puritanism. About 1580, Robert Browne gathered around himself a small band of artisans and laborers who rejected outright the authority of the state over the church. Since they would separate entirely from the Church of England and permit each congregation to govern itself without state interference, they came to be known as Separatists or Independents. Here was a doctrine which, followed to its logical conclusion, led straight to religious freedom and to government by consent — to democracy in both church and state.

The three major contending groups in the religious controversies of early-seventeenth-century England played leading roles in the colonization of America, and each exercised a profound influence on the colony or colonies that it established or dominated. Anglicans, always loyal to the aristocratic tradition in government, religion, education, and society generally, dominated the early colonization of the South and became an important element in other colonies, notably New York, Maryland, and Pennsylvania. Wherever the Anglican went, he was likely to be a strong defender of upper-class English ideals and institutions, and he held tenaciously to the belief that education was a private or religious function and no proper concern of the state. The Separatists, feared because of their dangerous beliefs, clearly not in accord with monarchical principles, and despised because of their lowly origin, were for the most part effectively silenced in England. A number of them fled to Holland in 1607 and 1608 in order to escape James's requirements of conformity and to worship as they chose. Finding life in Holland economically hard and fearing that their children would lose their English identity, they decided to go to America. Aided by the Virginia Company, in 1620 they set sail to establish a new colony in Virginia. After a long and difficult crossing, they landed at Plymouth, well north of the Virginia grant, and thus became the founders of the first permanent colony in New England. In the new setting, the Separatists were unable to carry their ideals to a logical conclusion, but their influence on the development of American institutions was out of all proportion to the small numbers engaged in the enterprise of establishing the Plymouth Colony.[3]

The Puritans, a far more powerful group and one which stood in closer relation to the main currents of English political and economic life, and the vast majority of whom were to remain in England to engage in the struggle between Parliament and the crown, dominated most of New England and made their influence felt in other colonies, particularly in those north of Virginia. No other group in colonial times was so active or influential in the development of educational institutions at all levels. The bourgeois character of Puritanism was a factor, too, in the development of New England into an important trading and business community in which many forces could more easily converge in support of education at all levels.

THE INHERITANCE OF THE RELIGIOUS TRADITION IN EDUCATION

At the opening of the seventeenth century, religion was still a dominant intellectual interest in England and on the Continent. We moderns may find it difficult to understand why men were so deeply concerned with one another's religion, why they were not willing to let others go their respective ways, worshiping how and when they pleased. But it must be remembered that institutionalized religion was the focal point of many aspects of life, that the religious garb cloaked many interests — political, economic, and social. Religion was a powerful instrument of social control and direction, an instrument scarcely less important than the state itself. It was a means of controlling thought, attitudes, and loyalties, of getting and keeping political power, of fixing or breaking up the scheme of economic arrangements, and of defining the relation of social classes.

The tradition that the school was a handmaiden of the church, that education at all levels should serve the ends of institutionalized religion, had been long established when the first colonies were planted in America. Everywhere in Europe, in Catholic and Protestant countries alike, the

[3] For an account, by Plymouth's second and many-times governor, of the English persecutions of the Separatists, their exile in Holland, and the first twenty years of the Colony, see William Bradford, *History of Plymouth Plantation,* Prepared for the Massachusetts Historical Society (Boston: Little, Brown & Co., 1856), or a new edition in modern English, Samuel Eliot Morison (ed.), *Of Plymouth Plantation, 1620–47* (New York: Alfred A. Knopf, Inc., 1952). For background on the Puritan migration, see Robert C. Winthrop (ed.), *Life and Letters of John Winthrop* (2 vols.; Boston: Ticknor and Fields, 1864, 1867); James Kendall Hosmer (ed.), *Winthrop's Journal, "History of New England"* (2 vols.; New York: Charles Scribner's Sons, 1908).

chief purpose of the vernacular elementary school was to inculcate in youth an acceptance of the religious beliefs of the particular sectarian group responsible for the school's existence. Everywhere, too, the various religious groups into which the peoples of Europe were divided regarded the secondary school as an agency for the training of leaders in the church. Religious ends were not the only objectives of secondary education, but they were the most important. And in the universities theology still held the center of the stage.

Nowhere was the religious tradition in education more deeply rooted than in England. An examination of the statutes of the founders of the Latin grammar schools makes it perfectly clear that the central purpose in the establishment of these schools was the desire to further the cause of religion. The same conclusion is inescapable when the curriculum of these schools is analyzed or when a study is made of the manner of their administration. In the early seventeenth century, none of the Latin grammar schools, whether supported by the church or not, was free of ecclesiastical control. Schools owed their very existence to the authority of the church, their teachers were licensed by it, and at all times they were subject to ecclesiastical visitation and inspection. And at Oxford and Cambridge the religious purpose in education was quite as obvious as in the Latin schools. To be a fellow in any of the colleges at Cambridge one had to be in holy orders. It is true that young men from the upper classes who did not intend to enter the ministry were beginning to frequent the universities in large numbers, but most who took degrees were looking forward to some kind of service in the church.

The religious tradition in education was transplanted to America in its full vigor and its roots struck deep in American soil. For more than a century, indeed during most of the colonial period, religion furnished education its dynamic motive. The content of the curriculum at all levels was profoundly affected by the religious ends education was made to serve, and the administrative control of education was directly or indirectly influenced by ecclesiastical authority.

Few Old World influences contributed more to the colonial migration and to the make-up of the settlers who found their way to the different colonies than the conflicts that had their bases in the religious beliefs that came to be held by different groups of post-Reformation Europeans; and few forces in American life have been so important in shaping educational policy and practice as the religious thought and tradition that had their origin in the Protestant Reformation.

The Class Structure of Society

The class structure of society which the colonies inherited from Europe was one of the most important Old World influences in American educational thought and practice during the colonial period. Educational policy differed considerably, to be sure, from colony to colony; but everywhere — in New England, the Middle Colonies, and the South — it reflected that arrangement of social classes which, long maintained in England and on the Continent of Europe, was now transplanted to American soil. The motives which prompted men and women to seek their fortunes in the New World were many and varied. Each hoped, of course, to better his own condition in life, to secure for himself a more satisfactory status, but few individuals, if any, came with the conscious intent of establishing a democratic social order.

THE ENGLISH BACKGROUND OF THE COLONIAL SOCIAL STRUCTURE

The class-based social structure which the colonists brought with them across the Atlantic had its roots deep in English, indeed in European, history. In England, as elsewhere, the relation of the social classes to one another was conditioned largely by the economic structure of society. For at least a century and a half before 1600, English economic life had been undergoing a momentous revolution, the essential feature of which was the transition from a feudal to a bourgeois economy.

In medieval England, as in other parts of Europe, power — economic, political, and social — was vested in a relatively small element of the population. The hands that operated the power controls were the hands of king, feudal lord, and priest, particularly those of the latter two. While the crown, the nobility, and the Church were engaged in a long and bitter struggle for place and power, the rest of the population had to remain content as tillers of the soil or as artisans or merchants in the few straggling towns that had come into being. The most powerful element in the population was the class of feudal lords, men whose vast manorial estates, worked by serfs, spread over the countryside of England. Scarcely less important were the members of the clergy. They were guardians of the life of the spirit, monarchs of the world of thought, dispensers of learning and wisdom, and as officials of the Universal Church possessors of no mean part of this world's goods.

As the Middle Ages wore on, however, a new social class developed, destined to challenge the supremacy of king, feudal lord, and priest. Slowly, towns developed and in them manufacturers, merchants, and bankers accumulated fortunes and rose to positions of place and power. New hands now began to reach for the power controls in society. Members of the rising bourgeoisie were dissatisfied with the existing order of things, an order which restricted their freedom of action and thought and denied them the recognition they were entitled to receive. At first lowly and despised, this class bided its time, entrenched itself behind its money bags, found an ally in the smaller landed gentry, and finally forced its representatives in greater number into the House of Commons.

The rise of towns and of a burgher class was accompanied by new social classifications in the open country. Trade and commerce brought money into circulation, and a money economy gradually undermined the feudal order. Serfs were able, by selling surplus produce to the townspeople, to accumulate small savings. With money in their pockets, they were in a position first to commute their services to the lord of the manor into money payments, and then to become tenants, or even acquire small holdings of their own. Before the rising power of the burgher middle class, the old feudal aristocracy began to go down, and, with the passing of feudalism, the smaller landed gentry and the yeomen — the owners of small farms — rose to positions of greater importance.

Feudal lords were not the only ones to whom the rising bourgeoisie threw down the gage of battle. In England, as in other parts of Europe, the sixteenth century saw the middle class rise in revolt against the power of the Church in a movement known as the Protestant Reformation. The concern of Protestantism with theological tenets should not be allowed to obscure the fact that the great revolt was in no small measure an uprising of the bourgeoisie against the power of the Church, against tithes and taxes, and against restraints, in one form or another, on the freedom of individual thought and action. Nor was the English monarchy to go unchallenged by this new middle class. The spirit of business enterprise was wholly incompatible with an arbitrary and capricious government; men who risked their fortunes in business ventures insisted not only on knowing but on determining the rules of the game. Restraint on government — constitutional law — was a natural accompaniment of the emergence of a business class. It is not surprising, therefore, that in the second third of the seventeenth century the bourgeoisie and their allies, the landed gentry, were able to challenge successfully the arbitrary government of the Stuart monarchy and send Charles I to the scaffold. And somewhat later, it will be recalled, after the Cromwellian period and a short-lived reaction, they forced James II to yield to the rising power of Parliament and to seek safety in flight from his kingdom. The Glorious Revolution of 1688–89 marked the triumph of the bid for power of these new elements in the English social structure. Henceforth the crown was to be subordinate to Parliament, and in Parliament the representatives of the burgher class were to play a leading role.

In the process of passing from a feudal to a bourgeois economy, the old scheme of social classification had been greatly disturbed; a new pattern of social grouping had emerged. It was this new class structure of society that was to have an important influence on American institutions.

The structure of English society at the opening of the seventeenth century. The landed aristocracy, on the eve of the colonization of America, constituted the most important element in English society. Members of this class owed their position very largely to the crown, especially to Henry VIII, who had conferred upon his favorites vast tracts of land confiscated from the Church. The landed aristocracy, moreover, had not overlooked the opportunities afforded by the enclosure movement to strengthen its position. From whatever source this element of the population had accumulated its titles or its lands, it was the most powerful politically, enjoyed the greatest social esteem, and perhaps possessed the greatest wealth. It was represented in the House of Lords and generally gave loyal support to the Anglican Church and to the crown.

The second class in the descending social scale was composed of the landed gentry, country gentlemen or squires, whose names were not adorned with titles but whose acres were many and whose influence was great. The social position of the landed gentry, however, was being challenged by the rising capitalistic class, by merchants, manufacturers, and traders, some of whom were now able to purchase estates and to live in a manner beyond the means of many of the country gentry themselves. The influence of the ideals and manner of life of the English country gentry on Virginia and Carolina planters of a later date would be hard to overestimate.

At the opening of the seventeenth century, the merchant-capitalists constituted one of the most vigorous and important elements of the population. No longer content to export raw wool, they were now flooding the markets of the world with woolen cloth. Nor was that all. England was in the midst of a commercial revolution that seemed to have no bounds. Great trading companies were being formed to exploit the markets of such distant lands as Russia, the Levant, Morocco, and India. Men who risked their capital in trade often realized handsome profits, sometimes as much as 200 or 300 per cent. And if profits were not to be had in lawful trade, freebooters like Drake and Hawkins might overhaul a Spanish galleon returning from Mexico or Peru and bring home a prize of gold or silver equal to a king's ransom. The merchant-capitalist was making his bid for riches and position, and the future was his.[4]

In the open country, next in importance to the landed aristocracy and the country gentlemen and squires were the yeomen, men whose thrift had enabled them to purchase small farms of their own. Below the yeomen in importance were the great masses of farm tenants, artisans, journeymen, day laborers, and servants, most of whom were struggling to eke out a bare subsistence.

Lowest in the social scale was the very large class of dependent poor, "sturdy beggars and paupers," criminals, vagabonds, and thieves, with which the countryside was infested. The most important factor in creating this numerous dependent class was the disruption of the agricultural econ-

---

[4] Louis M. Hacker, *The Triumph of American Capitalism* (New York: Simon and Schuster, Inc., 1940), pp. 65–67.

omy of England. As the markets for English wool expanded, vast acreage of farm lands was turned into pasture, and thousands of agricultural workers — whole families, and even whole villages — were set adrift without work or needed skills and, in a period of increasingly hard times, with little prospect of finding employment of any kind.[5] Everywhere the case of the helpless poor was a staggering burden; in some areas at least one-third of the population were on relief rolls.

The colonists who migrated to America during the opening decades of the seventeenth century were perfectly familiar with the class distinctions that had long characterized English society. Most of them were drawn from the middle and lower classes and, in general, they were disposed to accept without important modifications the social class structure to which they were accustomed. The establishment of a democratic society was not their purpose in coming to America; they hoped, rather, to secure for themselves a more favorable position within the framework of the old established order. In some instances, in fact, as in Maryland under the Calverts, in New York under the Dutch Patroons, and in the Carolinas under the Lords Proprietors, conditions were established which were a throwback to feudalism. As events turned out, in America as in England, a superior social class emerged, composed mainly of ministers, magistrates, merchants, and planters. As in England, too, men of position, influence, and wealth were able to dominate the state, make it an instrument of power, and shape public and social policy to serve their own ends. There was little equalitarianism in early America; it required time and the force of circumstance on a new continent to transform an essentially aristocratic society into one based on democratic principles.

A Two-Class Educational System

A no less important Old World influence on American education was the transplanted two-class educational system, which reflected unmistakably the prevailing system of social classes in seventeenth-century England.

THE UNIVERSITY IN THE ENGLISH SOCIAL ORDER

At the apex of the system were the ancient universities of Oxford and Cambridge, devoted as they long had been primarily to theology and auxiliary studies. Since the clergy was drawn in relatively small numbers from the higher social classes, these institutions were originally less exclusive than they were to become later. Already, however, the Renaissance ideal of a gentleman's education had made its influence widely felt in

[5] Bailey, *op. cit.,* p. 11. See also Hacker, *op. cit.,* pp. 60–61.

England, and, although none but a cleric was supposed to attend the colleges of Oxford and Cambridge, the sons of the wealthy were now flocking to them in increasing numbers.[6] From about the middle of the sixteenth century, protests were made against this influx of the sons of the upper classes into the universities. Theology still dominated the intellectual life of Oxford and, especially, of Cambridge, but the "poor scholar" who was preparing for a place in the service of religion was now rubbing elbows with the sons of gentlemen — young men whose chief interest lay in polite literature and in activities in no wise connected with the church. We owe the much-used phrase "a gentleman and a scholar" to this comingling of the "poor scholar and the squire's son" which had its inception in the sixteenth century.[7]

When viewed with respect to the social classes from which they drew their students, the English universities of the early seventeenth century cannot be regarded as highly aristocratic. But this is not the only test; one has to consider also the functional aspects of the universities. Their purpose was to prepare a relatively small element in the population for service in the church, or for those activities in which the members of the upper classes engaged during their mature years. Neither those Englishmen who remained in England nor those who migrated to America thought of colleges and universities as popular institutions. The function of their higher educational institutions was to prepare a select group of youth for places of leadership in society. Although the universities drew their students in large numbers from the middle class, they served fundamentally the needs of an intellectual elite. Even in America, despite the democratization of higher education, the modern college with its "liberal-arts" curriculum still, in some cases, bears the hallmarks of its aristocratic origin.

The Latin Grammar School and the Education of a Directive Class

The education of an intellectual elite in Elizabethan England was by no means confined to Oxford and Cambridge. A network of Latin grammar schools spread over the country, providing some opportunity, at least, for bright youth from all social classes to get a humanistic education. The contemporaries of Shakespeare exhibited a remarkable zeal for learning. Noblemen, gentry, merchants, yeomen — individuals of means from every social class — religious and guild organizations, and other agencies participated in the founding of grammar schools. By the close of the sixteenth century, there were open to English youth no fewer than 361 such

---

[6] Lunt, *op. cit.*, p. 296.
[7] Samuel Eliot Morison, *The Founding of Harvard College* (Cambridge, Mass.: Harvard University Press, 1935), pp. 54–57.

schools, one for about every 12,500 of the population.[8] It has been estimated that about 12,000 boys were attending the grammar schools of England at the opening of the seventeenth century, at which time, it has been stated, "every boy, even in the remotest part of the country, could find a place of education in his own neighborhood competent at any rate to fit him to enter college."[9] Although this claim must be an exaggerated one, it remains that approximately one in every 375 of the population was attending a grammar school,[10] and it is clear that the Latin grammar schools were widely established and, as compared with later ages, remarkably well attended before the English colonization of America began.

These schools were designed to provide for poor boys as well as for those in the middle and upper classes. Most of the founders took special pains to make it clear that the schools they were establishing should be open to the children of the poor. It is clear, too, that the grammar schools did not draw their pupils exclusively from the aristocratic class. But it is also certain that relatively few of the really poor attended these schools. To be sure, an occasional "poor scholar," a bright boy from the lower classes, was selected and trained for service in church or state — made into a cleric or a lawyer — but, by and large, and probably with a decreasing number of exceptions, the grammar schools were attended by boys from the middle and upper classes. An analysis by Watson of the occupations of parents who in 1643 sent their sons to the Colchester Grammar School, probably typical of most grammar schools, reveals that a large proportion of the pupils were sons of gentlemen, clergymen, and tradespeople. Among the last group were tanners, grocers, tailors, linen drapers, a goldsmith, a dyer, an ironmonger, and a chemist.[11]

The Latin grammar schools were not highly selective or aristocratic institutions in the sense that they closed their doors to boys of the lower classes. Like the universities, however, they served the needs of a society that was still essentially undemocratic. The grammar schools prepared a select few to take their places in the ranks of the directive classes. It was here that the future ministers, lawyers, merchants, country gentlemen, scholars, and diplomats — men of affairs in one area of life or another — received their preparation for university study.

[8] J. Howard Brown, *Elizabethan Schooldays: An Account of the English Grammar School in the Second Half of the Sixteenth Century* (Oxford: Basil Blackwell, 1933), p. 7.

[9] J. and J. A. Venn, Alumni Cantabrigienses I, xv, as quoted in Samuel Eliot Morison, *The Puritan Pronaos: Studies in the Intellectual Life of New England in the Seventeenth Century* (New York: New York University Press, 1936). Published also in paperback under the title *Intellectual Life of New England* (Ithaca, N.Y.: Cornell University Press, 1956).

[10] Brown, *op. cit.*, pp. 7–8.

[11] Foster Watson, *The English Grammar Schools to 1660: Their Curriculum and Practice* (Cambridge: University Press, 1908), p. 531.

THE EDUCATION OF THE LOWER CLASSES

For the great mass of English children there was little or no opportunity to attend schools of any kind. After the Reformation, the control of education for the masses remained in the hands of the new church, as it had remained in the hands of the Universal Church for centuries before. Anglicans everywhere, whether they stayed in England or migrated to America, held tenaciously to the view that education, not a function of the state, was to be provided for in the home or in private, religious, and philanthropic institutions. In practical operation, this policy resulted in great neglect of the education of the masses of children. Most parents were not financially able to educate their children and the endowed schools were nearly all Latin schools. It is true that vernacular elementary schools were not unknown. In fact, some parishes maintained schools of this kind and supported them in part out of public funds. But, even so, few English children were provided even the rudiments of an education. And where vernacular elementary schools were provided, they were regarded as essentially for the lower classes, as instruments for inculcating proper religious and social attitudes. The gulf which separated the Latin grammar schools and the universities from the vernacular schools for the masses was wide and could be spanned only by the exceptionally bright and ambitious boy.

As has already been pointed out, economic conditions in England were such as to produce a numerous pauper class. Parliament was constantly confronted with the problem of providing the means to keep the poor from starving and of making provision for the support and care of numerous pauper children. During the latter half of the sixteenth century, England formulated its policy for dealing with the poor in a succession of statutes which culminated in the famous Poor Law of 1601. Two principles established in this act were to be influential at a later date in America. The first of these was embodied in the requirement that all property-owners in a parish should be taxed for the care of the poor in that parish. The New England colonists had long been familiar with the crushing burden of poor relief, and it is not strange that they should have sought to escape this burden by passing laws, as in Massachusetts in 1642, which required that all boys and girls be trained for useful employment. Even more important, perhaps, was the provision of the same Poor Law of 1601 that dependent children should be apprenticed and that masters should teach their apprentices a trade. This practice was transplanted to America and expanded upon. As will be pointed out in greater detail later, apprenticeship in the colonies was commonly employed as a means of providing not only vocational but also religious and academic training for poor children. In some colonies, all children who were not being taught a trade and the elements of reading were to be apprenticed in order that these ends might be accomplished.

The Inherited Class System of Education

From England, then, and to some extent from the continent of Europe, the colonists inherited a class system of social arrangements and an educational system which reflected those arrangements. In the colonies, as in the Old World, secondary and higher education — Latin grammar schools and colleges — served primarily the needs of a small directive class. Schools concerned with the teaching of reading and writing in English — where they existed at all — were primarily terminal schools for the masses. They were designed to teach the children of the common people to read, to grasp the principles of some religious sect, and to conform to the existing principles of social organization.

A democratic school system in America was neither an inheritance nor, as often supposed, a gift of Puritan New England. It has been an achievement, perhaps the most significant cultural achievement, of the American people. It springs from, and is part of, the democratic way of life. Through the centuries it has taken its form and expanded its purposes to meet the needs of an evolving democracy.

Educational Institutions and Practices

American educational institutions, like many others, were cast in Old World molds. The types of schools established in the colonies — dame school, writing school, and Latin grammar school — were all built on Old World models. Likewise, Harvard College was as near an imitation of Emmanuel College, Cambridge University, as conditions in a pioneer society would permit. Textbooks were English importations and the methods employed in teaching differed little, if any, from those of the old country. Apprenticeship, an institution for the care and trade training of the poor in England, was developed in America still further and made an instrument for providing both academic and vocational education for poor and neglected children and, in some colonies, for all children whose education was not being provided for otherwise. It had long been a practice in England for philanthropic men of means to leave legacies for the endowment of schools, and in America this practice was continued. Land was plentiful and often public lands were set aside for the endowment of schools. It is not unreasonable to suppose that this early habit of giving land for the use of schools found expression at a later date in the federal grants of land for the support of education. It is possible, too, that educational philanthropy in this country, which has resulted in a more liberal support of education by individuals than in any other nation in the world, is but a continuation of an ideal and attitude long established in England before Jamestown was settled.

The Rise of Capitalism and Parliamentary Government

The forces that influenced American life and culture that have been discussed were, in the main, deeply rooted in the long-established customs and traditions of England; they represented, to a considerable degree, the heritage from the Middle Ages transformed and modified by the Renaissance and the Reformation. The class structure of society, the two-class educational system, the religious tradition in education, and the reliance placed upon the writings of classical antiquity as the source of humanistic values were conservative forces which contributed to the maintenance of the established order of things in both society and education. In some respects, both the Renaissance and the Reformation were reactionary movements. At the close of the Middle Ages, when the thought of Europe had been so long dominated by theology, the Revival of Learning had much to contribute by making available the art, philosophy, literature, and science of the ancients. But humanism looked to the past and not to the future and humanists were too often disposed to be hostile to, if not contemptuous of, the dynamic forces of their own day. The Reformation was also, although to a lesser extent, a throwback to the past, in that it tended to make religion once more the dominant intellectual interest of men. But as the seventeenth century opened, forces were gathering momentum in Europe which were to create a new economy and a new culture. Two of these new forces were the rise of capitalism and the establishment of parliamentary government.

From the beginning, the American colonies were an integral part of the great commercial and colonial empire established by the daring and foresight of English merchants and statesmen. It would be a mistake to regard the colonies as isolated outposts, uninfluenced by the changing intellectual interests of the age. And the fact cannot be overlooked that the British Empire was being wrought out by a capitalistic middle class, and that the motivation of empire-building is to be found, in large measure at least, in the desire for material gain. It is true that patriotism and religion were also impelling motives in the building of the Empire, but the profit motive was stronger than either. Nor were Americans content that Englishmen should reap all the profits of their colonial enterprise. From the outset, American civilization was profoundly influenced by economic interests and motives. Whatever their purposes may have been in coming to America, the colonists soon turned their attention to the exciting task of accumulating worldly goods. In the process of building up landed estates or of accumulating fortunes in the markets of the world, men lost much of their religious zeal and their enthusiasm for the literature of classical antiquity. And slowly but surely American education began to be emancipated from the dominance of religion and classicism; in purpose and content it began to reflect the demands of a new society built upon a broad foundation of business enterprise.

In a very real sense, the development of constitutional law and of the republican form of government is the product of the rise of a capitalistic society. As may profitably be pointed out, regularity in government is but a counterpart of accounting in business. And the struggle for parliamentary government in seventeenth-century England on the part of successful businessmen and the country gentry was not lost on the American colonists. From Maine to Georgia, merchant, planter, and yeoman, though their interests might at times conflict, were no less concerned with bending government to their will than were the men who forced James II to abandon his throne. Free political institutions in America, in part an English inheritance and in part the product of forces operating in American life, came in time to be the most powerful factor in shaping educational policy and practice.

Science and Rationalism

In the long history of Western culture, one of the most important and exciting movements was the development of science during the period extending from the middle of the sixteenth to the middle of the eighteenth century. In 1543, Copernicus published his great work on astronomy, *On the Revolutions of the Heavenly Orbs.* In the same year appeared Vesalius' *On the Structure of the Human Body,* and two years later Cardan published his treatise on algebra under the title *The Great Art.* As Preserved Smith observes, these are "three of the most momentous works of science that the world has ever seen," and they initiated a brilliant era of scientific discovery.[12] In astronomy, the pioneer work of Copernicus was carried forward by Kepler and Galileo to the triumphs of Newton and Laplace. Perhaps no scientific discoveries have so changed man's concept of the universe in which he lives or his relation to it as these discoveries in astronomy.

One cannot in brief space even catalogue the important scientific discoveries which now followed one another in rapid succession. Discoveries in physics were scarcely less significant than those in astronomy. William Gilbert (1540–1603) did pioneer work in magnetism. Kepler made some advance in the study of optics, to be followed by Snell and Descartes, who, working independently, discovered the fundamental law of refraction. Galileo's contributions to a knowledge of mechanics and dynamics were perhaps more important than anything he did in the field of astronomy. To quote Preserved Smith again, Galileo "found this branch of

[12] Preserved Smith, *A History of Modern Culture,* I: *The Great Renewal, 1543–1687* (New York: Henry Holt & Co., 1930), p. 18.

natural philosophy little but a mass of ignorance and error; he left it a well-built and comely science."[13] And, in less than a half-century after Galileo's death in 1642, Newton was to discover the law of gravitation.

The sixteenth and seventeenth centuries also saw remarkable advances in the science of mathematics. In his great work on algebra (1545), already referred to, Cardan made a fundamental contribution to an understanding of the theory of equations. The Dutch mathematician Stevin invented decimals as a method of notation in 1585. Soon after the opening of the next century, Napier came forward with the invention of logarithms, and his work was expanded upon and refined by other mathematicians, notably Gunter, Kepler, and Briggs. Notable work was done on the theory of numbers by Descartes, Pascal, and Fermat; in trigonometry by Pitiscus, Napier, Vieta, and others; and in analytical geometry by Descartes and Fermat. And, building on the work of earlier mathematicians, Newton (1642–1727) and Leibniz (1646–1716) were able independently to invent the infinitesimal calculus.[14]

While scholars were exploring the mysteries of astronomy, physics, and mathematics, adventurous souls were setting sail for new lands. Soon they were to sail the seven seas and open the vistas of new continents and strange lands. From almost every point of the compass new knowledge was accumulating about the earth, its size, its shape, its continents, and its seas, and about the manners, customs, and institutions of its peoples. This new knowledge stirred the imagination and forced a reconstruction of old beliefs, attitudes, and values. The work of the explorers paved the way for a more scientific geography; it also made possible notable advances in zoology and botany.

During the Middle Ages, for a knowledge of anatomy and medicine men had relied almost exclusively on the writings of Galen or Aristotle, or some other of the ancients. But in 1543 Vesalius, in his great work, *On the Structure of the Human Body,* broke with tradition and presented in detail the results of his own studies made with the dissecting knife. Nearly a century later (1628), Harvey made his momentous discovery of the circulation of the blood. Gradually, too, through the work of Redi, Leeuwenhoek, and others, the age-old belief that plant and animal life are generated spontaneously from decaying matter was dispelled.

For our purposes, the importance of the remarkable advance in science from the reign of Elizabeth to the American Revolution lies in its effect on the thought pattern of the age. Men always seek to establish a body of fundamental principles, a value system, that will serve as a touchstone to behavior, to thought and action in all areas of life. During the Mid-

---

[13] *Ibid.,* p. 69.

[14] William Cecil Dampier, *A Shorter History of Science* (New York: The Macmillan Co., 1944), pp. 46–91. Also published in paperback (Cleveland, Ohio: Meridian Books, Inc., The World Publishing Co., 1957).

dle Ages the core values of society, the body of "absolute principles" which would guide men in their daily life, were found in revealed truth and in the writings of Aristotle, the Church Fathers, and the more important medieval philosophers. The Renaissance sought its core values in the writings of classical antiquity, and in the age of the Reformation the Protestants turned once more to revealed truth, with each individual more or less free to exercise his own individual judgment. But as scientific discoveries multiplied, a profound change came about in the thinking of the intellectual class in Europe.

The accumulation of new knowledge and the development of new ways of obtaining it were basic elements in the definition and growth of the Enlightenment (see pages 187–190), a movement whose underlying idea was the conviction that human understanding is capable, by its own power and without reliance upon divine assistance, of comprehending not only the order of nature but of the entire system of the world, and that this new way of understanding the world in all its aspects would lead to a new way of gaining mastery over it. In the eighteenth century, reason was exalted and men sought to find in science the basic principles of human nature, of society, and of the universe itself. It was the age of rationalism; reason became the touchstone by which all institutions and practices were to be evaluated. Man was no longer regarded as depraved by nature, but innately noble and capable of perfectibility. The dynamic concept of progress now took form, and men came to entertain the belief that if human action could be given a rational basis old abuses and injustices in church and state, and in society generally, would be done away with.

The development of science and the increasing reliance on reason did not have a very immediate and direct effect on educational policy and practice. Slowly, however, the twin guardians of the citadel of learning, classical antiquity and institutionalized religion, had to retreat before the new forces released by the spirit of scientific inquiry.

Summary

If one is to bring the American colonies into the proper focus during the one hundred and seventy years which elapsed between the settlement of Jamestown and the Revolution, one must view them, not as isolated settlements fringing the wilderness of a great continent, but as parts of a world order. The colonies were planted and developed during an age of great events, not only in the history of Europe, but in the history of mankind. And colonial institutions and thought were profoundly affected by the course of events in the world outside.

At the opening of the seventeenth century, the peoples of Europe were in the midst of a long and bitter religious controversy which was ultimately to resolve itself in religious freedom. For another century, however, religion was to continue as a dominant, if not the dominant, intellectual interest of Europe. Closely associated with the effort to achieve freedom of individual judgment in religion was the rise of the bourgeoisie and the consequent change in the class structure of society. In England, and to some extent on the Continent, a middle class composed of prosperous merchants, capitalists, and artisans was challenging the supremacy of the old nobility. It was this new middle class that was supplying the capital necessary to develop a world-wide commerce, to plant colonies, and to wage a titanic struggle for empire. In England it was this middle class, too, that was establishing the principles of parliamentary government. Both in England and on the Continent representatives of the middle class were making momentous scientific discoveries and formulating a philosophy of rationalism.

The age from Elizabeth to George III was a great age. It witnessed the substantial achievement of religious liberty, the rise of the middle class to a position of pre-eminence, a rapid development of capitalism, the establishment of colonies and the conquest of empire, the triumph of parliamentary government in England, the accumulation of a vast store of scientific knowledge, and the formulation of a rationalistic philosophy which aimed to emancipate mankind from the abuses of ignorance and injustice. It is against this background of European thought and action and institutional change that American colonial history must be viewed.

Old World influences on American education during the colonial period were many, one of the most important of which was the class structure of society. Class distinctions were transplanted to America and they operated very definitely in the shaping of educational policy and practice. A two-class school system was a natural outgrowth of prevailing social classifications in Europe; it constituted an important Old World borrowing, which, as time was to prove, was extremely difficult to modify. More important still, perhaps, was the religious tradition in education. Schools and colleges alike, certainly during the early colonial period, were thought of as serving primarily religious ends. The objectives of education, the content of instruction, the means of support, and the organs of control were all profoundly affected by the prevailing view that education should serve the ends of institutionalized religion. The classical tradition in education — an influence of the Renaissance — was scarcely less important than the religious tradition. Latin and other ancient languages were long to occupy a dominant position in the curriculum of the secondary schools and colleges. The types of educational institutions established, the textbooks used, and the methods of instruction employed were in the main Old World borrowings.

These influences were backward-looking; they tended to perpetuate tradition and long-established custom. There were, however, other Old World influences which were forward-looking and dynamic, although their effect on education was less immediate and direct. These new forces were the rise of a capitalistic society, the development of representative government, the growth of science, and the added importance assigned to reason in the direction and control of human affairs. As we shall see, these forces went far to mold the theory and practice of education in the colonial and later periods.

Questions and Problems for Study and Discussion

1. The institutions of the colonists were shaped to a considerable extent by Old World influences. Evaluate each of the Old World influences on early American education. Which do you regard as having been the most important? Why?

2. In your opinion, which of the Old World influences that shaped colonial education has been most persistent? What present-day issues does it raise?

3. How do you account for the regional differences in American life that began to appear shortly after the first settlements? Discuss the factors that made for these differences.

4. How do you account for the different views with respect to the state's responsibility for education entertained by the Puritans and the Anglicans?

5. Evaluate the statement that it is difficult to determine which has more influence on the other, the environment on men or men on the environment.

6. In attempts to define the proper relation of the school to the American social order it has been suggested: (a) that the schools should aim at the creation of an essentially new order; (b) that the schools should cultivate in youth an unqualified attachment to the presently accepted pattern of economic, social, and political arrangements; (c) that, while the schools should accept the core values of American society, they should also seek to develop in youth a critical understanding of the workings of our political, economic, and social arrangements, essential for participation in making public policy. Which of these propositions most nearly conforms to your point of view? Indicate what would be the effect on the curriculum of the adoption of this point of view; of the adoption of each of the other points of view.

Selected References for Further Reading

Beard, Charles A., and Beard, Mary R. *The Rise of American Civilization,* I: *The Agricultural Era.* New York: The Macmillan Co., 1927. Pp. viii + 824.

Boorstin, Daniel J. *The Americans: The Colonial Experience.* New York: Random House, 1958. Pp. xii + 434.

Brown, J. Howard. *Elizabethan Schooldays: An Account of the English Grammar School in the Second Half of the Sixteenth Century.* Oxford: Basil Blackwell, 1933. Pp. x + 174.

Butts, R. Freeman, and Cremin, Lawrence A. *A History of Education in American Culture.* New York: Henry Holt and Co., 1953. Pp. x + 628.

Clark, G. N. *The Seventeenth Century.* Oxford: Clarendon Press, 1929. Pp. xii + 372. Also published in paperback (New York: Oxford University Press, Inc. [Galaxy Books], 1961).

Cubberley, Ellwood P. *Readings in the History of Education: A Collection of Sources and Readings to Illustrate the Development of Educational Practice, Theory, and Organization.* Boston: Houghton Mifflin Company, 1920. Pp. xxii + 684.

Eggleston, Edward. *The Transit of Civilization from England to America in the Seventeenth Century.* New York: D. Appleton & Co., 1900. Pp. viii + 344. Also published in paperback (Boston: Beacon Press, 1961).

Haller, William, *The Rise of Puritanism.* New York: Columbia University Press, 1938. Pp. viii + 464. Also published in paperback (New York: Harper & Brothers [Torchbooks], 1957).

Knight, Edgar W. *A Documentary History of Education in the South Before 1860, I: European Inheritances.* Chapel Hill, N.C.: University of North Carolina Press, 1949. Pp. ix + 744.

Leach, Arthur F. *English Schools at the Reformation, 1546–48.* Westminster, England: Archibald Constable & Co., 1895. Pp. 346.

Morison, Samuel Eliot. *The Founding of Harvard College.* Cambridge, Mass.: Harvard University Press, 1935. Pp. xxvi + 472.

Morison, Samuel Eliot. *The Puritan Pronaos: Studies in the Intellectual Life of New England in the Seventeenth Century.* New York: New York University Press, 1936. Pp. vi + 282. Also published in paperback under the title *Intellectual Life of Colonial New England* (Ithaca, N.Y.: Cornell University Press [Great Seal Books], 1956).

Notestein, Wallace. *The English People on the Eve of Colonization, 1603–30.* New York: Harper & Brothers, 1954. Pp. xvii + 302. Also published in paperback (New York: Harper & Brothers [Torchbooks], 1962).

Parrington, Vernon Louis. *Main Currents in American Thought: An Interpretation of American Literature from the Beginnings to 1920, I: The Colonial Mind, 1620–1800.* New York: Harcourt, Brace & Co., 1927. Pp. xvii + 414. Also published in paperback (New York: Harcourt, Brace & Co. [Harvest Books], 1954).

Rossiter, Clinton. *Seedtime of the Republic: The Origin of the American Tradition of Political Liberty.* New York: Harcourt, Brace & Co., 1953. Pp. xiv + 558. Also published in paperback, in abridged form, under the title *The First American Revolution* (New York: Harcourt, Brace & Co. [Harvest Books], 1956).

Rowse, A. L. *The Elizabethans and America.* London: Macmillan and Co., Ltd., 1959. Pp. xiii + 221.

Smith, Preserved. *A History of Modern Culture, I: The Great Renewal, 1543–1687.* New York: Henry Holt & Co., 1930. Pp. xii + 672.

Smith, Preserved. *A History of Modern Culture,* II: *The Enlightenment, 1687–1776.* New York: Henry Holt & Co., 1934. Pp. viii + 704.

Stowe, A. Monroe. *English Grammar Schools in the Reign of Queen Elizabeth.* New York: Teachers College, Columbia University, 1908. Pp. 200.

Tawney, R. H. *Religion and the Rise of Capitalism: A Historical Study,* Holland Memorial Lectures, 1922. New York: Harcourt, Brace & Co., 1926. Pp. x + 338. Also published in paperback (New York: New American Library of World Literature, Inc. [Mentor Books], 1961).

Watson, Foster. *The English Grammar Schools to 1660: Their Curriculum and Practice.* Cambridge: Cambridge University Press, 1908. Pp. x + 548.

Wertenbaker, Thomas Jefferson. *A History of American Life,* II: *The First Americans, 1607–1690.* New York: The Macmillan Co., 1927. Pp. xx + 358.

Wright, Louis B. *The Cultural Life of the American Colonies, 1607–1763.* New York: Harper & Brothers, 1957. Pp. xiv + 292.

Wright, Louis B. *Middle-Class Culture in Elizabethan England.* Chapel Hill, N.C.: University of North Carolina Press, 1935. Pp. x + 733.

2

The School in an Ecclesiastical Rural Social Order: Seventeenth-Century New England

The attempt of the New England Puritans to establish and maintain a new social order in which they could realize their religious ideas and carry into effect the social institutions they envisioned was destined to fail in the end. Even so, Puritanism profoundly affected nearly every aspect of American life. One does not realize the full impact of Puritanism upon American ideals and institutions until one attempts to unravel the warp and woof of our common culture and trace the several strands to their respective origins. Puritanism bequeathed a legacy of religious, spiritual, and moral values that long influenced patterns of conduct and behavior. Indeed, our present attitudes toward individual worth, freedom under law, the dignity of labor, and the form and functions of local government have been profoundly influenced by the New England Puritan.

It was, however, in the cultivation of the intellectual life that the genius of New England found its fullest expression. The Massachusetts Bay Colony had hardly been established when a printing press was put into operation and a college was opened. Nor had many years passed before the New England colonies generally enacted laws requiring a form of compulsory education and compulsory maintenance of schools. It was at this early date that the New England colonies began to implement the fundamental principle that a system of public schools is essential in a well-ordered state. To be sure, the state was acting in the interests of institutionalized religion, but, even so, for the first time in the English-speaking world education was being recognized as a fundamental responsibility of government. In many respects, the stern New England Puritan

was an unlovely figure. In the standards of behavior he adopted for himself and which he attempted to force upon his followers, and in the kind
of society he tried to establish, we moderns may find much that impresses
us as restrictive and undemocratic in purpose. Nevertheless, it was from
New England that we inherited many of our most important ideas and
practices.

The Founders of a New Society in New England

The founding of New England needs to be viewed against the background of contemporary events in England. By the opening years of the
seventeenth century the movement to transform English society from a
feudal to a bourgeois economy was well under way. This transformation
was largely responsible for the realignment of social classes and for a sharp
definition of both religious and political issues. A prospering middle class
and a small landed gentry drew together to challenge vigorously the traditional rulers of England, landed noble, priest, and king. The issues
touched nearly every aspect of English life. In the struggle were involved
the determination of the locus of authority in church and state and also
the structural organization of both of these important institutions. The
shifting fortunes of groups participating in the struggle had far-reaching
effects. It was two of the parties in this struggle which, despairing of success at home, undertook to establish a new society in New England.

PARTIES TO THE STRUGGLE FOR POWER IN
CHURCH AND STATE — ANGLICANS, PURITANS, AND SEPARATISTS

Three major parties emerged in the struggle. At the extreme right
stood the Anglicans, members of the Established Church of England,
who held tenaciously to the principles of absolutism in church and state.
Christian and subject owed unquestioning obedience to "bishop and
king," whose authority was of God. This union of absolutist church and
absolutist state was well designed to keep power over men's lives — over
their thought and action — in the hands of the hereditary rulers of
England.[1]

But many of the smaller landed gentry and their burgher allies, conscious of their growing importance, wealth, intelligence, and, if of nothing
else, their superior morality, were little disposed to let the Anglicans have
their way without a struggle. Both their economic and religious interests

---

[1] Vernon Louis Parrington, *The Colonial Mind, 1620–1800, Main Currents in
American Thought* (3 vols. in one; New York: Harcourt, Brace & Co. 1927), I,
p. 8. Also published in paperback (New York: Harcourt, Brace & World, Inc.
[Harvest Books], 1961).

led them to challenge the principle of absolutism and to set over against it the principle of an elective stewardship. Thus there emerged a second party, the Puritans, whose position represented a compromise between the extremes of the political and religious thought of contemporary England. Beginning with the moderate demands that the Anglican Church be purified of such "Roman" practices as wearing of the surplice or making the sign of the cross at baptism, the Puritans, in time, raised the issue of the source of authority in church and state.[2] Over against the principle of divine right, they set the principle of representation; over against anointed bishop and king, they set the synod and the Parliament. They were by no means champions of a pure democracy, but in synod and Parliament they had discovered institutions admirably adapted to serve their own class interests. One misses altogether the spirit and purpose of English Puritanism if one regards it merely as a movement to remove certain abuses in the Anglican Church. The Puritans aimed at nothing less than domination of the church and strict imposition of their beliefs upon others. They were equally intent on influencing, if not controlling, the course of political events. If they had had their way, Parliament would have been made an instrument to checkmate the crown and it would have increasingly reflected the growing strength of Puritanism.

The third articulate religious group produced by the controversies of the day was known as Separatists. In the main, the Separatists were humble folk, small farmers, laborers, and artisans whose instructors were contemptuously described by the Bishop of London as "cobblers, tailors, felt-makers, and such-like trash." The good Bishop appears to have been misinformed or sparing with the truth; as a matter of fact, the leaders of the movement were well-educated Englishmen, some of them graduates of Cambridge University. But it is true that the Separatists as a group were made up primarily of persons who "had only been used to a plaine countrie life & yᵉ inocente trade of husbandrey,"[3] and they came to constitute the extreme left wing of English Protestantism. They espoused the radical doctrine that each individual has the right to worship God in his own way and to formulate his own religious creed. And, what was more, desiring religious freedom for themselves, they were willing to accord it to others.[4] Moreover, the Separatists did not believe in an established church; since all people could not be expected to be of the same mind,

[2] Marcus Wilson Jernegan, *The American Colonies, 1492–1750* (New York: Longmans, Green & Co., 1929), p. 124. Also published in paperback (New York: Frederick Ungar Publishing Co., Inc., 1959). See also Oliver Perry Chitwood, *A History of Colonial America,* Third Edition (New York: Harper & Brothers, 1961), p. 9.

[3] William Bradford, *History of Plymouth Plantation,* first printed for the Massachusetts Historical Society (Boston: Little, Brown, & Co., 1856), p. 11.

[4] Carl Lotus Becker, *Beginnings of the American People* (Boston: Houghton Mifflin Company, 1915), p. 88. Also published in paperback (Ithaca, N.Y.: Cornell University Press, 1961).

those who did not agree should be permitted to form congregations of their own and to worship free from outside compulsion. Less aggressive than the Puritans, the Separatists wished neither to purify nor to dominate the Church of England. They were content to separate from it and to go their own way. Here were doctrines that struck at the existing pattern of political, ecclesiastical, and social arrangements in England. When transplanted to the New World by the Pilgrim Fathers who crossed on the *Mayflower,* they became a creative force in the making of a new society.[5]

Neither Queen Elizabeth nor the early Stuarts, James I and Charles I, had any notion of letting the Puritans and the Separatists have their way in England. It is unnecessary here to give a detailed account of the means adopted by the English sovereigns to force religious conformity or to stamp out the dangerous political and social doctrines entertained by the nonconformists. James I bluntly asserted that he would make the Puritans conform or else harry them out of the kingdom. Under the whip of religious persecution and in the face of a growing absolutism in government, many nonconformists lost hope of working out in England the kind of society they envisioned and turned to America as the place where they could carry into practical operation their ideas of social organization. In fact, to many it appeared that in the American wilderness God had prepared a special place for his chosen people to carry out their great experiment. As the future was to disclose, the Puritan migration was not to be the last time when men, defeated in purpose and dissatisfied with the arrangements of the established order, turned westward to the frontier in the hope of starting anew and of working out for themselves a new world and a new destiny.

THE SETTLEMENT OF NEW ENGLAND — THE IDEALS AND PURPOSES OF THE EARLY LEADERS

It is necessary to get a somewhat closer view of the men who were directing the venture of establishing a new society in New England, to understand their purposes, and to envision the kind of society they were endeavoring to build. As we shall see later, the school was to play an important role in their total plan of social organization.

The few score persons who in 1620 established the first permanent colony in New England have enjoyed a place in the esteem of all succeeding generations of Americans. This small band of Separatists, whose religious and political principles we have previously commented upon, was made up, in the main, of small farmers, artisans, and laborers, but their

[5] Chitwood, *op. cit.,* pp. 90–101; also, Curtis P. Nettels, *The Roots of American Civilization* (New York: F. S. Crofts & Co., 1938), p. 71. For the major source for the history of Massachusetts Colony up to 1646, see Bradford, *op. cit.* (also published as one volume in the series *Original Narratives of Early American History* [New York: Charles Scribner's Sons, 1908]).

devotion to a high ideal was such that under competent leadership they were able to endure persecution in England and economic hardships in Holland, and to overcome the privations and dangers of the American wilderness. Their devotion to the ideal also made for a larger measure of disciplined and generally willing cooperation than would have been likely to characterize a differently motivated group. It was their plan, on leaving England, to settle in Virginia, where they had made arrangements to go. But a storm — or, as some may say, destiny — forced them out of their course and they found themselves afloat along the shores of New England without a charter, without any legal authority to establish a settlement, and without any agreed-upon plan of political or social organization. But before going ashore they came together to sign a compact, the famous Mayflower Compact, whereby they agreed to establish a civil society and to abide by laws duly made. Thus, they put into practical operation the principle that government derives its just authority from the consent of the governed. And, in establishing the congregational form of church organization, they applied the same democratic principle. The lowly Pilgrim was not an impressive figure when compared with the Massachusetts Puritan or the Virginia planter, but it was given to these Pilgrim Separatists to catch a vision of the day when government would be responsive to the popular will and when the state would not be accorded the authority "to compell religion, to plant churches by power, and to force a submission to Ecclesiastical Government by lawes and penalties."[6]

The men who directed the Puritan migration to Massachusetts were men of a different temper. They were drawn from the great middle class of English society. Some of them were country squires with large landed estates and many servants — men who had relatively large if somewhat dwindling incomes. Some were merchants who had succeeded in accumulating substantial fortunes, and not a few were scholars who held their degrees from English universities. Massachusetts was not two decades old before one hundred and thirty university graduates, mostly ministers, had joined the Puritan movement out of England. The rank and file of the settlers, however, were small merchants, yeomen, tenants, artisans, and servants of the gentlemen who were directing the movement. And among these the great majority were persons of little wealth or none at all.

The motives which prompted the Puritan migration were many and varied. The fact has been frequently underemphasized or overlooked altogether that many who joined the Puritan exodus, including some of the leaders themselves, were influenced by the hope of material gain. In the southeastern counties of England, where Puritanism was the strongest, a severe depression in the textile industries had set in about 1625, and it

[6] Becker, *op. cit.,* p. 88; see also Bradford, *op. cit.*

continued for a number of years, creating economic unrest among all classes.[7] Poor crops added to the sufferings of the unemployed. As a contemporary expressed it:

> This Land growes weary of her Inhabitants, soe as man, whoe is the most pretious of all creatures, is here more vile & base then the earth we treade upon, & of lesse prise among us then an horse or a sheepe: Masters are forced by authority to entertaine servants, parents to maine-taine there owne children, all townes complaine of the burthen of theire poore, though we have taken up many unnessisarie yea unlawfull trades to mainetaine them. . . .
>
> We are growne to that height of Intemperance in all excesse of Riott, as noe mans estate allmost will suffice to keep saile wth his æqualls: & he whoe failes herein, must live in scorne & contempt. . . .[8]

No less a person than John Winthrop himself was feeling the "pinch of hard times." He gave as one of his reasons for considering going to America the fact that his means in England were so reduced that he was unable to continue his present "place and employment." His fortunes had declined to the point that he could write: "I owe more already than I am able to pay, without sale of my land."[9] But however strong the economic motive may have been, it seems clear that with most colonists it was less impelling than the religious motive, than the desire to establish a society in which the church could not be brought to desolation nor could the "ffountaines of Learning and Religion" be corrupted.[10] This was especially true of the leaders of the movement. It may be, as Carl Becker concludes, that "few would have come for religion's sake alone,"[11] that the rank and file came with the expectation that the doors of economic opportunity would open in the American wilderness. But men like Winthrop, and Dudley, and Cotton had caught the vision of a new society, a society of which they themselves would be both the architects and the builders.

[7] Chitwood, *op. cit.*, p. 104.

[8] Robert C. Winthrop, *Life and Letters of John Winthrop, Governor of the Massachusetts-Bay Company at Their Emigration to New England, 1630* (Vol. I of the two-volume *Life and Letters of John Winthrop*) (Boston: Ticknor and Fields, 1864), pp. 309–310.

[9] *Life and Letters, op. cit.*, p. 286. See also the letter from John Winthrop to his wife, May 15, 1629, *ibid.*, p. 296.

[10] *Ibid.*, p. 310. See also page 309: "It will be a service to the Church of great consequence to carry the Gospell into those parts of the world . . . & to raise a Bulworke against the kingdome of the AnteChrist. . . . All other churches of Europe are brought to desolation, & o^r sinnes, for wch the Lord beginnes allreaddy to frowne upon us & to cutte us short, doe threatne evill times to be comminge upon us, & whoe knowes, but that God hath provided this place to be a refuge for many whome he meanes to save out of the generall callamity, & seeinge the Church hath noe place lefte to flie into but the wildernesse, what better worke can there be, then to goe & provide tabernacles & foode for her. . . ."

[11] Becker, *op. cit.*, p. 94. See also Chitwood, *op. cit.*, pp. 104–105.

The Structural Design of a New Society

To understand clearly the educational policy of early New England, one must view it against the background of the total cultural pattern; to appraise it properly, one must take account of the role the educational system was made to play in the maintenance of the social order. Too often historians have viewed the schools of early New England in the light of later developments and have attributed to the men who were engaged in laying the foundations of the educational system motives and principles which they themselves would have regarded as strange and even dangerous. It is certain that one must have some insight into the nature and structure of the social order the leaders were undertaking to build if one is to understand the future significance of the educational policies they put into force. For example, the builders of the Massachusetts Bay Colony would have been shocked and alarmed if they had thought that their school system would ever contribute to the establishment of a democratic state, because to them democracy was the meanest and most contemptible form of political organization man had yet devised or proposed.

RELIGION AND GOVERNMENT

One misses entirely the spirit of early New England unless one keeps in mind the important fact that religion was the dominant intellectual interest. In all New England, if one excepts Rhode Island, the men who were directing the course of events were primarily concerned with the establishment of Bible commonwealths, with the maintenance of an ecclesiastical social order firmly buttressed by the civil authority and by a class-structured society.

The Puritans endowed their God with many of the attributes of an ancient despot. He was a God of authority, and more often a God of wrath than a God of love. To some he extended his grace and elected them unto salvation; toward others he hardened his heart and turned his face from them. It was the duty of the elect, God's vice-regents on earth, to obey his will and to enforce his law, which he extended over every aspect of life, secular as well as ecclesiastical. This type of religious belief, introduced into New England by the followers of John Calvin, the unmitered pope of Geneva, was a fit instrument for the establishment in Massachusetts of an oligarchy of ministers and magistrates. For the first sixty years of its history, Massachusetts was a Bible commonwealth, in which church and state were but reverse sides of the same thing. The state was the executive arm, the handmaiden, of the church. It stamped out, so far as it could, religious dissent; it suppressed freedom of thought and of speech; and it established schools and a college to develop in youth an attachment to the existing order.

The following quotation from Parrington describes with penetrating insight the early church-state in Massachusetts:

> It was an oligarchy of Christian grace. The minister was the trained and consecrated interpreter of the divine law, and the magistrate was its trained and consecrated administrator; and both were chosen by free election of the Saints. If unfortunately the Saints were few and the sinners many, was not that a special reason for safeguarding the Ark of the Covenant from the touch of profane hands? Hence all legislative experiments by annually elected deputies, no matter how exactly those experiments might fall in with the wishes of the majority, were sternly frowned upon or skillfully nullified. Not only were such popular enactments, it was held, too often prompted by the carnal desires of the natural man, but they were no better than an insult to God, as implying the insufficiency of the Scriptures to every temporal need. Unregenerate and sinful men must have no share in God's work. The Saints must not have their hands tied by majority votes. This explains, quite as much as mere love of power, the persistent hostility of the leaders to every democratic tendency. Such institutions as grew up spontaneously out of the necessities of the situation, were sharply hedged about by restrictions. The town meeting, which was extra-legal under the charter, was safeguarded by limiting the right of voting to freemen, except in a few trivial matters; and the more popular deputies, who inclined to become self-willed, were forced to accept the principle of magisterial veto on their actions.[12]

The attitude of Puritan leaders toward democracy.   There was little equalitarianism in New England Puritanism. In the seventeenth century few outstanding leaders in New England looked with favor upon democracy in any form. Certainly they did not believe in popular political institutions. John Winthrop, long the governor of the young colony, was outspoken in his disapproval of democracy. The same was true of John Cotton, the most influential spiritual leader in the early history of Massachusetts. The democratic state had no warrant in Scripture, and Winthrop did not propose to see it established in Massachusetts. Winthrop argued that "the best part is always the least, and of that best part the wiser part is always the lesser,"[13] and later agreed that democracy represented the worst form of government.[14]

[12] Parrington, *op. cit.*, p. 21.

[13] James Kendall Hosmer (ed.), *Winthrop's Journal, "History of New England," 1630–1649*, Original Narratives of Early American History (New York: Charles Scribner's Sons, 1908), I, p. 290.

[14] Robert C. Winthrop, *Life and Letters of John Winthrop from His Embarkation for New England in 1630, with the Charter and Company of the Massachusetts Bay, to His Death in 1649* (Boston: Ticknor and Fields, 1867), II, p. 430. Winthrop wrote:

In the following passage, John Cotton concisely expressed his conception of church and state and of the location of authority in both.

> It is better that the commonwealth be fashioned to the setting forth of Gods house, which is his church: than to accomodate the church frame to the civill state. Democracy, I do not conceyve that ever God did ordeyne as fitt government eyther for church or commonwealth. If the people be governors, who shall be governed? As for monarchy, and aristocracy, they are both of them clearly approoved, and directed in scripture, yet so as referreth the soveraigntie to himself, and setteth up Theocracy in both, as the best forme of government in the commonwealth, as well as in the church.[15]

Winthrop and Cotton and the small group of ministers and magistrates who dominated early Massachusetts, it must be remembered, had grown up in a semifeudal society, they had a long tradition of aristocracy behind them, and they believed sincerely that they were the special recipients of God's grace and will. Add to all this the self-interest and the will to power which most men have, and that theocracy in church and state which Cotton lauded becomes intelligible.

Restrictions on the right of suffrage and the subordination of state to church. If political power was to be exercised by God's chosen few, a way must be found to limit the suffrage and to render ineffective the growing insistence of common folk that they be permitted to take a hand in things. For the first sixty years in Massachusetts the right to vote for representatives to the General Court, as the colonial legislature was called, was restricted to church members. However, to become a church member was no easy matter. First of all, one had to obtain the approval of the minister, who took care that those who were opposed to the existing order were excluded. Having secured the approval of the minister, one must then appear in person before the congregation prepared to lay bare before the public eye the innermost depths of one's soul. To enter the church, as Carl Becker has vividly put it, "was an ordeal which the average man will not readily undergo, involving, as an initial procedure, a confession

---

"Now if we should change from a mixt Aristocratie to a meere Democratie: first we should haue no warrnt in scripture for it: there was no such Goverm^t in Israell.

"2: we should heerby voluntaryly abase o^rselues & deprive o^rselues of that dignitye, wch the providence of God hath putt vpon us: wch is a manifest breach of the 5th Com^t: for a Democratie is, among most Civill nations, accounted the meanest & worst of all formes of Goverm^t: & therefore in writers, it is branded wth Reproachfull Epithits as *Bellua mutoru capitū,* a monster, &c: & Historyes doe recorde, that it hath beene allwayes of least continuance & fullest of troubles."

[15] John Hutchinson, *The History of the Colony of Massachusetts-Bay, From the First Settlement Thereof in 1628. Until Its Incorporation with the Colony of King William and Queen Mary in 1691* (Boston: New England: Printed by T. & J. Fleet, at the Heart and Crown in Cornhill, 1764), I, p. 467.

of faults and a profession of faith, a public revelation of inner spiritual condition, an exposure of soul to the searching and curious inspection of the sanctified."[16] How many sensitive persons shrank from the ordeal, from renouncing "all private spiritual possessions," and from giving their "intimate convictions into the keeping of others," cannot be known, but for this reason, and perhaps more compelling ones, church membership and full enjoyment of the franchise were possessed by a relatively small minority.

In all the other New England colonies, except Rhode Island, there was in the seventeenth century a close relationship between church and state; care was taken not to let political power slip into the hands of those who would use it to challenge the existing order of religious and social arrangements. In Plymouth, the liberalism implicit in Separatism prevented, for a while, the establishment of a state church and the suffrage was more widely extended than in Massachusetts. But even there "liars, drunkards, swearers," Quakers, and other "opponents of the 'true worship of God' " were denied the ballot. Moreover, to be a "freeman" one required an estate of twenty pounds. It has been estimated that after 1640 not more than a third of the adult males were "freemen." It is true that certain non-freemen, known as inhabitants, were permitted to vote, but only freemen could serve as members of the legislature or cast a vote for the governor and assistants.

Similarly, in Connecticut political institutions were somewhat more liberal than in Massachusetts. Thomas Hooker, the founder of the colony and a liberal of the first rank, had taken sharp issue with the theological oligarchy in Massachusetts, and in Connecticut there was no established church. The suffrage was not conditioned on church membership, but only freemen could vote and only the General Court could admit one to the status of freeman.[17] The restriction on the suffrage was probably not so severe as in Massachusetts; nevertheless, political power was jealously guarded by the favored few. In 1692, the non-freemen were described as being many times the greater number of people. In the colony of New Haven the theocracy was about as strongly entrenched as in Massachusetts. Here, also, church membership was required for voting and a small group of religious leaders, as in Massachusetts, were able to hold office from year to year.[18]

Luckily, Roger Williams and Anne Hutchinson succeeded in establishing in Rhode Island a haven for all who found Puritanism oppressive. Rhode Island was not, to be sure, a democracy, but there was religious freedom and separation of church and state.

16 Becker, *op. cit.*, p. 114.
17 Nettels, *op. cit.*, p. 174.
18 *Ibid.*, p. 175.

The New England town. A clear understanding of the town is essential for the student of social institutions in New England. Many factors — geographical, economic, and social — operated to bring about this form of community life. Nature had decreed that agriculture in New England should not, as a rule, be carried on in large plantation units, as in the South, but on small farms. Neither the climate nor the soil was conducive to the cultivation of staple crops. For the most part, the soil was thin and stony, although it yielded a fair return to careful husbandry. The intensive form of agriculture which had been adopted contributed to the town form of local social organization. The compact type of settlement was also stimulated by the policy of granting land to community groups rather than to individuals, by the desire of religious leaders to keep congregations from becoming dispersed, and by the existence of good harbors, which soon enticed New Englanders to the sea for fishing and commerce.

Usually a town embraced an irregular area of some twenty to forty square miles. If a group of people, a congregation or part of one, wanted to settle a new town, they petitioned the legislature. If the petition was granted, the boundaries of the town would be laid off and the title to the land vested in a group known as the proprietors. The town became in reality a corporate entity with the right to send its representatives to the colonial legislature and to manage its own local affairs in town meeting and through its own elected officers. The village site would be laid off, and the land, still held in common proprietorship, would be portioned out in town meeting to the families of the proprietors and to other inhabitants. Each head of a family was usually assigned a home plot ranging from an acre or less to twenty-five or thirty acres. Here he built his home and his barn and perhaps a blacksmith shop or a tannery. If a farmer, he would also be allotted strips of land in the surrounding fields for the cultivation of his crops. All these the individual held as his own, but the woodlands, meadows, and pastures were reserved for common use. The unoccupied land was held for later distribution to newcomers.

The open town meeting was a public forum for the conduct of local affairs. Here the town officials, the selectmen, were elected, committees of one kind or another appointed, land tracts apportioned to newcomers, and funds voted for the support of schools. In the management of town affairs the democratic spirit was more in evidence than in the management of the affairs of the colony, but, even so, it would be a mistake to suppose that all could participate in the determination of local policy. In Massachusetts, for example, during most of the seventeenth century the town suffrage was bestowed upon all "English-men, that are settled inhabitants and House-holders in any Town, of the age of *twenty-four years,* and of honest and good Conversations, being Rated at *eighty pounds* Estate in a single Country Rate. . . ."[19] This latter provision was enough to disqualify a large percentage of the inhabitants.

The waning power of the theocracy.   For a while the religious leaders of New England were able to maintain an ecclesiastical social order in which the civil authority was used to carry out the policy of the church, but almost from the beginning one notes a popular dissatisfaction with the rule of the few and with the strict regulation of nearly every aspect of private and public life. In a frontier society it was impossible to repress the spirit of democracy and individualism, however much leaders in church and state might invoke divine sanction of their rule. Gradually, power — political, economic, and social — slipped from the hands of the ministers, magistrates, and gentlemen, who were the early leaders, to the hands of new and important elements in the population, namely, merchants, farmers, and artisans. As the seventeenth century drew to a close, the old order collapsed in Massachusetts, and elsewhere it was undergoing a transformation. As we shall see later, a powerful merchant class had developed which was quite as much interested in its account book as in its Bible and which was out of sympathy with the intolerance and restricted point of view of Puritanism. It was two merchants, Thomas Brattle and Robert Calef, who had the courage to raise their voices in denunciation of the witchcraft persecutions. More important still, perhaps, was the development of a large class of small farmers, the solid core of New England society. This New England yeomanry was essentially democratic and it became increasingly conscious of its strength and importance. As men became busily engaged in building their homes in well-kept, elm-shaded villages, in improving their acres and adding to them, in making in home and shop the articles of everyday use, in building ships, and in competing for profits in the markets of the world, they lost much of the old religious fervor which had impelled their fathers across the sea. The ministers and their magisterial supporters were losing their moral, as well as their political, influence. The banishment of Roger Williams and Anne Hutchinson in order to stifle freedom of thought; the sight of Quakers tied to the tail-ends of carts, stripped to the waist, and beaten on their bare backs as they trudged through village streets; the hangings during the witchcraft hysteria; the love of power of the Puritan clergy — all these, although they might be paralleled in other parts of the world, tended to turn men away from a religious faith which condemned so many of their friends and neighbors, if not themselves, to eternal punishment.

The ministers, unyielding to the last, were fully aware of the change that was coming over New England life. As Cotton Mather expressed it:

[19] W. H. Whitmore (ed.), *Colonial Laws of Massachusetts* (Boston, 1889), pp. 147–148, as quoted in John Fairfield Sly, *Town Government in Massachusetts (1620–1930)* (Cambridge, Mass.: Harvard University Press, 1930), pp. 75–76.

I saw a fearful *degeneracy,* creeping, I cannot say, but rushing in upon these churches; I saw to multiply continually our dangers, of our losing no small points in our *first faith,* as well as our *first love,* and of our giving up the *essentials* of that church order, which was the very end of these colonies. . . . I saw a visible *shrink* in all orders of men among us, from that *greatness,* and that *goodness,* which was in the *first grain* that our God brought from *three sifted* kingdoms, into this land . . . . in America . . . those parts which were at first peopled by the *refuse* of the English nation, . . . sensibly amend in regards of sobriety and education, [while] those parts which were *planted with a more noble vine* . . . give a prospect of affording only the *degenerate plants of a strange vine.*[20]

Similarly, in 1674, Samuel Torry lamented:

Truely, so it is, the very heart of New-England is changed and exceedingly corrupted with the sins of the Times. [He complained of a] Spirit of Profaneness, a Spirit of Pride, a Spirit of Worldliness, a Spirit of Sensuality, a Spirit of Gainsaying and Rebellion, a Spirit of Libertinism, a Spirit of Carnality, Formality, Hypocrisie and a Spiritual Idolatry in the Worship of God.[21]

The heart of New England was changing. Merchants and small farmers were quietly taking over the control of things and shaping the course of events. Cotton Mather might still be an impressive figure warning Boston that no town was ever more liable to be laid in ashes "through the wickedness of them that sleep in it,"[22] and Jonathan Edwards at a somewhat later date might temporarily stir the emotions of men to their very depths. But the New England theocracy was definitely in its twilight. As the eighteenth century opened, the age-old struggle in which men seek to lay hands on and to operate the power controls of society had moved to another terrain and new combatants had appeared on the scene. Merchants and farmers were now to fight it out for place and power.

The rule of the theocracy in Massachusetts came to a definite end with the granting of a new charter in 1691 which guaranteed religious freedom to all Protestants and extended the franchise. The right to vote was never again to depend upon church membership. Henceforth to the Revolution all adult males who possessed a forty-shilling freehold or forty or fifty pounds of property could exercise full suffrage. By industry and thrift

[20] Cotton Mather, *Magnalia Christi Americana; or, The Ecclesiastical History of New-England; from its First Planting, in the Year 1620, unto the Year of Our Lord 1698* (Hartford: Silas Andrus and Son, 1855), I, p. 249.
[21] In his election sermon of that year at Weymouth, Massachusetts. Lindsay Swift, "The Massachusetts Election Sermons," Colonial Society of Massachusetts, *Publications,* I, 402, as quoted in Thomas Jefferson Wertenbaker, *The First Americans, 1607–1690* (New York: The Macmillan Co., 1927) p. 110. Used by permission of The Macmillan Co.
[22] Cotton Mather, "The Boston Ebenezer," *Magnalia Christi Americana, op. cit.,* p. 92.

many could now force open the door to active citizenship, a door which had hitherto been bolted by a severe test of religious orthodoxy. The moderate property qualifications contained in the charter made for a material widening of the political base. Brown, on the basis of his study of the suffrage in colonial Massachusetts after 1690, concluded that "not many adult men were excluded from voting because of property qualifications."[23] In the rest of New England, as in Massachusetts, political power was slipping into the hands of merchants, farmers, and thrifty artisans and mechanics who were able to meet the property qualifications required to vote.

Social Structure and Economic Organization

The men who planned the Bible commonwealth in Massachusetts were as jealous of social status as of political power; they were as bent upon maintaining a due subordination of social rank as upon enforcing a conformity of religious belief. Themselves the product of a semifeudal social order, in which class lines were rigidly drawn, they dreamed of establishing in New England an aristocratic society not unlike that of the mother country. To be sure, in the new order they were designing there would be no titled nobility, because few of their own number were possessors of titles. But with the upper nobility, the traditional enemy of the smaller landed gentry and the bourgeoisie, eliminated, the social structure which they hoped to establish would closely resemble that of the England they had left. New England, if its early leaders had had their way, would have soon presented a picture of large landed estates cultivated by laborers and tenants and interspersed with the small holdings of a not-too-numerous yeomanry.

Climate and soil in Massachusetts and elsewhere in New England prevented the rise of a numerous landed aristocracy, but they did not prevent the establishment of a society characterized by sharp class distinctions. In the beginning, the dominant social class was made up of ministers and magistrates together with a sprinkling of the smaller landed gentry who had joined the Puritan migration out of England. Most of the members of this class were able, intelligent, and well educated. But in the course of a very few years a merchant class put in its appearance and prosperous merchants were able to force their way into the tightly closed ranks of the social elite.

The glacial soil, for the most part stony and thin, offered little opportunity for the accumulation of fortunes, but good harbors, timber in

[23] Robert E. Brown, *Middle-Class Democracy and the Revolution in Massachusetts, 1691–1780* (Ithaca, N.Y.: Cornell University Press, 1955), p. 37. The original charter (1691) required fifty pounds of property for suffrage; the copy sent the colonists provided forty. The evidence favors the conclusion that the general practice was to require forty rather than fifty pounds.

abundance for the building of ships, and nearby waters teeming with cod, herring, and whale called men to the open sea and challenged them to trade and traffic in the markets of the world. Beginning as early as 1631,[24] shipbuilding rapidly expanded to supply colonial needs and within a few years New England-built ships were being sold in England; and it was fishing, next to agriculture, upon which the economic life was founded. The building of ships was stimulated by fishing, but fish constituted the basic commodity of New England commerce. As early as 1641, some 300,000 dried fish were sent to market,[25] and long before the close of the century hundreds of vessels and thousands of fishermen were engaged in the industry.[26] New England merchants found it difficult to find a market for what they had to sell in England, but the planters of the West Indies were glad to exchange their sugar, molasses, indigo, and cotton for New England fish, provisions, horses, and lumber. The fur trade also yielded a neat profit, and New England merchants found it worth their while to exploit the markets of their southern neighbors.

Within a few decades of the planting of the first colonies, a merchant-capitalist class appeared which constantly expanded its economic, social, and political influence. John Holland of Dorchester, for example, left an estate in 1652 valued at 4000 pounds.[27] Edward Randolph, an Englishman sent out to Massachusetts in 1676 to investigate the condition of trade, listed 230 vessels of fifty tons or more, all of which were owned in Massachusetts. About thirty merchants, according to his estimate, were possessors of fortunes ranging from 10,000 to 20,000 pounds.[28] The clergy might and did look with misgivings upon the rise of a prosperous merchant class, which signaled the change of New England life from an ecclesiastical to a secular basis, but they were powerless to prevent it. As merchants expanded the volume of their trade and added profit to profit, their influence increased wherever they desired to exercise it.

The members of the dominant social class — minister, magistrate, and merchant — employed all the devices at their command to maintain their social position and to keep all below them in due subordination. Indians were enslaved, although, for various reasons, Indian slavery never became important, and Negro slaves were imported by the few who could profitably use them. Numerous laws, one as early as 1633, were enacted to keep down the wages of artisans and laborers.[29] One had to be of superior social position to bear the title of "Gentleman" or to be addressed

---

[24] *Winthrop's Journal, op. cit.,* I, p. 65.

[25] *Winthrop's Journal, op. cit.,* II, p. 42.

[26] See Chitwood, *op. cit.,* pp. 384–385.

[27] Thomas Jefferson Wertenbaker, *The First Americans, 1607–1690* (New York: The Macmillan Co., 1927), p. 71.

[28] William B. Weeden, *Economic and Social History of New England, 1620–1789* (Boston: Houghton Mifflin Company, 1890), I, p. 265.

[29] Wertenbaker, *op. cit.,* p. 69; *Winthrop's Journal, op. cit.* I, p. 112.

as "Mister." The pews in the village church were assigned on the basis of position, wealth, age, and social status; and on the Sabbath morning each worshiper took his place in the pew that had been assigned him. One of the perplexing problems of village life, and one requiring an almost endless meeting of committees, was to appraise the official position, wealth, and age of the various inhabitants in order that all might be seated in the proper order of precedence. The law was ready with heavy fines to punish any who might see fit to intrude into the pews which belonged to their betters.

Class distinctions were also reflected in the manner of dress permitted. It was not enough that clothes should hide one's nakedness and keep one warm; they must also reveal the social class to which one belonged. And when men and women of "mean condition" began to dress like their superiors, began to wear long hair, silken hose, and golden buttons, men in place and position took alarm and promptly enacted laws to put a stop to this tendency to disturb the well-ordered ranks of society. Thus, in 1651, an act of the General Court of Massachusetts expressed the attitude of the ruling class as follows:

> We declare our utter detestation and dislike that men and women of meane Condition should take upon themselves the garb of gentlemen, by wearing gold or silver lace or buttons, or points at their knees or to walk in bootes or women of the same rancke to weare silke or tiffany horlles or scarfes, which though allowable to persons of greater estates, or more liberal education, yet we cannot but judge it intollerable in persons of such like condition.[30]

The court records contain many instances of prosecutions for violation of laws against extravagant dress. In 1673, thirty women in the towns of Springfield, Northampton, Hadley, Hatfield, and Westfield were indicted as "persons of small estate who use to wear silk contrary to law." Three years later, thirty-eight women and thirty young men were brought into court, "some for wearing silk, some for long hair, and other extravagancies."[31]

Second in social rank in seventeenth-century New England was a large middle class composed of small farmers and skilled artisans. Working their own small farms themselves or plying their trade as carpenters, blacksmiths, wheelwrights, millers, weavers, fullers, tailors, coopers, and bricklayers, the members of this class were not only the most numerous, but in many respects the most important, element in New England society. Industrious, ambitious, and unashamed to work with their own hands, they were giving labor a dignity it had not known before. As the years

[30] As quoted in Jernegan, *op. cit.*, pp. 179–180.
[31] As quoted in Weeden, *op. cit.*, I, p. 289.

passed, they achieved an economic well-being and a self-respect that could not be ignored, and when the suffrage was changed to a property basis, many of them were in a position to participate directly in shaping public policy. This growing middle class, with its insistence on its importance and its rights, was an unwelcome intruder into the ranks of the society planned by the early leaders of New England, but it was destined to give New England life its essentially democratic character.

Below the yeomen and skilled artisans were the tenant farmers and wage earners. The latter consisted of such persons as journeymen, farm or dock hands, and unskilled laborers in general. Denied the right to vote and usually addressed by the Christian name alone, members of this class constituted a definitely dependent and inferior group. Below them were the indentured servants, and, at the very bottom of society, the Indian and Negro slaves. Members of these two lowest classes were never exceedingly numerous because, as a rule, they did not possess the skill which the New England economy demanded of workers.

The Development of an Educational System

CONFLICTING VIEWS OF THE EARLY SYSTEM OF EDUCATION IN NEW ENGLAND

The various appraisals of the educational policies and practices of seventeenth-century New England have reflected their authors' views regarding the motivations of the Puritans. They have reflected, too, in many instances, the tendency to regard the education of the period as the "cornerstone" of later American education and the colonies as a "wilderness citadel" of the ancient learning. A "cornerstone" Puritan education may have been, but it was first an integral part of the evolving society in which it developed and which it served.

Historians disagree sharply with respect to the essential purposes of education in early colonial New England, the extent to which it was made available to children and youth generally, and the influence of New England upon later educational development in other parts of the nation. Thus, Professor Morison views the establishment of schools and colleges in colonial New England as a heroic effort of a pioneer people to cultivate the intellectual life, to perpetuate the ideals of a liberal education, and to keep the flame of humanism from being extinguished by the demands of sheer physical survival. "It was no small feat to keep alive the traditions of classical antiquity in a region that had never known the grandeur that was Rome, the glory that was Greece. The New England schools and colleges did just that; and handed down a priceless classical tradition to the eighteenth and nineteenth centuries. . . ."[32] He also maintains that "the purpose of the first New England college was higher education in the broadest sense, not a specialized training in Protestant theology."[33]

The Beards, however, regarded the famous Act of 1647 which required the maintenance of schools as designed to impose on all children the Puritan creed.[34] Professor Edgar W. Knight likewise viewed the Act of 1647 as "an effort to . . . impose the Puritan creed upon this first generation of native-born New Englanders."[35] Professor Merle E. Curti regards education in New England, as elsewhere in the colonies, as serving primarily the ends of institutionalized religion and the class structure of society.[36]

Similar disagreement exists with respect to the actual workings and accomplishments of the educational system. "In popular education," wrote Professor E. Benjamin Andrews, "New England led not only the continent but the world, there being a school-house, often several, in each town. Every native adult in Massachusetts and Connecticut was able to read and write."[37] However, contemporary documents reveal the persistence of a considerable amount of illiteracy as measured by the ability to sign one's name, and Professor Charles M. Andrews has written that the laws designed to provide for universal literacy were more honored in the breach than in the observance, and that, when the laws were honestly enforced, the results were not noteworthy.[38]

To one group of historians our system of public, free, democratic educational institutions stems from New England Puritanism; in the early legislation relating to education and the schools, some see the design of things to come, the essential principles of a democratic school system. Thus Martin discovered in the Massachusetts laws of 1642 and 1647 the principles upon which all subsequent Massachusetts school history rests.[39] Professor Cubberley saw in the Massachusetts Act of 1647 "the cornerstone of our American state school systems." He attached great importance

[32] Samuel Eliot Morison, *The Puritan Pronaos: Studies in the Intellectual Life of New England in the Seventeenth Century* (New York: New York University Press, 1936), pp. 15–16. Also published in paperback under the title *Intellectual Life of Colonial New England* (Ithaca, N.Y.: Cornell University Press, 1956).

[33] *Ibid.,* p. 30.

[34] Charles A. Beard and Mary R. Beard, *The Rise of American Civilization*, I: *The Agricultural Era* (New York: The Macmillan Co., 1927) p. 179.

[35] Edgar W. Knight, *Education in the United States,* Third Revised Edition (Boston: Ginn & Company, 1951), p. 85.

[36] Merle Curti, *The Social Ideas of American Educators, with a New Chapter on the Last Twenty-five Years* (Paterson, N.J.: Pageant Books, 1959), a reprint of the tenth volume of the Report of the American Historical Association Committee on the Social Studies in Schools, first published by Charles Scribner's Sons in 1935, with a chapter added.

[37] E. Benjamin Andrews, *History of the United States,* Revised Edition (New York: Charles Scribner's Sons, 1894), I, p. 128.

[38] See Morison, *op. cit.,* p. 55.

[39] George H. Martin, *The Evolution of the Massachusetts Public School System* (New York: D. Appleton & Co., 1923), pp. 14–15.

to the fact that the state in New England was the active agent in compelling the establishment and maintenance of schools. "It can be safely asserted," he wrote, "in the light of later developments, that the two laws of 1642 and 1647 represent the foundations upon which our American state public-school systems have been built."[40] This interpretation has had wide acceptance, but there have also been opposing views. The Beards warned that the unwary might easily be misled by this contention. They wrote:

> Unquestionably the first of these acts was conceived partly in the spirit of the English poor law; while the second flowed from a great desire to impose on all children the creed of the Puritan sect. The fact that education was ordered by "the state" was of no special significance, for the state and church were one in Massachusetts at the time; indeed, if the Mathers were to be believed, the church was superior to the state.[41]

Professor Edgar W. Knight likewise failed to discover in the Act of 1647 a foundation stone upon which the American educational system was later constructed:

> Into the provisions of this act . . . strange meanings have been tortured. It has been claimed that here are the beginnings of those secular features which now characterize the American school system. In no American sense, however, does this appear to be a provision for public schools. The authority asserted was that of the Puritan congregation, which was identical with the state but was more powerful than it . . . But it may be seriously questioned whether the "old deluder" act [Act of 1647] was not an obstacle instead of an aid to free, universal, secular education.[42]

Education in seventeenth-century New England, as always and everywhere, was anchored in the society of which it was a part; it operated within the purposes and ideals of the contemporary social order. As we have seen in the preceding sections of this chapter, the founders of New England were primarily concerned with the establishment of ecclesiastical commonwealths buttressed by the authority of the civil state. They had in mind a definite way of life and they proposed to use the state, which they themselves controlled, to carry it into effect. One will fail to see the broader significance of educational legislation in the early years of the history of New England unless one views this legislation as a part of the whole body of laws employed by the founders to give effect to their ideas with respect to religion, government, and the arrangement of social

[40] Ellwood P. Cubberley, *The History of Education* (Boston: Houghton Mifflin Company, 1920), p. 366.
[41] Beard and Beard, *op. cit.,* pp. 179–180.
[42] Knight, *op. cit.,* pp. 105–107.

classes. In Massachusetts, especially, laws were enacted to regulate nearly every aspect of life, private and public, spiritual and material. Resort was had to the civil authority to enforce religious orthodoxy, to persecute and drive out heretics, to control the press, to keep wages down, to maintain class distinctions through the regulation of dress, and to regulate manners and morals in the greatest detail. In a society in which the spirit of authoritarianism was so strong, it would have been strange if no attempt had been made through institutionalized education to socialize youth in terms of the core values of the existing order.

The leaders of early New England saw very clearly that education could be a powerful agency of social control and direction, that "the good education of children is of singular behoof and benefit to any Commonwealth." Accordingly, they used the state as a means of requiring the establishment and maintenance of schools to promote the interests of church and commonwealth, which were but the reverse sides of the same thing. But it must not be supposed that either church or commonwealth was democratic in the modern sense — democracy was not yet the order of the day either in the American colonies, in England, or elsewhere. It is clear that those responsible for the enactment of the educational legislation in early New England were not consciously promoting the interests of a democratic society, for, as we have already seen, they regarded democracy as the meanest form of political organization. Education and the schools would serve the interests of the commonwealth, but it was the Puritan commonwealth and not the democratic state of later years they had in mind.

Fundamental principles of social policy have a way of outliving the particular circumstances in which they develop. So it was with the principle that "the good education of children is of singular behoof and benefit to any Common-wealth," whether the commonwealth be democratic or otherwise. It must be said to the credit of New England, and especially of Massachusetts, that this important principle was put into practical operation and passed on as a legacy to future generations. That every well-ordered state, regardless of the ideology governing its organization, should maintain an efficient system of public schools became firmly fixed in the New England tradition. As time passed and the New England commonwealths emancipated themselves from aristocratic and clerical control and became more democratic, this old principle in a new setting became a dynamic force in the development of American democracy.

Another contribution of New England is scarcely less important. It is that the state should be concerned with the education of all children whether rich or poor, that the school should be open to all the children of the community. Here, again, the founding fathers wrought better than they knew. Their purpose was not equalitarianism; schools were not designed to open the doors to social and political opportunity, but to bring youth to a willing acceptance of the prevailing pattern of religious, political, and social arrangements. In the kind of social order the leaders had planned, it was essential that schools be established and that all have an opportunity to attend. This principle, too, outlived the circumstances of its origin. As democratic commonwealths emerged during the national period in New England and elsewhere, early New England practice was not without its influence in the establishment of the policy of opening the schools to all, regardless of class background or economic condition.

THE ESTABLISHMENT OF COLONY-WIDE SYSTEMS OF COMPULSORY EDUCATION

During the period from 1642 to 1671, all the New England colonies except Rhode Island were brought under the operation of statutes designed to insure that all children acquire the minimum education regarded as essential in the Puritan commonwealth. None of these statutes requiring compulsory education, it must be kept in mind, made any reference to the maintenance of schools or to attendance in schools. The state prescribed the minimum educational standards, but the responsibility for meeting the standards was placed squarely on the home. If the home failed, then the institution of apprenticeship was relied upon as a means of accomplishing the desired ends. All the compulsory-educational legislation of New England had this one thing in common: If parents or masters did not teach the child to read, or to write, or the principles of religion, or a trade, as the statutes might require, the child was to be taken away from the parent or master and apprenticed to someone who would carry out the intent of the law.

This compulsory-educational legislation was clearly an extension of the poor laws of England as embodied in the statutes of 1562 and 1601. The Statute of Artificers (1562), among other things, made provision for a nation-wide system of apprenticeship. But the poor continued to increase, and in the Poor Law Act of 1601 special attention was given to the apprenticeship of poor children. In each parish, the justices of the peace were required to nominate overseers of the poor, who, together with the church wardens and certain other householders, had the duty of placing out poor children as apprentices. The main intent of the law, in this respect, was to provide for the maintenance of children rather than to insure that they be taught a trade, or otherwise be educated.[43] But in the New England colonies, and, as we shall see later, in other colonies as well, the English Poor Law was enlarged upon and extended so as to provide both vocational and academic education.

In 1642, the General Court of Massachusetts enacted a statute which

[43] Marcus Wilson Jernegan, *Laboring and Dependent Classes in Colonial America, 1607–1783* (Chicago: University of Chicago Press, 1931), p. 177.

obliged all parents and masters to see to it that the children under their care be taught a trade and the elements of reading. The selectmen of the several towns were required, under penalty of a fine, to determine whether parents and masters were teaching their children and apprentices some calling or trade and whether the children were being taught to read sufficiently well to enable them to understand "the principles of religion and the capital lawes of the country." It was also the duty of the selectmen, with the consent of any court or magistrate, to put out as apprentices the children of such as were not "able and fit to employ them and bring them up" as the law required. Of course, persons to whom children were apprenticed were required to teach them a trade and the elements of reading.

This act remained in force until 1648, when it was modified in some respects. It was still the duty of the selectmen to see to it that children and apprentices be taught to read, in order that they might be able to read "perfectly" the English tongue and thereby arrive at a knowledge of the capital laws. Children and apprentices were also to learn an orthodox catechism and be able to answer questions propounded to them in regard to it. And, finally, all parents and masters were required to "bring up their children and apprentices in some honest lawful calling, labor, or employment." Again, as in 1642, the selectmen could, with the help of two magistrates or the county court, take children and apprentices from families in case the requirements of the law were not being met and apprentice them to someone who would carry out the intent of the law. Boys were to be apprenticed until twenty-one years of age and girls until eighteen.[44]

Three distinct motives underlay these laws requiring universal education. The economic motive is very obvious. In a frontier society such as this there was great need for skilled labor, the price of labor was high, and the general tendency was for artisans to become small farmers. One sees, too, the desire to prevent the development of a numerous pauper class such as infested the parishes of England and raised the cost of poor relief. In some respects the Act of 1642 was a poor-relief measure, in that it shifted the burden of caring for poor and neglected children from the town government to the masters to whom the children were apprenticed. The religious motive is so obvious as to require little comment. It was fundamental that all children be taught to read in order that they might understand the principles of religion upon which the whole social experiment was based. And, finally, the political motive is reflected in the requirement that all be taught to read in order that they might understand the capital laws. This provision in the Act had reference to a broadside published in Cambridge in 1642 under the title "Capital Lawes."[45] This insistence that youth be able to read and acquire a knowledge of the capi-

---

44 *Ibid.*, pp. 91–92.
45 Morison, *op. cit.*, p. 63.

tal laws takes on added significance when one recalls how the state undertook to regulate so many details of the individual's life.

The Massachusetts Act of 1642, as amended in 1648, became a model for all the other New England colonies except Rhode Island. In its Code of 1650, Connecticut adopted almost verbatim the Massachusetts Act of 1648. New Haven, which was an independent colony from 1638 until its union with Connecticut in 1665, provided for a system of compulsory education in 1655.[46] The act made no reference to training for a trade, as the Massachusetts and Connecticut acts had done, but it went further than either of them in its provision for education of an academic type. The deputies of the court in each plantation, or other officers in public trust, were ordered to see to it that children and apprentices "attain at least so much as to be able duly to read the Scriptures and other good and profitable printed books in the English tongue . . . and in some competent measure to understand the main grounds and principles of Christian religion necessary to salvation."[47] Parents and masters failing to give the children under their care the required education were to be warned, and if that did not bring the desired results they were to be subject to a fine. And if the system of fines proved ineffective, the proper officers were authorized to apprentice the neglected children to someone who would carry out the intent of the law. Five years later, in 1660, the law was amended so as to require that all boys be taught to write a legible hand. By 1660, then, New Haven had developed the most comprehensive system of compulsory education to be found in New England, or, for that matter, in any other place in the world. Of course, after Connecticut absorbed the New Haven colony in 1665, the Connecticut Act of 1650 became operative throughout the enlarged colony.

Plymouth was the last of the New England colonies to adopt the policy of compulsory education. Its Act of 1671 embodied a number of the provisions of the Massachusetts acts of 1642 and 1648, together with some of the provisions of the New Haven Act of 1655. Children and apprentices were to be taught to read, to have a knowledge of the capital laws, to understand the principles of the Christian religion necessary for salvation, and to be given training in some lawful calling, labor, or employment. The deputies and selectmen were authorized to warn and fine neglectful parents and masters, and, where necessary, to take children from parents and apprentice them to masters who would carry out the requirements of the law.

With the enactment of the Plymouth law of 1671, all of New England except Rhode Island came under the operation of a compulsory-education

---

[46] Jernegan, *Laboring and Dependent Classes in Colonial America, op. cit.,* p. 95.

[47] Charles J. Hoadly (ed.), *Records of the Colony or Jurisdiction of New Haven from May, 1653, to the Union* (Hartford, 1858), pp. 583–584. Elsie W. Clews, *Educational Legislation and Administration of the Colonial Governments* (New York: The Macmillan Co., 1899), p. 79.

act. New Hampshire was a part of Massachusetts from 1641 to 1679, as was Maine from 1652 to the end of the colonial period. Rhode Island, with its emphasis upon religious and political freedom, was always the "land of the other-minded." Compulsory socialization of youth in terms of a dominant religious or political ideology was no part of its public policy.

The enforcement of compulsory-education legislation. These early compulsory-education statutes were by no means paper laws; the statutes themselves contained adequate provisions for their enforcement, and surviving town and court records indicate that a serious attempt was made to enforce them. The records disclose that, in some instances at least, parents and masters were brought into court for failure to carry out the requirements of the statutes, and sometimes, too, the selectmen of the town were indicted for neglect of duty in enforcing the compulsory-education acts. Just how well these laws were enforced it is difficult to say. In 1690, the General Court of Connecticut complained that many persons were unable to read the English language and thereby incapable of reading "the holy word of God or the good laws of the colony."[48] Of course, small, pioneer farming communities could scarcely be expected to possess the material or intellectual resources necessary to enable them to realize the high ideal of universal literacy. But that popular education was materially advanced by these early New England statutes does not appear to be open to doubt.

Declining interest in compulsory education. During the closing quarter of the seventeenth century, conditions in New England were such as to bring about a substantial modification of legislation requiring compulsory education. Soon after the opening of the eighteenth century, there was no place in New England where the law required that all children be taught to read.[49] A number of factors help to explain this change in policy. For one thing, religion was beginning to lose its dynamic force in New England life; as the second and third generations of New Englanders came on the scene, they were much less disposed to follow the leadership of the ministry than had been the case with their fathers. Then, too, in 1675 the Indian wars broke out with a severity that disrupted to a considerable extent all economic and social life. These wars accompanied, if they did not occasion, a general lowering of the old standards of behavior. The General Court of Connecticut found it necessary to legislate against some of the contemporary evils which it alleged had been produced by the Indian wars. Among the conditions to be corrected were:

> prophanation of the Sabboth; neglect of cattechiseing of children and servants, and famaly prayer; young persons shakeing of the government of

48 Jernegan, *Laboring and Dependent Classes in Colonial America, op. cit.,* p. 125.
49 *Ibid.,* p. 115.

parents or masters; boarders and inmates neglecting the worship of God in the famalyes where they reside; tipleing and drincking; uncleaness; oppression, in workemen and traders.[50]

The Indian wars and their disruptive consequences were followed by what is known as the Andros regime. From 1686 to 1689 all the New England colonies, it will be recalled, were united in one dominion under the governorship of Sir Edmund Andros. The old colonial charters were revoked and laws made for all New England by the governor and a single council. During the Andros regime all laws relating to the compulsory education of children were in effect repealed.[51] The closing years of the seventeenth century marked a decline in the zeal for compulsory education and, as we shall see in the next chapter, during the eighteenth century the policy of compulsory education for all was completely abandoned.

Compulsory Maintenance of Schools

The statutes requiring compulsory education, as was pointed out previously, contained no provisions with respect to compulsory school attendance. In fact, no mention was made in them of schools at all; the whole responsibility for the education of children was placed upon parents and masters. Whether children were taught in the home or sent to an organized school, if such a school existed, was a matter which parents and masters would have to decide for themselves. It soon became apparent, however, that schools would have to be maintained if children and youth were to receive the amount and kind of education deemed essential by the leaders of church and commonwealth.

Voluntary establishment of town schools paved the way for compulsory-school legislation. Beginning in 1635, a number of the towns in Massachusetts and in some of the other New England colonies took measures to establish schools, even though there was no law as yet which required them to do so. The town records of Boston disclose that in 1635 one Philemon Pormont was entreated to become schoolmaster in that town, and many writers have dated the founding of the Boston Latin School from the date of that invitation. It is not known, however, whether Pormont accepted the invitation or whether a school was actually opened. In fact, the records do not disclose whether the town of Boston appropriated funds for the support of any kind of school before 1643.[52] It is true that in 1636, at a meeting of the richer inhabitants of Boston, a subscription was taken for the maintenance of a "free school," but if the

[50] *Ibid.*, p. 102.   [51] *Ibid.*, p. 103.
[52] *Boston Town Records,* Second Report of the Record Commissioners of the City of Boston, 1877 (Boston: the Record Commissioners, 1877), p. 82.

school was actually opened it must have been supported for a number of years by contributions and tuition fees. The records do disclose, however, that in 1644 the town of Boston appropriated eight pounds toward the keeping of a school during the previous year, and a statement by John Winthrop under date of the fifth month, third day, 1645 (July 3, 1645 o.s.), although unsupported by any known record of an action of the General Court which he claims was taken, or any action reported in the *Town Records,* indicates a variety of possible sources without necessarily precluding tuition fees. He wrote:

> Divers free schools were erected, as . . . at Boston (where they made an order to allow forever 50 pounds to the master and a house, and 30 pounds to an usher, who should also teach to read and write and cipher, and Indians' children were to be taught freely, and the charge to be by yearly contribution, either by voluntary allowance, or by rate of such as refused, etc., and this order was confirmed by the general court ——). Other towns did the like providing maintenance by several means.[53]

Winthrop was probably referring to an earlier action and the school referred to was probably the Boston Latin School (but, it may be pointed out in passing, the origin of the Boston Latin School is shrouded in uncertainty despite the many positive assertions that it was established in 1635 by the action of the town meeting).

By 1647, as Professor Marcus Wilson Jernegan has shown, eleven of the sixty towns in New England had "voluntarily established, managed, and supported town schools."[54] The methods adopted to support these schools were many and varied. In some instances, land belonging to the town was set aside as an endowment, as in Boston and Dedham; or land belonging to private individuals was donated, as in Dorchester; or taxes were levied on all property-holders, as in Charlestown. In most places those able to pay were charged tuition.

The voluntary action of these towns was paving the way for a new educational policy, namely, that of compulsory maintenance of schools on the part of all towns of a certain size. The same general motives which prompted the enactment of compulsory-education legislation also prompted the passage of laws requiring the maintenance of schools.

Legislative provisions for compulsory town schools. In carrying the policy of compulsory schools into operation, Massachusetts again took the initiative. In 1647, the General Court passed an act which was the basis of the public school system of Massachusetts for many years and which was influential in the establishment of the public school systems of other

---

[53] James Savage (ed.), John Winthrop, *The History of New England from 1630 to 1649* (Boston: Little, Brown and Co., 1853), I, p. 264.
[54] Jernegan, *Laboring and Dependent Classes in America, op. cit.,* p. 82.

New England colonies as well. As previously indicated, some have seen in this statute the beginning of the American free public school system; others see in it only an attempt to impose the Puritan faith on the upcoming generation.

After setting forth in the preamble the religious motive for requiring the establishment of schools, the act required that towns of fifty householders should provide for instruction in reading and writing and went on to indicate possible ways and means of financing the venture. The act further required that all towns of one hundred families or householders should set up a grammar school to prepare youth for Harvard College. Neglect or refusal to obey the law was punishable by a fine of five pounds. This act is of such importance that we quote it in full (with the spelling modernized).

It being one chief object of that old deluder, Satan, to keep men from the knowledge of the Scriptures, as in former times by keeping them in an unknown tongue, so in these latter times by persuading from the use of tongues, that so at least the true sense and meaning of the original might be clouded by false glosses of saint-seeming deceivers, that learning may not be buried in the grave of our fathers in the Church and Commonwealth, the Lord assisting our endeavors,

It is therefore ordered, That every township in this jurisdiction, after the Lord hath increased them to the number of fifty householders, shall then forthwith appoint one within their town to teach all such children as shall resort to him to write and read, whose wages shall be paid either by the parents or masters of such children, or by the inhabitants in general, by way of supply, as the major part of those that order the prudentials of the town shall appoint: *Provided,* Those that send their children be not oppressed by paying much more than they can have them taught for in other towns; and

It is further ordered, That where any town shall increase to the number of one hundred families or householders, they shall set up a grammar school, the master thereof being able to instruct youth so far as they may be fitted for the university: *Provided,* That if any town neglect the performance hereof above one year, that every such town shall pay five pounds to the next school till they shall perform this order.[55]

This act, with some modifications, remained in force during the rest of the seventeenth century. In 1671, the fine was increased to ten pounds and later (1683) to twenty pounds in the case of towns of two hundred families. The act was so amended in 1683 as to require all towns of five hundred families to maintain two reading and writing schools and two

[55] As quoted in Knight, *op. cit.,* p. 105. For text with contemporary spelling and punctuation, see *Records of the Governor and Company of the Massachusetts Bay in New England,* II, p. 203; also Ellwood P. Cubberley, *Readings in Public Education in the United States* (Boston: Houghton Mifflin Company, 1934), pp. 18–19.

Latin grammar schools. After Massachusetts became a royal province, the law was re-enacted with some modifications. Towns of fifty families must now be constantly provided with a schoolmaster to teach children to read and write and every town of one hundred families was required to set up a grammar school and procure for it "a discreet person of good conversation and well instructed in the tongues."

The Massachusetts Act of 1647 became the basis of legislation in other New England colonies. Connecticut adopted it practically verbatim in 1650. New Haven passed no act requiring towns to establish schools, but when it was annexed to Connecticut in 1665 the Connecticut Act became operative there. Soon after the two colonies were united, the law was changed so as to require only one grammar school in each of the four counties. In 1677, the General Court complained that the law in regard to the maintenance of Latin grammar schools was not being obeyed and the fine was increased to ten pounds. The following year the law was also made stricter with respect to reading and writing schools. Now all towns of thirty families were required to keep a reading and writing school. After the overthrow of the Andros regime, to which attention has been called, only two towns in Connecticut, Hartford and New Haven, were required to maintain Latin schools.

Partly, perhaps, because among its leaders there were fewer university graduates and, perhaps, because schools were less essential to the achievement of the aims of its founders than was the case in Massachusetts and Connecticut, Plymouth was somewhat slow in getting its program of public education under way. As early as 1658, the General Court recommended to the towns that they consider securing schoolmasters to teach children to read and write. In 1673, the General Court set aside thirty-three pounds annually from the profits arising from the Cape Cod fisheries for the maintenance of a grammar school. Later, in 1677, all towns of fifty families or more which maintained a grammar school were to receive from five to ten pounds from the proceeds of the fisheries, and all towns of seventy families which did not maintain a grammar school were required to pay five pounds annually to the next town that did maintain one.[56] After Plymouth was incorporated into Massachusetts in 1691, the Massachusetts laws, of course, governed the enlarged colony.

Maine, New Hampshire, and Vermont were part of Massachusetts and subject to its laws relating to compulsory schools. New Hampshire became an independent colony in 1679, but it failed for a number of years to place on its statute books any requirements for the maintenance of schools. There is some uncertain evidence, however, that an act was passed in 1693 requiring all towns (Dover excepted) to provide a schoolmaster

[56] David Pulsifer (ed.), *Records of the Colony of New Plymouth in New England* (Boston: Press of William White, 1861), pp. 246–247.

under a penalty of ten pounds fine.[57] As we have already seen, Rhode
Island refused to pass any legislation establishing compulsory education.
Similarly, it never required any of its towns to establish and maintain
schools. This is not to be taken to mean, however, that Rhode Island
lacked institutionalized education.

Motives for the enactment of compulsory-school legislation. The body
of legislation requiring the maintenance of schools enacted by the New
England colonies during the seventeenth century was indeed remarkable.
Nowhere else in the English-speaking world, and perhaps in no other
place at all, had the state or any other social agency taken such vigorous
measures to provide schools for the education of children and youth. The
reason for the enactment of these laws has sometimes been found in the
intense religious zeal of the early New England leaders, in the desire to
bring education to serve institutionalized religion. Such a generalization is too facile, the explanation too simple. It is no doubt true that the
religious motive was stronger than any other, but the spirit of humanism
was also present. Certainly, there was some appreciation of "good literature" for its own sake, some regard for the humanizing and liberalizing
influence of the great writers of classical antiquity. As the General Court
of Plymouth expressed it in 1677, in the preamble to the law providing
funds to towns maintaining grammar schools, "the Maintenance of good
litterature doth much tend to the advancement of the weale and flourishing estate of societies and Republiques."[58] Finally, the fact must not be
overlooked, and this is of great importance, that the founders of New
England had a planned society in mind; the social design was worked out
in detail. This design included not alone the establishment of the true
church; it included also the relation of church and state, the location of
religious and political authority, and the orderly arrangement of social
classes. The leaders knew well the essential elements in the cultural pattern they were trying to establish, and they hoped to give these elements a
permanency and a stability. Life in nearly all of its aspects was to be
lived according to an ordered pattern; practically every stimulus was to
have its definite and known response. Not only was one to know the kind
of behavior expected of him; one was enveloped by a multitude of legal
sanctions aimed to enforce obedience. Under such circumstances it was
highly important that all be able to read the "capital lawes." It is to the
credit of New England leaders that they had the acumen to discern that
institutionalized education is an important instrument for inducting the
individual into his culture. Also, it was important to the future develop-

[57] This statute seems not to have been published in the laws and there is some
doubt that it was ever passed.
[58] Pulsifer, *op. cit.,* p. 246.

ment of public education in America that New England leadership utilized the civil state as a means of establishing and maintaining schools.

The enforcement of the law.   It seems clear that educational policy in seventeenth-century New England was formulated by a small group of educated leaders, most of whom were numbered among the clergy; it is not at all clear how well they succeeded in getting the masses to obey the laws they were able to put on the statute books. On this point historians have sharply disagreed. Some hold that the laws requiring the maintenance of schools were more honored in the breach than in the observance, while others hold that they were reasonably well enforced. As a matter of fact, sufficient documentary evidence, in the form of town and court records, does not exist to give one anything like an adequate picture of the operation of these laws. We do know, however, that enforcement, especially of the provisions relating to the maintenance of Latin grammar schools, was often inadequate. It is equally true that these laws were by no means dead letters. From the fragmentary town and court records, it is clear that many of the New England towns before 1700 undertook seriously to maintain schools; it is clear, too, that some were negligent of the matter and that some even exhibited great cleverness in evading the law.

The town records disclose that Boston began appropriating funds for the support of a school as early as 1644. This was probably a Latin grammar school from the beginning, and, so far as the town records disclose, it was the only school in Boston receiving public support until the opening of a writing school in 1684. It is not clear how the town of Boston met the legal requirement under the law of 1647 to maintain a school to teach children to read and write. Charlestown opened a school in 1636, agreeing with Mr. William Witherell to keep the school for twelve months at a salary of forty pounds.[59] In 1661, the famous Ezekiel Cheever was the master in Charlestown, which would seem to indicate that the school being kept was a Latin school. Ten years later, in the contract with Benjamin Thompson, it was agreed that he should "prepare such youth as are capable of it for the college."[60] In a town meeting in Cambridge in 1648, it was agreed that some of the town common land should be sold "for the gratifying of Mr. Corlett for his pains in keeping a school in the town . . . provided it shall not prejudice the cow common."[61]

Many other examples of town action in establishing schools might be cited. But not all the towns were obeying the law. The court records

[59] *Charlestown Archives,* Vol. XX; MS *Town Records,* 1629–64, II, ii, as adapted from Jernegan, *Laboring and Dependent Classes in Colonial America, op. cit.,* p. 73.
[60] Walter Herbert Small, *Early New England Schools* (Boston: Ginn & Company, 1914), p. 4.
[61] *Ibid.,* pp. 5–6.

of Essex County show that during a period of forty-four years six towns were indicted for failure to obey the law, although only one was actually fined. One of these six towns, Haverhill, was presented on three different occasions.[62] Failure to keep the statutory schools seems to have become more common during the last thirty years of the century. Writing in 1672, Thomas Shepard, a minister in Charlestown, said: "There is a great decay in Inferiour Schools; it were well if that also were examined, and the Cause thereof removed, and the Foundations laid for Free-Schools [Latin grammar], where poor Scholars might be there educated by some Publick Stock."[63] In 1689, Cotton Mather complained of the "too general Want of Education in the Rising Generation."[64] In 1667, the General Court of Connecticut raised the fine for failure to keep a Latin school from five to ten pounds, giving as its reason the neglect in some places to obey the law. And in Massachusetts, just after the turn of the century, in 1701, the General Court complained that many towns were neglecting to enforce the compulsory-school law.[65]

The evidence indicates that the Latin grammar schools received less popular support than the reading and writing schools. Professor Samuel Eliot Morison, of Harvard University, after a careful examination of the records, concludes that eleven towns in New England had Latin schools of one kind or another for an appreciable length of time during the seventeenth century.[66] Small, on the basis of town records, drew up a list of twenty-seven towns in which grammar schools were kept for a shorter or longer period of time. He makes the following significant generalizations about the Latin school of the seventeenth century:

> This list shows that in two generations as many as twenty-seven grammar schools were begun, and possibly seven others; and one was attempted but lacked popular support. At this time there were eighty-one towns in Massachusetts. It is unfortunate that the population of these towns cannot be ascertained, to enable us to know how fully they conformed to the law. The 1765 census in Massachusetts showed one hundred eighty-four towns, of which only eighty-one had over a thousand inhabitants. From this it might be inferred that the proportion of towns having grammar schools in 1700 was as large as it should have been; that, in fact, nearly all towns had complied with the law. Another view, however, is obtained from a list of polls given in by twenty towns in Middlesex county (Massachusetts) in 1708. Nine of the twenty showed more than one hundred families, but only five had attempted a grammar school, and but

---

[62] Morison, *op. cit.*, p. 69.

[63] *Eye-Salve* (Cambridge, 1673), quoted in Sibley, *Harvard Graduates*, I, 330; see Morison, *op. cit.*, p. 72.

[64] *The Way to Prosperity* (Boston, 1690), pp. 33–34, as quoted in Morison, *op. cit.*, p. 72.

[65] Morison, *op. cit.*, p. 73.   [66] *Ibid.*, pp. 96–97.

four had succeeded in its establishment. The list of Harvard graduates
from 1644 to 1700 shows that some towns credited with grammar schools
did not send a single student to the college, while other towns, for instance, Salisbury, Plymouth in 1646, Dedham, Ipswich, and Concord,
even before their schools were established, sent students, evidently prepared by the ministers of the towns. The great body of the college students came from the well-established and continuous schools at Boston,
Cambridge, Roxbury, and Charlestown. When all obtainable light has
been shed upon the subject but one conclusion can be reached: the grammar school was not a popular institution; it was conceived, supported,
and perpetuated by the few; its extension was slow; its course in most
towns was erratic; and yet, considering all the struggles of this period, it
was a marvelous institution, the bed rock of future educational systems.[67]

Schools and the Content of Instruction

The schools of early New England — the dame school, the writing
school, the Latin grammar school, and the college — were all definitely
imitations of the schools of England.

The dame school. It had long been the custom in England for some
woman in the community to gather a few children into her home and to
teach them, for a small fee, their ABC's and the rudiments of reading
while she carried on the routine work of the household. The dame school,
as this type of school was called, was early transplanted to New England.
Since dame schools were, as a rule, private ventures, not required by law
or supported by public funds, the records of their existence are very incomplete. There is reason to believe, however, that they were relatively
numerous in the seventeenth century. Since the Latin grammar schools
and even the town reading and writing schools usually required that pupils
entering them be able to read at least simple English, many children must
have begun their education in a dame school. In most New England
communities the dame school was supported by the small tuition fees
paid by the children's parents, but in some instances it was supported
partially or wholly by public funds. It may seem strange today that the
town schools proper were not open to beginning pupils, that the responsibility for the initial stage of the child's education should have been
placed on the home. But, after all, education in New England was primarily a family responsibility. As we have already seen, the whole body
of compulsory-education legislation was framed without reference to
schools or schooling; parents were left to their own devices to meet the
requirements of the law. And when town schools were established to
which children might be sent, the home was not relieved of the whole of
its responsibility. The dame school, kept by some woman in her home to

[67] Small, *op. cit.*, pp. 30–31.

teach the children of the community, and perhaps her own children as well, represented the first step in the development of a system of institutionalized education.

The curriculum of the dame school was a simple matter. Pupils were taught their ABC's, a little spelling, the rudiments of reading, and moral and religous precepts. Girls were frequently taught sewing and knitting and the making of samplers. An occasional dame might undertake to teach her wards a little writing and counting, but as a rule these were activities to be carried on in more advanced types of schools. Both boys and girls could attend the dame school, and the boys, after having learned to read words of two or three syllables, could go on to the town reading and writing school or the Latin school. But for girls the dame school marked the end of formal education, unless, perchance, some member of the family or a private tutor carried them further along the road of learning.

The public elementary school. The writing school was a second type of educational institution brought over by the colonists. It gave special attention to writing and arithmetic, although instruction in reading was frequently provided for boys who needed it. The teaching of writing and arithmetic required special ability; it also required special equipment, such as pens, paper, and ink. It was, perhaps, due to these special requirements that the writing school had developed as an institution separate from the reading school. In this country, however, the tendency was for the town vernacular elementary school to give instruction in all three subjects — reading, writing, and arithmetic, although the teaching of arithmetic in the seventeenth century was not particularly common outside commercial centers. The law requiring towns to maintain schools at the lower levels usually required that provision be made for teaching children to read and write. Although children were supposed to have made some progress in reading before entering the town school, and in some instances were excluded if they had not done so, instruction in reading and writing was commonly provided in the town elementary school, regardless of its name. In Boston, for example, there were only two types of public schools, the Latin school and the writing school. But in 1684, when the first writing school was opened, the master was appointed to teach children to read and write.[68] Although the separate writing school was not unknown and in some instances writing and arithmetic were taught by a special "scrivener" who moved about from place to place, the writing school never became very popular. Sometimes, as in Boston, the town elementary school was known as the writing school, but it afforded instruction in reading as well as in writing and arithmetic. In common practice, the private, or semipublic, dame school initiated the child into the mysteries of reading, and

[68] Robert Francis Seybolt, *The Public Schools of Colonial Boston, 1635–1775* (Cambridge, Mass.: Harvard University Press, 1935), p. 5.

when the pupil went on to the public town school, he continued his reading and took up writing and perhaps arithmetic also. Thus, the typical American elementary school of the three R's gradually took form.

The Latin grammar school. The classical tradition was one of the most powerful influences on the development of education in New England. The Puritans were the children of the Reformation; they were also the heirs of the Renaissance, more so than they themselves suspected. The secondary schools of sixteenth-century England, on the model of which the Latin grammar schools of New England were constructed, were in large measure the product of two great movements; from the Reformation they drew their religious purpose and from the Renaissance their classical content. In the Latin schools of England, the scholars studied little but Latin and Greek for seven years or so. The ideal was to teach boys to read, write, and speak Latin as a living language and to ground them in the rudiments of Greek. Some attention, of course, was given to religious instruction, but none to mathematics, science, history, or modern languages. For seven years the youthful scholars struggled with the intricacies of Latin grammar or the reading of such classic Latin authors as Cicero, Terence, Caesar, Livy, Vergil, and Horace. After a grounding in Greek grammar, they took up the study of Isocrates, Hesiod, or Homer.[69]

A striking fact about education in colonial New England was the closeness with which the curriculum followed that of the mother country, and of no institution does this seem to have been more true than of the Latin grammar school. It is true that we have no exact account of the curriculum of any of the Latin schools of seventeenth-century New England,[70] but from the entrance requirements of Harvard College and from the curriculum of the Boston Latin School in 1712, it seems reasonable to suppose that the English model was followed very closely. The Latin schools, it will be remembered, were designed to prepare pupils for entrance to Harvard and the entrance requirements of the college in 1642 are probably a reliable index of the content of the Latin-school curriculum at that time and for some years to come. The entrance requirements were as follows:

> When any Schollar is able to understand *Tully,* or such like classicall Latine Author *extempore,* and make and speak true Latine in Verse and Prose, *suo ut aiunt Marte;* And decline perfectly the Paradigim's of *Nounes* and *Verbes* in the *Greek* tongue: Let him then and not before be capable of admission into the Colledge.[71]

[69] Morison, *op. cit.,* p. 84. [70] *Ibid.,* p. 101.
[71] *New England's First Fruits* (London, 1643), *Mass. Hist. Col.,* 1792, I, pp. 242–246, as quoted in Cubberley, *Readings in Public Education in the United States, op. cit.,* p. 292.

We have also an exact account of the program of instruction in the Boston Latin School in the year 1712. There is evidence that the curriculum had been in effect under Ezekiel Cheever, master of the school for many years preceding his death in 1708. Morison describes and comments on the curriculum of the Boston Latin School as follows:

> The three first years were spent in learning by heart an "Accidence" or Beginning Latin Book, together with the *Nomenclator,* a Latin-English phrasebook and vocabulary called *Sententiae Pueriles,* and for construing and parsing the *Distichia* attributed to Dionysius Cato, a collection of maxims popular since the early Christian era. Corderius's Colloquies and Aesop's Fables were also read, in Latin. The fourth year began Erasmus's Colloquies, continued Aesop, studied Latin Grammar, and read Ovid *de Tristibus.* The fifth continued Erasmus and Ovid, including the *Metamorphoses,* and began Cicero's *Epistolae,* Latin prosody, and Latin composition with Garretson's "English Exercises for School-Boys to Translate." The sixth year began Cicero *de Officiis,* Lucius Florus, the Aeneid, and Thomas Godwyn's excellent English treatise on Roman history and antiquities, which had been used at the University of Cambridge in John Harvard's day; they continued the *Metamorphoses,* made Latin verse, dialogues, and letters, and began Greek and Rhetoric. The seventh and last year, boys of fourteen to sixteen began Cicero's Orations, Justin, Virgil, Horace, Juvenal, and Persius, made Latin dialogues, and turned 'a Psalm or something Divine' into Latin verse, with a Latin theme every fortnight. In Greek, they read Homer, Isocrates, Hesiod, and the New Testament. And from Cotton Mather's statements, it seems probable that infant prodigies like himself (who finished school at the age of eleven) began Hebrew as well.[72]

The Boston Latin School, however, can scarcely be regarded as typical of the Latin schools of the seventeenth century. A few towns, like Boston, had a separate Latin school with a more or less permanent master devoting practically all of his time to the teaching of Latin and Greek. In schools of this kind, the master might have an assistant to teach the younger pupils Latin grammar as well as English and writing. But many Latin schools, so-called, were not separate from the school which gave instruction to younger children in reading, writing, and arithmetic.

Frequently, the Latin-school master devoted most of his time to the teaching of reading, writing, and arithmetic and gave the remainder of his time to the preparation of a few boys for entrance to Harvard. The law requiring towns to keep a Latin school was usually regarded as having been met if a town could show that it employed a master who was qualified to teach Latin and who taught it to such boys as resorted to him. If no pupils desiring instruction in Latin turned up, that was no fault of the town; the master could then devote his time to the teaching of other sub-

[72] Morison, *op. cit.,* pp. 102–103.

jects. Nor is this merely a hypothetical situation; instances could be cited of masters who held themselves in readiness to teach Latin to the youth of the town, but no youth appeared for instruction. The law of 1647 in Massachusetts, requiring the larger towns to maintain a Latin school, really meant that the towns falling in this class would have to employ a college graduate to teach the town school; it did not mean that the town would have to support a separate grammar school. Apparently, in many towns the requirements of the law were met by a single master who taught the three R's to the masses of the children in the town and Latin to the few boys who were preparing for entrance to Harvard College.[73]

The college.   Since the social order which the founders of New England were building was buttressed by the church, provision for the appropriate education of ministers was of great importance. Among those who came over from England during the early years of the Puritan migration were many ministers who held their degrees from English universities. It soon began to appear, however, that New England must take measures to educate its own ministers.

In 1636, the General Court, or colonial legislature, of Massachusetts appropriated four hundred pounds for the establishment of a college. Soon thereafter the authorities of the Bay Colony were faced with the thorny problem of dealing with Mistress Anne Hutchinson and her heretical followers. Mistress Hutchinson and her fellow Antinomians placed their faith in revealed truth and were, therefore, opposed to the higher learning. But once this revolt against orthodoxy was suppressed, Mistress Hutchinson banished, and, incidentally, a severe blow dealt to freedom of thought, it was possible to go forward with the work of establishing the college. In the summer of 1638 the first freshman class took up its studies in a dwelling-house which had been purchased by the Board of Overseers for the use of the college.[74] A few months later, John Harvard bequeathed to the college half of his estate — the total being somewhat less than eight hundred pounds — and the whole of his library of some four hundred volumes. The name of the college was now changed in recognition of its benefactor.

The founders of the little college had to face many problems before they were able to establish it on a firm foundation. They found it necessary or expedient to dismiss the first two heads of the institution, for reasons we cannot go into here. The funds which had been appropriated by the General Court and which were derived from Harvard's bequest were used to erect a college building.[75] The college did not receive very much support from public funds, although after 1654 the General Court did pay the president's annual salary of some one hundred or one hundred and

[73] *Ibid.,* p. 89.   [74] *Ibid.,* p. 27.
[75] *Ibid.,* p. 35.

fifty pounds. But the people of New England rallied to the support of the college, some giving it farm produce, some bales of cloth, and some small grants of money. Even so, around 1650 the total college income, including tuition fees, was no more than two hundred and fifty pounds annually.[76] Meager funds meant that the college could employ only three or four young tutors, who were constantly being drawn off into the ministry by the offer of better salaries. It was not possible to maintain a permanent teaching force until the last two decades of the century.[77]

The number of students attending Harvard in the seventeenth century was relatively small. Not many parents were able to provide the fifty to seventy-five pounds necessary to see a boy through a college course.[78] Moreover, the college was not regarded as a popular institution; its function was to train a few leaders for service in church and commonwealth. The total number of students who had studied at Harvard before the year 1700 amounted to fewer than six hundred; the total number of graduates during the seventeenth century was four hundred and sixty-five.[79]

The main purpose in establishing and maintaining Harvard College was to provide the churches with a learned ministry — ministers both learned and loyal to the core values of the Puritan commonwealth. On a gate in the Harvard Yard is now engraved the opening statement of *New England's First Fruits,* the first commencement program of the college, published in 1643. It reads:

> After God had carried us safe to *New England,* and wee had builded our houses, provided necessaries for our livli-hood, rear'd convenient places for Gods worship, and setled the Civill Government: One of the next things we longed for, and looked after was to advance *Learning* and perpetuate it to Posterity; dreading to leave an illiterate Ministery to the Churches, when our present Ministers shall lie in the Dust.[80]

In reading this first account of Harvard College, it is easy to underline the dread of an illiterate ministry and to conclude that the chief, if not the sole, function of the college was the training of ministers. It is equally easy to underline the advancement of learning and the perpetuation of learning to posterity and thus see in this statement a kind of "charter for academic liberalism." Neither interpretation would be wholly correct.

It would be a grievous error to hold that Harvard College in the early days was merely a theological seminary designed to teach ministerial students the principles of the Puritan faith. Nor can one accept without

[76] *Ibid.,* p. 36.
[77] *Ibid.,* p. 38.
[78] *Ibid.,* p. 33.
[79] *Ibid.,* p. 54.
[80] As quoted in Perry Miller, *The New England Mind: The Seventeenth Century* (New York: The Macmillan Co., 1939), p. 75. Permission Harvard University Press. Also published in paperback (Boston: Beacon Press, 1961).

some qualification the statement of Morison that "the purpose of the first New England college was higher education in the broadest sense, not a specialized training in Protestant theology."[81] As Perry Miller points out, Puritanism was a piety, but "it was at the same time an intellectual system, highly elaborated and meticulously worked out."[82] As a piety, Puritanism was solidly based on the belief that the highest truth was revealed in clear and unmistakable terms in God's Word. The seeker after the truth would not find it by the exercise of "carnal reason," nor by the study of heathen poets or medieval philosophers. The key that unlocked the doors of truth was revelation, not reason. Justification by faith and reliance on revelation might well lead to the repudiation of the intellectual inheritance. In fact, the left wing of the Puritan movement did just that. Led by such men as Dale and Webster in England and by Mistress Anne Hutchinson in New England, the Antinomians opposed university training for the clergy, and as Perry Miller points out:

> Unsophisticated laymen could never understand, after they had been taught that the natural mind was abysmally incompetent and that God had uttered the truth in clear and simple dicta, why they should still need ministers skilled in the sciences, in rhetoric, logic, and physics, in order to hear and comprehend the explicit word of God. They argued with a naïve plausibility that since regeneration infused God's own substance into the elect, then a regenerated man thereafter required no other mentor than the Holy Ghost, no other instruction than its ever-present promptings. "For it is *only* the *Inspiration of God,* that inables a man to know the *things of God,* and not a mans *study* or *Humane Learning* . . . No man can know *Christ* and His *Gospel* . . . but by the most *present Teaching* and *Revelation* of God himself by his *Spirit.*" From the time of the Anabaptists at Münster, Protestant theologians strove with might and main to keep justification by faith from becoming a justification of illiteracy.[83]

However, the men who were responsible for the social design in New England were not of a mind to pay attention to the left-wing radicals of the Puritan movement, to those who would make of it little more than a piety. Opposition to an educated clergy meant two things. It represented an attack on the well-ordered ranks of society, the undermining of the prestige, place, and position of the holders of university degrees. More than that, it represented a repudiation of that body of knowledge and learning of which the ministry had long been the especial custodians. Despite the protests of the Antinomians or the misgivings of the unsophisticated who might place reliance on revelation, the more responsible New England leaders were determined to provide for an educated ministry; they would not permit the control of their theocratic state to fall into

[81] Morison, *op. cit.,* p. 30.   [82] Miller, *op. cit.,* p. 67.
[83] *Ibid.,* p. 73.

the hands of the unlettered; and they would not suffer their class interests to be jeopardized. As a speaker at a Harvard commencement once put it, without the college "the ruling class would have been subjected to mechanics, cobblers, and tailors; the gentry would have been overwhelmed by lewd fellows of the baser sort, the sewage of Rome, the dregs of an illiterate plebs which judgeth much from emotion, little from truth."[84] Moreover, men are never, it seems, entirely satisfied with the passive acceptance of revealed truth — with dicta and authority. They may accept it, as did the New England leaders, but they seek to find the reasons for it; they try to put a rational underpinning beneath the superstructure of dogma. In New England this was no less true than it had been with the Schoolmen of the Middle Ages.

Harvard College, then, was designed and founded by men whose chief concern was the education of the ministry; but the program was broadly conceived — perhaps as broadly conceived as the programs of either Oxford or Cambridge. Authorities differ with respect to the proportion of Harvard graduates who entered the ministry, the estimate for the seventeenth century ranging from fewer than half to a large majority.[85] The undergraduate program did include a large measure of theology, but all professions, whether the ministry, the law, or statecraft, required a thorough grounding in theology as well as in arts. At Harvard, as at Cambridge, the intellectual fare of the undergraduate consisted of the liberal arts — grammar, logic, rhetoric, arithmetic, geometry, and astronomy; ethics, metaphysics, and natural science; and Hebrew, Greek, and ancient history. Many of the Latin authors had been read in the grammar school and Latin was the language of instruction in the classroom. Of course, considerable time was given to the study of the Bible and to Protestant theology.[86]

In devising a curriculum for the college, elements were drawn from classical antiquity, from the Middle Ages, and from the Renaissance and the Reformation. In short, the Puritans adapted to their purposes the intellectual inheritance of the race, rejecting only those portions which did not support or conform to their religious views. "They were first and foremost heirs of Augustine, but also they were among the heirs of Thomas Aquinas and the pupils of Erasmus."[87]

THE SUPPORT OF SCHOOLS

The early legislation in New England specifying compulsory education placed the cost of this endeavor entirely upon the family — on parents

[84] *Ibid.*, p. 84.

[85] Morison, *op. cit.*, p. 39; Bailey B. Burritt, *Professional Distribution of College and University Graduates*, U.S. Bureau of Education Bulletin No. 19, 1912 (Washington, D.C.: Government Printing Office, 1912); Samuel E. Morison, *The Founding of Harvard College* (Cambridge, Mass.: Harvard University Press, 1935), pp. 247–248.

[86] Morison, *op. cit.*, pp. 39–40.   [87] Miller, *op. cit.*, p. 66.

or masters of apprentices. Neither the state nor any of its political sub-divisions assumed any part of the responsibility of providing means for the support of the program. But when it became apparent that schools were necessary to supplement or to take the place of the home in providing educational opportunities, legislation was enacted which authorized the local communities to support their schools by taxation, or such other means as might be deemed satisfactory. In some instances, indeed, provision was made for colony-wide taxes as a source of school revenue.

The Massachusetts Act of 1647 placed on the several towns the responsibility for seeing that schools were kept, but each town was left free to decide for itself the method of school support it would adopt. The schoolmaster's salary was to be paid "either by parents or masters of such children, or by the inhabitants in general, by way of supply, as the major part of those that order the prudentials of the town shall appoint."[88] Thus, the selectmen of the town were empowered to support the schools by taxation or by tuition fees, or, if they deemed it advisable, to rely upon a combination of the two.

Connecticut, in its Code of 1650, copied verbatim the provisions of the Massachusetts Act of 1647 relating to methods of school support. Nearly a quarter of a century later, in 1672, Connecticut modified its requirements with respect to the maintenance of Latin grammar schools. Henceforth, only the four county towns of Hartford, New London, New Haven, and Fairfield were required to keep a school of this type. Each of these county towns was granted six hundred acres of land to be used for the benefit of the Latin school to be maintained in it.[89] A few years later, in 1677, the broadest kind of discretion was bestowed on the towns with respect to the manner of school support. It was ordered by the General Court that, "where schools are to be kept in any town, whether it be the county town or other, what shall be necessary to the maintaining the charge of such schools, it shall be raised upon the inhabitants by way of rate, except any town shall agree upon some other way to raise the maintenance of him they shall employ in the aforesaid work. . . ."[90] Later legislation in Connecticut continued the policy of bestowing on the officials of the town a broad discretion in the matter of ways and means of school support. In New Hampshire, after it became a royal province, the selectmen were given ample authority to support the town schools by taxation.

The town records reveal that relatively few schools in the seventeenth century were open to pupils free of tuition. The two most common sources of school revenue were tuition fees and town taxes. Frequently, a town would set aside certain public lands for the benefit of the

[88] As quoted in Small, *op. cit.*, p. 188.   [89] Clews, *op. cit.*, pp. 92–93.
[90] James Hammond Trumbull and Charles J. Hoadly (eds.), *The Public Records of the Colony of Connecticut*, II (Hartford: 1850–90), pp. 307–308.

school, and many public-spirited individuals made donations or left legacies for the maintenance of schools. In some instances, as in Boston, the schools were supported almost entirely at public cost. In other places, the town would agree to pay the schoolmaster a fixed sum and allow him to supplement it as best he could by charging specified tuition fees. Again, it might be agreed that the master should charge certain tuition fees, the town to make up the difference between the amount thus raised and the sum agreed upon in the contract. In some instances, a tuition fee was charged of all boys of a certain age, whether they attended school or not. A fairly typical arrangement was that of Northampton in 1687: "The town agreed to pay in general by way of rate the above named sum of £40, that is so much of it as the scholars, readers at 3d. per week and writers at 4d. per week, did lack of amounting to the above said sum. . . ."[91] Watertown, in 1667, agreed to pay the schoolmaster a specified sum, less the amount that might be derived from tuition fees charged pupils living outside the town. Pupils living in the town could attend free of charge.[92] Lynn, in 1702, guaranteed the schoolmaster ten pounds to be paid by the town. Over and above this he was to have what would be derived from tuition fees, "2d. per week for such as are sent to read, 3d. per week for them that are sent to write and cypher, and 6d. per week for them that are sent to learn Latin, to be paid by parents and masters."[93] The following interesting arrangement was made for the support of its school by Dedham in 1685:

1   that the one half of the Schoole charges as well for quality as quantity Shall be raised upon the ratable Estate of our inhabitants whether nearer the school or further of.

2   that all such persons as dwell within one mile an A quarter from the School haveing male children Shall pay for each Such child five Shillings A year from six years old to twelve years old.

3   that those that dwell within two miles and A half of the Schoole, and beyond the mile and quarter Shall pay two Shillings Six pence A year for their male children from Seaven years old to twelve years old.

4   that gramer Scholors Shall be rated and pay to the Schoole five Shillings pr head mor then English Scholers that dwell within A mile and a quarter of the Schoole.

5   that those inhabitants that dwell mor than two miles and A half from the Schoole Shall be freed from all charges by rates upon their childrens heads for the Schools until they Shall receive benifit thereby, and then Shall be rated and pay as those within A mile and quarter: all wayes prouided that such childrin be taken care of, so that they shall be Sufitiantly taught to read and wright.

6   that the one halfe of the Schoole charge Shall be raised upon the

heads of the children according to those rules of proportion mentioned above.[94]

It was a common practice to remit the tuition fees of pupils whose parents were too poor to pay. Thus, in Brookline in 1687, the master's salary was to be paid in part by tuition fees "laid equaly on the scholars heads save any persons that are poor to be abated wholly or in part."[95] And in Braintree, in 1702, it was provided "that any poor persons in this Town who shall send any children to sd school & find themselves unable to pay upon application to the Select men it shall be in their power to remit a part or ye whole of ye sum."[96]

That many New England towns were taxing themselves to provide a substantial part of the cost of maintaining schools is clear from the record; it is equally clear that the picture, so often drawn, of every town with its school free and open to all is without foundation in fact. It must be said, however, that the poor child was seldom, if ever, turned away from the school because of the inability of his parents to pay the required tuition rates.

Questions and Problems for Study and Discussion

1. Indicate in some detail the kind of society the Puritans desired to establish in America.
2. How did the educational system established by the New England Puritans differ from the educational system with which they had been familiar in England?
3. How did the educational ideals and practices of the early settlers in New England resemble those found in England?
4. What objectives did the Puritans have in mind in the establishment of Harvard College? Account for the fact that the College was established only a few years after their arrival.
5. What was the relation of the elementary school to the Latin grammar school in early New England?
6. It has been said that the educational policy and practice in the early New England colonies laid the foundations upon which our later educational system was built. Evaluate this statement.
7. Formulate a brief statement summarizing the essential elements in the educational policy of seventeenth-century New England. How and why did educational policy in New England differ from educational policy in England?

[94] *Dedham Records*, V, 164, as quoted in George Leroy Jackson, *The Development of School Support in Colonial Massachusetts* (New York: Teachers College, Columbia University, 1909), pp. 45–46.
[95] As quoted in Jackson, *op. cit.*, p. 31.   [96] *Ibid.*, pp. 31–32.

Selected References for Further Reading

Adams, James Truslow. *The History of New England,* I: *The Founding of New England.* Boston: Little Brown & Co., 1921. Pp. xii + 482.

Bailey, Thomas A. *The American Pageant: A History of the Republic,* Second Edition. Boston: D. C. Heath & Company, 1961. Pp. xix + 1037.

Baxter, William Threipand. *The House of Hancock: Business in Boston, 1724–1775.* Cambridge, Mass.: Harvard University Press, 1945. Pp. xxvii + 321.

Beard, Charles A., and Beard, Mary R. *The Rise of American Civilization,* I: *The Agricultural Era.* New York: The Macmillan Co., 1927. Pp. viii + 824.

Boorstin, Daniel J. *The Americans: The Colonial Experience.* New York: Random House, 1958. Pp. xii + 434.

Butts, R. Freeman. *The American Tradition in Religion and Education.* Boston: Beacon Press, 1950. Pp. xiv + 230.

Chitwood, Oliver P. *A History of Colonial America,* Second Edition. New York: Harper & Brothers, 1948. Pp. xix + 874.

Clews, Elsie W. *Educational Legislation and Administration of the Colonial Governments,* Columbia University Contributions to Philosophy, Psychology, and Education, Vol. VI, Nos. 1–4. New York: The Macmillan Co., 1899. Pp. xii + (7–524).

Crouse, Nellis M. "Causes of the Great Migration, 1630–1640," *New England Quarterly,* V (January, 1932), 3–36.

Cubberley, Elwood P. *Readings in Public Education in the United States: A Collection of Sources and Readings to Illustrate the History of Educational Progress in the United States.* Boston: Houghton Mifflin Company., 1934. Pp. xviii + 534.

Curti, Merle. *The Growth of American Thought,* Second Edition. New York: Harper & Brothers, 1951. Pp. xvii + 910.

Curti, Merle. *The Social Ideas of American Educators, with a New Chapter on the Last Twenty-five Years.* Paterson, N.J.: Pageant Books, Inc., 1959. Pp. xliv + 613.

Haskins, George Lee. *Law and Authority in Early Massachusetts: A Study of Tradition and Design.* New York: The Macmillan Co., 1960. Pp. 298.

Jackson, George Leroy. *The Development of School Support in Colonial Massachusetts,* Teachers College Contributions to Education, No. 25. New York: Teachers College, Columbia University, 1909. Pp. 96.

Jernegan, Marcus Wilson. *Laboring and Dependent Classes in Colonial America, 1607–1783: Studies of the Economic, Educational, and Social Significance of Slaves, Servants, and Poor Folk.* Chicago: University of Chicago Press, 1931. Pp. xiv + 256.

McKinley, Albert Edward. *The Suffrage Franchise in the Thirteen English Colonies in America,* Publications of the University of Pennsylvania, Series in History, No. 2. Boston: published for the University, Ginn & Company, 1905. Pp. vi + 518.

Mather, Cotton. *Magnalia Christi Americana; or, The Ecclesiastical History of New-England; from its First Planting, in the Year 1620, unto the Year of our Lord 1688,* I. Hartford, Conn.: Silas Andrus & Son, 1855. Pp. xiii + 625.

Meriwether, Colyer. *Our Colonial Curriculum, 1607–1776.* Washington, D.C.: Capital Publishing Co., 1907. Pp. 302.

Miller, Perry. *The New England Mind: The Seventeenth Century.* New York: The Macmillan Co., 1939. Pp. xiv + 528. Also published in paperback (Boston: Beacon Press, 1961).

Miller, Perry. *Orthodoxy in Massachusetts, 1630–1650.* Cambridge, Mass.: Harvard University Press, 1933. Pp. xvi + 353. Also published in paperback (Boston: Beacon Press, 1961).

Morison, Samuel Eliot. *Harvard College in the Seventeenth Century.* 2 vols. Cambridge, Mass.: Harvard University Press, 1936.

Morison, Samuel Eliot. *The Puritan Pronaos: Studies in the Intellectual Life of New England in the Seventeenth Century.* New York: New York University Press, 1936. Pp. xii + 282. Also published in paperback under the title *Intellectual Life of Colonial New England* (Ithaca, N.Y.: Cornell University Press [Great Seal Books], 1956).

Morris, Richard B. *Government and Labor in Early America.* New York: Columbia University Press, 1946. Pp. xvi + 557.

Nettels, Curtis P. *The Roots of the American Civilization: A History of American Colonial Life.* New York: F. S. Crofts & Co., 1938. Pp. xx + 748.

Parrington, Vernon Louis. *Main Currents in American Thought: An Interpretation of American Literature from the Beginnings to 1920,* I: *The Colonial Mind, 1620–1800.* New York: Harcourt, Brace & Co., 1927. Pp. xviii + 414. Also published in paperback (New York: Harcourt, Brace & Co. [Harvest Books], 1954).

Perry, Ralph Barton. *Puritanism and Democracy.* New York: The Vanguard Press, 1944. Pp. xvi + 688.

Rossiter, Clinton. *Seedtime of the Republic: The Origin of the American Tradition of Political Liberty.* New York: Harcourt, Brace & Co., 1953. Pp. xiv + 558. Also published, in abridged form, in paperback under the title *The First American Revolution* (New York: Harcourt, Brace & Co. [Harvest Books], 1956).

Seybolt, Robert Francis. *The Public Schools of Colonial Boston, 1635–1775.* Cambridge, Mass.: Harvard University Press, 1935. Pp. x + 102.

Sly, John Fairfield. *Town Government in Massachusetts (1620–1930).* Cambridge, Mass.: Harvard University Press, 1930. Pp. x + 244.

Small, Walter Herbert. *Early New England Schools.* Boston: Ginn & Company, 1914. Pp. x + 402.

Stokes, Anson Phelps. *Church and State in the United States,* I. New York: Harper & Brothers, 1950. Pp. lxix + 936.

Suzzalo, Henry. *The Rise of Local School Supervision in Massachusetts, the School Committee, 1635–1827,* Teachers College Contributions to Education, No. 3. New York: Teachers College, Columbia University, 1908. Pp. viii + 154.

Updegraff, Harlan. *The Origin of the Moving School in Massachusetts,* Teachers College Contributions to Education, No. 17. New York: Teachers College, Columbia University, 1908. Pp. 186.

Weeden, William B. *Economic and Social History of New England, 1620–1789.* 2 vols. Boston: Houghton Mifflin Company, 1890.

Wertenbaker, Thomas Jefferson. *A History of American Life,* II: *The First Americans, 1607–1690.* New York: The Macmillan Co., 1927. Pp. xxii + 358.

The School in an Emerging Capitalistic Social Order: Eighteenth-Century New England

As has been indicated in the preceding chapters, the founders of New England considered themselves a "chosen people" and willingly accepted the heavy responsibility which their selection imposed upon them. The men who founded New England, who led Pilgrim and Puritan across the seas to establish Bible commonwealths in the wilderness, had worked out, in their own minds at least, a definite social design. God had provided the time and the place for the building of a spiritual city far removed from the heresies and abuses of the Old World; he had sifted three kingdoms for choice grain for the planting of his church in the wilderness; and he had selected the leaders, who were to be the special recipients of his grace and the custodians of his will. The social order designed by the leaders was a closely knit church-state. According to the reading the leaders of New England gave their history, sacred and profane, God had never looked with favor on the rule of the many, in either church or commonwealth. Consequently, they proposed the establishment and maintenance of a social order in which the popular will would be permitted only limited expression. With political power in the hands of the few — in the main, the same relatively small group which governed the church — it was possible to employ the state to carry into effect the social design of the founders. And the state was extremely active. All manner of laws were enacted to enforce acceptance of, and conformity to, the political, religious, economic, and social ideals of the leaders. Education, above all other means perhaps, was regarded as the best way to accomplish these ends. Outside Rhode Island, the educational systems of the early New England colonies were designed, among other things, to socialize youth in terms of the ideology underpinning the prevailing social order. Through instruction in the home, in the school, and in the college, youth, it was hoped and believed, would be led to accept the religious principles of the founders, the concentration of political and economic power in the hands of the few, and a well-ordered arrangement of the social classes.

Winthrop and Cotton and other New England leaders labored valiantly and long to maintain the Puritan social order, but, almost from the first, forces developed which were in the end to defeat their experiment. New England was not two generations old before the foundations of the Puritan commonwealth began to show signs of crumbling. By the opening of the eighteenth century, New England society was taking on a purpose and a form very different from that of the original design. As the century progressed, significant changes occurred in the economic order, social conflicts developed out of which the middle and lower classes registered significant gains, and shifting currents of thought and feeling swept many away from a religious to a more secular view of life. A society modeled on that of England and modified to suit the purposes of Puritan leadership was slowly being reshaped by forces distinctly American in origin. Moreover, as the economic foundations of society changed, as shifts occurred in the locus of both political and social power, and as new attitudes and values emerged, it was only natural that certain modifications should take place with respect to both the purpose of education and the means of its diffusion. However, before taking up in any detail what these changes in education were, it is necessary to consider more fully some of the significant movements in New England life.

Changes in the Economic Order

One of the distinguishing features of eighteenth-century New England was the growth of a class of merchant-capitalists and large landowners. Capital, of course, was scarce in the early days of settlement, although from the very first one could find an occasional person of some means, especially in Massachusetts. It was not long, however, before men gave up the hope of deriving much more than a moderate living from the thin and stony soil, and many of the more ambitious turned to the sea in search of profits from commercial ventures. As we have already seen, even in the closing decades of the seventeenth century, men of considerable means began to appear in New England. As the eighteenth century opened, a merchant class was emerging as one of the most important elements, perhaps the most important element, in New England society. As time passed, merchant princes in the coast towns, men like the Faneuils, Browns,

Bowdoins, and Phillipses, accumulated large fortunes, built imposing city homes, and played a role in the life of New England quite as important as that of the larger planters in the life of the tobacco colonies in the South. One misses altogether the main currents of New England life unless one understands something of the varied and far-flung activities of these merchant-capitalists who were transforming the social order to its very foundations. Theirs were the hands which, in very large measure, were operating the power controls in New England from the opening of the eighteenth century to the outbreak of the Revolution.

THE VARIED ACTIVITIES OF THE MERCHANT-CAPITALISTS

The New England merchant was likely to be a man of many enterprises, a kind of general capitalist. He sent his ships far and wide in search of profitable trade. He carried the enormous catch of the Newfoundland fisheries to the ports of southern Europe and to the English and French planters in the West Indies. He exported the surplus commodities of New England — lumber, livestock, meat, wheat, and flour — to the West Indies, where he exchanged them for specie, bills of exchange, molasses, or other produce of the West Indian planters. He bought and sold in England; but there he bought more than he sold, because England herself produced many of the commodities New England had for sale. The quantity of goods New England could buy from the mother country was conditioned in large measure by the bills of exchange her merchants were able to obtain in commerce with the West Indies. The New England merchants also trafficked with their fellow colonists to the south whenever and wherever they could drive a bargain. Though many of their descendants were to look upon slavery with horror, they themselves plied the slave trade with both vigor and profit. Each year their ships carried thousands of gallons of rum to the African coast to be exchanged for slaves; the slaves were then sold to planters in the West Indies or the southern colonies and the proceeds exchanged for molasses for the making of more rum in New England for the purchase of more slaves. The slave trader, however, did not always find things easy; at times he had to face severe competition. Thus, James Brown in 1736 received the following complaint from his brother on the Guinea Coast:

> There never was so much Rum on the Coast at one time before . . . Slaves is very scarce: we have had nineteen sails of us at one time in the Rhoad, so that those ships that used to carry pryme slaves off is now forced to take any that comes.[1]

[1] Quoted by G. S. Kimball, *Providence in Colonial Times* (Providence: 1912), p. 248, as quoted in James Truslow Adams, *Provincial Society, 1690–1763* (New York: The Macmillan Co., 1927), p. 230.

Even Peter Faneuil, whose charity made possible the building of Faneuil Hall, the cradle of liberty, was not above employing his ship *The Jolly Bachelor* as a slaver — in which there was seen no inconsistency by most of his contemporaries. During the eighteenth century, American ships in considerable number were engaged in the slave trade. Just before the Revolution between sixty and seventy vessels were plying that trade, many of them from the ports of Boston, Newport, Salem, and New York.[2]

The merchant-capitalist often invested his money in ships. Craft of many kinds were required. By the middle of the century, some four hundred vessels were employed in the fishing industry of Massachusetts alone.[3] Ships were needed in large numbers to carry New England commerce to all parts of the world and ships were made and sold to England. As early as 1724, shipbuilders in England were complaining to the government that they were being ruined by the competition of New England. At the outbreak of the Revolution, about one-third of England's merchant marine had been built in America, chiefly in New England.[4]

Men with surplus capital had a weather eye out for any enterprises that would yield a neat profit and many of them invested their savings in rum distilleries. By the middle of the century, the manufacture and sale of rum was playing an extremely important role in the economic life of New England. Distilleries were to be found in large numbers in Boston, Newport, and Medford, and in smaller numbers in lesser seaport towns. In 1750, an agent reporting to the "Lords Commissioners of His Majesty's Treasury" stated that there were sixty-three distilleries in Massachusetts making molasses into rum,[5] the output being no less than one and a half million gallons annually. Twelve years later, Newport, Rhode Island, had twenty-two distilleries. Weeden comments on the importance of rum in the economic life of New England as follows:

> In whatever branch of trade we find ourselves now, we are impressed by the immense prevalence and moving power of rum. Negroes, fish, vessels, lumber, inter-colonial traffic in produce, all feel the initiative and moving impulse of rum. . . . It was merchandise in Guinea, on the banks of Newfoundland, in the Southern colonies, in exchange for furs

[2] Oliver Perry Chitwood, *A History of Colonial America* (New York: Harper & Brothers, 1961), p. 345; Curtis P. Nettels, *The Roots of American Civilization: A History of American Colonial Life* (New York: F. S. Crofts & Co., Inc., 1938), pp. 435–436. In colonial days there was not much active opposition to slavery on moral grounds except among the Quakers. Even George Whitefield, the great evangelist, owned slaves and endorsed slavery.

[3] Marcus Wilson Jernegan, *The American Colonies, 1492–1750* (New York: Longmans, Green & Co., 1929), p. 371. Published also in paperback (New York: Frederick Ungar Publishing Co., 1959).

[4] Chitwood, *op. cit.*, pp. 353, 378.

[5] William B. Weeden, *Economic and Social History of New England, 1620–1789* (Boston: Houghton Mifflin Company, 1890), II, pp. 640–641.

with the Indians, and "as store for the consumption of about 900 vessels engaged in the various branches of their trade at sea."[6]

Quantities of rum were consumed by the people generally, especially by the lower classes, who could not afford the more expensive liquors and wines. Rum was served at public gatherings and festive occasions — at weddings and funerals and even at ordinations of the clergy. Common laborers were often allowed portions of rum as a part of their rations and, as John Adams observed, in the evenings one could find the taverns frequented by people drinking drams of flip and toddy.[7]

The merchants of New England also found a rich opportunity to multiply their profits in their dealings with the small farmers, who composed, of course, the bulk of the people. It was not always easy, as is often supposed, for the small farmer to make a go of it. In the first place, it was becoming more difficult for him to get land to work. In the early period, the title to land was vested in the proprietors of each town, who allotted part of the land to themselves and part to non-proprietors or inhabitants, and held part of it for later division. As the older towns filled up, the descendants of the original proprietors laid claim to the undivided land and began to sell it. High-priced land in the older settlements, crowded conditions, and soil exhaustion were forcing people to move out to the frontier to form new settlements. In this situation, the merchants, land speculators, and men of means and influence of one kind or another in the coastal towns saw their opportunity. They proceeded to buy up huge tracts of land in advance of the settlers and to hold it for high prices. After 1735, Connecticut and Massachusetts adopted the policy of selling whole townships to the land speculators.[8] In 1737, six townships were sold at public auction in Connecticut, and somewhat later Massachusetts sold a whole township to a single person.[9] When the actual settlers moved in and performed the arduous labor of developing the town — felling forests, building roads, and the like — the capitalists in the eastern towns reaped the gains of unearned increment on lands not yet sold. Worse than that, not infrequently the actual settlers were denied the rights of local government, the management of the affairs of the town, including taxation, being vested in the grantee capitalists.[10]

Land speculation was but one way in which the merchant class derived profits in its relations with farmers. The farmer was often in need of capital to buy his land, to build his house, or to purchase livestock and supplies. He borrowed the necessary funds from the merchant-capitalist on a short- or long-term loan or bought on credit what he needed from

---

[6] *Ibid.*, p. 641.   [7] Jernegan, *op. cit.*, pp. 412–413.
[8] *Ibid.*, p. 359; Chitwood, *op. cit.*, p. 366.
[9] Chitwood, *loc. cit.*
[10] *Loc. cit.*; Adams, *op. cit.*, pp. 247–248.

the merchant. When the farmer harvested his crops, he undertook to pay off his debts, but again he found himself at a disadvantage, because he had no control over prices. The markets were likely to be flooded, and the merchants were usually able to keep prices down. Once caught in the meshes of debt, the farmer often found it extremely difficult to extricate himself. Frequently he ended up by losing his farm and was forced to start all over again.[11] Year by year, many of the small farmers, especially those farther to the west, saw a large part of the gains from their labor flow into the coffers of the land speculators and the merchant-capitalists. It was but natural that many among the yeomanry, especially those nearest the frontier, should come to look with bitterness upon the eastern capitalists, whom they regarded as responsible for their plight. "Wall Street" had become a reality before it had been given a name.

It is not necessary to detail further the various activities of the merchant-capitalists; enough has been said to give some indication of the way they were transforming the New England economy and of the dominant role they played in the economy they were helping to create. It was an economy, as we shall see later, which the transplanted European educational system was ill designed to serve. But, before taking up the specific educational changes which the new order of things was making necessary, we must examine further certain other changes in the economic, social, and intellectual life of New England in the eighteenth century.

Social Conflicts and the Gains of Democracy

In their far-flung and varied enterprises, the merchant-capitalists were creating the capital necessary for a more advanced civilization. At the same time, they embodied another important movement in eighteenth-century New England, namely, the rise of a new, conservative, aristocratic class in little sympathy with democratic liberalism. In the social processes which had transformed the Puritan into the Yankee, little had happened to make him more democratic in his outlook on life. In the frontier settlements that fringed the New England coast in the early days, when there was little accumulated capital and few were able to escape the drudgery of hard labor, Puritan leaders found the basis of their superiority in the conviction that they were God's elect, special agents for the accomplishment of his great design. Leaders of a later day were no less concerned with the hallmarks of a specially favored class, but they were entirely willing to substitute the possession of worldly goods for more intangible evidence of superiority. Imposing homes, rich apparel, imported wines, domestic slaves — these were tangible and unmistakable badges of one's social superiority. The colonial governors and the members of the

11 Chitwood, *op. cit.,* p. 366; Nettels, *op. cit.,* pp. 413–415.

small cliques that surrounded them, or true aristocrats of the Old World, might exhibit some disdain for the rising capitalists, but the New England Puritan, turned merchant prince, was in no wise abashed in their presence.

New England merchants were no less at home in manipulating colonial politics than in directing their commercial ventures or in establishing their claim to social superiority. When laws were required to protect or to promote their interests, they knew how to exercise their great influence; in most crucial matters they were able to have their way without too much opposition from lesser folk. They were able to dominate the colonial councils, the upper branches of the legislatures; their influence in the more popular assemblies was by no means negligible; and even in the town meetings they were often able to secure the passage of desired measures.

It would be a mistake, however, to assume that the upper classes in New England had their way without any opposition. Paralleling the development of a small directive group was another movement of no less significance, the rise of the common man to a place of economic and political importance. After all, it was the farmers and artisans who constituted the bedrock of New England society; it was they who were laying the foundations on which a democratic social order was to be erected. As we saw in the preceding chapter, most of the leaders of early New England looked with disfavor on democracy in church and commonwealth and in society generally. But men who had been social underlings in Europe — peasants, artisans, tenants, and day laborers — were not disposed to remain social underlings in America; they resisted any attempt to prevent social mobility, to confine them to the social stratum in which they had been born. The suffrage might be denied them, laws might be enacted requiring them to wear clothes indicative of their social status, on the Sabbath morning they might be seated in church pews according to their rank, and in daily life they might be addressed as Tom or Dick or as Goodman or Goodwife; but they would not accept such an arrangement of things as final. At the opening of the eighteenth century New England was not a democracy, but the class structure of society inherited from Europe, and buttressed by the efforts of minister, magistrate, and merchant to maintain it, was slowly breaking up in the face of the development of an independent yeomanry. The tide of a rising democracy had set in.

Many forces were sweeping men along toward a more democratic way of life. The congregational form of church organization, instituted by the Separatists in Plymouth and, not without some reluctance, adopted in Massachusetts, represented from the beginning a more democratic form of religious life.[12] In the earlier years of the seventeenth century, Roger

---

[12] The plan of church government finally adopted in Massachusetts represented a compromise between the Presbyterian and Congregational systems. After 1798 the Connecticut Congregationalists placed themselves "under a system not unlike that of the Presbyterians."

A

PLATFORM OF
CHURCH DISCIPLINE

GATHERED OUT OF THE WORD OF GOD:
AND AGREED UPON BY THE ELDERS:
AND MESSENGERS OF THE CHURCHES
ASSEMBLED IN THE SYNOD AT CAMBRIDGE
IN NEW ENGLAND

To be prefented to the Churches and Generall Court
for their confideration and acceptance,
in the Lord.

The Eight Moneth Anno 1649

Pfal: 84. 1. How amiable are thy Tabernacles O Lord of Hofts?
Pfal: 26. 8. Lord I have loved the habitation of thy houfe & the
place where thine honour dwelleth.
Pfal: 27. 4. One thing have I defired of the Lord that will I feek
after, that I may dwell in the houfe of the Lord all the
days of my life to behold the Beauty of the Lord & to
inquire in his Temple.

Printed by S G at Cambridge in New England
and are to be fold at Cambridge and Boston
Anno Dom: 1·6 4 9 .

American Puritanism in the seventeenth century: agreed upon by the Synod and maintained by law.

Jonathan Edwards (1705–1758), America's greatest Puritan theologian of the eighteenth century.

Cotton Mather (1663–1728), clergyman, scholar, author of religious books, and defender of New England Puritanism.

William Penn (1644–1718), founder of Pennsylvania.

Peter Stuyvesant (1592–1672), Dutch director-general of New Netherlands.

Brouwer Street, New Amsterdam, in 1659.

Charles Town (now Charleston), the most important city and seaport in the southern colonies as it appeared in the early eighteenth century.

Strange virtues were ascribed to tobacco, but the demand for Virginia's chief export was not based upon its medicinal value.

PANACEA;
OR
The Universal Medicine,
BEING
A DISCOVERY
of the
Wonderfull Vertues
OF
Tobacco
Taken in a Pipe,
WITH
Its Operation and Use both in
Physick and *Chyrurgery.*

By Dr *EVERARD*, &c.

LONDON,
Printed for *Simon Miller* at the Star in St *Pauls*
Church-yard, near the West-end, 1659.

Wealthy southern planters adopted the English practice of hiring a tutor to instruct their children. Often classes were held in a small school building near the plantation house.

The Boston Latin School, establis
during the first decade of the Ma
chusetts Bay Colony, as it appeare
the close of the seventeenth cent

Harvard (below), founded in 1636,
as it appeared in 1725–26, and Dartmouth (left), founded in 1770, the
first and last of the nine colonial colleges to be established.

Williams in Rhode Island and Thomas Hooker in Connecticut had struck powerful blows in defense of democratic liberalism and their influence continued to be felt. Some of the clergy, like John Wise, of Ipswich, were now espousing the popular cause. It is true, also, that New England felt to some extent the impact of liberal thought from eighteenth-century Europe. However, above all else, it was the wide diffusion of landownership that gave vigor and vitality to democratic impulses. On the surface of things, the New England farmer of the eighteenth century did not appear to be a very dramatic figure in New England life, but he was far more important than he seemed. As he went about his daily tasks, tilling his own acres and adding to them as time and circumstance permitted, as he mingled with his fellow townsmen and argued with them in town meetings over the management of local affairs, as he taught his children to be ambitious and self-respecting, he was quietly and unobtrusively injecting into the mores ideals and attitudes that were to become the core values of our democratic society.

But farmers were not always quiet and unobtrusive; in fact, as a class they were becoming articulate. Many of them owned enough property to entitle them to vote, and in the assemblies, the lower branches of the legislatures, their representatives were in a position to champion the farmers' cause. It is not necessary to detail the conflicts that developed between the farmers, especially on the frontier, and the eastern capitalists with respect to such matters as the ownership of land or the control of the currency. It is important, however, to remember that the farmer was beginning to insist upon his right to take a hand in the direction of social policy and that in the struggle that ensued definite gains were registered for democracy.

Allied with the farmers in their struggles against the ruling classes were the artisans, tenants, and day laborers. In a number of the more populous centers some of the artisans had accumulated enough capital to own their own tools and to set up shops of their own in which they employed a number of journeymen. Not an inconsiderable number of these master artisans had accumulated sufficient property to entitle them to vote in the election of members to the colonial assemblies. Many others of the artisan class — blacksmiths, fullers, bricklayers, shipwrights, weavers, shoemakers, and carpenters — had little property of their own and sought work where opportunity afforded. They belonged to the disfranchised class, as did, of course, large numbers of tenants, fishermen, sailors, peddlers, small shopkeepers, day laborers, and indentured servants. In local political affairs, however, the common people were beginning to make their influence felt. Thus, Governor Shirley of Massachusetts complained that a Boston town meeting might be "called together at any time upon the Petition of ten of the meanest Inhabitants, who by their constant attendance there generally are the majority and outvote the Gentlemen, Merchants, Substantial Traders, and all the better part of the Inhabitants; to whom it is Irksome to attend at such meetings, except upon very extraordinary occasions."[13] As the colonial period drew to a close amidst the distant rumblings of revolution, the common people of New England were ready to follow the lead of Samuel Adams in his determination to put an end to the rule of an aristocratic minority and to establish a state really based upon popular sovereignty.

Shifting Currents in Thought and Feeling

Much of the thought of early New England, certainly much of the recorded thought, was theological to the core. The world of nature and of man, even in its simplest manifestations, was explained in terms of divine will if not of divine providence. It is not strange that this was so, because for a thousand years and more the intellectual life of Europe had been cast in the religious mold; except for the comparatively brief interlude of the Renaissance, the clergy had been able to hold the citadel of learning against all assaults. Add to this the deep conviction of the Puritan leaders that New England was the appointed place for the ultimate reformation of the true church, and it is not difficult to understand the religious framework within which most of early New England thought was cast. But for two reasons, if no others, thought in New England was tending to become more secular. First of all, men who undertake to establish homes in the wildernesses of an underveloped continent are almost sure to become engrossed in the prosaic but essential business of making a living; however high their spiritual aspirations may be, they are likely to be swept along in the direction of material things. In the second place, Puritanism was in no small measure a bourgeois movement; no amount of theological robing could altogether hide the bourgeois in the Puritan.

One is not surprised, therefore, that, slowly at first and later more swiftly, the currents of thought in New England swept away from the piety that was Puritanism toward the materialistic conception of life that was capitalism. As the second and third generations came upon the scene, economic interests assumed a new importance; the spiritual light in the city builded upon a hill began to fade; seed which God had sifted for planting in the wilderness began to grow strange fruit — bitter fruit for men like Cotton Mather, whose hearts were fixed on the maintenance of the old order. If Mather may be believed, the Glory of the Lord was departing from New England, and there is abundant evidence to indicate that after about 1670 a revolt had set in against the strict Puritan moral

[13] Charles Henry Lincoln (ed.), *Correspondence of William Shirley, Governor of Massachusetts and Military Commander in America, 1731–1760* (New York: The Macmillan Co., 1912), I, p. 418.

code. It is always dangerous to take too seriously contemporary complaints about the moral decadence of a people, but it is clear that there was a lowering of moral standards during the last thirty years of the seventeenth century. In 1692 Cotton Mather complained that "some of our Rising Generation have been given up to the most abominable Impieties of Uncleanness, Drunkenness, and a Lewd, Rude, Extravagant sort of Behaviour. There are the Children of Belial among them, and Prodigies of Wickedness."[14] Whether many of Mather's contemporaries should be regarded as "Children of Belial" may be questionable, but at any rate not a few of them were given to frequenting taverns, to drinking rum and brandy, to mixed dancing, to playing cards, and to attending theatres. One thing seems certain: The cold winter of Puritanism was passing into the warm springtime of human nature. An ecclesiastical society was being transformed into one of deepening secular interests.

Evidence of a more secular order of things could be seen on every hand. The influence of the clergy, especially in political matters, was definitely on the decline; it was no longer that force which in the old days had moved heaven and earth. It was a far cry from John Cotton to those ministers who, just before the Revolution, spoke apologetically when dealing with political issues. The law and medicine were opening the doors to professional careers and the law might now lead to political preferment. Cotton Mather might continue to produce heavy and learned religious tomes and Jonathan Edwards in his theological writings might demonstrate that his was one of the great intellects of the age, but other books were appearing which had to do with secular things. Thomas Prince, of Boston, in writing his history of New England was attempting to apply rigorous standards of historical scholarship. Not infrequently one could find a man like Samuel Adams who was deeply read in the political classics of Europe, in the works of Locke, Vattel, Rousseau, Hume, Montesquieu. Moreover, the scientific writings of such men as Copernicus, Galileo, Newton, Gilbert, Kepler, Descartes, and Leibniz were not without their influence on New England thought. As the eighteenth century progressed, a small number of New Englanders were giving their attention to the study of natural phenomena. Some of them were members of the Royal Society in England and prepared data for its publications. John Winthrop, the leading man of science in New England and perhaps "the most competent teacher of mathematics in his generation," was made professor at Harvard in 1738, an appointment that he held until his death in 1779.[15]

[14] As quoted in Thomas Jefferson Wertenbaker, *The First Americans, 1607–1690* (New York: The Macmillan Co., 1927), p. 197. For Mather's resounding indictment of the people of Boston, see Cotton Mather, *Magnalia Christi Americana; or, The Ecclesiastical History of New-England* (Hartford: Silas Andrus and Son, 1855), I, pp. 90–104.

[15] Theodore Hornberger, *Scientific Thought in American Colleges* (Austin, Texas: University of Texas Press, 1945), pp. 49–51.

The secular spirit was also manifesting itself in the rise of newspapers and in the formation of numerous clubs of like-minded individuals to discuss scientific and philosophical questions or the news of the day. The cultivation of the fine arts, like the appearance of new forms of amusement and sport, was also indicative of the increasing secularization of life.

School and College in the New Order

The changes taking place in the economic, political, social, and intellectual life of New England were naturally reflected in educational policy and practice. As we have seen, religion was losing its grip on the intellectual life; the stream of men's interests was broadening. More and more, both thought and activity were directed toward the improvement of economic conditions. The state was no longer primarily an instrument of religious policy; men composing the various social groups now saw in it a powerful means of promoting or maintaining their economic interests. It was but natural, therefore, that political power should slip from the hands of the clergy into the hands of the agents of the British government, the merchant-capitalists, and the farmers and artisans. The theocratic state was giving place to the secular state, and politics was becoming a more absorbing interest as contending groups maneuvered to gain positions of strategic advantage. Puritan opposition to the aesthetic was breaking down and the spirit of the Enlightenment was penetrating the New England mind.

One may discern certain broad movements in education in the eighteenth century. First of all, those now in charge of the state had less regard for the school as a means of accomplishing their ends than was the case in the early days of settlement. Men were less convinced than of old that there should be a system of public education in every well-ordered state. The early Puritans had transplanted and modified somewhat the educational institutions of England, institutions that had been shaped to a great extent by influences growing out of the Renaissance and the Reformation. They regarded these educational institutions as extremely important in the accomplishment of their ends. But their ends were not the ends of the merchant-capitalists and the small farmers of the eighteenth century. To be sure, eighteenth-century New Englanders were not yet ready to discard or to reorganize thoroughly the educational system they had inherited from their fathers. Neither were they disposed to support it with vigor and enthusiasm. An educational order designed primarily to serve the interests of institutionalized religion and the class structure of society, established during the early period of Puritan leadership, was not well suited to serve the interests of the eighteenth century. The educational system, if it may be called a system, underwent some modification, particularly at the elementary level, in an attempt to make it serve more adequately the needs of the children of the common people. At the secondary level, change was extremely slow. The Latin grammar school, possessing a long tradition and record of accomplishment, could not expand its program to meet the needs of all the children and youth who wanted to extend their education beyond the acquisition of the rudiments, and as time went on a smaller and smaller proportion of such students were found in Latin schools.[16]

The development of private schools to meet new needs was a significant development of the eighteenth century. In the town elementary schools, children could learn to read and write and they might gain some proficiency in arithmetic. In the Latin grammar schools they could learn the Latin language and get some insight into classical thought. In all types of town schools, due care was taken of religious instruction. But there were many things which a considerable number of the youth of New England needed and desired to learn that were not taught in any of the town schools. Private teachers, however, were not backward in sensing the drift of things and they began to offer instruction in all manner of subjects, both practical and cultural. In the private schools that were springing up in most of the commercial centers one detects the beginning of the academy movement, which was to gather momentum toward the end of the century.

Abandonment of Compulsory Education for All

In the preceding chapter it was pointed out that by 1671 all New England except Rhode Island was under a system of compulsory education. School attendance was not compulsory, but parents or masters were required to see to it that their children or apprentices were taught reading and in some instances a trade as well. It was also pointed out there that, during the brief existence of the Dominion of New England, an act was passed in 1687–88 which in effect repealed all legislation in New England relating to compulsory education. After Andros had been overthrown and the New England colonies had regained charters, they were free to deal once more with the matter of compulsory education. The General Court of Massachusetts in 1692 passed an act designed to validate all laws which had been in force in Massachusetts and New Plymouth at the time the charters had been revoked.[17] The effect of this act would

---

[16] W. N. Small, the meticulous historian of early New England schools whose work, although old (1904), still represents the best scholarship devoted to the subject, stated that by the end of the Revolution there was "scarcely a Latin grammar school worthy of the name existing anywhere in New England." Small, *op. cit.*, p. 29.

[17] Marcus Wilson Jernegan, *Laboring and Dependent Classes in Colonial America, 1607–1783* (Chicago: University of Chicago Press, 1931), p. 103.

have been to revive the statutes dealing with compulsory education. Under the new charter which had been granted to Massachusetts in 1691, however, acts of the General Court were subject to disallowance by the Privy Council in London. The Act of 1692, which would have kept the compulsory educational legislation in force in Massachusetts, was disallowed by the Privy Council.

After the Act of 1692 was disallowed, Massachusetts never again during the colonial period undertook to enforce a policy of compulsory education for all children. The General Court in 1692 enacted a statute which gave authority to the selectmen or the overseers of the poor to bind out as apprentices "any poor children." Henceforth to the Revolution, no laws were passed requiring that children be apprenticed in case they were not being taught to read or write; the town officers could, at their discretion, bind out as apprentices poor children, but no others. When the children of the poor were bound out, the law required that their masters see to it that they be taught to read and write. A later statute, however, in 1710, did not include the requirement that girl apprentices be taught to write; it was enough for girls to be taught to read "as they respectively may be capable."[18] From the beginning of the eighteenth century to the Revolution, Massachusetts made no attempt to provide through compulsory measures for the academic, religious, or trade education of all children.

During the eighteenth century, the provisions of the compulsory-education statutes in Connecticut were somewhat different from those of Massachusetts, but here, too, one notes a weakening of the law. In 1690, soon after the charter had been restored, the General Court of Connecticut passed an act which indicated that it proposed to enforce with vigor its former policy of compulsory education. In the preamble to the act, it was stated "that notwithstanding the former orders made for the erudition of children and servants, there are many persons unable to read the English tongue, and thereby uncapable to read the holy word of God, or the good laws of the colony." To remedy this condition the act ordered

> that all parents and masters shall cause their respective children and servants, as they are capable, to be taught to read distinctly the English tongue, and that the grand jurymen in each town do once in the year at least, visit each family they suspect to neglect this order, and satisfy themselves whether all children under age and servants in such suspect families can read well the English tongue, or be in a good procedure to learn the same or not, and if they find any such children and servants not taught as their years are capable of, they shall return the names of the parents or masters of the said children so untaught, to the next county court, where the said parents or masters shall be fined twenty shillings for

[18] *Ibid.*, p. 105.

each child or servant whose teaching is or shall be neglected, contrary to this order. . . .[19]

In its Revised Code of 1702, Connecticut, however, introduced a provision in the section dealing with compulsory education which greatly weakened the requirements. It was still the duty of parents and masters to see to it that their children and apprentices were taught to read, but those unable to do this could avoid the penalty of the law by showing that they had required their children or apprentices to memorize "a short orthodox catechism."[20] Later, this provision, making it possible to substitute the commitment to memory of an orthodox catechism for ability to read, was made more explicit. Clearly, this loophole in the compulsory-education law was sufficiently wide for all to slip through who were disposed to take advantage of it. From the opening of the eighteenth century, then, down to the Revolution, Connecticut, like Massachusetts, had no statutes in force which required that all children be taught to read.

New Hampshire, it will be recalled, was embraced within the territory of Massachusetts until 1679. For a number of years after it had become a separate colony, no compulsory legislation was in force, but in 1712 the selectmen of the various towns were authorized to examine all youth above ten years of age to see if they had been taught to read. Children who were not being taught to read might, at the discretion of the selectmen and a justice of the peace, be bound out as apprentices, and in such instances the masters were required to teach their apprentices to read and write. This act cannot properly be regarded as one establishing compulsory education because there was nothing in it compelling the selectmen to act. Later, in 1766, New Hampshire passed an act which authorized the town selectmen, or the overseers of the poor, with consent of the justices of the peace, to bind out as apprentices children whose parents were unable to maintain them. Children bound out in this way were to be taught to read and it was required that boys be also taught to write.

During the whole colonial period, Rhode Island enacted no statute establishing compulsory education. Nowhere, then, in eighteenth-century New England did the law make book education mandatory for all children. This policy was in sharp contrast with that which had been put into opera-

[19] *The Public Records of the Colony of Connecticut from August, 1689, to May, 1706, Transcribed and Edited in Accordance with Resolutions of the General Assembly, by Charles J. Hoadly* (Hartford: Press of Case, Lockwood & Brainerd, 1868), p. 30. The quotation in modernized English is from Elsie W. Clews, *Educational Legislation and Administration of Colonial Government*, Columbia University Contributions to Philosophy, Psychology, and Education, VI, Nos. 1–4 (New York: The Macmillan Co., 1899), pp. 95–96.

[20] *Acts and Laws of His Majesty's Colony of Connecticut in New England . . .* Boston, 1702. See Jernegan, *Laboring and Dependent Classes in Colonial America, op. cit.,* p. 109.

tion in the period from 1642 to 1671. However, in appraising this change of policy with respect to compulsory education, one must not overlook the fact that in most of the colonies laws existed which required the towns to maintain schools. As these schools were supported more and more at public expense, the older type of compulsory-education legislation may not have appeared so necessary as it had earlier.

Compulsory Town Schools

The first Provincial Assembly in Massachusetts, after the restoration of charter government in 1691, passed an act which required all towns of fifty families or more to be "constantly provided of a schoolmaster to teach children and youth to read and write." Towns of one hundred families were also required to maintain a grammar school taught by a "discreet person of good conversation, well instructed in the tongues."[21] Towns failing to obey the law were subject to presentment to the justices in quarter sessions. Conviction of disobedience involved a fine of ten pounds. This act was amended from time to time so as to increase the fine on the towns which failed to obey it, but otherwise it remained in force until the end of the colonial period.

Connecticut followed much the same policy as Massachusetts, requiring certain of the larger towns to maintain Latin grammar schools and the smaller communities to maintain reading and writing schools. In 1690, the year following the resumption of charter government, the General Court, "considering the necessity and great advantage of good literature," ordered that two Latin grammar schools be "kept and maintained in this colony," to teach all such children as might attend "reading, writing, arithmetic, the Latin and Greek tongues."[22] Pupils would not be admitted, however, unless they were already able to read the Psalter. Hartford and New Haven were the towns designated as the ones in which the Latin schools should be maintained. The necessary funds for the maintenance of these schools were to be derived in part from county-wide taxes, in part from donations, and in part from town taxes and tuition fees. Towns of thirty families or more were required to keep for six months each year a school in which children could be taught "to read and write the English tongue." The time the school was to be kept each year was no longer than six months because the court was mindful of the "necessity many parents or masters may be under to improve their children and servants in labor for a great part of the year."[23]

[21] Ellis Ames and Abner Cheney Goodell (eds.), *The Acts and Resolves, Public and Private, of the Province of the Massachusetts Bay* (Boston, 1869–1922), I, p. 66.

[22] *The Public Records of the Colony of Connecticut . . . , op. cit.,* IV, pp. 30–31.

[23] *Ibid.,* IV, p. 31.

In 1700, the General Court of Connecticut took additional steps to insure the maintenance of both Latin and reading and writing schools. It was now required that four Latin grammar schools be maintained, one in each of the four county towns of Hartford, New Haven, New London, and Fairfield. It was ordered that these Latin schools be "constantly kept." This act also reveals the strong intent of the legislature to maintain a system of town schools for the teaching of reading and writing. Towns of seventy families or more were ordered to "keep from year to year, a public and sufficient school for the teaching [of] children to write and read." Towns of fewer than seventy families were required to keep a reading and writing school "for one-half of the year." These schools were to be supported in part by a tax of "forty shillings upon every thousand pounds of the public list of persons and estates unto the several towns of this colony, and proportionably for lesser sums." Towns failing to obey the law were to suffer the penalty of having their share of this colony-wide tax withheld.[24]

In interpreting the statutes of Connecticut, and for that matter of any of the New England colonies of the eighteenth century, one should be careful not to be misled by the provision that schools be "constantly kept," or that they be kept for any definite term. As will be pointed out in greater detail later, the eighteenth century had not progressed far before New England towns began to break up into parishes or districts. Soon these subdivisions of the town began to insist that the town school be kept in them part of the time. Commonly, the town school would be kept in a half-dozen or more places during the course of the year. If the sum total of these terms equaled twelve months, then the school had been constantly kept within the meaning of the law. The point is that children in any given community seldom, if ever, had the opportunity of attending school for a term equal to that prescribed in the statutes.

The one remaining important act passed by the colonial legislature in Connecticut imposing on the local communities the duty of maintaining schools took cognizance of the dispersion of population and the rise of district schools. This act was passed in 1715 and made more stringent in 1717 by providing "that every society or parish within the colony shall be obliged to keep a school; where there are seventy families in any parish, the school shall be there kept at least eleven months in a year; and where there is a less number of families, not less than half the year."[25] Apparently the penalty remained as before, namely, the withholding of any share in the colony funds raised for the support of schools.

Legislation in New Hampshire with respect to the compulsory maintenance of schools was much like that in Massachusetts and Connecticut. In 1693, the legislature passed an act which required all the towns in the province, except Dover for the duration of the war, to "provide a schoolmaster for the supply of the town." These schoolmasters were evidently

[24] *Ibid.*, IV, pp. 331–332.   [25] *Ibid.*, V, p. 10.

to teach reading and writing. Failure to obey the law involved a penalty of ten pounds.[26] Since no Latin grammar school had yet been established in the province "for the Encouragement of Learning and Vertue," the legislature in 1708 provided for the establishment of such a school in Portsmouth. The several towns in the province were required to contribute fifty pounds for the support of the schoolmaster, who was to keep a school for "writers, Readers and Latinists."[27] The only other acts passed during the colonial period requiring towns to maintain schools were those of 1719 and 1721. The first of these was very similar to the old Massachusetts Act of 1647 except that the penalty for failure to obey the law was more severe. It provided that all towns of fifty families should be constantly provided with "a schoolmaster to teach children and youth to read and write," and that all towns of one hundred families should set up and keep a Latin grammar school. The penalty for failure to obey the act was set at twenty pounds. Apparently the people in the various towns were not well disposed toward the maintenance of Latin schools. Two years later, in 1721, the legislature complained that "the selectmen of sundry towns within this province often neglect to provide grammar schools for their respective towns." To remedy the situation, the law was amended to require not only every town but every parish of one hundred families in the province to "be constantly provided with a grammar school." Moreover, if any town or parish required by law to maintain a grammar school failed to do so for more than a month each year, the selectmen were to be personally liable for a fine of twenty pounds.[28]

Rhode Island, during the eighteenth century, adhered to its earlier policy of passing no legislation requiring towns to maintain schools. Historians, who have based their accounts of education overly much on legal enactments, have fallen into the error of assuming that Rhode Island was especially backward in the matter of education. As a matter of fact, an examination of town records discloses that numerous towns in Rhode Island were on their own volition undertaking to maintain schools.[29]

Enforcement of the Law Requiring the Maintenance of Schools

It is always dangerous to assume that the conditions prescribed by law actually exist in fact. If one were to examine none too critically the edu-

[26] There seems to be some doubt with respect to the enactment of this law. See Clews, *op. cit.*, p. 165.

[27] Eugene Alfred Bishop, *The Development of a State School System: New Hampshire* (New York: Teachers College, Columbia University, 1930), p. 22.

[28] *Acts and Laws of His Majesty's Province of New Hampshire in New England* . . . (Portsmouth: printed by David Fowle, 1761), p. 120. Also see Clews, *op. cit.*, pp. 167–168.

[29] See Charles Carroll, *Public Education in Rhode Island,* Rhode Island Education Circulars (Providence, R.I.: Published Jointly by the State Board of Education, the

cational legislation of New England, one might well come to the conclusion that most of the smaller communities were provided with a reading and writing school and that in most of the larger towns Latin schools were to be found. Certainly there was no dearth of legislation; if the laws had been well enforced, the children and youth of New England would have been provided with remarkable educational facilities. But in the preambles to these acts one meets unmistakable evidence that the laws were not being well enforced; in fact, if one may believe the lawmakers themselves, the provisions they were writing into the statute books were being disregarded in many towns, and the establishment and maintenance of schools "shamefully neglected." Thus in 1701 the General Court of Massachusetts stated in the preamble to its new educational act that the former "wholesome and necessary law is shamefully neglected by divers towns, and the penalty therefore not required, tending greatly to the nourishing of ignorance and irreligion."[30] Popular opposition to the law requiring towns to keep grammar schools seems to have been particularly strong. In 1718 once again the General Court of Massachusetts registered a complaint:

> Whereas, notwithstanding the many good and wholesome laws of this province for the encouraging of schools, and the penalty, first of ten pounds, and afterwards increased to twenty pounds, on such towns as are obliged to have a grammar schoolmaster, and neglect the same; yet by sad experience it is found that many towns that not only are obliged by law, but are very able to support a grammar school, yet chose rather to incur and pay the fine or penalty than maintain a grammar school,
>
> Be it enacted by his excellency the Governor, Council and Representatives in General Court assembled, and by the authority of the same, that the penalty or forfeiture for non-observance of the said law henceforth shall be thirty pounds on every town that shall have the number of one hundred and fifty families, and forty pounds on every town that shall have the number of two hundred families, and so, *pro rata,* in case the town consist of two hundred and fifty or three hundred families, to be recovered, paid and employed in manner and to the use as by the law is directed; any law, usage or custom to the contrary notwithstanding.[31]

Nor were complaints of the neglect of the law confined to Massachusetts. In 1721, the legislature of New Hampshire stated that "the selectmen of sundry towns within this province often neglect to provide grammar schools for their respective towns, whereby their youth lose much of their

Commissioner of Public Schools, and the Trustees of the Rhode Island Normal School, 1918), Chap. I.

[30] Ames and Goodell, *op. cit.,* I, p. 470.
[31] *Ibid.,* II, pp. 67–68.

time, to the great hindrance of their learning."[32] The increase in the severity of the penalties imposed for failure to obey the law is also indicative of the difficulty in getting the statutes carried into effect.

Town and court records afford a much better picture than do the statutes of actual conditions with respect to the establishment and maintenance of schools. In general, it may be said that popular opinion was much more favorable toward the maintenance of reading and writing schools than toward the support of Latin grammar schools. Many towns simply neglected to establish schools as the law required, hoping that they would not be presented and fined. And even if they were fined, it would be cheaper than hiring a schoolmaster. Some towns resorted to subterfuges to evade the law, as, for example, employing a master for a short time while the court was in session or arranging with the local minister for the teaching of Latin to any pupils who might resort to him, it being generally understood that few or no pupils would resort. It was perhaps this practice that led to the enactment of a law in Massachusetts in 1701 which prohibited towns from employing ministers as schoolmasters.

The lack of accurate census data with respect to population and the incompleteness of town records make it impossible to ascertain precisely the extent to which the laws requiring the maintenance of schools were enforced. Evidence is sufficient, however, to make it clear that the Latin grammar school was never a popular institution. The county of Middlesex in Massachusetts in 1708 contained twenty towns, nine of which had one hundred families or more. Only four of these nine had lived up to their legal obligations.[33] The town records show that in not a few towns the people were definitely opposed to the law requiring them to maintain a Latin school. Thus, in 1704, the inhabitants of Braintree, Massachusetts, agreed to pay the Latin schoolmaster thirty pounds a year "dureing the time he perform the work, untill the present Law refering to schools be Repealed."[34] The inhabitants of Worcester, Massachusetts, in 1767 instructed their representative to the General Court as follows: "That you use your endeavors to relieve the people of the Province from the great burden of supporting so many Latin grammar schools, whereby they are prevented from attaining such a degree of English learning as is necessary to retain the freedom of any state."[35] The preference here expressed for schools to teach children to read and write English was not uncommon.

Presentments of towns for failure to obey the law were numerous, and more often than not the towns were able to escape conviction. The laxity

---

[32] *Acts and Laws of His Majesty's Province of New Hampshire, op. cit.,* p. 121.

[33] Walter Herbert Small, *Early New England Schools* (Boston: Ginn & Company, 1914), p. 33.

[34] Samuel A. Bates (ed.), *Records of the Town of Braintree* (Randolph, Mass.: Daniel H. Huxford, 1886), p. 58.

[35] Small, *op. cit.,* pp. 42–43.

of the courts in the enforcement of the law no doubt reflected popular attitudes. The defenses offered by the towns when presented are often very revealing. Two of them are presented here. The first is the answer the selectmen of Andover, Massachusetts, made to an indictment in 1713.

This may certify any to whom it may concern, that the selectmen of said town have taken all the care and pains they could for to procure a schoolmaster for our town for the year last past, but could not obtain one; first, we agreed with Mr. Obediah Ayers of Haverhill for half a year, only he expected liberty if he had a better call or offer, which we thought would be only for the work of the ministry; but, however, he was pleased to take it otherwise and so left us; whereupon we forthwith applied ourselves to the college to the president for advice, and he could tell us of none, only advised us to the Fellows to ask them; and they advised to Mr. Rogers of Ipswich, for they could tell us of no other; and we applied ourselves to him and got him to Andover. But by reason our Rev. Mr. Barnard could not diet him, he would not stay with us, and since we have sent to Newbury and Salisbury and to Mistick for to hire one and cannot get one; and we do take the best care we can for to bring our children to reading by schooldames, and we have no grammar school in our town as we know of, and we are now taking the best care we can for to obtain one, therefore we pray that we may be favored so far as may be, for we cannot compel gentlemen to come to us, and we do suppose they are something afraid by the reason we do lie so exposed to our Indian enemies. Pray consider our great extremity in that regard and we shall do our uttermost to answer to the true intent of the law in that behalf. So we rest your humble petitioners.[36]

The selectmen of the town of Medfield made the following reply to a presentment:

Whereas the town of Medfield having been presented for some deficiency in a school according to law, we, whose names are underwritten, being selectmen of the said town of Medfield, do certify your honors that for several years past, we have had a constant schoolmaster who is very capable to learn to read and write &c in English, and is very inclinable for that work; and we have not at any time been without such a school except it were a small space of time last July, when the schoolmaster was taken ill and incapable of that work; we, the selectmen, did quickly seek out another to supply that place, and we have been constantly supplied to this time, till the same schoolmaster hath been recovered and is now engaged in that work. And may it please your honors, we are certain that we had such a school when the presentment was made. And as for the number of householders or families in our town, referring to a grammar school, indeed in former years we had such a number of families and had

[36] *Ibid.*, p. 38.

a grammar school some years before Medway was taken from us, and is a distinct town; we were ready to conform to our duty in the law; but now may it please your honors, our town falleth short considerably of 100 householders or families, we having sufficient knowledge of every family within the town bounds, which bounds contains no more than three miles one way and four miles the other way; and to the best of our understandings, we have reckoned up all the families in the town, and find but ninety-four families.[37]

In 1765 a census was taken in Massachusetts which shows the population of the several towns. By an examination of town records and histories it is possible to get a fairly accurate picture of the status of Latin grammar schools at that date. The picture is not complete because in many instances available information does not indicate whether a town was maintaining a Latin school. In 1765 there were one hundred and forty towns in Massachusetts with a population of one hundred families or more, and all of these under the law were required to maintain a Latin school. Forty-eight of these it is definitely known were meeting the legal requirement.[38] It is possible, indeed probable, that other towns were maintaining schools, even though the evidence in the study from which these data are drawn does not reveal it. Still it seems a fair conclusion that the grammar-school law in Massachusetts was not being complied with in many communities. Small, after a detailed examination of many town records in Massachusetts, came to the following conclusion with respect to the popular attitude toward the Latin grammar school in the eighteenth century: "The whole century is marked by indifference to the law, or open defiance of it. More and more the conviction is forced upon us that this form of school existed not by popular will but by force of law."[39]

The Declining Interest in Popular Education

The evidence with respect to both compulsory education and compulsory maintenance of schools indicates that from about 1690 on there was a general decline in popular interest in education, at least in the kind of education represented by the town schools. It is not difficult to understand why the fourth and fifth generations of New Englanders did not have the enthusiasm for education that characterized the founding fathers.

[37] *Ibid.*, pp. 40–41.
[38] Mary Adalene Hope, "The Rise and Decline of the Grammar School in Massachusetts, 1635–1765" (Master's thesis, Department of History, University of Chicago, 1938), p. 88.
[39] Small, *op. cit.*, pp. 36–37.

First of all, as we have already seen, there had been a decrease in religious zeal. In the early days, religion had been the principal integrative force in New England life, the dominant unifying force in society. To no small degree the early educational program had been made possible by unity of religious purpose. But, as the years passed, the integrating force of religion was lost to a considerable degree. It was lost partly because life was becoming more secular and partly because of the growing toleration of various religious faiths. As Anglicans and Baptists began to establish themselves and as dissensions appeared in the ranks of the Puritans, there was some loss of social solidarity, which reflected itself in attitudes toward education. Still other forces were contributing to the social disintegration of the New England towns. Among these the dispersion of population and the decentralizing tendency of democracy were the most important. As population spread from the central village to all parts of the town, one detects the development of the spirit of individualism and localism. Antagonisms developed between groups in the same town and there was less tendency to follow a united leadership. Moreover, the theocratic state was giving place to the civil state, but the civic values inherent in a system of popular education were not yet fully apprehended. As the economic interest in life grew stronger, the tendency was to evaluate education in terms of its contribution to social and economic ends. Hence it was only a comparatively small group of leaders who saw any great value in the Latin grammar school. In a frontier society, such as New England still was, even the ability to read in the vernacular was not very important if one were no longer greatly concerned with the reading of the Scripture. Finally, the first generation of educational leaders who had come over in the great migration had passed on and their passing had marked an intellectual decline from which New England did not easily recover.

Financing the Cost of Education

During the eighteenth century down to the Revolution, no significant changes occurred in the law governing the support of schools. Each separate town was still permitted to follow its own policy about as it pleased. One does note, however, a fundamental change of practice on the part of most communities. There was a definite tendency to increase materially the share of the cost of education borne by the town in its corporate capacity. This tendency to shift the burden of school support from individual parents and masters to the town definitely reflects the growth of democracy, the rise of small farmers and artisans to a place of greater importance.

School Administration

From the earliest days in New England, the principle that education is a function of the state rather than the local community was accepted and put into practical operation. The General Court, the colonial legislature, was the source of authority and control. It determined whether the towns should be required to maintain schools, the kinds of schools to be maintained, the length of the school term, the possible means of support, and the qualifications of teachers.

THE TOWN AS THE LOCAL UNIT

The colonial legislatures generally made use of the town as the unit of local school administration. The town must not be confused with the central village or any aggregation of people. It was simply a civil subdivision of the state, usually embracing from twenty to forty square miles irregularly laid off.

The town meeting, where those who had the right to exercise the local suffrage met to elect town officers and reach decisions in the management of the town's affairs, was the source of authority for the administration of schools locally. In open town meetings decisions were reached with respect to such matters as whether the town would have a school or pay the fine imposed upon it for neglect to do so, the method of raising funds for school support, the location of the school, and the choice of a teacher. As time passed, however, matters of this kind were to a considerable degree delegated by the town meeting to the selectmen, the regularly elected town officers.

THE RISE OF THE DISTRICT SYSTEM

A great deal of importance attaches to the rise of the district system of school administration. It was significant because it represented a high degree of decentralization of school control. It was equally significant because it marked the separation of school and municipal administration, a separation which has continued, in the main, to the present day. The development of the district system was due largely to the dispersion of population and the growth of the spirit of democracy and localism. In the early days, people built their homes around a village center in one part of the town. Here was located the village church and the schoolhouse, if the town had one. Early New England towns were distinctly village-centered. In time, however, as population increased, families moved out into the various parts of the town and new villages or settlements sprang up. These outlying settlements came to be known as quarters, squadrons, ends, skirts, or districts. It was not long until the people in these outlying settlements began to demand the right of local self-government. They demanded their own church, and thus the district would become a parish. They might also demand that their settlement become a road district, or a district for recruiting the militia. In time, these outlying settlements began to insist on having their own schools. They began to have a dame school in the summer and a private school of their own kept by a master in the winter. The result was a severe crippling of the town school located in the original village. The law required the town to maintain a school, but the people from the outlying districts were not much disposed to tax themselves to support a school to which it would be difficult to send their children because of the distances involved. The people in the central village, on the other hand, were not disposed to support the town school entirely by tuition fees. The outcome was a compromise, namely, the moving school, supported in the main by town taxes. The schoolmaster now moved from one community in the town to another, spending a few weeks in one or a few months in the other, depending, as a rule, upon the amount of taxes each settlement had paid into the town treasury for school purposes.

The following record of the moving school in the town of Harwich illustrates how this type of institution operated. In 1725 there were six places in the town in which the master taught for varying lengths of time. The following arrangement was worked out for the "removes" of the master:

> First remove, 16 families, 29 children,
>   school 6 months 1 week
> Second remove, 25 families, 55 children,
>   school 8 months 3 weeks
> Third remove, 22 families, 56 children,
>   school 8 months 3 weeks
> Fourth remove, 25 families, 47 children,
>   school 8 months 1 week
> Fifth remove, 14 families, 32 children,
>   school 4 months
> Sixth remove, 26 families, 35 children,
>   school 6 months 1 week
> The school shall begin at the
>   westernmost part of the town
>   first, and so remove eastward.[40]

Under this plan the master would make the circuit of the town every three and one-half years. Perhaps the children welcomed these long vacations from school of from two to three years, but it must have been dis-

[40] *Ibid.,* p. 64.

astrous to their learning. The law, which required a town to keep a school constantly, was, of course, complied with if a school was kept at all times in some one settlement in the town.

The moving school proved unsatisfactory. In time, the various districts within a town where the school was kept from time to time began to demand their quota of the town school taxes and the right to employ their own master and to run the school as they pleased. The following extract from the records of the town of Swanzey in 1775 indicates what had been going on throughout New England for many years:

> We, the subscribers, living very remote from any district where we might be convenient to a school for our children, do humbly petition that the town would vote us off as a district and grant that the money which we pay towards maintaining a school in this town may be laid out for school in the said district as near the center as may be convenient. . . . Voted the above request be complied with during the town's pleasure.[41]

It is clear that, although the town was still the local unit contemplated in the statutes, the district had become the unit actually employed in the practical operation of the schools. All that was needed to establish the district system was to enact statutes legalizing the practice. A step was taken in this direction in Connecticut in 1766 when the General Court authorized the towns "to divide themselves into proper and necessary districts for keeping their schools, and to alter and regulate the same from time to time."[42] Soon after the Revolution, Massachusetts legalized the district system and in time other states in and outside New England adopted it as the form of local organization.

The development of the district system reflects the rise of the middle class to a position of greater importance in New England life. Small farmers and artisans were insisting that their children share in whatever opportunities for schooling the town might afford. The moving school and the small school district were means of achieving a high degree of equality of educational opportunity; they also meant that schooling was spread extremely thin.

The school district was a democratic institution. Without it, many children would have had no opportunity to attend school at all. It fitted into the pattern of rural life in the United States. Even when cities began to develop, most of them were for some years divided into more or less independent school districts, with their own governing bodies. And when the districts embraced in a city were consolidated into a single city-wide district, the newly created school district usually had a board of trustees

[41] As quoted *ibid.*, p. 73.
[42] *The Public Records of the Colony of Connecticut, op. cit.*, XII, pp. 497–498.

separate and distinct from the municipal government. It appears that the American policy of separating school and municipal administration is more the result of historic circumstance than of any well-considered educational policy.

The Content of Instruction, Methods, and Teachers

The eighteenth century witnessed the combination of the dame school and the reading and writing schools to form a single elementary school for the teaching of the three R's. The town English school was primarily concerned with teaching children reading and writing and, in some instances, the fundamentals of arithmetic. Of course, children still were surrounded by a somber religious atmosphere. Nearly all the reading matter put into their hands was of a religious nature. In the elementary school, the *New England Primer,* "The Little Bible of New England," was used almost universally. One has to read this little book to realize how thoroughly it was permeated from cover to cover with religious doctrine and to realize what a stern and cruel God was held up before the Puritan child. The catechism was the most important part of the *Primer,* and it was etched into the child's memory in the school, in the home, and at church. It was regarded as a fit instrument for making sure that children, "young vipers, and infinitely more hateful than vipers to God," according to Jonathan Edwards, would attain that happy state of being mortally afraid they "should goe to Hell" and would be "stirred up dreadfully to seek God." Once the child had finished the *Primer,* with all its moralizing, catechism, religious poetry, and commandments, he was then ready to proceed to the reading of the Psalter, the Testament, or the Bible. Toward the end of the colonial period, spelling books began to appear which were somewhat less religious in content. That by Thomas Dilworth, *A New Guide to the English Tongue,* published in 1740, became the most popular in America. It was really a speller and reader combined. The doors of history, geography, and science were closed to the child; he was not even aware of their existence. After about 1725, most town elementary schools included some instruction in arithmetic. As a rule, neither teacher nor pupil had the benefit of an arithmetic text. Traditional rules and operations were recorded by the child in a manuscript and examples were set to which the rules and operations were to be applied. In time, the child produced for himself the same kind of manuscript the teacher had produced when he was a child.

The curriculum of the Latin grammar school underwent little change during the eighteenth century. In some towns, like Boston, where the Latin grammar school was kept separate and distinct from the English elementary school, boys were put through seven years of rigorous drill in

Latin and they were also given instruction in the rudiments of Greek. Latin occupied three-fourths or even more of the pupil's time; he was expected to read, write, and even speak Latin with some degree of ease. The religious atmosphere was quite as evident in the Latin school as it was in the elementary English school. The master prayed regularly with his pupils and quizzed them thoroughly on the sermons they heard each Sabbath morning.

It would be a mistake, however, to assume that all the Latin grammar schools were of the high quality of that of Boston and of some of the other more populous towns. Many schools passed as Latin grammar schools in the eyes of the law which were in fact nothing more than English elementary schools with a few boys in them receiving instruction in Latin.

The individual method of instruction was employed in both the elementary and the Latin grammar schools. It was not until the next century that the class method of instruction came to be the common practice. Pupils were called up one by one before the master to "recite" their lessons, and woe unto him whose memory was bad or who for some other reason had failed to "learn" what he was supposed to know. Rare was the master who failed to use the rod as an aid to learning. The "ferule" and the whipping post were regarded as essential items in the school's equipment and not a few masters were positively ingenious in devising novel ways of punishment.

The following quotation from the autobiography of Samuel Griswold Goodrich, or "Peter Parley" as he called himself on the title pages of his numerous books, is revealing with respect to the kind of education a child in rural Connecticut received in the last years of the eighteenth century:

The schoolhouse chimney was of stone, and the fireplace was six feet wide and four deep. The flue was so ample and so perpendicular that the rain, sleet, and snow fell directly to the hearth. In winter the battle for life with green sizzling fuel, which was brought in lengths and cut up by the scholars, was a stern one. Not infrequently the wood, gushing with sap as it was, chanced to let the fire go out, and as there was no living without fire, the school was dismissed, whereat all the scholars rejoiced.

I was about six years old when I first went to school. My teacher was "Aunt Delight," a maiden lady of fifty, short and bent, of sallow complexion and solemn aspect. We were seated upon benches made of slabs — boards having the exterior or rounded part of the log on one side. As they were useless for other purposes, they were converted into school benches, the rounded part down. They had each four supports, consisting of straddling wooden legs set into auger holes.

The children were called up one by one to Aunt Delight, who sat on a low chair, and required each, as a preliminary, "to make his manners," which consisted of a small, sudden nod. She then placed the spelling-book before the pupil, and with a pen-knife pointed, one by one, to the letters of the alphabet, saying, "What's that?"

I believe I achieved the alphabet that summer. Two years later I went to the winter school at the same place kept by Lewis Olmstead — a man who made a business of ploughing, mowing, carting manure, etc., in the summer, and of teaching school in the winter. He was a celebrity in ciphering, and Squire Seymour declared that he was the greatest "arithmeticker" in Fairfield County. There was not a grammar, a geography, or a history of any kind in the school. Reading, writing, and arithmetic were the only things taught, and these very indifferently — not wholly from the stupidity of the teacher, but because he had forty scholars, and the custom of the age required no more than he performed.[43]

The town schools were taught by persons varying a great deal in both learning and force of character. The masters of some of the Latin grammar schools, as, for example, Ezekiel Cheever and John Lovell of Boston, were men of outstanding classical scholarship who left a deep and lasting impression on their pupils. Many of the masters in the grammar schools were Harvard or Yale graduates. During the hundred years from 1671 to 1771, the town of Plymouth had twenty-eight schoolmasters and all but two were college graduates.[44] It was not unusual for a master to teach for many years in the same community. Thus, Samuel Savil was the master in Braintree for twenty-three years, and in the town of Sandwich John Rogers and Silas Tupper each taught for more than a quarter of a century.[45] Frequently, however, the grammar-school master taught for only a few years, while he was waiting for a call to the ministry. In many towns the local minister also served as the master in the grammar school, and this practice continued in Massachusetts even after the law prohibited it.

The scholastic requirements for teaching were far from rigorous. Of course, the grammar-school master was expected to have a knowledge of Latin and perhaps some Greek, and the masters and dames who taught elementary school had to know how to read and write and in most instances be able to teach simple arithmetic. Diligent care was taken that the schoolmaster be sound in the faith and of "sober and good conversation." Commonly, he was required to have a certificate signed by the minister of the town in which he proposed to teach and by the minister in one or more of the adjacent towns. A certificate issued in Wenham in 1743 read:

> Mr. Jonathan Perkins, having been agreed with to keep school in our town for six months, we being well satisfied of his ability for that service

[43] As quoted in Clifton Johnson, *Old-Time Schools and School-Books* (New York: The Macmillan Co., 1904), pp. 116–117. See also Mary Crawford, *Social Life in Old New England* (Boston: Little, Brown & Co., 1914), pp. 36–38.
[44] Small, *op. cit.*, p. 114.   [45] *Ibid.*, p. 103.

and his sober and good conversation, do approbate the said Jonathan Perkins to keep a school in our town for the time agreed on, he continuing in such conversation.[46]

The ministers granted the certificate to teach; they also kept a close supervision over the school to see to it that the teachers remained sound in the faith and of good conversation. The selectmen and committees of prominent citizens also paid periodic visits to the school to make sure that it was being satisfactorily conducted.

The New England College in the Eighteenth Century

While the Latin grammar school was declining in popular favor and the town elementary school of the three R's was being brought close to the people by the spread of the district system, higher education was increasing in importance, and at Harvard, at least, it was beginning to emancipate itself from sectarian control. During the closing years of the seventeenth century, Harvard appears to have suffered a decline both in the number of students and in the quality of its work. Two Dutch travelers visited Harvard in 1680, where they found fewer than twenty students in attendance. And, rightly or wrongly, they placed a low estimate on the scholastic attainment of the students. The first group of young men they encountered gave them the impression they were in a tavern rather than a college. The students, they reported, could hardly speak a word of Latin. Nor were they any more favorably impressed with the library, "where there was nothing particular."

But soon after the turn of the century, the little college fell on better days. College enrollment soon reflected the peace and prosperity that followed the Treaty of Utrecht in 1713. By 1718 there were no fewer than one hundred and twenty-four students in attendance, counting candidates for the Master's as well as the Bachelor's degree.[47] More important than growth in numbers, however, was the refusal of Harvard to permit its intellectual life to be entirely circumscribed by the narrow tenets of Puritanism. Located in Cambridge, at the very heart of the intellectual life of Massachusetts, Harvard could not escape the influence of the secular interests and the growing liberalism of Boston merchants and men of affairs. Some of the ministers, like the two Mathers and Jonathan Edwards, and many of the farm folk in towns removed from the seacoast might still be held in the grip of Puritanism, but this was no longer true of many of the outstanding leaders in Boston. Moreover, it was the merchant class that was providing Harvard with a large percentage of its

---

[46] *Ibid.*, p. 91.

[47] Samuel Eliot Morison, *Three Centuries of Harvard, 1636–1936* (Cambridge, Mass.: Harvard University Press, 1936), p. 59.

students and some of its instructional staff. It was possible, therefore, for Harvard presidents, notably John Leverett and Edward Holyoke, to prevent the college from being merely a sectarian institution. During the course of the eighteenth century, the religious thought of Harvard moved slowly away from Puritanism toward a broad Unitarianism or Deism.

The curriculum and the activities of the students reflected this partial emancipation from Puritan thought. In 1728, Isaac Greenwood was installed as the first professor of mathematics and natural philosophy. Ten years later, he was succeeded by Professor John Winthrop, who continued to teach until 1779. Of his work Nettels has the following to say:

> The first creative scientist in academic circles was John Winthrop, professor of mathematics and natural philosophy at Harvard between 1738 and 1779. As the son of a Boston merchant, Professor Winthrop was in touch with that element among the colonial capitalists which was turning from Puritan dogma to science, and his appointment was viewed with misgivings by the theologians. He established the first laboratory of experimental physics in an American college, using the best available scientific apparatus to demonstrate the laws of heat, light, and mechanics, and in 1751 he introduced the study of calculus at Harvard. He made observations of sunspots, studied electricity, and proved that earthquakes are the result of natural forces, not of divine anger. In 1761 he led an official expedition to Newfoundland to observe the transit of Venus over the sun. His scientific contributions were printed in the *Transactions of the Royal Society* — the main channel of publication for the papers of colonial scientists.[48]

French was not a regular study in the curriculum, but after 1750 it was customary to license a French teacher to give private instruction to Harvard students who might desire it. New books, such as Locke's *Essay Concerning Human Understanding*, were being introduced into the classrooms, and the curriculum was undergoing a rather thorough reorganization.

Student activities and the subjects selected by students for commencement theses also reflected the broader intellectual life at Harvard. In 1721 the first college periodical, *The Telltale,* made its appearance. Student clubs were organized, and many of the subjects brought up for discussion in them, as, for example, "Whether There Be Any Standard of Truth," were indicative of the wide departure from the Puritan outlook on life.[49] Although many commencement theses still reflected the spirit of Scholastic

[48] *The Roots of American Civilization,* by Curtis P. Nettels. Copyright, 1938, F. S. Crofts & Co., Inc. By permission of Appleton-Century-Crofts, Inc. For information concerning Winthrop, his background, his methods of teaching, and his scientific interests and excellence, see Theodore Hornberger, *Scientific Thought in the American Colleges, 1638–1800* (Austin, Texas: University of Texas Press, 1945), pp. 49–61.

[49] Morison, *op. cit.,* pp. 62–63.

theology, some of them clearly revealed the new currents of thought. From those reflecting the religious interest and the older point of view, the following topics have been selected:

Is the act of creation eternal? (1660, 1755, 1768)

Does a good intention suffice to make an action good? (1692, 1716, 1743, 1755, 1791)

Was the eclipse of the sun at the time of Christ's Passion a natural occurrence? (1678, 1708)

Do the angels have matter and form? (1680, 1682, 1693, 1694, 1703)

If Adam had not sinned, would original righteousness have been communicated to his descendants? (1731)

Were the Hebrew prophets of divine origin? (1681 [Cotton Mather])

Did Adam have an umbilical cord? (1765 [Jeremy Belknap])

When Balaam's ass spoke, were there any changes in its organs? (1731 [Josiah Quincy])

If Lazarus, by a will made before his death, had given away his property, could he have legally claimed it after his resurrection? (1738, 1754, 1769)

Is there an order of rank among the demons? (1714)

When the shadow went back on the sundial of Hezekiah, did the shadows go back on all sundials? (1769, 1771)

Is original sin both sin and punishment? (1674 [Samuel Sewall])

Does the will always follow the last dictate of the intellect? (1675, 1686, 1692, 1700, 1716, 1722, 1739)[50]

The theses in the following list were argued no doubt in much the same way as the theses in the foregoing one, but they are of a different order and reflect the growing secularization of thought:

Is civil government absolutely necessary for men? (1758 [John Adams])

Is it lawful to resist the supreme magistrate, if the Commonwealth cannot otherwise be preserved? (1743 [Samuel Adams])

Are we bound to observe the mandate of kings, unless they themselves keep their agreements with their subjects? (1738)

Does civil government originate from compact? (1743, 1747, 1751, 1761, 1762)

Can the new prohibitory duties, which make it useless for a people to engage in commerce, be evaded by them as faithful servants? (1765 [Elbridge Gerry])

---

[50] *Subjects for Master's Degree in Harvard College, 1655–1791.* Translated and Arranged, With an Introduction and Notes, by Edward J. Young. Reprinted from the *Proceedings of the Massachusetts Historical Society,* June, 1880 (Cambridge: John Wilson & Son, University Press, 1880). See *Proceedings . . .* (Boston: published by the Society, 1881), pp. 123–151.

Is it wrong to smuggle goods for the purpose of withholding revenue from the king? (1725)

Is there a circulation of the blood? (1660, 1699)

Are the causes and cures of all natural diseases mechanical? (1731, 1747, 1758, 1762)

Is the man who has an ardent passion for accumulating riches a greater injury to the state than the spendthrift? (1761)[51]

It appears that the curriculum of Harvard was undergoing some expansion and a measure of liberalization, but it is easy to overestimate the extent of the changes that had taken place. After all, only a beginning had been made in the study of mathematics and science. Little systematic attention was given to English writers — to Shakespeare, Ben Jonson, Addison, Swift, or Pope. And those studies which deal with human society — history, economics, sociology, geography, and anthropology — were almost wholly neglected. Harvard did not have a chair of history until the nineteenth century.

The second college to be established in New England, and the third in the English colonies, was Yale. It has often been said that Yale was established as a reaction to the growing liberalism of Harvard. This is only partly the case. John Davenport and other leaders in Connecticut had long been interested in founding a college, but they felt that the colony was not financially able to support one. There can be no doubt, however, that the establishment of Yale in 1701 was in part due to the feeling that Harvard was becoming unsound in the faith. From the beginning, Yale kept in the strict and narrow path of Congregationalism; it may be regarded as a strictly sectarian institution. The same was true of Dartmouth, founded in 1769. Like Yale, it was a Congregationalist college and was in large measure the product of the religious revival known as the Great Awakening, a remarkable movement centering in New England in the early 1740's but reaching all the colonies by 1750.

Ventures in Adjusting Education to Social Needs — the Rise of Private Schools

Too often the history of education in colonial New England has been written as though an account of the town schools and colleges comprised the whole of it; the attention of historians has been too narrowly confined to colonial laws and town records as sources of information. The examination of other sources reveals that there were other schools of very great importance. As we have seen, the town schools were dominated by influences growing out of the Renaissance and the Reformation, by classical and religious traditions. It is perhaps no exaggeration to say that they were

51 *Ibid.*

always exotic in the American climate and they tended to become more so as the eighteenth century progressed. The educational opportunities they afforded were too narrow and restricted to meet the needs of a large element in the population. Many youth who wanted to engage in one or another of the business enterprises of the day, or who desired to cultivate a certain refinement of taste, found it necessary to turn away from the town schools and seek a more practical education elsewhere. This need for a type of education that would be more functional was met by the private teacher. Unfortunately, the records do not disclose anything like so much as we should like to know about these private schools. But an examination of newspaper advertisements does enable one to patch together a fairly accurate picture of the work these schools were doing.[52]

The contrast in the spirit and purpose of the town and the private schools is brought out vividly, perhaps too vividly, by the two following quotations. The first, a quotation from the preface of a school text published in Boston about the middle of the eighteenth century, may be taken as more or less indicative of the spirit of the town schools:

> Lord what is man: Originally dust, engendered in sin, brought forth in sorrow, helpless in his infancy, extravagantly wild in his youth, mad in his manhood, decrepid in his age; his first voice moves to pity, his last commands grief.[53]

The second is an advertisement which appeared in the *Boston Gazette* in 1739.

> Such as are desirous of learning any Parts of the Mathematicks whether Theoretical, as the demonstrating Euclid, Appollonius, &c. or Practical, as Arithmetic, Geometry, Trigonometry, Navigation, Surveying, Gauging, Algebra, Fluxions, &c. Likewise any of the Branches of Natural Philosophy, as Mechanics, Optics, Astronomy, &c. may be taught by Isaac Greenwood, A.M. &c. at the Duke of Marlborough's Arms in King-Street, over against the Golden Fleece, Boston, where Attendance is given from 9 to 12 A.M. and 3 to 6 P.M.
>
> N.B. If any Gentlemen, or particular Company of such, are desirous of more private Instruction relating to the Premises at their respective Places, Attendance will be given out of the aforesaid Hours of teaching.[54]

From the opening of the eighteenth century, and possibly earlier, in the larger commercial centers private teachers were giving instruction in

---

[52] For a pioneer work on the private schools in colonial America see Robert Francis Seybolt, *Source Studies in American Colonial Education: The Private School*, Bureau of Educational Research Bulletin No. 28; University of Illinois Bulletin, XXIII, No. 4 (Urbana, Ill.: University of Illinois, 1925). Also see Seybolt, *The Private Schools of Colonial Boston* (Cambridge, Mass.: Harvard University Press, 1935).

[53] From a textbook published in Boston in 1757 under the title *Youth's Instructor*.

[54] *Boston Gazette*, March 26–April 2, April 2–April 9, 1739, as quoted in Seybolt, *The Private Schools of Colonial Boston, op. cit.*, pp. 26–27.

almost any subject for which there was a demand. Interest in vocational subjects was especially strong. Youth who wanted to enter the business world found it necessary to study arithmetic, bookkeeping, and accounting; those who wanted to learn navigation or surveying would have to give attention to a variety of subjects, including geometry, trigonometry, and geography.[55] There was a demand, too, for "dialling, gauging, fortification, gunnery, and optics, as well as . . . navigation and surveying." As Professor Seybolt points out, "for such courses algebra, geometry, logarithms, mensuration, trigonometry, conic sections, and calculus were necessary."[56] But it is not to be supposed that the demand for instruction given by these enterprising private teachers was limited to vocational subjects. They were also teaching Latin, French, geography, music, dancing, painting, and "the genteelest manner."

The work of these private teachers is revealing with respect to the education of girls. Some of the schools they conducted were coeducational and some were designed for girls only. The latter type specialized in reading and writing, French, music, dancing, painting, embroidery, sewing, millinery, and hairdressing.

The private schools were commonly kept in the home of the teacher or that of someone with whom the teacher lived. The hours for instruction were arranged to meet the convenience of the pupils. Evening schools were not uncommon. In some instances the teachers, in their advertisements, indicated that they were conducting boarding schools. Private schoolmasters in colonial America have been described as a generally poor and incompetent lot. Some were, no doubt, of little competence; some, perhaps, in their efforts to provide instruction in too many of the subjects in demand, pretended to competencies that they did not possess; some were intemperate, and no doubt some held unorthodox views and beliefs. In fact, three of the masters whose advertisements are reproduced in these pages were dismissed by Harvard on account of intemperance or dangerous beliefs. However, in Boston masters had to obtain leave to teach, which presumably all three were able to do. Many private schoolmasters in Boston, and perhaps in most of the other larger colonial cities, were college graduates and on the whole no less capable than the teachers in the town or district schools.

The following advertisements selected by Seybolt from many which appeared in the Boston newspapers of the eighteenth century illustrate the wide range of subjects being taught by private teachers.

(1709) Opposite to the Mitre Tavern in Fish-street near to Scarlets-Wharff, Boston, are Taught Writing, Arithmetick in all its parts; And also Geometry, Trigonometry, Plain and Sphaerical, Surveying, Dialling, Gaug-

[55] Seybolt, *Source Studies in American Colonial Education, op. cit.,* p. 35.
[56] *Ibid.,* p. 61.

ing, Navigation, Astronomy; The Projection of the Sphaere, and the use of Mathematical Instruments: By Owen Harris.[57]

(1713) AT THE HOUSE of Mr. George Brownell in Wings-Lane, Boston, is taught Writing, Cyphering, Dancing, Treble Violin, Flute, Spinnet, &c. Also English and French Quilting, Imbroidery, Florishing, Plain Work, Marking in several sorts of Stiches and several other works, where Scholars may board.[58]

(1720) AT THE HOUSE formerly Sir Charles Hobby's are taught Grammar, Writing after a free and easy manner, in all the hands usually practiced, Arithmetick Vulgar and Decimal in a concise and Practical Method, Merchants Accompts, Geometry, Algebra, Mensuration, Geography, Trigonometry, Astronomy, Navigation and other parts of the Mathematicks, with the use of Globes and other Mathematical Instruments, by Samuel Grainger.

They whose Business won't permit 'em to attend the usual School Hours, shall be carefully attended and instructed in the Evenings.[59]

(1734) THIS is to Notify any young Gentlemen who are desirous to learn the French Tongue, That Mr. Langloiserie will keep his French School Three Days in the Week at Cambridge, and Three Days in Boston, at the House of Mr. Benjamin Bridge in King Street. . . .[60]

(1743) THESE may inform the Publick, that Nathan Prince Fellow of Harvard College proposes, on suitable Encouragement, to open a school in this Town for the instructing young Gentlemen in the most useful Parts of the Mathematicks, Natural Philosophy and History. Particularly in the Elements of GEOMETRY and ALGEBRA; in TRIGONOMETRY and NAVIGATION: in GEOGRAPHY and ASTRONOMY, with the Use of the Globes and the several Kinds of Projecting the Sphere: In the Arts of SURVEYING, GAUGING and DIALING; and in the General Rules of FORTIFICATION and GUNNERY. . . .[61]

(1754) AT THE WIDOW ROBINS's at the North-End near Mr. Gledden's Ship-Yard, is kept a School by JOHN LEACH, from LONDON, who teaches the following Branches, viz. Arithmetick, common, vulgar and decimal: Geometry, Trigonometry; Navigation and Journal keeping in a practical Method . . . Mensuration of Superficies, Solids, Heights, and Distances . . . Gauging . . . Surveying . . . Drawing, as far as it is useful for a compleat Sea-Artist . . . &c.&c. With the Use and Construction of each Instrument us'd in the above Science. N.B. He keeps an Evening

[57] *Boston News-Letter*, March 14–21, 1708/9, as quoted in Seybolt, *The Private Schools of Colonial Boston, op. cit.*, p. 11.
[58] *Boston News-Letter*, March 21–28, 1708/9, as quoted *ibid.*, p. 12.
[59] *Boston Gazette*, March 21–22 (Supplement), 1719/20, *ibid.*, p. 15.
[60] *Boston Gazette*, July 8–15, 15–22, 22–29, 1734, *ibid.*, pp. 21–22.
[61] *Boston Weekly News-Letter*, March 3, 10, 1742–43, *ibid.*, p. 30.

School from 6 to 9 P.M. during the Winter Season. — Also, surveys Land, draws Plans, &c.[62]

(1772) [The English Grammar School] Is Now OPEN for the Instruction of Youth; where Gentlemen and Ladies may have their Children taught Reading, Spelling, English-Grammar, Arithmetic, Letter-Writing, and Composition in general. Also Logic, Rhetoric, Oratory, the Knowledge of the Globe, Geography, History, Chronology, Natural and Moral Philosophy; the Nature of Civil Government, and other Parts of Knowledge that are necessary to form the Minds of Youth for entering on the Stage of Life with Advantage, and to make an amiable Figure in the World.

From 11 o'clock to 12 in the Morning, the School will be kept for those who go to the free Schools, and cannot attend at other Hours.

Boys who are deficient in Reading, and Pronunciation, will be perfected in a short Time. . . .

Joseph Ward.[63]

The town schools of colonial New England were designed to meet the needs of a Puritan social order. These schools did change in response to the forces that impinged upon them, but it is clear that the pattern was so rigid, and the schools were so firmly anchored in a glorious tradition, that they did not yield readily to the pressures of an emerging capitalistic society. The Latin grammar schools maintained by the towns continued to perform their tasks as before, but they enrolled a relatively smaller number of the youth. In a number of towns the enrollment actually declined. The reading and writing school maintained by the town was brought closer to the children of farmers and artisans, but its efficiency was greatly impaired in the process. Although the colleges continued to prepare ministers for the Congregational churches, at Harvard the religious liberalism and the expanding intellectual needs of merchants and men of affairs were making themselves felt, in some measure, throughout the eighteenth century. In larger measure, it was left for the private teachers to sense the demands that a changing society was making upon the lower schools. Their success depended to a considerable degree on how well they anticipated the public demand. They were experimenting with new content and new methods, and before the close of the period the work that they were doing had become institutionalized in the academy, a form of school which was to occupy a dominant place in education for more than a century.

[62] *Boston Weekly News-Letter,* October 3, 10, 17, 1754, *ibid.,* pp. 37–38. Note the evening session.

[63] *The Boston Gazette and Country Journal,* October 26–November 2 (Supplement), 9, 1772, *ibid.,* p. 69. Note the provision made for boys attending the town schools.

Questions and Problems for Study and Discussion

1. How did educational policy and practice differ in seventeenth- and eighteenth-century New England?
2. How did the rise of a merchant-capitalist class affect education in New England?
3. How did the declining importance of the New England clergy as a social force in the community affect education?
4. How did the changes that occurred in the arrangement of the social classes in New England affect education? Did the rising importance of the yeomanry have significant educational consequences? If so, what?
5. How do you account for the abandonment of the policy of universal compulsory education in eighteenth-century New England?
6. How were the schools of colonial New England supported? Were there discernible trends? If so, how do you account for them?
7. What needs were served by the private schools of New England that were not served by the Latin grammar school that had been inherited from the Old World?
8. Evaluate the contribution of colonial New England to the theory and practice of school administration. What do you consider New England's greatest contribution to American education? Why?

Selected References for Further Reading

Adams, James Truslow. *Provincial Society, 1690–1763. A History of American Life,* III. New York: The Macmillan Co., 1927. Pp. xx + 374.

Bailyn, Bernard. *Education in the Forming of American Society.* Chapel Hill, N.C.: University of North Carolina, 1960. Pp. xvi + 147.

Bailyn, Bernard. *The New England Merchants in the Seventeenth Century.* Cambridge, Mass.: Harvard University Press, 1955. Pp. viii + 249.

Baxter, William Threipand. *The House of Hancock: Business in Boston, 1724–1775.* Cambridge, Mass.: Harvard University Press, 1945. Pp. xxvii + 321.

Beard, Charles A., and Beard, Mary R. *The Rise of American Civilization,* I: *The Agricultural Era.* New York: The Macmillan Co., 1927. Pp. xviii + 824.

Boorstin, Daniel J. *The Americans: The Colonial Experience.* New York: Random House, 1958. Pp. xii + 434.

Bridenbaugh, Carl. *Cities in Revolt: Urban Life in America, 1743–1776.* New York: Alfred A. Knopf, Inc., 1955. Pp. xiii + 433.

Bridenbaugh, Carl. *Cities in the Wilderness: The First Century of Urban Life in America, 1625–1742.* New York: The Ronald Press Company, 1938. Pp. xiv + 500.

Brown, Robert E. *Middle-Class Democracy and the Revolution in Massachusetts, 1691–1780.* Ithaca, N.Y.: Cornell University Press, 1955. Pp. ix + 458.

Brubacher, John S., and Rudy, Willis. *Higher Education in Transition, 1630–1956.* New York: Harper & Brothers, 1958. Pp. vii + 496.

Clews, Elsie W. *Educational Legislation and Administration of the Colonial Governments,* Columbia University Contributions to Philosophy, Psychology, and Education, Vol. VI, Nos. 1–4. New York: The Macmillan Co., 1899. Pp. xii + (7–524).

Curti, Merle. *The Growth of American Thought,* Second Edition. New York: Harper & Brothers, 1951. Pp. xvii + 910.

Jernegan, Marcus Wilson. *Laboring and Dependent Classes in Colonial America, 1607–1783: Studies of the Economic, Educational, and Social Significance of Slaves, Servants, and Poor Folk.* Chicago: University of Chicago Press, 1931. Pp. xiv + 256.

Johnson, Clifton. *Old-Time Schools and School-Books.* New York: The Macmillan Co., 1904. Pp. xxii + 382.

Meriwether, Colyer. *Our Colonial Curriculum, 1607–1776.* Washington. D.C.: Capital Publishing Co., 1907. Pp. xviii + 301.

Miller, Perry. *The New England Mind: From Colony to Province.* Cambridge, Mass.: Harvard University Press, 1953. Pp. xi + 513. Also published in paperback (Boston: Beacon Press, 1961).

Morison, Samuel Eliot. *Three Centuries of Harvard, 1636–1936.* Cambridge, Mass.: Harvard University Press, 1936. Pp. viii + 512.

Nettels, Curtis P. *The Roots of American Civilization: A History of American Colonial Life.* New York: F. S. Crofts & Co., 1938. Pp. xx + 748.

Perry, Ralph Barton. *Puritanism and Democracy.* New York: The Vanguard Press, 1944. Pp. xvi + 688.

Rossiter, Clinton. *Seedtime of the Republic: The Origin of the American Tradition of Political Liberty.* New York: Harcourt, Brace & Co., 1953. Pp. xiv + 558. Also published in paperback, in abridged form, under the title *The First American Revolution* (New York: Harcourt, Brace & Co. [Harvest Books], 1956).

Seybolt, Robert Francis. *The Private Schools of Colonial Boston.* Cambridge, Mass.: Harvard University Press, 1935. Pp. x + 106.

Seybolt, Robert Francis. *Source Studies in American Colonial Education: The Private School,* Bureau of Educational Research Bulletin, No. 28; University of Illinois Bulletin, XXIII, No. 4. Urbana, Ill.: University of Illinois, 1925. Pp. 110.

Small, Walter Herbert. *Early New England Schools.* Boston: Ginn & Company, 1914. Pp. x + 402.

Subjects for Master's Degree in Harvard College, 1655–1791. Translated and Arranged, with an Introduction and Notes, by Edward J. Young. Reprinted from the Proceedings of the Massachusetts Historical Society, June, 1880. Cambridge, Mass.: John Wilson & Son, University Press, 1880. Pp. 28.

Suzzalo, Henry. *The Rise of Local School Supervision in Massachusetts (the School Committee, 1635–1827)*. Teachers College Contributions to Education, No. 3. New York: Teachers College, Columbia University, 1908. Pp. viii + 154.

Sweet, William Warren. *Religion in Colonial America*. New York: Charles Scribner's Sons, 1942. Pp. xiii + 368.

Updegraff, Harlan. *The Origin of the Moving School in Massachusetts*, Teachers College Contributions to Education, No. 17. New York: Teachers College, Columbia University, 1908. Pp. 186.

Weeden, William B. *Economic and Social History of New England, 1620–1789*. 2 vols. Boston: Houghton Mifflin Company, 1890.

The School
in an Aristocratic Rural Social Order:
The Colonial South

The Beginnings of Southern Society

THE ENGLISH HERITAGE

If any region in the New World was to bear the name "New England," it should have been the area stretching from the Chesapeake Bay southward rather than the northeastern corner of what is now the United States. The colonists who settled along the estuaries and the lower reaches of the rivers of the southern coastal plain and the men back home who were sponsoring colonization in that area were in no revolt against the existing order of things in England. They accepted with little reservation prevailing notions of law and government and the fundamental principles of English liberty, although the various groups entering into the colonization enterprise were willing to modify those notions and principles to make them serve their own ends. The structure of government at both the colonial and local level was fashioned after the English model; governor, council, assembly, county, sheriff, and justice of the peace — all these found their more or less exact counterpart in England. It is equally true that the southern colonists accepted without serious question the class structure of society so characteristic of seventeenth-century England. Each sought to better his own economic status and to open wider for himself the door to social esteem and preferment, but few would disturb the well-ordered ranks of society. The social ideals of the English country gentry were in fact an important influence in molding the emerging social order in the South.

The Englishmen who migrated to Virginia had embraced a much less thoroughgoing Protestantism than had those who sought refuge in New England. By and large, they had no quarrel with the Anglican Church, and few of them were impelled to cross the sea by the desire for religious freedom. Although religious, they were prompted with no thoughts of founding a "Wilderness Zion," and the Puritan regime would have been as distasteful to them as it was to some in New England who were forced to endure it. Whereas New Englanders generally accepted the doctrines of John Calvin, with the implications that such acceptance entailed with respect to the establishment of a religious state and the obligations of the state to serve the church in the performance of its religious and educational functions, the early settlers of the South were, on the whole, content to accept the Established Church and the arrangements whereby it assisted the state in meeting the obligations which might properly be delegated to an official religious establishment. Even so, the transplanted Anglican Church never took very deep root in southern life except in certain limited areas. It did not thrive in the sparse population which characterized the plantation economy. It was never liberally supported, and it did not draw out of England any large number of outstanding intellectual leaders. On the whole, the Anglican clergy in the South were not an impressive lot. Their influence on political development was relatively slight; they tended to follow rather than to shape social policy. As we have already seen, a numerous, well-educated, and determined clergy provided New England in the early days with an intellectual leadership of a high order. It was this group, by and large, that shaped and carried into effect the educational policies of New England in the early years of the seventeenth century. In the South, the clergy played no such important role. The Anglican Church, with its decorous and non-emotional ritual, its sympathy with an aristocratic type of social organization, and its undemocratic form of government, fitted well into the order of life desired by southern planters, but as an agency of intellectual and cultural advance its role was of no great importance.

Educational ideals and practices.   The educational ideals and practices of the southern colonists were only slightly changed by the transit to America. No phase of southern life reflected more truly its English origin than did education. At the opening of the seventeenth century, the Protestant theory of education as essential to a godly life still persisted in England, and almost universally the church continued to be looked upon as an agency which should play a large part in establishing, controlling, and maintaining the educational program. A militant middle class was demanding education, but this demand reflected the growing importance of the class rather than the development of any marked democratic or liberal tendencies. Members of this expanding and power-seeking group looked upon education as a means of enhancing prestige and assuring worldly success, but there were as yet few to argue that children generally should be provided with more training than required to fit them to participate, at levels proper to their social stations, in the political, economic, and religious life of the day. Scientists and scholars in many fields were making progress in dispelling the darkness which closed from view the nature of man and of the world about him, but the great majority of persons, educated and uneducated alike, retained almost absolute confidence in the classics as constituting the proper curriculum for a liberal education. The southern colonists, like other Englishmen, accepted the religious tradition in education, a class structure of social and educational organization, the classical ideal, and, in general, the "theories, forms, practices, and machinery connected with the various agencies and processes of education" as they were operative in England in the opening years of the seventeenth century. In 1671, more than sixty years after the founding of Virginia, Governor Berkeley, in answer to a query from the Board of Trade as to what course was taken about the instruction of the people in the colony, replied: "The same that is taken in England out of towns; every man according to his own ability instructing his children."[1] This to him, and to Virginians generally, appeared to be an entirely satisfactory program.

FORCES IN THE DEVELOPMENT OF A NEW SOCIAL ORDER

The development of southern institutions, including education, cannot be entirely explained, however, in terms of the ideas, ways of thinking, and patterns of behavior which went to make up the cultural heritage of the colonists. In time, a distinctive social order was to emerge in the South, and it was this peculiar type of social organization that gave education its bent and direction for more than a hundred years. An understanding of the development of southern society is to be found in the motivations and drives of the individuals and groups that took a hand in the colonization enterprise, in the struggles of those individuals and groups to exploit the resources of the area to their economic and social advantage, and in the influence of geography. Southern society took form as the various and sometimes conflicting elements of the population of England and Europe sought in one way or another to improve their fortunes in this particular region of the New World.

The actors in the drama of southern life were many and varied. First, there were the great nobles and lords of England, among them George

[1] As quoted in Elmer Ellsworth Brown, *The Making of Our Middle Schools* (New York: Longmans, Green & Co., 1918), pp. 49–50. For a complete statement, see William W. Hening, *The Statutes-at-Large*, II (Collection of Laws of Virginia).

Calvert, Lord Baltimore; Arthur Hyde, Earl of Clarendon; Anthony Ashley Cooper, Earl of Shaftesbury; George Monck, Duke of Albermarle; Sir William Berkeley; Lord Thomas Culpeper; and a long list of others of greater or lesser prominence. Of course, few of these upper-class Englishmen ever migrated to the colonies, but through their great political influence they were able to obtain large grants of land which they sought to develop into semifeudal estates worked by tenants and servants. The greater and lesser merchants of England also took a hand in southern affairs. Some of them, like Martin Noell and Thomas Povey, joined the English nobility in the attempt to carve out large landed estates; others were content to multiply their profits in the exploitation of southern commerce. Middle-class Englishmen with some surplus capital saw in the southern tobacco and rice fields an opportunity to build up landed estates not afforded them in England, and not a few of them migrated to one or another of the southern colonies. Many sturdy yeomen and artisans in England were able to pay for their passage to Virginia, Maryland, or the Carolinas, where they, too, hoped to get possession of land as independent owners. Still others with no means at all were willing to serve as indentured servants in America in order to pay their transportation over, and not a few of the inmates of English prisons were hustled off to Virginia to labor as indentured servants in the tobacco fields. As the seventeenth century drew to a close, the interests of British and New England slave traders and of southern planters were merging to bring into the colonies thousands of unfortunate African blacks, whose presence was to revolutionize the social order. And as the plantation economy based on slavery was fastening itself on the coastal plain, thousands of poverty-ridden German peasants and hard-pressed Scotch-Irish Presbyterians from North Ireland were moving into the valleys of the back-country South all the way from Pennsylvania to South Carolina. Out of the struggle for place and position, for the ownership of land and the exploitation of labor, of all these varied elements — the English landed nobility, middle-class farmers and merchants, tenants and artisans, land-hungry German peasants, Scotch-Irish, and a merchant class that developed in the colonies — the southern social order took form. In order to understand the educational ideals and practices which developed in this social order, we must subject it to a somewhat more detailed examination.

The Southern Economy

The aims of the promoters of early colonization were only partially realized. Certainly, the economic order they planned failed to materialize. The London merchants and capitalists who supplied the necessary funds to launch the settlement at Jamestown had no idea of developing an agricultural economy based upon the production of a staple crop. Had they had their way, Virginians would have devoted themselves to the making of iron and glass, to the growing of hemp, to the production of potash, silk, and wine — things much needed in the English economy. But in spite of well-intentioned efforts on the part of both the London Company and the English government to develop a diversified economy, the success and prosperity of the Virginia colonists became inseparably linked with the production of a single staple crop.

TOBACCO AND THE DEVELOPING ECONOMY

Jamestown was not a decade old before it was discovered that the soil and climate of Virginia were admirably suited to the production of tobacco. The cultivation of tobacco began in 1612, and it spread so rapidly that within a few years Governor Dale was obliged to order that no man should be permitted to plant the weed until he had put down two acres in corn. The quantity of tobacco exported annually increased rapidly, from 20,000 pounds in 1619 to about 40,000,000 pounds at the beginning of the eighteenth century, and to more than 71,000,000 pounds in 1771.

The requirements for the production and marketing of tobacco more than anything else, perhaps, determined the social order that was to prevail in Virginia. The cultivation of tobacco affected profoundly both the land and labor systems. The planter needed a large tract of land, partly because tobacco was very exhaustive of the soil and partly because the larger his enterprise, the greater his profits. Land hunger came to possess Virginians from the royal governor down to the indentured servant; and for the first half-century at least, land was relatively easy to acquire. Favorites of the king or of the royal governor, or members of the colonial council who were in a position to exercise influence, might without too much difficulty secure patents to thousands of acres. And the headright system, whereby one could secure title to fifty acres of land by showing that he had paid the passage of an indentured servant from England, made it possible for the lesser planters to add to their holdings.

The plantation system did not, however, develop very rapidly; until near the end of the seventeenth century, Virginia was still, in the main, a land of relatively small planters. It has been estimated that, around 1700, more than 60 per cent of the whites in Virginia did not own slaves or have indentured servants.[2] To be sure, one could find here and there a large plantation like that of Ralph Wormeley, Robert Beverley, John Carter, William Fitzhugh, or the first William Byrd. The fact is that

---

[2] James Truslow Adams, *Provincial Society, 1690–1763* (New York: The Macmillan Co., 1927), p. 217. See also Philip Alexander Bruce, *Economic History of Virginia in the Seventeenth Century: An Inquiry into the Material Condition of the People* . . . (2 vols.; New York: The Macmillan Co., 1896).

more than cheap land and a favorable climate were required to make possible the development of a plantation economy. A bountiful nature was not enough. Dense forests had to be cleared; crops had to be planted, cultivated, and harvested. For these tasks human hands were needed — many hands, if not skilled ones. A plentiful supply of workers was essential for the development of an agrarian economy based upon the production of tobacco.

THE LABOR SYSTEM

In England at the opening of the seventeenth century there was almost an endless supply of laborers. English parishes were filled with idle men. Many of those who were employed found their wages entirely inadequate to purchase food and clothing at the prevailing prices. The burden of the support of the idle poor rested heavily upon the taxpayers, many of whom were finding it increasingly difficult to maintain themselves. It was hoped that the colonies would draw off large numbers of the dependent class, and it is true that America offered extraordinary inducements. Compared with what it was in England, the price of labor in the colonies was dear, and the opportunity to obtain land was infinitely greater. The English laborer could make what must have appeared, at the time, very good terms if he would migrate to America. Lacking funds to pay his passage to the New World and to establish himself once he had arrived, the worker could bind himself out for a period of service in payment for transportation, maintenance during his period of servitude, and sometimes land or other remuneration at the end of his term of indenture.

At the very outset of colonization, the London Company sent a number of indentured servants to Virginia. Colonists who could afford to do so immediately followed the lead of the Company. The introduction of these servants was effected by various means. Many, the so-called redemptioners, were brought over by shipmasters and given a few days to sell their services on the best terms possible. Others before leaving England signed contracts whereby it was agreed that the shipmaster was to sell them into a term of servitude. Children were gathered up from the parishes of England and dispatched to the colonies. Kidnaped persons and others forced into service, among them convicts and political prisoners, added to the labor supply of tobacco planters. Estimates as to the number of convicts sent to the plantations vary considerably.[3] Jefferson placed the figure at about two thousand for Virginia; others have stated

[3] The practice of seizing persons and selling them into service was known as "spiriting" victims. Channing states that "in 1670 as many as ten thousand persons were spirited from England in one year." Edward Channing, *A History of the United States* (New York: The Macmillan Co., 1909), II, p. 369. Children were the chief victims. See Oliver Perry Chitwood, *A History of Colonial America,* Third Edition (New York: Harper & Brothers, 1961), pp. 340–342.

that as many as fifty thousand prisoners were sent to America by English judges. It has been suggested that American genealogists have, in passing over the archives of Newgate and the Old Bailey, neglected a mine of untapped material. The harsh laws of England, however, probably resulted in sending over few convicts whose offenses were more than petty crimes growing out of poverty, helplessness, and wretchedness. All in all, white servants constituted the chief labor supply for the plantations during the entire seventeenth century. It has been estimated that to Virginia alone came 1500 to 2000 annually from 1635 to 1705 — a total of 100,000 to 140,000 for the seventy-year period.

So long as the Virginia planter had to rely on indentured servants as a source of labor supply or till his acres with his own hands, the plantation system did not develop very rapidly. Indentures usually ran for only four or five years. Consequently, an increasing stream of arrivals was required to maintain an adequate servant population. As Pennsylvania and other colonies came to offer greater opportunity to the migrant, and as economic conditions in England improved, it became increasingly obvious that a plantation economy would have to be based upon some other form of labor than white servitude. Moreover, after his term of enforced labor was over, the indentured servant was free to establish himself as a small planter, and he often succeeded in doing just this. Not a few ex-indentured servants became leaders of the Virginia yeomanry and were elected to serve in the House of Burgesses. It must be remembered, too, that the small-planter class was constantly being augmented by immigrants who were able to pay their own transportation to Virginia.

Professor Thomas Jefferson Wertenbaker through careful research has dispelled the long-accepted picture of seventeenth-century Virginia as a land of large plantations. Writing of Virginia of about 1700, he says:

> Even a cursory examination of the rent roll is sufficient to dispel the old belief that Virginia at this time was the land of the large proprietor. As one glances down the list of plantations he is struck by the number of little holdings, the complete absence of huge estates, the comparative scarcity even of those that for a newly settled country might be termed extensive. Here and there, especially in the frontier counties, is listed a tract of four or five or even ten thousand acres, but such cases are very rare. In Middlesex county there is but one plantation of more than 2500 acres, in Charles City county the largest holding is 3130, in Nansemond 2300, in Norfolk county 3200, in Princess Anne 3100, in Elizabeth City county 2140, in York 2750, in Essex 3200.
>
> On the other hand the rolls reveal the existence of thousands of little proprietors, whose holdings of from 50 to 500 acres embraced the larger part of the cultivated soil of the colony. Thus we find that in Nansemond, of 376 farms 26 were of 50 acres or less, 66 were between 50 and 100 acres, 110 between 100 and 200 acres, 88 between 200 and

400 acres, 78 between 400 and 1000 acres, and only eight over 1000 acres. In Middlesex county out of 122 holdings eleven were of 50 acres or less, 33 between 50 and 100 acres, 32 between 100 and 200 acres, 25 between 200 and 500 acres, 19 between 500 and 2500 acres, one of 4000 acres and one of 5200 acres. Of the 94 plantations in Charles City county 26 were of 100 acres or less, 21 between 100 and 200 acres, 25 between 200 and 500 acres, 19 between 500 and 2500 acres and three more than 2500 acres. . . .[4]

Thus vanishes the fabled picture of Seventeenth century Virginia. In its place we see a colony filled with little farms a few hundred acres in extent, owned and worked by a sturdy class of English farmers. Prior to the slave invasion which marked the close of the Seventeenth century and the opening of the Eighteenth, the most important factor in the life of the Old Dominion was the white yeomanry.[5]

The statistics presented by Wertenbaker serve to correct an erroneous view concerning the nature of the total agricultural economy. However, they confirm the existence of many large estates that could not be worked without a large supply of agricultural labor. One plantation of a thousand acres, if fully worked, required a considerable number of servants, and a sprinkling of large estates was sufficient to keep the servant population at a relatively high level, and to create a situation in which it became increasingly difficult for small holdings to be worked profitably.

The Rising Tide of Negro Slavery

During the closing years of the seventeenth century, the Virginia yeomanry began to go down before the rising tide of Negro slavery. There had long been a demand for slaves, but neither the English nor the New England merchants had been able to break the grip of the Dutch on the slave trade. Slaves were present in Virginia from 1619, but their number increased slowly. In 1671, there were two thousand Negroes, as compared with six thousand white servants in the colony. It was not long, however, before the number of Negro slaves began to increase markedly, and this was especially the case after the Treaty of Utrecht in 1713 opened the African slave markets to English and American slavers. By 1715, one-fourth of Virginia's population of some ninety-five thousand were Negroes, and around the middle of the century the ratio of slaves to whites was about two to three.

The impact of Negro slavery on the economic and social order in Virginia was immediate and profound. The small farmer could not com-

[4] Thomas Jefferson Wertenbaker, *The Planters of Colonial Virginia* (Princeton, N.J.: Princeton University Press, 1922), pp. 52–53. See also Harold Underwood Faulkner, *American Political and Social History,* Sixth Edition (New York: Appleton-Century-Crofts, Inc., 1952), p. 58.

[5] Wertenbaker, *op. cit.,* p. 59.

pete with slave labor. The day was virtually over when eastern Virginia offered opportunity to Englishmen without means to establish themselves as members of an independent yeomanry; the number of indentured white servants coming over from England fell off suddenly; henceforth the ships that dropped anchor in the Virginia rivers and estuaries were to be laden with hopeless Africans rather than Anglo-Saxons who looked forward to the time when they would be masters of their own small farms. Slavery dried up the source of English migration; it also forced the Virginia yeomanry to retreat before it or to adjust to it. Many small farmers, reduced to poverty by competition with slave labor, gave up the fight and moved on to the frontier or into western Pennsylvania and Maryland. Many of them took refuge in North Carolina, where slavery was less common. Others were able to adjust to the new situation by becoming small slaveholders themselves. Some sank into the poverty and despair of "poor whites," and were despised by all who could own a slave and held in contempt by the blacks themselves. Numerically, the small slaveholders came to be the most important element in the slaveholding population, but here and there one could find a large plantation worked by scores of slaves. Thus, in 1782, of the 633 slaveholders in Dinwiddie County, "95 had one only, 66 had two, 71 three, 45 four, 50 five, making an aggregate of 327, or more than half of all the slave holders, who possessed from one to five Negroes."[6] But there were also many who numbered their slaves by the score. In Dinwiddie the following year the tax lists show that no fewer than sixty owners had twenty-one or more slaves.[7] Occasionally the records reveal the possession of more than a hundred Negroes. Truly, the introduction of African slavery had wrought a revolution in the economic life of Virginia. An aristocratic social order, based upon a plantation economy which had begun to take form even before the rapid growth of Negro slavery, had now fastened itself on tidewater Virginia.

THE SPREAD OF THE PLANTATION ECONOMY

Much the same course of events was transpiring in Maryland, where, also, tobacco was the staple crop. Originally, Lord Baltimore had hoped to establish a manorial system in Maryland not unlike that of England, but he soon discovered that the Englishmen who came to America were bent upon obtaining a freehold of their own. Consequently, he adopted the policy of granting land in fee simple in relatively small tracts. During most of the seventeenth century in Maryland, as in Virginia, indentured servants constituted the major part of the labor supply. Maryland, too, was essentially a land of small independent farmers, a condition which was to change rather rapidly after the turn of the century. Here, too, the

[6] *Ibid.*, p. 153.　　　　[7] *Ibid.*, p. 158.

yeomanry were unable to stand their ground against Negro slavery, or against the favored position of the men of wealth, who were able to bring their influence to bear on proprietors and crown officials to secure large grants of land. The proportion of slaves in the population increased from about one-sixth in 1715 to around 29 per cent in 1755. Men of means, especially in the Western Shore counties, developed large estates worked by slaves,[8] and some, like Charles Carroll, Daniel Dulany, and Thomas Brerewood, were able to obtain large tracts of land which they peopled with Irish and German tenants. As the eighteenth century progressed, the ranks of the independent yeomanry in Maryland, as in Virginia, gave way before the steady advance of a plantation economy.

To the south of the tobacco colonies, in what are now the two Carolinas, the little group of Englishmen who dominated English colonial policy in the sixteen-sixties sought personal possession of huge tracts of land which they hoped to develop into ducal estates. As lords proprietors of Carolina, they were able to dispose of the land much as they pleased — to hold large tracts for themselves or to grant it to their friends and favorites or other entrepreneurs. It was soon discovered, however, that the settlers in Carolina were in no frame of mind to be exploited in the interest of absentee proprietors. Those who had taken refuge in Albermarle, the northern part of Carolina, from the rising tide of slavery and aristocracy in Virginia insisted upon establishing freeholds for themselves and upon managing their own affairs much as they pleased. Those who settled in and around Charleston — Englishmen, French Huguenots, planters from the East Indies, Irish, Welsh, Swiss, Germans, and Dutch — were soon engaged in carving out for themselves large rice plantations worked by slave labor or in exploiting the trade of the huge area of which Charleston was the commercial capital. After 1740, indigo as well as rice became a staple crop. The importance of rice as an export is indicated by the fact that in 1754 more than 100,000 barrels of this grain were shipped from Charleston. Within five years after the cultivation of indigo was introduced, more than 200,000 pounds of the cake made from the dried liquid of the plant were exported to England. Rice and indigo fields were cultivated almost exclusively by slave labor, and each decade saw the number of slaves rise with startling rapidity. In 1715, approximately five-eighths of South Carolina's 16,000 inhabitants were Negro slaves. In 1769, there were about 45,000 whites and 80,000 blacks in the population of the colony.[9] Some Carolina planters numbered their slaves by the hundreds, as, for example, Ralph Izard, who employed 594 Negroes to cultivate his eight plantations.[10]

[8] Lewis Cecil Gray, *History of Agriculture in the Southern United States to 1860* (Washington, D.C.: Carnegie Institution of Washington, 1933), I, p. 354.

[9] Leila Sellers, *Charleston Business on the Eve of the American Revolution* (Chapel Hill, N.C.: University of North Carolina Press, 1934), p. 15.

[10] *Ibid.,* p. 26

Charleston was one of the great centers of colonial commerce. Its merchants, in the value of their trade and the size of their fortunes, could rival any to be found in America. Indian traders exploited the fur trade into the back-country for a thousand miles and for a while deerskins rivaled rice and indigo as an article of export. The commanding importance of Charleston as a commercial center is witnessed by the fact that shortly before the Revolution more than four hundred ships were entering its harbor annually.[11] In 1773, Carolina exports, most of which were cleared through Charleston, were valued at 456,513 pounds. This was considerably more than the total value of exports to Great Britain from all the colonies north of Maryland.[12]

Social Consequences of the Plantation Economy

As the colonial period drew to a close, the plantation system based upon African slavery had come to dominate most of the coastal plain stretching from the Chesapeake Bay region to Florida. The plantation economy and the factors which promoted its development profoundly influenced every aspect of southern life — economic, political, social, and educational. Everywhere, the better lands came to be concentrated in the hands of an aristocracy of increasing numbers. In Virginia, primogeniture tended to prevent the break-up of large estates once they had been established. Although small farms in the tidewater South continued to exist, the plantation system precluded the possibility of a society of small freeholders.

As the size of the plantation increased and free labor gave place to slave labor, there was a definite hardening of the class structure. The freeman, particularly after 1700, who attempted to establish himself as a planter found the odds heavily against him, and the owner of a small freehold found it increasingly difficult to compete with neighbors possessed of large resources of land and slave labor. The inherited class structure, which had weakened considerably in the early seventeenth century under the leveling influence of the frontier, had become more rigid than ever. The yeomanry was not completely wiped out, but the large planter who owned huge tracts of land, commanded large resources of capital and credit, and owned many slaves came to dominate the economic, political, and social life of the southern colonies. The line between these two planter groups, which during the seventeenth century had not been clearly drawn, became more distinct as the opportunity decreased for the small planters to rise to places of wealth and prominence. The aristocracy of the southern plantations was neither so pretentious nor so arrogant as that of England, but it knew well enough how to keep lesser people in their place, how to exercise political power in its own class interest, how to

11 *Ibid.*, p. 11.   12 *Ibid.*, p. 10.

exploit economic resources to the limit, and how to give thought and sentiment the direction desired. As we shall see a little later, the aristocratic tendencies of this society were reflected in the arrangements made for the education of the young.

The plantation economy affected very definitely the growth of population and the pattern of its distribution on the land. The baneful influence of the southern type of economic organization upon the growth of population has been discussed by many writers. It should be pointed out, however, that, after approximately ninety years of colonization, the combined population of the tobacco colonies, Virginia and Maryland, was at least three-fourths of that of all New England. And at the time of the taking of the first census in 1790, three-eighths of the white population was found south of the Mason-Dixon line. It was not so much the size of the population as it was the manner in which it was distributed that influenced the development of the cultural and intellectual life of the South. Plantations were large and in many instances separated from one another by poor or abandoned lands. Transportation, except by boat, was difficult and distances were great. For much of the colonial period the great plantations tended to cluster along the rivers and estuaries that threaded the coastal plain. In 1724, the average size of twelve typical parishes, the smallest units of government, was five hundred and forty-five square miles, an area larger than the average midwestern county of today and almost twenty times larger than the average New England town of the period. It has been estimated that the majority of the members of a parish were obliged to travel five to ten miles to attend church. In the twelve parishes mentioned above, there was, on the average, less than one family to the square mile. Under circumstances such as these vigorous community life was almost impossible. Comparatively few areas possessed a sufficient number of children to make the establishment of schools an economical procedure. Organized efforts to provide schools were commonly made in those areas in which cooperation was possible. In other communities, the education of children of necessity was achieved, if at all, through other means. Thus, the pattern of population distribution as well as the type of social organization was reflected in the educational program.

One of the most conspicuous results of the plantation system was the almost complete non-existence of town life. In New England, even in agricultural communities, the bulk of the population lived in compact settlements, the majority dwelling within a comparatively short distance of the church. The New England village-centered community did not have its counterpart in the South. As late as the beginning of the eighteenth century, there was hardly so much as a village in Virginia. Few persons could be induced to settle in towns. Even county seats consisted, in most instances, of the public buildings with perhaps an inn or a store. It is said that Thomas Jefferson, prior to his matriculation at William and Mary in 1760, had never seen so many as a dozen houses grouped together. As late as the middle of the eighteenth century Williamsburg was a village of about two hundred houses, and at the close of the Revolution Richmond had fewer than four thousand inhabitants. Norfolk, the largest town in colonial Virginia, had a population of about six thousand in 1776. Baltimore did not develop into a place of great importance until after the Revolution. Towns did not develop even for commercial purposes so long as seagoing vessels could dock at the wharves of the great plantations that lay along the banks of the navigable rivers.

Charleston, in South Carolina, was an exception. As we have already seen, it rivaled Boston, New York, and Philadelphia as a great center of trade. Its merchants maintained close relations with the other colonies and with England. Planters, many of them masters of a hundred slaves, built town houses in Charleston and filled them with furniture, silver plate, and china imported from England or the Continent. Here was to be found the most cavalier, and perhaps the most attractive, social life in America. Music, art, drama, and education were encouraged. From 1762 on, concerts were given under the auspices of the far-famed Saint Cecilia Society. Josiah Quincy of Massachusetts, a graduate of Harvard, visited Charleston in 1775 and recorded the following impression of it in his journal:

> The town makes a most beautiful appearance as you come up to it, and in many respects a magnificent one. I can only say in general, that in grandeur, splendour of buildings, decorations, equipages, numbers, shippings, and indeed in almost everything it far surpasses all I ever saw, or ever expected to see, in America.[13]

Government and Religion

Public policy, as it found expression in legal enactment, was by and large determined by the great planter class, and in South Carolina by a combination of planter and merchant. It would not be far wrong to regard the colonial councils, the upper branches of the legislature, as special committees representing the interests of the plantation and merchant aristocracy — of the Carrolls, Byrds, Carters, Lees, Washingtons, Middletons, Laurenses, and Pinckneys. Royal and proprietary governors often found it necessary or expedient to yield to the demands of the wealthy and influential planters even to the point of granting them patents to large tracts of lands. The assemblies, the lower branches of the legislature, were more representative of the common people, but property qualifications for voting excluded the lower elements in society from participating in government. Even in the management of local affairs, in county and parish, the landed aristocracy exercised an influence out of all proportion to their numbers.

[13] *Journal of Josiah Quincy*, pp. 72–73, as quoted *ibid.*, p. 17. See also Faulkner, *op. cit.*, pp. 171–172.

The five southern colonies, like the other English colonies in America, were settled largely by Protestants, but, more important in explaining their subsequent educational development, the Anglican Church was established by law in each of them. The English Church, established on the principle of the union of church and state, expressed the spirit of the upper classes, who, through self-perpetuating vestries, as in Virginia, or elected vestries, as in South Carolina, and through the close relationship in which they stood to the colonial governments, sought to make the church an instrument of social control and direction. The Anglican Church in America reflected the attitude of the English upper classes toward popular education. The need for education among the people generally was not keenly felt by persons in authority. The movement of Englishmen into the South was motivated by no burning desire to perpetuate particular religious ideals or to establish a new social order. All English institutions, including education, were acceptable to them and were modified only as positive needs developed.

The church, as in England, was not entirely unmindful of the importance of popular education. The Bishop of London, as the diocesan of the colonial church, sent over commissaries charged with, among other things, the promotion of religious education. Thomas Bray, noted for the establishment of parish libraries, and James Blair, who secured the charter for William and Mary College, were the two outstanding representatives of the Bishop of London[14] in the colonial South. The educational interests of the southern colonies were also promoted by the work of the Society for the Propagation of the Gospel in Foreign Parts. This organization, established in 1701 as an auxiliary of the Anglican Church, was active in promoting education in all the southern colonies except Virginia. However, neither the church nor any of its agencies was destined to become a vital force in the spiritual and cultural life of the masses. Governors neglected their ecclesiastical duties; no American bishop was appointed and the Bishop of London was too far removed from the scene to exert much influence; the ministers were too few in number,[15] and, of that number, too many exhibited little zeal for their religious duties. There were in 1697 "not a half dozen Anglican ministers outside of Maryland and Virginia, and less than fifty in all the colonies."[16] North Carolina had only six Anglican churches in 1775, and it was asserted that the amount of state aid voted in fifty years would have supported only two ministers for one year. In 1769, eleven years after the establishment, there were only two Anglican churches in Georgia. In South Carolina, the state of the church was somewhat better, but the Anglicans in the population probably never exceeded one-third of the total. The church did not flourish,

[14] Before about 1673, the colonial church was directly under the jurisdiction of the Archbishop of Canterbury.

[15] In the absence of a bishop in America, ministers could be ordained only in England. This hindered the development of a native ministry.

[16] Chitwood, *op. cit.*, p. 427.

even in Virginia, where, at least during the seventeenth century, a majority of the people adhered to the established faith. Most of the Anglican ministers in America were in Virginia, but even so the shortage of clergy in that colony was acute. And of this meager supply too many were morally or temperamentally unsuited for their high calling. Sustained by law but generally dependent upon a virtually self-perpetuating vestry for appointment, and upon local taxes for their meager stipends, they were too often actuated by expediency and subservient to the local and provincial administration. There was always the temptation to identify themselves with, and minister mainly to, those persons who possessed influence, power, and wealth. But the failure of the Anglican church to gain "strength in America commensurate with the efforts made in its behalf" should be attributed, for the most part, to the policies of the religious authorities in England, the royal government, geography, and other factors which were operating to increase religious dissent within the colony.

The southern colonies, settled largely by persons who were seeking to advance their economic position, attracted a diversity of religious groups. From the beginning of the eighteenth century on, Scotch-Irish, German, and other groups were pouring into the back-country through Pennsylvania and western Maryland. The Anglican governments were more interested in having settlers on the frontier than in enforcing religious conformity. The Anglican Church neither met the needs of the newcomers nor sought to convert them. The dissenters — Presbyterians, Baptists, Methodists, Lutherans, German Reformed, and others — were bitterly opposed to the union of church and state and vigorously objected to taxes for the support of an established church.

It is difficult to measure the influence of the Anglican Church upon education in the South. It provided, at least indirectly, education of a sort for many children who otherwise would have been totally neglected. On the other hand, the leaders of the church reflected the indifference of the upper class toward the education of the poorer classes. The existence of an established church was responsible for such legislation as the Schism Act of 1714, which aimed to prevent the establishment of schools by dissenters by requiring teachers to be licensed by the Bishop of London. The attitude of the church and its leaders was not conducive to educational development, but the difficulties confronted in organizing a system of public education were rooted, not only in the religious, but also in the social, economic, and political conditions of the colonial South.

Tidewater versus Back-Country — a Conflict of Cultures

The type of society which took form in the tidewater, or "low-country," South was strikingly different from that which developed on the frontier, back of the fall line in the Piedmont region, or in the "back-country," as it was called. The Piedmont and the western valleys, stretching from Pennsylvania to Georgia, were peopled in part by the younger sons of the eastern aristocracy, by indentured servants who had won their freedom, and by small farmers and tenants who had been forced to retreat before the rising tide of Negro slavery. Here the poor and dispossessed from the East, along with some who were better off, met a stream of European migrants — Scotch-Irish, Germans, Irish, Swiss, and Welsh — moving southward from Pennsylvania and Maryland. Thousands of German peasants, especially from the Palatinate, who had been repeatedly harried by war and persecuted for their religious faith, sought a refuge in Pennsylvania. To Pennsylvania, too, came other thousands of Scotch-Irish from northern Ireland, seeking an escape from the poverty and hopelessness into which they had sunk as a result of the events following the English Revolution of 1688–89.[17] Soon after 1725, these Germans and Scotch-Irish were pressing their way southward from Pennsylvania and western Maryland, through the Great Valley of Virginia, and into the Piedmont of the Carolinas.

In this frontier, back-country South, a society developed which was far more democratic than that which had taken form in the tidewater low country. In the East, an aristocratic society had been firmly built on a plantation economy, Negro slavery, primogeniture, entail, and an established church. To all these, most back-country folk were strongly opposed. The West was made up of small farmers, though here and there a sizable plantation might be found. Slaves were not unknown, but they were relatively few, and perhaps as late as 1820 the people in the back-country would have voted to abolish slavery if they had been given the opportunity. The Scotch-Irish and others who settled on the frontier had been conditioned by their experiences in Europe to fear government and an established church, to hate landlordism, and to oppose taxation.

As the years passed, a deep-seated conflict developed between the two ways of life represented by the aristocratic tidewater and the democratic frontier. Planters and merchants along the seaboard were disposed to look upon the back-country settlers as intruders whose interests and social ideas made them a threat to the survival of the social order of which tidewater Virginia and South Carolina had been the architects. Certainly these back-country folk must not be given proportional representation in the colonial legislatures, not, at least, until they had come around to the support of slavery and to the acceptance of the ideology underpinning the low-country aristocracy.[18] Since the government was already under the control of eastern planters, it was not too difficult to devise ways by which

---

[17] Adams, *op. cit.*, p. 171.

[18] See Samuel Eliot Morison and Henry Steele Commager, *The Growth of the American Republic*, Fourth Edition, enlarged and revised (New York: Oxford University Press, 1950), I, pp. 166–172.

the growing West could be deprived of its proportionate representation in political affairs. In passing, it may not be amiss to note that the doctrine of nullification merely represented the application to national politics of a principle long in operation in South Carolina. Of course, the frontier yeomanry bitterly resented their partial disfranchisement. Presbyterians, Baptists, Methodists, and other dissenters all but refused to support the Anglican Church as the law required. Back-country folk in general disapproved of primogeniture and entail, and they were particularly bitter toward the large planters and speculators who had bought up western lands and now held them for high prices. When the American Revolution broke, it is not surprising that the western yeomanry rallied to its support, not so much because many of them had no reason to love England as because they saw in the movement an opportunity to right some of their old grievances against the low-country aristocracy. The Revolution was really a revolution within a revolution; the cause of America against England was also the cause of the back-country farmers against the tidewater planters.

The unsettled and exacting conditions of life in the back-country South were not conducive to the development of public education. Yet the intellectual nurture of youth was not wholly neglected. In well-populated communities, schools were maintained in connection with churches, and by the close of the colonial period a few academies and classical schools had been established. It was, however, this more democratic back-country which was to supply the South with a large part of its educational leadership at a later day. Thomas Jefferson, a back-country man, gave America its first well-thought-out plan for a complete system of public education, and to this day it is a noteworthy fact that most institutions of higher education in the Southeast are located west of the area dominated by the plantation aristocracy of the eighteenth century.

Education and the Intellectual Life in the Southern Colonies

The forces which determined the course of educational development in the South are reasonably clear. First of all, the southern colonists, unlike those who migrated to New England, had not set their hands to the building of a new social order; consequently, they did not look upon education as an essential means of developing in youth an acceptance of a new social design. They were no more and no less religious, perhaps, than the rank and file of their fellow countrymen in England, and they were, by and large, entirely satisfied with the religious establishment they had brought across the seas. The Anglican Church, to which they officially adhered, was not indifferent to education. But in sharp contrast to the attitude of the Puritans, Anglicans did not look with too great favor upon the state as an agency for providing schools. The church would take steps to provide itself with an educated clergy and it would devise ways and means to extend some educational opportunities to the poor and neglected, but for the great mass of children education was an obligation resting upon home and parent. More important still, perhaps, was the dispersion of population and the absence of community life resulting from the development of a plantation economy. Finally, a planter aristocracy, amply able to educate its own youth and occupying a dominant position in politics as well as in matters economic and social, was little disposed to champion the cause of popular education.

Although the influence of tradition, organized religion, and the class structure of society were all conducive to the acceptance in the Anglican colonies of the principle that education was not a public or primarily a religious matter, but one which was private and individual, conditions required some modification of this attitude in the direction of placing responsibility for the training of youth upon the state. The entire course of action which was followed in providing education at all levels and for all social classes, however, disturbed the inherited pattern as little as possible.

EDUCATION THROUGH APPRENTICESHIP

The presence in Virginia and the other southern colonies of a large class of poor and dependent persons made feasible the early introduction of the apprenticeship system, which had developed in England during the preceding hundred years. In time, the state, particularly in Maryland and Virginia, and to a lesser degree in the Carolinas, felt obliged to employ apprenticeship as a means of making compulsory some education for those children who would otherwise be neglected. The motive, no doubt, was in part religious and humanitarian, but the major interest of the colonial governments was economic — to prevent pauperism, to lighten the burden of poor relief, and to increase the industrial efficiency of the colony. In this connection, it must be noted that even in Virginia, where arrangements for education through apprenticeship were more complete than in any other southern colony, the laws relating to compulsory education dealt, with one exception, not with all the children, but with special classes — orphans, poor children, and those of illegitimate birth, including mulattoes born of white mothers.

Orphans were the first dependents to become the subject of legislation in Virginia. Jernegan has found at least seventeen acts relating to this class of children, beginning with the legislation of March, 1642/43, and spaced throughout the colonial period. Most of those acts involved the principle of compulsory education. They provided that orphans should be educated as well as their estates would permit; that those whose estates were insufficient should be apprenticed and "educated according as their estates will beare" (1656); and, after 1705, that apprenticed boys be taught to read and write. A later act, effective in 1751, extended the provisions of the law to include apprenticed girls.[19]

Jernegan also cites eight important laws which were passed between 1646 and 1769 relating to "religious, industrial, or book education of poor children of various classes." He concludes that five of the eight acts "contemplated some form of book education, and that four of them can be properly classed as compulsory laws."[20] It was not, however, until 1727 that compulsory book education was provided by law for poor apprenticed boys. A later act, effective in 1751, resembles closely the famous Massachusetts Act of 1642. Where parents were neglecting to take "due care" of the education of their children or were incapable of bringing them up "in honest courses," it was within the authority of the county court to apprentice the children to someone who would teach them to read and write. Literally construed, this act applied to all children whose parents neglected to take "due care" of their education. Some children were apprenticed under the authority of this law apparently for no other reason than that their education was being neglected, but it is clear that such action was exceptional and that few children of parents able to provide food and shelter were apprenticed. It may be noted, too, that there were statutory enactments requiring the religious education of all children, poor and rich alike.

It would be a serious mistake to accept, as has been done, the laws of colonial Virginia as evidence of the existence of a system of compulsory education that involved any large portion of the population. The word "poor" was used in the acts, not to denote persons of little means, but to designate the relatively small number of dependent poor — that is, paupers. The children receiving education under the acts relating to the poor were probably no more numerous than those making up the body of orphans whose apprenticeship and education were ordered in the series of laws referred to in a preceding paragraph. Records extant for two Virginia parishes indicate that only some one hundred and sixty-three children of those two parishes were apprenticed during a forty-year period beginning shortly after 1740. Of the children apprenticed, sixty-two were designated as orphans, sixty-four as poor children, seventeen as of illegitimate birth, and twenty as mulattoes born of white mothers. The fact that the number of "poor" children apprenticed in these two parishes was less than twice the number of white and part-Negro illegitimates would seem to indicate that only a very small part of the actually poor children fell under the provisions of the laws.

In all, there were some ten laws which made masters responsible for

---

[19] Marcus Wilson Jernegan, *Laboring and Dependent Classes in Colonial America, 1607–1783* (Chicago: University of Chicago Press, 1931), pp. 144–145.

[20] *Ibid.*, pp. 147–148.

some book education of apprenticed dependents — orphans, poor children, and those of illegitimate birth. There is little evidence as to how much education was actually provided. In the two Virginia parishes referred to previously, the indentures specified reading and writing in sixty-one instances; reading in eighteen; reading, writing and ciphering in three; instruction for eighteen months in one and for two years in seven; and as the law allows, etc., in eighteen. No education was required in forty-two instances.

Compulsory education, when provided for in the southern colonies other than Virginia, also centered around the training of dependents through apprenticeship. In Maryland, orphans without means for an education were to be bound out to learn a trade (1663). A later act (1715) provided that justices of county courts should require from a jury a report on whether apprentices were taught trades or turned to common labor.

In North Carolina, no legislation concerning apprenticeship was passed for many years. In 1715, it was ordered that orphans without estates be apprenticed, and later (1755) provision was made that the masters of all orphans should teach them to read and write. This law was later (1760) extended to include "all free base born children and every such Female Child being Mulattoe or Mustic."

Apprenticeship in South Carolina and Georgia was probably less common than in the other southern colonies. A law passed in South Carolina in 1695 provided that poor children be bound out. Georgia, settled late and slow to grow, did not pass legislation requiring education through apprenticeship, but, as in South Carolina, children were apprenticed, and there can be no doubt that apprenticeship was a means to at least a measure of industrial training.

Apprenticeship as a means of training dependents and promoting the prosperity of the several colonies fitted into the arrangements of the social organization of the seventeenth and eighteenth centuries. In the southern colonies, where class lines were more distinctly drawn than in New England or the Middle Colonies, the only compulsory education provided was through the agency of apprenticeship. There were in these colonies no laws similar to those in New England requiring the establishment of schools or providing for their support by taxation. Nor was there any law which permitted the authorities to interfere with respect to the education of other than dependent children, unless the Virginia law of 1748 may be interpreted as having made such provision. In this connection, it should be remembered, however, that after 1692 no law was passed in Massachusetts involving the compulsory education of all children in either religious or book education. Such laws as were passed in Massachusetts after 1692 referred exclusively to poor apprenticed children, and after 1710 the law provided only that apprenticed males were to be taught to read. Thus, it appears that after the downfall of the Puritan regime in Massachusetts compulsory-education legislation in Virginia was not greatly different from that of New England.

PUBLIC EDUCATION

The colonial governments in legislating with respect to the poor were primarily concerned with the dependent poor — that element in the population from which those on the relief rolls were drawn and were likely to continue to be drawn. For this class, industrial training through apprenticeship was provided by legislation in all the southern colonies except Georgia; and in two, Virginia and North Carolina, some instruction in reading and writing was added. It appears, however, that the number of poor children apprenticed, except perhaps during the earliest years of the Virginia colony, has been grossly overestimated and the number of apprentices who received instruction in the rudiments during any part of the colonial period has been somewhat exaggerated. Furthermore, a large majority of the parents in all the colonies during the seventeenth and eighteenth centuries were persons who, although not dependents, were unable to provide privately for the education of their children. Since apprenticeship legislation affected these children only as they became or threatened to become paupers, the education of the great majority had to be undertaken in other ways, or, as was often the case, go by default.

In some instances, the colonial governments took measures for the establishment and support of schools, and where this was done provision was usually made for the free instruction of a limited number of poor pupils. The Virginia Company encouraged philanthropic efforts made in 1619 and 1624 to establish schools of the charity type. In South Carolina, an act passed in 1710 provided that various bequests that had been made for the establishment of a free school should be placed under the control of a board of trustees which was empowered to build a school and employ a master capable of teaching Latin, Greek, and the useful parts of mathematics. Since nothing was accomplished under this act, two years later the legislature gave life to it by providing that one hundred pounds should be appropriated annually from public funds in payment of the master's salary. Twelve pupils were to be admitted free of tuition and the others were to pay tuition at the rate of four pounds a year.[21]

Interest attaches to this school because it provides one of the very first examples of a radical modification of the old Latin-grammar-school program. Its course of study was very much like that of the later academies. In fact, in the act establishing the school it was referred to as "said school or academy." In addition to a master to teach Latin and Greek, provision was made for an usher "to teach writing, arithmetic, and merchants' ac-

[21] Brown, *op. cit.*, pp. 96–97.

counts, and also the art of navigation and surveying, and other useful and practical parts of mathematics." The usher's salary of fifty pounds was to be paid out of the public funds, and he was required to teach free of charge such persons as were "appointed to have their learning free."[22] The Act of 1712 also authorized the vestry in each parish in the colony to draw upon colony funds to the amount of twelve pounds for the building of a schoolhouse and ten pounds per annum was to be allowed toward the payment of the master's salary. In this colony, a later act (1722) gave the justices of the county and precinct courts authority to purchase lands and erect free schools in each county or precinct and to assess the lands and slaves of each jurisdiction for the support of its school. Ten poor children were to be taught annually if sent by the justices.[23]

The North Carolina legislature in 1745 ordered the construction of a school at Edenton, but the school probably was not built. In 1766, it voted to establish a school at Newbern and to give for its maintenance certain revenues derived from the importation of liquors. The school was to educate ten poor children annually. In Maryland, an atttempt was made in 1696 to found a number of Latin grammar schools throughout the colony. A corporation including the governor and other colonial officers was created to receive donations and bequests for the establishment of schools and to have general control of them. A few years later, duties were imposed upon certain exports and imports, the revenues derived therefrom to be used to supplement the funds received as gifts. Only one such school was established under this act, King William's School at Annapolis, which was later to grow into Saint John's College. In 1723, the legislature of Maryland passed an act for the establishment of a system of county schools wherein as many poor pupils should be taught gratis as the visitors might require. The schools contemplated in the law — one in each county — seem to have been generally established.[24] The records extant for one of these schools in Queen Anne's County indicate that in curriculum and equipment it was ahead of the times. It gave instruction in geography and navigation and provided opportunity for advanced study in mathematics. The collection of maps, charts, and globes was unusually good, as was also the collection of Latin and Greek texts and treatises.[25] Although some fifteen of these county schools were established, in general they found it difficult to survive, and by the time of the Revolution their usefulness was about over. It is true, however, that Maryland was the only colony outside of New England that made any very

[22] *The Statutes at Large of South Carolina* (compiled by Thomas Cooper and David J. McCord, Columbia, S.C., 1836–41), II, pp. 389–396.

[23] Elsie W. Clews, *Educational Legislation and Administration of Colonial Governments* (New York: The Macmillan Co., 1899), p. 465.

[24] Brown, *op. cit.*, p. 76.

[25] Charles M. Andrews, *Colonial Folkways* (New Haven, Conn.: Yale University Press, 1919), p. 134.

serious effort to establish what might properly be called a state system of schools.

After 1754, when Georgia became a royal colony, two schoolmasters and a minister who had previously been maintained by the Society for the Propagation of the Gospel in Foreign Parts were paid salaries or allowances out of Parliamentary grants made for the support of the civil government of the colony.[26]

No legislation of the southern colonies, however, contemplated the establishment of public schools free and open to all. When the founding of schools was ordered, they were expected to be tuition schools. Very few children were or could have been provided for in the few schools that received a measure of their support from the colonial governments.

ENDOWED, CHARITY, AND DENOMINATIONAL SCHOOLS

In England, as a partial remedy for the terrible condition of the poor, endowments had been created for the support of charity schools or to provide for the maintenance of poor children in tuition schools. In a number of instances philanthropically disposed persons in the southern colonies followed the English precedent. Attempts to establish schools which would receive indigent children, particularly Indian youth, were made early in the history of Virginia. A considerable sum of money was raised for the projected East India School, which was to be primarily a tuition school, but which, no doubt, would, in keeping with the custom in England, have received a number of non-paying students. These attempts came to nought, and the first endowed school was not established until some time after the will of Benjamin Symms, dated February 1634/35, set aside two hundred acres of land and other property to found a free school in Elizabeth City County. This school was alluded to near the middle of the century as follows:

> I may not forget to tell you we have a Free-School, with two hundred Acres of Land, a fine house upon it, forty milch Kine, and other accommodations to it: the Benefactor deserves perpetual memory: His name Mr. Benjamin Symes, worthy to be Chronicled, other petty schools also we have.[27]

The establishment of free schools (generally endowed schools with free places for poor scholars) was neither rapid nor considered necessary by all persons. In 1671, Governor Berkeley in a report to the home govern-

[26] Robert Lawrence McCaul, "A Documentary History of Education in Colonial Georgia" (Doctor's thesis, University of Chicago, 1953).

[27] As quoted in Guy Fred Wells, *Parish Education in Colonial Virginia,* Teachers College Contributions to Education, No. 138 (New York: Teachers College, Columbia University, 1923), p. 33.

ment wrote: ". . . I thank God there are no free schools nor printing, and I hope we shall not these hundred years, for learning has brought disobedience and heresy and sects into the world and printing has divulged [them] and libels against best government. God keep us from both." Even though the development of free schools was slow, the statement does not, as it has often been assumed to do, accurately describe educational conditions throughout Virginia at the time. There were at the time of this report two and probably more flourishing free schools in the province. Berkeley was perhaps refusing to place these schools in the category of some of the larger "free schools" of England. Be that as it may, schools that might be referred to as "public" or "free schools" were never numerous, and the slowness with which they increased is indicated by the replies to a questionnaire addressed to the parish clergy in Virginia by the Bishop of London in 1724. He asked: "Have you in your Parish any Public School for the instruction of youth? If you have, is it endowed? and who is the Master?" By "public" the Bishop probably meant a school not operated privately for gain, at which at least some of the children of the community were admitted without charge. Of the twenty-nine parishes from which replies were received, only four reported having endowed schools. A typical reply was that from Saint Peter's Parish in New Kent County. "We have no Public Schools but some private, wherein children are taught to read, write, etc."[28] Altogether, five "public" schools were reported. Between 1724 and the Revolution, probably four more endowed schools were added. These nine "public" schools, located in seven of Virginia's ninety parishes, offered, with the possible exception of the Eaton School, instruction in elementary subjects only. These schools accomplished at least in part, the ends toward which the endowments aimed, in that they received some children who could not pay for their education. It is also probably true that the lower tuition rates made possible by the endowment resulted in the enrollment of some children whose parents could not pay higher rates. It was of such schools as these that Beverley, the historian of Virginia, wrote in 1705:

> There are large tracts of land, houses, and other things granted to free schools for the education of children in many parts of the country, and some of these are so large that of themselves they are a handsome maintenance to a master; but the additional allowance which gentlemen give with their sons render them a comfortable subsistence. These schools have been founded by the legacies of well-inclined gentlemen, and the management of them hath commonly been left to the direction of the county court or to the vestry of their respective parishes.[29]

[28] *Ibid.*, p. 32.
[29] *History of Virginia*, as quoted in Lyon G. Tyler (ed.), "Education in Colonial Virginia," Part III: "Free Schools," *William and Mary College Quarterly Historical Magazine*, VI (October, 1897), 71.

Although these schools were primarily tuition schools, and at least on one occasion complaint was made that the children of those who could pay received attention to the neglect of the children for whom the schools had been established, they did enroll many children who might not have been provided for otherwise. The number of these schools in proportion to the population, however, was small, and the part played by them in the total educational plan, and particularly in the education of the poor, is easily exaggerated.

The people of South Carolina were especially generous in their donations for the endowment of schools. For example, a Mr. Whitmarsh left five hundred pounds to a free school in Saint Paul's Parish. Mr. Ludlam left an estate valued at two thousand pounds for the same purpose in Saint James's Parish. In Saint Thomas's Parish, Richard Beresford bequeathed one-third of the yearly profits of his estate, which amounted to sixty-five hundred pounds, to the support of one or more schoolmasters and the other two-thirds "for the support, maintenance, and education of the poor." James Childs bequeathed six hundred pounds for a free school in Saint John's Parish, and other inhabitants contributed an additional twenty-four hundred pounds.[30] The size of these donations is impressive when it is recalled that John Harvard's gift to Harvard College was only about eight hundred pounds. Not only were "free" schools established through the benevolence of individuals, but also by organizations such as the South Carolina Society of Charleston and the Winyaw Indigo Society. All these schools provided a number of free places for poor children. South Carolina surpassed the other southern colonies, and perhaps all the other colonies, in the liberality of its educational endowments.

Probably a larger number of poor children were educated in the charity schools maintained by the Society for the Propagation of the Gospel in Foreign Parts than in the endowed schools. This society was the most important religious and philanthropic agency operating in the American colonies. It maintained schools in all the southern colonies except Virginia. Although its chief purpose was to give religious training, it provided instruction in reading, writing, and the elements of arithmetic. Knight states that the schools established by this missionary society furnished the nearest approach to a public school organization found in the South before the Revolution.

Schools were established in connection with the various churches.[31] Covenanters, Scotch Presbyterians, and Anglicans maintained schools which, although primarily tuition schools, probably geared their rates to what a considerable number of the people could pay and perhaps, as had

[30] Edward McCrady, Jr., *Education in South Carolina Prior to and During the Revolution*, Collections of the South Carolina Historical Society, IV, p. 11.

[31] Edgar W. Knight, *Public Education in the South* (Boston: Ginn & Company, 1922), p. 26.

been the age-long practice in the religious schools of Europe, taught some of the poor "for God's sake." The Moravians, before leaving Georgia for Pennsylvania in 1738, founded mission schools for the religious instruction of Indian youth. Other religious groups, no doubt, made provision for the instruction of their own children in the true faith and, to some extent, in the rudiments of learning. The educational highway was not entirely closed to the poor. A considerable number could progress a short way; a few might hurdle the almost insurmountable obstacles to journey a little further; but, on the whole, the educational programs of the upper and lower classes were sharply differentiated.

PRIVATE EDUCATION

In a social order in which it was accepted as a principle that education was a personal matter and that competent parents would see to it that their children were trained according to their proper stations in society, education at private expense and privately controlled was bound to loom large.

The English practice of employing a private tutor found favor among the large planters and others of the richer inhabitants. The tutors, although not all of the same quality, were usually competent persons, often keeping the plantation accounts as well as teaching the children. Tutors were recruited from among the candidates for the ministry who had been trained abroad or in such American colleges as William and Mary or the College of New Jersey. There were also among them a goodly number of indentured servants — oftentimes persons of some culture who, fleeing the hopeless conditions of England, Scotland, or North Ireland, sold themselves into service for a period of years.

The tutors were sometimes called upon to teach not only the children of the family, but also those of the planters' kinsmen and neighbors. A school building was not uncommonly found on the plantations of the great landowners. The evidence which remains with respect to the subjects taught indicates that a restricted curriculum was not necessarily characteristic of the instruction provided by the tutor in the home.

COMMUNITY SCHOOLS

Many children were educated in the community schools, later known as "old field schools." This name was applied because these schools, set up at convenient points by the people of the various neighborhoods, were frequently erected in some neglected or abandoned field. Beverley, writing of these schools in 1705, stated: "In all other places, where such endowments [for free schools] have not already been made, people join and build schools for their children where they may learn on very easie terms."[32]

Some of these schools enjoyed a long life of usefulness; others were ephemeral. Usually, reading and writing and sometimes ciphering were taught, but here and there advanced studies were offered. Some few became academies in the later years of the period. Many of the early teachers were local ministers or lay readers of the Anglican Church who sought to supplement their meager incomes by tuition fees. Schools recognized by the Established Church were taught by teachers who held licenses from the Bishop of London or from the governor. In Virginia, at least, an attempt was made to require certification of all teachers. In 1686, for example, schoolmasters were ordered to attend the meeting of the General Assembly in Jamestown to be examined and to receive licenses from the governor. The crown, apparently, was more solicitous with respect to this matter than were the planters, some of whom protested that many teachers ceased teaching rather than make the trip. This law, when enforced, curtailed the educational programs of dissenting groups.

PRIVATE-VENTURE SCHOOLS

The schools which were purely private in nature must have been fairly numerous. Remaining records allude to many schools kept by ministers who taught, and sometimes boarded, a few boys who were preparing for college, and to schools of other masters maintained as private ventures. Among the private teachers of note were Thomas Martin, who prepared James Madison for entrance into Princeton College, and the Reverend James Mayre, Jr., the teacher of Washington and other prominent Virginians.

Private schools of all grades were found in all cities during the later half of the colonial period. These schools taught the elementary subjects, the higher branches, and the "businesses of sea and air." Several such schools were located in Charleston and some in Norfolk and Savannah. In the preceding chapter it was shown how private teachers appeared in eighteenth-century New England to meet the needs of an emerging capitalistic society. Much the same kind of thing was taking place in the South, especially in Charleston. Knight has found that "from 1733 to 1774 more than four hundred advertisements relating to schools and schoolmasters appeared in the *South Carolina Gazette,* which was published in Charleston."[33] Jernegan, after a careful examination of vestry books, wills, and

[32] As quoted in Marcus Wilson Jernegan, *The American Colonies, 1492–1750* (New York: Longmans, Green & Co., 1929), p. 106. Also published in paperback (New York: Frederick Ungar Publishing Co., Inc., 1959).

[33] Knight, *op. cit.,* p. 41.

the files of the *South Carolina Gazette,* concludes that the development of the private school in Charleston "was far ahead of that in any other city in the Colonies." The files of the *South Carolina Gazette* "show that between 1760 and 1770 at least seventy different schools were in operation for a longer or shorter period, many of them covering the whole period in question." Jernegan also says: "It is believed that not less than twenty-five private schools were in operation in Charleston every year from 1760 to the Revolution."[34] The private teachers, like those in New England and the Middle Colonies, were giving instruction in a great variety of subjects: French, English, Latin, writing, arithmetic, Spanish, bookkeeping, navigation, surveying, needlework, and drawing.

HIGHER EDUCATION

The development of institutions for higher learning in the South was retarded by the practice of sending young men to English, Scotch, and Continental schools and universities to complete their education. The Byrds, Fitzhughs, Lees, Pinckneys, Gadsdens, Middletons, and many other leading families, anxious to maintain their contact with Europe and to educate their children in the European social tradition as well as in humanistic learning and the professions, sent their sons and sometimes their daughters abroad, especially to the schools and universities of England and Scotland. Tyler has prepared a long list of Virginians, including seven members of the Lee family, who received their education in whole or in part in English schools and universities. At least one headmaster of an English school thought it worth his while to advertise in the *Virginia Gazette* as follows:

> At the Academy in Leeds, which is pleasantly situated in the county of York, in England, young gentlemen are genteely boarded and diligently instructed in English, the classicks, Modern Languages, Penmanship, Arithmetick, Merchant Accounts, Mathematicks, Modern Geography, Experiential Philosophy, and Astronomy. . . . Drawing, Musick, and Dancing are extra charges.[35]

During the period from 1754 to 1778, more than a score of Virginia physicians had studied at the University of Edinburgh.[36] The practice of sending boys to England to complete their education seems to have been

---

[34] Marcus Wilson Jernegan, "Factors Influencing the Development of American Education Before the Revolution," *Proceedings of the Mississippi Valley Historical Association for the Year 1911–12* (Cedar Rapids, Iowa: Torch Press, 1912), V, p. 205.

[35] Lyon G. Tyler, "Education in Colonial Virginia," Part IV: "The Higher Education," *William and Mary College Quarterly Historical Magazine,* VI (January, 1898), 175.

[36] *Ibid.,* 176.

even more common in South Carolina than in Virginia. The list of Southerners educated abroad is imposing, but it should not be permitted to obscure the fact that the practice was confined to a relatively few wealthy families. It is true, however, that persons educated in foreign universities did provide the South with a small group of extremely able leaders.

The early attempts (1619, 1624, 1660) to establish a college in Virginia were unsuccessful, and it was not until 1692 that the College of William and Mary at Williamsburg received its charter. James Blair, who had gone to England to obtain the charter, was highly successful in securing donations for the new college. The government granted it 1985 pounds, a group of English merchants contributed three hundred pounds, and a like sum was "donated" by a group of pirates who were making their settlement with the government. The college was also to receive funds accruing from an export tax on tobacco from Virginia and Maryland. The fees from the land surveyor's office were also to go to the college, and it was the recipient of a grant of ten thousand acres of land. The General Assembly in Virginia allocated to the college the export duties on skins and furs and, after 1726, for a period of twenty-one years appropriated two hundred pounds annually to the college. This second institution of higher learning to be established in the English colonies enjoyed exceptionally liberal financial support.

William and Mary, like Harvard and Yale, was established primarily to provide the church with an educated ministry. The college was divided into three departments, the grammar school, the school of philosophy, and the divinity school. The college proper did not begin operation until about 1712, and it was not until 1729 that all the six professorships provided for in the charter were filled. The curriculum in the philosophy department was much like that of the other colleges of the day — rhetoric, logic, ethics, physics, metaphysics, and mathematics. As time passed, the sons of Virginia planters exhibited an increasing interest in the political and natural sciences and William and Mary tended to break away from the traditional curriculum. In 1779, partly as the result of Jefferson's influence, the curriculum of the college was reorganized into perhaps the most remarkable one in the United States. The grammar school and the divinity school were abolished and in their places were established "a school of modern languages, a school of constitutional and court law, and a school of medicine." The faculty now consisted of a professor of natural philosophy and mathematics; a professor of law and "police"; a professor of anatomy and medicine; a professor of moral philosophy, the law of nature and nations, and of the fine arts; and a professor of modern languages.[37] As the colonial period drew to an end, William and Mary had freed itself from the trammels of medieval ecclesiasticism.

[37] *Ibid.,* 180–181.

On the whole, the institutional arrangements for education in the southern colonies were English in their origin, and in their development they reflected the inherited traditions and customs of the colonists as well as the dominant economic, social, and political conditions of the period. Apprenticeship, the private tutor, charity schools, endowed free schools, private schools, and a college fitted into the colonial scene in Virginia, South Carolina, and the other southern colonies as they did into the stratified social system of England. Changes were wrought in America by the forces of geography and isolation, but during the colonial period educational practices and theories in the South never lost their resemblance to those from which they derived.

Questions and Problems for Study and Discussion

1. How important were the differences in the motivations of the colonists who settled New England and the southern colonies in explaining the differences in the educational and other social arrangements of the two regions?
2. Explain how geography, climate, soil, and topography affected the structure of southern society. Evaluate the influences of the physical environment as compared with other factors in determining the nature of southern society.
3. Why was educational development in the southern colonies more influenced than that in New England by English traditions, theories, and practices?
4. How did the class structure of southern society affect the development of education in the South? How did the prevalence of white servitude and the introduction of slavery affect education in the southern colonies?
5. What were the educational consequences of the conflict between the tidewater and back-country cultures in the South?
6. Indicate the relative importance of church and state in the development of southern education during the colonial period.
7. Describe the system of education in the southern colonies and show how and to what extent it reflected the southern social structure.

Selected References for Further Reading

Adams, James Truslow. *Provincial Society, 1690–1763. A History of American Life,* III. New York: The Macmillan Co., 1927. Pp. xx + 374.

Andrews, Charles M. *Colonial Folkways: A Chronicle of American Life in the Reign of the Georges,* The Chronicles of America Series, IX. New Haven, Conn.: Yale University Press, 1919. Pp. x + 256.

Bell, Sadie. *The Church, the State, and Education in Virginia.* Philadelphia: Science Press Printing Co., 1930. Pp. xii + 796.

Boorstin, Daniel J. *The Americans: The Colonial Experience.* New York: Random House, 1958. Pp. xii + 434.

Bowes, Frederick. *The Culture of Early Charleston.* Chapel Hill, N.C.: University of North Carolina Press, 1942. Pp. x + 156.

Bridenbaugh, Carl. *Myths and Realities: Societies of the Colonial South.* Baton Rouge, La.: Louisiana State University Press, 1952. Pp. x + 208.

Brubacher, John S., and Rudy, Willis. *Higher Education in Transition: An American History, 1636–1956.* New York: Harper & Brothers, 1958. Pp. vii + 494.

Bruce, Philip Alexander. *Economic History of Virginia in the Seventeenth Century: An Inquiry into the Material Condition of the People; Based upon Original and Contemporaneous Records.* 2 vols. New York: The Macmillan Co., 1896.

Bruce, Philip Alexander. *Institutional History of Virginia in the Seventeenth Century: An Inquiry into the Religious, Moral, Educational, Legal, Military, and Political Condition of the People, Based on Original and Contemporaneous Records.* 2 vols. New York: G. P. Putnam's Sons, 1910.

Bruce, Philip Alexander. *Social Life in Virginia in the Seventeenth Century: An Inquiry into the Origin of the Higher Planting Class, Together with an Account of the Habits, Customs, and Diversions of the People.* Richmond, Va.: printed for the author by Whittet and Shepperson, 1907. Pp. 268.

Clews, Elsie W. *Educational Legislation and Administration of the Colonial Governments,* Columbia University Contributions to Philosophy, Psychology, and Education, Vol. VI, Nos. 1–4. New York: The Macmillan Co., 1899. Pp. xii + (7–524).

Dabney, Charles William. *Universal Education in the South,* I. Chapel Hill, N.C.: University of North Carolina Press, 1936. Pp. xvi + 568.

Dodd, William E. "The Emergence of the First Social Order in the United States," *The American Historical Review,* XI (January, 1935), 217–31.

Dodd, William E. *The Old South: Struggles for Democracy.* New York: The Macmillan Co., 1937. Pp. viii + 312.

Gray, Lewis Cecil. *History of Agriculture in the Southern United States to 1860,* I. Washington, D.C.: Carnegie Institution of Washington, 1933. Pp. xx + 568.

Heatwole, Cornelius J. *A History of Education in Virginia.* New York: The Macmillan Co., 1916. Pp. xviii + 382.

Hindle, Brooke. *The Pursuit of Science in Revolutionary America, 1735–1789.* Chapel Hill, N.C.: University of North Carolina Press, 1956. Pp. xi + 410.

Jernegan, Marcus Wilson. *Laboring and Dependent Classes in Colonial America, 1607–1783: Studies of the Economic, Educational, and Social Significance of Slaves, Servants, and Poor Folk.* Chicago: University of Chicago Press, 1931. Pp. xiv + 256.

Knight, Edgar W. *A Documentary History of Education in the South before 1860,* I: *European Inheritance.* Chapel Hill, N.C.: University of North Carolina Press, 1949. Pp. x + 744.

Knight, Edgar W. *Public Education in the South.* Boston: Ginn & Company, 1922. Pp. xii + 482.

Morgan, Edmund S. *Virginians at Home: Family Life in Eighteenth Century.* Williamsburg, Va.: Colonial Williamsburg, Inc., 1952. Pp. ix + 99.

Sellers, Leila. *Charleston Business on the Eve of the American Revolution.* Chapel Hill, N.C.: University of North Carolina Press, 1934. Pp. xii + 260.

Smith, Abbott. *Colonists in Bondage: White Servitude and Convict Labor in America, 1607–1776.* Chapel Hill, N.C.: University of North Carolina Press, 1947. Pp. viii + 435.

Wells, Guy Fred. *Parish Education in Colonial Virginia,* Teachers College Contributions to Education, No. 138. New York: Teachers College, Columbia University, 1923. Pp. 96.

Wertenbaker, Thomas Jefferson. *The Old South: The Founding of American Civilization.* New York: Charles Scribner's Sons, 1942. Pp. xiv +364.

Wertenbaker, Thomas Jefferson. *The Planters of Colonial Virginia.* Princeton, N.J.: Princeton University Press, 1922. Pp. 260.

Wright, Louis B. *The First Gentlemen of Virginia: Intellectual Qualities of the Early Colonial Ruling Class.* San Marino, Cal.: Huntington Library, 1940. Pp. xii + 374.

5

Education in
a Diversity of Cultural Patterns:
The Middle Colonies

The Middle Colonies were "middle" in the sense that they were located between the colonies of New England and those of the plantation South. Historians have pointed out that they also occupied a position between New England and the South with respect to the size of landholdings, the nature of local government, the extent of industrial development, and other factors that influence the nature of educational arrangements and practices. It appears to be impossible, however, to fit education into this pattern of the "middle way." Education in the Middle Colonies, particularly in those colonies which had an extended educational history, was greatly influenced by distinctions which the colonies had in their own right, and which in some instances were almost unique to one of them.

As the transplanted Europeans in the Middle Colonies strove, no less mightily than those in New England and the South, to maintain the old and familiar culture in new surroundings, they, too, were subjected to the molding influences of geography and the frontier. However, the lack of a common inheritance of tradition, language, religious beliefs, and political theories, together with the conditions peculiar to the individual colonies, delayed the development of a common culture or of a situation that would contribute to cooperative endeavor in the building of institutional arrangements.

Educational development in each of the colonies established between New England and Maryland was retarded by the disorganizing influences of clashing cultures. In no other section were the people so sharply divided in social origin or in social outlook. In no other section did the

Protestant theory of the personal relationship between God and man find such varied expression as in the divided and constantly dividing religious affiliations of the inhabitants. In no other section was the population so heterogeneous with respect to nationality. All northern Europe contributed to the population and the only non-English peoples to found settlements within the limits of the original thirteen colonies established them in this middle region.

The Middle Colonies differed not only from the other American colonies, but also from one another. In this region, educational development had its setting in scenes which, although similar in their broader aspects, varied considerably as to the arrangement and relative importance of significant elements. For example, the culture of New Netherland, in spite of the presence in that colony of many national and religious groups, was predominantly Dutch; and the Dutch Reformed Church was the state church. The period after the English conquest was marked by a fusion of cultures, with the English slowly gaining ground. In Pennsylvania, because of large-scale and long-continued immigration, the great diversity of the early population with respect to race, religion, economic status, and cultural background increased as the period progressed. The educational histories of New York and Pennsylvania, therefore, must be traced separately. New Jersey, to a certain extent, followed the pattern set by New York. Delaware, small and unimportant as an independent colony, had a meager educational history.

New Netherland and New York

The slow progress of education in New Netherland may be attributed to several causes. In the first place, the colony was founded, and, until the English occupation, controlled, by the Dutch West India Company. The colonization of the Hudson Valley was only one, perhaps a minor, item in this corporation's ambitious program to promote trade and other Dutch interests "between the tropic of Cancer and the Cape of Good Hope, in the West Indies, and on the coasts of America between Newfoundland and the Straits of Magellan."[1] The educational needs of a few struggling communities in the American wilderness, although in part a responsibility of the Company and given consideration by it, were of less consequence to that gigantic monopoly than were its more purely commercial and military affairs. Then, too, the extremely backward political development in New Netherland created little motive for education beyond religious and civic

---

[1] Ellis H. Roberts, *New York: The Planting and Growth of the Empire State* (Boston: Houghton Mifflin Company, 1887). See also Samuel Eliot Morison and Henry Steele Commager, *The Growth of the American Republic,* Fourth Edition, revised and enlarged (New York: Oxford University Press, 1950), I, pp. 59–61.

conformity. Educational progress was certainly not stimulated by the existing pattern of political arrangements.

POLITICAL, ECONOMIC, AND SOCIAL DEVELOPMENT UNDER THE DUTCH

In granting the charter to the West India Company, the Dutch government retained a very limited authority.[2] The control of the Company was vested in five chambers of directors, the general assembly of which was to be made up of nineteen members, called the College of the XIX. The Amsterdam chamber furnished eight members to the College; the other chambers together provided ten; and the States-General, the legislative branch of the Dutch government, was represented by only one member. The College of the XIX delegated the direct supervision of the colony to the Lords Directors of the Amsterdam chamber.[3]

Arbitrary government. The States-General reserved the right of approving the director-general, the chief executive officer of the Company in the colony, and of reviewing his instructions. From time to time it intervened to correct the most flagrant abuses in the government of the colony. Even so, the Company, unfitted as it was by its military and commercial character to govern a colony, enjoyed almost a free hand in directing the affairs of New Netherland. Moreover, most of the authority vested in the Company was delegated to the director-general, who exercised not only executive but legislative and judicial powers as well. The director-general was assisted by a council, but as a rule he was able to control or ignore it altogether. Little restrained by a distant board of directors or by fear of the States-General, he administered the affairs of the colony as autocratically as he pleased. To aggravate the situation, the colony, from Minuit's recall in 1632 to the end of its history as a Dutch possession, did not have one properly qualified governor. The director-generals, jealous of their authority and possessing little judgment in exercising it, kept the internal affairs of the colony in a constant state of turmoil. Stuyvesant, the last and, in some respects, the best of the lot, was a narrow-minded, bigoted, tyrannical, blustering bully whose term was marked by oppressions and persecutions which in the light of Dutch policy and the instructions of the Company were more unreasonable and far less understandable than those which characterized the government of his Puritan neighbors. In rejecting the petition of leading and respected citi-

[2] Oliver Perry Chitwood, *A History of Colonial America,* Third Edition (New York: Harper & Brothers, 1961), p. 162.
[3] William Heard Kilpatrick, *The Dutch Schools of New Netherland and Colonial New York,* Reprint from United States Bureau of Education Bulletin No. 12, 1912 (Washington, D.C.: Government Printing Office, 1912), p. 11.

zens to investigate the conduct of his predecessor, he made evident his position. If, he said, petitions were received from private persons against a former magistrate, "will not these cunning fellows, in order to usurp over us a more unlimited power, claim and assume in consequence even greater authority against ourselves and our commission, should it happen that our administration may not square in every respect with their whims?" He ended by stating, "It is treason to petition against one's magistrates, whether there be cause or not."[4] Stuyvesant not only supported his predecessor, but, instigated by him, prosecuted and convicted the petitioners for seditious attack on the government. When one of the unjustly convicted men asked for grace until his case could be presented in Holland, Stuyvesant, much excited by the contempt involved in an appeal from his judgment, furiously declared: "If I knew . . . that you would divulge our sentence . . . or bring it before Their High Mightinesses, I would cause you to be hanged at once on the highest tree in New Netherland." In another case, it is said the Director declared: "It may during my administration be contemplated to appeal; but if anyone should do it, I will make him a foot shorter, and send the pieces to Holland and let him appeal in that way."[5] It is clear that such a director would oppose any development in the direction of popular government. In fact, he was able, in the main, to prevent the inhabitants from enjoying fully even those rights and privileges which the Company saw fit or was obliged to accord them.

Opposition by the burghers to certain taxes proclaimed by Stuyvesant forced him to make concessions which admitted the people to a semblance of a share in the government. In 1647, he ordered the election of a board of nine men, which was to be presided over by the director. Three members of this advisory body were to sit in rotation to judge civil cases, the litigants having the right to appeal to the council. In each year six were to retire and their places were "to be taken by six others, to be appointed by the director from a list of twelve of the 'most notable citizens' named by the Commonalty."[6] The board could be dispensed with at the pleasure of the director. Its establishment, however, furthered the development of the principle of representation in government. The nine men became a center of opposition and were able to carry their complaints directly to the States-General, which, after some years, forced much-needed reforms upon the Company. Among these, the organization of municipal govern-

---

[4] As quoted in Bayard Tuckerman, *Peter Stuyvesant, Director-General for the West India Company in New Netherland* (New York: Dodd, Mead & Co., 1893), p. 65. See Henry H. Kessler and Eugene Rachlis, *Peter Stuyvesant and His New York* (New York: Random House, 1959).

[5] As quoted in Maud Wilder Goodwin, *Dutch and English on the Hudson*, Vol. VII, *The Chronicles of America*, Copyright Yale University Press (New Haven, Conn.: Yale University Press, 1920), p. 69.

[6] Tuckerman, *op. cit.*, p. 68. For acts of Stuyvesant's regime, see Isaac Newton Phelps Stokes, *The Iconography of Manhattan Island* (New York: R. H. Dodd, 1915), I, pp. 25–113.

ment in New Amsterdam was perhaps the most important. A charter was granted which placed the city government in the hands of five schepens, two burgomasters, and a schout or sheriff. These officers were to be elected by the citizens, but Stuyvesant, with fine disregard for the orders of the States-General, proceeded to appoint them. In 1658, he made a small concession toward representative government by conceding to the schepens and burgomasters the right to nominate twice as many candidates as there were offices to be filled, from which list the director was to choose. Even in what appears to have been purely municipal affairs, Stuyvesant did not hesitate to interfere, reserving the right to make regulations contrary to the wishes of the city officials and without consulting them. On one occasion, he issued an order forbidding the playing of a particular game in connection with the celebration of the feast of Bacchus. On learning that the magistrates felt aggrieved that this unpopular order should have been issued without consulting them, he made reply in his usual arrogant manner:

> Aggrieved, forsooth! . . . because the director-general had done this without their consent and knowledge! As if without the knowledge and consent of the burgomasters and schepens no order can be made, no mob interdicted from celebrating the feast of Backus; much less have the privilege of correcting such persons as tread under foot the Christian and holy precepts, without the knowledge and consent of a little bench of justices! Appreciating their own authority, quality, and commission better than others, the director and Council hereby make known to the burgomasters and schepens that the institution of a little bench of justices under the name of the schout, burgomasters, and schepens, or commissioners, does in no wise diminish aught of the power of the director-general and councillors.[7]

In spite of the liberalization of municipal government and the administrative reforms which were granted from time to time as the Company sought to attract settlers or as complaints from the colony aroused sentiment against the Company in Holland, it is evident that New Netherland came to an end without evolving a representative form of government and without even devising a plan whereby the inhabitants, as a group, could express themselves on educational or other matters.

Attempts to organize a feudalistic colonial society. The arbitrary government of the Company and the generally poor administration of its officers, together with its shortsighted commercial policy, checked the growth of the colony. Grudgingly granted reforms, such as the removal of certain trade restrictions, the establishment of municipal government in New Amsterdam as already noted, or minor concessions granted to

[7] As quoted in Tuckerman, *op. cit.,* p. 127.

the villages with respect to self-government, did not appreciably stimulate immigration. In an attempt to bring about a more rapid growth of the colony, the Company in 1629 issued a charter of privileges, an elaborate plan to encourage the stockholders to finance the settlement of colonists in quasi-feudal patroonships. Each stockholder who planted a colony of fifty persons over fifteen years of age was to acquire land sixteen miles in length if situated on one side of a navigable stream, or eight in length if situated on both sides, and extending into the interior for an indefinite distance.[8] The owner, or patroon, was to possess the hereditary rights of a feudal noble, with power to make laws, establish courts of justice, and "to control hunting, fishing, and the grinding of grains, subject only to allegiance to the States-General." Only five men took up patroonships and only one succeeded. Only two patroonships actually developed to the point, either in organization or population, that made possible any considerable educational history. In fact, the system was doomed to failure from the beginning. Goodwin, after careful study of the history of these ventures, states:

> As we study the old documents we find a sullen tenantry, an obsequious and careworn agent, a dissatisfied patroon, an impatient company, a bewildered government. . . . The reason for the discontent which prevailed is not far to seek, and all classes were responsible for it, for they combined in planting an anachronistic feudalism in a new country, which was dedicated by its very physical conditions to liberty and democracy. The settlers came from a nation which had battled through long years in the cause of freedom. . . . No sane mind could have expected the Dutch colonists to return without protest to a medieval system of government.[9]

Slow growth under the Dutch. In spite of these and other efforts on the part of the Company, the population increased slowly. By 1630, the Dutch possessions could have been little more than trading posts, and to a considerable degree they retained that character throughout the entire period. In 1630, the population, according to the best estimate, was only 500 persons. It increased to 1000 in 1640, 3000 in 1650, and 6000 in 1660. By the latter date the inhabitants of Massachusetts numbered approximately 25,000 and those of Virginia some 33,000. Little Connecticut had perhaps a larger population during the entire period than did New Netherland.[10] New Amsterdam remained small, having in 1628 about 270 inhabitants; in 1643, some 400; in 1652, about 700; in 1656, by actual count, 120 houses and 1000 souls; in 1664, about 1500 inhabi-

---

[8] Chitwood, *op. cit.*, p. 162.
[9] Goodwin, *op. cit.*, pp. 46–47.
[10] United States Bureau of the Census, *A Century of Population Growth* (Washington, D.C.: Government Printing Office, 1909), p. 9.

tants. Fortunately for education, because otherwise progress would have been even slower, a majority of the inhabitants lived in a comparatively small area centering in New Amsterdam and embracing Manhattan Island, parts of Staten and Long islands, and the west bank of the lower Hudson. Many of these inhabitants, however, and most of the remaining population, which was scattered from Fort Orange (later Albany) to outposts on the Delaware and Connecticut Rivers, were living under the isolated and primitive conditions of the frontier. Under such conditions, there was in New Netherland, as under similar circumstances elsewhere, little educational development.

Diversity of race and religion. Both the sparseness and the heterogeneous character of the population were factors retarding educational progress. The Dutch were not a migrating people. Few advantages, political, religious, or economic, were offered by New Netherland that they did not enjoy at home. The population of New Netherland was drawn from many countries. Even the first colonists sent out by the Company were not Dutch, but French-speaking Walloons, Protestant exiles from the lower Netherlands, which had remained Catholic. It is said that in 1644 eighteen languages were spoken in or near New Amsterdam, although Dutch was the one in most common use. English settlers, however, were in a majority on Long Island, and on the Delaware the Swedes predominated. French, Walloons, Norwegians, Danes, Jews, Irish, Scotch, and Germans added to the cosmopolitan character of the colony.

Religious sects were even more numerous than national or racial groups. The colony from the beginning followed, in the main, the same liberal policy with respect to religious refugees that had been followed in Holland, which, after gaining independence from Spanish control, had provided asylum to many persecuted religious sects of Europe. The States-General in 1661 invited "Christian people of tender conscience, in England or elsewhere oppressed," to migrate to New Netherland.[11] French Huguenots, Baptists, Quakers, Presbyterians, Lutherans, Mennonites, and other denominations found in New Netherland much greater freedom than was generally consistent with seventeenth-century ideals. Most of the attempts to restrict religious freedom must be charged to an irascible, bigoted Director who found it almost impossible to tolerate disagreement in anything. In 1656, the Director forbade preachers not "called by ecclesiastical and temporal authority" to hold meetings, but the Company, more liberal than it had been in 1654, at which time it had upheld the Director in his refusal to permit the Lutherans to build a church, rebuked him and declared its purpose to let those outside the Dutch Reformed Church "enjoy all calmness and tranquility." The clergymen in New Amsterdam were warned by the authorities in Holland against new forms and an

11 Roberts, *op. cit.*, p. 79.

"overbearing preciseness" which might prevent keeping Lutherans within the fold.[12] Unable to distinguish between freedom of worship and contempt of government, Stuyvesant continued his persecutions, particularly of the Quakers. This heresy frightened and angered the old governor. His treatment of the members of this sect became a scandal in New Amsterdam and a matter of concern to the Company, which wrote to Stuyvesant:

> Let every one remain free as long as he is modest, moderate, his political conduct irreproachable, and as long as he does not offend others or oppose the government. This maxim of moderation has always been the guide of our magistrates in this city, and the consequence has been that people have flocked from every land to this asylum. Tread thus in their steps and we doubt not you will be blessed.[13]

The old Director perhaps saw little prohibition in the rebuke. Those who disagreed with him were neither modest and moderate nor, in political conduct, irreproachable. The fact must not be lost sight of, however, that, on the whole and judged by the standards of the day, the policy of New Netherland with respect to religious freedom was liberal. New Netherland offered asylum to the oppressed and persecuted of Europe and New England. Although the many religious groups found in New Netherland were, as a rule, friendly toward education, particularly at the elementary level, the force of a well-knit social organization was not exerted in its behalf.

EDUCATION IN NEW NETHERLAND

As has been indicated, the development of public education was retarded by the sparseness of the population and therefore, indirectly, by factors retarding immigration; by the many diverse elements in the population; by the quality and nature of the early immigration; by the great variety of religious beliefs; and by the almost complete lack of representative government, either local or provincial. On the other hand, there were factors present in the situation which were favorable to education and gave direction to its development. Among these, the acceptance of Calvinism, with its implications for state-church cooperation in education by the racially and politically dominant group, was, perhaps, the most important. In Holland, as was the rule in countries in which Calvinistic doctrines prevailed, "the public authorities, partly civil and partly ecclesiastical, provided the school, examined, and licensed the teacher, paid him a salary, and by law regulated what he should teach, what books he should use, and the conditions under which he should in general conduct his school."[14] The great synods showed a concern for education and for the

[12] *Ibid.,* pp. 78–89.   [13] *Ibid.,* p. 80.   [14] Kilpatrick, *op. cit.,* p. 38.

support of schools, but the articles, rules, and regulations relating to education of the synods and lesser church bodies could be enforced only by civil authorities, who in many instances found enforcement inexpedient. The schools of Holland throughout the. period "remained the joint concern of both church and state, with the state the dominant party."[15]

Church and school relationships. As in the homeland, so in New Netherland throughout its history, the school and the church were closely knit together. In Holland the principal function of the school was the teaching of religion, and Dutch colonists could conceive of no other way by which their children could receive the essentials of religious teachings. "This fact," states Kilpatrick, "will account for the presence of schools in struggling frontier villages of Holland America, where, without this religious zeal, interest in education alone would not have sufficed to maintain adequate schools."[16] Inasmuch as the state was interested in promoting the recognized religion, it lent its support to elementary education. In New Netherland, the obligation of the Company, which represented the state, to provide education was recognized from the beginning. The Company paid the salaries of the teachers of the official school, although, as elsewhere, it appears that the teacher's income was largely derived from the tuition fees which were commonly charged. In theory, if not always in practice, the patroons bore the same relationships to schools in their patroonships that the Company bore to the schools in the colony proper.

Although the obligation of maintenance rested upon the Company, the classis of Amsterdam, representing the Dutch Reformed Church, exercised considerable authority in the educational affairs of New Netherland through the privileges which it enjoyed of selecting ministers, schoolmasters, and other church officials. Although governors and dominies might quarrel, and although Stuyvesant was a quarrelsome, egotistical, oversensitive despot, it appears that there was little interference with the church in the exercise of its educational functions, and the relations between the Company in Holland and the classis of Amsterdam seem to have been without friction. One of the last ordinances of the Dutch government in America required that children be publicly catechized on Wednesday and Saturday by the schoolmaster and the minister.

In New Netherland, as definitely as in Massachusetts, the obligation to provide schools rested upon the state (the Company). In Massachusetts, where the town served as a unit of administration as well as of local government, the state placed the obligation of support upon the inhabitants of the towns to be provided as one of the expenses of government or otherwise as the towns deemed fit. In New Netherland a portion of the costs of maintenance was paid as a part of the costs of government either by the lords directors in Amsterdam or, in the colony, by the director-general.

[15] *Ibid.,* p. 24.   [16] *Ibid.,* p. 35.

The city government of New Amsterdam provided quarters for the school and for one year, in return for certain license fees, assumed the support of the minister and the schoolmaster.

Educational opportunities provided. Probably seven of the nine villages chartered by the Dutch government established schools before the English occupation. Their establishment, for the most part, however, was late in the period. In 1657, a report by the ministers of New Amsterdam to the classis stated "that so far as we know, not one of all these places, Dutch or English, has a schoolmaster, except the Manhattans, Beverwyck, and now also Fort Casimer on the South River."[17] In the villages, as well as in New Amsterdam, the elementary schools appear to have been the joint concern of church and state. In three villages the director and council assisted the villages in paying the schoolmaster. Quite likely, the village revenues were generally drawn upon to provide the master with a house and whatever income he received in addition to the fees that were derived from tuition and from his performing certain duties assigned to him as the reader, psalm-setter, and sexton of the church. Schoolmasters who were also church officials, as was usually the case, were of necessity acceptable to both church and state. In fact, in the villages as well as in New Amsterdam, state-church cooperation in educational affairs is clearly discernible.

The schools were generally small and primitive. School was often held in the home of the master. In New Amsterdam, during a part of the period, the school was housed in a building provided by the municipality. The curriculum was extremely limited, providing instruction in reading, writing, and sometimes the simplest parts of arithmetic. Religion was always emphasized. The offerings for girls were even more restricted. Night schools for teaching the elements were not unknown, but for the great mass of children only a meager education was contemplated. Some children were taught by private tutors, and private schools were maintained, at least in New Amsterdam, during the greater part of the period. A Latin school was not established until near the end of the Dutch regime. It appears to have been supported and controlled in much the same way as the elementary school, the main differences being, as pointed out by Kilpatrick, that no ecclesiastical body is mentioned in connection with the certification or selection of either of the two masters who, in succession, served the school, and that, while the city provided only quarters for the elementary schoolmaster, it paid a large share of the salaries of the masters of the Latin school. In spite of the high hopes of the authorities, the school did not prosper, probably never enrolling at a given time more than twenty to twenty-five students.

In New Netherland, we have a situation unique in American colonial

17 As quoted *ibid.,* p. 124.

history. It was not the only colony in which educational development was conditioned by a great diversity of racial and religious groups, but in no other colony of this nature was there one group, homogeneous as to race and religion, so completely dominant in the social, economic, and political life of the colony. Without serious interference from or offense to other groups, the Dutch were more or less free to provide education as they pleased. Naturally, they reproduced as nearly as circumstances would permit the educational arrangements of the fatherland.

DUTCH SCHOOLS UNDER ENGLISH CONTROL

Elementary schools. The Dutch school in New Amsterdam was permitted by the English to continue with little change until about 1674, after which the municipality contributed nothing to the support of either the Dutch school or church. The school was made dependent upon the church for support and came to be entirely under church control. During the eighteenth century, the school in New York (city) came to be an instrument to preserve the Dutch tongue in a society that was becoming definitely English. As such, the school was little more than a charity institution for a limited number of poor Dutch.

In the Dutch villages, old and new, the English influence was not so overwhelming as in New Amsterdam. The schools continued in the Dutch tradition, the local government and the church working together in ordering the educational arrangements. The officials of the two generally selected the master, furnished him a house, and paid part of his salary. The master, often as a minor church official, received a portion of his income from the church. A part of his income might also be charged to his serving as court messenger or town clerk. For a time, at least, the school was controlled jointly by the church and the local magistracy.

On the whole, the Dutch colony, as inadequate as its educational provisions were, compared favorably with its contemporaries in the matter of providing schools for its children. In evaluating the influence of the educational activities of the Dutch on American education, Monroe has made the following summary statement:

> The significant fact in regard to this system of parish schools is the marked contrast which it offers to the villages or towns where English customs prevailed. In all of these Dutch settlements a community school existed as one essential part of the structure of society and of the local system of government. While church and town government co-operated, these were essentially town schools supported as a town charge. To the Dutch a church was essentially a part of the local government scheme. The "church masters" were selected by the town government. So while the school was immediately under the church, it was essentially a town school. In the early national period these schools continued to form the

basis or nucleus of a system of public schools. Undoubtedly the tradition represented by these state-church or parish schools, and the actual working system which they presented were a leading factor in the establishment of the first system of public schools created after the Revolution (New York, 1795).[18]

SOCIAL STRUCTURE AND CLASS CONFLICTS IN NEW YORK

The English conquered New Netherland in 1664 and the king conferred the province on his brother, the Duke of York. In due time the name of the colony was changed to New York. The new proprietor had authority to govern and dispose of the colony about as he pleased, and he soon began to encourage the development of the aristocratic class which had already begun to take form under the Dutch regime. He confirmed the land grants which the Dutch Company had made to certain wealthy families. These holdings often included hundreds of thousands of acres. Soon, too, the Duke or his governors began to issue new patents with a generous hand. Individuals who were able to exercise the proper influence in official circles found no great difficulty in securing title to an estate of one hundred thousand acres or more. It took time, of course, to bring these immense tracts of land under cultivation, but in the eighteenth century one could find many large estates with broad arable fields and meadows tended by tenants in true English fashion. One of these, Rensselaerswyck, with Albany as its center, included 700,000 acres. The great Van Cortlandt, Livingston, and Beekman manors ranged in size from 140,000 to 240,000 acres.[19] Other large holdings — Morrisania, Pelham, Fordham, Scarsdale, Claverack — were the seats of an agricultural aristocracy not unlike that of the tobacco colonies to the south and rivaling the landed gentry of England.

In New York City a merchant class was rising to an importance comparable to that of the manorial aristocracy of the Hudson Valley. Even in the early days, New Amsterdam had been a commercial center of considerable importance, and New York, under the English, continued to expand the volume of its trade. Its leading merchants, often in their own ships, exported the flour and other surplus products of the agricultural hinterland. Like the merchants of New England, they reaped handsome profits from the rum and slave trade. They speculated in land, supplied the small farmers and the large manorial estates with the goods they required, and were beginning to invest surplus capital in small manufacturing enterprises. Frequently, the owners of large landed estates engaged in commercial enterprises and merchants in their turn invested in land.

---

18 Paul Monroe, *Founding of the American Public School System* (New York: The Macmillan Co., 1940), I, p. 82. Used by permission of The Macmillan Co.
19 Nettels, *op. cit.*, p. 308. See Morison and Commager, *op. cit.*, pp. 61–62.

Thus, an aristocracy based on land and trade came to occupy a dominant position in the life of the colony. This upper class supplied most of the political, social, and intellectual leadership. As we shall see later, this leadership was not greatly interested in the development of a system of popular education.

Landed proprietors and merchants were not, however, to have their way without opposition. Small farmers, lesser tradesmen, and artisans drew together to assert their rights.[20] They lacked any great political power, however, because, of all the English colonies in the seventeenth century, New York had the most undemocratic form of government. The Duke of York held full power to govern the colony through an appointed governor and council. He could make laws, levy taxes, appoint officials — in fact, govern the colony in practically every detail — without the aid of a popular assembly.[21] It was against this despotic government that the democratic party took up the gage of battle, demanding a share in the government. Under the leadership of Jacob Leisler, the farmers and the city "rabble" actually appealed to force in 1689. The revolt was put down and Leisler executed, but in 1691 a popular assembly was established. The suffrage was then extended to possessors of a forty-shilling freehold, and eight years later it was broadened to include also those with a personal estate of forty pounds.[22] Many were still disenfranchised, but yeomen, small traders, and better-to-do citizens were now in a stronger position to defend their rights. In most of the crucial matters, however, the merchants and large landholders were still able to have their way and to shape public and social policy along the lines they desired. In New York, as elsewhere, as the colonial period drew to an end, there was a sharp cleavage between the aristocratic and democratic parties. Social and economic distinctions, political controversy, and diversity of national groups — all these prevented New York from achieving any great degree of social unity and cohesion.

Religion was never a very powerful positive factor in the educational history of colonial New York. As we have seen, the Dutch were Calvinists and, like Calvinists elsewhere, they displayed some interest in the maintenance of schools. After the English took over, an attempt was made to make the Church of England the state church, but Anglicanism was not established at all until 1693, and then in only four counties.[23] At the outbreak of the Revolution, only about one in fifteen of the population was a communicant of the Anglican faith.[24] Many of these, however,

[20] Nettels, *op. cit.*, p. 343.   [21] *Ibid.*, p. 344.

[22] James Truslow Adams, *Provincial Society, 1690–1763* (New York: The Macmillan Co., 1927), p. 20.

[23] Marcus Wilson Jernegan, *The American Colonies, 1492–1750* (New York: Longmans, Green Co., 1929), p. 233. Also published in paperback (New York: Frederick Ungar Publishing Co., Inc., 1959).

[24] Nettels, *op. cit.*, p. 478.

were among the most influential persons in the colony and they were instrumental in the establishment of King's College (Columbia). Many of the upper class, too, belonged to the Dutch Reformed Church, which was responsible for the establishment of Rutgers College in New Jersey. Other religious groups were extremely numerous; among them were the Quakers, Anabaptists, Presbyterians, Independents, and Jews. At a time when one of the chief purposes of education was commonly regarded as being to serve religious ends, this multiplicity of religious faiths practically precluded any state action in the maintenance of schools.

EDUCATIONAL POLICY UNDER ENGLISH RULE

English charity schools. Following the English practice, the colonial government of New York engaged in few educational activities other than providing for general oversight of poor children and apprentices and asserting its right with respect to the licensing of teachers. The government, however, did encourage the work of the Society for the Propagation of the Gospel in Foreign Parts, an auxiliary of the Established Church founded in 1701 to convert the heathens and strengthen the national church, which felt itself threatened at home as well as abroad. The Society, particularly interested in the colonies directly under royal control, found New York, with a heterogeneous population of French Calvinists, French Lutherans, Quakers, Sabbatarians, Anti-Sabbatarians, Anabaptists, Independents, Mennonites, Moravians, Dunkers, Seceders, New Lights, Covenanters, and others, a fertile field for missionary work.

As a part of its program of colonial evangelization, this organization, until it withdrew during the Revolution, continuously supported from five to ten schools in the province of New York. For the most part, the schools maintained by the Society in New York City were charity schools. Outside the city, one-half to three-fourths of the enrollment was made up of paying scholars.[25] These schools failed to enlist the support of the better-to-do English colonists, who had a long tradition of educating their children by private tutors, nor were the sectarian groups friendly toward them. They were established, however, in a number of English villages,[26] in which, in some instances, they competed with the Dutch schools.

These English charity schools enjoyed the patronage of the governor, public officials inspected them, the Church of England examined the teachers, its great missionary society supported them, and the governors licensed their teachers. As Kemp states, the movement represented "a

[25] William Webb Kemp, *The Support of Schools in Colonial New York by the Society for the Propagation of the Gospel in Foreign Parts* (New York: Teachers College, Columbia University, 1913), pp. 276–277.
[26] Monroe, *op. cit.*, p. 87.

most praiseworthy attempt to adapt the system of English charity-schools to the needs of the province."[27] The schools supported by the Society in New York, however, continued throughout the period to be of the meanest sort. They were not greatly unlike the Dutch schools, providing only the most meager instruction in reading, writing, sometimes the elements of arithmetic, and always the catechism and religious exercises. As poor as they were and as few persons as they reached, it has been claimed that they provided "the nearest approach to a public school system that was to be found among the English colonists in New York."[28] This claim has been disputed by persons unable to reconcile charity schools with public schools, no matter how extensively the former may have been provided.

Elementary schools of other religious groups. A number of other religious groups maintained schools as best they could. The Quakers, although feared and heartily disliked by the Established Church and the government alike, were able to organize schools in connection with their churches. That these schools were tolerated can be explained only by the conflicting interests of that unsettled time.

Secondary schools. With respect to secondary education, the English colonial government also pursued a policy of indifference. The Latin school, established a few years before the close of the Dutch regime, is said by some writers to have continued under English rule for a few years.[29] Whether it expired with the English occupation or somewhat later, many years passed before the government showed an interest in secondary education beyond possibly licensing private teachers. A bill for the encouragement of a "Grammar Free-School in the City of New York," to be taught by a master "Elected, Chosen, Lycensed, Authorized, and appointed" by the authority of the "Governor and Council and Representatives," was passed in 1702. French and Dutch, as well as English, boys were to be instructed in the "Languages or other Learning usually taught in Grammar Schools." The act was to be in force for a period of seven years, during which period fifty pounds was to be "Assessed, Levyed, Collected and paid" for the maintenance of the master in the same way that the minister's salary was provided.[30] No record of the establishment of such a school is found until 1704, and when the act expired by its own limitation there seems to have been no effort made to revive it. Almost

---

[27] Kemp, *op. cit.*, p. 276.   [28] *Ibid.*, p. 277.

[29] A. Emerson Palmer, *The New York Public School* (New York: The Macmillan Co., 1905), p. 8.

[30] Daniel J. Pratt, *Annals of Public Education in the State of New York from 1626 to 1746* (Albany: Printed for the Regents of the University of the State of New York, 1871), pp. 76–77.

a generation was to pass before the colonial government made another move.

In 1732 the General Assembly passed an "Act to encourage a Public School in the City of New York for teaching Latin, Greek and Mathematicks." For forty pounds annually, derived from certain provincial license fees, the master was to teach without charge twenty children, ten of whom were to be drawn from New York City and County, the others from other counties. This school is notable in that its curriculum represented a departure from the narrow classical studies typical of the Latin grammar school. Instruction was offered in Latin, Greek, geometry, algebra, geography, navigation, and "Merchants Book-keeping."[31] It did not, however, have a very long life. The government's bounty, which by the act lapsed in 1737, was extended for one year. After 1738 nothing further concerning the school is known.[32] With the exception of encouraging the establishment of a preparatory school in connection with King's College sometime after the middle of the century, the government gave no further aid to secondary education during the colonial period.

Private schools. The neglect of schools by the government and the factors which explain that neglect resulted in the development of private schools on a large scale. Advertisements in the newspapers published in New York City during the eighteenth century reveal that private schools were very numerous and that they afforded instruction in a great variety of subjects for both boys and girls. For those who wanted to learn French, Italian, Portuguese, and Spanish, there appears to have been no dearth of teachers. A typical advertisement was that which was published in the New York *Gazette* in 1735:

> This is to give Notice that over against the Sign of the black Horse in Smith street, near the old Dutch Church, is carefully taught the French and Spanish languages, after the best Method that is now practised in Great Britain which for the encouragement of those who intend to learn the same is taught for 20s per Quarter.[33]

Some of the teachers conducted French boarding schools, and at least one was open to both "young Gentlemen and Ladies."

As was the case in Boston, Philadelphia, Charleston, and other cities, private teachers in New York provided instruction in a great variety of vocational subjects, such as navigation, surveying, and bookkeeping. Be-

[31] *Ibid.,* pp. 632–643, 672–687. See also Elmer Ellsworth Brown, *The Making of Our Middle Schools* (New York: Longmans, Green & Co., 1918), p. 94.

[32] Pratt, *op. cit.,* p. 141.

[33] Robert Francis Seybolt, *Source Studies in American Colonial Education: The Private School,* Bureau of Educational Research Bulletin No. 28; University of Illinois Bulletin, XXIII, No. 4 (Urbana, Ill.: University of Illinois, 1925), pp. 11, 133.

tween 1709 and 1776 at least nineteen teachers advertised themselves as teaching navigation, twenty as teaching bookkeeping, and eleven as teaching surveying. Others were teaching geography, music, mensuration, and the various branches of mathematics, such as algebra, geometry, and trigonometry.

Private schools were of special importance in relation to the education of girls, as Professor Seybolt has made evident in his excellent study. Some of these schools were open to both sexes, some were available to girls at special hours, and many were for girls exclusively. Instruction for girls was made available in a great variety of subjects, including reading, writing, arithmetic, music, needlework, history, and Latin. Certainly, old notions with respect to the limited educational opportunities afforded girls during the colonial period need to be revised, at least as far as middle- and upper-class girls in New York and other cities were concerned.

Benjamin Franklin is often credited with having broken with tradition in establishing the academy in Philadelphia about the middle of the eighteenth century. As a matter of fact, private teachers had long been giving instruction in many if not most of the subjects included in the curriculum of Franklin's academy. The following account of a school advertised as being in operation in New York City in 1723 shows how closely some of the earlier private schools resembled the later academies:

> There is a School in New York, in the Broad Street, near the Exchange where Mr. John Walton, late of Yale-Colledge, Teacheth Reading, Writing, Arethmatick, whole Numbers and Fractions, Vulgar and Decimal, The Mariners Art, Plain and Mercators Way; Also Geometry, Surveying, the Latin Tongue, and Greek and Hebrew Grammers, Ethicks, Rhetorick, Logick, Natural Philosophy and Metaphysicks, all or any of them for a Reasonable Price. The School from the first of October till the first of March will be tended in the Evening. If any Gentlemen in the Country are disposed to send their Sons to the said School, if they apply themselves to the Master he will immediately procure suitable Entertainment for them, very cheap. Also if any Young Gentlemen of the City will please to come in the Evening and make some Tryal of the Liberal Arts, they may have opportunity of Learning the same things which are commonly Taught in Colledges.[34]

King's College (Columbia). No provision was made for higher education in the colony of New York until near the end of the colonial period. A few young men went abroad to pursue their studies in law, medicine, or divinity, and now and then one turned up at Harvard or Yale. It was rare, however, to meet a college graduate in New York. As late as the

[34] *American Weekly Mercury,* Oct. 17–Nov. 7, 1723, as quoted in Seybolt, *op. cit.,* p. 99. A much more detailed statement of another similar school, the English Grammar School conducted by Thomas Byerley and Josiah Davis, is reproduced *ibid.,* pp. 96–98.

middle of the eighteenth century, it is estimated that not more than ten persons in the entire province, excluding clergymen, were holders of a college degree.[35] The Anglican Church, however, insisted on trained ministers, and in 1754 adherents of this faith obtained a charter for King's College (later Columbia University). While plans were being laid to establish the college under the auspices of the Anglican Church, William Livingston came forward with a vigorous proposal that the college be established instead by the *state*. He insisted that higher education inescapably affected the public weal and could not possibly be regarded as merely a private concern.[36] Livingston lost his fight, but his proposal foreshadowed the establishment of state universities. The new college, though sectarian in spirit and control, had a curriculum that was comparatively liberal. In 1767 a medical department was added and in 1773 a law professorship was established, the first in any American college. The college was closed from 1776 to the end of the Revolutionary War, when it reopened under the name of Columbia College.[37]

New Jersey

In 1665 the Duke of York, who held all of the Dutch colony of New Netherland, granted that part lying between the Hudson and the Delaware to his friends Berkeley and Carteret, naming it New Jersey. Berkeley retained his interest only ten years and then sold it to a Quaker or to Quaker interests. The colony was then divided, Carteret retaining East New Jersey and the new owners taking over West New Jersey. In time, East New Jersey also came partly under the control of the Quakers. West New Jersey, which had a few Dutch and Swedish settlements at the time of the original grant, was peopled afterward largely by Quakers. Many New Englanders migrated to East New Jersey, where this element in the population became increasingly strong. Scotch and Scotch-Irish elements also increased rapidly. The two provinces were united in 1702 and ruled by the governor of New York until 1738, after which the territory had its own governor. During all these troublesome and stormy years, the government, whether that of a proprietary or royal colony, failed to take action with respect to education except to pass a short-lived act authorizing the establishment of town schools at the pleasure of the inhabitants. The legislature two years later took action which authorized the control of schools by the church groups. This, perhaps, was the only solution at the time. To most of the settlers of New Jersey, as elsewhere, the chief function of the school was religious instruction. For the most part, education which served other than religious ends or was sponsored

---

[35] Brown, *op. cit.*, pp. 283–284.   [36] *Ibid.*, p. 285.
[37] Chitwood, *op. cit.*, p. 469.

by any save a religious group was regarded with cold indifference by a heterogeneous population concerned largely with securing a living and maintaining its rights against proprietors, landlords, and royal governors.

A notable event, however, in the history of education in New Jersey was the establishment in 1747 of the College of New Jersey (later Princeton), which was designed primarily to train ministers for the Presbyterian Church. It was largely the product of the Great Awakening, an intense religious movement that swept the colonies during the late seventeen-thirties and early seventeen-forties. The College of New Jersey was definitely sectarian in spirit and loyal to the classical tradition. It soon began to draw students not only from New Jersey and Pennsylvania, but from the Scotch-Irish Presbyterian settlements that extended along the whole back-country of the South. In the course of years, numerous "Log Colleges" were established along the frontier from Pennsylvania to Georgia, one of their chief purposes being to provide young men with the classical education required for entrance to Princeton.

Pennsylvania

The influences which led to the founding of Pennsylvania and which contributed to its subsequent development sprang from the social, economic, and religous conditions which characterized seventeenth-century Europe. In Europe during this period, the great forces making for colonization were hope for personal gain on the part of members of all classes of society, ambition to advance national interests, and the desire of those persecuted on account of their religious beliefs to find a place where they could worship as they pleased. As Greene has pointed out, there was in William Penn, the founder of Pennsylvania, a curious meeting of these forces.

> By birth and family connections he belonged to that ruling class in England which was eager to exploit the economic resources of the New World, for themselves as well as for their country. Yet by his own choice Penn was also associated with a group of radical enthusiasts, quite outside that ruling circle, who looked to America as a refuge from intolerable conditions at home and as the scene of a hopeful experiment in religion and government.[38]

THE QUAKERS

The Quakers or Friends, as these religious and social radicals were called, were regarded, wherever found, as dangerous citizens whose very

[38] Evarts Boutell Greene, *The Foundations of American Nationality* (New York: American Book Co., 1922), pp. 165–166.

presence constituted a serious menace to an orderly society. Accepting
without reservation the religious theory of early Protestant reformers,
which postulated a Christianity that derived "its authority solely from
the voice of God speaking to the individual conscience," they rejected
"forms and ceremonies, priesthoods, and temples built with human
hands."[39] They therefore rejected not only the ecclesiastical hierarchies of
the established churches, but, since God was revealed without the inter-
position of earthly mediators, they also rejected the idea of a formally ordained and paid ministry for themselves. Paying tithes to support the
clergy of other churches became, therefore, not only an unwelcome financial burden, but a matter of conscience as well. They regarded taking
oaths and military services as contrary to the teachings of Christ. Their
stubborn insistence upon wearing their hats in the presence of authority,
their custom of addressing social and political superiors with the singular
thou instead of the more polite *you,* and other seemingly superficial pecu-
liarities attracted attention to their fundamental belief that all men are
given alike the gift of God's Spirit. This belief, which implied that all
artificial distinctions, including those of rank and wealth, should be leveled, not only threatened the existing social order, based as it was on rank
and privilege, but also provided a "religious as well as intellectual basis for
a true democracy."[40] It is not strange that the teachings of these social
revolutionists should have been considered the greatest menace of the
time and that well-meaning citizens and zealous seventeenth-century
Christians should have considered persecution of Quakers to be in the
interests of the public welfare and to the glory of God.

Founding a Quaker Refuge

Quakers early considered the establishment of a refuge in America, and
Penn, together with others, made a beginning in West New Jersey. It was
soon realized, however, that protection against interference, which only a
royal charter could give, was necessary to the development of a refuge
where Quakers might work out their experiment in religion and government.

There can be little doubt but that Penn believed that the well-being of
the colony required a program of education under provincial authority.
His statements on the subject of education indicate that he was fully aware
of the importance of education to the state as well as to the individual.
Commenting on the relation of education to the state, Penn said:

[39] *Ibid.,* p. 167; Chitwood, *op. cit.,* pp. 201–213; Morison and Commager, *op.
cit.,* p. 73.
[40] James Pyle Wickersham, *A History of Education in Pennsylvania, Private and
Public, Elementary and Higher* (Lancaster, Pa.: published for the author by the
Inquirer Publishing Co., 1885), p. 21.

Upon the whole matter I undertake to say that if we would preserve our government, we must endear it to the people. To do this, besides the necessity of presenting just and wise things, we must secure the youth: this is not to be done, but by the amendment of the way of education. . . . I say the government is highly obliged: it is a sort of trustee for the youth of the kingdom; who, though minors, yet will have the government when we are gone. Therefore, depress vice, and cherish virtue, that through good education, they may become good.[41]

It is not strange, therefore, that in the Frame of Government drawn up in England before his departure for Pennsylvania, Penn clearly accepted the theory of education as a function of civil authority.[42] This idea may be found in the first three frames adopted by the province and in other provisions made by the Assembly.

Little more than a month after Penn's arrival in Pennsylvania, the first General Assembly met and passed what has been known as the "Great Law," one section of which may be interpreted as having implications for education. It was provided:

That the Laws of this Province, from time to time, shall be published and printed, that every person may have knowledge thereof: and they shall be one of the books taught in the schools of this Province and Territories thereof.

The second frame, accepted in the spring of 1683, contained the following provision:

And to the end that poor as well as rich may be instructed in good and commendable learning, which is to be preferred before wealth, *Be it enacted, etc.,* That all persons in this Province and Territories thereof, having children, and all the guardians and trustees of orphans, shall cause such to be instructed in reading and writing, so that they may be able to read the Scriptures and to write by the time they attain to twelve years of age; and that then they be taught some useful trade or skill, that the poor may work to live, and the rich if they become poor may not want: of which every County Court shall take care. And in case such parents, guardians, or overseers shall be found deficient in this respect, every such parent, guardian, or overseer shall pay for every such child, five pounds, except there should appear an incapacity in body or understanding to hinder it.

The third frame, the last to mention education, contained provisions much like those of Penn's first frame. It provided:

41 As quoted in Wickersham, *op. cit.,* pp. 33–34.
42 Thomas Woody, *Early Quaker Education in Pennsylvania,* Teachers College Contributions to Education, No. 105 (New York: Teachers College, Columbia University, 1920), p. 42.

That the Governor and Council shall erect and order all public schools and encourage and reward the authors of useful sciences and laudable inventions in the said Province and Territorities.[43]

Penn and the council in 1683 invited Enock Flower to become a schoolmaster in Philadelphia to teach reading, writing, and the casting of accounts, and agreed with him on the amounts that might be charged for tuition. The school established as a result of this action was, to a degree, under public authority, although not fully supported by the government.[44] In the same year, it was proposed in the council that a school of arts and sciences be established. The Friends' Public School, now known as the William Penn Charter School, was opened in 1689, incorporated by the council in 1697, and formally chartered by Penn in 1701. The charter provided for the establishment of other schools as they became necessary. It appears that several branch charity schools were provided later. Although the school was known as a public school and children of all denominations were admitted, the school was a private institution managed by a group of leading Quakers.[45]

Articles relating to education in the various frames, laws enacted by different provincial assemblies, and the activities of the Quakers in establishing schools indicate that education was considered important in furthering the main ends toward which the colony had been established and suggest that the Quakers contemplated the establishment of a system of education under public authority.

Penn's advanced position with respect to education was not maintained by his successors, nor even by Penn himself. He evidently became impressed in a few years with the impossibility of realizing his educational purposes in a situation created by the presence in Pennsylvania of a population representing the greatest diversity with respect to nationality, religious belief, political philosophy, and general culture. Education also suffered from conditions arising from the inharmonious relations between the proprietor and the English government, from strife growing out of Penn's efforts to found a democracy and yet remain a feudal lord, and from other clashes of opposing interests and principles. Also, in a day when religion and education were so closely associated, full religious liberty and a public school system were incompatible, a state school implying an established church. Even the topography of the country was a retarding influence in educational development. The last Charter of Privileges granted by Penn in 1701, which continued in force to the end of the colonial period, did not contain a single section on education.

[43] As quoted in Wickersham, *op. cit.*, pp. 38–40.

[44] Louise Gilchriese Walsh and Matthew John Walsh, *History and Organization of Education in Pennsylvania* (Indiana, Pennsylvania: published by the authors, 1930), p. 4.

[45] Woody, *op. cit.*, pp. 49–52.

The only general acts relating to education passed under the last charter dealt with the right of Protestant congregations or societies to purchase lands for building schools and other purposes, to receive gifts, and to hold the properties thus acquired. Pennsylvania accepted the only solution compatible with the religious and social ideas of the time and relinquished all control of schools to the many churches and religious organizations, to a smaller number of volunteer community organizations, to the home, and to private enterprise.

EDUCATION OF NATIONAL AND RELIGIOUS GROUPS

As heterogeneous as was the population of Pennsylvania in the seventeenth century, it became more so in the eighteenth. Unlike New York, where the fusion of the Dutch and English went on with the Dutch steadily losing ground before increasing numbers of the politically dominant English, in Pennsylvania the large-scale immigration of the eighteenth century greatly increased the population of non-English people. For reasons not difficult to find, it was through Pennsylvania rather than New York that the persecuted and economically crushed hordes of Germany, Ireland, Switzerland, and other European countries sought asylum in America.

To the English, Swedes, Dutch, Welsh, and Germans of Penn's time were added thousands upon thousands of European peasants and workers to whom, crushed as they were by poverty, war, and religious persecution in the Old World, the New appealed almost irresistibly. The emigration from Germany to America reached such proportions that it has been likened to the great migratory movements of the Germans at the beginning of the Middle Ages.[46] So great was the influx of the "Scotch-Irish" and English from northern Ireland that in 1729 the scholarly Secretary of the Province wrote in alarm, "It looks as if Ireland is to send all its inhabitants hither." Southern Ireland, Scotland, and Switzerland also sent forth a considerable, if smaller, number of emigrants, many of whom settled in Pennsylvania. The moving forces were economic or religious, or, more often, both.

The Germans, suffering from the results of a century of warfare and internal dissensions, from demoralized agriculture, industry, and commerce, from disrupted economic and social life, and from the oppression of princely governments, felt also, in many sections, the weight of religious persecution. Catholic governments persecuted Protestants; Protestant governments persecuted Catholics; and both governments persecuted small dissenting Protestant groups. The Quakers early offered refuge to pacifist sects like themselves, and, almost from the beginning of the colony, these groups were important elements in the population.

[46] Nettels, *op. cit.*, p. 384.

Also, the English in 1702 began a policy of settling America with poor Germans and for a time managed to send over thousands each year. These Germans, reduced to the direst poverty in the homeland, sometimes persecuted for their religious beliefs, mistreated by dishonest shipowners and labor agents, exploited by the English government, and generally misunderstood wherever they might go, poured into Pennsylvania, many as servants bound for a term of years to pay their passage. They were suspicious of all other national and religious groups and resentful and fearful of even well-intentioned interference, either from government or from any other source.

Among the Germans to settle in Pennsylvania, the Lutherans and German Reformed (Calvinists) were the most numerous, although they did not arrive in force until near the end of the 1730's. The non-resistant sects which migrated have, however, attracted more attention. In the words of Fisher:

> The first great increase of alien population came from Germany, which was still in a state of religious turmoil, disunion, and depression from the results of the Reformation and the Thirty Years' War. The reaction from dogma in Germany had produced a multitude of sects, all yearning for greater liberty and prosperity than they had at home. . . . The German mind was then at the height of its emotional unrestraint. It was as unaccustomed to liberty of thought as to political liberty and it produced a new sect or religious distinction almost every day.[47]

These sects were known under an almost unending variety of names — Moravians, Mennonites, Amish, Dunkers, Seventh-Day Adventists, Schwenkfelders, New Born, Inspired, Separatists, Depellians, River Brethren, and many others. It has been stated that between twenty and thirty of these religious groups were to be found in Lancaster County alone. They generally opposed the union of church and state; refused to engage in lawsuits or hold civil office; opposed war, and in other ways were not greatly different from the Quakers, with whom, however, they could not cooperate in matters that touched the soul. In fact, the German immigrants, although they at times gave their support to the Quakers as the least obnoxious of the political groups, were generally indifferent to political responsibility. With the exception of the later Lutherans and German Reformed (Calvinists), they tended to live in isolated communities and to remain aloof from those who spoke other than the German language, to which, along with their old customs and traditions, they tenaciously clung. Their interest in education stemmed almost entirely from their religious beliefs, and, to the extent that their religious spirit waned, education became less important. Whatever education was pro-

[47] From Sydney G. Fisher, "The Quaker Colonies," Vol. VIII, *The Chronicles of America,* Copyright Yale University Press (New Haven, Conn.: Yale University Press, 1920), pp. 41–42.

vided was in the German language and under the control of their own clergy.[48] Like the Quakers, they were generally distrustful of higher education. The more permanent and larger of the German groups, however, provided elementary schools for their children.

At the beginning of the eighteenth century, there was as much hopelessness and bitterness in northern Ireland as in Germany. Oppressive trade regulations, long-continued economic depression, and a series of disasters brought about the financial ruin of the Scots and English who, with the aid of England, had settled in Ireland during the seventeenth century. The attempt to force these Scotch-Irish Presbyterians to accept and support the Church of Ireland, an offshoot of the Church of England, added to the general despair and helped swell the tide of immigrants who "left Ireland with bitter hatred of England in their hearts."[49]

The Scotch-Irish, whatever their good qualities as settlers in a new country, were as intolerant of the religion of others as were enthusiastic followers of Calvin elsewhere. They probably liked the Quakers no more than did the Calvinists of New England, and the kindliness and tolerance of the Quakers were hardly sufficient to make them understand, much less love, these vigorous and outspoken Scotch-Irish Presbyterians.[50] The Scotch-Irish were among those who pushed to the frontier, with which they were well able to cope. There, without effective checks by the provincial government, they developed a highly individualistic society, intensely disliking and vigorously opposing any control over local affairs by the central government. Between them and other groups, especially the Quakers, there could be little cooperation in matters pertaining to education.

As Calvinists generally were, however, they were devoted to education. They prized an educated ministry and emphasized the necessity of reading the Bible as a means to salvation. Reading became, therefore, a part of the religious education of each child and some means of training ministers became a necessity.

Closely related, in spirit at least, to these Presbyterians were the settlers from Connecticut and other parts of New England who, shortly before the Revolution, moved into the Wyoming Valley of northeastern Pennsylvania. They brought with them from the older settlement, as their forefathers had brought from Europe, their old institutions and ideals. As pawns in Connecticut's attempt to assert ownership of the land, these people lived a harried and extremely difficult life until after the Revolution, when Pennsylvania's title was acknowledged. The region, however, was largely occupied by the New Englanders, who as early as 1768 had decreed that nine hundred and sixty acres in each township should be set aside for the use of the church and schools, and had elected for each dis-

[48] Walsh and Walsh, *op. cit.*, p. 55.
[49] Adams, *op. cit.*, p. 172.   [50] Walsh and Walsh, *op. cit.*, pp. 60–61.

trict a school committee charged with the employment of a teacher, the supervision of instruction, and the collection of a rate bill.

Among other important religious groups to establish themselves in Pennsylvania were Episcopalians, Baptists, Catholics, and, shortly before the Revolution, Methodists. Prominent among the Episcopalians were the descendants of Penn, the deputy-governors, and other members of the proprietary party. This group never gave up, during the colonial period, the hope that its church would become the established church in the colony, as was the case in England. They retained the traditional English attitude toward education. Schools under the control of the Anglican Church were established early in the history of the colony, and the Society for the Propagation of the Gospel in Foreign Parts, an auxiliary of the Established Church of England, also was active in promoting education and the interests of the church. The Baptists, whose first settlement in Pennsylvania was made in 1684, probably established schools rather generally in connection with their churches. They supported the founding of Brown University in Rhode Island, the state from which the first Baptists made their way to Pennsylvania. There were few Catholics in the province, probably not more than two thousand at the close of the colonial period. Their presence, however, added to the heterogeneity of population and their insistence upon controlling the education of their children led to the establishment of church schools and helped to promote further the parochial-school idea. The Methodists, who established their first church in Pennsylvania in 1769, did not become numerous until after the war. For this reason, and because of their poverty and lack of interest in building a church organization, they alone of all the religious groups who found refuge in Pennsylvania failed to develop parochial schools."[51]

PAROCHIAL SCHOOLS

Except for the religious affiliation and the language of instruction, the parochial schools of the various denominations and sects were much alike. Elementary education was religious in purpose and seldom went beyond the barest rudiments. The Scotch-Irish did quite often develop more advanced schools, usually, however, around their ministers. The Moravians, one of whose bishops, Comenius, had been the leading educational thinker of the early seventeenth century, had a long tradition of education. Arriving in America near the middle of the eighteenth century, they established a communal system of which schools were a part. They established a number of institutions, particularly boarding schools, not only for boys and girls, but for infants as well. Several of these schools enjoyed a long history and have had a lasting influence on American education.

[51] *Ibid.*, pp. 72–73.

The quality of the instruction in most of the parochial schools must have been poor. After the first years of colonization, most teachers were natives and commonly selected from the neighborhood in which they taught. Although the names of many have come down to us, only one made a lasting impression by his teaching alone. Christopher Dock, "the Pious Schoolmaster on the Skippack," came to America between 1710 and 1714 and shortly engaged in teaching school, which he continued, with a ten-year interlude, to his death in 1771. Saur, the Germantown printer and leader of the Germans in Pennsylvania, impressed by the great teaching skill and ability of the humble Mennonite, urged him to write a treatise on the organization and conduct of a school. Dock was averse to presenting his methods because, he said, "it would appear as though I were trying to build up for myself a reputation, testimonial or unsavory monument, which, if it were indeed true, would deserve before God and all pious, Christian people, not honor, but rather ridicule and shame, and could not conduce to my soul's welfare and salvation. It would only be food for self-love."[52] Dock was persuaded, however, to prepare the manuscript, which he completed in 1750. It was given to Saur with the understanding that it was not to be printed during the author's lifetime. Shortly before Dock's death some twenty years later, friends overcame his scruples, and the younger Saur, who had succeeded his father, published the treatise, often said to be the first work on education published in America. A second edition was brought out less than a year after the first. Through the entire book "runs the modest schoolmaster's love of his work and of his pupils, with many shrewd observations as to methods and devices. Some of these have a decidedly modern sound." For example, when he was teaching three days each week in two different schools, he had the pupils of the two schools exchange letters as a means of education and as motivation for learning reading, writing, and spelling.[53] Dock, like the other teachers of the time, emphasized instruction in religion, and a considerable part of the *Schul-Ordnung* is devoted to questions found useful in teaching "the fear of God . . . through many excellent Scripture passages."

CHARITY SCHOOLS

In addition to the purely parochial schools and those aided by the Society for the Propagation of the Gospel in Foreign Parts, there was for a brief period a small and totally inadequate system of charity schools under

[52] From the *Schul-Ordnung* by Christopher Dock, as quoted in Martin G. Brumbaugh, *The Life and Works of Christopher Dock* (Philadelphia: J. B. Lippincott Co., 1908), pp. 99–100. The entire *Schul-Ordnung* is reproduced in German and again in translation in this excellent work.

[53] Walsh and Walsh, *op. cit.,* p. 57.

the auspices of the Society for the Propagation of Christian Knowledge among the Germans in Pennsylvania. Although not a sectarian organization, its membership consisted largely of Englishmen of wealth and position, a majority of whom were Anglicans. The utterances and actions of Doctor William Smith, Provost of the College of Philadelphia and leader of the Anglican party in Philadelphia, confirmed the belief of Saur and other members of the German sects that the real purpose back of providing charity schools was political; that it was all a part of a project to array the organized religions, the Anglicans, Lutherans, and Reformed, against the groups having no formal ecclesiastical organization; that the promoters were less interested in the minds and culture of the Germans than in promoting the interests of the war party; and that designs were entertained, not only against the German tongue, but also against their religion. At least twenty-five schools were planned; probably only a dozen were established. After a languishing existence of less than ten years, the system failed completely in 1763, leaving all education to private, church, and neighborhood schools.[54]

PRIVATE EDUCATION

A discussion of the educational opportunities provided must include some statement with respect to private education, which was, perhaps, in Pennsylvania and other colonies as well, the dominant type of education during the entire period. Many children on the farms received all of their education from their parents, a neighbor, or some person employed by their parents. There were many private schools in Philadelphia. During the latter part of the colonial period, these schools provided instruction in bookkeeping, surveying, navigation, mathematics, Latin, modern languages, and many other subjects — elementary, secondary, and vocational.

The private schools in Philadelphia were fully as numerous and as varied in their program of instruction as those of Boston and New York, to which reference has been made at considerable length in preceding chapters of this volume.[55] One of these schools, however, deserves special comment. About the middle of the eighteenth century, Benjamin Franklin and a few other liberal-minded citizens founded an "academy" and secured for it a charter of incorporation. This institution was important for two reasons. First, its curriculum included many modern subjects, reflecting Franklin's liberal views on education. The breadth of the program of instruction may be seen from the following advertisement in the *Pennsylvania Gazette* announcing the opening of the school:

[54] The history of this movement is admirably set forth in Samuel Edwin Weber, *The Charity School Movement in Colonial Pennsylvania* (Philadelphia: Press of George F. Lasher, 1905).

[55] See also Seybolt, *op. cit.*

NOTICE is hereby given, That the Trustees of the ACADEMY of Philadelphia, intend (God willing) to open the same on the first Monday of January next; wherein Youth will be taught the Latin, Greek, English, French, and German Languages, together with History, Geography, Chronology, Logic, and Rhetoric; also Writing, Arithmetic, Merchants Accounts, Geometry, Algebra, Surveying, Gauging, Navigation, Astronomy, Drawing in Perspective, and other mathematical Sciences; with natural and mechanical Philosophy, &c. agreeable to the Constitutions heretofore published, at the Rate of Four pounds per annum, and Twenty Shillings entrance.[56]

In the second place, the Philadelphia Academy has commonly been regarded as initiating the academy movement, a movement which was to dominate the field of secondary education for more than a century. In a sense, this is true, inasmuch as it was the first chartered academy and one which was widely influential. In another sense, Franklin's academy merely represented the institutionalization of the private-school movement, which had been under way in practically all American cities for a generation and more.

HIGHER EDUCATION

Higher education was slow to develop in Pennsylvania. Religion had always been one of the principal moving forces in the establishment of institutions of higher learning, and in Pennsylvania the religious groups were too small and too poor to support a college, and some would not have supported one had the means been available. It was not long, however, after the opening of the academy in Philadelphia before steps were taken to develop it into a college. The Reverend William Smith, a distinguished clergyman and graduate of the University of Aberdeen, was added to the faculty of the academy and began to give instruction to the older students in "logic, rhetoric, and natural and moral philosophy." In 1755, four years after the academy was opened, a new charter was obtained which designated the institution as the College, Academy, and Charitable School of Philadelphia. Henceforth, the English and mathematical divisions of the school were known as the Academy, and the Latin and philosophical divisions constituted the College. Some years later, in 1779, the College of Philadelphia was reincorporated as the University of Pennsylvania.[57]

The College of Philadelphia was a private institution and entirely free from denominational control. In this respect it was unique among colonial institutions of higher learning. The curriculum represented a revolt against the religious traditions and to some degree a revolt against the

---

[56] *Pennsylvania Gazette*, Dec. 18, 1750, as quoted *ibid.*, pp. 98–99.
[57] Brown, *op. cit.*, p. 288.

classical tradition as well. Provost Smith's curriculum drawn up for the College in 1756 has been regarded as the first and most significant expression of the new utilitarian tendency in American higher education.[58] At the end of the colonial, and during the early years of the national, period, the College of Philadelphia shared with William and Mary the distinction of having moved furthest in the direction of a modern curriculum. This is not strange because these two colleges reflected, respectively, the influence of the two great American liberals of the age, Benjamin Franklin and Thomas Jefferson.

Basically, however, the curriculums of these two schools reflected the advancing knowledge and changing thought that had been forcing alterations in college curriculums generally throughout the entire century.[59] As previously noted, philosophers and political theorists such as John Locke were gaining a hearing. It is worthy of note that the proposition that civil government originates in social compact was debated in theses for the Master's degree at Harvard in 1743, 1747, 1751, 1761, and 1762. Science and mathematics were making a strong bid for greater recognition and had gained some notable victories.[60] However, much of the thought relating to science, and particularly to its utilitarian applications, was taking place in America, as in Europe, outside institutions of higher learning. In fact, only two or three of the fifteen American colonials elected fellows of the Royal Society of London before the Revolutionary War held regular teaching positions in colleges.

The growth of scientific thought and the increasing interest in science led to the organization of societies designed to advance and disseminate the learning. The first of these groups to have a wide influence and the only one to have a continuous existence to the present time was established in Philadelphia. It, as well as the college, profited from the guiding genius of Franklin.

The American Philosophical Society.   In 1743, Franklin, with the encouragement of John Bartram and others, published his *Proposal for Promoting Useful Knowledge Among the British Plantations in America.*[61] He proposed that a society should be formed, in Philadelphia as the most central place, made up "of *virtuosi* or ingenious men residing in the several Colonies, to be called *The American Philosophical Society,* who are to maintain a constant correspondence." The broad scientific and utilitarian interests of Franklin and his associates are indicated by the following statement of the Society's purpose:

[58] Theodore Hornberger, *Scientific Thought in American Colleges, 1638–1800* (Austin, Tex.: University of Texas Press, 1945), p. 55.
[59] *Ibid.*   [60] *Ibid.*, pp. 22–34.
[61] Brooke Hindle, *The Pursuit of Science in Revolutionary America, 1735–1789* (Chapel Hill, N.C.: University of North Carolina Press, 1956), pp. 68–69.

That the subjects of correspondence be: all new-discovered plants, herbs, trees, roots, their virtues, uses, etc.; methods of propagating them and making such as are useful, but particular to some plantations, more general; improvements of vegetable juices, as ciders, wines, etc.; new methods of curing or preventing diseases; all new-discovered fossils in different countries, as mines, minerals, and quarries; new and useful improvements in any branch of mathematics; new discoveries in chemistry, such as improvements in distillation, brewing, and assaying of ores; new mechanical inventions for saving labor, as mills and carriages, and for raising and conveying of water, draining of meadow, etc.; all new arts, trades, and manufactures that may be proposed or thought of; surveys, maps, and charts of particular parts of the sea-coasts or inland countries; course and junction of rivers and great roads, situation of lakes and mountains; nature of the soil and productions; new methods of improving the breed of useful animals; introducing other sorts from foreign countries; new improvements in planting, gardening, and clearing land; and all philosophical experiments that let light into the nature of things, tend to increase the power of man over matter, and multiply the conveniences and pleasures of life.[62]

The Society grew very well at first, but even Franklin's untiring efforts and personal leadership did not suffice to prevent its decline. After languishing for twenty years or more it was revived in 1768, and its first meeting was announced by a reprinting of Franklin's proposal of 1743.[63] Shortly after its revival, it was reorganized to include a rival organization, The American Society, and, even before the Revolution, several of its achievements were recognized throughout America and abroad.

The Slow Development of Education in the Middle Colonies

Educational development at all levels was slow in the Middle Colonies, including New Jersey, whose educational development followed the pattern set by New York, and Delaware, which was settled by the Swedes, held for a short time by the Dutch, and finally, in 1682, turned over to William Penn. After that date, the educational development of Delaware was not unlike that in Pennsylvania. The trend in the Middle Colonies, if there was one, was away from state control or support. A small beginning was made by the Dutch in the direction of public education, but after the English conquest the traditional English attitude toward educa-

---

[62] "A Proposal for Promoting Useful Knowledge Among the British Plantations in America," Philadelphia, May 14, 1743, as taken from Thomas Woody (ed.), *Educational Views of Benjamin Franklin* (New York: McGraw-Hill Book Co., Inc., 1931), pp. 59–60.

[63] *Ibid.*, p.132.

tion prevailed. The Dutch schools became purely parochial and the English schools were maintained by a recognized auxiliary of the Anglican Church. In New Jersey, an early act had authorized the inhabitants of a town to establish schools, but two years later church groups were made secure in their control of education.

One of Pennsylvania's early requirements was that parents should see to it that their children learn to read and write and be taught some useful trade. This auspicious beginning, however, was unable to survive the conditions created by clashing principles and cultures. The state, in its weakness, ceased to be interested and the responsibility for education was assumed by families, churches, and philanthropic and religious organizations. The parochial school became definitely predominant in elementary education, while secondary education, with the exception of that provided by the Scotch-Irish, owed its development largely to private enterprise.

In the area of private and higher education, considerable progress was made. Over the Middle Colonies, as elsewhere in America, the Renaissance and the Reformation cast long shadows; for many years the classical and religious traditions held education firmly in their grip. As a result, education was, in large measure, divorced from the realities of American life except as it served religious ends or the purposes of a small aristocratic class. In no adequate way did it interpret for youth either the world of nature or the world of man. Slowly, however, the influence of classicism and ecclesiasticism weakened, and education began to play a more dynamic role in the social, economic, and intellectual life of the people. In this movement, the activities of enlightened men acting independently and collectively should not be discounted; but, in the main, it was the private schools and the colleges which served as the avenues leading away from the heritage of European traditions, and nowhere were these institutions more liberal than in the Middle Colonies.

Questions and Problems for Study and Discussion

1. How do you explain the differences in educational policy and practice in colonial New England and colonial Pennsylvania? Colonial New York?

2. Indicate the efforts made in the Middle Colonies to make education a function of government. Why did these efforts fail?

3. Did education in the Middle Colonies contribute to the development of cultural unity or did it tend to retard the development of social cohesion? Defend your position.

4. Had the pattern of education developed in colonial Pennsylvania prevailed, how would American society have been affected?

5. Appraise Benjamin Franklin's contribution to American education.

6. What contributions did the private schools in the Middle Colonies make to the development of secondary education?

Selected References for Further Reading

Adams, James Truslow. *Provincial Society, 1690–1763. A History of American Life,* III. New York: The Macmillan Co., 1927. Pp. xx + 374.

Boorstin, Daniel J. *The Americans: The Colonial Experience.* New York: Random House, 1958. Pp. xii + 434.

Bridenbaugh, Carl. *Cities in Revolt: Urban Life in America, 1743–1776.* New York: Alfred A. Knopf, Inc., 1955. Pp. xiii + 433.

Bridenbaugh, Carl. *Cities in the Wilderness: The First Century of Urban Life in America, 1625–1742.* New York: The Ronald Press Company, 1938. Pp. xiv + 500.

Bridenbaugh, Carl, and Bridenbaugh, Jessica. *Rebels and Gentlemen: Philadelphia in the Age of Franklin.* New York: Reynal and Hitchcock, 1942. Pp. xvii + 393.

Brumbaugh, Martin G. *The Life and Works of Christopher Dock: America's Pioneer Writer on Education, with a Translation of his Works into the English Language.* Philadelphia: J. B. Lippincott Co., 1908. Pp. 272.

Burnaby, Andrew. *Travels through the Middle Settlements in North America, in the Years 1759 and 1760,* Third Edition, revised and enlarged. London: T. Payne, 1798. Pp. xix + 209. Also published in paperback (Ithaca, N.Y.: Cornell University Press [Great Seal Books], 1960).

Carmen, Harry J., and Syrett, Harold C. *A History of the American People,* I: To 1865. New York: Alfred A. Knopf, Inc., 1957. Pp. xxiv + 746 + xxi.

Fisher, Sydney G. *The Quaker Colonies: A Chronicle of the Proprietors of the Delaware,* The Chronicles of America Series, VIII. New Haven, Conn.: Yale University Press, 1920. Pp. x + 244.

Franklin, Benjamin. *The Autobiography of Benjamin Franklin & Sections from His Writings.* New York: A. S. Barnes & Co., Inc., 1944. Pp. xix + 264. Also published in paperback under the title *Autobiography of Benjamin Franklin* (New York: Washington Square Press, Inc., 1961).

Gegenheimer, Albert Frank. *William Smith: Educator and Churchman, 1727–1803.* Philadelphia: University of Pennsylvania Press, 1943. Pp. viii + 234.

Goodwin, Maud Wilder. *Dutch and English on the Hudson: A Chronicle of Colonial New York,* The Chronicles of America Series, VII. New Haven, Conn.: Yale University Press, 1920. Pp. x + 244.

Greene, Evarts Boutell. *The Foundations of American Nationality.* New York: American Book Co., 1922. Pp. xii + 614 + xiii–xl.

Hindle, Brooke. *The Pursuit of Science in Revolutionary America, 1735–1789.* Chapel Hill, N.C.: University of North Carolina Press, 1956. Pp. xi + 410.

Kemp, William Webb. *The Support of Schools in Colonial New York by the Society for the Propagation of the Gospel in Foreign Parts,* Teachers College Contributions to Education, No. 56. New York: Teachers College, Columbia University, 1913. Pp. viii + 280.

Kilpatrick, William Heard. *The Dutch Schools of New Netherland and Colonial New York.* Reprint of United States Bureau of Education Bulletin, No. 12, 1912, Whole No. 843. Washington, D.C.: Government Printing Office, 1912. Pp. 240.

Mark, Irving. *Agrarian Conflicts in Colonial New York, 1711–1775.* New York: Columbia University Press, 1940. Pp. vii + 237.

Nettels, Curtis P. *The Roots of American Civilization: A History of American Colonial Life.* New York: F. S. Crofts & Co., 1938. Pp. xx + 748.

Palmer, A. Emerson. *The New York Public School: Being a History of Free Education in the City of New York.* New York: The Macmillan Co., 1905. Pp. xxx + 440.

Pratt, Daniel J. *Annals of Public Education in the State of New York, From 1626 to 1746.* Albany, N.Y.: Printed for the Regents of the University of the State of New York, 1871. Pp. viii + 152.

Roberts, Ellis H. *New York: The Planting and Growth of the Empire State,* I: *American Commonwealths.* Boston: Houghton Mifflin Company, 1887. Pp. xii + 358.

Rossiter, Clinton. *Seedtime of the Republic: The Origin of the American Tradition of Political Liberty.* New York: Harcourt, Brace & Co., 1953. Pp. xiv + 558. Also published in paperback, in abridged form, under the title *The First American Revolution* (New York: Harcourt, Brace & Co. [Harvest Books], 1956).

Seybolt, Robert Francis. *Source Studies in American Colonial Education: The Private School,* Bureau of Educational Research Bulletin, No. 28; University of Illinois Bulletin, XXIII, No. 4. Urbana, Ill.: University of Illinois, 1925. Pp. 110.

Smith, H. Shelton, Handy, Robert T., and Loetscher, Lefferts A. *American Christianity: An Historical Interpretation with Representative Documents,* I: *1607–1820.* New York: Charles Scribner's Sons, 1960. Pp. xv + 615.

Soule, George, and Carosso, Vincent P. *American Economic History.* New York: Dryden Press, 1957. Pp. xvii + 654.

Tolles, Frederick B. *Meeting House and Counting House: The Quaker Merchants of Colonial Philadelphia, 1682–1763.* Chapel Hill, N.C.: University of North Carolina Press, 1948. Pp. xiv + 292.

Walsh, Louise Gilchriese, and Walsh, John Matthew. *History and Organization of Education in Pennsylvania.* Indiana, Pa.: published by the authors, 1928. Pp. xvi + 412.

Weber, Samuel Edwin. *The Charity School Movement in Colonial Pennsylvania* (Thesis presented to the Faculty of Philosophy of the University of Pennsylvania). Philadelphia: Press of George F. Lasher, 1905. Pp. 74.

Wertenbaker, Thomas Jefferson. *The Golden Age of Colonial Culture.* New York: New York University Press, 1942. Pp. 171. Also published in paperback (Ithaca, N.Y.: Cornell University Press [Great Seal Books], 1959).

Wickersham, James Pyle. *A History of Education in Pennsylvania, Private and Public, Elementary and Higher: From the Time the Swedes Settled on the Delaware to the Present Day.* Lancaster, Pa.: published for the author by the Inquirer Publishing Co., 1885. Pp. xxii + 684.

Woody, Thomas. *Early Quaker Education in Pennsylvania,* Teachers College Contributions to Education, No. 105. New York: Teachers College, Columbia University, 1920. Pp. 288.

Wickersham, James Pyle, A History of Education in Pennsylvania, Private and Public, Elementary and Higher, From the Time the Swedes Settled on the Delaware to the Present Day, Lancaster, Pa.; published for the author by the Inquirer Publishing Co., 1885, Pp. xvii + 683.

Woody, Thomas, Early Quaker Education in Pennsylvania, Teachers College Contributions to Education, No. 105, New York; Teachers College, Columbia University, 1920, Pp. 258.

PART TWO

The School and the Emergence of
the Democratic National State, 1776–1860:
Preview

The period extending from the Revolution to the Civil War was characterized by a number of significant movements and developments: by the formulation and, more or less, acceptance of the principles of democratic liberalism; by humanitarian strivings and the building of a more democratic social structure; by the growth of a feeling of national unity; by the rise of the common man to a position of political importance; and by the bitter struggle to control the national state on the part of southern planter interests and the rising industrial East. As new forces transformed American life, it became apparent that the educational arrangements designed to meet the needs of colonial society were no longer satisfactory. A few farsighted leaders saw at an early date that a system of education publicly supported and controlled and free and open to all was required to meet the needs of the emerging democratic state. This point of view, however, found slow acceptance in practice. Religious, private, and philanthropic agencies through the ages had been looked upon as the appropriate ones to provide education, and most men were loath to abandon them in favor of the political state. As time passed, however, and repeated efforts failed to provide adequate educational facilities through the traditional agencies, sentiment developed in favor of education as a function of government. By the close of the period (1860), material progress had been made, although somewhat less than has commonly been supposed, in the development of state systems of public education.

Chapter 6 appraises some of the more important intellectual trends observable during the early decades of the young Republic, explains the rearrangement of social classes that occurred, and recounts the clash of interests that led to the formulation of the principles of democratic liberalism and the founding of a new political order. Chapter 7 records educational progress down to 1828, revealing how the universalization of education was slowly coming to be widely regarded as a necessary and proper function of government, despite one last grand effort to provide through philanthropy the education needed by citizens of the Republic. In Chapter 8 attention is directed to the economic, ideological, and political rivalries of the major sections — South, East, and West — between 1828 and 1860, as economic revolutions transformed life in each region, and to the social, political, and educational adjustments that were brought about as the democratic state emerged. Chapters 9 and 10 recount the struggle for public education and record the achievements down to the outbreak of the Civil War.

6

Education and the Struggle
for Freedom and Equality:
Intellectual and Social Trends, 1776–1828

The severance of the political connection with England was only one of the fundamental changes which brought to an end the old colonial social orders that have been described and which marked the beginning of the reorganization of American society on the broad bases of social and political democracy. These changes, economic, social, intellectual, and religious, although interrelated, did not all occur simultaneously with the political upheaval. In fact, some of them had been effected, in no small measure, before the war began, while others were not completed until well into the national period. The previous chapters have indicated that the fundamental characteristics of the old society which had the greatest implications for education were (1) the political relationship with the mother country, (2) the inherited culture and the close connection maintained with England, (3) the aristocratic class organization of society, and (4) the religious tradition in education, as modified in the educational arrangements of Puritan New England and as exemplified in the educational development of the Middle Colonies and in the practices of the Anglicans in the South and elsewhere. When the political ties with England were finally cut; when an upsurging democracy gave evidence of gathering from contemporary intellectual, philosophical, religious, and political movements sufficient strength to challenge successfully the aristocratic concept of societal organization; and when religion became, at best, a secondary determinant of the kind of culture into which youth were to be inducted, a revolution had taken place which touched every aspect of American life — "its class arrangements, intellectual concerns, aesthetic interests, provisions for the promotion of knowledge and encouragement of the arts."[1]

The new order was not born without pain. The period of transition was marked by interminable conflicts, bitter struggles, and almost incomprehensible contradictions. Old and conservative theories and practices gave way but slowly before liberal thought and tendencies. The concept of government as founded on authority and force and having as its supreme function the protection of property yielded very reluctantly to the theory of government as established in the consent of the governed and existing to promote the general welfare. The antagonistic motives of men arising, on the one hand, from unconscious habit, from unreasoned sentiment, and from vested interests in the old order, and, on the other hand, from the growing conviction that institutions could fulfill their proper functions only when kept flexible enough to permit growth, created conflicts between groups and strange inconsistencies within individuals. It was a period of uneven development, of great advances followed, in many instances, by almost equally great recessions. But slowly the old order yielded to the forces which were shaping the new. An educational program which had received its sanctions in the earlier society and which had served as a powerful force in preserving old values could not satisfactorily serve a society which saw fresh visions and sought new goals. A new educational program eventually would need to evolve, a program reflecting the new order and bearing the marks of the impact of new social forces. The culture of the period was to be reflected, at least in part, in its educational arrangements.

The Changing Intellectual Climate

The thought pattern of an age, the outlook on life, the essential elements of a people's ideology, are always important. In subtle ways they condition the quality of individual living, give color and tone and motif to the day-by-day problems which men face, and in the end are powerfully reflected in the institutional forms which men achieve. During the decades immediately preceding and immediately following the Revolution, the ideological basis of American life underwent profound changes. Pent-up revolutionary energies cracked the hard core of custom and tradition, and new conceptions emerged with respect to such fundamental matters as the nature of man, the destiny within his power to achieve, and the political and social institutions best suited to the achievement of that destiny.

[1] Charles A. Beard and Mary R. Beard, *The Rise of American Civilization,* I: *The Agricultural Era* (New York: The Macmillan Co., 1927), p. 437.

The Enlightenment

The culture of the Revolutionary period derived not only from a heritage rooted in the past, but drew also from contemporary European movements. Of these latter influences the Enlightenment, a movement growing out of the slow accumulation over a century or more of new knowledge and out of the persistent, if uneven, development of scientific method, was perhaps the most important. The writings and researches of Newton (1642–1727), Harvey (1578–1657), Boyle (1627–1691), Descartes (1596–1650), and Bacon (1561–1626) were the source of a stream of scientific thought which was both widened and deepened during the eighteenth century by the epoch-making researches of Rutherford (1749–1819), Cavendish (1731–1810), Bergman (1735–1784), Priestley (1733–1804), Lavoisier (1743–1794), Galvani (1737–1798), and Volta (1745–1827). It was the researches of these men and others who labored in the same field "which swept into the discard innumerable inherited traditions, superstitions, and vagaries"[2] and which in the long run could not but influence the thinking of mankind, even though it had been habituated to centuries of restraint, first by restrictions imposed by the Church and later by the almost equally repressive authority of humanism.

Scientific thought, however, could but slowly influence the institutions which had served so long to preserve the cultural heritage, the old values, and ancient virtues. Universities resisted change, and lower schools, from the nature of their accepted function and organization, could make little use of the new ideas until they found a wide, if not general, acceptance. The medical faculty of the University of Paris protested the teaching of the circulation of the blood as contrary to Aristotle fifty years after Harvey had demonstrated that phenomenon, and the matter was debated in true Scholastic manner in a Master's thesis at Harvard during the last year of the seventeenth century. During the eighteenth century, degrees were granted on the basis of theses which settled in the affirmative the existence of sympathetic powder, a substance supposedly of therapeutic value when applied to blood that had issued from a wound. And two candidates, not even deigning to argue the existence of this remedy, established in true medieval style the lawfulness of employing it. Other theses established, on the basis of equally valid evidence, that the earth is not the center of the universe (1717); that the enlargement of the pores caused by smallpox prevents the return of that disease (1738); that

[2] See J. A. Wolf, *History of Science, Technology and Philosophy in the 16th and 17th Centuries* (New York: Harper & Brothers, 1961, Harper Torchbooks); E. J. Dijksterhuis and R. J. Forbes, *History of Science and Technology,* I: *To the End of the Seventeenth Century;* II: *18th and 19th Centuries* (Baltimore: Penguin Books, Inc., 1960).

the vocal chords did not change in Balaam's ass when it spoke (1731); that heavenly bodies produce changes in the bodies of animals (1762); that American reptiles descended from those preserved by Noah (1769); and that a comet appearing after many years is no more a foreboding of divine wrath than is a planet which appears daily (1770). Even scientists, then as now, could but slowly overcome the authority of tradition, religion, and superstition in matters that lay outside the sphere of their own scientific activities. The horoscopes cast by the leading astronomer of the seventeenth century were probably considered by university-trained persons of the eighteenth century as valid as the fundamental laws formulated by that same scientist. Few persons, educated or illiterate, sensed any incongruity in the recommendation by Robert Boyle, the father of modern chemistry, of the healing ministrations of one of the greatest charlatans of all time, or in a sermon by a college professor of physics which demonstrated the probability that birds escaped the rigors of the Massachusetts winter by migrating annually to the moon. Little wonder that in 1782 a Harvard undergraduate, Harrison Gray Otis, was impatient to "bid adieu to the sophisticated Jargon of a superstitious synod of pensioned bigots."[3] Although some excellent scholarship, even in science, was to be found in the colleges, Franklin could have, with some justification, looked upon them and exclaimed, like Petrarch of old, "Gloomy nests of ignorance."

The new knowledge could but slowly diminish the authority of tradition, superstition, narrow humanism, and ecclesiastical dogma, but as it accumulated, liberal scholars everywhere organized it for use in their struggle against all the restraints which held the minds and persons of men in bondage — in their attack on unreasonable authority in whatever form and wherever it might be found, in the church, state, "empty ceremonial, or blighting superstition." Liberals, in America as elsewhere, were the apostles of reason, which they made the touchstone of all institutions and values. They urged that science be made to solve the problems of men and of nations. The greatest advances, as might be expected, were apparent in the interests and achievements of the few, and in America the work of Franklin (1706–1790), Rittenhouse (1732–1796), Colden (1688–1776), and Catesby (1679?–1749)[4] was perhaps equal in quality to that of their European contemporaries. The American Philosophical Society, established in Philadelphia in 1769, could be compared without apology with similar French and English institutions.

Although relatively few persons were actively engaged in formulating and disseminating the new thought, it would be a mistake to think that scientific and cultural influences upon American life were negligible. By the middle of the eighteenth century, bookshops were offering for sale a wide selection of the works of European scholars and writers. By the

[3] Beard and Beard, *op. cit.,* I, p. 492.
[4] Catesby, a native of England, was active during his prolonged residence in America, 1712–14, 1722–25.

end of another seventy-five years, respectable beginnings had been made in literature and the arts. For the masses, American presses were turning out newspapers (twenty-seven by 1809), magazines, repositories, almanacs, sermons, and tracts of various kinds. Although it is true that the spirit of science failed to affect deeply the lives of many people, it is also true that no sphere of human activity was left entirely untouched by it. A culture based on science was spreading and, in a much diluted form, was reaching far down the social and economic scale. Although slow to affect the educational program of America, its influence was reflected to a considerable degree by the reorganized course offerings of colleges and by the curriculums of many private schools and newly established academies. More important for education, perhaps, was the fact that on the basis of the new learning there was being formulated a philosophical or theoretical justification for a democratic system of schools.

New Social Dynamics: the Appearance of the Idea of Human Progress

As knowledge accumulated and the practical applications of the laws of science were discovered, the imagination of man was freed from the fetters of tradition, superstition, Aristotelianism, and ecclesiastical dogma. Faith in the power of knowledge came to dominate the thinking of the day. Knowledge was the force that would make men whole. Science was the means by which the mysteries of the universe would be solved, human institutions perfected, and nature harnessed to serve the material needs of man. French philosophical thought, reflecting definitely the influence of the new emphasis on science, gave formulation to the idea of human progress, a new concept in the history of mankind and a concept which was to supply the most dynamic social theory man had yet evolved. In 1737, the French philosopher Abbé de Saint-Pierre published his epoch-making work, *Observations on the Continuous Progress of Universal Reason.* "Here," says Professor J. B. Bury, in his stimulating volume on the history of the idea of progress, "we have for the first time, expressed in definite terms, the vista of an immensely long progressive life in front of humanity."[5] Strange as it may seem, the idea of progress, the belief that man through his own institutions can move forward, had not been entertained either by the ancients or by the men of medieval Europe. In the ancient world, time was considered the enemy of man; he had fallen from a high estate in some golden age in the remote past and it would never be possible for him again to attain that exalted condition. In the Middle Ages, men lifted their eyes from this world, which was at best a

[5] As quoted in Beard and Beard, *op. cit.,* I, p. 445. See also John Bagnell Bury, *The Idea of Progress: An Inquiry into Its Origins and Growth* (New York: Dover Publications, Inc., 1955).

valley of sorrow, to the heavenly city, to which death alone held the key. Thus men sought escape from the present, not by the painful and slow processes of human betterment, but by taking refuge in the thought of some idealized past or in the hope of some brighter future after death. The existence of vistas of progress, which might lead on and on through the countless centuries, was obscured by concepts of man's own depraved nature, by beliefs with respect to the capricious moods of nature, and by the equally capricious and arbitrary character with which man endowed his God. But as science moved forward from one advanced position to another, it became apparent that, after all, nature is not capricious but something definitely predictable. Slowly the idea developed that, if there is law and order in the natural world, man can discover it and thereby subdue nature to his own ends.

The development of the idea of progress also depended upon the secularization of thought, upon the growing confidence of men that they could become, in a measure at least, masters of their own destiny. God had created a universe governed by law and he had endowed man with reason sufficient to discover that law. Secularization of thought did not rule God out of his universe, but it did immeasurably extend the range of man's free will and the area of his creative activity. The idea of progress also implied emancipation from a narrow and restrictive humanism and at least some repudiation of the authority of classical antiquity. Certainly, the development of science pushed back the confines of supernaturalism and discredited to some extent the sanctions of Greek and Roman thought. And, finally, the idea of progress — the continued improvement of man and his condition in this world — rested on new conceptions of the nature of man himself. Man, the philosopher now said, is neither inherently bad nor innately depraved. Ignorance had depraved and enslaved him. Knowledge would make him free, lord not only of nature but of himself as well. Man was not only inherently good, but under conditions favoring his development he was capable of indefinite perfectibility.

The new idea of progress took deep root in the thought of eighteenth-century America. Here of all places, it was felt, man could move steadily forward, perfecting himself and his institutions. This new and stimulating doctrine struck at the very roots of the old aristocratic social order — at class and economic distinctions, at theological absolutism, and at the concentration of political power in the hands of a small governing group.

The Secularization of Thought and Feeling

As we have already seen, as the eighteenth century progressed religion began to lose some of its dominance over the intellectual life. Old colonial America had been relatively static, cautious in its ways, little given to conscious experimenting with social values or institutional forms,

But the shock of the American Revolution, and especially of the War of 1812, broke the bonds that held men in their old ways. To quote Parrington:

> It needs no uncommon eyes, surely, to discover in the swift changes that came to America in the wake of the second English war, the seed-bed of those ebullient romanticisms which in politics and economics, in theology and literature, turned away so contemptuously from the home-spun past. Of a sudden America was becoming a new world with potentialities before undreamed of; and this new America was no longer content with the narrow ways of a more cautious generation.[6]

In religion, as well as in politics and economics, men were in an experimental state of mind. At the outbreak of the Revolution, in nine of the colonies there was an established church,[7] but within a few years America had achieved the ideal of a secular state. In New Hampshire, Connecticut, and Massachusetts, Congregationalism lingered on as the established faith, but elsewhere in the new commonwealths and in the new nation religious toleration and freedom were the order of the day. Moreover, the problems which men inescapably had to face in the Revolutionary and early national period served to deepen secular interests. Theirs was the task of fashioning new governments, state and national, of steering the new republic through the rough sea of international relations, and of repairing and expanding an economy suffering from the ravages of war. The development of the secular state and the attainment of religious freedom were necessary forerunners of the establishment of democratic, secular systems of public education.

Individualism and the Ideals of Social Equality and Mobility

One of the outcomes of the American Revolution was the opening up of vast new lands for settlement in the West. The urge to the frontier, which had been present from early colonial days, resulted, once the mountain barriers were overcome, in a vast movement westward. If the census figures did not confirm them, the statements made by eyewitnesses of this great folk movement would be almost incredible. More than a million persons had moved beyond the mountains by the turn of the

[6] Vernon Louis Parrington, *Main Currents in American Thought: An Interpretation of American Literature from the Beginnings to 1920,* II: *The Romantic Revolution in America, 1800–1860* (New York: Harcourt, Brace & Co., 1927), p. iv. Also published in paperback (New York: Harcourt, Brace & Co. [Harvest Books], 1961).

[7] J. Franklin Jameson, *The American Revolution Considered as a Social Movement* (Princeton, N.J.: Princeton University Press, 1926), p. 130. Also published in paperback (Boston: Beacon Press, 1961).

century, and by 1820 the western population had increased to two and one-half million — a fourth of the population of the United States and a million more persons than were to be found in all New England.

A frontier society commonly turns out to be a solvent of custom and tradition. Certainly on the American frontier, in each succeeding West, men tended to cast off inherited notions with respect to such matters as arbitrary political power, religious establishments, and class distinctions. More important still, the West developed its own values, its own ways, which were basically democratic. As it turned out, men could not pit their strength against nature on a raw continent and subdue it to their ends without developing in themselves a spirit of self-reliance and individualism. It was not an accident that the man who penned the immortal words, "We hold these truths to be self-evident, that all men are created equal; that they are endowed by their Creator with certain inalienable rights," was born on the frontier in western Virginia. It was in the West more than anywhere else that men accepted the premises with respect to the nature of man which are basic to any democratic political or social system. As men toiled in isolation, or, as it sometimes happened, together, to introduce the ways of civilization into the wilderness, they came to believe that man is not depraved by nature, that he is capable of achieving a sense of justice and good conscience, a dignity and a worth which all should respect. When reaction threatened the extinction of the principles of the Declaration of Independence and the Revolution, it was the West, now extended to include new states, each with as many senators as the most populous of the older states, that reasserted the principles of democracy and defeated the efforts of those who openly expressed disbelief in the common man and bent their efforts mightily to suppress him. Here, too, in the West, where land was cheap or to be had for the taking, was developed and to some extent realized the ideal of a classless society. Each succeeding West was usually poor, and suffered the evils of a debtor economy. The conditions of life, at best, were rigorous. But men in the West were not content to remain poor and underprivileged. They believed in social mobility; they felt that the way to place and power, wealth and prestige, should be open to youth of ability and energy regardless of inheritance. And, as Professor Craven has pointed out, all the American frontiers and Wests have had one thing in common:

> They have been thwarted and bitter. They have been regions of protest. They have been conscious of their own merits, sensitive to their rights, and resentful of neglect. They have constituted a more or less permanent region and interest which have wielded the democratic ideal as a weapon. Out of the American West have come the men and the movements which, after the days of Thomas Jefferson, have kept strong the democratic faith. Far more important than their simple practice of American democracy have been their protests and their revolts. From

Andrew Jackson to Abraham Lincoln and William Jennings Bryan they have fought their own fights, but they have kept the democratic dogma alive in doing so.[8]

It is easy to idealize the West and to overlook its shortcomings — its worship of material gain which pointed in the direction of an aristocracy of wealth, its rigorous enforcement of conformity to its own standards of behavior, and its general lack of devotion to any abstract ideals of democracy.[9] Nevertheless, it was the West more than any other force in American life that gave expression to and kept alive the essential elements of the faith of democratic liberalism — the love of freedom, self-reliance, respect for personality, equality of opportunity, and social mobility.

The Rearrangement of the Social Classes

Class distinctions in the American colonies were less sharp and less rigid than in Europe, but they still existed. The lofty idealism of the Declaration of Independence with respect to the equality of men must not be taken as an expression of historical fact but as a social theory which men hoped, or at least some men hoped, might in time be spelled out in the lives of men. As a matter of fact, American life down to the outbreak of the Revolution was largely dominated by an aristocracy of official position, wealth, and talents. The royal governors, judges, army officers, and others representing the British government in America never forgot, nor did they permit the common man to forget, that they were members of an upper social class. The same was true of the southern planters, many of whom had been educated abroad, and of the rich merchants, whether in Charleston, Philadelphia, New York, or Boston. Notions of social superiority and inferiority were still deep-rooted. No doubt many in the lower classes would have agreed with Devereaux Jarratt: "We were accustomed to look upon what were called gentlefolks as being of a superior order."[10] And even in the year following the signing of the Declaration of Independence, John Adams remarked in the Continental Congress:

> It is of no consequence by what name you call the people, whether by that of freemen or slaves; in some countries the laboring poor are called freemen, in others they are called slaves; but the difference as to the state is imaginary only. What matters it whether a landlord employing

---

[8] Avery Craven, *Democracy in American Life: A Historical View* (Chicago: University of Chicago Press, 1941), p. 52.

[9] *Ibid.*, Chap. II.

[10] Marcus Wilson Jernegan, *The American Colonies, 1492–1750: A Study of Their Political, Economic and Social Development* (New York: Longmans, Green & Co., 1929), p. 399. Also published in paperback (New York: Frederick Ungar Publishing Co., Inc., 1959).

ten laborers on his farm gives them annually as much money as will buy them the necessaries of life or gives them those necessaries at short hand? . . . The condition of the laboring poor in most countries — that of the fishermen particularly of the Northern states — is as abject as that of slavery.[11]

The Enlightenment ideals of liberty and equality and the western movement, to which attention was called in the preceding section, were powerful forces in bringing about a new arrangement of social classes — in shifting the locus of economic and social prestige. The leaders of the Revolution early realized that, if the war was to be won, an appeal had to be made in terms of social equality. A long time was to elapse, it is true, before the democracy proclaimed by the signers of the Declaration of Independence was even to approximate actuality. Great social gains, however, were among the immediate results of the Revolution.

In a very real sense the Revolution was a leveling movement. A large proportion of the members of the ruling and aristocratic class remained loyal to the crown and either chose to leave the country or were driven into exile. J. Franklin Jameson, in his excellent treatment of the Revolution as a social movement, points out that in 1775 the Tory party comprised probably more than half "of the most educated, wealthy, and hitherto respected classes" of New England.[12] When Lord Howe evacuated Boston he was accompanied by eleven hundred persons who refused to renounce their allegiance to the British crown. Later a thousand others joined them. As Jameson suggests, this exodus "bore away perhaps a majority of the old aristocracy of Massachusetts." Certainly the three hundred odd persons who were banished by the Massachusetts legislature in 1778 were representative of many of the most distinguished families in the history of the colony. In New York, too, the Tory party probably composed the bulk of the property owners.[13] And in Pennsylvania, where a majority of the population remained loyal to the crown, the Tory element included many persons of superior social status. The Virginia planters were, in the main, supporters of the Revolution, but farther south the Loyalists were relatively numerous, although frequently they were not members of the upper classes.

Naturally enough, the supporters of the Revolutionary cause were none too considerate of those who remained loyal to the crown. High Tories were driven out of power, many out of the country. A large number of the ruling class of colonial days — royal governors, judges, agents, and their supporters — were exiled. Among the Tories were also merchants, capitalists, and owners of large properties. New state legislatures wiped out many huge Tory estates by confiscation. Such was the fate of some

[11] As quoted in Beard and Beard, *op. cit.,* I, p. 132. Used by permission of The Macmillan Co.

[12] Jameson, *op. cit.,* p. 21.   [13] *Ibid.,* p. 22.

three hundred square miles of land belonging to the Phillipse estate in New York; of the estate of fifty thousand acres of Sir John Johnson in the Mohawk Valley; and of the estate of Sir William Pepperell, extending about thirty miles along the coast of Maine. From Maine to Georgia, estate after estate was confiscated, aggregating a total value of some three million pounds sterling.[14] Confiscated lands were commonly sold in small parcels to yeomen, in some instances a single estate being broken up into as many as two hundred and fifty separate holdings. This breaking up of "baronial estates" was accompanied by less violence than was the case during the revolution which was soon to occur in France, but it was perhaps no less complete and no less significant in its broad social consequences.

The American Revolution, then, accomplished far more than just the formulation of a creed of democratic liberalism. In no small measure it liquidated the old aristocracy and opened the way for men in the lower social strata to rise to places of importance and esteem. New men with new principles, if sometimes of little competence, took the places vacated by the erstwhile ruling class. As the Beards point out, the class which had the least regard for the common man, which would have supported a state church, which believed that education was nothing more than Christian benevolence bestowed by generous souls upon the poor, and which looked upon primogeniture and entail as requisites of a well-ordered society, was thoroughly discredited. And some of the new men with new principles who were now coming into power were bent upon preventing the re-establishment of large semifeudal estates. Less than a year after the signing of the Declaration of Independence, Jefferson had pushed through the Virginia legislature a bill abolishing the entail of estates. Within ten years entail was practically unknown in America, and within fifteen years all the states had abolished primogeniture. Although it must be admitted that the Revolution failed to achieve all that its leaders had promised, it is true that reforms were produced within a period of a few years that were not accomplished in England for another hundred. A fundamental change had occurred in the arrangement of the social classes, and the gains were clearly on the side of the yeomen and artisans who had given the Revolution a full measure of support.

A New Political Order

In the closing years of the colonial period the weight of political power rested with a comparatively small group of seaboard aristocrats — with

---

14 *Ibid.*, pp. 51–53. For a brief statement concerning the Loyalists and their plight, see Thomas A. Bailey, *The American Pageant: A History of the Republic,* Second Edition (Boston: D. C. Heath & Co., 1961), pp. 109–111.

the royal governors and officials sent out from England, New England merchants, the holders of great manorial estates in New York, Quaker merchants in Pennsylvania, and tobacco and rice planters in the South. The Revolution was in no small measure a revolt of disfranchised artisans, mechanics, and back-country farmers against the dominance of the wealthy and well-born who, in the main, determined public and social policy from their seaboard estates or imposing city homes. The issues of the Revolution were scarcely joined, however, before plain people began to draw together for the purpose of forcing a recognition of their rights. And one price they demanded for their support of the Revolution was the right to vote and to hold public office. This struggle between the traditional possessors of power and a rising democracy is strikingly described by Van Tyne:

> . . . a new class, formed within a decade, growing rapidly in numbers, was rising to power. In Pennsylvania, as in a number of other colonies, it consisted of small farmers in the back country, Scotch-Irish and German immigrants, reënforced by the voteless laborers and artisans of Philadelphia or other seaboard cities. . . . For over a decade this rising democracy had struggled for power against the little seaboard aristocracy of wealth and accepted social leadership. . . . The colonial masses could no longer be controlled by reverence for the high-born. The Quaker merchants of Philadelphia, the holders of manors on the Hudson, the tobacco and rice planters of Virginia and South Carolina, and even the great merchants, clergy, and professional men of New England, could no longer rule without question their social inferiors. . . . Thus, in 1774, came the climax in the struggle between rich and poor, East and West, those with a vote and those who were voteless, between privilege and the welfare of the common man. The two classes might work in harmony or might clash on the question of resistance to Great Britain, but they were pretty sure to be in opposition on the issue of individual rights. A merchant . . . might welcome the support of the mechanics and small shopkeepers against a grievous tax by the British Government, but the price, a right to vote and to hold office, he was sure to resent, and he grew more and more alarmed as the pressure became more insistent.[15]

It is not to be supposed, of course, that many leaders of the Revolution looked with favor upon popular government or that the Revolution in fact resulted in the immediate transfer of political power to the masses. In the Convention that framed the Federal Constitution "not one member represented in his immediate personal economic interests the small farming or mechanic classes."[16] In the Federal Constitution, and in the first state

[15] Claude H. Van Tyne, *Causes of the War of Independence* (Boston: Houghton Mifflin Company, 1922), pp. 424–426.
[16] As quoted in Allen Johnson, *Union and Democracy* (Boston: Houghton Mifflin Company, 1915), p. 29.

constitutions as well, the propertied classes were able to protect their interests against a too-numerous democracy. In none of the states was universal manhood suffrage the rule, and property qualifications still barred men of small means from most important public offices. Yet the Revolution did bring about a material extension of political power to the masses. It removed the authority of the English government, which had been a powerful influence in limiting the development of self-government and of a democratic social organization. In some instances, too, the suffrage requirements were materially lowered.

> The freeholder, or owner of real estate, was given special privileges in four of the new state constitutions, two others widened the suffrage to include all owners of either land or personal property to a certain limit, and two others conferred it upon all taxpayers.[17]

Small farmers, shopkeepers, and prosperous artisans were now in a position to make their voices heard in state legislatures to a degree unknown before. On every hand, during the years intervening between the end of the war and the adoption of the Federal Constitution, one heard the complaint that matters were going from bad to worse because of too much democracy. Elbridge Gerry, one of the Founding Fathers, discovered in the "excess of democracy" the source of many of the country's ills. Governor Edmund Randolph of Virginia felt that something should be done to escape the "turbulence and follies of democracy." Alexander Hamilton firmly believed that those who owned the country should govern it because the mass of the people "seldom judge or determine right." In the Constitutional Convention Gouverneur Morris favored a senate founded upon an aristocracy of wealth, which would serve to "keep down the turbulence of democracy." John Adams was convinced that "democracy never has been and never can be so desirable as aristocracy or monarchy, but while it lasts, is more bloody than either." Democracy, he maintained, "wastes, exhausts, and murders itself." The people, he argued, are not to be trusted as keepers of their own liberties. "They are the worst conceivable, they are no keepers at all; they can neither judge, act, think, or will as a political body."[18]

During the closing decade of the eighteenth century it appeared on the surface of things that a conservative reaction had set in, that the leveling tendencies of the Revolution had been checked. But common men had found in Thomas Jefferson a leader who was intellectually qualified to give philosophic expression to the creed of democratic liberalism and at the same time sufficiently astute as a politician to organize and make

[17] Jameson, *op. cit.*, p. 26.
[18] Vernon Louis Parrington, *op. cit.*, I: *The Colonial Mind, 1620–1800*, p. 316. See also C. F. Adams (ed.), *Works of John Adams, Second President of the United States* (Boston: Little, Brown & Co., 1856), VII, p. 211.

articulate the democratic elements in American life. Jefferson's election to the presidency in 1800 did not mean that political democracy had become a reality; a large part of the population was still disfranchised and many men in the lower classes who had the right to vote still looked upon government as a matter for their superiors. It did, however, signify that the battle for political democracy would go forward, that Jefferson's faith in man's capacity to govern himself would be the framework within which our political institutions would be set. Drawing upon the great liberal thinkers of the past and interpreting the currents of American life, Jefferson was able to formulate the basic assumptions on which democracy must rest. Common men everywhere — the poor, the underprivileged, and the dispossessed — then and later, were to use the creed of democratic liberalism which Jefferson and his associates formulated as a powerful weapon in their struggle to attain a more equitable status in society.[19]

The principle of political democracy received powerful support in what had been the back-country, or the West, before the Revolution, and in the new states which were admitted to the Union. Before 1800 Vermont and Kentucky entered the Union with full manhood suffrage. Mississippi was the only state admitted after the War of 1812 which did not confer the right to vote on all white males.[20] Moreover, it was not long before the influence of the West began to make itself felt in the more conservative original states. By 1810, the reformers had achieved notable victories in Maryland and South Carolina.[21] Connecticut in 1818 discarded its old charter for a new constitution which extended the right to vote to all who paid a state tax or served in the militia.[22] In New York, where the suffrage had been especially restricted, the struggle for full manhood suffrage was won by 1826. About the same time, Massachusetts, despite the opposition of Daniel Webster, extended the suffrage to all male citizens who had paid any state or county tax. To be a state senator, however, one still had to be a person of some means.[23]

The Revolution, then, marked the beginning of a new political order; slowly, the balance of power shifted from men of fortune to small farmers, shopkeepers, and artisans. A new theory of the state, a new conception of the function of government, was taking form. The old conception of the state had been well expressed by John Locke: "The great and chief end, therefore, of men uniting into commonwealths and putting themselves under government, is the preservation of their property."[24] This

---

[19] Craven, *op. cit.*, p. 12.   [20] Johnson, *op. cit.*, p. 303.

[21] John Spencer Bassett, *A Short History of the United States* (New York: The Macmillan Co., 1913), p. 473.

[22] Johnson, *op. cit.*, p. 304.   [23] Bassett, *op. cit.*, pp. 473–474.

[24] John Locke, *Second Treatise on Civil Government*, Chap. IX, as quoted in Parrington, *op. cit.*, I, p. 270.

theory, that the chief end of government is the protection of property rights, had long been entertained by English statesmen by the time of the outbreak of the Revolution and it continued to be the view of most statesmen in the young republic. The fear of the turbulence of democracy expressed by Hamilton, Morris, and Randolph, and in fact by most men of wealth, was the fear that popular government would jeopardize the rights of property. No one can deny that this fear was real and well justified. When the masses of men won the right to vote and began to exercise it, a new conception of the state began to take form. Government was to serve the ends of common men as well as to protect property rights; government was to become an instrument to promote the common good, the general welfare. The end of society was the happiness of the individual; men were above institutions, and government, like other institutions, was but a means to help men achieve their common goals. The old theory of the state was that governments are instituted among men to secure life, liberty, and the rights of property. Jefferson gave expression to a very different theory when he proclaimed that government is instituted to secure life, liberty, and the pursuit of happiness. Few men who signed the Declaration of Independence were willing to accept the full implications of this new conception of government. Slowly, however, a new political order did emerge, democratic in form and relatively democratic in spirit and purpose. In time, the development of the democratic state was to be the most powerful factor in shaping the course of our educational history.

THE CLASH OF ECONOMIC INTERESTS AND THE GROWTH OF DEMOCRATIC LIBERALISM

Political theories and social philosophies are seldom, if ever, intellectual abstractions; they are usually weapons forged by articulate groups in society as they struggle either to maintain or to advance their own interests. Such was certainly the case during the early life of the Republic. The clash of economic interests was sharp, and each of the contending parties formulated a political and social theory which it hoped would constitute justification of and defense for practical programs of political action.

Even before the Constitution was adopted, a conflict of interest between the capitalistic and agrarian classes was clearly discernible. President Washington was not long in office before the capitalistic and agrarian forces were aligned in a struggle to capture the national government. Alexander Hamilton led the Federalists in their fight to carry through a legislative program to promote the interests of bankers, merchants, and manufacturers. Hamilton had little regard for the processes of democratic government and little sympathy for the interests of common men, whether farmers or artisans.

> The American villager and farmer he never knew and never understood; his America was the America of landed gentlemen and wealthy merchants and prosperous professional men, the classes that were most bitterly anti-agrarian. And it was in association with this group of conservative representatives of business and society that he took his place as directing head in the work of reorganizing the loose confederation into a strong and cohesive union.[25]

Hamilton's program was brilliantly designed to promote the interests of the northern and eastern financiers, merchants, and manufacturers. First, the national debt was refunded at its face value, both principal and interest. Most of this debt was no longer held by the original subscribers but had been bought up by speculators, chiefly in the North and East, at only a small fraction of its face value. The national government also assumed the debts of the several states. These two measures immensely benefited northern financiers and speculators, and they increased the national debt enormously. More important still, as Hamilton well knew, they resulted in the creation of a large volume of fluid capital which could be used to stimulate business enterprises. As Beard says:

> The upshot of the whole procedure, from an economic point of view, was the transformation of a well-nigh worthless public paper into substantial fluid capital to be employed in commerce, manufacturing, and the development of Western lands. It was not merely the payment of the debt that Hamilton had in mind; on the contrary the sharp stimulation of capitalism — banking, commerce, and manufactures — was an equally fundamental part of his system.[26]

A third measure was designed to further the same end. A national bank was established, three-fourths of whose stock might be purchased with the recently issued government securities. The bank could issue its notes, which could also be used to stimulate commerce or build factories. Here were measures which would provide sufficient liquid capital to meet the needs of the expanding business community. A fourth measure in Hamilton's program was a protective tariff, designed, of course, to promote the interests of the rising manufacturing group in the New England and Middle Atlantic states.

All these measures of Hamilton and his fellow Federalists for the promotion of a capitalistic economy were enacted by Congress. It was not long, however, before a determined agrarian opposition began to challenge

[25] Parrington, *op. cit.,* I, p. 293.
[26] Charles A. Beard, *Economic Origins of Jeffersonian Democracy* (New York: The Macmillan Co., 1915), p. 116. Used by permission of The Macmillan Co.

Hamilton's program item by item. Southern planters and western farmers alike rallied around Thomas Jefferson, the acknowledged leader of the agrarian interests. Farmers resented all the fiscal policies of the Federalists: the refunding measures, which created many large fortunes at what they regarded their own expense; the creation of a huge national debt, the burden of which would fall mainly on them; the establishment of a national bank, a design "conjured up by law" for erecting an aristocracy of wealth at the expense of farmers and laborers; the imposition of protective tariffs, which farmers would have to pay to promote industry. The legislature of Virginia in a famous resolution set forth its own point of view, as well as that of most other agrarian interests, with respect to Federalist fiscal policies.

> In an agricultural country like this, therefore, to erect and concentrate and perpetuate a large moneyed interest is a measure which your memorialists apprehend must, in the course of human events, produce one or other of two evils; the prostration of agriculture at the feet of commerce, or a change in the present form of Federal government fatal to the existence of American liberty.[27]

It is not our purpose here to appraise the merits of the points of view of the two contending parties — the northern and eastern capitalists on the one hand and the southern and western planters and farmers on the other. Both were driving hard to promote their own interests. But, out of the conflict, political and social theories were developed which were important to American democracy. It is essential that these theories and their implications be understood.

Hamilton and John Adams were among the most outstanding representatives of the Federalist point of view. Though Adams was more liberal than Hamilton, both believed that men are motivated by self-interest rather than by reason or a sense of justice and humaneness; both felt that government should be especially solicitous of the rights of property, and neither could conceive of a society without an aristocracy of talent and wealth. Parrington has illuminatingly stated the basic principles of Hamilton's philosophy — principles, we may add, which were entertained by a very large part of the upper classes in the closing years of the eighteenth century.

> Accepting self-interest as the mainspring of human ambition, Hamilton accepted equally the principle of class domination. From his reading of history he discovered that the strong overcome the weak, and as they grasp power they coalesce into a master group. This master group will dominate, he believed, not only to further its interests, but to prevent the spread of anarchy which threatens every society split into factions and

[27] *State Papers: Finance*, I, Chap. VII, p. 90, as quoted *ibid.*, p. 124. Used by permission of The Macmillan Co.

at the mercy of rival ambitions. In early days the master group was a
military order, later it became a landed aristocracy, in modern times it
is commercial; but always its power rests on property. "That power
which holds the purse-strings absolutely, must rule," he stated unequivocally. The economic masters of society of necessity become the political
masters. It is unthinkable that government should not reflect the wishes
of property, that it should be permanently hostile to the greater economic
interests; . . .[28]

Hamilton's views with respect to the proper political and social organization are best expressed in his own words:

> All communities divide themselves into the few and the many. The
> first are the rich and well-born, the other the mass of the people. The
> voice of the people has been said to be the voice of God; and, however
> generally this maxim has been quoted and believed, it is not true to fact.
> The people are turbulent and changing; they seldom judge or determine
> right. Give, therefore, to the first class a distinct, permanent share in the
> government. They will check the unsteadiness of the second; and as they
> cannot receive any advantage by a change, they therefore will ever main-
> tain good government. Can a democratic assembly, who annually revolve
> in the mass of the people, be supposed steadily to pursue the public good?
> Nothing but a permanent body can check the imprudence of democracy.
> Their turbulent and ucontrollable disposition requires checks.[29]

John Adams was careful to set down his notions of political and social
organization at great length. He did not hold with Hamilton that "the
people is a great beast" but he did agree with Machiavelli "that all men are
bad by nature; that they will not fail to show that natural depravity of
heart whenever they have a fair opportunity."[30] Since men are moved by
interest and not by reason or humaneness, and since nature endows men
with different capacities, it follows that society will always be divided
into classes — the rich and the poor, "gentlemen" and "common people."
An aristocracy of the rich, the well-born, and the educated is inescapable.
And, finally, he agreed with Locke that the chief end of government is the
protection of property. "The moment the idea is admitted into society, that
property is not as sacred as the laws of God, and that there is not a force
of law and public justice to protect it, anarchy and tyranny commence."[31]
Adams favored the kind of political order that would protect the aristocracy from despoliation at the hands of the lower classes and at the same

[28] Parrington, *op. cit.*, I, p. 299.
[29] As quoted *ibid.*, p. 302.
[30] C. F. Adams (ed.), *Works of John Adams, Second President of the United
States* (Boston: Little, Brown & Co., 1856), IV, p. 408.
[31] "Defence of the Constitution of Government of the United States of America,"
ibid., VI, p. 9. See Parrington, *op. cit.*, I, pp. 316–317.

time prevent the rich and well-born from utterly crushing the poor and weak.

Before the Revolution, the American colonies had been governed in such a way as to make them contribute to the prosperity of the growing capitalistic class in England. Laws regulating trade, navigation, and manufacturing in the colonies were designed to promote the interests of the merchants, manufacturers, and landed gentry who were in fact governing England and her empire. If Hamilton and Adams and their fellow Federalists had had their way, the general situation would have continued, except that the government of the United States would have been substituted for the British government, and the bankers, manufacturers, and merchants of America would have taken the place of those of England. During the administrations of Washington and John Adams the drift of things was certainly in this direction. But Jefferson now came forward with another program, based upon other principles. He made his appeal directly to the southern planters and to the ever-expanding farm communities in the West. It was as spokesman of agrarian America that Jefferson formulated the essential principles of our creed of democratic liberalism. "For the first time democracy became the weapon of an important element in American life for the purpose of giving shape to the political-economic structure."[32]

Jefferson differed sharply with the defenders of aristocracy on the matter of the nature of man. He had a deep and abiding faith in human nature. With Jefferson, democracy was something more than a political system, a form of economic organization, or a pattern of class arrangements. Over and above all these, it was a great faith, a faith in the humanity of man. Jefferson held that man is not depraved by nature, that he is capable of achieving a sense of justice, equity, and good conscience, that he is capable of achieving a humaneness, a dignity, and a worth which all men should respect. This faith led him to proclaim that all men are created equal and possessed of inalienable rights. No one knew better than this son of a small back-country planter the long story of the tyranny of government by the privileged, of the repression and exploitation of common men by the possessors of economic and political power. He, therefore, proposed that men be free to govern themselves and, above all, that they be free in thought and conscience. If properly enlightened, men could be trusted to abandon the rule of force for that of reason and truth. "I have sworn," he said, "upon the altar of God eternal hostility against every form of tyranny over the mind of man."[33]

To Jefferson the happiness of the individual was the supreme goal of

[32] Craven, *op. cit.*, p. 18.
[33] As quoted in Parrington, *op. cit.*, I, pp. 355–356. See also Gordon C. Lee, *Crusade Against Ignorance: Thomas Jefferson on Education,* Classics in Education, No. 6 (New York: Bureau of Publications, Teachers College, 1961), pp. 1–26.

mankind — it was the touchstone of men and measures. This emphasis on the happiness of the individual led to freedom of conscience, of intellect, and of speech; if followed as a principle, it would free men from the grip of a dead past, of old political forms and social customs; it would place men above institutions, in the sense that institutions would be made to serve the needs of the masses of men; it would set the individual over against or above the social caste; and it would make of government an instrument to aid men in the pursuit of happiness. Here were principles, too, which led to popular systems of democratic education.

No wonder that Jefferson's name was anathema to the large element in America who were still thinking in terms of the old colonial or European system of class arrangements and of government. To many of the staunch old Federalists — men of "talent, property, reputation, and influence" — the rise to power of this "leveler from Virginia" marked the end of much that was good, and true, and beautiful in American life. They could scarcely understand how such a thing had happened. They could refuse to associate on equal terms with Jefferson's "democrats," but they could not ignore the fact that out of the clash of capitalistic and agrarian forces a new social philosophy had been formulated and to some extent put into practical operation.

Significant changes — revolutionary changes, in fact — were taking place in American life during the decades just before and immediately following the War of Independence. The thought pattern of the age was perceptibly, if slowly, becoming scientific. Men had accepted and were putting into practical operation the dynamic idea of progress. The secularization of thought and feeling had gone far enough to permit the creation of the secular state — the separation of government and religion. A new arrangement of social classes was taking place; an ambitious and self-assertive middle class was advancing on a very wide front; more and more, political power was shifting to the hands of common men. Out of the clash of interest between capitalism and agrarianism had come a formulation of the democratic dogma which was to play such an important role in future years. Out of these and other changes there evolved during the period a society that in many ways stood in sharp contrast to the society in which the Founding Fathers had been nurtured and had moved.

Questions and Problems for Study and Discussion

1. Summarize the most important intellectual trends in the United States during the period from the Revolution to the election of Andrew Jackson in 1828.
2. How do you account for the important political and social changes that took place during the first forty years of our national life? Which of these changes had the greatest effect on education?

3. How much importance for the development of education should be attached to the emphasis on social equality and mobility during the period immediately following the Revolution?

4. Discuss and evaluate the most significant influences contributing to the development of the idea of human progress. How has this idea influenced the development of education?

5. What ideals of social and political life did the West contribute to American life during the early nineteenth century?

6. By 1830, the American people were ready to accept the principle of greater state responsibility for education. How do you account for this change in attitude?

Selected References for Further Reading

Adams, James Truslow. *Revolutionary New England, 1691–1776.* Boston: Atlantic Monthly Press, 1923. Pp. xiv + 470.

Beard, Charles A. *Economic Origins of Jeffersonian Democracy.* New York: The Macmillan Co., 1915. Pp. x + 474.

Beard, Charles A., and Beard, Mary R. *The Rise of American Civilization,* I: *The Agricultural Era.* New York: The Macmillan Co., 1931. Pp. 824.

Becker, C. L. *The Declaration of Independence: A Study in the History of Political Ideas.* New York: Alfred A. Knopf, 1942. Pp. xii + 286. Also published in paperback (New York: Random House [Vintage Books], 1961).

Billington, Ray A., and Hedges, James B. *Westward Expansion: A History of the American Frontier.* New York: The Macmillan Co., 1949. Pp. xiii + 873.

Bowers, Claude G. *Jefferson and Hamilton: The Struggle for Democracy in America.* Boston: Houghton Mifflin Company, 1927. Pp. xviii + 532.

Chinard, Gilbert. *Thomas Jefferson, the Apostle of Americanism.* Boston: Little, Brown & Co., 1929. Pp. xviii + 548. Also published as an Ann Arbor Paperback (Ann Arbor, Mich.: University of Michigan Press, 1957).

Counts, George S. *The Prospects of American Democracy.* New York: The John Day Company, 1938. Pp. xii + 370.

Craven, Avery. *Democracy in American Life: A Historical View.* Chicago: University of Chicago Press, 1941. Pp. xii + 150.

Cunliffe, Marcus. *The Nation Takes Shape, 1789–1837,* Chicago History of American Civilization Series. Chicago: University of Chicago Press, 1959. Pp. 222. Also published in paperback (Chicago: University of Chicago Press, 1961).

Curti, Merle. *The Growth of American Thought,* Revised Edition. New York: Harper & Brothers, 1943. Pp. xviii + 910.

Dangerfield, George. *The Era of Good Feelings.* New York: Harcourt, Brace & Co., 1952. Pp. xiv + 525.

Douglass, Elisha P. *Rebels and Democrats: The Struggle for Equal Political Rights and Majority Rule during the American Revolution.* Chapel Hill, N.C.: University of North Carolina Press, 1955. Pp. xiv + 368.

Ekirch, Arthur A. *The Idea of Progress in America, 1815–1860.* New York: Columbia University Press, 1944. Pp. 305.

Gabriel, Ralph Henry. *The Course of American Democratic Thought: An Intellectual History Since 1815.* New York: The Ronald Press Company, 1940. Pp. xii + 452.

Greene, Evarts Boutell. *The Revolutionary Generation, 1763–1790.* New York: The Macmillan Co., 1943. Pp. xviii + 488.

Jameson, J. Franklin. *The American Revolution Considered as a Social Movement.* Princeton, N.J.: Princeton University Press, 1926. Pp. xii + 105. Also published in paperback (Boston: Beacon Press, 1956).

Jefferson, Thomas. *Autobiography.* New York: G. P. Putnam's Sons, 1914. Pp. xlii + 162. Also published in paperback (New York: G. P. Putnam's Sons [Capricorn Books], 1959).

Jensen, Merrill. *The New Nation: A History of the United States during the Confederation, 1781–1789.* New York: Alfred A. Knopf, Inc., 1950. Pp. xvii + 433.

Johnson, Allen. *Union and Democracy.* Boston: Houghton Mifflin Company, 1915. Pp. x + 346 + xviii.

Knight, Edgar W. *A Documentary History of Education in the South before 1860, II: Toward Educational Independence.* Chapel Hill, N.C.: University of North Carolina Press, 1949. Pp. ix + 603.

Malone, Dumas. *Jefferson and the Rights of Man, II: Jefferson and His Time.* Boston: Little, Brown & Co., 1951. Pp. xxix + 523.

McDonald, Forrest. *We the People: The Economic Origins of the Constitution.* Chicago: University of Chicago Press, 1958. Pp. 436.

Miller, John C. *The Federalist Era, 1789–1801* (New American Nation Series). New York: Harper & Brothers, 1960. Pp. 304.

Morgan, Edmund S. *The Birth of the Republic, 1763–1789,* Chicago History of American Civilization Series. Chicago: University of Chicago Press, 1956. Pp. 176.

Nye, Russell B. *The Cultural Life of the New Nation, 1776–1830.* New York: Harper & Brothers, 1960. Pp. xii + 324.

Parrington, Vernon Louis. *Main Currents in American Thought: An Interpretation of American Literature from the Beginning to 1920* (3 vols. in one), I: *The Colonial Mind, 1620–1800* (pp. xviii + 414); II: *The Romantic Revolution in America, 1800–1860* (pp. xxii + 494). New York: Harcourt, Brace & Co., 1927. Also published in paperback as Harvest Books Nos. 4 and 5 (New York: Harcourt, Brace & Co. [Harvest Books], 1961).

Rossiter, Clinton. *Seedtime of the Republic: The Origin of the American Tradition of Political Liberty.* New York: Harcourt, Brace & Co., 1953. Pp. xiv + 558. Also published in paperback, in abridged form, under the title *The First American Revolution* (New York: Harcourt, Brace & Co. [Harvest Books], 1956).

Shannon, Fred Albert. *America's Economic Growth,* Third Edition. New York: The Macmillan Co., 1951. Pp. x + 967.

Sweet, William. *Religion in the Development of American Culture, 1765–1840.* New York: Charles Scribner's Sons, 1952. Pp. xiv + 358.

Sydnor, Charles. *The Development of Southern Sectionalism, 1819–1847.* Baton Rouge, La.: Louisiana State University Press, 1948. Pp. xii + 400.

7

Education and the Struggle for Freedom and Equality: Public versus Private and Philanthropic Education

Educational thought and practice were materially affected by the changes that occurred in American life during the years between the American Revolution and the election of Andrew Jackson to the Presidency in 1828. The election of Jackson, as we have already noted, marked the rise of the common man to a prominent, if not dominant, position in the political life of the young nation. During the years between 1776 and 1828 the changing conditions in American society described in the preceding chapter were largely responsible for four major lines of development in American education.

First of all, there was a growing recognition of education as a legitimate and necessary function of government. Educational statesmanship was turning to the secular state as the only agency that could be relied on to provide a system of popular education. Plans for a national system of education by noted publicists, advocacy of public education on the part of political leaders, grants of land for the aid of education by the federal government, provisions relating to education in state constitutions, state aid for education in varied forms, legislative enactments in regard to public schools, the establishment of a number of state universities — all these gave evidence of growing sentiment in favor of state intervention in the field of education. Even so, the period came to an end with the people in most of the existing states still unwilling to resort to direct taxation as a means of school support.

The second aspect of educational development of importance was the widespread attempt to extend the benefits of education to larger numbers through various philanthropic agencies. Education had generally been regarded, in England and in most of the English colonies, as a matter to be taken care of primarily through private, religious, or philanthropic effort. In the early years of the republic men were slow to abandon this pattern; they made one last grand effort to make it work. A few leaders saw clearly the need for public, tax-supported schools, but the great majority preferred to rely on philanthropy, hoping that it would provide adequate education for the poor and underprivileged. Sunday schools, schools supported by subscription societies, the infant school movement — all these were part of the last great effort to build an educational system on the basis of philanthropy. The almost unbelievable enthusiasm with which Joseph Lancaster's monitorial system of instruction was received can be explained in large measure in terms of the interest in education through philanthropy. The monitorial system, it was hoped, would make education so cheap that it could be supported wholly through philanthropic agencies of one kind or another.

The third major trend in American education during this period was the increased emphasis on private educational institutions. Academies multiplied in number and came to dominate the field of secondary education. At the elementary level, too, private effort was extended. This was true even in New England, where persons of means and social position were prone to look upon the traditional town schools as schools for the less privileged.

The fourth, and an extremely important, area of educational development was that of the new educational objectives now envisioned and the new instructional content introduced to achieve these objectives. Schools and colleges were assigned enlarged social and political obligations. More and more, education was made to serve secular ends, although the religious purpose was by no means discredited. The classical tradition showed signs of growing weaker in the face of a rising interest in science. Religion and classical antiquity were losing their grip on the intellectual life — Greece and Rome and the Middle Ages were in retreat, although they still had in them a good deal of fight. Most important of all, perhaps, education was coming to be regarded as a means of safeguarding and advancing America's experiment in democratic political and social institutions. Formal education was coming to be looked upon, too, as having a broader function in preparing young people to take their place in the expanding economic life of the day. Necessarily, new instructional content was provided to accomplish the new and extended functions of education.

These four trends in educational development were sometimes complementary and sometimes contradictory. Even though chief reliance was still placed upon philanthropic, religious, and private agencies, the civil state was assuming increased responsibility. The academies were in the main private and denominational institutions, but many of them were also recipients of the state's bounty. The state universities charged tuition, and in some of them denominational influence was strong. In the curriculum of both the academies and the colleges the classics occupied a commanding position, but new subjects were beginning to challenge their supremacy.

The following sections of this chapter will be devoted to a more detailed discussion of the four major lines of educational development that characterized this period.

The Development of Education as a Function of Government

PLANS FOR PROMOTING A NATIONAL SYSTEM OF EDUCATION

At the close of the Revolution no one could have foreseen that education would come to be regarded as one of the essential functions of government. At that time it was also uncertain whether the national government or the governments of the several states would play the more important role in case the people should decide that the state was the necessary agency to provide an adequate educational program. Conditions in the young republic were, however, such as to give rise to a considerable volume of sentiment in favor of a national system of education. The successful conclusion of the conflict with England had brought independence to the colonies, but the lack of any real national unity was painfully evident. It appeared to many that republican institutions were to be wrecked by the ignorance and stupidity of the electorate and by the failure to achieve a measure of national unity based upon "some force other than external constitutional control."[1] To some of the outstanding thinkers of the day, the proper remedy for the situation was to be found in a fundamental reorganization of the educational program on a national basis. Some fear was expressed that a national system of education would tend to perpetuate the existing order, that it might not permit the flexibility that should exist in republican institutions. The prevailing feeling, however, among the small but extremely articulate group of leaders was that, because the older forms of education might perpetuate the tradition of monarchy, a system of national education should be established.

The advocates of a system of education organized to serve national ends were by no means content to rest their case on general discussions. Be-

[1] Allen Oscar Hansen, *Liberalism and American Education in the Eighteenth Century* (New York: The Macmillan Co., 1926), p. 79.

tween 1786 and 1800 such outstanding leaders as Benjamin Rush, Robert Coram, Samuel Knox, Samuel Smith, James Sullivan, Noah Webster, Nathaniel Chipman, and Du Pont de Nemours published essays setting forth in more or less detail their plans for a system of education. Two of these essays, one by Samuel Knox and the other by Samuel H. Smith, shared the prize offered by the American Philosophical Society for the best essay on a "system of liberal Education and Literary Instruction, adapted to the genius of the Government, and best calculated to promote the general welfare of the United States: comprehending also a plan for instituting and conducting public schools in this country on the principles of the most extensive utility."[2]

The plan of Robert Coram published in 1791 illustrates a type of thinking not uncommon among those who were advocating a national system of education. He insisted that the chief end of education was to promote intelligent citizenship, true democratic control of government, maximum individual achievement, and social integration. Democratic principles and the obligations of government were to be taught. No modes of faith, systems of manners, or foreign or dead languages were to be included in the curriculum. There could be no true democracy if education was "left to the caprice or negligence of parents, to chance, or confined to the children of wealthy parents." Glaring inequalities in educational opportunity existed, particularly as between country and town. Equal educational opportunity would make possible the development of leadership and at the same time prevent the few from learning "to cheat the rest of their liberties." Education was a state function — every citizen suffered for the failure of anyone to meet the demands of democracy. Property, he said, was to be considered chiefly as of social value — a social trust to be used for the common good, rather than for the acquisition of personal power. There could be no valid objection to providing for schools by general taxation throughout the nation, and there could be no equality of opportunity — no democratic education — unless schools were so provided. Coram recommended that a school be established in the geographical center of each district, which was to be six miles square. His plan went so far as to prescribe the nature of the school building, fix the salaries of the instructor and his assistant, and suggest the taxing procedures that would provide the needed revenues.[3]

The various essays setting forth plans for a system of education had their points of difference, but in all a certain common philosophy is discernible. As Hansen has stated, these "various efforts to create a national

---

[2] See Samuel Knox, *An Essay on the Best System of Education, adapted to the Genius of the Government of the United States* (Baltimore, Md.: Warner and Hanna, 1799). See also Samuel Harrison Smith, *Remarks on Education: Illustrating the Close Connection between Virtue and Wisdom* (Philadelphia: printed for John Armrod, 1798); see also Hansen, *op. cit.,* p. 110.

[3] Hansen, *op. cit.,* pp. 63–78.

system of education . . . were largely attempts to make the principles of the eighteenth century liberal movement the determining force in the development of American character and institutions."[4] The belief was reiterated that man is a perfectible being and that his nature is favorable to continued improvement. Science, it was believed, could determine the lines of human progress. Education was a function of government, the primary concern of which was the welfare of the individual and of society. If institutions were to promote progress, they must be kept flexible. They must be based upon utility rather than the accident of circumstance. Among the various institutions created by man, the school should exist primarily to provide training to enable youth to become citizens in whose hands the future of democracy would be safe. The nation was thought to be the most effective unit through which to work for individual and social betterment. The establishment of a national system of education would make possible equal support of education of all grades, equality of educational opportunity between rich and poor, and universal support of the program. It was argued that if education were on a national basis, trained personnel could be more easily obtained and the entire program more effectively and economically administered. It was practicable to provide education from birth and to continue it as long as it was profitable to the individual and the state. In fact, with a national system, the expense of education would be less. Such a system would promote human progress and shape a nation which would be, in the words of an English liberal, the "seat of liberty, science, and virtue, and from whence . . . sacred blessings will spread, till they become universal and the time arrives when kings and priests shall have no more power to oppress."[5]

THE ATTITUDE OF POLITICAL LEADERS TOWARD EDUCATION

Essayists and theorists were not the only ones to espouse the national interest in education. Some of the outstanding political leaders of the time expressed similar views, although they were more cautious and less specific in their statements, and few of them would have made education generally a charge upon the national government. A common theme, that of the dependence of republican government upon the enlightenment of all citizens, was discernible in the expressions of all these leaders, but with respect to the philosophy underlying their ideas of how to achieve universal education, there was no clear agreement. John Jay, the first Chief Justice of the Supreme Court, wrote that he considered "knowledge to be the soul of the republic" and urged that everything should be done

4 *Ibid.*, p. 256.
5 Richard Price, *Observations on the Importance of the American Revolution* (1784), p. 2, as quoted *ibid.*, p. 262.

to provide to all classes the opportunity of obtaining a proper degree of education "at a cheap and easy rate." General Francis Marion of South Carolina vigorously urged the value of schools to the nation; but his urgings reflected the acceptance on his part of the pauper-school philosophy.[6] All of our first four presidents urged the necessity for the widest propagation of education — no matter what, individually, their views may have been regarding the need for either national or state systems of public education. John Adams, however, did state that "the instruction of all people ought to be the care of the public" and "that schools for the education of all should be placed at convenient distances and maintained at public expense."[7] In a letter to W. T. Barry in 1822 Madison expressed his conviction, long held, that "A popular Government, without popular information, or the means of acquiring it, is but a Prologue to a Farce or a Tragedy; or, perhaps both." He went on to state: "Knowledge will forever govern ignorance: and the people who mean to be their own Governors, must arm themselves with the power which knowledge gives."[8] Jefferson, whose educational ideas will be discussed more fully in later pages, wrote to George Wythe in 1786:

> Preach, my dear Sir, a crusade against ignorance; establish and improve the law for educating the common people. Let our Countrymen know that the people alone can protect us against these evils, and that the tax which will be paid for this purpose is not more than the thousandth part of what will be paid to kings, priests and nobles who will rise up among us if we leave the people in ignorance.[9]

President Washington urged upon Congress the desirability of establishing a national university, as did Jefferson, Madison, and Adams, and otherwise stressed the importance of learning and its broad dissemination. In his speech to both Houses of Congress on January 8, 1790, in what is now regarded as his first annual message, he wrote:

> Nor am I less persuaded, that you will agree with me in opinion, that there is nothing which can better deserve your patronage than the pro-

---

[6] Last interview of General Peter Horry with General Marion in 1795, as quoted in United States Office of Education, *Expressions on Education by Builders of American Democracy*, Bulletin 10, 1940 (Washington, D.C.: Government Printing Office, 1941), p. 79.

[7] Charles Francis Adams (ed.), *The Works of John Adams, Second President of the United States: With A Life of the Author, Notes, and Illustrations* (Boston: Little, Brown, & Co., 1851), VI, p. 16.

[8] Gaillard Hunt (ed.), *The Writings of James Madison, Comprising his Public Papers and his Private Correspondence, including Numerous Letters and Documents now for the First Time Printed* (New York: G. P. Putnam's Sons, 1910), IX, p. 14.

[9] Letter to George Wythe, dated October 13, 1786, Paris, and quoted in Gordon C. Lee (ed.), *Crusade Against Ignorance: Thomas Jefferson and Education*, Classics in Education, No. 6 (New York: Bureau of Publications, Teachers College, Columbia University, 1961), p. 100.

motion of science and literature. Knowledge is in every country the surest basis of public happiness. In one, in which the measures of government receive their impression so immediately from the sense of the community, as in ours, it is proportionably essential. To the security of a free constitution it contributes in various ways; by convincing those who are intrusted with the public administration that every valuable end of government is best answered by the enlightened confidence of the people, and by teaching the people themselves to know, and to value their own rights; to discern and provide against invasions of them; to distinguish between oppression and the necessary exercise of lawful authority, between burthens proceeding from a disregard to their convenience and those resulting from the inevitable exigencies of society; to discriminate the spirit of liberty from that of licentiousness, cherishing the first, avoiding the last, and uniting a speedy but temperate vigilance against encroachments, with an inviolable respect to the laws.[10]

In his Farewell Address, published in 1796, Washington urged the promotion of education in the national interest: "Promote, then, as an object of primary importance institutions for the general diffusion of knowledge. In proportion as the structure of government gives force to public opinion, it is essential that public opinion should be enlightened."[11]

Although the attitudes of public leaders, including those of the presidents, differed in important ways, on one issue there was no disagreement. All related education to the public welfare, and all considered the universalization of education the means toward, and a safeguard of, good government. The concern of great men of high office, extending over many years, must have been a factor in the awakening of what Cubberley has called the educational consciousness of the nation.

THE FEDERAL GOVERNMENT AND EDUCATION

Why, it may be asked, did not the new nation, born of revolution and dedicated, in a measure at least, to democratic principles, show greater concern for education, which was generally recognized by the liberal thinkers of the time as the means by which the individual might be improved and institutions perfected? Why did neither the Articles of Confederation nor the Constitution recognize the national interest in education? There are several reasons. In the early years, a national government as a positive force was envisaged by relatively few persons. The results of distant control over the affairs of the colonies were still fresh

[10] Jared Sparks (ed.), *The Writings of George Washington; Being his Correspondence, Addresses, Messages, and Other Papers, Official and Private, Selected and Published from the Original Manuscripts: With a Life of the Author, Notes, and Illustrations* (New York: Harper & Brothers, 1848), XII, pp. 9–10.

[11] From "Washington's Farewell Address"; see United States Office of Education, *Expressions on Education by Builders of American Democracy, op. cit.*, p. 3.

in the minds of those who had fought a war to escape the restraints of England's imperial policy. The Articles of Confederation were drawn up under circumstances which did not promote consideration of comparatively remote issues. The Republic was founded in a time of storm and stress. The colonies, which in the face of a common enemy had cooperated in the solution of common problems, now, as states, sought to protect their individual interests — which too often ran counter to those of their neighbors. The older view, developed by Fiske and others, that for lack of a strong central government the nation under the Articles was always on the verge of disruption — unable to keep the peace, to arrest decline in the economy, or to resist foreign aggression — was overdrawn.[12] The United States under the Articles of Confederation was certainly more than a geographical expression (as one historian, paraphrasing Metternich's description of Italy before the unification, called it). However, the fact remains that its government was subjected, on various accounts, to severe conflicting pressures and that the issue of the extent of central authority divided even those men who drew up the Constitution under which the new federal union was formed.

Furthermore, the more conservative supporters of the Revolution were able to exercise great influence under the Articles, in the Constitutional Convention, and in the new government under the Constitution. There is little reason to think that many of the men who met in Philadelphia to draw up a new constitution were dissatisfied with the existing educational arrangements. They themselves were products of an educational system that was not without its merits, at least for the training of leaders. The character of the constituency of the Constitutional Convention was proof in itself that some success had attended the efforts of the old system. In most of the states from which the delegates to the Convention came, the people did not regard education as a proper function of government, state or federal. In the circumstances it is not strange that educational development under the Articles of Confederation was slow and that the Constitution made no mention of education at all.

Under the Articles of Confederation, the government was unable to organize education within the states. Nevertheless, it took action which recognized the importance of education and the desirability of establishing schools. During this period a national land policy was formulated which was to affect education very vitally.

Soon after the Revolution, the states asserting title to lands beyond the Alleghenies ceded their claim to the national government. A large na-

[12] Merrill Jensen, *The Articles of Confederation: An Interpretation of the Social-Constitutional History of the American Revolution, 1774–1781* (Madison, Wis.: University of Wisconsin Press, 1948; also published in paperback, Madison, Wis.: University of Wisconsin Press, 1961), and *The New Nation: A History of the United States during the Confederation, 1781–1789* (New York: Alfred A. Knopf, 1950).

tional domain was formed out of which future states were to be carved. The war was scarcely over before prospective settlers were demanding the right to buy these lands. Before sale could be made, a survey was needed. Congress in 1785 adopted a rectangular survey, under which the lands were laid out in townships six miles square, each township being divided into sections one mile square. The sections in each township were numbered one to thirty-six, and the sixteenth section was "reserved" for the support of education. In 1787 and 1788 two large tracts were sold to land companies, and Congress, as a part of the bargain, granted each company a township for a future college, Section Sixteen of every township for schools, and Section Twenty-seven for religion. When Ohio was admitted in 1802, Congress gave the new state the sixteenth section of land in every township for the maintenance of schools, Ohio agreeing not to tax lands belonging to the federal government or lands sold by it until five years after the date of sale. Each new state admitted since, except Texas, Maine, and West Virginia, has received section grants from the federal government for the support of schools. Beginning with California, in 1850, the grant was increased to two sections; and three southwestern states containing much arid and semi-arid land have each received four sections, one-ninth of the total area, of each township. Other grants have increased the total amount of land given by the federal government to the states for educational purposes to nearly a quarter-million square miles.

Although these grants, particularly the section grants of the early national period, should not be considered evidence that the government had adopted a policy of providing education to all its citizens, their importance cannot be lightly dismissed. They formed a basis for permanent school funds in the new states and stimulated the older states to set aside lands and to create permanent school funds. The revenues derived from these lands helped build support for schools. It is also clear that in this land policy the government recognized the importance of extending educational opportunities to the western settlers and of transplanting the culture and institutions of the older established regions to the new settlements. Possessing greater freedom of action with respect to the national domain than it enjoyed in the sovereign states, the national government voiced the sentiments of enlightened leaders everywhere in the official act (1787) which incorporated the Northwest Territory.

> Religion, morality, and knowledge being necessary to good government and the happiness of mankind, schools and the means of education shall be forever encouraged.

This clause, although not mandatory, recognized the importance of education to the individual and to democratic institutions, even though it failed to place the responsibility for education upon the government.

STATE GOVERNMENTS AND EDUCATION

Since the Constitution of the United States provides that all powers not conferred upon the federal government are retained by the states, and inasmuch as education is not expressly mentioned in the Constitution, it has been often supposed that it was the purpose of those who drafted the Constitution to make education a function of the governments of the several states. As a matter of fact, at the time the Constitution was drafted education was not commonly regarded as a function of government at any level. It seems reasonably certain that the great majority of those who drew up the document, and of those who voted to adopt it, did not envision the development of comprehensive systems of public education. The failure of the Constitution to mention education in express terms probably does not reflect the intention of the Founding Fathers to make public education a function of the state governments; rather, it probably reflects the widespread sentiment of the time that education was a private, religious, or philanthropic function. Moreover, the authority conferred upon Congress to promote the general welfare may have appeared to many to be entirely adequate, as was actually the case at the time, to enable the national government to support a program of education.

In any event, as sentiment developed in favor of public schools, the people turned to their state governments as the proper agents to provide them. The slowness and the caution with which the movement toward public schools took place is well illustrated, however, by Thomas Jefferson's failure to persuade his own state to accept his educational proposals.

Jefferson's plan for education in Virginia.   Jefferson's program for education in Virginia, even though unacceptable to the people of that state, was important — so important that one biographer has written that "nothing else that he did or proposed during his entire career showed him more clearly to be a major American prophet."[13] In his proposal Jefferson elaborated his central ideas on education, which remained constant throughout his life. The clearest expression of the public importance of education that had been written, the proposal defined the responsibility of the state to seek out talent, no matter where it might be found, and to develop that talent at public expense. Jefferson envisioned an articulated and complete state system, and he brought the weight of his great name to the support of public education throughout the nation.

The plan is embodied in *A Bill for the More General Diffusion of Knowledge,* drawn up by Jefferson and Wythe, acting for a committee appointed three years earlier, and reported in 1779, a few days after Jefferson was elected governor of Virginia. The proposed law was for Virginia,

[13] Dumas Malone, *Jefferson the Virginian* (5 vols.; Boston: Little, Brown, & Co., 1948), I, *Jefferson and His Times,* pp. 280–281.

but the thoughts expressed were universally applicable. After declaring education to be the most effectual means of preventing government from being perverted to tyranny and of insuring the happiness of all, the preamble of the Bill goes on to elaborate:

> . . . . And whereas it is generally true that that people will be happiest whose laws are best, and are best administered, and that laws will be wisely formed, and honestly administered, in proportion as those who form and administer them are wise and honest; whence it becomes expedient for promoting the publick happiness that those persons, whom nature hath endowed with genius and virtue, should be rendered by liberal education worthy to receive, and able to guard the sacred deposits of the rights and liberties of their fellow citizens, and that they should be called to that charge without regard to wealth, birth, or other accidental condition or circumstance; but the indigence of the greater number disabling them from so educating, at their own expence, those of their children whom nature hath fitly formed and disposed to become useful instruments for the public, it is better that such should be sought for and educated at the common expence of all, than that the happiness of all should be confided to the weak or wicked.[14]

Under the plan provided for in the Bill, three aldermen were to be selected in each county to divide the county into "hundreds" of such size that all children living in the subdivisions could conveniently attend the school which was to be established in each. After the electors of each hundred had decided upon a site for the school, the aldermen were to have a schoolhouse erected and kept in repair. The expenses involved in erecting and maintaining the schoolhouses and in paying the teachers' salaries were to be provided in such manner as the other county expenses were by law directed to be provided. In each of the schools, reading, writing, and arithmetic were to be taught. The books used to teach reading were also to be used to provide instruction in Greek, Roman, English, and American history. All free children, girls as well as boys, residing in their respective hundreds were to attend school for three years without paying tuition, "and as much longer, at their private expense, as their parents, guardians, or friends thought proper." An overseer for every ten of the schools was to be appointed annually. He was to be a person "eminent for his learning, integrity, and fidelity to the commonwealth," and it would be his duty to appoint teachers and have general supervision of the work of the schools.

Jefferson's plan provided also for a state-wide system of secondary schools. Twenty districts, each embracing from two to seven counties, were to be organized and a grammar school was to be erected in each. The school was to be built of brick or stone and located on a plot of one hun-

---

[14] Julian P. Boyd (ed.), *The Papers of Thomas Jefferson* (Princeton, N.J.: Princeton University Press, 1950), II, pp. 526–527.

dred acres. There were to be a schoolroom, dining room, four rooms for the master and usher, and ten or twelve rooms for lodging students. The expense of establishing and equipping these schools was to be paid out of the public treasury. The curriculum was to include Latin, Greek, geography, English grammar, and "the higher part of numerical arithmetick." A board of visitors, composed of one member from each county making up the district, was to have general supervision of the school.

The plan provided for the free education of a number of promising poor boys. Each overseer of the "hundred" schools was to appoint, annually, from the ten schools under his supervision, one promising boy whose parents were too poor to provide him further education, to be sent, at public expense, to the grammar school. Each September one-third of the boys sent to the grammar school by appointment of the overseers the preceding year were to be sent home, and of the appointees who had been in school two years, only one was to be kept on at state expense for the four remaining years of the grammar-school course. At the end of six years' instruction, one-half of the remaining scholarship students were to be discontinued and the other half, ten in number, of the "best learning and most hopeful genius and disposition," were to be authorized by the visitors to proceed to William and Mary College, "there to be educated, boarded, and clothed, three years," at the expense of the state.[15]

Viewed from the perspective of the present, the provisions of the Bill may appear mild indeed. Each primary school, on the average, was to be permitted to send one poor boy to its grammar school in a period of ten years. One-third of the free scholars admitted to the grammar school were to be sent home after one year, and nearly all were to leave at the end of two years, only twenty in all Virginia being retained for the four senior years. Of those twenty, only ten were to have the opportunity to attend William and Mary College for three years at state expense. Some critics have cited the Bill as evidence that Jefferson's ideal was an educated elite based upon a broad foundation of mere literacy. Such was not the case. Jefferson was not proposing a program for all time. More than most of his contemporaries, he believed that each generation could be trusted to frame its own laws and order its own institutions. (See the excerpt from Jefferson's letter to Governor Plumer, p. 231.) The Bill did provide a clear expression of the democratic rationale for the public interest in and responsibility for universal education. The philosophy underlying the Bill is clearly set forth in its preamble (and in numerous other statements made by Jefferson) and this theoretical foundation should not be confused with his conception of the political realities of 1779.

[15] See *The Writings of Thomas Jefferson;* collected and edited by Paul Leicester Ford (New York: G. P. Putnam's Sons, 1893), II, pp. 220–237; Roy J. Honeywell, *The Educational Work of Thomas Jefferson,* Harvard Studies in Education, No. 16, published under the direction of the Graduate School of Education (Cambridge, Mass.: Harvard University Press, 1931), pp. 201–205.

Nearly forty years after submitting this bill, Jefferson drafted a second one, *A Bill for Establishing a System of Public Education* (1817), which incorporated many features of the earlier proposal. Certainly it was no more liberal, nor did it provide for a larger measure of universal education.[16] The fact that the second bill, like the earlier one, failed to pass the legislature was indicative of the slowness with which sentiment in favor of universal education developed.

Educational provisions in the state constitutions. In this early period, the presence or absence of some provision in the state constitution relating to education reflected the attitude of the people toward education as a proper function of the government of the state. In the constitutions of only seven of the sixteen states comprising the Union in 1800 was any mention made of education. In a majority of the states, apparently, the idea of universal and free education still pertained to the field of theory rather than to politics. Moreover, in some of the constitutions the educational provisions were very weak or general. In its constitution of 1790, Pennsylvania clearly expressed the pauper-school idea in an article which read, in part:

> The legislature shall, as soon as conveniently may be, provide, by law, for the establishment of schools throughout the State, in such manner that the poor may be taught *gratis*.[17]

Relatively liberal provisions, on the other hand, were written into the constitutions of New Hampshire, Vermont, and Massachusetts. A section of the Massachusetts Constitution, which was changed only slightly in the Constitution adopted by New Hampshire in 1784, read:

> Chap. V, Sec. 2. Wisdom and knowledge, as well as virtue, diffused generally among the body of the people, being necessary for the preservation of their rights and liberties; and as these depend on spreading the opportunities and advantages of education in the various parts of the country, and among the different orders of the people, it shall be the duty of the legislatures and magistrates, in all future periods of this Commonwealth, to cherish the interests of literature and the sciences, and all seminaries of them; especially the university at Cambridge, public schools, and grammar-schools in the towns; to encourage private societies and public institutions, by rewards and immunities, for the promotion of agriculture, arts, sciences, commerce, trades, manufactures, and a natural history of the country; to countenance and inculcate the principles of humanity and general benevolence, public and private charity, industry

[16] See Honeywell, *op. cit.*, pp. 244–247.

[17] Ellwood P. Cubberley, *Readings in Public Education in the United States: A Collection of Sources and Readings to Illustrate the History of Educational Practice and Progress in the United States* (Boston: Houghton Mifflin Company, 1934), p. 110.

and frugality, honesty and punctuality in their dealings; sincerity, good humor, and all social affections and generous sentiments among the people.[18]

Between 1800 and 1820, seven new states were admitted to the Union. The constitutions of these new states included general statements concerning the necessity of diffusing knowledge among the people, in order that morality might be promoted and liberty preserved. Of all the constitutions adopted before 1820, that of Indiana probably approached most nearly the democratic ideal in its provision which directed the general assembly "to provide by law for a general system of education, ascending in a regular gradation from township schools to a State university, wherein tuition" should be "gratis, and equally open to all." This same section, however, paid tribute to reality with the qualifying clause, "as soon as circumstances will permit."[19]

Early state legislation. Laws, because they are often mandatory, constitute, in general, a much better index of a state's interest in promoting education than do constitutional provisions. By 1820, ten states had been added to the original thirteen and in most of these states, old and new alike, the legislatures had sketched partial programs of education. But these were, at best, vague foreshadowings of democratic school systems. It is true that the New England states, Rhode Island excepted, entered the Union with a tradition of public education and what might be considered systems of public schools, but, generally, too much significance has been attached to these early beginnings. However, the law in New England did require the towns or districts to maintain schools, and public schools of a kind were widely distributed as a result of legislation. In fact, if the number of laws passed were taken as a measure of progress, the period might be regarded, as far as New England was concerned, as one of rapid development. The laws in New England commonly prescribed the subjects to be taught, granted aid to local districts, gave towns and districts the right to tax or render rate bills, ordered the erection of buildings, required the towns and districts to examine the qualifications of prospective teachers, and fixed the length of the school term. As we shall see later, however, these laws did not result in effective systems of public education.

In most of the older states outside New England, the old colonial theory that competent parents would provide suitable education for their children without state intervention still persisted. New York made some noteworthy progress in the development of its public schools, but in the other original states legislation tended to deal primarily with means and methods of providing instruction for the dependent poor.

[18] *Ibid.*, p. 109.
[19] Cited in Clement T. Malan, *Indiana School Law and Supreme Court Decisions* (Terre Haute, Ind.: Teachers College Press, 1931), p. 451.

State administration and supervision.   Some progress was made during this period in the development of state agencies for the administration and supervision of education. New York came the nearest to creating an effective system of state administration. This state, which had failed to mention education in its constitution of 1777, a few years later provided for a Board of Regents of the University of the State of New York, which was to exercise general control over secondary and higher education. The Board was reorganized in 1787, but its functions remained substantially the same throughout the period, with education above the elementary grades subject to its rules and regulations. New York was also active in the field of elementary education. In 1811, five commissioners were appointed by the governor "to report a system for the reorganization and establishment of common schools." In 1812, the system recommended by the commissioners' report was adopted. The same year Gideon Hawley was appointed the first superintendent of common schools. Not under the control of the Regents, he exercised authority only in matters relating to elementary education. In this field, it was stated by a contemporary, he reduced near chaos to order. He is said, however, to have offended the legislators, who abolished the office and designated, in 1821, the secretary of state to act as superintendent, ex officio.

Other beginnings in the development of state administration may be noted (1) in the Connecticut Act of 1810, which provided for a commissioner of school funds, whose duties were entirely fiscal; (2) in Virginia's creation, in 1815, of a state board charged with the duty of supervising the Literary Fund; and (3) in the adoption by Georgia, Louisiana, and Michigan of a form of state administration along the lines of that of New York. The state university chartered by Georgia in 1785, however, never exerted any considerable measure of control over the schools of the state. Nor did the regents of the university in Louisiana acquire so much authority over the educational system as did the Board of Regents in New York. The Catholepistemiad, or the University of Michigan, created near the close of the period (1817) to provide instruction in the higher branches and to administer the entire educational system of the Territory, failed to make more than a fleeting impression before 1827, at which time a new school law provided for a different type of administration for the common schools. Although significant beginnings were made in the development of state agencies of control, no marked progress was recorded outside New York. By initiating programs of state support of education, however, the states laid the foundation upon which administrative and supervisory control was to rest.

State aid for education.   Before the end of the period, nearly all the states had created permanent school funds, the income of which was designated to supplement local support in maintaining schools. In some instances the funds originated in the sale of public lands, but they were also derived from various other sources, such as fines, licenses, special taxes, and lotteries.

Several years before Vermont became the fourteenth state in 1791, she had provided some state aid. In 1750, Connecticut had created a permanent school fund out of revenue received from the sale of western lands. This fund was increased to $1,200,000 in 1795 by the sale of the Western Reserve. In 1796, Delaware started a school fund from the receipts of tavern and marriage licenses. After 1817, one thousand dollars a year was granted to each of the three counties for the instruction of the poor. Maryland began a school fund in 1812 by levying a tax on banks, and some aid was extended to institutions of higher education and later to academies in each county in the state. South Carolina made the beginning of a state system in 1811, providing aid for one or more free schools in each electoral district. Pennsylvania after 1802 granted aid for the education of pauper children. Virginia established its Literary Fund in 1810, the income of which was used to educate the children of the poor. Kentucky made numerous land grants to academies between 1798 and 1808. Massachusetts appropriated townships of land in the interior and northerly part of Maine for the encouragement of academies, although these tracts proved to be of little financial value. After 1811, Louisiana granted aid for the erection and maintenance of an academy in each parish. Aid was not extended to common schools, however, until 1827. For a five-year period beginning in 1795, New York appropriated annually fifty thousand dollars from the revenues of the state "for the purpose of encouraging and maintaining schools in the several cities and towns." These grants were discontinued in 1800, but the foundation of a permanent school fund was laid in 1805, when the legislature voted to appropriate the proceeds from the sale of five hundred thousand acres of land as a permanent fund for the support of common schools. In 1819 one-half the amount to be received from quitrents, the net proceeds of all lands escheating to the state in the military tract, and certain fees and other moneys were forever appropriated to the school fund.

Although in some states the aid granted was considerable in the total amount and not negligible when computed on the basis of pauper children, it was insignificant in terms of the entire child population except in Connecticut, in New York during a few years of this period, and in one or two other states. The value of the grants made by the states, however, is not easily measured. Small sums distributed as aid not only enabled the states to exercise beneficial supervision, but also led to increased local revenue.

The prevalence and characteristics of the public schools. Despite the efforts described in the preceding sections to make education more definitely a function of government, the programs of the several states at the close of the period here under consideration gave only faint promise of developing into systems of free public schools, adequate to meet the needs of the democratic society that was emerging. The very term "public school" did not have the meaning we attach to it today: It was used to denote schools that were entirely free and open to all, schools that were free for a part of the session, and schools that were subsidized in order that children might be taught cheaply and the poor gratis. In New England the law required the towns or districts to maintain schools, and this they did, although the schools were generally of poor quality and maintained at the lowest possible cost. The public Latin grammar school, moreover, was giving way to the private academy. The development of the district system had undermined the resources of towns for maintaining public secondary schools. In Massachusetts the towns were failing to maintain Latin schools as required under the law of 1789. In New York, too, by the end of the period, there existed what might properly be called a system of public schools. Outside New England and New York, in the older states, public support of schools was confined, in the main, to providing some degree of education for the children of the poor. The newer states in the West made use of land grants to provide some public education, but they were still unwilling to resort to taxation to provide even meager facilities.

Free education, even when not pauper education, was commonly confined to the elementary level. Universal education at public expense may have appealed to educational philosophers and liberal statesmen as "the heart of the republic," the "bulwark of our liberties," the "palladium of our freedom," the "protector of republican institutions," the means of insuring the success of the democratic experiment in government, and the most powerful of all forces contributing to the happiness of the individual. But in actual practice there was little evidence, other than public utterances, that schools were generally considered as necessary means of solving political, economic, and social problems of the day. A great majority of the children who attended school were sent to learn to read, write, and master as much arithmetic as might prove useful in the commonplace activities of everyday life. With respect to opportunity beyond this, the masses were generally indifferent. A proposal to offer a more advanced program free of charge and open to all would have been regarded, at least by the wealthy and politically powerful, as an extravagance, a waste, a step toward national bankruptcy, a threat to the social order, and even perhaps a downright robbery which placed a penalty upon thrift and which encouraged indolence.

Even where so-called public schools existed, they were poorly housed, their curriculums were severely restricted, and the teachers were, in the main, ill-prepared. In New England, where the tradition of free schools was the longest and conditions were most advanced, school buildings were, for the most part, still primitive. Concerning them, the winner of a prize offered by the American Institute of Instruction for the best essay on the construction of schoolhouses wrote:

> From the earliest period in the history of New England up to the year 1831, we are not aware that much had been said or done in regard to the improvement of schoolhouses. . . . They consisted, with few exceptions, of a single room, with a chimney at one end, on one side of which was the door and entrance. . . . There were generally no outhouses of any kind whatever. Even the wood lay exposed to the snow and rain. The furniture consisted of a chair, a table, a few benches, and a writing desk; and the latter was usually attached to the walls, on three sides of the room. The benches consisted of slabs, with pegs for their support; and they were without backs. The schoolroom was in general so small that the pupils were obliged to economize as much as possible in regard to space, at the risk of crowding and jostling each other, and a thousand other evils.
>
> This, we say, was the general state of things.[20]

As already indicated, the curriculum of the public elementary schools, even in New England, was severely restricted. Massachusetts, which, in spite of many defects in her program, was probably the most advanced educationally of all the states, in the law of 1789 required no more than the teaching of reading, writing, orthography, English language, arithmetic, and decent behavior. This, in its day, and judged by standards elsewhere, was no doubt a liberal course. New demands, however, were beginning to be made upon the schools. New textbooks by Noah Webster, Morse, Murray, and others reduced new content to teachable form, making possible the introduction of geography, grammar, and some history into the curriculum. These subjects, however, were added slowly. Outside the cities, it was a long time before the enrichment provided by the new subjects, or the improvement of instruction which the texts made possible, affected the education of any considerable number of children. In the meantime, bored and unruly children were stimulated to self-improvement only through harsh discipline administered, in the main, by poorly prepared and unimaginative teachers.

In spite of numerous exceptions, the teachers of the elementary school were a poor lot, whose meager qualifications were matched by the low esteem in which they were held. In sections in which the only free schools were pauper schools there were perhaps fewer exceptions. In one state, the governor declared that willingness to teach was prima facie evidence of inability to do anything else. Probably the better teachers were to be found in New England, but even there salaries as low as two and three dollars per month, supplemented as they might be by board and

[20] "New England Schoolhouses," *American Annals of Education and Instruction,* VII (June, 1837), 241.

sometimes laundry, did not often attract capable teachers. Carter in his *Essays upon Popular Education* gave testimony of the poor quality of teachers in Massachusetts and also of the shortcomings in the methods of selecting them:

> To whom do we assign the business of governing and instructing our children from four to twelve years of age? . . .
>
> The teachers of the primary summer schools have rarely had any education beyond what they have acquired in the very schools where they begin to teach. Their attainments, therefore, to say the least, are usually *very moderate*. But this is not the worst of it. They are often very young, they are constantly changing their employment, and consequently can have but little experience; and, what is worse than all, they never have had any direct preparation for their profession. . . .
>
> They are a class of teachers unknown in our laws regulating the schools. . . . No standard of attainments is fixed . . . so that anyone *keeps school* . . . who wishes to do it, and can persuade, by herself, or her friends, a small district to employ her. . . . The farce of an examination and a certificate from the minister of the town, for it is a perfect farce, amounts to no efficient check upon the obtrusions of ignorance and inexperience. As no standard is fixed by law, each minister makes a standard for himself, and alters it as often as the peculiar circumstances of the case require. And there will always be enough of peculiar circumstances to render a refusal inexpedient. . . .
>
> Many of the above remarks upon the character and qualifications of the teachers of the summer schools apply with equal force to the young men, who undertake the instruction of the primary winter schools, which now constitute the highest class of schools, to which the whole population of the state have free access. . . . What are the acquirements of these young men? . . . We have a catalogue . . . of branches of knowledge, which the laws suppose the candidates . . . to be possessed of. But who knows that they come up to established standard? And who knows that they are fully possessed of the knowledge, which the laws require? . . . The laws provide that the minister and the selectmen of each town shall assure themselves, that their teachers possess the prescribed qualifications. The minister. Which minister? . . . .
>
> The young man who lays down his axe and aspires to take up the "rod" and rule in a village school, has usually, in common with other young men, a degree of dignity and self-complacency, which it is dangerous to the extent of his power to disturb. And when he comes to his minister, sustained by his own influence in the parish, and that of a respectable father and perhaps a large family of friends, and asks of him the legal approbation for a teacher, it is a pretty delicate matter to refuse it. . . . And martyrs in ordinary times are rare.
>
> It is the intention of the school-law to secure good, moral characters . . . by requiring the approbation, as to this qualification, of the selectmen of the town, where the school is to be taught. . . . If a young

man be moral enough to keep out of the State Prison, he will find no difficulty in getting approbation for a schoolmaster.[21]

Carter's enthusiasm for improved teacher education, no doubt, impelled him to make the best possible case for it, but he was subject to whatever restraints may have been imposed by the knowledge that his readers, as well as the members of the many audiences which he addressed, were not entirely unaware of the conditions that existed.

Educational developments of great later import. The criticisms of the existing educational arrangements made by Carter and other persons bent on reform, and the failure of the government in some states to respond to, or to take more than feeble action in response to, the recommendations of educational and political theorists and leaders, have been cited to support the invalid conclusion that no real expansion of public education occurred until late in the period — until after the nation had recovered from the effects of the War of 1812. It is true that Jefferson's plan for a state system of education, providing a modicum of universal education at public expense, was unacceptable to the people of Virginia at the close of the period, as it had been in 1779; that progress was slow, halting, and very uneven throughout the nation; that the contemporary criticisms were, by and large, justified. But these facts should not obscure the important truth that developments had taken place which made possible and understandable the occurrence of three events during the later years of the period that may well be considered landmarks in the progress of American public education. These events were the establishment of a system of public primary schools in Boston in 1818, the founding, in 1821, of a public high school (Boston Classical School, renamed English High School in 1824), and the enactment of the Massachusetts law of 1827 requiring the establishment of high schools in cities, towns, and districts of 500 families or more.[22] The high school extended public education upward for youth who had completed the elementary school but who lacked the inclination or, perhaps, the ability to follow the program of the Latin Grammar School. The establishment of primary schools extended public education downward to children of ages and levels of advancement not previously provided for in town schools, and certainly these schools were sorely needed.

In 1817 a survey was made which revealed that there were enrolled in all the publicly supported schools of Boston, including the Latin Grammar School, the African School, and the Alms House School, 2365 students. All except a few of the pupils in the Alms House School were

---

[21] James G. Carter, *Essays upon Popular Education: Containing a Particular Examination of the Schools of Massachusetts and an Outline of an Institution for the Education of Teachers* (Boston: Bowles & Dearborn, 1826), pp. 35–40.

[22] For the rise of the high school, see pages 356–359.

seven years of age or older. A total of 3767 pupils were enrolled in 154 dame schools and other private schools. Probably more than 40 per cent, perhaps half, of the private-school pupils were under seven years of age. It was reported that about 500 children between the ages of four and seven were not enrolled in any school.[23] The enrollment in the public primary schools numbered about 3400 in 1828 and rose to more than 5000 a decade later. By placing these schools under a special committee that functioned under the direction of the town, Boston built her educational structure. The management of the primary schools, however, remained separate from that of the other town schools until they were combined under one school committee in 1854.[24]

By 1828, the outlines of the major components of an American educational system were beginning to take form in the developments in Massachusetts and the other New England States — developments that were to culminate in an articulated, comprehensive public educational system.

Discontent with religious control of higher education. With the waning of religious influence and the development of secular interests during the late colonial period, dissatisfaction with the nature of higher education and with its administration was expressed in many quarters. For centuries it had been generally assumed that the primary responsibility for higher education rested upon the church, but now the sentiment came to be expressed with growing frequency that higher education was rightfully a function of the state. With the spread of the liberal philosophy of the Revolutionary period, the conviction was voiced that higher educational institutions, freed from the control of religion and the interests vested in it, and organized to disseminate knowledge and develop learning, particularly in the field of science, would be a beneficent influence upon government, promote individual well-being, and contribute to the national prosperity. This view was entertained not only by theorists, but by practical statesmen as well. The desirability of founding a national university was in the minds of at least several members of the Constitutional Convention. Among the early presidents of the United States, Washington, Jefferson, Madison, and John Quincy Adams urged upon Congress the establishment of such an institution.[25]

Although Congress failed to act, state governments by various means

---

[23] Joseph M. Wightman (ed.), *Annals of the Boston Primary School Committee from Its First Establishment in 1818 to Its Dissolution in 1855* (Boston: George C. Rand and Avery, City Printers, 1860).

[24] *Ibid.*

[25] Edgar Bruce Wesley, *Proposed: The University of the United States* (Minneapolis, Minn.: University of Minnesota Press, 1936), pp. 8–10; David L. Madsen, "History of an Idea: The University of the United States" (Doctor's thesis, Department of Education, University of Chicago, 1961).

indicated their determination to relate higher education more closely to the contemporary political and social philosophy. Their efforts were first directed toward transforming existing colleges into institutions that would be more responsive to what they considered the needs of the new era. Attempts were made, with varying degrees of success, to change self-perpetuating boards of trustees to boards on which all or a specified number of places were to be filled by state officers, by appointees of state officers, or by persons elected by the legislature. In other instances, the state attempted to accomplish its ends by creating boards of overseers which were to exercise control over the corporations, or, in case such a board already existed, by legislation designed to secure representation from the state on the board. Pressure was also exerted by threatening to withhold the appropriations which a college received from the state or by expressing an interest in the establishment of a competing institution. Six of the nine colleges founded during the colonial period were subjected to attempts on the part of the new state legislatures to bring them more closely under the control of the state.

Attempts to control private colleges. Several years before the outbreak of the Revolution, a number of appeals were made to the legislature of Connecticut for changes in the Yale charter of 1701 which would give the colonial government a greater measure of control over the affairs of the college. The proposals were strenuously opposed and no action was taken.[26] Shortly after the close of the war, a petition was presented to the state legislature demanding that either the charter granted by the state to the college be altered to give the state representation on the college board or that a new institution, under control of the state, be established. No immediate action upon the petition was taken, but a reorganization was effected in 1792, and provision was made for a measure of state representation by making the governor, the lieutenant governor, and "six state officials" members ex officio of the corporation. Yale, by this concession, escaped further legislative interference.[27]

The College of Philadelphia, the only colonial college initiated under non-sectarian influence, in time came to reflect the interests of the Tory party and the Anglican Church. In 1779, after a charge that the college was conducted "with a general inattention to the authority of the State," the Assembly voided its charter and created a new corporation, "The Trustees of the University of the State of Pennsylvania."[28] After the col-

---

[26] Elbert Vaughan Wills, *The Growth of American Higher Education: Liberal, Professional, and Technical* (Philadelphia: Dorrance & Co., 1936), pp. 24–26.

[27] Donald G. Tewksbury, *The Founding of American Colleges and Universities before the Civil War: With Particular Reference Bearing upon the College Movement* (New York: Bureau of Publications, Teachers College, Columbia University, 1932), pp. 144–145.

[28] Wills, *op. cit.*, p. 25.

lege protested, the original charter was reinstated in 1789, but the university was retained as a separate corporation. The two institutions were merged under a single board in 1791. The state was represented on the new board only by the Governor, whose membership was ex officio. In New York, King's College, rechristened Columbia, was reorganized in 1784 and again in 1787, and, although left with a self-perpetuating board, it was placed under the nominal supervision of a newly created body, "The Regents of the University of the State of New York." The Harvard Board of Overseers had, during the colonial period, included ex officio representatives of the government and had been subject to a measure of legislative control. In 1810, the legislature attempted to change, subject to the ratification of the board, the membership from an ex officio basis to one largely elective. The action was opposed by the corporation on the grounds that a change in the body which controlled it was a violation of its rights under the Constitution of 1780. The question of the exercise of visitorial power over the college by the legislature was raised at subsequent dates, but Harvard was able to escape serious curtailment of her earlier privileges. Attempts to transform William and Mary College into a state institution failed, partly because the college, which had been closely associated with both the colonial government and the Established Church, was unwilling to break its connections with the church. Since no action was taken upon a bill introduced in the legislature in 1779 to make the college more responsive to the public will, Jefferson and his friends lent their further efforts toward the establishment of a rival institution, the University of Virginia.

The most outstanding and by far the most highly publicized attempt to alter the status of a former colonial college came in 1816. The charter of Dartmouth College, which had been established in 1769 under Congregational influence, provided for state representation on the board of trustees only to the extent of making the governor a member ex officio. The state legislature made no serious effort to change the charter of the college, so long as Congregational interests dominated both. As time went on, however, the more liberal and democratic elements in the state — followers of Thomas Jefferson in the main — supported a movement for the reorganization of Dartmouth. President Wheelock associated himself with the Democratic movement, and the board of trustees, staunchly Federalist in its sympathies, removed him in 1815. The Democrats (Jefferson's party, i.e., Republicans) secured control of the legislature the following year and passed an act that changed the designation of the college to Dartmouth University and placed over the board of trustees a board of overseers, composed of certain state officials and appointees of the governor. The stage was set for a political and legal battle that was to attract wide attention. The *Salem Gazette,* far removed from the scene, commented: "The Act of the Legislature is political proof of the evils of the Democrats."[29] The trustees, amid the applause of their supporters, maintained that the act was unconstitutional. For a while, two rival institutions were in operation, one Dartmouth College and the other Dartmouth University. In time, the authority of the legislature to change the charter of the college was questioned in the supreme court of the state of New Hampshire, which sustained the authority of the legislature to modify the charter. An appeal was taken to the Supreme Court of the United States, which rendered its decision in 1819. The decision of the state court was reversed, and the action of the New Hampshire legislature was declared unconstitutional and void because it violated that section of the Federal Constitution which prohibits a state from impairing the obligation of a contract. The charter, the Court held, was a contract between the state and the college. "The decision was a complete victory for the Federalist and Congregationalist interests represented at Dartmouth College."[30] And it might be added that Chief Justice John Marshall, who rendered the decision, was as staunch a Federalist as could be found anywhere in the nation.

Jefferson, representing the liberal view, had written to Governor Plumer in 1816:

> The idea that institutions established for the use of the nation cannot be touched or modified, even to make them answer their end, because of rights gratuitously supposed in those employed to manage them in trust for the public, may, perhaps, be a salutary provision against the abuse of a monarch, but it is most absurd against the nation itself. Yet our lawyers and priests generally inculcate this doctrine, and suppose that preceding generations held the earth more freely than we do; had a right to impose laws on us, unalterable by ourselves; and that we, in like manner, can make laws and impose burdens on future generations, which they will have no right to alter; in fine, that the earth belongs to the dead, and not to the living.[31]

But the philosophy of Jefferson was not to prevail. In the "contest between conservatives and liberals, Federalists and Republicans, John Marshall and Thomas Jefferson, the former in each instance had won."

It has often been argued that the states, prevented by the Dartmouth College decision from transforming private colleges into state institutions, turned with renewed effort to the establishment of state universities. Tewksbury has presented evidence and a most convincing argument that, on the contrary, the decision contributed in no small measure to checking the development of state universities for at least half a century.[32]

---

[29] As quoted in Vera M. Butler, "Education as Revealed by New England Newspapers Prior to 1850" (Doctor's thesis, Temple University, 1953), p. 92.
[30] Tewksbury, *op. cit.*, p. 150.   [31] *Ibid.*, pp. 150–151.   [32] *Ibid.*, 152.

The establishment of state universities. During the fifty years that
followed independence, some eight or ten states laid the foundations of
future state universities. It is to be understood that none of these institutions, with the possible exception of South Carolina College, in its
early development was entirely under the control of the state. Even
in those instances in which laws provided for almost complete control, denominational interests were able to exert strong influence upon the
universities. The University of North Carolina, chartered in 1789 and
opened for instruction in 1795, had under its original charter a self-
perpetuating board of trustees. The charter was amended in 1804, 1805,
and 1821 so that in the end all the trustees were elected by joint ballot
of the legislature.

Georgia in 1784 set aside forty thousand acres of land for a university,
which was chartered in 1785. The charter provided for a system of
schools at all levels, headed by a university, which was to give instruction
in the higher branches and also to supervise the work of the inferior
schools. By 1800 eight academies had been established and in 1801 instruction began in the college. Strong religious and political interests almost nullified the considerable measure of control that the state was to
exercise under the charter.

South Carolina in 1801 chartered its university, which was opened as
a degree-granting institution in 1805. This institution was placed entirely under the control of the state, the original charter providing for
the election of all members of the board of trustees by the legislature.
Maryland was only partially successful in establishing a university under
the control of the state. The only other of the thirteen original states to
establish a university during this period was Virginia. Jefferson's leadership over a period of more than forty years finally culminated in the establishment of the most advanced and complete type of state institution
founded for a generation to come. The charter emphatically stated that
the institution "should in all things and at all times be subject to the control of the legislature."[33] But even in Virginia, religious forces were able
to exercise considerable influence upon the legislature.

To the foregoing five southern states of the original thirteen may be
added two more, Alabama and Tennessee. Alabama provided for a state
university under the direct control of the legislature. The charter was
granted in 1821, but instruction did not begin until a decade later. Tennessee established two colleges, which might be classified as semi-state
institutions.

Vermont was the only new state to establish a university without the
aid of large grants of land. The right of this institution to be classified

[33] *Revised Code of Virginia,* Chap. XXXIV, Sec. 9, as quoted *ibid.,* p. 181.

as a state university has been questioned.[34] Ohio established two state colleges in the early nineteenth century. Charters granted to the older of these in 1802 and 1804 provided for effective state control. Neither institution, however, was entirely to escape sectarian influences, and both were to suffer severely from denominational competition. Indiana, after experimenting with a Territorial college, established Indiana College as a degree-granting institution in 1828.

In Ohio, Alabama, and Indiana, the establishment of universities was encouraged by the federal township grants. In Tennessee one hundred thousand acres of land were set aside for the support of two universities. It is doubtful, because of the bitter and narrow sectarianism of the period, if it would have been possible to establish the state universities without such land grants. The injunction laid upon the states by the federal government and the possession of a source of revenue were probably fundamental considerations in the establishment of state universities in all four of these states.

Sectarianism and the establishment of denominational colleges were deterring factors in the development of state universities. Several state institutions, in fact, came to reflect Congregational and Presbyterian interests almost as distinctly as did private institutions of those faiths. This was the case, however, only in those instances in which a religious group dominated not only the university but the entire state government as well.

Many state institutions of higher learning bore the name of university, but most of them were no more than small colleges. Although they received financial support from the state, they all charged tuition. In perspective they appear more important for what they were to become than for what they were. Even so, their importance is not to be underestimated. They prepared many young men for the professions and for leadership in state and nation; and, more important still, they were the beginnings of a democratic movement in higher education that was to develop far beyond anything the world had yet seen.

The Movement to Provide Education through Philanthropic Effort

As indicated in the preceding sections, interest in education as an obligation of the state and a function of government manifested itself slowly, particularly outside New England. The practice of supporting schools through philanthropic effort, which had been popular in both

[34] Ellwood P. Cubberley, *Public Education in the United States: A Study and Interpretation of American Educational History,* Revised and Enlarged Edition (Boston: Houghton Mifflin Company, 1934), p. 115.

England and America during colonial times, continued far into the national period. The church-charity school had been a familiar institution
throughout America. In several colonies the Society for the Propagation of
the Gospel in Foreign Parts had maintained schools as a part of its missionary effort among the poor, but after the Revolution the Society withdrew
from the field. Churches generally found their efforts inadequate to meet
the increased demands for education. Many persons, truly concerned with
the sad plight of the ignorant poor, were willing and anxious to do by
philanthropic effort what they refused to consider a duty of the state.
Every man in a democracy should walk in the light of learning, through
his own efforts if possible, and if not, as the recipient of philanthropy,
which had the added virtue of ennobling and warming the soul of the
donor. In states where the tradition of public education was weak or non-
existent, philanthropy represented one stage through which education was
to pass on its way to state support. It was only with the failure of philanthropy that education at public expense could be established. A period of
groping within the old and familiar framework was first necessary before
education at public expense would be seriously considered.

If the effort to build a satisfactory educational system on the basis of
philanthropy was to succeed, means would have to be found to make
education as cheap as possible. During the period under consideration,
numerous attempts were made to provide cheap mass education. One of
the first of these was the Sunday-school movement.

SUNDAY SCHOOLS

The Sunday school as a means of teaching the catechism and religious
exercises was old, even in America, when Robert Raikes, an Englishman,
moved by the misery and shocked by the boisterousness of the child factory operatives of Gloucester, employed four women at a shilling each to
conduct Sunday classes in reading and the catechism, so that the children
might be improved and the "deplorable profanation of the Sabbath"
checked. In 1783 Raikes published a description of his plan. Within a
year, it is reported, a union society, established at Stockport near Man-
chester, had a school of five thousand "scholars." Besides instruction in
the Scriptures these children, who for the most part had no other means of
education, were taught reading, writing, and elementary bookkeeping.[35]
The cheapness of the instruction and the opportunity offered for easily
satisfying philanthropic impulses led to the usual English practice of organizing a society — in this case, the Society for Promoting Sunday
Schools throughout the British Dominions.

When the idea was brought to America, Sunday schools were organized

[35] Asa Bullard, *Fifty Years with the Sabbath Schools* (Boston: Lockwood, Brooks
& Co., 1876), pp. 29–30.

in great numbers. It is claimed that Bishop Asbury organized a school of this kind in Hanover County, Virginia, in 1783, and there is a record of a Sunday school in that county in 1786. The First-Day, or Sunday-School, Society, was organized in Philadelphia in 1791. It is said that by 1800 there had been admitted to the several schools of the Society more than two thousand "scholars." The instruction was confined to reading — after 1793 from the Bible — and writing. Schools were established in Charleston, South Carolina (1787), New York (1793), Paterson (1794), Hudson, New York (1803), Pittsburgh (1809), and a large number of other cities in the middle and southern states.

A student at Brown University upon the suggestion of Samuel Slater opened a school in Pawtucket, Rhode Island, in 1797. New England, however, appears to have had little to do with the movement in its early stages. Beginning about 1816, however, newspapers in Connecticut and Massachusetts began to carry frequent notices of the establishment of Sunday schools, as well as reports of their success in numerous New England towns. By 1825 the Salem Sunday schools, organized in 1816, enrolled 750 pupils and had a total of 166 teachers. Many schools were opened in Boston under the Society for the Moral and Religious Instruction of the Poor. In 1826 Boston reported twenty-two schools, with four hundred teachers; and in 1827 on one occasion "five thousand children marched in procession and then listened to an address and exercises, the whole meeting lasting for a space of three hours."[36]

Several attempts were made to obtain state aid for Sunday schools[37] and arguments were advanced that they merited assistance more than did the pauper schools supported by the state.[38] When the school commissioners in Richmond granted aid they commented:

> The Sunday School holds out flattering promises of future usefulness to the state for the diffusion of knowledge. . . . It has been remarked that a pupil learns more on that day in the Sunday school than in the common school in a week.[39]

It was the church, however, and not the state which was to capture the Sunday school. By 1820 all the leading denominations were fostering them. Under ecclesiastical control, the Sunday schools gradually came to emphasize religious education to the complete neglect of secular instruc-

[36] Butler, *op. cit.*, p. 250.

[37] Cubberley, *Public Education in the United States, op. cit.*, p. 123.

[38] See Sadie Bell, *The Church, the State, and Education in Virginia* (Philadelphia: University of Pennsylvania, 1930), pp. 336–337.

[39] Second Auditor, *House Journal*, 1826, quoted in William Arthur Maddox, *The Free School Idea in Virginia before the Civil War: A Phase of Political and Social Evolution*, Teachers College Contributions to Education, No. 93 (New York: Teachers College, Columbia University, 1918), p. 38.

tion. Whatever importance or influence they may have continued to possess was in an entirely different field.

The schools, as poor and makeshift as they were, and representing, as they did, the dying gasps of the ideal of universal education through philanthropic effort, served a useful purpose. Through them many persons attained what may be termed literacy and achieved perhaps a greater self-respect. The total enrollment in these schools has been estimated in the millions. The *Springfield Republican* estimated that in a single year, late in the period, more than two hundred thousand children were receiving the benefits of Sunday-school instruction.[40] In a number of children there may have been awakened a desire to learn something more of that to which they had been introduced. Perhaps the general indifference of the ignorant poor to education was to some extent overcome. Maddox stresses the significance of the Sunday school in the development of the free-school idea in Virginia:

> The new movement indirectly promoted the political ideal of common schools by bringing the children of all classes together in the name of religion on terms of perfect equality. Certainly it involved no political theory nor suggested change in government. It is not curious then that the Sunday school was a prime factor in drawing the attention of the rich to the actual educational needs of the poor with an impressiveness that political theory could never have for the conservative. At the same time it accustomed a neighborhood to schools. It was particularly effective in the country districts, where it must have done much toward suggesting the practicability of a system of country schools.[41]

One may well wonder about the success of these schools in bringing many children of all classes together on "terms of perfect equality," in Virginia or elsewhere, but there can be no doubt that in a number of states these schools enlisted the services of public-spirited, influential men — judges, lawyers, senators, mayors, and governors. Once the assistance of some of these men in teaching and conducting Sunday schools had been enlisted, it may well have been later extended to participation in the struggle for public education.

Schools Supported by Subscription Societies

The greatest achievement of the philanthropic movement in attempting to make education universal was the organization of voluntary school societies, designed to provide educational opportunity of a sort to the rapidly growing group of "wretched, ignorant, and friendless children." So successful were these societies that they have been given, rightfully perhaps,

[40] Butler, *op. cit.*, p. 251.
[41] Maddox, *op. cit.*, pp. 31–32.

a large measure of credit for helping to awaken "an educational conscious-ness." It should be pointed out, however, that their aim was to adapt the pauper system to new conditions and that their success in doing so was probably responsible for delaying the establishment of public school sys-tems.

Earlier means and methods employed "to give the poor the power to read" proved entirely inadequate in the rapidly expanding urban centers, in which the evils of poverty, crime, illiteracy, and child delinquency were not only appalling, but could not be hidden from the public view. Alarmed by threatened social deterioration, public-spirited persons in numerous cities organized societies to provide a modest education for children who were without other means of instruction.

New York City was perhaps the most fertile field for the new endeavor. This city was slow to recover from the Revolutionary War. When, with the coming of peace, the churches again became active, they found them-selves unable to cope with the much-aggravated situation. Their charity schools, open to the children of indigent members, failed to reach more than a small part of the poor. In 1805 only four denominations are known to have maintained schools, and the number of children attending the most successful of these was only about one hundred.[42] The failure of these schools to reach large elements in the population led to the establishment of benevolent associations organized to administer to the needs of these neglected groups. As early as 1785 the "Manumission Society" was or-ganized to promote the liberation of slaves, to protect Negroes who had been freed, and to give them the elements of an education. Schools spon-sored by this Society, and aided by several small grants from both the city and the state, provided instruction for thousands of Negro children. In 1834 the schools of the Society were taken over by the Public School Society. In 1801 a school was opened by the Association of Women Friends for the Relief of the Poor to provide for another special category of children, those whose parents belonged to no religious group and who for one reason or another were not admitted to the charity schools of the city. A number of schools were added and, aided by a share in the Com-mon School Fund, they provided instruction for thousands of girls (750 in 1823) before being deprived of further state aid in 1824.[43]

The most famous of the school societies was the Free School Society of the City of New York (founded 1805), which was reorganized in 1826 under the title Public School Society of New York (1826–53). From the first, this organization enlisted the services and support of prominent men,

---

[42] Directory, 1805, as cited in New York City Board of Education, *Public Edu-cation in the City of New York: Its History, Condition, and Statistics,* An Official Report to the Board of Education by Thomas Boese, Clerk of the Board (New York: Harper & Brothers, 1869), p. 24.

[43] A. Emerson Palmer, *The New York Public Schools: Being a History of Free Education in the City of New York* (New York: The Macmillan Co., 1905), p. 14.

such as its first president, De Witt Clinton. Among its trustees were five Motts, four Ogdens, five Underhills, two Van Rensselaers, three Palmers, and other notables such as Robert Cornell, Peter Jay, James Roosevelt, and Hamilton Fish.[44] The original purpose of the Society was strictly charitable. In 1805, when it was established, there were in New York City only one hundred and forty-one teachers in a population of some seventy-five thousand, and almost all of these were engaged in private schools. Before the Society changed its title in 1826, nine schools had been provided, and for several years the attendance had been approximately four thousand.[45]

After the reorganization of the Society, the pay system was introduced, based on a small charge made to all who could afford to pay. The high reputation of the schools attracted some children of middle-class families who had formerly patronized pay schools, but on the whole the experiment was a failure, and the enrollment dropped. Although a considerable portion of the students were designated as pay students, great difficulties were encountered in collecting tuition. Some churches, by opening their schools to all at cheap tuition, drew off large numbers. A committee appointed to investigate the causes for the decline in enrollment came to the following significant conclusion:

> Your committee believe that the only true and legitimate system of our Public Schools would be to open our doors to *all* classes of our citizens free from any expense, and that all deficiencies should be defrayed by a public tax.[46]

Following this report, the schools abolished tuition charges, and subsequently their enrollment increased.

The Society had received aid from both the state and the city. In 1829 it was granted a tax of one-eighth mill. Two years later this tax was raised to one-half mill. When the Society gave up its charter in 1853 and turned over its properties to the public school department of the city, which had been established in 1842, it had spent more than $3,500,000 and had provided instruction for children whose total attendance aggregated almost five hundred thousand pupil years.[47]

Subscription societies also established and maintained schools in Baltimore, Washington, Albany, Philadelphia, Providence, and numerous other cities. The education of the children of the dependent poor was promoted in Philadelphia by the Philadelphia Society for the Free Instruction of Indigent Boys,[48] which within a few years of its establishment in 1799

[44] William Oland Bourne, *History of the Public School Society of the City of New York* (New York: Wm. Wood & Co., 1869), pp. xxvii–xxxi.

[45] *Ibid.,* p. xxxii.

[46] New York City Board of Education, *op. cit.,* p. 47.

[47] Bourne, *op. cit.,* p. xxxii.

[48] Cubberley, *Readings in Public Education, op. cit.,* pp. 134–135.

changed its name to the Philadelphia Society for the Establishment and Support of Charity Schools. In 1807, the Philadelphia Association for the Instruction of Poor Children was established. These and other organizations provided as best they could for the education of the poor. In 1818, Philadelphia was permitted by the legislature to organize a school system. Free schools, as they now exist, were not, however, contemplated by the law. Philadelphia schools were no less pauper schools than those established under the general law of 1809. There was no provision to educate any child at public expense except orphans or children of indigents. Under responsible officers, these schools, it has been claimed, came to resemble closely free schools, but there were no free schools open to rich and poor alike until 1836.

The work of these societies in New York, Philadelphia, and other cities provided some schooling for a large number of children who otherwise would have been neglected. The societies did good work in a way that was acceptable to the socially and politically dominant group of the period. They no doubt stimulated interest in education, but one might well argue the case that they had the immediate effect of delaying the development of public school systems.

EXTENDING EDUCATION DOWNWARD

Another early-nineteenth-century movement which had its roots in philanthropy and which aimed at alleviating the distressing condition of the poor was the infant-school movement. This unusual product of the English factory system originated in New Lanark, Scotland, where Robert Owen, touched by the sordid life of the community, instituted a number of successful social reforms. He established schools in which the children of the community, including some five hundred pauper apprentices from three to ten years of age, were given moral, physical, and intellectual training through games and well-devised instruction. Coming as it did years before the first great factory law prohibited the employment of children under nine years of age in the textile industry, the Owen plan created much favorable comment. It was seized upon by reformers, who generally attempted to improve upon it by introducing formal methods and a course of study entirely unsuitable for young children.

The first infant schools introduced into the United States were of the formal type. The *Connecticut Courant* some years later indicated the nature of these schools in an article describing the Hartford school:

> On Wednesday forenoon last, there was an exhibition of the Infant School, in this city, in the Centre Church. The house was filled with one of the most respectable assemblies, both of our own citizens, and of strangers, that we have ever seen on any public occasion. The Governor,

Lieut. Governor, and most of the members of the two branches of the
Legislature, were present. . . .

We have not time to give a minute description of the various lessons
which were recited. The scholars read and spelt, and showed that they
understood the elementary principles of arithmetic, and of the most
simple ones of geometry. They were examined with regard to their knowledge of religious truth, and of moral obligation, and manifested that this
was not a mere repetition by rote. . . . They were questioned, also . . .
on the history of our own State, with which they showed an accuracy
of knowledge with regard to facts, the names, and dates, that was truly
surprising.[49]

That the work of this school was too advanced and formal for the children is suggested by the fact that only two or three of the "scholars" had
reached the ripe age of six. Elsewhere, too, the infant schools introduced
into the United States reflected the formal curriculum of their English
prototypes.

The infant schools in America were largely an urban development. As
the laboring element in the cities increased rapidly and was augmented by
immigrants from Europe, more and more children were without opportunity for schooling, even of the lowest level or meanest type. In many
cities which maintained public schools, no public provision was made, as
we noted in the case of Boston, for children who had not learned to read.
Infant schools were organized, in part, to provide instruction in the rudiments, and they were organized in many cities. In time, they generally
became the primary grades of the common schools. In the various cities
the infant-school idea was modified in each case to fit the existing arrangements and needs. Where education at public expense had been provided,
as in Boston, the infant schools were more likely to be incorporated into
the public school at an early date. (See pages 227–228.) Where town
schools were not provided, infant schools, if not provided under private
auspices, were supported by charity. In both instances, infant schools extended educational opportunity downward, and even those that not only
had their origins in philanthropy but continued to be maintained for varying periods of time by it, served to help awaken interest in public education.

EXTENDING OPPORTUNITY THROUGH CHEAPER METHODS

Another innovation of the early nineteenth century was the "system of
mutual instruction," a development which had its roots in poverty, and
which was nurtured by philanthropic efforts to make education more
nearly universal without challenging the prevailing social and political

[49] Butler, *op. cit.*, pp. 262–263.

theories. The essential feature of the plan, the use of older, brighter, and more advanced children to teach the younger and less competent under the supervision of a master, was not new. Never before, however, had the practice been viewed as anything but the cheap makeshift that it was, and never before had an educational administrator, with the assurance which only ignorance can give, seized upon the idea and built around it a system founded upon what at least appeared to be a rational basis. Even so, it is almost unbelievable that a plan hit upon by one person to reduce the cost of instruction in an orphan asylum in India and independently developed by a young Quaker schoolmaster in England to provide teaching assistance for which he could not pay should have attracted so much attention, spread so rapidly and so widely, and enlisted the support of so many well-intentioned men. The popularity of the plan is to be explained, in part, by the fact that the crowding of the population into industrial centers had resulted in bringing together, under almost inconceivable conditions, large numbers of children. The sordidness of their existence made the procedure for introducing some order into their lives appear as divinely inspired to a public which was becoming increasingly conscious of the possibilities of mass production. Violent quarrels developed between the Anglican supporters of Bell, one of the innovators, and the dissenting friends of Lancaster, the other originator of the plan, for the somewhat similar methods of the two men engendered loyalties such as spring only from strife centering in religious belief.[50] The movement spread throughout the British Isles to the Continent, to Asia, to Africa, and to the Americas.

In 1806, Lancaster's system was introduced into the United States, which, perhaps excepting England, was to prove the most fertile soil for its growth. As in England, it was hailed as of greater importance than any discovery that had been made since the alphabet.[51] Governor Clinton, President of the Free School Society of New York, compared its operation in education to that of labor-saving machinery in the useful arts.[52] The trustees of the Lancasterian school in Georgetown accepted the system as a sign that God had not "forgotten to be gracious."[53]

Lancaster's plan was made the official system of the Free School Society of New York on the establishment of the Society's first school in

[50] David Salmon, *Joseph Lancaster* (London, England: published for the British and Foreign School Society by Longmans, Green & Co., 1904), pp. 25–52.

[51] *Westminster Review* (January, 1824), as cited in John Franklin Reigart, *The Lancasterian System of Instruction in the Schools of New York City* (Teachers College Contributions to Education, No. 81 (New York: Teachers College, Columbia University, 1916), pp. 7–8.

[52] Reigart, *op. cit.*, p. 8.

[53] *The British System of Education: Being a Complete Epitome of the Improvements and Inventions Practiced by Joseph Lancaster: To Which Is Added, A Report of the Trustees of the Lancaster School at Georgetown, Col.* (Washington: published by William Cooper; and Georgetown: Joseph Milligan, 1812), p. 123.

1806 and was continued until 1853, at which date, it will be recalled, that organization gave up its charter. Lancaster came to the United States in 1818 to devote most of the remaining years of his life to promoting the system. He was received with acclaim. In fact, his visits to the larger cities took on somewhat the appearance of a triumphal tour. In Washington, Clay yielded him the Speaker's chair. Many cities in all parts of the United States followed the lead of New York in establishing Lancasterian schools and societies. Statesmen, including governors and congressmen, urged the general adoption of the plan. Roberts Vaux, Chairman of the Committee on Public Schools of the Pennsylvania Society for the Promotion of Public Economy, eloquently urged the system and in the outline of a bill for the education of children at public expense in Philadelphia provided for its adoption "in its most complete character."[54]

The success of monitorial schools in Philadelphia City and County, which became the "First School District" of the state under a law passed in 1818, was the subject of considerable comment in the newspapers and journals of the day. A state system was proposed in North Carolina but not adopted by the legislature. Maryland provided for a state system in 1826 but abandoned the idea soon after. Outside Massachusetts scarcely a voice was raised to question Clinton's words spoken in 1809 which were prophetic of the general attitude toward the system for the succeeding twenty years or more.

> His [Lancaster's] tree of knowledge is indeed transplanted to a more fertile soil and a more congenial clime. It has flourished with uncommon vigor and beauty; its luxuriant and wide-spreading branches afford shelter to all who require it; its ambrosial fragrance fills the land, and its head reaches the heavens![55]

The plan developed by Lancaster provided for the collection of as many as a thousand children in one schoolroom, the sorting of the children into groups of approximately equal attainment, the seating of the children in rows of six to ten, and the assignment of a previously taught boy to instruct each group. There were monitors to take attendance, monitors to teach the various subjects, monitors to keep order, monitors to care for equipment, and monitors in charge of monitors. This high degree of organization extended also to the course of study and the teaching procedures. Lancaster turned out numerous publications outlining exact procedures.[56] He

[54] *Report of the Committee on Public Schools to the Pennsylvania Society for the Promotion of Public Economy,* Read at its Meeting, on November 10, 1817 (Philadelphia: printed for the Society, 1817), p. 10.

[55] De Witt Clinton, Address to the Free School Society, New York, 1809, as quoted in Reigart, *op. cit.,* p. 8.

[56] Joseph Lancaster, *Hints and Directions for Building, Fitting Up, and Arranging School Rooms on the British System of Education* (London, England: printed by the author, 1809); Joseph Lancaster, *Improvements in Education; Abridged; Containing a Complete Epitome, of the System of Education, Invented and Practiced by the Author* (London: printed by the author, 1808).

The Gift of
FRANKLIN

JACK and *Gill*
Went up the Hill,
To fetch a Pail of Water ;
Jack fell down
And broke his Crown,
And *Gill* came tumbling after.

Adjudged
by
the School Committee
as
A Reward of Merit
to
John Collins Warren.
1792

Maxim.

The more you think of dying, the better
you will live.

ARISTOTLE'S

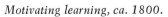

Foolishness punished, 1792.

Merit rewarded: Franklin medals.

Motivating learning, ca. 1800.

This certifies that the bearer Mr. W^m E Coult is a young Gentleman of good moral character has been a member of the school under my superintendency for several months during which his deportment and improvement were commendable — and he is hereby recommended as a person well qualified to teach an English school. — Lyme March 6th 1817 Jonathan Dodge. PS

1817

Requirements for certification became more formal and specific in Old Lyme, Connecticut, but certification continued to be a function of local authorities.

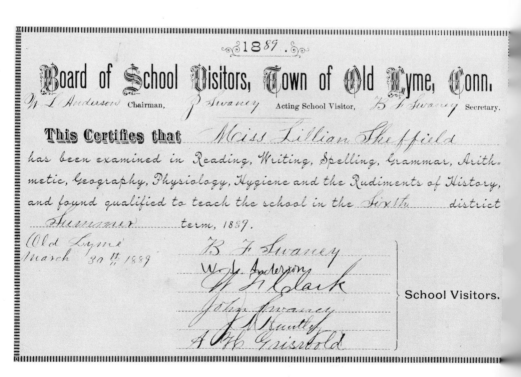

1889.

Board of School Visitors, Town of Old Lyme, Conn.

W. I. Anderson Chairman, J. Swaney Acting School Visitor, B. F. Swaney Secretary.

This Certifies that Miss Lillian Sheffield has been examined in Reading, Writing, Spelling, Grammar, Arithmetic, Geography, Physiology, Hygiene and the Rudiments of History, and found qualified to teach the school in the Sixth district Summer term, 1889.

Old Lyme
March 30th 1889

B. F. Swaney
W. I. Anderson
W. H. Clark
John Swaney
J. A. Huntley
A. H. Griswold

School Visitors.

"The Country School," by Winslow Homer, 1871. The one-room school was dominant in public education throughout the nineteenth century.

Horace Mann (1796–1859), "Father of the American Public School."

QUARTER CARD OF DISCIPLINE AND STUDIES IN MR. ALCOTT'S SCHOOL FOR THE WINTER TERM CURRENT 1837.

THE TUITION AND DISCIPLINE ARE ADDRESSED IN DUE PROPORTION TO THE THREEFOLD NATURE OF MAN.

THE SPIRITUAL FACULTY.	THE IMAGINATIVE FACULTY.	THE RATIONAL FACULTY.
MEANS OF ITS DIRECT CULTURE.	MEANS OF ITS DIRECT CULTURE.	MEANS OF ITS DIRECT CULTURE.
Listening to Sacred Readings on Sunday Morning. Conversations on the GOSPELS. Keeping Journals. Self-Analysis and Self-Discipline. Conversations on Study and Behaviour. Government of the School.	Spelling and Reading. Writing and Sketching Maps. Picturesque Geography. Writing Journals, Epistles, and Paraphrases. Illustrating Words. Conversations and Amusements.	Defining Words. Analysing Speech. Self-Inspection and Self-Analysis. Demonstrations in Arithmetic. Reasonings on Conduct, and Discipline. Review of Conduct and Study.

The Subjects of Study and Means of Discipline are disposed through the Week in the following general Order.

TIME.	SUNDAY.	MONDAY.	TUESDAY.	WEDNESDAY.	THURSDAY.	FRIDAY.	SATURDAY.
IX	SACRED READINGS with Conversations on the TEXT (BEFORE CHURCH) with Readings and Conversations at Home.	WRITING JOURNALS and Studying Lesson.	WRITING JOURNALS and Studying Lessons.	WRITING JOURNALS and Studying Lesson.	WRITING JOURNALS and Studying Lesson.	WRITING JOURNALS and Studying Lessons.	PREPARING JOURNALS AND BOOKS For Examination.
X		SPELLING with Illustrative Conversations on the Meaning & Use of WORDS.	RECITATIONS in GEOGRAPHY, with Conversations and Illustrations.	CONVERSATIONS on the GOSPELS as a means of Spiritual Growth.	ANALYSING SPEECH Written and Vocal with Conversations on the Principles of GRAMMAR.	RECITATIONS in ARITHMETIC with Demonstrations Written and Mental.	CONVERSATIONS on STUDY and BEHAVIOUR as means of Personal Improvement.
XI							
XII		READINGS from Class-Books.	WRITING Paraphrases.	CONVERSATIONS on NATURE.	WRITING EPISTLES.	READINGS from Class-Books.	REVIEW of Studies and Conduct.
	RECREATION ON THE COMMON OR IN THE ANTE ROOM.						
	INTERMISSION FOR REFRESHMENT AND RECREATION.						
III		STUDYING LATIN LESSON with Recitations.	STUDYING FRENCH LESSON with Recitations.	RECREATIONS and DUTIES At Home.	STUDYING LATIN with Recitations.	STUDYING FRENCH with Recitations.	RECREATIONS and DUTIES At Home.
IV							

*** CONVERSATIONS ON SPIRITUAL CULTURE on Friday Evening of each week, at the School Room No. 7, in the Temple; commencing at 7 o'clock.
*** Teachers of Classes in Sunday Schools, Parents, and others interested in Spiritual Culture, are respectfully invited to attend.
Children of both sexes, between the ages of four and fourteen, are admitted to the exercises of the School.

Program of Studies of Amos Bronson Alcott's school, 1837. The better schools were most often not the public schools.

had worked out the lessons in the most minute detail. (His procedures suggest a type of programed instruction, with the monitors serving the role of the electronic and other devices of more recent times.)

The mechanical aspects of the system extended even to the disciplining of the pupils. Lancaster abhorred the use of the rod, more, perhaps, than many of his disciples, but he designed a carefully organized system of rewards and punishments, including the use of placards, shackles, and yokes. He also suggested that children be suspended from the roof in baskets or be left tied up in blankets in the schoolroom overnight to reflect on their misdeeds. However, the mechanical activity, the obedience to rules engendered by the system, and the pervading air of mild militarism were not entirely bad in a day when, it is reported, three hundred schools were closed in one state in a single year because teachers could not manage the unruly pupils.

The beneficial results of the Lancasterian or monitorial system have been enumerated at length. It helped awaken an interest in education. It presented an organized scheme of classification and promotion. It pointed to the need of teacher-training. The work of the teacher was made more dignified. Above all, its cheapness made possible some training for thousands of children who would, otherwise, have had less or none. Also, through the use of the system some communities were gradually led to assume the expense of public education. On the other hand, the "spell of Lancaster . . . hindered all reform movements. Pestalozzian methods . . . were cast in the Lancasterian mould. The imparting of information rather than training in observation and eliciting of thought became the aim." The maintenance of the system became the main end of its sponsors in many cities. In the words of the secretary of the Public School Society, the constant aim of the trustees was "to preserve, in all its integrity, a scheme of popular education rendered eminently honorable by the names of distinguished men who had been interested in it from its inception, and to hand it down to their successors in a form massive and enduring, and as faultless as practical wisdom, enlightened philanthropy, and liberal endowment could make it."[57]

The failure of the system of monitorial instruction to make greater headway in Boston was not due, as has been suggested, to that city's complacency and dislike of the unorthodox; Boston had already had wide experience with a better system. There it was generally conceded that the plan might be well adapted to those cases "where the object was to confer a very limited degree of instruction, at the least possible expense, to those entirely ignorant." Continuing the argument, the *Boston Advertiser* stated:

It will be found on examination, to be principally in use in the most unenlightened and uneducated parts of Europe, as a means of giving a

[57] Bourne, *op. cit.*, pp. 527–528.

degree of knowledge, preferable only to total ignorance. In New York, there are about 12,000 children who attend no school whatever. It is not strange, then, that anything which has the appearance of instruction, should there be considered as success.[58]

This statement is a fair evaluation of the system, whose only real virtue was that it reduced the costs of instruction. Lancaster at one time expressed the hope of being able to reduce the cost to four shillings per pupil per year and to complete the education of a majority of the children in twelve months. His system did stimulate a widespread interest in popular education, but it soon outlived its usefulness and became a hindrance to the healthy development of universal education at public expense.

The Further Development of Private and Denominational Agencies

This period of cautious movement in the direction of public support of education and of intensified philanthropic effort was also characterized by a continued emphasis on denominational schools and a marked expansion of private educational agencies. At the elementary level, the various denominations, especially in the Middle Atlantic states, maintained numerous parochial schools. Private elementary schools were also fairly numerous. Even in New England private schools were commonly patronized by those who could afford it, and the once highly regarded public schools were beginning to take on something of a pauper taint. As one well-informed contemporary put it in commenting upon the lower schools of New England:

The country schools are everywhere degraded. They stand low even in the estimation of their warmest friends. It is thought a mean thing for a man of competent estate, or for any but the mechanic, the artisan, or the laborer, to send their children to them for their education.[59]

It was, however, in the field of secondary education that private schools thrived most vigorously. Each year saw the private or semiprivate academy take on increased importance. In higher education the pre-eminent position of the denominational college, as we have already seen, was being challenged by the rise of state institutions.

THE RISE OF ACADEMIES

Although it has been customary to date the academy movement in America from the establishment of Franklin's academy in Philadelphia

[58] As quoted in "Monitorial Instruction," *American Journal of Education,* III (May, 1828), 314.
[59] *Remarks upon Mr. Carter's Outline of an Institution for the Education of Teachers* (Boston: Bowles & Dearborn, 1827), p. 9.

near the middle of the eighteenth century, it has been generally recognized that somewhat similar schools had been in existence long before and that many schools known as academies could not have been readily distinguished from these earlier institutions.[60] By the beginning of the national period academies were to be found throughout the entire nation. By 1820, or before, they provided almost exclusively the opportunities for instruction at the secondary level. These schools, to a considerable degree, took the place of the old town grammar schools in New England, and great numbers of them sprang up in all sections of the country.

The academies were a product of the age. While the country was new and the vast majority of people were forced to bend every effort to the task of carving a precarious foothold on the edge of three thousand miles of wilderness, the Latin grammar school had provided, more or less satisfactorily, the preliminary classical education for the small, select number of youth who sought admission to Harvard, William and Mary, Yale, and the other colonial colleges. The Latin grammar schools had served primarily the interests of the upper class, of youth who looked forward to entering the professions or to taking their place in the ranks of planters or merchants. But gradually, as the frontier was pushed westward, a new kind of social and economic life evolved and a growing middle class emerged. Young persons other than prospective ministers and the sons of planters and merchants began to manifest an interest in obtaining education beyond that provided in the dame school, the old-field school, or the reading-and-writing school. Moreover, they wanted an education more practical than that offered in the Latin schools, which were still dominated by classical tradition and religious purpose. As was pointed out earlier, private teachers began to meet the needs of the rising middle class by offering instruction in surveying, navigation, modern languages, mathematics, and a great variety of other subjects. The Latin schools were unable to adapt themselves to the needs of the rising middle class. This failure to adjust to new needs was not wholly the result of inability to break with the traditional curriculum. In fact, a number of Latin schools did materially modernize their curriculums. Perhaps the real reason why Latin schools were unable to adjust to the new demands on secondary education is to be found in their method of support. The Latin grammar schools, particularly in New England, where they were most numerous, were town schools, and they were supported in large measure out of town funds. The establishment of a sufficient number of secondary schools to provide the training demanded by the new clientele probably would have required more funds than could have been made available under existing and acceptable plans of taxation. Certainly such a program would have resulted in a tax burden which would have been

[60] Two examples are the Free School in Charleston, South Carolina, established in 1712, and the Public School of New York, established in 1732.

intolerable to a people not yet convinced that education beyond the merest rudiments was a function of the state and a legitimate charge upon government.

The academies, however, were, in the light of contemporary theory and practice, generously supported. State, county, and town governments encouraged the establishment of these institutions. They were given rights and immunities under state charters. Their properties generally were made exempt from taxation. They were privileged to receive endowments and to raise money by subscription and quite often by lottery. They were sometimes given the receipts from the sale of confiscated lands and certain types of fees collected by state offices. In Pennsylvania, Maryland, New York, and other states, they received aid in the form of money grants. For example, ten academies in New York in 1793 received amounts ranging from $215 to $515. In 1828, fifty academies received nearly $10,000, prorated at about $6.12 per student enrolled in the classical or higher English courses.[61] Land grants were made to the academies in several states. By 1800, twenty-four academies in Kentucky had each been endowed with six thousand acres of land and permission had been granted to twenty-three of them to raise one thousand dollars by subscription or lottery. In other states academies received funds from varied sources: state aid, endowments, gifts, subscriptions, and tuition.

Some academies were established as private stock companies; many sprang from the generosity of wealthy donors; a considerable number were founded by churches and religious organizations. Among the religious groups, the Scotch-Irish Presbyterians, noted for their favorable attitude toward education and for their insistence upon an educated ministry, were particularly active in founding and maintaining academies. Many such institutions originated as strictly private ventures. An enterprising teacher sought out a likely location, provided himself with a schoolroom, and solicited the patronage of the neighborhood. All schools, chartered or unchartered, whether aided by the state, sponsored by a religious denomination, or established by an individual, were tuition schools. All who attended were expected to pay, except those who were received on scholarships, which were set aside, particularly in the state-aided schools, for the poor.

The states generally exercised little control over the organization and management of academies. Chartered institutions were usually under the control of boards of trustees which possessed corporate powers and

[61] "Abstract of Reports Made for 1828 to the Regents of the Universities of Academies Incorporated by Them or Subject to Their Supervision," *Journal of the Senate of the State of New York at Their Fifty-second Session*, January 6, 1829. Many features of the academy and of the academy movement — founding, financing, control, curriculum, teachers, students — are treated in Harriet Webster Marr, *The Old New England Academies Founded before 1826* (New York: Comet Press Books, 1959).

were, in the main, self-perpetuating. In some instances certain requirements with respect to such matters as the subjects taught, the location,
and the number of free places reserved for the poor had to be satisfied
before institutions became eligible for state aid; but for the most part they
were permitted the greatest freedom. Not bound by tradition, they provided instruction to girls at the secondary level as well as in the common
branches. Sometimes separate institutions were established for girls, but
quite often girls were instructed in "female departments" of coeducational
academies. Instances in which boys and girls, except the very youngest,
were taught in mixed classes are, however, difficult to find. The practice
may not have been uncommon in some of the smaller one-teacher institutions. Each academy was, within limits, free to develop in its own way.
In the field of the curriculum, particularly, there were few restrictions.

Whatever else may be said of the academies, they were in accord with
the developing spirit of American democracy. They were, however,
tuition schools and therefore closed to many children. In describing the
conditions of education in Massachusetts in 1824, Carter forcefully called
attention to their shortcomings in this respect:

> The decline of popular education among us, or rather the compara-
> tively retrograde motion of the principal means of it, has been more per-
> ceptible, during the last twenty or thirty years, than it ever was at any
> former period. And in the meantime, there has sprung up another class
> of schools, more respectable, indeed, in their character, and better an-
> swering the demands of a portion of the public, but not free. The acad-
> emies are *public*, but not *free* schools. They are open to the whole com-
> munity, under certain conditions. But those conditions exclude nineteen-
> twentieths of the people from participating in the advantages which they
> are designed to afford.[62]

The academies were largely independent of the colleges, and, although
they usually provided a preparatory course, they sought to give a substantial education to students whether they wished to go to college or not.
They were therefore able to enter the neglected field of education for
women. As the number of elementary schools increased, academies were
called upon to assume a teacher-training function, which they did with
reasonable success. When the history of the academy movement is
adequately written, the contribution of these institutions to American
education will loom large.

THE GROWTH OF DENOMINATIONAL COLLEGES

Despite the rise of a considerable number of state colleges and universities, higher education continued to be dominated by private and

[62] Carter, *op. cit.*, p. 23.

248 *The School and the Democratic State*

TABLE 1: GRADUATES OF SELECTED COLLEGES AND UNIVERSITIES, 1823–1827*

Colleges	Graduates in 1823	Graduates in 1824	Graduates in 1825	Graduates in 1826	Graduates in 1827
Waterville College	3	3	3	3	14
Bowdoin College	31	13	37	31	32
Dartmouth College	34	28	26	37	38
Vermont University	8	9	13	13	14
Middlebury College	17	24	16	19	15
Williams College	7	15	19	24	31
Amherst College	3	17	23	32	23
Harvard College	37	67	58	53	47
Brown University	27	41	48	27	38
Yale College	73	68	68	100	79
Union College	67	79	62	71	68
Hamilton College	34	17	23	28	23
Columbia College	29	22	21	24	34
Princeton College	36	47	38	29	28
Dickinson College	10	24	19	14	22
University of Pennsylvania	23	14	14	8	15
16 Colleges	448	488	488	517	521

* Data for the first four years are taken from an article, "View of Colleges in the United States," *American Journal of Education,* I (November, 1826), 692. The article gives the *New York Observer* as its authority. The figures for 1827 are taken from an article, "Colleges in the United States," *American Journal of Education,* III (January, 1828), 65–66. The *Richmond Visitor* is given as the source.

denominational institutions. Most of the approximately fifty new colleges established between 1780 and 1829 belonged to this latter class. The expanding number of new colleges marked a tendency to popularize higher education, but, even so, private and public colleges alike continued to be extremely selective. They administered to the needs of a very small part of the population. Cubberley has reproduced figures on attendance which indicate that in 1815 the graduating classes numbered: Harvard, 66; Yale, 69; Pennsylvania, 15; South Carolina, 37; Princeton, 40; and Williams, 40.[63] Table 1 indicates that, with the exception of South Carolina, for which the later figures are not available,[64] these colleges, which had a total of 230 graduates in 1815, graduated only two hundred in 1827.

Other evidence reveals relatively small enrollment in colleges during

[63] Cubberley, *Public Education in the United States, op. cit.,* p. 114.

[64] According to Edwin L. Green, *A History of the University of South Carolina* (Columbia, S.C.: State Co., 1916), pp. 432, 437, there were enrolled 114 students in 1827. Thirteen of them graduated; twenty-four seniors were expelled.

this period. In 1826 the *New York Observer* estimated that the 488 graduates of sixteen colleges represented two-thirds of the whole number of graduates in the entire United States.[65] Two years later the *Richmond Visitor,* on the basis of the number of graduates reported for the same sixteen institutions, plus nine additional colleges and universities, estimated that the total for all the colleges in the United States was not fewer than eight hundred. The whole number of students enrolled was estimated at something over 3200.[66]

Changes in the Curriculum

During the fifty years following the Revolution the curriculum at all levels underwent considerable expansion and enrichment in response to the changing conditions of American society. In the elementary schools the teaching of spelling and reading was materially improved by the publication of new texts by Noah Webster and Caleb Bingham. Webster's famous "blue-backed" speller, published in 1783, soon replaced the New England Primer as a school text. The teaching of arithmetic was also popularized by the appearance of new texts by Nicholas Pike (1788) and Warren Colburn (1821). The publication of Lindley Murray's *Grammar* in 1795 and of Caleb Bingham's *The Young Lady's Accidence* of about the same date did much to make English grammar a common-school subject. Morse's *Elements of Geography* (1795) and Goodrich's *A History of the United States* (1822) stimulated the introduction of these subjects into the elementary schools. It should be pointed out, however, that these new subjects — grammar, geography, and history — were added slowly. Outside the cities it was a long time before the enrichment provided by them affected the education of any considerable number of children.

Changes in the curriculum at the secondary level were especially significant. The curriculums of the academies, designed to meet the needs of an upsurging middle class, were extremely flexible. The academies, like the Latin grammar schools before them, prepared students for college, but they also provided education to an increasing number of youth to whom a college education was either unattractive or too expensive and time-consuming. A single academy might offer as many different subjects as were demanded by the students. In 1828, for example, the Albany Academy offered Latin, Greek, English grammar, geography, Kane's criticism, algebra, descriptive geometry, engineering, natural philosophy,

---

[65] "View of Colleges in the United States," *American Journal of Education,* I (November, 1826), 692.

[66] "Colleges in the United States," *American Journal of Education,* III (January, 1828), 65–66.

trigonometry, rhetoric, Roman antiquities, Euclid, surveying, French, United States history, bookkeeping, mapping, physical geography, Grecian antiquities, composition, and declamation. Although each academy could choose its offerings from a wide range of courses, it appears that the more substantial ones taught at least a small core of more or less common subjects. An examination of the curriculums of nineteen academies (all in New York) of the second half of the eighteenth century reveals that Latin was offered in all of them; Greek in eighteen; English grammar in eleven; geometry, arithmetic, and geography in ten; writing in nine; logic in seven; and reading, oratory, composition, mathematics, surveying, navigation, trigonometry, and philosophy in more than three and fewer than seven. Twenty-two other subjects, including French, algebra, history, astronomy, commerce, music, and dramatics were taught in one or two of the institutions. During the next half-century many new subjects appeared. The report made in 1828 to the Regents of the University of the State of New York on academies incorporated by them, or subject to their visitation, reveals that in that year approximately fifty subjects were offered in the fifty academies of the state which received state aid. Latin, Greek, English grammar, geography, and arithmetic were offered in each of the fifty; algebra, composition, and declamation in forty; natural philosophy in thirty-five; rhetoric and philosophy in thirty-two; surveying in thirty; bookkeeping in twenty-eight; United States history in twenty-five; French in nineteen; chemistry in eighteen; logic in sixteen; astronomy in thirteen; and about thirty other subjects in twelve or fewer instiutions. When one compares these offerings with those of the eighteenth-century academies, the increasing popularity of history and the scientific subjects is to be noted. An examination of other courses of study of the period indicates that the subjects taught in the New York academies were typical of those offered by the better types of academies elsewhere.

Although there were numerous examples of well-staffed schools, probably a majority of them were one-teacher institutions, and certainly a relatively small number had more than two instructors. In most academies located in small villages and the open country, a single teacher held forth in all the common branches, plus as many higher studies as his students requested and his own scholastic attainments permitted. Some teachers, no doubt, restricted themselves to a more specialized curriculum. The Derby Academy, located in Hingham, Massachusetts, was probably more nearly typical of the academies found in the more settled areas. An account of this school appearing in 1826 described its course and organization:

> The number of instructors is three; the preceptor, preceptress, and her assistant....
>
> The present number of male scholars is thirty-eight.... The number of females in winter is about forty, in summer forty to fifty-five.... Fe-

males may enter the institution and stay at pleasure: males not intended for college, at twelve years of age; if for college, younger at discretion. The studies . . . are "for males, the Latin, Greek, English, and French languages, and the sciences of Mathematics and Geography; and for females, writing, and the English and French languages, Arithmetic, and the art of needlework in general." To these may be added reading, orthography, history, rhetoric, philosophy, astronomy, and composition. . . .

About two fifths of the male scholars are not classed, except in reading. These are such as enter the institution for the purpose of attending almost exclusively to one object of study, in arithmetic, navigation, or surveying, for example. The scholars are . . . admitted at any time . . . and for as short a period as three months.

There has been very little use of corporal punishment in the institution. . . .

The institution is supported, principally, by funds furnished by Mrs. Derby. . . .[67]

There were, of course, among the academies, many that were competently staffed and well organized, and that offered work in some subjects not inferior to that of many higher institutions. The Round Hill School, founded by George Bancroft, the historian, and Joseph Cogswell in 1823, staffed by twelve instructors, was one of these. Concerning it, the *American Journal of Education* said in 1826:

The whole number of boys at the school is one hundred and twelve. Of these thirty-three pursue the study of Greek in seven classes. . . .

There are ninety-five who pursue the study of Latin, in twelve classes. . . .

One hundred and ten attend to French, in thirteen classes. . . .

Fifty-four learn the Spanish, for which are arranged ten classes. . . .

In the two German classes there are twelve. . . .

A small class in the Italian language has just been formed.

The whole number pursue mathematical studies in thirteen regular classes, of which six are engaged with Arithmetic, and the rest have courses in Algebra, Geometry, Trigonometry, and the Application of Algebra to Geometry.

The English Language is made a subject of study to all. Exercises in Grammar, Reading, Declamation, and Writing . . . constitute the course.

For English Grammar and Composition the school is divided into two parts. . . .

For reading the School is divided into sixteen classes. . . .

Besides these regular classes, there are several which are organized for the furtherance of particular views. . . .[68]

[67] "Derby Academy, Hingham, Massachusetts," *American Journal of Education,* I (July, 1826), 433.

[68] "Round Hill School," *American Journal of Education,* I (July, 1826), 437–438.

The Round Hill School represented a conscious attempt to capture the values of the German *Gymnasium* and the English public school, with both of which Bancroft and Cogswell were familiar. In spite of its excellent buildings, wealthy clientele, superior staff, the blessing of Harvard (from which it secured a loan to purchase its plant), excellent leadership, and an academic program that went beyond that of many colleges, the Round Hill School survived for only a decade. It may have been, in part, a victim of its high standards and its rigorous, German-inspired academic program.

During this period the college curriculum also underwent a considerable change. At the end of the colonial period the colleges confined their efforts, in the main, to providing instruction in Latin; Greek; Hebrew; mathematics, including elementary arithmetic, algebra, geometry, conic sections, and the arithmetic of infinities; philosophy; and very elementary aspects of science.[69] Soon after the Revolution, however, forces that have already been discussed contributed greatly to accelerating the expansion of the scope of the college curriculum and rendering it more practical in the light of contemporary needs. Divinity continued, however, to be the crowning glory of the curriculum. A surprisingly large part of the college graduates entered the ministry far into the national period. Latin and Greek retained their position of importance throughout the entire period, but the scope of instruction in mathematics and the sciences was extended. Physics, chemistry, and mineralogy took form from natural philosophy. Modern languages were made regular subjects of instruction in an increasing number of institutions. Political economy was introduced at William and Mary and other colleges. John Quincy Adams, at Harvard in 1806, became, said the *Salem Gazette,* the "first professor of Rhetorick and Oratory which New England has ever known."[70] When the University of Virginia opened for instruction in 1825, it offered a program of courses which fully represented the development that had taken place in the college curriculum during the preceding hundred years. This program provided instruction in the ancient languages; modern languages, including French, Spanish, Italian, Anglo-Saxon, and, if required, Danish, Swedish, "Hollandish," and Portuguese; mathematics, including architecture; "physico-mathematics," including astronomy; physics, chemistry, and mineralogy; botany and zoology; anatomy and medicine; government; municipal law; and ideology, including ethics, rhetoric, and fine arts.[71] The solution of the problem arising from the multiplicity of courses was attempted by the introduction, for the first time in an American college, of

[69] See Edgar W. Knight, *Education in the United States,* New Edition (Boston: Ginn & Company, 1934), p. 116.

[70] *Salem Gazette,* June 20, 1806.

[71] See Charles F. Thwing and William T. Foster, "The American College," in Paul Monroe (ed.), *A Cyclopedia of Education* (New York: The Macmillan Co., 1911), II, pp. 64–65.

the elective system. Another recourse was the establishment of special types of schools.

The expanding scope of instruction had necessitated separating divinity from the regular college course. Several professional schools of divinity were established in connection with existing colleges and before the end of the period several theological seminaries were founded, three before 1800. Medicine and law developed slowly. The first medical school was established in connection with the College of Philadelphia in 1765; King's Medical School was founded in 1767; the Harvard Medical School was organized in 1782; instruction in medicine was first given at Dartmouth in 1797; the College of Medicine of Maryland and the College of Physicians and Surgeons of New York were established in 1807; the Medical Institution of Yale College, chartered in 1810, was opened in 1813; and several other institutions were established before the close of the period. The medical instruction given in all these institutions was meager and in some it was extremely poor. For a long time to come, the practice of medicine was to be learned in the main by "reading" under the direction of practicing physicians. Early instruction in law was offered at William and Mary (1779), Pennsylvania (1790), Columbia (1797), and Transylvania (1799). A law faculty was organized in the University of Maryland in 1812 and a law school was opened at Harvard in 1817, and, a few years later, at Yale and at the University of Virginia. The earliest and most famous of the private law schools was conducted at Litchfield, Connecticut, by practicing lawyers and jurists. Between 1784 and 1833, this school instructed more than one thousand students, among whom were John C. Calhoun, Aaron Burr, Horace Mann, and other persons destined to become important public figures. Higher technical education, which may be said to have begun with the establishment of the United States Military Academy in 1802, and also agricultural education are rightfully to be considered in the development of the succeeding period. When the program of higher education in 1825 is compared with that of the colonial period, it is evident that the fundamental changes in the curriculum, as well as in the organization of higher education, were inevitably influenced by the basic changes which were taking place in society.

Questions and Problems for Study and Discussion

1. During the decades following the Revolution down to the election of Andrew Jackson in 1828, there were two trends in education that ran counter to each other. Indicate what these trends were and explain the causes of each.
2. During the period covered by this chapter, there was increasing state activity in education. In what ways were state governments assuming a larger

The School and the Democratic State

responsibility for the development of education? Evaluate the contribution of the federal government to this movement.

3. Summarize Jefferson's ideas on education as reflected by his efforts to establish public schools in Virginia. Speculate with respect to the possible effects had Jefferson's proposals of 1779 been adopted and fully implemented.

4. Evaluate the education efforts of the period down to about 1830 in terms of the availability of education and the quality of that which was available.

5. Summarize the major trends in higher education during the first half-century of our national life. Do you think that the efforts to bring private colleges under some degree of state control were justifiable? What in your opinion is the proper relation of the state to the private college?

6. What were the major steps taken by philanthropists and private agencies to meet educational needs following the Revolution down to about 1828? Why did the intensive efforts of so many thoughtful and well-intentioned men fail to provide adequately the educational program that was needed?

7. Indicate the major trends in secondary education for the period of this chapter. Cubberley has described the academy as a transitional institution. What did he mean?

8. What were the major changes in the curriculums of American schools and colleges during the period? How do you account for these changes?

Selected References for Further Reading

Bell, Sadie. *The Church, the State, and Education in Virginia.* Philadelphia: University of Pennsylvania, 1930. Pp. xii + 796.

Bourne, William Oland. *History of the Public School Society of the City of New York.* New York: Wm. Wood & Co., 1869. Pp. xxxii + 768.

The British System of Education: Being a Complete Epitome of the Improvements and Inventions Practiced by Joseph Lancaster: To Which is Added, A Report of the Trustees of the Lancaster School at Georgetown, Col. Washington: published by William Cooper; and Georgetown: Joseph Milligan, 1812. Pp. xx + 130.

Brubacher, John S., and Rudy, Willis. *Higher Education in Transition, 1630–1956.* New York: Harper & Brothers, 1958. Pp. vii + 496.

Bullard, Asa. *Fifty Years with the Sabbath Schools.* Boston: Lockwood, Brooks & Co., 1876. Pp. 336.

Butler, Vera M. "Education as Revealed by New England Newspapers Prior to 1850." Doctor's thesis, Temple University, 1935. Pp. x + 504.

Butts, R. Freeman. *The American Tradition in Religion and Education.* Boston: Beacon Press, 1950. Pp. xiv + 230.

Butts, R. Freeman. *The College Charts Its Course: Historical Conceptions and Current Proposals.* New York: McGraw-Hill Book Co., Inc., 1939. Pp. xvi + 464.

Butts, R. Freeman, and Cremin, Lawrence A. *A History of Education in American Culture.* New York: Henry Holt and Co., 1953. Pp. xi + 628.

Carter, James G. *Essays upon Popular Education: Containing a Particular Examination of the Schools of Massachusetts and an Outline of an Institution for the Education of Teachers.* Boston: Bowles & Dearborn, 1826. Pp. iv + 60.

Cubberley, Ellwood P. *Readings in Public Education in the United States: A Collection of Sources and Readings to Illustrate the History of Educational Practice and Progress in the United States.* Boston: Houghton Mifflin Company, 1934. Pp. xviii + 534.

Green, Edwin L. *A History of the University of South Carolina.* Columbia, S.C.: State Co., 1916. Pp. 476.

Hansen, Allen Oscar. *Liberalism and American Education in the Eighteenth Century.* New York: The Macmillan Co., 1926. Pp. xxvi + 318.

Honeywell, Roy J. *The Educational Work of Thomas Jefferson,* Harvard Studies in Education, XVI. Cambridge, Mass.: Harvard University Press, 1931. Pp. xvi + 296.

Knight, Edgar W. *A Documentary History of Education in the South before 1860: Toward Educational Independence.* Chapel Hill, N.C.: University of North Carolina Press, 1949. Pp. ix + 603.

Lancaster, Joseph. *Hints and Directions for Building, Fitting Up, and Arranging School Rooms on the British System of Education.* London: printed by the author, 1809. Pp. 32.

Lancaster, Joseph. *Improvements in Education; Abridged: Containing a Complete Epitome, of the System of Education, Invented and Practised by the Author.* London: printed by the author, 1808. Pp. viii + 88 + xii.

Lancaster, Joseph. *The Lancasterian System of Education, with Improvements.* Baltimore, Md.: published for the author, 1821. Pp. xvi + 34.

Maddox, William Arthur. *The Free School Idea in Virginia before the Civil War: A Phase of Political and Social Evolution,* Teachers College Contributions to Education, No. 93. New York: Teachers College, Columbia University, 1918. Pp. vi + 226.

Madsen, David L. "History of an Idea: The University of the United States." Doctor's thesis, Department of Education, University of Chicago, 1961.

Manual of the Lancasterian System, of Teaching Reading, Writing, Arithmetic, and Needle-Work, as Practiced in the Schools of the Free-School Society, of New York. New York: published by order, and for the benefit, of the Free-School Society, 1820. Pp. 63.

New York City Board of Education. *Public Education in the City of New York: Its History, Condition, and Statistics,* An Official Report to the Board of Education by Thomas Boese, Clerk of the Board. New York: Harper & Brothers, 1869. Pp. 228.

Palmer, A. Emerson. *The New York Public School: Being a History of Free Education in the City of New York.* New York: The Macmillan Co., 1905. Pp. xxx + 440.

Reigart, John Franklin. *The Lancasterian System of Instruction in the Schools of New York City,* Teachers College Contributions to Education, No. 81. New York: Teachers College, Columbia University, 1916. Pp. vi + 106.

Salmon, David. *Joseph Lancaster.* London: published for the British and Foreign School Society by Longmans, Green & Co., 1904. Pp. vi + 76.

Sweet, William. *Religion and the Development of American Culture, 1765–1840*. New York: Charles Scribner's Sons, 1952. Pp. xiv + 358.

Tewksbury, Donald G. *The Founding of American Colleges and Universities before the Civil War: With Particular Reference Bearing upon the College Movement*. New York: Bureau of Publications, Teachers College, Columbia University, 1932. Pp. x + 254.

Wesley, Edgar Bruce. *Proposed: The University of the United States*. Minneapolis, Minn.: University of Minnesota Press, 1936. Pp. x+ 84.

8

The Clash of Interests:
Sectional, Ideological, Economic, and
Political Rivalry, 1828–1860

Economic Progress and Social Conflict

In many ways the year 1828 marked a significant change in American history. The elevation of Andrew Jackson to the presidency was, as it has been noted, a result rather than a cause of the rise of democracy; but his election represented the emergence of the democratic state as a form of political organization and served notice that the common man had moved and was moving toward claiming his birthright, demonstrating the vitality that was to be one of the forces which made the thirty-two years between Jackson's election and the onset of the Civil War a period packed with significant change — political, social, and economic.[1] The tides of migration swept with increasing volume beyond Illinois and Michigan into Wisconsin, Iowa, Kansas, and Nebraska. Manifest destiny had set its stamp upon the land-hungry western expansionists, and neither plains nor desert nor mountains could stop them. Backed by fur-trading interests in the East and by New England merchants who were already exploiting the commerce of the Pacific, they pushed on into the Oregon country and forced Britain to compromise her claims. No less romantic and no less

[1] Richard Hofstadter, *The American Political Tradition* (New York: Alfred A. Knopf, 1948); also published in paperback (New York: Random House [Vintage Books], 1954). Other works on and interpretations of the Jacksonian period are reviewed in Harry Stevens, "Jacksonian Democracy, 1825–1849," in William H. Cartwright and Richard L. Watsen, Jr. (eds.), *Interpreting and Teaching American History,* Thirty-first Yearbook of the National Council for the Social Studies (Washington, D.C.: the Council, 1961), pp. 75–86.

imperious were the slaveholders of the lower South. They relentlessly drove the Indians from the fertile lands of Georgia and Alabama, took over Texas from Mexico, and extended the cotton kingdom to the banks of the Rio Grande. The Mexican War resulted in the acquisition of New Mexico, Arizona, and California.

This epic of western expansion meant far more than the annexation of an imperial domain and the reshuffling of people in search of economic and social opportunity. No aspect of American life — political, economic, or cultural — could escape the impact of the ideas, attitudes, and interests which took form as men pushed steadily westward. Men who were living on what had only recently been the frontier took their places in the political councils of the nation and not infrequently dominated them with characteristic western forcefulness. Nor did the exploitation of the resources of the great Ohio and Mississippi valleys have any less influence on the expanding national economy. Most important of all, however, were the conflicting ideals that emerged with respect to the desirable forms of political and social organization. As we shall see later, the cotton planters of the deep South came to repudiate Jeffersonian liberalism. In time, the mantle of Jefferson was to fall on the ungainly form of Lincoln of Illinois. In the upper Mississippi basin democratic liberalism found a congenial climate. There men may not have been deeply devoted to democratic ideals in the abstract, as Jefferson and his closest followers had been, but they used democratic principles as a powerful weapon in their battle against the rising capitalistic aristocracy of the East and the slavocracy of the South. In fact, these western farmers and small businessmen made such telling use of the ideals of democratic liberalism that thenceforth men were forced to give lip service at least to these ideals and appear to make programs of action square with them.

The Northeast was also feeling the impact of social and economic revolution. The old merchant-capitalist class which had held high sway for so long was being forced to retreat in the face of the rising power of industrial capitalism. A household and domestic economy was giving way to the factory system. Men whose fathers had gone down to the sea in ships and reaped a fortune in far-flung commercial ventures were now searching the fall line of the rivers for factory sites for power-driven machines. A great technological revolution was beginning which was finally to sweep aside agrarian opposition and move forward in seven-league strides. In the meantime, factory towns mushroomed overnight in the Northeast, bringing in their wake the exploitation of child and woman labor, poverty and pauperism, juvenile crime and delinquency, bitterness and strikes among workingmen, socialistic experiments, a broad humanitarianism that sought to soften the harshness of the new industrialism, and a demand for public education. The eastern farmers, caught in competition on the one hand with the rising industrialism of the East and on the other with the more prosperous farmers of the West, began to lose a pre-eminence in American life they were never again to recover. The intellectual leaders of New England were turning from the stern God of their Puritan forebears to the God of love and comradeship of the Unitarians and Transcendentalists. Here was a social order shot through with dynamic change. With each passing year industrial capitalism entrenched itself more securely. It is not strange, in such a society, that public education should have made a wide appeal. Under its banners were enlisted such diverse elements as agrarians, workingmen, humanitarians, intellectuals, and capitalists. As will be noted later, progress was not so great as has commonly been supposed, but, even so, education, like democracy, was on its way to become something to which all men at least professed allegiance.

No section of the country was caught in the grip of a more thoroughgoing economic and social revolution than the southern states. As the demand for cotton to supply the needs of mill owners increased both in England and in New England, planters in the South revived a dying plantation and slave system and spread it imperiously from Virginia to Texas. History affords no more romantic and dramatic chapter than that which recounts the rise and fall of the Cotton Kingdom, with its millions of slaves, its dream of empire, its aristocratic ways, its ceaseless struggle with the rising forces of eastern capitalism, its ideal of a Greek democracy, and its vain efforts to defy the rising moral sentiments of the Western world. Southern leadership undertook to devise a political order, a social philosophy, and a pattern of cultural arrangements that would conform to the realities of southern economic life. As long as the planter South was able to hold the allegiance of the West, the other great agrarian interest of the nation, it could prevent the control of the national government from falling into the hands of the industrial capitalists of the East. But the South was facing a force perhaps more powerful than the moral sentiment of the Western world; it was opposing the advance of technological revolution. And when the Civil War finally came, industrial capitalism was able to defeat its ancient enemy and to move forward in its conquest of a continent, despite the ineffective opposition on the part of agrarian interests.

Enough has been said to make it clear that during the period under consideration the United States was divided into three great competing sections — South, East, and West. Each of these sections was undergoing an economic and social revolution, each sought to modify its culture to meet the demands of economic forces, and each sought to bend national policy to the protection of its own interests. The development of education during this period, to be understood, must be viewed against the background of economic and social change, of sectional rivalries, of competing ideologies, of the clash of economic interests. Broadly conceived, the moving forces of the period were not new; they represented a continuation of the old struggle between agrarianism and capitalism, between democracy and aristocracy, between common men and the possessors of wealth, power, and prestige. And education then, as always, was in large measure the product of the social order in which it developed. But before taking up the specific educational changes of the period, it will be helpful to examine more carefully the transformations that were taking place in each of the major sections.

The Planter South:
The Bid of King Cotton for Power

The South over which Jefferson Davis assumed the presidency was a far different South from that which had sent Thomas Jefferson to Washington in 1800. The invention of machinery for the spinning, weaving, and ginning of cotton and the consequent growth of cotton mills in England and New England had the effect of disrupting the economic life of the South and of establishing it on a new basis. In the early nineteenth century tobacco and rice were still the great staple crops, but nature had set narrow limits within which rice could be cultivated and the demand for tobacco was not such as to make it the basis of support of a far-flung planter aristocracy. In the eastern counties of Maryland, Virginia, and the Carolinas, and to some extent in what had been the back-country before the Revolution, one could still find large plantations worked by numerous slaves. But most southern whites were not slaveowners, and it appeared that the small farmers of western Virginia and the Carolina piedmont would carry their system of small holdings into Kentucky and Tennessee and into the virgin lands of the deep South. True aristocrats there were in Virginia and South Carolina, but one could not travel far to the westward without encountering small farmers who were deeply devoted to democratic ways. Slavery in Virginia was no longer highly profitable. Indeed, many felt that it was not profitable at all. Moreover, Jefferson and many of the Virginia gentry had drunk more deeply at the springs of French humanitarian liberalism than any other group in America. To them the Declaration of Independence was more than a political platform; the principles of democratic liberalism were more than a weapon to be used in defense of one's own special interest. They did what men seldom dare to do: They espoused the principles of democracy as a program of broad social action. True, Jefferson and the Virginia aristocrats like him were owners of slaves, but the system under them was highly patriarchal. What was more important, most people in the South regarded slavery as doomed to eventual extinction and few could be found who would defend it as a positive good. Jefferson sought to overthrow it until his dying day.

He almost succeeded. In 1831, a few years after his death, the legislature of Virginia seriously considered a plan of emancipation and the measure failed in the committee to which it was referred by only a single vote. This near did the Old Dominion come to the realization of the dream of its great leader.[2]

Already, however, the economic life of the South was responding to a new force that was forging more firmly the bondsman's chains. Broad acres planted in cotton were infusing new life into the institution of slavery. Between 1820 and 1860 the production of cotton increased fourteen-fold, from about 160,000,000 pounds to 2,200,000,000 pounds, and the export of cotton increased in about the same ratio, from about 128,000,000 to 1,768,000,000 pounds. For the period 1840 to 1860, the value of the cotton exported amounted to one-half or more of the value of all exports.[3] Practically the whole natural increase of population, white and black, of the older, settled South was moving into the cotton belt, which in time was to extend from North Carolina to eastern Texas and up the lower reaches of the Mississippi Valley. Men who had been small farmers "back home" in the Carolinas or Georgia were soon to become the masters of a hundred slaves and owners of plantations in the rich river bottoms of Alabama and Mississippi. Many planters in Virginia who no longer found it profitable to grow tobacco on exhausted soil sold their land for whatever it would bring and joined the migration to the cotton country. First families in Charleston, if they did not themselves move into the Southeast, frequently invested their surplus capital in slaves and plantations in Mississippi and Louisiana. There in the deep South King Cotton ruled over a veritable El Dorado, where, although generally under heavy economic pressure, men of ambition and intelligence were making fabulous fortunes in the course of a few years. Nor were Southerners the only ones who joined in this exploitation of Negro slaves and fertile soil. Shortly before the Civil War no fewer than a hundred ships of New York registry were engaged in the illegal business of supplying southern planters with slaves fresh from Africa. Not a few Northerners also migrated to the South and became slave and plantation owners, among them Sargent Prentiss from distant Maine, who is said to have received fifty thousand dollars as a lawyer's fee in a single case. Others who remained in the North invested surplus capital in cotton lands and Negroes or married into wealthy southern families. The Barnwells of

[2] William E. Dodd, *Statesmen of the Old South* (New York: The Macmillan Co., 1911), p. 80.

[3] Chester W. Wright, *Economic History of the United States* (New York: McGraw-Hill Book Co., Inc., 1941), p. 370; also Thomas A. Bailey, *The American Pageant: A History of the Republic*, Second Edition (Boston: D. C. Heath & Company, 1961), pp. 356–357. For cotton exports in relation to other exports, 1821–60, see John R. Craf, *Economic Development of the United States* (New York: McGraw-Hill Book Co., Inc., 1952), pp. 196–198.

South Carolina and the Roosevelts of New York were closely linked by family ties, and Douglas, the Little Giant of Illinois, married a North Carolina heiress who numbered her slaves by the scores.

It must not be supposed, however, that all white Southerners came to be large slaveholders and the owners of large plantations, or, for that matter, that all plantations were prosperous and all large planters solvent. Most Southerners remained small farmers, owning no slaves at all, or, at the most, only three or four. (See Table 2, page 263.) In 1850 only 347,000 families owned slaves and only half that number owned five or more, while three-fourths of the population belonged to families who possessed no slaves at all.[4]

Gray summarizes the situation in 1860 with respect to slavery and slaveholding as follows:

> . . . in 1860 half the people of the South were slaves or members of slaveholding families. In the border States less than two fifths of the people were slaves and slaveholders, but in the lower South they were nearly two thirds. In the South as a whole only a little more than one fourth of the free population belonged to slaveholding families. Even in the lower South the population comprised in such families was only a little over a third of the entire free population, and in the border states only one fifth. . . .
>
> In 1860 the plantation population (persons connected with families holding ten or more slaves) was only 7.4 per cent of the total free population; in the border States 4.7, and in the lower South 12.1. . . .
>
> If we consider the large, or upper class, planters as those with 50 or more slaves, the number of holdings included in 1860 was 10,993, comprising 0.75 per cent of the total free population, but owning more than a fourth of all slaves. In 1860, only one slaveholding reported more than 1000 slaves. It was located in South Carolina. There were 14 holdings of 500 and under 1000, nearly all in South Carolina and Louisiana, and 74 holdings of 300 and under 500. The total number of holdings of 100 or more was 2358.
>
> What we may call the middle-class planters, those with from 10 to 50 slaves each, numbered 99,895. About two thirds of them had under 20 slaves, and more than two fifths under 15. The entire group of middle-class planters comprised about 6.6 per cent of the free population, but controlled approximately one-half of the entire slave population.[5]

Economic power in the South came to be highly centralized. In 1850 a thousand families in the cotton states "received over $50,000,000 a year, while all the remaining 666,000 families received only about

[4] Bailey, *op. cit.*, pp. 359–360. See also Robert D. Patten, *The American Economy* (Chicago: Scott, Foresman & Company, 1953); also Craf, *op. cit.*, pp. 220–221.

[5] Lewis Cecil Gray, *History of Agriculture in the Southern United States to 1860* (Washington, D.C.: Carnegie Institution of Washington, 1933), I, pp. 481–483.

TABLE 2: PER CENT OF SLAVE POPULATION TO TOTAL POPULATION,
SLAVEHOLDING POPULATION TO TOTAL FREE POPULATION,
AND COMBINED SLAVE AND SLAVEHOLDING POPULATION
TO TOTAL POPULATION, 1860*

States	Per Cent of Slave Population to Total Population	Per Cent of Slaveholding Population to Total Free Population	Per Cent of Combined Slave and Slaveholding Population to Total Population
Alabama	45.1	35.1	64.4
Arkansas	25.5	19.4	40.0
Delaware	1.6	2.9	64.1
Florida	44.0	36.0	65.1
Georgia	43.7	38.0	4.5
Kentucky	19.5	22.8	37.9
Louisiana	46.9	32.2	64.0
Maryland	12.7	12.6	23.7
Mississippi	55.2	48.0	76.7
Missouri	9.7	12.5	21.0
North Carolina	33.4	28.8	52.5
South Carolina	57.2	48.7	78.1
Tennessee	24.8	24.3	43.1
Texas	30.2	28.5	
Virginia	30.7	25.9	50.1
			48.7
Southern States	32.3	26.1	50.0
Border States	22.3	20.8	38.5
Lower South	44.8	35.6	64.5

* Adapted from Lewis Cecil Gray, *History of Agriculture in the Southern United States to 1860* (Washington, D.C.: Carnegie Institution of Washington, 1933), I, p. 482.

$60,000,000."[6] With wealth came political control and social prestige. In all important matters of public policy — local, state, and national — small farmers and poor whites alike looked to the great statesmen of the South for guidance and leadership. The planter economy required that certain national policies be kept in force — which meant that the South must control the national government. In any event, the control of the government must not be permitted to fall entirely into the hands of the industrial East, the South's great economic antagonist.

The planter aristocracy saw clearly the economic foundations of the state. Consequently, they formulated a clear-cut political program and

6 William E. Dodd, *The Cotton Kingdom: A Chronicle of the Old South* (New Haven, Conn.: Yale University Press, 1920), p. 24. From *The Cotton Kingdom*, Vol. XXVII, *The Chronicles of America.* Copyright Yale University Press.

pushed it relentlessly to its logical conclusion. The Constitution must be so construed as to make it a shield for the protection of slavery and to justify the right of secession in case such a measure became necessary. There must be no high protective tariffs, which would lay tribute on the southern planters in the interests of the eastern manufacturers. The federal government must not launch upon a program of internal improvements, because this might lead to a policy of broad construction of the Constitution and to a demand for a protective tariff to supply the necessary funds. The western lands, the great public domain, must not be given away to the prospective settlers, because this might create an economy of small farmers, whose interests would probably conflict with those of the South. And, finally, the national government must adopt an expansionist program to acquire new lands for southern planters. The acquisition of Texas and California from Mexico was not enough. In the 1850's southern leaders were casting covetous eyes on Cuba, Mexico itself, and the republics of Central America. Here was an ambitious program, grounded firmly on the rock of economic realism. To carry it into effect there could be no division in the ranks of the Southerners. They must be brought to act as a unit, to share common ideals, to have the same deep loyalties. As we shall see later, southern leaders were shaping educational policy to make it conform to their broader strategy. But it would not be enough to have a solid South. Political support must come from one of the other great sections, the capitalistic East or the farmer West. Not a few financial and commercial leaders in the East gave their support to southern interests, and a considerable number of small farmers in that region still voted the Democratic ticket, unaware that the party of Jefferson and Jackson had become the organ of vested interests. Even so, the industrial East was the great protagonist against which the South was girding its loins. Since the farmer West held the balance of power, the success of the South depended on holding the West in line. This it was able to do during most of the time from Jackson to Lincoln.

During the four years preceding 1860 southern leaders were proudly confident. The President in the White House, though a northerner, was subservient to their interests; Jefferson Davis of Mississippi was the mastermind of the cabinet; the Supreme Court was under their control and consistently interpreted the Constitution to their liking; and the Democratic party commanded a majority in Congress. In the South itself opinion was united in defense of the existing social order. A system of education was evolving designed to socialize youth in terms of existing institutional arrangements. The volume of cotton produced within the decade was to double, while tobacco and sugar were still substantial crops. Four million slaves were laboring in the fields. The three great crops of cotton, tobacco, and sugar were worth about $300,000,000 annually,[7] a sum

[7] William E. Dodd, *Expansion and Conflict* (Boston: Houghton Mifflin Company, 1915), p. 194.

only slightly less than the output of the iron, cotton, and wool manufacturers of the East.[8] The South was furnishing about two-thirds of the exports of the nation, although the great volume of these goods cleared through northern ports.[9]

But the bid of the planter economy for national dominance was about to fail. As we shall see a little later on, the contest for economic power was being won by the industrial East, whose demands could no longer be compromised. By 1860, the East had become the great manufacturing, financial, and shipping center of the nation.

> When Lincoln was inaugurated, the capital invested in industries, railways, commerce, and city property exceeded in dollars and cents the value of all the farms and plantations between the Atlantic and the Pacific — a fact announcing at last the triumph of industry over agriculture. The iron, boots, shoes, and leather goods that poured annually from the northern mills alone surpassed in selling price all the cotton grown in southern fields.[10]

The South produced no great financial and manufacturing institutions of its own. It relied on the North to market its agricultural products abroad and to supply it with manufactured goods. And in the process much of the wealth created on southern plantations remained in northern pockets in the form of profits, tariffs, freight charges, commissions, and interest. In reality the South had become a colony of the industrial North. Nor were southern leaders ignorant of the fact. One of them, speaking before a southern commercial convention to promote railroads and manufactures, asked:

> How much does the North receive from us annually in the support of her schools and her colleges, her editors, her authors and her clergy, her Saratogas and her Newports? . . . I think it would be safe to estimate the amount which is lost to us annually by our vassalage to the North at one hundred million dollars. Great God! Does Ireland sustain a more degrading relation to Great Britain? Will we not throw off this humiliating dependence, and act for ourselves? What a country would be the South, could we retain this money at home — What ships and navies we should have — What dense and metropolitan and magnificent cities — What manufacturing establishments. . . . What schools and colleges, in which our sons should be reared to fidelity to their native South?[11]

The South was losing the contest with the East for economic supremacy, and at the same time its political alliance with the West was becom-

---

8 *Ibid.,* p. 187.   9 *Ibid.,* p. 194.

10 Charles A. Beard and Mary R. Beard, *The Rise of American Civilization* (New York: The Macmillan Co., 1927), I, p. 635. Used by permission of The Macmillan Co.

11 Herbert Wender, *Southern Commercial Convention, 1837–1859* (Baltimore, Md.: Johns Hopkins Press, 1930), pp. 84–85.

ing more tenuous. When the Republican party came into power and was skillfully made the carrier of the economic interests of both the industrial East and the agricultural West, and when its great leader rallied the really democratic forces of the nation by taking seriously again the principles of Jefferson, the South was isolated. It chose secession, and the Civil War was to be fought to decide whether America was to be ruled by agrarian or capitalistic interests.

The spread of slavery and the plantation system, after about 1825, produced a new social philosophy in the South. With $100,000,000[12] invested in slaves, Virginia planters had never been quite able to bring themselves to square facts with the principles of the Declaration of Independence, and when slavery became more profitable, around 1825, men began to turn from the "humanitarian idealism" of Jefferson to the "economic realism" of Calhoun.[13] The voice of those who had made apology for slavery grew silent and men began to assert boldly that the institution was a positive good, divinely sanctioned, and basic to the highest form of civilized life. Thomas R. Dew, a professor at William and Mary and only recently returned from study in Germany, was the first to formulate an able defense of slavery. Chief Justice John Marshall and John Randolph also lent the weight of their great names to the defense of the South's "peculiar institution." Chancellor William Harper of the Supreme Court of South Carolina came forward with a treatise even more forceful in its arguments than that produced by Dew. Calhoun, who had grown up as a boy in back-country South Carolina, where slavery was unpopular, now became its ablest spokesman. Lesser men everywhere — lawyers, ministers, and college professors — were its ardent supporters.

Slavery, it was asserted, had the sanction of divine authority. It was in conformity with natural law. Said Harper:

> It is the order of nature and of God that the being of superior faculties and knowledge, and therefore of superior power, should control and dispose of those who are inferior. It is as much in the order of nature that men should enslave each other as that animals should prey upon each other.[14]

Servitude, moreover, was the essential basis of all great civilizations, as the history of the past clearly revealed. Was not the greatness of Athens, some argued, the product of slave labor? And, finally, as Calhoun em-

[12] Andrew C. McLaughlin, William E. Dodd, Marcus Wilson Jernegan, and Arthur P. Scott, *Source Problems in United States History* (New York: Harper & Brothers, 1918), p. 389.

[13] Vernon Louis Parrington, *Main Currents in American Thought,* II: *The Romantic Revolution in America, 1800–1860* (New York: Harcourt, Brace & Co., 1927), p. 61. Also published in paperback (New York: Harcourt, Brace & Co. [Harvest Books], 1961).

[14] McLaughlin, Dodd, Jernegan, and Scott, *op. cit.,* p. 415.

ployed the logic of his great mind to prove, did not the Constitution of the United States give the slaveholder legal protection to his property? Thus the defense of slavery stood foursquare: It had the authority of the Bible behind it, it was in harmony with the law of nature, it had the support of history, and it had the sanction of the supreme law of the land. Moreover, it was profitable.

The social philosophy of the South, however, embraced far more than a mere defense of slavery; it laid the theoretical base of a well-articulated social order. Southern leaders repudiated outright the principles of democracy as they had developed in America and as they had taken concrete form in the Declaration of Independence, and they embraced with ardor and conviction the principles of aristocracy. As George Fitzhugh put it, the Declaration of Independence and the Virginia Bill of Rights were "wholly at war with slavery" and "equally at war with all government, all subordination, all order."[15] Jefferson was not merely in error, he was "exhuberently false, and arborescently fallacious."[16] Southern society was to consist of three main orders: the upper class of true aristocrats, who would have the wealth and the leisure to develop the finest fruits of civilization; a middle order of professional men, yeomen, traders, and mechanics; and, at the bottom, the Negro slaves — the mudsill of the entire edifice. But the feudalistic principles of southern social theory were tempered by the presence of the great mass of non-slaveholding whites, men upon whom the frontier had left its stamp and who did not propose to have the door of opportunity closed to them. Consequently, the southern social philosophy moved steadily in the direction of a Greek democracy. Although the members of the white race would be divided into social ranks, all would be members of a superior social class and all would profit by the labor of slaves.

SOCIAL THEORY AND EDUCATIONAL POLICY

This view that all whites should be regarded as members of a superior ruling caste profoundly affected educational policy and practice. It meant that all whites should be educated at public expense and that they should be taught to uphold the basic principles upon which the southern social order rested.

In the eighteen-forties and fifties, public education was coming to be an important element in the strategy of southern social policy. An educational renaissance was under way, and it was not, as might be supposed, a mere imitation of a similar movement in the northern states. It had its

15 George Fitzhugh, *Sociology for the South: Or the Failure of Free Society* (Richmond, Va.: A. Morris, 1854), p. 175; also in George Fitzhugh and H. R. Helper, *Antebellum: Classic Writings on Slavery in the Old South,* ed. Harvey Wish (New York: G. P. Putnam's Sons [Capricorn Books], 1960).

16 As quoted in Fitzhugh, *op. cit.,* p. 182.

own social origin and its own peculiar objectives. By 1860 it had acquired a momentum far greater than has been commonly supposed. The following resolutions adopted at the Southern Commercial Convention held in New Orleans in 1855 reveal something of the spirit in which the program of education was to be carried out:

> 1. That the convention is gratified to see the several state institutions of the South prosper in the cause of education. 2. That parents and guardians be earnestly recommended to consider that to neglect the claims of their own seminaries and colleges, and patronize and enrich those of remote states is fraught with peril to the sacred interests of the South. 3. That governors and legislatures of Southern States be requested to support the establishment of normal schools for the free admission of such persons of both sexes as might wish to become teachers. 4. That the legislatures should encourage the production of Southern books by the offer of suitable prizes to authors. . . . 6. That a committee be appointed to prepare a report on the subject of the book trade of the South.[17]

George Fitzhugh, the author of the influential treatise *Sociology for the South,* also set forth a view on education that was coming to have wide acceptance:

> As ours is a government of the people, no where is education so necessary. The poor, too, ask no charity, when they demand universal education. They constitute our militia and our police. They protect men in possession of property, as in other countries; and do much more, they secure men in possession of a kind of property which they could not hold a day but for the supervision and protection of the poor.
>
> Free schools should at once be established in all neighborhoods where a sufficient number of scholars can be collected in one school. Parents should be compelled to send their children to school. The obligation on the part of government, to educate the people, carries with it the indubitable right to employ all the means necessary to attain that end. . . .[18]
>
> Educate all Southern whites, employ them, not as cooks, lacqueys, ploughmen, and menials, but as independent freemen should be employed, and let negroes be strictly tied down to such callings as are unbecoming white men, and peace would be established between blacks and whites. The whites would find themselves elevated by the existence of negroes amongst us. Like the Roman citizen, the Southern white man would become a noble and privileged character, and he would then like negroes and slavery, because his high position would be due to them. Poor people can see things as well as rich people. We can't hide the facts from them. It is always better openly, honestly, and fearlessly to meet danger, than to fly from or avoid it. The last words we will utter

17 Wender, *op. cit.,* p. 157.
18 Fitzhugh, *op. cit.,* pp. 144–145.

on this subject are, — The path of safety is the path of duty! Educate the people, no matter what it may cost![19]

Religious zeal as well as social theory stimulated the development of education, especially at the higher level. Indeed, institutionalized religion, as has often been the case, became an important carrier of social theory. The Methodist, Baptist, and Presbyterian churches, essentially Puritan in spirit, had all but replaced the old Episcopal establishment, and the generous religious sentiments of such men as Jefferson and Doctor Thomas Cooper were giving place to a rigid orthodoxy. Ministers of these evangelical faiths — William A. Smith, Basil Manly, A. M. Poindexter, James P. Boyce, John H. Thornwell, Richard Fuller, Benjamin Palmer — were as zealous in their advocacy of higher education as their spiritual prototypes had been in Massachusetts at an earlier day. These advocates of collegiate training for youth found in the aristocratic South a fruitful field for their labor. The result was the establishment of a number of denominational colleges in all of the southern states and a state university in most of them. During the decade 1850–60 scarcely a college in the South failed to double its enrollment.[20] Dodd describes the situation with respect to higher education as follows:

> Twice as many young men per thousand of the population were in colleges in the lower South or in some of the Eastern institutions as were sent from similar groups in other parts of the country. Eleven thousand students were enrolled in the colleges of the cotton States, while in Massachusetts, with half as many white people as were found in all the cotton states, there were only 1733 college students. Illinois, with a population of 1,712,000, or more than half as many white people, had three thousand young men in her colleges. The income of all the higher institutions of the lower South in 1860 was $708,000, which represented an increase of more than a hundred per cent over the figures for 1850. The six New England States, with the best public school system in the world outside of Germany and with an accumulated wealth far in excess of that of the cotton region, spent only $368,469 per year in collegiate education, and their population of 3,235,000 sent only 3748 young men to college.[21]

Nor was education at the secondary and elementary levels neglected. Academies appear to have been more numerous in the South than elsewhere, but many institutions which bore this name were, in the South as in other sections, in reality no more than elementary schools. Educational leaders such as Ruffner in Virginia, Wiley in North Carolina, and Perry in Alabama, and statesmen like Yancey in Alabama and Brown in

[19] *Ibid.,* pp. 147–148.
[20] Dodd, *The Cotton Kingdom, op. cit.,* p. 111.   [21] *Ibid.,* pp. 111–112.

Georgia, were creating public sentiment in favor of state support of popular education. The educational system was far from being highly effective, but in both 1850 and 1860 the South was spending more per capita of the free population on education than any other section. The percentage of white children of school age attending school in the South was, however, lower than in the other sections. Dodd describes the situation of the cotton states with respect to the support of common schools as follows:

> Although the states were not so liberal in their grants to lower schools as to colleges and universities, yet there were 425,600 children in the schools of the cotton States in 1860. This showed that one child in every seven of the white population in the lower South was in school at least for a short term. In the remainder of the country the ratio was one to five or five and a half. In the cotton States $2,432,000 was expended each year upon common schools and $1,383,000 in the maintenance of academies and private schools. Comparison with Eastern conditions or with those of the Northwest shows once again that the planters were not far behind in actual performance and that they were in the lead in the ratio of progress.[22]

The East: the Rise of an Industrial Economy

While the institutional life of the South was being transformed by the spread of cotton culture and the plantation system, a revolution no less important was taking place in the eastern section of the United States. At the beginning of the national period, the New England and Middle Atlantic states were peopled in the main by small farmers and mechanics, although, as we have seen, political power and the advantages of wealth and social position still rested in large measure in the hands of the great merchants in Boston, New York, Philadelphia, and other seaboard cities. The nineteenth century was not far advanced, however, before the East was caught in the grip of an industrial revolution that was to bring about a shift in the locus of economic power, create political issues of national import, undermine the position of small farmers, call new social classes into being, change the pattern of social values, and transform the means for cultural and intellectual growth.

A number of influences stimulated industrial development in the young republic. The breaking of the political ties with England and the War of 1812, with its restrictions on commerce, forced the people of the United States to rely more and more on their own manufactures. The mechanical inventions which were producing an industrial revolution in England found their way to the United States and were developed and improved by American inventors. The phenomenal increase of population of about

[22] *Ibid.*, p. 115.

35 per cent each decade — from 9,600,000 in 1820 to 31,400,000 in 1860[23] — created a rapidly expanding market. And, finally, a protective tariff, though not always so high as manufacturers desired, placed American producers at an advantage in competition with foreign rivals.

Household and domestic manufacture was slow, however, to give place to the factory system of production. As late as 1820 about two-thirds of all textiles were still produced by domestic industry, and home manufacture probably outranked factory production until well after 1830, continuing to be important, particularly in the West and South, up till 1860.[24] As early as 1814, however, the first modern factory in this country had been built at Waltham, Massachusetts, for the making of cotton cloth. Not many years were to pass before New England capitalists were seeking sites for cotton factories wherever water power was available. Industrial cities sprang up along the falls of the Merrimack River and in the Fall River district. The twenty-four spindles constructed by Slater in 1790 were the first of more than 5,000,000 in operation in 1860,[25] and New England was the great center of the industry. By 1860, cotton manufacturers were employing more than 122,000 workers and producing goods valued at almost $116,000,000.[26] Profits of 10 per cent or more a year were not unusual. Samuel Slater, starting as an English immigrant with almost no capital, was able to amass a fortune of $700,000 in forty years.[27] Woolen mills were also numerous in New England, Pennsylvania, and New York. The value of their products in 1860 was about $8,000,-000.[28] The iron industry was confined largely to the valleys of northern rivers — the Hudson, Monongahela, Lehigh, Delaware, and Schuylkill. Pennsylvania took the lead in producing the 600,000 tons which represented the nation's output in 1850.

By 1860 an industrial belt had developed, much smaller in size but stronger in economic power than the cotton kingdom. Says Dodd:

> The East had developed her manufactures beyond all expectation, and the great mill belt stretched from southeastern Maine to New York City, its center of gravity, thence to Philadelphia and Baltimore, and from these cities westward to Pittsburgh. Another belt ancillary to this began in western Massachusetts and extended along the Erie Canal to Buffalo, thence to Cleveland, Detroit, and Chicago. In these areas, or in the industrial belt as it may be termed, there lived about 4,000,000 mill operatives, whose annual output of wool, iron, and cotton manufac-

---

23 Wright, *op. cit.*, p. 306.
24 *A History of American Economic Life,* by Edward C. Kirkland. Third edition copyright 1951, Appleton-Century-Crofts, Inc.
25 Wright, *op. cit.*, p. 388.
26 Kirkland, *op. cit.*, p. 304.
27 Fred Albert Shannon, *America's Economic Growth* (New York: The Macmillan Co., 1951), p. 234.
28 Wright, *op. cit.*, p. 390.

tures alone was worth in 1860 $330,393,000 as compared to the $58,000,000 of 1830.[29]

In 1860, the three great southern crops of tobacco, cotton, and sugar were valued at about $300,000,000.[30] Thus the industrial East was already outdistancing the agricultural South. Moreover, since the southern planter owned his own labor, the capital investment of the South was markedly greater than that of the East.

Business enterprise in the East was by no means limited to the manufacture of textiles, iron, and other commodities. The shipping of the country was largely concentrated in the hands of eastern capitalists. The tonnage of the East increased from 500,000 in 1830 to 5,000,000 in 1860.[31] Although the South provided far more than half the nation's exports, these goods were carried abroad chiefly in northern bottoms. Merchants in New York, Philadelphia, Boston, and other eastern cities reaped rich profits by supplying southern planters with a large part of the goods they consumed from abroad or from northern factories.

It was but natural that eastern capitalists should seek to tie in the markets of the great agricultural West and South with Middle Atlantic and New England cities through the development of means of transportation. At first canals were employed, but by 1828 railroad rails were being laid. By 1840 almost 2800 miles of railroads threaded eastern and southern cities, and during the next decade the mileage was more than tripled. It was not, however, until shortly after 1850 that the railroads extended their lines to tap the rich agricultural markets of the West. By 1860, thirty thousand miles had been built; the industrial East was extending its roads to Chicago and St. Louis and dreaming of spanning the continent to the Pacific. As railroads opened up the eastern markets for the products of western farms, the West began to shift its political allegiance from the South to the East. In fact, the West was beginning to develop industries of its own and to become a part of an expanding industrial economy.

The East was also the area in which were concentrated the great banking and financial interests of the country. Since Hamilton's day banking had been highly concentrated in the Middle Atlantic and New England states. Around 1830, the East had 414 of the 502 banks of the nation.[32] Despite Jackson's attack on the National Bank, eastern capitalists were able to keep their grip on the financial structure of the country. In 1860, the East had about two-thirds of all banking capital; New York alone did a business of some $7,000,000,000 each year.[33]

Thus, each decade from 1830 to 1860 saw the East become increasingly the center of the nation's industry, its commercial interests, its

29 Dodd, *Expansion and Conflict, op. cit.,* p. 187.
30 *Ibid.,* p. 194.   31 *Ibid.,* p. 187.
32 *Ibid.,* p. 45.   33 *Ibid.,* p. 189.

transportation system, and its financial institutions. As Dodd points out, there was a certain similarity between the cotton belt and the industrial belt. In the one was the plantation, in the other the factory; in the one about 4,000,000 slaves, in the other about 4,000,000 mill operatives.[34] The economy of both sections was frankly grounded on the exploitation of labor, but the Southerners claimed that their system of exploitation was the more humane. In the South the principle of aristocracy was frankly accepted and the principles of the Declaration of Independence were openly rejected; in the East, an aristocracy of wealth was rising and the prosperous manufacturers and merchants entertained much the same social philosophy as the southern planters. Of this eastern aristocracy, Professor Schlesinger of Harvard has the following to say:

> In the North at the same time a pretentious aristocracy was rapidly establishing itself socially, confined largely to the great cities of the Atlantic seaboard. Men of that section who had made money out of land speculation and the nascent manufacturing industries were beginning to coalesce into a special caste although as yet there were few millionaires to be found among their number outside of the Astors, the Girards and the Longworthys. Distinguished visitors in America became aware of the growing importance of social distinctions. The English historian, Harriet Martineau, was told much about the "first people" of Boston, New York and Philadelphia when she visited the United States in the thirties; and in the last-named city she discovered a sharp social cleavage between the ladies of Arch Street whose fathers had made their own fortunes and the social leaders of Chestnut Street who owed their wealth to their grandfathers. Compared with the corresponding social class in the South, the upper stratum of northern society constituted an upstart aristocracy, based upon fluid capital rather than upon land, and destitute of traditions or culture or negro vassals. Condemned by the southern patricians as *nouveaux riches,* this aspiring group were destined to be the forerunners of the class that was to supplant the southern aristocracy in the period after the Civil War and become the modern conservators of the aristocratic tradition.[35]

The dominant group in any society seeks to control the state as a means of promoting and protecting its own interests. During the period between 1820 and 1860, the three great sections of the nation — South, East, and West — were waging a great triangular battle to control the federal government. Each expressed nationalist sentiments when in control of the government and each used the threat of secession when it felt its own interests too greatly in jeopardy. The industrial East insisted first of all upon high tariffs to keep out competitors from the rapidly expanding

[34] *Ibid.,* Chap. X.
[35] Arthur Meier Schlesinger, *New Viewpoints in American History* (New York: The Macmillan Co., 1922), pp. 91–92. Used by permission of The Macmillan Co.

American markets, although many northern merchants, farmers, and some financiers steadfastly voted with the South in opposition to the tariff. Naturally, the East favored a liberal immigration policy that would result in abundant and cheap labor, internal improvements in the form of roads and canals, subsidies to railroads, and a monetary system that would both safeguard debts and permit the eastern capitalists to dominate the credit structure of the nation. Although the East had a staunch ally in Chief Justice John Marshall of the United States Supreme Court, who always interpreted the Constitution in the interests of industrial capitalism, from the election of Jackson to 1860 the agrarian South and West were able most of the time to dominate national policy. But, as we have seen, the East, even without excessively high tariffs, was able to forge ahead in the struggle for economic power. And in 1860 it was able, by making the newly formed Republican party the conveyer of its interests, to break the political alliance between South and West. The Republican platform of 1860 offered a protective tariff to the industrial East and to rising industrialists in the West; it also promised a free homestead to western farmers and to dispossessed laborers in the East. As the Beards point out, the rallying cry to the masses of the West and the East was, "Vote yourself a farm," and to the manufacturers, "Vote yourself a protective tariff." "The hour for the transfer of the public domain to private persons without compensation and the creation of protective safeguards for American industry was at hand."[36] The new party of Lincoln not only united East and West on great economic interests; it also appealed to common men in the North, many of whom had come to entertain a bitter hatred of the slaveholding southern aristocrats. The new party, skillfully tying together the economic interests of the eastern capitalists, the mill operatives, and the western farmers and appealing to deep-seated emotional drives of men east and west, won the election of 1860 and left the South as isolated as New England had been in 1812. And the South, like New England, began to think in terms of secession. To be sure, Lincoln was no radical. As Hacker puts it:

> The fact is, as his Abolitionist enemies within his own party were soon to learn, Lincoln did not believe in equality for the Negro, or indeed, in emancipation. There was to be no federal interference with the institution in the states; he favored the enforcement of the fugitive-slave law; and he was willing to approve of a constitutional amendment protecting slavery in those states where it already existed.[37]

[36] Beard and Beard, *op. cit.,* pp. 692–693.

[37] From *The Triumph of American Capitalism* by Louis Hacker, pp. 336–337. Copyright 1940 by Simon and Schuster, Inc. By permission of Simon and Schuster, Inc. Also published by Columbia University Press (New York), 1947 and (Fourth Printing) 1959.

The South exaggerated its fear of Lincoln. What he was determined to prevent was the extension of slavery into free territory and the dissolution of the Union. Southern leaders were wrong if they thought they saw in the election of Lincoln the immediate extinction of slavery. They were right when they recognized in the party of Lincoln the successor of the party of Hamilton, Webster, and Clay. What they should have seen, but did not, was that in the long struggle between Hamiltonianism and Jeffersonianism, between industrialism and agrarianism, the former had won. Quite regardless of the fortunes of political campaigns, America had become a great industrial nation. But southern leaders had too long dominated the national government to yield. A great civil war was to be fought to decide whether the planter South or the industrial East was to direct the destiny of the nation. But, as the Beards have pointed out, before hostilities began the issue had already been decided in terms of bank deposits and ledger entries.

THE RISE OF ORGANIZED LABOR AND THE DEMAND FOR STATUS

If the profits of cotton manufacturers, exclusive of salaries, often amounted to 10 per cent or more a year, or if iron manufacturers sometimes declared dividends of from 40 to 100 per cent[38] the result was not wholly due to the genius of men of business enterprise. The prosperity of the East was based upon an exploitation of labor scarcely more humane than that of the planter South. As industry expanded, a definite labor class developed. At first mill hands were drawn largely from the rural hinterland of the rising industrial centers, but in the late forties a stream of immigrants began to flood the country. Hamilton had urged that manufacturing establishments would render women and children more useful than they would otherwise be,[39] and the New England industrialists viewed the matter in the same light. Large numbers of women were employed in the making of boots and shoes, in the ready-made clothing industry, and especially in the cotton mills. As early as 1831 women constituted four-fifths of the workers in the textile mills of Massachusetts. Women and girls, it was estimated, comprised in the same year 68 per cent of the labor force of the cotton mills of New England. By 1860, the percentage had dropped to about 60.[40] More important for its influence on education was the extensive use made of the labor of young children. Says Curti, in regard to child labor:

In 1833 a report of a committee of the New England Association of Farmers, Mechanics and other Workingmen exposed the fact that two

38 Shannon, *op. cit.*, p. 234.   39 Kirkland, *op. cit.*, p. 314.   40 *Ibid.*, p. 317.

fifths of all persons employed in New England factories were children between seven and sixteen; that hours were from daylight to eight in the evening; and that the only opportunity for them to obtain an education was on Sunday, or after eight on week days. At Hope Factory in Rhode Island, workers, more than half of whom were children, toiled fifteen or sixteen hours a day. In the same state, where conditions were worse than in Massachusetts, small, half-clothed children went to work and came home by dark, and as late as 1853 their numbers were increasing.[41]

In the eighteen-thirties, a normal day's work was twelve or more hours and wages were barely above what was required for existence. Standards of living and moral conditions were shockingly bad. Shannon describes the general status of the working class in the following statement:

The factory system was particularly baleful in its influence on wages and hours of labor. Skill was supplanted by machinery, and painstaking tasks were replaced by monotonous routine which could be entrusted to women, children, poorhouse inmates, homeless orphans, and baffled immigrants at pitifully low wages. Mathew Carey estimated in 1830 that 20,000 women in Boston, New York, Philadelphia, and Baltimore were employed for 16 hours a day at wages of no more than $1.25 a week. By 1837 other figures showed women in the needle trades receiving less than $60 a year for full time, or below $36 if their attention was divided by the care of children. At the same time the average in the cotton mills was about $2.50 a week.

Wages varied widely in different sections, usually being in inverse ratio to other costs of production. In many cases the whole family was employed in the same mill to make a bare living. Nearly three fifths of the cotton-mill operatives from New England to Virginia were women, and 7 per cent were children under 12 years of age. In 1832 an estimate showed two fifths of all employees in Massachusetts factories under 16 years. Men who operated spinning mules received as much as $7.50 or $8.50 a week before 1830, but the period of wage-cutting had already begun.

Laborers at heavy tasks, even when paid in money instead of truck, got little more than starvation wages. Workers on the Pennsylvania Canal in 1831 were given bed and board and from $10 to $12 a month, except in the coldest months, when they were lucky to get just their board and bunk. Carey calculated that such a worker could by no means support a wife and two children. The wife might make a pittance, but if eight cents a day was allowed for food for the wife and each child, with other necessities in proportion, the man would be $30 in debt at the end of the year. Since no such laborer could get that much credit, he would have to

[41] Merle Curti, *The Social Ideas of American Educators, with a New Chapter on the Last Twenty-five Years* (Paterson, N.J.: Pageant Books, Inc., 1959) (a reprint of the tenth volume of the American Historical Association Committee on the Social Studies in Schools [first published New York: Charles Scribner's Sons, 1935], with a chapter added).

cut the clothing allowance for the family from $40 to $10. But about half of the men so employed returned to their homes in the winter, broken in health by malaria. City workers making 75 cents a day were hardly any better off, even when their rent was figured at 50 cents a week. When such men struck for a living wage, their disturbances were referred to as riots, and it was no uncommon thing for them to be quieted by a well armed militia. Many Southern slaves had a larger money income than they. Even skilled craftsmen did little better. Philadelphia shoemakers were getting only 94 cents a day after a successful strike in 1835, and had to furnish their own tools and findings. At the same time New York carpenters got $1.37½ for a day of from 15 to 17 hours.

The great stream of immigrants in the eighteen-forties and following added to the distress of the laboring classes. Between 1847 and 1854 a total of 2,676,000 arrived, including 1,187,000 from Ireland alone. The aliens, accustomed to hard lives, were submissive under a régime of from 14 to 16 hours a day at almost any rate of pay they were offered. Their presence in the Eastern cities had such a depressing effect on wages as to cause the first organized protests of American workingmen against unrestricted immigration.

Slum conditions were a natural result of this situation. An enumeration made by the chief of police of New York in 1850 showed 18,456 people living underground in 8141 cellars. Sometimes the "flophouse" system was found where a bedding of loose straw cost two cents a night or bare floor space one cent. In such places black and white people, men, women, and children, were "mixed in one dirty mass." Bedrooms were found "without air, without light, filled with damp vapour from the mildewed walls, and with vermin; they are the most repulsive holes that ever a human being was forced to sleep in." Numerous other like situations were revealed where people with steady employment had to live far below a decent plane of existence. Small effect did the much vaunted limitless expanse of public land have in improving the situation. Transportation charges to the regions of cheap land were heavy, the lifetime savings of a whole family often not being enough to pay the cost, much less leaving a surplus to pay for the land, equipment, and sustenance needed before a crop could be grown.[42]

It was only natural that the working class should seek to improve its status through forms of cooperative action. In the early years of the nineteenth century skilled craftsmen — shoemakers, printers, hatters, masons, and the like — began to organize locally. In time all these craft societies in a single city coalesced into a single "Trades Union." The first of these was organized in New York in 1833, and in a few years they were to be found in many industrial cities. A few craft unions became national in scope, and attempts were made to organize a national trades union.[43]

---

[42] From *America's Economic Growth* by Fred Albert Shannon. Third Edition copyright 1951 by The Macmillan Company, and used with their permission.
[43] *Ibid.*, p. 351. See also Hacker, *op. cit.*, pp. 267–279.

Labor was becoming articulate, even if its ranks were not very tightly closed or its organization very powerful or permanent. The efforts of workingmen to improve their condition and status took various forms. Strikes to obtain a ten-hour day were numerous and usually unsuccessful. Many sought an escape from the hard realities of an industrial society in socialistic experiments of one kind or another. Toward the end of the period there was a throwback to earlier agrarian ideals and free home-steads in the West were regarded as a means of improving the condition of the laboring masses.

For our purpose it is more important to note that workingmen were quite as much interested in status as in shorter hours and higher wages. The upper classes had long had a substantial monopoly of education and had used it to protect their favored position. The spokesmen of labor now undertook, through political action, to break down this monopoly and to establish systems of tax-supported, non-sectarian schools. In this they were perhaps more successful than in any other of their endeavors.

HUMANITARIANISM, ROMANTICISM, LIBERALISM

The French revolutionary philosophy, which had done much to inspire Jefferson and his fellow agrarians in their struggle for political democracy, found little favor in New England. Emerson was perhaps too drastic a critic when he said of Massachusetts: "From 1790 to 1820 there was not a book, a speech, a conversation or a thought in the state." But new currents of thought and emotion were forming which were to result, among other things, in a great humanitarian movement. Puritanism had always had a deep ethical content at its core and now this spiritual and ethical quality, in the lives of a few great intellectual leaders, was breaking through the crust of Calvinistic theology and bourgeois acquisi-tiveness. At long last Puritanism was coming to flower in the God of love of Channing and other Unitarians and in the sensitive social con-science of Emerson and his fellow Transcendentalists. Other forces were also operating to create a social conscience, to accent the divinity in man. German idealism was being grafted on to the native spiritual and ethical qualities of Puritanism. Sensitive souls could not remain indifferent to the social wreckage that acquisitive industrialism was leaving in its wake — to the grinding labor of women and children, to juvenile delinquency, to pauperism, to intemperance, to the disintegration of family life, and to all the other social ills to be found in rising urban centers. As Emerson observed, a "restless, prying, conscientious criticism broke out in unex-pected quarters."[44] "It was a day," said John Morley, "of ideals in every camp." Some organized to suppress intemperance; some championed the rights of women; others struck at the criminal codes; many became abo-

[44] Henry Steele Commager and Allan Nevins (eds.), *The Heritage of America* (Boston: Little, Brown & Co., 1939), p. 415.

litionists. To these crusaders for righteousness public education made a strong appeal, and humanitarians in general struck hands with organized labor in the struggle for tax-supported schools.

THE RISING SENTIMENT FOR PUBLIC SCHOOLS

As we have seen, southern planters were giving education a social orientation in terms of a caste system based on Negro slavery — in terms of their ideal of a Greek democracy, which represented a compromise between the principle of feudalism and the frontier spirit of freedom and equality. Similarly, in the East an educational policy took form as a result of the conditions and forces we have been considering. Many diverse elements of the population were brought to support more adequate tax-supported schools, although there was no general agreement with respect to the ends education should accomplish. Among all classes, though not by all members of each class, there was a widespread acceptance of the view that popular education was essential to the preservation of republican political institutions. This argument was tellingly used over and over again by intellectuals, publicists, and spokesmen of labor. Schools, it was also asserted, would teach respect for law and authority, they would make labor more productive, they would alleviate pauperism and prevent crime, they would be conducive to political honesty — in short, they would promote the general welfare.

But those who supported the cause of education often differed with respect to more specific ends. Among men of property, talent, and social position there was much misgiving with respect to the social disturbances of the day — the gains of democracy, the agitation and strikes of laborers, the insistence of common men that they climb the ladder of economic and social opportunity and find a place for themselves at the top. Men of wealth had two choices: They could oppose public education or they could support it with the view of making it a means of giving permanence and stability to the new order of things created by expanding industry. Some chose the first alternative, opposing education on the ground that it was unjust to tax one man for the education of the children of another and that free schools would destroy the self-respect of the poor. Some took the position that free public education would break down class distinctions and promote an undesirable growth of the democratic spirit. Like the southern planters, they held that cultural accomplishment is made possible by a small leisure class, which in turn depends on wealth. It was insisted, too, that the "only way to get along with such ignorant people [the working class] is to keep them from mischief by keeping them constantly employed."[45]

Others among the industrial and commercial leaders saw in free

[45] *American Annals of Education and Instruction,* III (June, 1833), 257–258, as quoted in Curti, *op. cit.,* p. 88.

schools a means of creating a more productive labor force and of checking social unrest. Men like Abbott Lawrence insisted that an intelligent working class was essential if American manufacturers were to compete successfully with their English competitors. "Let your common school system," he said, "go hand in hand with the employment of your people; you may be quite certain that the adoption of these systems at once, will aid each other."[46] Horace Mann, it will be recalled, was at great pains to convince employers that educated workingmen were more efficient and productive than those who were left in ignorance.

Education, it was also urged, would serve to develop loyalties to the existing pattern of social and economic arrangements. It could be made a conservative force to create respect for law and order, to allay social unrest, to check revolutionary tendencies, and to protect property rights. Says Professor Curti:

> But it was not only prosperity that the industrialists were led to expect from public education. Anxious to wring support for public schools from propertied interests then opposed to taxation for that purpose, educational spokesmen warned them of the dangers to property rights from universal suffrage, Jacksonian democracy, and even, possibly, revolution — any of which might result if the masses were left undisciplined by education. If the rich would enjoy security against hostile legislative attacks on corporation franchises; if they would put an end to the mob violence which was already attacking property; if they would curb 'men of warm passion and little reason,' vindictive and dangerous workingmen, restless and vicious frontiersmen — they could do no better than to lend support to the movement for free public schools. A writer in the conservative *North American Review* drew from Dorr's rebellion the lesson that the security of the established order depended on whether the masses were instructed or remained untaught, saying that the manufacturers might well tremble in the presence of the large masses of uninstructed population which were growing up around them, and see it written everywhere with a distinctness which none could comprehend as well as they, that it was only by educating this population that their business would prosper and their lives and property be secure. This is by no means an exceptional statement. . . .[47]

The position of these men indicates that the movement for the education of the masses was not merely a democratic movement peculiarly at home in republican America. It was in part a product of the industrial capitalism rapidly becoming dominant throughout the western world. We tend today to think of our American system of public schools as having been founded out of a great zeal for the welfare of the plain people. But actually this zeal was tempered by zeal for the welfare of the employers of labor, by zeal for maintaining the political and social *status quo*. These economic motives were frankly recognized in the days of the

[46] As quoted in Curti, *op. cit.*, p. 77.   [47] *Ibid.*, pp. 79–80.

founding. Now, however, looking back, we tend to rationalize, and to recognize only the more idealistic motives, which were of course also operative.[48]

Others saw in education a different purpose. Humanitarians and labor leaders insisted that free public schools would salvage and even prevent some of the human wreckage which industrialism was leaving in its wake. Free schools would be a means of social mobility, of making class distinctions less sharp, and above all, perhaps, of improving the status of workingmen. Seth Luther, a spokesman of labor in Boston, said:

> In our review, we have seen a large body of human beings, ruined by a neglect of education, rendered miserable in the extreme, and incapable of self-government; and this by the grinding of the rich on the faces of the poor, through the operation of cotton and other machinery.[49]

The privileged few, it was said, had a monopoly on learning and employed this monopoly to keep the masses in an inferior social status. "Literature and education, thus affianced to opulence, naturally feel a strong repugnance to share their intellectual dominance with the mass of society."[50] Labor leaders were coming to look to education "for redress of that perverted system of society, which dooms the producer to ignorance, to toil, and to penury, to moral degradation, physical want and social barbarism."[51] The point of view of labor is well expressed in a report adopted by workingmen in Philadelphia in 1830:

> When the committees contemplate their own condition, and that of the great mass of their fellow laborers; when they look around on the glaring inequality of society, they are constrained to believe, that, until the means of equal instruction shall be equally secured to all, liberty is but an unmeaning word, and equality an empty shadow, whose substance to be realized must first be planted by an equal education and proper training in the minds, in the habits, and in the feelings of the community.[52]

Summing up the social tensions that centered around education in New England and New York in the period 1827-1842, Jackson says:

[48] *Ibid.,* p. 85.

[49] As quoted in Frank Tracy Carlton, *Economic Influences upon Educational Progress in the United States, 1820–1850* (Madison, Wis.: University of Wisconsin, 1908), p. 48. Reprinted with permission of the copyright owners, the Regents of the University of Wisconsin.

[50] Stephen Simpson, *A Manual for Workingmen* (1801), p. 201, as quoted *ibid.,* p. 49.

[51] Simpson, *op. cit.,* pp. 24–25, as quoted in Carlton, *op. cit.,* p. 49.

[52] As quoted in Kirkland, *op. cit.,* p. 335. Used by permission of Appleton-Century-Crofts, Inc.

The great problems before the intellectual leadership, in the New England and New York of the eighteen-thirties, was to parry the thrusts of Jacksonian Democracy. For American life had developed in a manner that seemed to them to make their position precarious. They wished to use the church, the school, and whatever other means of propaganda were at their disposal, to buttress the claims of the Elect, politically, and theologically. Yet the advances of the prevailing economic system, and the spirit and philosophy accompanying it, rendered their task most difficult. . . .

To meet this situation the educators offered improved common schools. By avoiding the conflict over the nature of man and every other ticklish issue that did not force its way into the discussion, they gathered the necessary support in at least three states — New York, Massachusetts, and Connecticut. The businessmen and property-owners generally were approached in the name of their own protection. The warring sects of Christendom were appeased with *Bible*-reading in "non-sectarian" schools. The workingmen and shopkeepers, who asked for a better living and for a realization of their theoretically enjoyed "equal rights," were given some concessions and the advice that education rather than political action would lead to the Promised Land.

Very little was said to the farmer, and he was more a hindrance than a help in the struggle for better schools. For he was suspicious of "book-farming," city people, and anything requiring cash out of his pocket. . . .

The youth of the colleges, on the other hand, received particular attention. For the intellectual leadership had to be perpetuated in ideas as well as in physical existence.[53]

The West — the Rising Power of Agrarian Democracy

In the triangular struggle for economic well-being and political power — for place, position, prestige, and cultural advance — which characterized the period from 1830 to 1860, western farmers were to measure their strength with southern planters and eastern capitalists. Then, as always, the West was a difficult geographical area to define, but the West which sent Jackson to the White House in 1828 may be thought of as comprising the Northwest and the Southwest, as well as the older western states of Tennessee, Kentucky, and Ohio. The Southwest was soon to be drawn within the orbit of the southern system — indeed, to become the heart of the cotton kingdom — but, for the moment, if voting for Jackson was a criterion, it stood solidly in the ranks of the West. Western in sentiment, too, if not in geographical location, were the large numbers

[53] Sidney L. Jackson, *America's Struggle for Free Schools: Social Tension and Education in New England and New York, 1827–42* (Washington, D.C.: American Council on Public Affairs, 1941), p. 172.

of small farmers in the back-country South and the western counties of the Middle and New England states. In time, the Southwest, as suggested above, became more southern than western in interests and sentiment, and the Northwest expanded to include Michigan, Iowa, Wisconsin, Minnesota, Kansas, and Nebraska.

THE CHARACTERISTICS OF WESTERN SOCIETY

While the spread of slavery and the plantation system was working an economic, social, and political revolution in the South, and while capitalistic enterprise and the factory system were bringing about a revolution no less important in the East, the West was attracting a multitude of small farmers. Before the opening of the Erie Canal (1825), New England had fought practically every measure calculated to promote western development, but despite this opposition each year saw thousands of new settlers pushing on into the land of the "western waters," buying cheap lands from the government or "squatting" without taking the trouble of securing a title. At first, the settlers came largely from the back-country South, where the principles of Jeffersonian democracy had taken deep root, from Kentucky and Tennessee, and from western Pennsylvania and New York. Later, thousands from New England and from Europe, especially Germany, joined the western movement. By 1830, some 4,000,000 of the 12,500,000 people comprising the population of the nation lived in the West, while another 2,000,000, in the western parts of New York, Pennsylvania, Virginia, the Carolinas, and Georgia, were in reality western in interests and sentiment.[54]

Although the plantation system was beginning to eat its way into the lower Mississippi Valley, the West in 1830 was essentially a land of small farmers. The small, family-sized farm was to continue to dominate the Northwest during the whole of the period. In 1850, for example, the average number of acres per farm in Ohio was 125 and the average number of improved acres per farm was 68.5. In no northwestern state did the average farm include more than 185 acres, nor did the number of improved acres per farm, on the average, exceed 70.[55] In 1830, life in the West was harder and less romantic than we now sometimes suppose. Land, to be sure, was fertile and relatively cheap in terms of dollars, but even so the average settler from the East was not able to obtain and develop a farm without great effort and hardship. Turner estimates that a pioneer who obtained title from the government of a 160-acre tract,

[54] Dodd, *Expansion and Conflict, op. cit.,* p. 28. See also United States Bureau of the Census, *Historical Statistics of the United States, 1789–1945* (Washington, D.C.: Government Printing Office, 1949).

[55] Frederick Jackson Turner, *The United States, 1830–1850: The Nation and Its Sections* (New York: Henry Holt & Co., 1935), p. 298.

built a log cabin, improved half of his tract, bought stock and tools, and sustained his family until the first crop was harvested would need about one thousand dollars.[56] And one thousand dollars was not easy to get. The farmer could grow plenty of food, and his log cabin and homespun clothes would keep him warm, but to get his hands on cash was another matter. Unless he lived near a river, it was next to impossible to find a market for his surplus wheat, corn, hogs, or cattle. Now and then, along with his neighbors, he would send a drove of cattle and hogs into the South and sell them to the cotton planters, or to Baltimore and Philadelphia or other eastern cities in search of a market. But the amount of cash that passed through his hands was small, rarely totaling more than ten dollars per capita each year.[57] Despite a crude plenty, the economic structure of the West was weak. The farmer was often in debt to the government for his farm or to the eastern bankers who had supplied him, directly or indirectly, with the necessary funds to get started. If he was a "squatter" he was haunted by the fear of dispossession. Until there was improvement in economic conditions, there would be little money for the support of schools or other agencies of cultural advance. Economic improvement depended upon markets, and markets could not be opened up without internal improvements in the form of turnpikes, canals, or railroads. Most Westerners, like Lincoln, had been born in a log cabin, and to them life was still hard. As we shall see, however, they developed a program, and every year saw them register a gain over the South and Northeast in numerical importance.

The western farmers entertained a political and social philosophy strikingly different from that of the eastern capitalists and southern planters. Many of them had come from a stock that had accepted the ideals of Jefferson, and frontier conditions had served to deepen their faith. Here men both believed in and practiced political democracy. In their daily lives they exhibited their loyalty to the ideals of equality of opportunity and social mobility. To be sure, the Westerner did not believe in equality of condition; like everyone else in America, he was exploitative and acquisitive. He knew that men of talent and energy would get ahead and he was determined that merit should have its reward. At a time when the southern planters were flouting the principles of the Declaration of Independence and the eastern capitalists, with much the same social philosophy, were devising ways and means to protect themselves from too much democracy, the western farmers were asserting the rights of the common man and rising in revolt against the pretensions of aristocracy. Nothing was so damaging to a candidate for public office as to have plain people feel that he belonged to a superior social class. Individualism was a high

[56] *Ibid.*, p. 297. See also Hacker, *op. cit.*, p. 202–203.
[57] Dodd, *Expansion and Conflict, op. cit.*, p. 31.

component of democracy; freedom from restraint of any kind was still considered an essential condition of democracy by most persons. If the plain people of the West were little given to abstract thinking about democracy, and if they exhibited no great concern about the condition of either the black slave of the South or the wage slave in the East, they nevertheless believed in democracy for themselves and they employed its principles and its dogma in their struggle with the other two great sections of the nation for economic advance and political power.

THE STRATEGY OF POLITICS

The election of Andrew Jackson to the presidency in 1828 represented the emergence of the democratic state, the passage of political power from the hands of men of prestige and property to those of the common people. The old general was not elected because his position on the important political issues of the day were widely known and approved. No one, perhaps not even Jackson himself, knew just where he stood. Southern planters supported him because they hoped he would be favorable to their interests, and because they saw that an alliance with the West was essential if the South was not to be isolated in the political life of the nation. Western men throughout the length of the Mississippi Valley and small farmers in the back-country South and Pennsylvania were bent on overthrowing the old Jeffersonian machine, which had become conservative, and on placing in the White House a man who, in their own minds at least, was the perfect embodiment of the common people. "King Numbers" had come into power and the West was the seat of his empire.

The West was not content to raise one of its sons to the presidency; it had its grievances and its interests, and it formulated a program no less specific than that of the South or the East. Above all else, perhaps, the West wanted legislation which would dispose of the public domain on easier terms for the settler. The price of land must be lowered, or, better still, homesteads be given to those who would come and take them. Laws were required, too, to confirm the rights of the squatter to the land he had taken and improved without legal title. The West was always imperialistic, always ready to join the South in extending our borders westward and in adding new acres to the national domain. It demanded internal improvements at national expense — roads and canals over which surplus commodities could find a market. The West was also in favor of a monetary policy that would provide cheap money, not to say inflation. Since farmers were commonly in debt to eastern banking interests, a bountiful supply of bank notes would raise prices and relieve their distress. Naturally enough, the farmers supported Jackson in his war on the United

States Bank and later approved a system of state banks that all but nullified the constitutional prohibition against a state's coining money or issuing bills of credit. And, finally, on the great issue of the tariff, the West, though not always unanimous, was disposed most of the time to go along with the South in favor of low duties. On most of the important issues of the day — tariffs, internal improvements, the disposition of western lands, banking policy, territorial expansion — the two great agricultural sections, the West and the South, had much in common. They did not agree on all issues, nor did the West maintain its allegiance to the South against the Northeast at all times. During most of the period, however, the southern planters and the western farmers found enough in common to cause them to work together to prevent the national government from falling into the hands of the eastern manufacturing and financial interests.

THE GROWTH OF ECONOMIC POWER AND THE SHIFT OF POLITICAL ALLEGIANCE

The development of transportation facilities in the West, together with the invention of machinery for the planting and harvesting of grain, brought an economic revolution comparable to that which was taking place in the South and the East. In 1825 the Erie Canal linked New York City with the Great Lakes region and provided an outlet for an ever increasing quantity of grain. When Jackson was elected President, the annual tonnage of the Great Lakes was less than 6000; by 1851, the value of the trade passing through the Erie Canal was $300,000,000.[58]

In 1834, the Pennsylvania system of canals connecting Philadelphia with the West was also completed.[59] Ohio, Indiana, and Illinois, in their turn, launched upon expansive programs of canal construction. But the railroad era was at hand. The Erie Canal made obvious the great commercial possibilities that lay in the expanding wheat fields of the West, and it was not long before eastern capitalists began to push their railroad lines in that direction. In 1851 the Erie Railroad connected New York City with Dunkirk on Lake Erie. The following year the Baltimore and Ohio pushed its line over the mountains to Wheeling, West Virginia.[60] During the decade 1850 to 1860, some seventy-five hundred miles of railroad were built in the Northwest. The eastern financiers and capitalists were bringing into the orbit of their economic system the rising cities of the Northwest — Cleveland, Detroit, Chicago, Milwaukee, St. Louis, Cincinnati, Indianapolis, and Columbus.

While the building of canals and railroads was opening up expanding markets for western grain, inventions of farm machinery in the

---

[58] Turner, *op. cit.,* p. 311.   [59] Beard and Beard, *op. cit.,* p. 636.
[60] Kirkland, *op. cit.,* p. 249. See also Hacker, *op. cit.,* pp. 231–234.

eighteen-forties — seed drills, reapers, and threshers — were making grain the great staple crop of the Northwest in much the same way that the invention of the cotton gin had made cotton the staple crop of the South. In the single decade between 1850 and 1860, the value of the wheat and corn crops of the Northwest increased from $80,000,000 to $225,000,-000.[61] In this connection, it may be well to recall that the value of the three great staple crops of the South in 1860 — cotton, tobacco, and sugar — amounted to about $300,000,000. During these years the Northwest was laying the economic basis on which the structure of a well-supported educational system was in time to be erected.

The upper Mississippi Valley had become the granary of the nation and a center for the production of hogs and cattle; it was also becoming industrialized. Eastern capitalists, bankers, and merchants saw in the West a profitable field for the investment of surplus capital. Not a few men in the West itself were turning from agriculture to industry. In 1850, Ohio stood second to Pennsylvania in the production of pig iron, and ten years later, one-fourth of the woolen factories in the nation were located in the West.[62] Cincinnati, St. Louis, and Chicago were already to be numbered among the nation's great urban centers, and many smaller places were beginning to pulsate with the vigor of industrial growth.

As canals and railroads opened up the eastern markets to western products and as the commerce of the West shifted from the South to the East, the upper Mississippi Valley was gradually drawn into the economic orbit of the East and into the pattern of cultural arrangements that an expanding industrial economy was weaving. The ties that had long bound the agricultural Northwest to the agricultural South were weakening. Until 1860 the Northwest continued, by and large, to vote the Democratic ticket, but the time for a political realignment was at hand. In that year, as we have already seen, the newly formed Republican party compounded the economic interests of the Northeast and the Northwest and became the carrier of deep-seated emotional drives of both sections against the South. The Civil War was to follow and in its wake came the passing of the dominance of rural America. An industrial society was about to come of age.[63]

THE SCHOOL AS AN AGENCY OF SOCIALIZATION

Education in the West was slow to develop on a large scale, but from the beginning its purposes and its ideals were more genuinely democratic than was the case in either the South or the East. There was nothing of

[61] Dodd, *Expansion and Conflict, op. cit.,* p. 201. See also Hacker, *op. cit.,* pp. 223–226.

[62] Turner, *op. cit.,* p. 306; Beard and Beard, *op. cit.,* p. 638.

[63] Hacker, *op. cit.,* pp. 400–405, 437–438.

the southern purpose to socialize youth to take their places in a democracy based on caste like ancient Athens, and there was little of the eastern purpose to make education a means of creating acquiescence on the part of the laboring classes to the existing pattern of economic arrangements. In the West there was greater emphasis on the preparation of youth to perform their civic duties in a democratic republic, and education was designed more than elsewhere to prevent the rise of social classes, to make social mobility a reality, and to release the moral and intellectual capacities of the individual.

Questions and Problems for Study and Discussion

1. In what sense is it true that the major regions of the nation — East, South, and West — underwent an "economic and social revolution" during the period 1828–1860?

2. How was the growing sectionalism of the period related to the social and economic changes, and what were its effects?

3. What changes did the economic revolution in the South bring about in the social philosophy of the section? How did the South's new social theory affect educational policy and practice?

4. In what ways did the rise of cities in the industrial Northeast stimulate the development of education? What were the motives of the supporters of public education in the Northeast?

5. Evaluate the influence of organized labor on the development of American education during the period.

6. Characterize the social outlook of the West during the period. Evaluate the influence of this outlook on education.

7. It has been stated that the period was characterized by the "rise of the common man." Discuss.

Selected References for Further Reading

Beard, Charles A., and Beard, Mary R. *The Rise of American Civilization,* I: *The Agricultural Era.* New York: The Macmillan Co., 1927. Pp. 824.

Carlton, Frank Tracy. *Economic Influences upon Educational Progress in the United States, 1820–1850,* Reprinted from the Bulletin of the University of Wisconsin, Economics and Political Science Series, IV, No. 1. Madison, Wis.: University of Wisconsin, 1908. Pp. 136.

Commager, Henry Steele. *The Era of Reform, 1830–1860.* Princeton, N.J.: D. Van Nostrand Co., Inc. (Anvil Books), 1960. Pp. 192.

Craven, Avery. *The Coming of the Civil War.* Chicago: University of Chicago Press, 1957. Pp. xvii + 491.

Craven, Avery. *The Growth of Southern Nationalism, 1848–1861,* History of the South Series. Baton Rouge, La.: Louisiana State University Press, 1953. Pp. xi + 433.

Curti, Merle. *The Growth of American Thought,* Second Edition. New York: Harper & Brothers, 1951. Pp. xvii + 910.

Curti, Merle. *The Social Ideas of American Educators, with a New Chapter on the Last Twenty-five Years.* Paterson, N.J.: Pageant Books, Inc., 1959. Pp. xliv + 613.

Dodd, William E. *The Cotton Kingdom: A Chronicle of the Old South,* The Chronicles of America Series, XXVII. New Haven, Conn.: Yale University Press, 1919. Pp. x + 162.

Dodd, William E. *Expansion and Conflict.* Boston: Houghton Mifflin Company, 1915. Pp. xii + 330 + xxiv.

Dulles, Foster R. *Labor in America: A History,* Growth of America Series. New York: Thomas Y. Crowell Company, 1949. Pp. 402.

Eaton, Clement. *A History of the Old South.* New York: The Macmillan Co., 1949. Pp. ix + 636.

Elkins, Stanley M. *Slavery: A Problem in American Institutional and Intellectual Life.* Chicago: University of Chicago Press, 1959. Pp. 247.

Fish, Carl Russell. *The Rise of the Common Man, 1830–1860,* A History of American Life, VI. New York: The Macmillan Co., 1927. Pp. xx + 392.

Fitzhugh, George. *Sociology for the South: Or the Failure of Free Society.* Richmond, Va.: A. Morris, 1854. Pp. vi + 310.

Gray, Lewis Cecil. *History of Agriculture in the Southern United States to 1860,* I. Washington, D.C.: Carnegie Institution of Washington, 1933. Pp. xx + 568.

Hacker, Louis M. *The Triumph of American Capitalism: The Development of Forces in American History to the End of the Nineteenth Century.* New York: Columbia University Press, 1947. Pp. 460.

Hugins, Walter. *Jacksonian Democracy and the Working Class: A Study of the New York Workingmen's Movement, 1829–1837,* Stanford University Studies in History, Economics, and Political Science, No. 19. Stanford, Cal.: Stanford University Press, 1960. Pp. 286.

Jackson, Sidney L. *America's Struggle for Free Schools: Social Tension and Education in New England and New York, 1827–42.* Washington, D.C.: American Council on Public Affairs, 1941. Pp. viii + 276.

Morison, Samuel Eliot, and Commager, Henry Steele. *The Growth of the American Republic.* New York: Oxford University Press, 1930. Pp. viii + 956.

Nevins, Allan. *The Ordeal of the Union.* 5 vols. I: *Fruits of Manifest Destiny, 1847–1852;* II: *A House Dividing, 1852–1857.* New York: Charles Scribner's Sons, 1959. Pp. xiv + 593; viii + 590.

Olmsted, Frederick Law. *The Cotton Kingdom: A Traveller's Observations on Cotton and Slavery in the American Slave States; based upon Three Former Volumes of Journeys and Investigations by the Same Author,* ed. Arthur M. Schlesinger, Jr. New York: Alfred A. Knopf, Inc., 1953. Pp. lxiii + 626.

Parrington, Vernon Louis. *Main Currents in American Thought: An Interpretation of American Literature from the Beginnings to 1920,* II: *The Romantic Revolution in America, 1800–1860.* New York: Harcourt, Brace & Co., 1927. Pp. xxii + 494. Also published in paperback (New York: Harcourt, Brace & Co. [Harvest Books], 1961).

Schlesinger, Arthur M., Jr. *The Age of Jackson.* Boston: Little, Brown & Co., 1945. Pp. xiv + 577. Also published in paperback (New York: New American Library of World Literature, Inc. [Mentor Books], 1961).

Soule, George, and Carosso, Vincent P. *American Economic History.* New York: Dryden Press, 1957. Pp. xvii + 654.

Sydnor, Charles. *The Development of Southern Sectionalism, 1819–1849.* Baton Rouge, La.: Louisiana State University Press, 1948. Pp. xii + 400.

Taylor, George R. *The Transportation Revolution, 1815–1860.* New York: Rinehart & Company, Inc., 1951. Pp. xvii + 490.

Turner, Frederick Jackson. *The United States, 1830–1850: The Nation and Its Sections.* New York: Henry Holt & Co., 1935. Pp. x + 602.

Van Deusen, Glyndon G. *The Jacksonian Era, 1824–1848,* New American Nation Series. New York: Harper & Brothers, 1959. Pp. 291.

Wender, Herbert. *Southern Commercial Conventions, 1837–1859.* Baltimore, Md.: Johns Hopkins Press, 1930. Pp. 240.

Wright, Chester W. *Economic History of the United States.* New York: McGraw-Hill Book Co., Inc., 1941. Pp. xxviii + 1120.

9

Education in the Emerging Democratic State: The Struggle for a System of Public Education, 1828–1860

The Opportunity for Education at the Beginning of the Period

Historians agree that the progress of public education during the three decades which preceded the Civil War was truly remarkable. However, considerable disagreement exists among them with respect to how deeply the several states, during the period or at its close, were committed to a system of tuitionless schools open to all children and fully controlled and supported by the state. An exaggerated view of the progress of the development of state school systems has resulted, partly from the tendency to assume that the acts of state legislatures and the provisions of state constitutions were immediately implemented. This exaggeration has been further fostered by failure on the part of some investigators to understand that the word "public" as used in reports of the period had various meanings and was, in many instances, used to describe schools supported almost entirely by tuition. In general, it appears that those states which made strong legal provisions for the establishment of state school systems have been credited with greater achievements than they actually attained. On the other hand, there has been, in some instances, a tendency to discount the educational programs of the states which failed to make strong statutory provisions for public schools. The states' educational arrangements were many and varied, and in their variety they reflected the many different stages through which education passed as it moved slowly toward full state support and jurisdiction. Although forces long at work had in most parts of the country created the general expectation that all children should learn to read and write, it was not accepted, even in New England, that education should be provided free to those children whose parents were able to pay for it. In fact, as late as 1840 only about one-half of the children of New England were provided free education, one-sixth of those of the West, and one-seventh of those of the Middle States.[1]

Although some states, particularly in New England, permitted districts to levy taxes for the support of schools, "public schools" were supported in the main by returns from rate bills levied against the patrons of the schools and from the meager revenues received from state-school funds. The most important of these was the permanent fund of Connecticut, which was derived largely from the sale of lands in the Western Reserve. In the West some legislation and much hope centered about the "sixteenth section" of land which had been set aside for education, but this section of unimproved land failed, in a country characterized by low land values, to provide schools or funds for schools in keeping with the expectations of optimistic thinking.

In all parts of the country, even in those areas in which tax support was permitted, the public schools were a reproach to the democracy which fostered them. Conditions in Massachusetts, a state in which school maintenance was required by law and perhaps provided to a greater degree by taxation than elsewhere, led a reviewer of Carter's *Essays upon Popular Education* to complain that the common schools were degraded, held in low esteem by their warmest friends, and considered worthy of attendance only by children of the artisan and laboring class.[2] Although more or less grudgingly supported by men of means, public schools were not commonly patronized by the upper classes; nor can it be stated that they found general favor among the poor. Schools, particularly primary schools, however, were accessible in Massachusetts and in other parts of New England to those who would attend. The total costs of operating these schools, approximately two dollars per week for summer schools and from six to ten dollars per week for winter schools, indicate the background for contemporary complaints that teaching positions were either considered as steppingstones to better-rewarded activities or as licensed refuges of the incompetent. An article, based largely on the *Report of the Committee of the Society for the Improvement of Common Schools in*

---

[1] *The Seventh Census of the United States: 1850 . . . Compendium*, pp. 150–151. See also Herman G. Richey, "Reappraisal of the State School Systems of the Pre-Civil-War Period," *Elementary School Journal*, XLI (October, 1940), 118–129.

[2] *Remarks upon Mr. Carter's Outline of an Institution for the Education of Teachers* (Boston: Bowles and Dearborn, 1827), p. 9.

Connecticut, 1828, and the *Report of the School Convention (Hartford), 1831,* stated:

> The average compensation, in addition to board, is about $11 a month for male teachers, and a dollar a week for females. Many females, however, of considerable experience, teach at 75 cents a week; and some whose experience is less at 62½, or even 50. Many board themselves and teach for one dollar; as it is generally supposed that a female instructor can earn enough at some other employment, during the intervals between school hours, to pay for her board. . . .
>
> One of the greatest evils which exist in connection with the common schools of Connecticut, is a *perpetual change of teachers.*[3]

In other parts of the country, with the possible exception of New York State, conditions with respect to public education were even worse. In New York City there was no provision for public schools, but there, as in Philadelphia and other large cities, philanthropic societies contributed toward the education in non-sectarian schools of children not provided for by the churches and church organizations. In 1800 New York was a city of some sixty-thousand population, but it had no schools other than those provided privately or by churches. Five years later, however, the New York Free School Society was organized, under the leadership of De Witt Clinton, and until its work was completed in 1853 it spent each year increasingly larger amounts on its system of Lancasterian schools, which provided a free, if extremely meager, education to thousands of children.

In Pennsylvania conditions varied considerably. Here the desire of each religious sect to provide instruction in its own faith led to the establishment of denominational schools wherever churches were financially able. Outside Philadelphia chief dependence was placed upon these parochial schools, some of which, such as those of the Quakers and Moravians, must be considered by the standards of the time as generally adequate. Even pauper education was not available on a large scale. Where it was available, it was often not acceptable to a large number of that part of the poor who were unable or unwilling to pay tuition charges. Whole communities were without educational facilities of any kind except those provided in homes in which the parents generally possessed the most meager academic background and little enthusiasm for intellectual attainments.

In the South the greatest diversity existed. From early colonial times the theory had prevailed in this region that parents, without compulsion, would educate their children to their proper station in life. Tutors were employed by persons of means, and considerable opportunity was provided through private schools for children whose parents could pay mod-

[3] "Common School System of Connecticut," *American Annals of Education and Instruction,* II (April, 1832), 202.

est fees. Some concern was shown for paupers and other dependents, but little provision was made for the ordinary poor who were unable or unwilling to pay for their education. When schools were organized for the poor, the children of the well-to-do did not attend.

In the West "a faith in and a tradition for education constituted the chief educational assets." Perhaps less opportunity to attend schools, private and public, was provided in this area than in any other section, the South included. The situation in the new states, aggravated as it was by frontier conditions, poverty, and an optimistic dependence upon the income from permanent funds and school lands, was such that most children went without any schooling and only a few were able to attain an education of substantial quality.

Throughout the country at the beginning of this period, opportunities for an education beyond the rudiments were thinly if rather widely distributed. Although satisfactory statistics are not available, it appears that the opportunities for secondary education, as in the case of elementary education, were most numerous in New England. In this region, however, as well as elsewhere, the great popularity of the academy is evidence of the widespread acceptance of the idea that the responsibility for education rested upon the parent. Here, however, were found the old Latin or grammar schools, with a history extending over two hundred years. Here also, beginning in the eighteen-twenties, a few high schools were established. The Massachusetts law of 1827 required towns of five hundred or more families to establish tax-supported high schools. By 1840 a few high schools had been established in New York, Vermont, Maine, Pennsylvania, South Carolina, and Connecticut, but the academies, seminaries, and other private schools were by far the most important secondary schools throughout the entire period. Although the many academies and private institutions which thrived in the more heavily populated centers taught many secondary, vocational, and higher subjects to a larger and larger number of youth, they were barely tapping the great reservoir of potential learners.

The opportunities for education above the secondary schools were generally poor in quality and limited in extent. Although more than twice as many colleges were established in the decade preceding 1830 as had been organized during the entire colonial period, the increase in numbers was more remarkable than the growth of any of these institutions. The great day of college building lay in the future. In 1830 most of the colleges were the result of denominational pride and, at least in theory, retained their original purpose of educating clergy in the true faith. The University of North Carolina had been brought under complete state control in 1821, Virginia had established its university in 1825, and in the western states land grants for the aid of higher education had stimulated the laying of the foundations upon which state universities were to rise;

but the period just beginning was to be noted for denominational rather than state activity. Whether state or denominational, the colleges were generally small and lacking in facilities. Fees were usually charged and, although they were not large, they were probably important factors in keeping down the enrollment. For the most part the courses were grounded in Latin, Greek, and mathematics. New subjects such as science and literature began to find a place, not so much by any fundamental reorganization of the curriculum as by the curtailment of the requirements in theology and logic. To offset this, theological seminaries were springing up to provide prospective ministers with the training which was not given in sufficient measure by the colleges. At the beginning of the period, professional training except for the ministry was still very largely a matter of apprenticeship. The organization of professional training, however, had begun. A few previously established law and medical schools, together with new ones now being opened in connection with a few of the colleges, were attracting students whose training gave them a certain amount of prestige over those who learned their profession by "reading law" in the office of a successful lawyer or by assisting in the routines of the medical practitioner. Here and there, particularly in Rensselaer and Franklin institutes, scientific and technical training was available, but for all except the very few such training was acquired through the more difficult and laborious means of apprenticeship and self-instruction. Trades were taught in private schools established in the larger towns and cities, but few persons destined for the trades ever had the advantages of such instruction. In 1830 no provision had been made for the education of women above the secondary level, but within three years the opening of Oberlin was to mark the beginning of a great coeducational experiment.

Urbanism and Humanitarianism

The leaders of the educational awakening of the fourth and fifth decades of the nineteenth century were motivated by the same humanitarianism which prompted an unusually large number of persons of that generation to strive against all the forces which were debasing man and to aid, with almost missionary zeal, in any movement which promised human betterment. Among these enthusiasts, some stressed the social benefits to be derived from the reform of the administration of penal institutions, some worked to promote temperance or abolition, some urged the training of the deaf and dumb, and still others engaged in one or more of the numerous reform activities of the day. Whatever their field of interest, nearly all the reformers had one thing in common. They were characterized by an almost blind faith in the power of education to improve the individual and to eliminate social evils, and almost to a man they were active supporters of the public school movement.

Although these reformers were spiritual descendants of the eighteenth-century liberals, their program, in regard to both direction and significance, to a considerable degree arose from a growing urbanism. Most of their support came, directly or indirectly, from the rapidly expanding towns and cities, in which an articulate middle class and a much larger group with middle-class aspirations were coming to be an increasingly important element. Nor did the reformers appear on the scene too soon. For decades changes had been occurring in the economic life of the nation creating problems of a social and political nature which necessitated sweeping modifications in the existing institutions.

The Industrial Revolution had changed more than long-practiced methods of production; it had also changed ways of living and thinking. In New England and the Middle States cities sprang up, rising in the midst of a type of squalor unknown to an earlier agricultural society. Farm boys and girls, men and women, were drawn from the farms to become operatives in the newly established mills and factories. But the factories were spreading more rapidly than the social insight needed to solve the problems which they created.

It was in the rapidly growing urban centers that the inadequacies of the institutions which had served the old order first became apparent. The disintegration of the old rural economy and the crowding of thousands of people into unsanitary and hideous factory towns and cities, with consequent loss of social restraints, created conditions which would have been generally recognized as a national disgrace if there had been a real social consciousness. Intemperance, poverty, sickness, disease, crime, and moral decay thrived in the new urban communities. Illiterate and unruly children roamed the city streets uncared for and considered only as potential workers in factories which took them at a tender age. The employers of young workers were looked upon as public benefactors because they kept small boys and girls from idleness and from succumbing to criminal tendencies during the ten to thirteen working hours of the day. Children were not the only economic assets. The mother also was likely to be employed at wages which, added to the income of the other members of the family, helped to provide a bare subsistence. At the same time, huge profits were rolled up on invested capital. The resulting conditions threatened a moral and social breakdown. To persons not "submerged in apathy or blinded by the prospects of rapidly acquiring wealth," far-reaching reforms seemed not only desirable but, on every consideration, necessary. Even in the field of politics there were persons who foresaw disaster if the quality of the slowly expanding electorate was not improved.

It was in the cities also that the accumulation of wealth made feasible reforms which required relatively large expenditures. Here, philanthropy, although failing, made its greatest bid to solve the educational problems of the new order, and here the first and most persistent demands for reform were heard. Reformers, statesmen, and other leaders who esteemed education as a means of curing the social, economic, and political ills came more and more, with each new evidence of the impotence of philanthropy, to demand free schools equally open to all as the only agency which could ameliorate these conditions.

It was also in the cities that the more articulate of the laboring classes, conscious of the strength which organization and the expanding suffrage gave them, added their voices in demanding a better education for their children than workers could finance privately. Moreover, the laboring classes were less and less inclined to accept education as a charity, even had this means of financing proved adequate. Between 1828 and 1832, the period of the workingmen's political parties, demands were heard for schools at public expense, for schools in which rich and poor would mingle on terms of equality, and for schools under boards directly responsible to the electorate. Labor leaders were also demanding competent teachers, infant schools, and some means for education beyond the rudiments.

So much have the demands of labor leaders and organizers impressed themselves upon the minds of historians that exaggerated claims have been made with respect to the influence of the laboring classes on the development of the American public school system. It has been claimed, for example, that "to the agitation of organized labor in the twenties and thirties . . . we owe the beginning of the public-school system"; that the public school system was created because of the insistence of the early trade-unionists; that "to this movement, more than to all other causes combined, is due the common school system"; and that "the vitality of the movement for tax-supported schools was derived, not from humanitarian leaders, but from the growing class of wage-earners."[4] The careful reader of Curoe's authoritative history of the educational attitudes and policies of organized labor in the United States must, however, be convinced that the workingmen's organizations were only contributing factors in a much wider movement for education and social reform. It is true that the workingmen's organizations did great service in educating "their own membership to the value of education, thus counteracting the inertia or cupidity of laboring parents, and changing apathy toward education into active interest"; in working "with other groups toward stirring up an interest in educational reform among the complacent members of legislatures and among the general public"; and in helping to develop "the idea that a voting citizen cannot discharge his obligations without a modicum

---

[4] As quoted in Philip R. V. Curoe, *Educational Attitudes and Policies of Organized Labor in the United States,* Teachers College Contributions to Education, No. 201 (New York: Teachers College, Columbia University, 1926), p. 31.

of education and some leisure for self-improvement."[5]   If these associations had accomplished no more than to move the indifferent in their own ranks toward an acceptance of public education, their contribution would have been considerable, for, as Noble has pointed out, free schools did not result from a proletarian upsurge.[6] The great masses were indifferent to education.[7] The men who led the fight for free schools had to battle the selfishness of the well-to-do, who were able to provide privately for their children and who looked upon taxation for social purposes as merely a legalized plundering of the rich for the benefit of the poor. More important still, perhaps, they had to overcome the apathy of the poor, who in protecting the "rights of the individual" — rights which they had never possessed — joined hands with the reactionaries to make the lot of children in the towns and cities scarcely less distressing than that of Negro youth born into another type of servitude. The battle for public education was half won when the masses had been educated to the point of insisting upon free schools open on equal terms to all children.

Although many of the social ills and maladjustments of the period were in a large measure the result of growing urbanism, it was the cities from which humanitarianism drew its strength, and it was in the cities that a class of persons was emerging from which members might be recruited in the struggle for education and reform. It was the influence of urbanism combined with the long-established tradition for education in New England and the presence there of the best educational programs existing at the time that account for the leadership of the East in advancing education. While it is true that the cities of the East made the greater progress, it is also true that all the cities were powerful forces and their influence extended far into the hinterland, in fact, throughout the entire length and breadth of the country. It was no accident that the "educational awakening" was first noted in the East, that New England, with a long history of state participation in education, yielded more readily to the impact of new forces, and that Massachusetts, which had dominated the larger part of New England from the early colonial period, led the way.

Preparing the Way for Free Public Schools

Many of the persons influenced by the humanitarian movement of the period followed strange enthusiasms with a tenacity deserving of a better

[5] *Ibid.*, pp. 190–191.

[6] Stuart G. Noble, *A History of American Education* (New York: Farrar and Rinehart, 1938), p. 150. One New England reformer of the period stated that the simplest way to disperse a mob would be to begin a speech on public schools. See also Adolphe E. Meyer, *An Educational History of the American People* (New York: McGraw-Hill Book Co., Inc., 1957), pp. 152–153.

[7] Edward H. Reisner, *Nationalism and Education Since 1789: A Social and Political History of Modern Education* (New York: The Macmillan Co., 1929), p. 378.

cause. Among the educational reformers there were those who mixed their zeal for public schools with hopes for millenniums to be achieved by many and varied means. Although not of single mind as a group, they were all but unanimous in voicing the great social and political heresy that education be liberally supported, even to the point of providing schools at public expense for all the children of the state. It was not easy to combat the sentiment against free public schools, whose enemies argued that education merely gave rise, on the part of those born to inferior positions, to futile aspirations; that class distinctions made for social cohesion; that the encouragement of indolence begot indolence; that the decrease of religious responsibility for education was not only unwise but immoral; that the rights of individuals should not be invaded, or parents divested of their natural authority; that no state could long withstand the financial strain involved in maintaining free schools; and that no lasting good was likely to result from implementing the dreams of impractical and sometimes agnostic visionaries. The drive which gave direction and strength to the movement, however, was provided by those persons whose fear of change had been replaced by an almost naïve faith in the power of education to reduce poverty and distress, to prevent child delinquency and crime, and to promote the well-being of the individual, the intelligent use of the suffrage, and the welfare and stability of the state.

Needless to say, the struggle for free schools was not won overnight. A generation was to pass before the idea became generally acceptable in the North. In the almost entirely agricultural South progress was even slower. Although rapid improvement was to be noted in all sections, particularly in the urban areas, the implementation of the ideal of free schools was largely the accomplishment of the last half of the nineteenth century. The work of promoting the cause of public education remained for a long time the task of an inspired minority, the members of which became expert proselytizers of their faith. They recruited influential personages as well as lesser persons, all of whom in the face of threatened social disintegration found the "struggle for schools an outlet for the pent-up feelings of foreboding disaster." They urged statesmen and public officials to positions in advance of those of their constituents. They made use of all means and methods to spread their faith — the daily press, journals, political parties, labor organizations, conventions, educational societies, and foreign examples.

With respect to the struggle to advance the cause of public schools, Cubberley makes the following summary statement:

> For this work of propaganda hundreds of School Societies, Lyceums, and Educational Organizations were organized; many conventions were held, and resolutions favoring state schools were adopted; many "Letters" and "Addresses to the Public" were written and published;

public-spirited citizens traveled over the country, making addresses to the people explaining the advantages of free state schools; many public-spirited men gave the best years of their lives to the state-school propaganda; and many governors sent communications on the subject to legislatures not yet convinced as to the desirability of state action. At each meeting of the legislatures for years a deluge of resolutions, memorials, and petitions for and against free schools met the members.[8]

THE AID OF PUBLIC OFFICIALS

The humanitarian influence of the times, the recognition of the new needs of society, and the pressure of educational reformers aroused men of influence to take advanced positions with respect to education. Most prominent among these were the governors of several states. Although the recommendations and demands of these governors for schools were not lacking in earlier years, they increased in frequency throughout the first third of the century. The extent to which such statements had become common by the beginning of the period is revealed by a quotation taken from an 1831 issue of the *Annals of Education*, the outstanding educational journal of the time.

We are happy to see that the governors of Maine, New York, Pennsylvania, Delaware, South Carolina, Ohio, and Illinois, in their recent messages to the Legislatures of those States, have adverted to common education: in some instances with peculiar emphasis. In addition to these, Gov. Trimble of Ohio, in his last message (Dec. 6, 1830) adverted with interest to the same subject.

The executive of Maine congratulates the members of the legislature on account of the progress and influence of "mental light and good morals among the people." Speaking of literary institutions generally, he says: "For the correct management and progressive improvement of these institutions we cannot feel too anxious, since on education depends so much of our happiness and the security of our free governments."

Gov. Throop, of New York, speaks in the most unqualified terms of the importance of general education to the happiness of a free people, and the very existence of free institutions. He rejoices that the public mind is beginning to awake on this great subject. After a recapitulation of the most important facts contained in the Superintendent's last Report, he says: "I feel confident that, under proper regulations, a vast amount of knowledge in arts and sciences, connected with agriculture and handicraft, which are simple in their principles and easily comprehended, might be taught to children during those years which are usually spent at common schools." He complains of a want of competent instructors, and of suitable books, for the purposes of the common schools.

Gov. Hamilton, of South Carolina, says that the only safe and effective

[8] Ellwood P. Cubberley, *Public Education in the United States: A Study and Interpretation of American Educational History*, Revised and Enlarged Edition (Boston: Houghton Mifflin Company, 1934), p. 167.

Agrarian system is the scheme of public education. This alone will secure to the poor their just rights; and he recommends the subject to the consideration of the legislature.

Gov. McArthur, of Ohio, insists that "intelligence alone is capable of self-government." He urges upon every member of the community, as a "solemn duty," attention to common schools.

The executive of Delaware urges in strongest terms the claims of primary education, from various considerations, especially from the fact that an enlightened public opinion is the only safeguard of a government like ours. He thinks, however, that legislation in that State has been carried far enough; and that an attempt to give further aid to the cause, by extending the system of taxation, would defeat the object intended.

Gov. Reynolds, of Illinois, suggests the importance of having our eyes fixed on the rising generation, in all our movements. His language on this subject is strong and emphatic, and his arguments incontrovertible. He speaks, especially, of the importance of having the intellectual growth "keep pace with the physical."

Gov. Wolf, of Pennsylvania, devotes a very considerable portion of his message to the same subject, taking a very liberal and extended view of its importance.[9]

Nor were governors the only public officials to advocate free schools. A number of the members of legislative bodies, both national and state, and men destined for even higher positions not only expressed their firm opinion on the subject, but also were often active in the organizations which were established to promote the wider diffusion of knowledge and the organization of state systems of education.

THE INFLUENCE OF EDUCATIONAL ORGANIZATIONS

Hundreds of organizations devoted to the promotion of free public schools sprang up in all sections and states of the nation. The direct influence of these educational societies and associations is difficult to measure, but fundamental educational reforms have been attributed to the efforts of several, such as the Pennsylvania Society for the Promotion of Public Schools and the American Institute of Instruction. Although the programs of these organizations varied somewhat in nature and in scope, all were directly focused upon spreading the free-school doctrine and upon the improvement of education. Among the scores of educational associations established, the two most important were the American Lyceum and the Western Academic Institute and Board of Education, later succeeded by the Western Literary Institute and College of Professional Teachers. These represented the organized propaganda for public education at its best, whether judged in terms of aims, organization, effective use of available means, or the character of the personnel of the proselytizing groups.

[9] *American Annals of Education,* I (March, 1831), 125.

The Western Literary Institute. In 1832 the Western Literary Institute and College of Professional Teachers succeeded the Western Academic Institute and Board of Education, which had been launched in Cincinnati in 1829 by Albert Pickett. The reorganized Institute was supported by such outstanding leaders as Lewis, Stowe, and Beecher. By 1835, auxiliary organizations had been established in Ohio, Indiana, Illinois, Missouri, Kentucky, Tennessee, Mississippi, and Louisiana. By 1840, auxiliaries had been formed in every state of the Union outside New England, with the exception of New York, New Jersey, Delaware, and Maryland. Each state organization was charged to form county associations within its state. Of this great society, it has been said by Cubberley:

> It raised money, employed an agent to visit the schools of the State, published its proceedings in good form, diffused information as to education, tried to elevate the character of teachers of the State, and repeatedly sent delegations to the legislature to ask for action. In addition it sent out lecturers to arouse the public, through its state auxiliaries it memorialized legislatures in behalf of schools, and enlisted the support of the newspapers for its work. For two years (1837–38) Pickett edited the *Western Academician and Journal of Education and Science,* which was published at Cincinnati as part of the propaganda work. It sent Professor Stowe to Europe to investigate education there, and on his return induced the legislature (1837) to print ten thousand copies of his *Report on Elementary Education in Europe* for distribution. . . . In 1836 it called a state convention in Ohio of the "Friends of Education," in 1837 induced the legislature to create the office of Superintendent of Common Schools, and in 1838 the culmination of its efforts came in what has been frequently called "the great school of law of Ohio." . . . It has been said of this institution that it was "the commencement of a new era in education in the West."[10]

The American Lyceum. The most widely known and perhaps the most useful of these organizations was the American Lyceum, organized by Josiah Holbrook in 1826 "for the improvement of its members in useful knowledge, and the advancement of popular education, by introducing uniformity and improvements in common schools, by becoming auxiliary to a board of education."[11]

Within two years of the Lyceum's foundation, the *Boston Advertiser* reported that more than fifty societies had been organized, and in 1829 Barnard noted that branches had been formed in nearly every state of the Union. It appears, however, that they were more numerous in New England than elsewhere.[12] On May 4, 1831, delegates from the state lyceums

[10] Cubberley, *op. cit.*, pp. 169–170.
[11] From a circular by Holbrook, as quoted in Cecil B. Hayes, *The American Lyceum: Its History and Contribution to Education,* United States Office of Education Bulletin 12 (Washington, D.C.: Government Printing Office, 1932), p. 3.
[12] Hayes, *op. cit.*, pp. 4–5.

of Maine, Massachusetts, and New York, together with representatives from Yale and Dickinson Colleges and of several county lyceums, met in New York City and organized a national lyceum.[13] By the time of the second annual meeting of this organization in May, 1832, it was reported that there were, in addition to numerous state and county lyceums, nine hundred such institutions in towns scattered throughout the United States. Although perhaps most of these were not large, memberships of two and three hundred were not uncommon. The Salem Lyceum, it is said, had twelve hundred members. Although they flourished in the East, they were also popular in the South and West. In 1832 Holbrook wrote concerning the importance of this institution in the western country, where he was then traveling, as follows:

> The lyceum system never presented itself to my view with so much grandeur or importance, as since my visit to Ohio, Indiana, Illinois, Missouri, Kentucky, and Tennessee, in each of which state meetings or conventions of the friends of education have been held, and measures adopted to organize State Lyceums, and to extend the system through the whole community. A unanimous opinion and strong feeling have been expressed, at every meeting, and by every individual, when any has been manifested upon the subject, in favor of the Lyceum, as peculiarly fitted to a new and thinly settled country; and it is perfectly evident, that nothing is wanting but a sufficient number of good agents, to act under the patronage of State and County Lyceums, to extend their operations and their blessings to nearly every family in this Western country while not more than a third part of them have the advantages of schools.[14]

As Hayes in his excellent study of the movement points out, neither the rather remote National Lyceum nor the state organizations functioned well as compared with the town lyceums, which touched intimately the lives of many people. The state and national organizations, however, were not without influence. The nine annual meetings of the National Lyceum were given over largely to a consideration of educational problems and of ways and means of promoting schools. A list of the chief topics presented to the first meeting for discussion is indicative of the interests and purposes of the organization:

1. What are the greatest desiderata in relation to the improvement of the common Schools?
2. What are the most eligible and practical means of advancing and perfecting the science of instruction?
3. To what extent is the monitorial system advisable and practicable in common Schools?

[13] *Ibid.*, p. 7.
[14] "Correspondence," *American Annals of Education and Instruction,* II (February, 1832), 110.

4. What is the most eligible plan of promoting education, by legislative enactments?

5. Ought manual labor Schools to be encouraged, and upon what general plan?

6. Should every boy who can devote his whole time to study until the age of 16, be put to the study of Latin and Greek, and if not, to what class should these languages be restricted?

7. To what extent may lectures be useful in common Schools?

8. To what extent can the natural sciences be advantageously introduced into common Schools?

9. The object and usefulness of town and district Lyceums?

10. What should be the object of County and State Lyceums, and how should they be formed?[15]

Throughout the entire existence of the National Lyceum, the problems of public education continued to be its chief consideration.[16] The ninth and last meeting was given over to a discussion of plans for a national educational convention, which met in Philadelphia in November, 1839.

Although after 1838 the lyceums more and more stressed adult improvement, they were active long after that date in the advancement of popular education. The service rendered the cause of public schools by the lyceum movement would be difficult to overestimate. The testimony is overwhelming that wherever local lyceums were established, interest in and concern for public education were soon manifested. Henry Barnard in 1838 wrote:

> The increase of active and well-conducted lyceums in this State [Connecticut] and at this season is much to be desired as one of the most direct and effectual means of directing the attention of the people to the importance of improving the schools.[17]

The lyceums aided in stirring parents from their general apathy toward education, long recognized as one of the most important obstacles to educational development. They also aided in resolving the conflicts of opposing groups. Holbrook wrote that they provided common ground on which, in the states north of the Ohio, the former Kentuckians, Tennesseans, Virginians, Carolinians, and Yankees could meet.[18] They were effective instruments in overcoming the hostility of the enemies of public education in Pennsylvania, where a vigorous public school movement was meeting the strong opposition of several powerful groups.[19]

[15] "American Lyceum," *American Annals of Education and Instruction,* I (June, 1831), 278–279.

[16] Henry Barnard, "The American Lyceum," *American Journal of Education,* XIV (September, 1864), 535–537.

[17] As quoted in Hayes, *op. cit.,* p. 37.

[18] "Correspondence," *American Annals of Education and Instruction, op. cit.,* 110.

[19] Henry Barnard, "Josiah Holbrook," *American Journal of Education,* VIII (March, 1860), 242.

Religious groups — Episcopalians, Methodists, Presbyterians, Quakers, Baptists, Catholics, and Lutherans — were able to cooperate in advancing the purposes of the lyceum and, at the same time, although incidentally, the interests of public education.

The cooperative action in support of education of persons of different habits, notions, philosophies, prejudices, and religious persuasions found expression in many ways. The lyceum attempted to find means by which the qualifications of teachers might be raised. It promoted the organization of teachers' associations. At least one county lyceum established a school for teachers. By various means, the necessity of providing better-trained teachers was kept constantly before the public. The lyceum was also a powerful force in promoting the establishment of state control over public education. Early in its existence, this organization was advocating state and county boards of education. State and county lyceums were attempting to perform some of the functions which the boards they sponsored performed after they had been organized. Many local lyceums in their constitutions expressed the idea that they would become auxiliary to the local board of education. Persons prominent in the affairs of the lyceum often became active in school affairs. The American Institute of Instruction was founded by such persons. Edward Everett, Governor of Massachusetts at the time of the creation of the State Board of Education, had been a vice-president of the National Lyceum from its founding. As already mentioned, this latter organization planned the national educational convention which met in Philadelphia in 1839. State and local branches supported and sometimes sponsored the educational conventions which were held in the various states and sections.

Educational conventions.   State conventions were held in Virginia, Tennessee, Indiana, Illinois, Kentucky, and other states. These conventions, although not following an exact pattern, engaged generally in one or several activities, among which the most common were preparing addresses to the people, developing plans of education, reporting on defects and needs of the schools, and preparing memorials to be submitted to the various state legislatures urging the more liberal support of education and the establishment of free schools.

EDUCATIONAL JOURNALISM

Necessary to the development of educational journalism was a professional-minded teaching group and a considerable measure of educational consciousness. Davis has gathered evidence to show that the reading public of the United States, during the first quarter of the nineteenth century, did not remain entirely ignorant of educational developments, either in Europe or at home.[20] Lay journals and newspapers treated a number of educational subjects, but of course they failed to go far enough beyond the interests of their readers to satisfy the ardent friends of education. These latter were witnessing the beginning of journalism in a number of special fields, none of which was, in their minds, so important as education.

Beginning with the *Academician* (1818–20) in 1818, some twenty educational journals were founded before 1840, but at this date only three were being published. Few continued publication more than a year or two. Notable exceptions were the *American Journal of Education* (1826–31), edited by William Russell; its successor, the *American Annals of Education* (1831–39), edited by W. C. Woodbridge; the *Common School Assistant* (1836–40), edited by J. Orville Taylor; Henry Barnard's *Connecticut Common School Journal,* published from 1838 to 1842 and revived in 1851; and the semimonthly *Common School Journal* (1839–52), edited by Horace Mann during the first ten years of its existence.

The educational journals of the period, although intended largely for teachers, aimed to interest a wider public in the extension of education. Along with discussions of methods of teaching and of school subjects, such as grammar, geography, and arithmetic, they presented articles advocating the education of girls, infant schools, mechanics' institutions, lending libraries, better-qualified teachers, and schools at all levels, both private and public. It appears, however, that in general their first consideration was the extension of common schools free to all children. Among the aims of these journals as stated by the editors may be found the purpose of awakening "the attention of our community to the frightful disproportion that exists between the want and the amount of education"; of securing "intelligent legislation upon the subject of common schools"; of improving and promoting the "elevated character of common schools"; of arousing "the community to a sense of the importance of education"; and of "disseminating among the masses" correct views with respect to the importance of education. It is obvious that educational journalism itself was in a large measure a product of the educational awakening. Nevertheless, it appears to have played at least a small part in promoting the cause of public schools.

THE INFLUENCE OF FOREIGN EXAMPLES

The acceptance of the public school idea, particularly its implications for a measure of state supervision, was further fostered by increased

[20] Sheldon Emmor Davis, *Educational Periodicals During the Nineteenth Century,* United States Bureau of Education Bulletin 28 (Washington, D.C.: Government Printing Office, 1919).

familiarity with European practices, which were becoming known in America largely through accounts in the newly established educational journals, but also through the reports of a number of Americans who had visited England, France, and the German states. The tendency to look to Europe for guidance is revealed in contemporary writings. For example, in 1828 one observer, who listed the advantages to be expected from the organization of a society for the improvement of education, wrote:

> Some measures for facilitating the extensive reception of *European works* on the various departments of education, and of transferring to our systems of instruction whatever might seem valuable in them, would be another object of attention with the society, and would afford opportunity of effecting extensive and permanent good.[21]

During the third decade of the nineteenth century, accounts by American travelers of the educational programs and arrangements of European countries, including the reforms of Pestalozzi and Fellenberg and the teachers' seminaries of Prussia, became available to teachers, educational reformers, and, in fact, the entire reading public. In 1832 there was published in France Victor Cousin's report to the French government on the condition of public education in Prussia and other German states — a report which influenced the reorganization of the French school system, and which was to become one of the most widely read documents in the history of education.[22] The part of Cousin's work which pertained to primary schools was translated into English and published in London in 1834 under the title *Report on the State of Public Instruction in Prussia.* This translation, republished in America, was described as "an account of the best school system in the world, by the first philosopher of the age."[23] Francis Bowen, Professor of Moral Philosophy at Harvard, called the American publication "a judicious and timely step, as the work contained the outlines, and even the minute details, of the most elaborate and complete system of common schools which had yet been devised in the civilized world."[24]

The *Report,* the first complete account of a European school system to be made available to Americans, came at a time when those who labored for the extension of state supervision and the improvement of the schools needed support in their efforts to limit the authority of the local district

[21] "Advantages to Be Expected from the Formation of a Society for the Improvement of Education," *American Journal of Education,* III (February, 1828), 84.

[22] Victor Cousin, *Rapport sur l'état de l'instruction publique dans quelques pays d'Allemagne, et particulièrement en Prusse* (Paris: Paul Renouard, 1835).

[23] "Notices of Books," *American Annals of Education,* V (April, 1835), 190.

[24] "Memoir of Edmund Dwight," *American Journal of Education,* IV (September, 1857), 14.

and to transfer some of its functions to the state. Not only did it give aid to those interested primarily in educational organization and administration, but also to those who saw the state-supported teachers' seminary as a necessary step toward the establishment of effective state systems.[25] The influence of the *Report* was widespread. There was scarcely an educational journal that did not reproduce large portions of it. Speakers also made use of it. Calvin Stowe, a member of an enlightened western group interested in improving instruction and promoting the establishment of schools, read a paper before a body of teachers in Columbus in 1836. In his lecture, which was published under the title "The Prussian System of Public Education and Its Applicability to the United States," he drew heavily upon Cousin's report. Walz, the historian of the German influence on American education, states that this lecture gave the clearest and most succinct account of the Prussian school system to be found in the literature at that time.[26] At the close of the paper, Stowe said of the Prussian system:

> It is impossible to contemplate the system without admiring the completeness and beauty of the plan — the wisdom, benevolence and good taste of its minutest regulations — and the promptness and efficiency with which every part of it is carried into execution.[27]

He was especially impressed with the provisions made in Prussia for the education of teachers, and in his lecture he urged the adoption of a similar policy in the United States. Partly due to Prussian example, American educators generally were coming to regard the training of teachers as essential in any adequate state program.

Stowe was instrumental somewhat later in making known to many Americans the essential features of the Prussian educational system. In 1836, the legislature of Ohio directed the governor to commission Stowe, who was going to Europe to buy a library for Lane Theological Seminary, to make a study of European school systems. Stowe made this study, and late in 1837 submitted a report to the legislature in which he dealt largely with the Prussian primary school and its counterpart, the teachers' seminary. Of the Prussian program he wrote that it was "in its great outlines, as nearly complete as human ingenuity and skill can make it; though undoubtedly some of its arrangements and details admit of improvement; and some changes will of course be necessary in adapting it to the circumstances of different countries."[28] This report was printed by the

[25] See Cubberley, *op. cit.*, pp. 357–359.
[26] John A. Walz, *German Influence in American Education and Culture* (Philadelphia: Carl Schurz Memorial Foundation, Inc., 1936), p. 18.
[27] *Ibid.*, p. 19.   [28] *Ibid.*, pp. 20–21.

legislature of Ohio and copies were sent to every school district in the state. Several other states also printed the document and circulated it widely.

Alexander D. Bache, sent to Europe by the trustees of Girard College, an institution for the care and education of orphans, after an extensive inspection of schools in Great Britain, Germany, Holland, France, Austria, and Switzerland was equally enthusiastic with respect to the German system, to which more than two hundred pages of his report, published in 1839, were devoted. Of the Prussian system of primary schools, he wrote:

> This is the most perfect of the centralized systems, allowing consider-able latitude in the arrangement of the individual schools, while all are subject to the influence of the central authority. It has not, as is com-monly supposed, recently sprung into existence, but has been the work of time, has been altered and amended, and is still in progress. Its pres-ent condition is the result of experience, and thus it commends itself to enlightened imitation, by which I mean that which, laying aside what is inapplicable to the political or social institutions of the country adopting it, would employ the large amount of useful material which it contains.[29]

Bache, Stowe, Taylor, and many other writers of the period did not share the fears of those who saw a threat to democracy in the adoption of the educational ideas of an absolute monarchy. In fact, American edu-cators expressed chagrin that a free government such as our own should in educational matters be so much less progressive than was the most absolute of European governments.

Of those to visit Europe, Barnard exerted perhaps the greatest influ-ence. For a full generation after his visit during the middle eighteen-thirties, he was ever outspoken in advocating the introduction "into our state school systems of the best European organizations and practices." As the most prolific writer on educational matters in the United States, he presented to the growing professional group, and to lay groups as well, excellent descriptions of educational organization in foreign states. Many of his articles which had appeared in magazine form were published in 1854 under the title *National Education in Europe*.

Among others to report on European systems of education, particularly the Prussian system, were Dr. H. Julius, Dr. Benjamin F. Smith, and Mann. Julius, at the suggestion of the Reverend Charles Brooks, appeared before the Committee on Education of the Massachusetts Legislature and gave a lucid account of the Prussian system. Smith, who had lived in Prus-

---

[29] Alex. Dallas Bache, *Report on Education in Europe, to the Trustees of the Girard College for Orphans* (Philadelphia: Lydia R. Bailey, 1839), pp. 171–172.

sia, at the request of Governor Campbell of Virginia prepared a report on the school system of that country. He drew both upon his own observations and upon those of others, particularly Stowe. Among other things, he dealt with the training of teachers, the machinery of administration, and general taxation for the support of education. Mann, who did not go to Europe until 1843, several years after the creation of the Board of Education in Massachusetts and the establishment of the state normal school, found much to admire in the Prussian system. His famous *Seventh Report*, in which he appraised what he had seen in such a manner as to place American practices in an unfavorable light by comparison, precipitated a bitter controversy with the Boston schoolmasters.

The amount of material dealing with the educational system of Prussia in the relatively new educational journals of the day is significant. The general diffusion of information concerning a system which was strongest in those very aspects in which American systems were least effective must have been an influential factor in the struggle to curb the power of local districts, provide state supervision, and establish state institutions for the training of teachers.

A GENERATION OF EDUCATIONAL STATESMEN

In listing the forces which promoted and gave direction to the public school movement, the influence of the group of educational reformers who went on to become educational statesmen would be difficult to overestimate. These persons, content to abandon the easier avenues of public service, instead dedicated their ability and capacity for leadership to blazing new trails that led to a more extended and better education for American children. Among these men, Mann, Barnard, and Wiley have received the greatest acclaim, but there were also others. In fact, in every section of the country there arose men of ability to give aid and direction to the movement for public schools.

James G. Carter. Perhaps more than any other person, James G. Carter prepared the way for the public school "revival" in Massachusetts and for its acclaimed leader, Horace Mann. After graduation from Harvard in 1820, Carter continued to teach and soon began to write on educational matters for the press. The leading thoughts of some of his articles written for the *Boston Transcript* were made the basis for a series of essays which appeared in pamphlet form in 1824 under the title *Letters to the Hon. William Prescott, LL.D., on the Free Schools of New England: With Remarks upon the Principles of Instruction.* In these essays Carter traced the history of educational legislation in Massachusetts, noted the decline of free schools, listed the causes of the impaired state of education, and made suggestions for the improvement of free schools.

He dealt at some length with the baneful and long-persisting influence of incompetent teachers, poor books, and an inadequate understanding of the science of education. "The success of our schools," he said, "depends as much on the principles by which they are governed, and the school books, as on the personal and literary qualifications of the instructor."[30] More specific proposals were made for the improvement of the educational system of Massachusetts in his widely read *Essays upon Popular Education,* which was published in 1826.

Carter presented a petition in 1827 to the legislature of Massachusetts asking for an appropriation for the establishment of a state normal school. A bill was introduced, but was lost in the Senate by one vote. He then opened a private school in Lancaster, but during the succeeding years he continued to work to arouse interest in the training of teachers. He was chosen a member of the House in 1835, served as chairman of the Committee on Education, and drafted the bill which created the State Board of Education. His name headed the list of the appointed members of the board. He was active in the organization of the American Institute of Instruction and for a time served as one of its officers.

Carter urged that education be considered a science. He stressed the importance of having pupils discover truth inductively and urged the views of Pestalozzi. His regard for Colburn's textbook on arithmetic led to a long discussion of it in the *Letters.*[31] He suggested inductive methods for the teaching of other subjects, particularly languages and geography. In collaboration with William H. Brooks, he attempted to apply the inductive method in an illustrated geography of Essex, Middlesex, and Worcester counties which was to lead up to the larger unit, the state.[32] His later years were spent in the eclipse of the more dynamic Horace Mann, who had been named secretary of the State Board of Education, a position for which, in the minds of most educators of the state, Carter was better fitted.

Horace Mann.   Horace Mann, more closely identified with the public school revival than any of his contemporaries, personified in many ways the social, educational, and moral movements arising from the ferment of the second quarter of the nineteenth century. The son of five generations of New England Puritans, he too was a Puritan, but one in whom the stern Calvinism of his early youth was sublimated in a zeal for human betterment and its corollary, an enthusiasm for education. Although by

---

30 James G. Carter, *Letters to the Hon. William Prescott, LL.D., on the Free Schools of New England: With Remarks upon the Principles of Instruction* (Boston: Cummings, Hilliard & Co., 1824), p. 60.

31 *Ibid.,* pp. 84–111.

32 See note on James G. Carter and William H. Brooks, *A Geography of Massachusetts; for Families and Schools,* in "Critical Notices," *American Journal of Education,* I (May, 1830), 211–213.

the age of ten he had learned the whole Calvinistic creed "and the dialectics by which it was maintained," at twelve he rejected the main tenets of that theology and later embraced Unitarianism as the better expression of his religious thought. His rejection of the Calvinistic theology was a step toward, and foreshadowed, his acceptance of the doctrine of the improvability of the human race, a belief clearly set forth in an oration, "The Gradual Advancement of the Human Species in Dignity and Happiness," delivered by Mann on the occasion of his graduation from Brown in 1819.[33]

Recent writers have contended, rightly, that Mann was entirely content to work within the framework of the existing capitalistic economy. It is unlikely that any other alternative presented itself to a reformer who believed implicitly in the revolutionary doctrine that through education man is an indefinitely perfectible being — a theory which was in the process of influencing, and which was destined to promote, wide-sweeping social change. Mann, convinced that most ills could be remedied by education, appealed, it is true, to his audiences with whatever arguments he thought most forceful to the occasion, but it should be noted that, although he urged education as a means of promoting industrial welfare and thus rather directly the welfare of the industrialists, he also urged, more emphatically and on more numerous occasions, education as a necessity for a republican form of government, as an instrument for equalizing opportunity, and as a means of saving people from vice, crime, and poverty. It was fortunate for the cause of public education that Mann never doubted certain generally accepted core values; never wavered in his esteem of knowledge; never joined with a minority group of contemporary reformers in seeking to escape the difficult social problems of the new order by attempting to re-establish the old, which had not been afflicted with the evils of industrialism; and never sought one of the shorter routes to Utopia, the "overgrown trails" which cross, but seldom parallel, the main path of social progress.

Mann appeared on the educational scene at the most opportune time. Industrialization, urbanism, and other kindred phenomena were creating new social conditions which made urgent, and at the same time possible, a new shaping of elementary education. It was fortunate that the indefatigable labors of Carter and others had prepared the way for Mann, even to the point of persuading the state legislature to create the State Board of Education in 1837. To be secretary of this board, Mann was called from a promising legal and political career, which had already brought

---

[33] See B. A. Hinsdale, *Horace Mann: And the Common School Revival in the United States* (New York: Charles Scribner's Sons, 1898); E. I. F. Williams, *Horace Mann, Educational Statesman* (New York: The Macmillan Co., 1937). Mann's wife gives the title of the oration as "The Progressive Character of the Human Race." See Mary Peabody Mann, *Life of Horace Mann,* Centennial Edition (Washington, D.C.: N.E.A., 1937), p. 28.

him to the presidency of the State Senate, but which he did not hesitate to renounce in favor of the opportunity to devote himself "to the supremest welfare of mankind upon earth," a service which was to occupy the twelve most active years of his life.

Although the cause of public education was nowhere strong, Massachusetts at the time Mann became secretary of the State Board of Education was threatened with the loss of her position of educational leadership. In fact, feeble developments in New York, recent permissive legislation in Pennsylvania, and the initial efforts of a few other states to adapt their educational programs to the needs of a society in which democracy was taking on new meaning threatened to make Massachusetts' pride in leadership nothing more than vain boasting of earlier glory. Within a few months after taking office, Mann disclosed the glaring defects in the system, which investigation at first hand had made apparent to him. He pointed to the poor quality of the school committees and charged that they were derelict in the performance of their duties. Little attention was paid to the laws concerning visitation and certification of teachers. One-third of the children dependent upon public schools for their education were absent in winter; two-fifths in summer. Inadequately trained teachers, teaching in schoolhouses unbelievably bad, and further handicapped by the apathy of the people, the multiplicity of texts, the lack of necessary facilities, the absence of libraries, and a term averaging less than seven months, created little enthusiasm for public schools, which were generally less highly regarded than private and sectarian ones.

Mann, fully aware that any long-term program of improvement would have to be based on popular acceptance, launched, immediately upon his acceptance of the secretaryship, the most intensive and sustained campaign for public education that had ever been engineered by one person. He made the most of the limited powers granted to the Board. He journeyed up and down the state, held educational conventions, promoted teachers' institutes, called upon men of prominence to support education, sponsored the establishment of the three first public normal schools, wrote twelve annual reports (which remain notable documents in the history of educational statesmanship), founded and edited for ten years the *Common School Journal,* and worked tirelessly for the improvement of the common schools. With respect to his accomplishments, his biographer wrote:

First, the campaign of education in Massachusetts that he conducted was thoroughly successful; the people of the State were converted again to that one of their ancient institutions in which their faith had most waned — their common schools. Secondly, the Board of Education and the Secretaryship were strongly entrenched in public confidence; before he laid down his office all serious danger of a backward step had passed away. Thirdly, the Normal schools, the teachers' institutes, the county associations, and school district libraries were founded and placed beyond the reach of hostile influences. Fourthly, the common schools made great material progress. The appropriations more than doubled; a sum in excess of $2,000,000 was spent in providing better schoolhouses and equipments; the wages of men teachers increased 62 per cent, of women teachers 51 per cent, while the relative number of women teachers had increased 54 per cent; a month was added to the average length of the school; the ratio of the private school expenditure to the public school expenditure fell from 75 per cent to 36 per cent; the compensation of school committees was made compulsory, and the supervision which they exercised over the schools improved in both quantity and quality; about 50 new high schools were established, thus restoring secondary teaching to large numbers of pupils. Fifthly, the schools improved in studies, in textbooks, in both the absolute and relative number of pupils in attendance, in methods of teaching and discipline, and, above all, in spirit.[34]

Henry Barnard. Mann's influence in stimulating and directing the public school movement was outstanding in a period characterized by able, aggressive leadership and great accomplishment in all parts of the country, but his contribution was perhaps in no way greater than that of his contemporary, Henry Barnard. Although Barnard, looking back to his earlier years, stated that, as far as he could remember, "the cause of true education, of the complete education of every human being without regard to the accidents of birth or fortune, seemed most worthy . . . of any sacrifice of time, money, and labor . . . ,"[35] there was little in his early experience to indicate that the promotion of the cause of public education was to be the consuming interest and work of his life. In fact, after graduating from Yale in 1830 and teaching for a year in a Pennsylvania academy, Barnard prepared himself for a legal career, was admitted to the bar, and engaged in local politics. From 1835 to 1837 he visited in Europe, where he spent much of his time studying schools, particularly those which reflected the Pestalozzian influence. On his return he became a member of the Connecticut Legislature. A bill to provide for the better supervision of schools, introduced by him in 1838 and passed unanimously by the legislature, created a state board of commissioners of common schools, of which he became a member and, after Gallaudet's refusal, the first secretary.

Conditions in Connecticut, as described in contemporary accounts, were even worse than those found by Mann in Massachusetts. As in Massachusetts, the towns had been largely divested of their educational responsibilities. Taxation for educational purposes was opposed, and the

---

[34] Hinsdale, *op. cit.*, pp. 275–276.
[35] Harris Elwood Starr, "Henry Barnard," *Dictionary of American Biography* (New York: Charles Scribner's Sons, 1928), I, p. 622.

public schools were operated by local societies, almost solely on the income derived from the permament school funds of the state. Few but the poor attended the free schools, others enrolling in the academies and other types of private schools. Teachers were generally untrained and inefficient, and, even so, underpaid; the turnover was appalling. School buildings and equipment, except in a relatively few instances, were almost indescribably bad. Barnard, like Mann in Massachusetts, set out to awaken the state to its obligations. He addressed letters to the people, organized conventions in every county, gathered information on the operation and defects of existing schools, prepared reports to the legislature pointing toward needed changes in the school laws, founded and edited the *Connecticut Common School Journal,* emphasized in speeches and writings the need for trained teachers, and established the first teachers' institutes to attempt seriously to improve the quality of teaching. After four years of unselfish service, dynamic leadership, and great accomplishment, Barnard was, for the time, removed from the scene by the enemies of public schools in the legislature, who legislated his office out of existence.

In 1843 he was called to Rhode Island, where conditions were even worse than those he had faced in Connecticut, and where opposition to state intervention in education was a tradition of two centuries' standing. Employed to collect and disseminate information regarding the defects and possible improvements in the school system and to awaken an interest in education on the part of the public, he launched a campaign similar in many respects to the one that he had carried on in Connecticut. In 1845, largely as a result of his labors, a good school law was passed which he as state commissioner of public schools (1845–49) put into operation before his resignation in 1849.

At this time, it is stated, he might have been appointed to a professorship in one of two colleges; the superintendency of Boston, New York, Cincinnati, or New Orleans; or the presidency of the state university of either Michigan or Indiana. In 1851, however, he accepted the principalship of Connecticut's newly established normal school (New Britain), by virtue of which action he became ex officio secretary of the State Board of Education. In this position, he spent most of his time promoting the public school cause — rewriting school laws, obtaining additional tax support, and curbing the power of the school societies.

When, in 1855, he resigned on account of his health and in order to devote himself to the publication of the *American Journal of Education,* he had already achieved some distinction as a writer and editor. He had edited four volumes of the *Connecticut Common School Journal* (1838–42) and three volumes of the *Journal of Rhode Island Institute of Instruction* (1845–49) and written an excellent work on school architecture, and, during his period of service as the chief state school officer in Connecticut and Rhode Island, a number of noteworthy reports. Among the latter, his first annual report (Connecticut) has been characterized as a "bold and startling document" containing "a minute, accurate, comprehensive, and instructive exhibition of the condition and operation of the common-school system."[36] His first printed report as commissioner of public schools in Rhode Island has often been called the first school survey report, and his 1853 report[37] as ex officio secretary of the Connecticut State Board of Education, which was a history of educational legislation in Connecticut, was a scholarly and significant study. His greatest contribution to educational leadership, however, was the *American Journal of Education*. This monumental work, brought out between 1855 and 1882 in thirty-two volumes of more than eight hundred pages each, treated, in encyclopedic fashion, nearly all phases of education from the earliest times to Barnard's own, and upon it his recognition as the "scholar of the awakening" is largely based. Although he took time from the *Journal* and his other writings to serve as chancellor of the University of Wisconsin from 1858 to 1860, as president of St. John's College for a short period during 1866–67, and as the first United States commissioner of education from 1867 to 1870, his great reputation as an educator rests largely upon his work in establishing the school systems of Connecticut and Rhode Island and his immeasurable contribution to American educational scholarship.

Leaders in the South and West. Not only in New England, but in almost every state in the Union, capable, enthusiastic persons were engaged in stimulating interest in public education and promoting the organization of state school systems, often in the face of greater obstacles than were confronted by Mann, Barnard, and their contemporary reformers in the relatively wealthy and urbanized states of Connecticut, Rhode Island, and Massachusetts. The campaigns for free public schools in the states of the South and the West followed, within limits, the pattern set in New England. But, although outside example was a factor of great influence, reformers everywhere were, perhaps, more deeply indebted to the pioneering work within their own states done by the leaders who had preceded them and but for whom the ideal of universal education, never very strong, would have entirely disappeared.

In North Carolina, the work of Calvin Wiley, the outstanding figure in the educational awakening, would have been less successful had it not been for the activities of such men as Braxton Craven, the founder of Trinity College, and President Caldwell, of the University of North

[36] James Kent's *Commentaries*, as quoted in Edgar W. Knight, *Education in the United States*, Third Revised Edition (Boston: Ginn & Company, 1951) p. 219.

[37] *History of the Legislation of Connecticut Respecting Common Schools Down to 1838*, Report of the Superintendent of Common Schools, to the General Assembly, May Session, 1853 (Hartford, Conn.: Printed by Order of the Legislature by Alfred E. Burr, State Printer, 1853), pp. 5–184.

Carolina. In the early thirties Caldwell pointed out the deterrents to educational advancement, "suggested plans for overcoming the State's educational backwardness, discussed the usual methods of school support, remarked freely on educational practices in the State, discussed the public-school systems of other States, . . . pointed out those features which would be practicable for conditions in North Carolina," and presented a plan to provide for the training of teachers which was considered as "a necessary feature of any system which the State should adopt. . . ."[38]

Although the foundation for a system of education had been laid by the school law of 1839 and a "fairly creditable educational plan was in operation"[39] when Wiley took office as state superintendent, he faced, as had Mann in Massachusetts and Barnard in Connecticut and Rhode Island, a situation characterized by negligence on the part of school officials, stubborn localism, poorly prepared teachers, primitive schoolhouses, inadequate facilities, and prejudice on the part of many people with respect to public education.[40]

As in the case of the two great New England reformers, there was little in Wiley's early life and training to indicate his particular fitness for the tasks of educational leadership which he was later to perform so ably. After graduating from the University of North Carolina in 1840, he studied law and was admitted to the bar in 1841. After ten years devoted to practicing law, to editing the *Oxford Mercury,* and to writing, he was elected to the state legislature in 1850. He urged and secured legal provision for a superintendent of common schools to be chosen for a two-year term by the legislature. Wiley was chosen the first superintendent under the act and entered on his duties in January, 1853. A Whig, he was, in spite of predominantly Democratic legislatures, reappointed until 1865, when, after the collapse of the Confederacy, his office was abolished. During his term of office, he worked steadily to reorganize and improve the educational program, never ceasing to attempt to stimulate a wider and deeper interest in it. He visited all parts of the state; made speeches before teachers, legislators, and other groups; prepared and presented annual reports; founded and edited the *North Carolina Journal of Education;* organized and headed the Educational Association of North Carolina; and helped promote the work of Normal College, the first teacher-training institution of a semipublic character in the state.[41]

That his achievement, as measured by change in the actual status of education, was, after all, relative and easily exaggerated is revealed by Wiley's report for 1860, the year immediately preceding the outbreak of

38 Edgar W. Knight, *Public Education in the South* (Boston: Ginn & Company, 1922), pp. 151–152.
39 Knight, *Education in the United States, op. cit.,* p. 223.
40 *Ibid.,* p. 224.
41 Jerome Dowd, *The Life of Braxton Craven: A Biographical Approach to Social Science* (Durham, N.C.: Duke University Press, 1939), p. 83.

the Civil War. On the basis of incomplete returns from the eighty-six counties, he estimated that more than 3000 schools had been in session during the year; that approximately 150,000 children, or nearly five-sevenths of those of school age, were enrolled; that perhaps $100,000 ($75,929.88 in sixty-five counties) had been collected by taxation; that the school term was nearly four months in length; and that the average salary paid to teachers was twenty-six dollars per month.[42] However, as modest as these achievements appear, North Carolina compared favorably with many northern states, and before the Civil War was fast becoming a center of educational reform in the South. Evidence that the foundations were well laid is the fact that both the state organization and the permanent school fund survived throughout the desolating war. Neither the state program nor the Literary Fund, however, could withstand the aftermath.

Every section of the country felt the impact of determined men firmly convinced of the regenerative power of education, and the social value of literacy. In Indiana, where the legislature had, with almost studied neglect, ignored the rather strong provisions of the constitution of 1816, education had reached a low ebb. The state and in turn the district had almost abdicated all responsibilities. Education had become an almost individual or parental matter; the dreary situation reflected the low state of group thinking and the helplessness of the individual. By 1840, one-seventh of the population was classified as illiterate. Only about one-half of the children between the ages of five and eighteen, it was said, could read, and fewer than one-sixth of those of school age were in any kind of school. The most illiterate of any free state, Indiana, in the ten years that followed, not only retained her unenviable position, but moved below some of the slave states.

Here, too, a voice arose to point the way out of the wilderness. Caleb Mills, born in New Hampshire and a graduate of Dartmouth College and the Andover Theological Seminary, took time from his duties at Wabash College to take a leading part in the educational affairs of the state and to exert a profound influence, for more than a quarter of a century, on the development of the public school system. In 1846 Mills published the first of a series of six annual "Addresses to the Legislature," in which he called attention to the deplorable conditions and the lack of educational opportunity, outlined needed reforms, and urged the state to accept its responsibilities. These addresses were issued on the opening day of sessions of the legislature, except the Fifth Address, which appeared in 1850, as the constitutional convention assembled. The sixth and last of

[42] *Report of the Superintendent of Common Schools of North Carolina, for the Year 1860* (Document 10), pp. 2–6, as quoted in M. C. S. Noble, *A History of the Public Schools of North Carolina* (Chapel Hill, N.C.: University of North Carolina Press, 1930), pp. 225–227.

these communications was published as the first legislature, under the new constitution, convened in 1851 to implement the provisions of the constitution. This address, recommending desirable educational legislation, was published by order of the legislature and circulated throughout the state.

These addresses reflect Mills's advanced views. The constitutional provisions for education and the school laws which were enacted reflect his influence. While he was state superintendent of public instruction, from 1854 to 1856, his reports provided further evidence of his advanced thinking, but they also indicated that progress was slow and halting. Another decade was to pass before the schools were placed upon a sound basis, and perhaps a longer period was to elapse before the title of "Father of the Common Schools of Indiana," which was later bestowed upon him, was one in which he might feel pride.

In other states, reformer-educators led campaigns which, although differing in their immediate ends, were ultimately designed to promote the cause of public schools. Their tasks were dictated by the particular needs of their state. Some made their greatest contribution in helping frame a state organization, in curbing a rampant localism, or in breaking the strangle hold of powerful sectarian interests; others devoted their energies largely to the task of obtaining taxation for the support of schools and of making the schools free; others labored for the improvement of instruction and a better-trained teaching force; but in every instance the ultimate goal was the same. Among the men "who helped fight through the battles of state establishment and state organization and control," Cubberley has given honorable mention to "Calvin Stowe, Samuel Lewis, and Samuel Galloway in Ohio; . . . Ninian W. Edwards in Illinois; John D. Pierce and Isaac E. Crary in Michigan; Robert J. Breckinridge in Kentucky; . . . John Swett in California," and others, including the leaders already discussed in some detail in this chapter.[43]

When the complete history of the public school movement is written, many forces will stand out as influential in giving it both impetus and direction, but few will be accorded greater importance than the work of the public-minded persons who sought to ennoble man and to equalize the conditions of his existence through universal education.

The Emergence of the Democratic State

Without in any way minimizing the role played in the so-called educational awakening by humanitarians, political leaders, educators, educational propaganda, and foreign example, we must seek the theme by which

[43] Cubberley, *op. cit.*, p. 229.

the unfolding drama is to be interpreted, not in one or all of these factors, but in the source of which these forces were no more than manifestations. The reformers and the activities sponsored by them were products of the time and had significance only from this relationship. Without the underlying current of social and economic change, there could not have been a generation of reformers pointing to the failure of old institutions — a generation intent upon providing a program of universal education through the establishment of state-controlled and publicly supported schools. Although to interpret the public school movement without reference to Mann, Barnard, and their contemporaries is to discount the influence of personalities to an extent to which careful students of history are not prepared to go, it is important to note that the dynamics of the new orientation which they sought sprang from an economic, social, and political movement, the nature of which has been indicated by terms such as the "triumph of Jacksonian democracy," the "rise of the common man," and the "emergence of the democratic state."

EXTENSION OF SUFFRAGE AND REPRESENTATION

The victory of American arms in the Revolutionary War had resulted in the permanent banishment of the monarchical-minded professional ruling cliques and the sending into exile or obscurity of the most vociferous defenders of the old order. The establishment of the Republic, proclaimed on democratic principles, both consolidated the products of a century's trend toward political and social equality and pointed in the direction of even greater gains to be achieved. But, although uneven progress continued to be made, at the close of the first quarter of the nineteenth century the control of government was still largely in the hands of men of property and privilege. Government remained the business of gentlemen, and the leaders of the organized protests against the rule of aristocracy and wealth, on gaining immediate and modest ends, grew conservative and became champions of the status quo.[44]

Universal manhood suffrage as the basis of representation was but slowly accepted. Of the thirteen original states, only New Hampshire, Pennsylvania, North Carolina, and Delaware, at the time of the adoption of the Federal Constitution in 1789, allowed full suffrage without the ownership of property; but even in these four states only persons who paid taxes were allowed to vote. It has been estimated that at this time less than one-fifth of the entire male population of the United States was in possession of the franchise. The often-expressed idea that government had first been instituted among men as a means of protecting property and that this was still its most important function was reflected in the suffrage regulations. These, for the most part, were ordered on the as-

[44] William E. Dodd, *Expansion and Conflict* (Boston: Houghton Mifflin Company, 1915), p. 3.

sumption that men without property should have no stake in government, being unfit either to make the laws or to administer them. The provisions regarding the right to hold office were, as a rule, even more restrictive than those which governed the suffrage. "The higher the office, the higher was the property qualification."[45]

Equally important in keeping the control of government in the hands of men of property were the constitutionally sanctioned arrangements within states which made it difficult for the electorate to express its will and which, in some of the older states, successfully minimized the influence of whole sections, whose population in some instances embraced a majority of all the voters in the state. Everywhere the power of property was accepted.

The slow progress made toward unrestricted manhood suffrage during the first quarter of the century following the Revolution was greatly accelerated during the second quarter. Up to the close of the War of 1812, only four states had removed all property and similar restrictions upon the suffrage. But by 1815, "new winds had begun to blow over the American people," and the democratic movement which sought to abolish political inequalities gained strength rapidly. The economic and social regime in the South resisted the development of democratic institutions, but, even so, Maryland in 1809 and South Carolina in 1810 abolished all tax and property qualifications.

With the exception of Ohio and Louisiana, the western states, both north and south, granted full or, in one or two instances, almost full, manhood suffrage from the beginning of statehood.[46]

As indicated in an earlier chapter, the democracy of the frontier states had, to use the words of Turner, "reactive effects of the highest importance upon the older States whose people were being attracted" westward.[47] Thus the eastern states were obliged to extend the suffrage and to give, at least in the case of New York and Virginia, the western counties a more equitable representation. However, the right to vote must have been more important in the minds of many persons who had gained the right than was the actual discharge of this civic duty. Old habits, ideas, and perhaps a sense of futility kept many from the polls who had the right of suffrage.[48] Nevertheless, under the surface, the ground swell of democracy was strong. With the election of Andrew Jackson to the presidency in

[45] Reisner, *op. cit.*, p. 330. Quoted by permission of the Bureau of Publications, Teachers College, Columbia University.

[46] Cubberley, *op. cit.*, p. 151. See also Carl Russell Fish, *The Rise of the Common Man, 1830–1850* (New York: The Macmillan Co., 1927), pp. 111, 164–166.

[47] Cubberley, *op. cit.*, p. 152.

[48] "In Virginia, with a white population of 625,000, only 15,000 had voted in the election of 1824; in Pennsylvania, whose population was over a million, only some 47,000 had taken the trouble to go to the polls; while in Massachusetts, where the 'favorite son' motive operated, just one man in nineteen exercised the right of suffrage." Dodd, *op. cit.*, p. 3.

1828, the changes which had taken place with respect to the franchise were translated for the first time into political action. There now came before the electorate a candidate who could stir the emotions of the common man. Jackson represented the democracy, the aspirations, and the prejudices of the frontier. "Let the people rule," the battle cry of the Jackson party, struck a responsive chord untouched by other issues. For the first time the great masses were aroused to use the political power which they possessed. The result constituted a political revolution which to the defenders of the special rights of property in government threatened to destroy not only property but laws and liberty as well. However, to persons unblinded by unreasoning emotion it was becoming increasingly evident that in the end the old claims to political superiority on the part of any class would be denied and that everywhere the remaining restrictions on suffrage would be abolished. The people, though they might be unskilled in steering, had seized the helm. To make government more directly responsive to their will, election by popular vote came to be the approved manner of filling public offices, particularly in the West, where even the chief state school officers were chosen at general elections, usually for short terms. The power of the state legislatures was limited, the time of meeting and the length of session being prescribed. Although it was thought that equality would be achieved when restrictions on the suffrage, long terms of office, ignorance, and related ills were abolished, the optimistic viewpoint of the time prevented serious thought of leveling society downward. Equality was the reward of striving, and the room at the top was believed to be almost unlimited. Fish, one of the foremost interpreters of the period, states:

> The limit was only the top. Nothing was to be dragged down. The struggle for equality aimed not at all at transferring one man's wealth to another; no important man thought of an equal division. Nor was there any purpose of limiting any man's liberty. The ideals — that some men's liberty should be restricted because they are not strong enough to use it for their own advantage; that some men's liberty, or at least the liberty of artificial men, corporations, should be restricted because dangerous to other individuals or to the body politic; that the body politic is more deserving of consideration than any of the individuals who comprise it — were never in America so weakly held or apologetically presented. Resources were limitless. Free men could be trusted to want what was right and to get it.[49]

The influence of wealth and the talent it represented continued to be a force in government, but with the election of Jackson few could fail to see that the old political order had passed and that only vestiges of it remained.

[49] Fish, *op. cit.*, pp. 11–12. Used by permission of The Macmillan Co.

THE EDUCATIONAL NEEDS OF A DEMOCRATIC STATE

The consequence of the emergence of the democratic state was, of course, the eclipse of the old order. This chapter and previous ones have indicated the steps in the process, something of the factors involved, and the fact that the transition, when all of its aspects are considered, was not abrupt. The changes had been gradual, but the culmination of many forces long at work resulted in the general recognition that political democracy had triumphed, and with this recognition came an awareness on the part of many persons that the educational arrangements which had served the old order well were no longer adequate for the new. No longer were the ends of society to be served by educating the few for leadership and the many to be good subjects and staunch, if unintelligent, supporters of a social system which denied them their just rights. No longer would the classics, traditionally considered the proper content of education, wholly satisfy the educational needs of a society which was coming to deny the prerogatives that birth and breeding had always given and to measure the value of the individual in terms of his ability to subdue a new country and to gain control of its resources. No longer could education for the masses aim at a literacy far below the functional level, nor could men long continue to feel neither loss nor shame in their inability to read and write. Yet, of all the institutions of the old order, none resisted change more than the school. A long history and the sanctions of religion had given to the content, method, and the arrangements for control and administration of education a vitality which led to the survival of a class system of education in a society which had repudiated class rule.

But education needed to be oriented around the concept of citizenship in the democratic state. Although this was not a simple task, men of vision, aware of this necessity, united in the effort to provide, freely and as a right which citizenship implied, adequate opportunity for all — opportunity which was neither the kindly offering of an altruistic church nor the contribution of hopeful, well-meaning philanthropists.

The change was not easily accomplished. Old traditions which resisted change had to be broken. Establishing a program of education designed to socialize youth in terms of the new and more democratic way of American life was to be the work of more than one generation. The history of the educational activity of the entire period here under consideration centers about the false starts, halting steps, and real progress toward that goal.

A program of education adequate to meet the needs of the new political order could be implemented only as rapidly as voters came to understand that the success of the great democratic experiment depended upon an enlightened citizenry and to believe that education was worth the cost which its provision entailed. There was little precedent for looking upon education as a matter of general concern. As long as the suffrage had been limited by property and sometimes by religious qualifications, children who were, in later life, to play a part in church and state were educated privately and without undue burden upon the parents. When the suffrage was granted to persons without means to provide for their children — who had neither a tradition of education nor, in many instances, an understanding of its worth — state intervention became a necessity. The state must intervene to require an educational program organized in terms of new political and social conditions — a program to give the state the stability which only an intelligent citizenry could make possible.

This meant that the support of education could not be left to private, religious, and philanthropic agencies, but must be provided out of public funds derived largely from taxation. Control could not be allowed to remain in the hands of persons or groups of persons blinded by their own particular interests, but had to be made responsive to the will of the entire public. Education at public expense had to be extended upward to provide the trained intelligence which the new order required. And, above all, a common education — the minimum essential for intelligent citizenship in a democratic state — had to be provided for, and even imposed upon, all. As Fish has pointed out, the exciting and vital educational problems of the period "revolved about the questions of equality of educational opportunity, tax-supported education, the functions of church and state in elementary education, and the organization of a system of schools adapted to American conditions."[50] That the widening of the base of education was recognized as of paramount importance is evidenced by the fact that the greatest amount of educational activity of the period was related to the establishment and development of common schools.

Democratizing the Support of Education

Corresponding stages in the progress toward acceptance of the idea of universal education supported by a tax on all property were reached at widely varying times in the different states and regions, but everywhere the movement was slow. Certain states moved more rapidly than others, but the differences between states with respect to this development were perhaps no greater than the differences found between communities within a single state. Educational historians have professed to see the origins of free schools in the legislation enacted in Massachusetts in the fourth and fifth decades of the seventeenth century — a series of laws which provided that the cost of government and church should be met by a tax upon the inhabitants according to their means (1638); that children should be taught to read (1642); and that towns of fifty house-

[50] *Ibid.,* pp. 216–217.

holders should provide a teacher of reading and writing and towns of a hundred householders should maintain a grammar school to fit youth for the university (1647). It should be noted, however, that the idea of taxing wealth for the support of church and state was not new; that the purpose of the law of 1638 was to compel all the inhabitants to support the Puritan Church; that schools were not contemplated under the law of 1642; that the law of 1647 did not require tax support for schools; and that no legislation of the period was based on the premise that free education should be provided to the children of parents who were able to pay.

The claims put forth that the right to tax for the support of schools open without charge to rich and poor alike and the several other principles upon which the present free, compulsory, and secular systems of education rest sprang from acts of the General Court of Massachusetts acting for the Puritan Church, even though they may have a small measure of validity, have tended to obscure the fact that these principles evolved slowly and painfully, and were only recognized and accepted in much later times. Outside Massachusetts and perhaps one or two other New England states, the principle of public support of education through taxation was rejected during the first half-century of the national period. It is true that the duty of society toward paupers was, as a rule, recognized, and some meager provision, which they generally scorned, was made for them. Even in Massachusetts, Carter and others were led to protest against the attitude of persons of means which was threatening to reduce what approximated a free school to a purely pauper institution. When such persons refused to send their children to the tax-supported schools, a stigma naturally attached to pupils attending them. Public, tax-supported education was accepted only after it was fully recognized that the education of all the people in a democracy was a matter of community concern; that the education which the lower economic groups could or were willing to pay for was entirely inadequate; and that philanthropy, though sanctioned by religion and the ages, could not carry the burden of providing even the minimum education needed by the greatly augmented number of children if they were to grow up as effective guardians of the new order.

SUPPLEMENTING THE FUNDS DERIVED FROM TUITION AND PHILANTHROPY

Long before the general public was willing to adopt the policy of school support by taxation — even in early colonial times — attempts were made to increase educational opportunities and to reduce tuition charges by supplementing the two long-accepted means of school support — tuition and philanthropy — by resorting to revenues derived from other sources. As the necessity for universalizing education became recognized, the supplementary methods of securing funds were adopted more widely than ever before and several new sources of revenue were found. Fines and forfeitures were set aside for the use of schools; lotteries were organized for their benefit, sometimes chartered by the states, sometimes organized in the cities without state sanction, and, in the case of the District of Columbia, authorized by joint resolution of Congress; state revenues from the sale of stocks of banks and of certain internal improvements were made available for educational purposes; fees for marriage licenses were used to provide funds for schools; and a motley assortment of indirect taxes, collected from slave traders, hawkers, auctioneers, owners of tenpin alleys and billiard tables, theater proprietors, bankers, and others with respect to whom the state might easily exercise its sovereign right, was added to the total.

Permanent school funds. For a long time it was generally expected that permanent school funds could be built up to the point where the income derived from them would provide an adequate educational program. Connecticut created a permanent school fund in 1750, to which in 1795 was added $1,200,000 received from the sale of the Western Reserve. By 1821 the income from this fund was so large that the law of more than a century's standing which required towns to levy a two-mill tax for schools was repealed. Virginia in 1810 established a permanent fund, the income to be used for the education of the poor only. Among the other older states to establish such funds were Maryland (1812), New York (1805), Delaware (1796), New Jersey (1816), Georgia (1817), New Hampshire (1821), Kentucky (1821), Vermont (1825), and North Carolina (1825).

With respect to the possibility of financing education through endowments, undue optimism was aroused and interest stimulated by the federal land grants for education in the new states carved from the national domain. The distribution of the federal surplus of more than $28,000,-000 to the twenty-six states then comprising the Union likewise created great expectations, not only in the West, but also in the older states, which had not received federal lands. The states, sharing in this deposit on the basis of their representation in Congress, received sums varying from slightly less than $300,000, as in Delaware, Michigan, and Arkansas, to something over $4,000,000 in New York. Although the states were free to make any use of the funds they saw fit, sixteen of them placed the money received in a special fund for educational purposes or added it to the permanent school fund. According to Swift, "the income, or a portion of it has reached the common schools in every state [then in the Union] except four: Michigan, Mississippi, South Carolina, and Virginia."[51]

[51] Fletcher Harper Swift, *Federal and State Policies in Public School Finance* (Boston: Ginn & Company, 1931), p. 34.

The funds never became so important as had been hoped. As the costs of education mounted, permanent funds played a steadily smaller part in financing education. In certain instances the existence of a permanent fund operated to inhibit the development of an adequate program. In some states, the restriction of the use of the income to the schooling of paupers fixed more firmly the idea that public-supported and pauper schools were one and the same thing. In others, the early optimism which attended the creation of such funds continued long after educational statesmen had discounted their importance in the total financial program. Contemporary writers blamed the low condition of Connecticut's schools on the existence of that state's exceptionally large and well-managed fund. In Massachusetts, opponents of the establishment of a permanent fund pointed to the sad results of Connecticut's efforts to escape taxation. In Connecticut the increasing costs of education led to a reduction in the quantity and quality of schooling offered, to the extended use of the rate bill as the only practicable means of securing the added funds needed, or to both.

On the other hand, these permanent school funds did serve a useful purpose. They were, in most instances, the "first stable sources of support given to free schools," and they fostered the idea of education as a public concern.

Since these funds could be granted or withheld by the state, they could be used to stimulate effort. Districts were granted funds if they fulfilled certain conditions set by the state. As one of these requirements, the state often specified that the local district should raise money to supplement the state funds received. The effectiveness of this requirement in breaking down opposition to local taxation and in otherwise influencing progressive action will be discussed in the following pages.

The Struggle for Tax Support

By the close of the first quarter of the nineteenth century it had become apparent to many that all measures for the support of schools short of taxation were futile. The breakdown of the traditional methods of financing education was most noticeable in urban areas, where changed conditions of life were creating serious social problems. In the city, also, was found a large and increasing body of voters who paid little or no direct taxes, and there, too, capital accumulated from which schools could be supported. The cities, unwilling to wait for the rural sections, often took the lead in demanding schools supported by taxation and the state legislatures responded, usually slowly and without enthusiasm, by granting permission to certain communities to organize themselves as school-taxing districts long before tax support was made mandatory throughout the state. For example, the city and county of Philadelphia were organized as the first school district of the state in 1818, and a system of Lancasterian schools was established. Although these non-tuition schools failed to enroll children of the upper economic groups and were therefore not entirely free from the pauper taint, they enrolled more than five thousand children in 1821 — as many as were being educated under the Poor-Law Act in all of Pennsylvania.

Permissive legislation. In spite of the option it provided, permissive legislation was bitterly contested at every turn and overcame opposition only slowly and with many backward movements. An Illinois law of 1825 provided for an optional district-school tax which, with the income from lands and the permanent school fund, would have maintained free schools in districts accepting the law. Two years later, however, the tax was made obligatory only in the case of those persons who consented in writing to the levy. In some instances only the poor were permitted to benefit from funds raised by taxation. In other instances more than a simple majority of the voters of the district had to unite in demanding taxation, as was the case under the Missouri law of 1824. Under that statute districts were permitted to levy taxes, provided two-thirds of the voters petitioned for the privilege. Permissive legislation was opposed, not only because it opened the way to mandatory taxation, but also on the principle that to permit the indolent, although constituting a majority in many districts, to place their burdens upon the thrifty was wrong. The more powerful and wealthy the person threatened by the tax or the more readily he could estimate the immediate and direct effect of the tax upon his own purse, the more likely he was to see the tax as a deathblow to the principles upon which American democracy had been established.

States differed widely in the patterns of their progress toward free, public, tax-supported systems of schools. In general, however, the movement was from the mildest type of legislation, by which permission was "granted to communities so desiring to organize a school-taxing district, and to tax for school support the property of those consenting and residing therein," to legislation which compelled general taxation by the local district.[52] The time required to progress from legislation which permitted taxing only within a special district (as that under which free schools were established in New York City, Cincinnati, New Orleans, Detroit, Baltimore, and numerous other cities), or taxing for the education of paupers only, to legislation which required the taxing of all property for the support of free schools varied widely, but roughly the transition required a quarter-century or more. At any given time, tax laws representing all stages of the development were being passed. But as state funds, derived sometimes from permanent funds and sometimes from a small state school tax, increased, and aid could be given to those communities

[52] Ellwood P. Cubberley, *State School Administration* (Boston: Houghton Mifflin Company, 1927), p. 414.

which were willing to tax themselves, sentiment in favor of taxation grew and states in increasing numbers made taxation for educational purposes mandatory upon all communities. This step, opposed by strong and articulate groups, was taken only haltingly and with misgivings. For example, after a long period of agitation for a general school-tax law, the matter was referred to the voters of Indiana in 1848. Although two-thirds of the counties and considerably more than half of the persons voting favored such legislation, the legislature timidly drew the new law to apply in only those counties in which it was accepted by the people, and a general state school tax was not voted until 1851. Other instances of slow and timid progress are numerous.

The struggle in Pennsylvania.   One of the most bitter and, in many ways, the most dramatic of all the struggles for free schools was waged in Pennsylvania, where the pauper-school idea was firmly established. In his volume on the history of the period, *The Rise of the Common Man, 1830–1850,* Professor Fish states that "this contest may be taken as the turning-point toward a public-school system free to all on equal terms."[53]

The dramatic aspects of this controversy and the importance of the victory to the cause of free schools in Pennsylvania and elsewhere justify a somewhat detailed account of the contest in this key state.

In Pennsylvania a pauper-school law enacted in 1802 carried out that mandate of the Constitution of 1790 which had provided that the legislature should as soon as convenient "provide, by law, for the establishment of schools throughout the State, in such manner that the poor may be taught *gratis.*"[54] No community took advantage of the law of 1802 and a supplemental act passed two years later was also ignored. A clearer law superseded this legislation in 1809. It was, however, purely a pauper law, requiring parents to stigmatize themselves as paupers before tuition for their children would be paid in the most convenient pay school. Obviously, public acknowledgement of inability to pay for education was grossly offensive to most parents. In light of this fact and the lack of zeal among the poor for schooling, it is not surprising that little was accomplished under the law, which remained in effect until 1834, except for a two-year interval following the enactment of a weak optional free-school law in 1824. By this date, several urban counties had been exempted from the pauper-school law and permitted to organize schools for the education of their own poor. Outside these urban centers only a few thousand children were enrolled annually as paupers, and in the entire state not more than one-half of the children between the ages of five and fifteen were enrolled at all.

Growing dissatisfaction with the results of existing arrangements and

53 Fish, *op. cit.,* p. 217.
54 As quoted in Cubberley, *Public Education in the United States, op. cit.,* p. 64.

an intensive campaign led by the friends of public schools resulted in the passage of a free-school law in 1834. Each of the 987 districts created was given the right to accept or reject the law in a school election to be held in the autumn of that year. Nearly one-half of the districts, in spite of pecuniary inducements offered, either voted outright against acceptance or refused to take any action with reference to the matter, thereby continuing under the old pauper law of 1809.

This partial victory for free schools, however, only served to arouse general opposition and indignation. The feeling against the law was intense and widespread.

> In many districts the contest between those in favor of accepting the new law and those determined to reject it became so bitter, that party and even church ties were for a time broken up, the rich arrayed themselves against the poor, and the business and social relations of whole neighborhoods were greatly disturbed. Cases are known in which father and sons took different sides, and in certain districts an outspoken free school man was scarcely allowed to live in peace and transact his ordinary business.[55]

The new law met with some favor in the northern counties, settled largely by people from New York and New England. It was not badly received in the western frontier counties. But in the southern, central, and southwestern portions of the state some of the more prosperous elements in the population, the Germans, and several religious denominations provided formidable opposition. The act became the main issue in the autumn elections and nearly all the "legislators were elected on a platform committed to repeal or received specific instructions to that end."[56]

Before the matter could be considered by the new legislature, so many petitions had been received by the House of Representatives that a special committee was appointed "to ascertain the number of petitions in each county of the Commonwealth, praying for the repeal or modification of the school law, and the number remonstrating against such repeal." The report of this committee, consisting of a single paragraph, is significant. It reads:

> That although the number who have petitioned for the repeal is deplorably large, yet it is but a small minority of the whole number of voters in the Commonwealth, to wit, about thirty-two thousand. Those who ask for a modification only are two thousand and eighty-four; those who have

[55] James Pyle Wickersham, *A History of Education in Pennsylvania, Private and Public, Elementary and Higher: From the Time the Swedes Settled on the Delaware to the Present Day* (Lancaster, Pa.: published for the author by the Inquirer Publishing Co., 1885), p. 318.

[56] Thomas Frederick Woodley, *Thaddeus Stevens* (Harrisburg, Pa.: Telegraph Press, 1934), p. 152. See also Samuel W. McCall, *Thaddeus Stevens* (Boston: Houghton Mifflin Company, 1899); Elsie Singmaster, *I Speak for Thaddeus Stevens* (Boston: Houghton Mifflin Company, 1947).

deemed it necessary to remonstrate against the repeal, two thousand five hundred and seventy-five. The Committee were pained to find among those who deem a general system of education unnecessary and ask for its repeal, sixty-six who are unable to write their own names, and who attached their signatures by making their marks; and according to the best conclusion to which the Committee could arrive, more than ten out of every hundred of the petitioners' names appear to be written by other hands than their own. Whether this arose from inability to write their own names, the Committee do not feel themselves called on to determine. The Committee would further remark, that in most of the petitions not more than five names out of every hundred are written in English, and the great mass of them are so illegibly written as to afford the strongest evidence of the deplorable disregard so long paid by the Legislature to the constitutional injunction to establish a general system of education.[57]

The Senate, on convening in 1835, lost little time in passing a bill repealing the law of the previous year. Members of the House, however, in spite of the opposition voiced by their constituents, were not so easily stampeded. They withstood with rare fortitude the strongly advanced arguments that the act violated the Constitution of 1790; that the old system must have had merit to continue for twenty-five years; that funds were not available; that under the system, as projected, schools could not be kept open two months a year; that the poor would be better off under the act of 1809; and that further taxation would compel the people to "leave the houses of their childhood and the graves of their fathers" and "migrate into the great unknown regions of the 'far west,' there to enjoy in peace and tranquility the well-earned reward of their labor and toil."[58] After a bitter struggle, the House refused to follow the Senate's action and was finally able to force the Senate to accept a bill stronger than the original act. For this victory perhaps equal credit is due to the adroitness of a stubborn minority group in the House, to Governor Wolf, who urged the retention of the free-school act and indicated that he would veto any repealing act passed by the legislature, and to Thaddeus Stevens, the acknowledged leader of the free-school forces, who by his unselfish and uncompromising stand in an oration against the repeal of the school law did much to persuade the House to maintain its strong position.

This speech, made by Stevens in support of a substitute measure for the repealing act of the Senate, said a contemporary, was "so convincing that the friends of education were brought in solid column to the support of the measure and thus saved the common school system." Another witness, commenting years later on the speech, stated: "The House was electrified. The wavering voted for the House sections and the school system was saved from ignominious defeat."[59] The Democratic *Pennsyl-*

57 Wickersham, *op. cit.,* p. 330.   58 As quoted *ibid.,* p. 329.
59 *Ibid.,* p. 333.

vania Reporter, ordinarily scathingly critical of Stevens, approved the speech and felt "assured that a more beautiful effort at oratory was never listened to within the walls of this or any other Legislative Hall."[60] Woodley quotes a contemporary historian who, although "politically opposed and unfriendly to Stevens" and although impugning Stevens's motive in defending the free-school system, said that

> . . . his speech had a magical effect upon the sentiments of members. . . . All, without distinction, whether enemies or friends, acknowledged the overpowering superiority of it. Many who had determined to favor repeal changed their opinions and voted to sustain the Law of 1834. This speech ranked its author henceforth, as one of the first intellects of Pennsylvania.[61]

Stevens, who had spoken from rough notes, was prevailed upon to set down the speech in full and portions of it were printed on silk by friends of the school system. He considered the speech his greatest single achievement. Fish, almost a hundred years after its delivery, called it one of the great orations of American history. The text of the speech can be found, at least in part, in many volumes, including several standard texts on the history of American education.[62]

The victory of the free-school forces was decisive. The new law provided for state aid, a measure of state control and supervision, and county and local taxation, but districts willing to forgo their share of the new state funds were free to reject the new law, and it was "not until 1873 that the last district in the State accepted the new system."[63] However, more ready acceptance was the rule. By 1838, the new law had been accepted by 84 per cent of the districts and at the close of the decade which followed only slightly more than 10 per cent continued to reject the law.

The repudiation of the pauper-school idea in Pennsylvania gave support to its enemies elsewhere. Within the next few years, New Jersey repealed its pauper-school legislation and attacks were made upon the system in other states, particularly in Virginia. By the close of the period, the position of the pauper schools was becoming increasingly precarious. They had been repudiated in their former strongholds; the West, where school facilities were perhaps the poorest, had never tolerated them; and in the South, wherever such schools existed, progress was being made toward their elimination.[64]

---

[60] *Pennsylvania Reporter,* April 15, 1835, as cited in Woodley, *op. cit.,* pp. 168.
[61] Alexander Harris, *Political Conflict in America,* p. 27, as cited in Woodley, *op. cit.,* pp. 168–169.
[62] See Wickersham, *op. cit.,* pp. 333–336; Knight, *Education in the United States,* Third Revised Edition, *op. cit.,* pp. 268–271; Cubberley, *Readings in Public Education,* pp. 179–181; Woodley, *op. cit.,* pp. 153–167.
[63] Cubberley, *Public Education in the United States, op. cit.,* p. 196.
[64] *Ibid.,* pp. 196–198.

The rate bill.   Although public school systems were generally established in the North and West and beginnings had been made in the South, equal educational opportunity for all children was slow to be provided. In fact, several states among the earliest to establish public school systems failed to make the "schools entirely free" during the period. The rate bill, a charge levied upon parents on the basis of the number of their children attending school, was resorted to quite generally to supplement the funds derived from public sources and to make possible an extension of the school term. In some states, public funds were not used for the purchase of supplies and fuel, and the cost of these items, although small, fell very heavily on the poor.

The rate bill, sanctioned by tradition in such states as Massachusetts and Connecticut, offering a compromise between private-pay and publicly financed schools, and regarded even by friends of education as the only feasible means of meeting mounting school costs, gave way only after bitter contests and heated controversy. Educational statesmen, however, were aware of the fact that a system which caused parents to keep children out of school in order to avoid payment of rate bills and encouraged men of means to patronize private schools defeated the very purpose for which public schools had been established.

Generally, with respect to the elimination of the rate bill, the cities were more advanced than the states in which they were located. Cubberley's careful analysis of the fight against the rate bill in New York indicates clearly the attitude of rural districts and their influence in retarding state-wide legislation. After many cities had eliminated the rate bill and after many demands had been made that general state taxation should provide for schools without the aid of rate bills, the legislature in 1849 ordered a referendum, which was carried by the free-school forces. Although more than 70 per cent of the some 340,000 ballots cast were favorable, the legislature refused to act and called for another referendum, to be held in the autumn of 1850. Again the results favored free schools, although by a much reduced margin. The legislature then took middle ground by authorizing the organization of "union districts" to provide schools by local taxation when demanded by the voters of the district and by increasing the state appropriation. The rate bill, however, was not abolished until 1867. Within four years after the abolition of the rate bill in New York, Connecticut, Rhode Island, Michigan, and New Jersey joined the other northern states which had eliminated it earlier.

In the North, although much remained to be done to provide equal opportunity to all children, the "battle for free state schools" may be said to have been won. In the South, the effects of a devastating war and a disastrous "reconstruction" had to be slowly overcome, for the promise of the antebellum period would not be fully realized until returning prosperity and the resolution of old issues made educational reorganization possible.

The Development of New Patterns of Control

Revenues for school purposes derived from state taxes, permanent funds, and other sources served not only as assistance and encouragement to communities to establish and maintain schools, but also as means of control, because the state legislature could fix the conditions under which the community might share in the distribution of funds. A growing awareness of the educational needs of the emerging democratic states led an increasing number of legislators, elected by small political units, to view education broadly, particularly as it related to the welfare of the entire state. They began to see with greater clarity that education, to perform its proper function, had to be subjected to a type of control which only the state could exercise.

In theory, there was no reason why the state legislature could not establish its control merely by passing laws, but in practice the problem was not so simple. The state had almost abdicated its right to control education. Members of the legislature were elected by voters whose first allegiance was to the local district or even perhaps to the church. Legislators who moved further or more rapidly than their constituents were, as a rule, soon returned to private life, replaced by persons committed to undo the work that had been done.

FORCES OPPOSING THE DEVELOPMENT OF STATE CONTROL

All efforts to create state supervision, even of the mildest sort, were opposed by powerful forces. First, any kind of compulsion or regulation by government was repugnant to a large part of the American people. Indeed, many of the reformers who sought the aid of government to effect needed improvements or changes in particular areas still recited the old Jeffersonian creed, which called that government best which governed least. Control of anything so intimately related to the life of the people as education, particularly by a body as far removed as the state legislature, was certain to be opposed. The older educational agencies, such as the church and other religious organizations, constituted a second center of opposition. For centuries, as long as religiously motivated morality had remained the main end toward which the education of the masses was directed, the church had been called upon to lead or, at least, to point the way. In some states, such as Pennsylvania, the church alone had been responsible for keeping alive, if but feebly, the ideal of universal education. Religious schools, good and bad, were strongly entrenched in their communities. They were rooted in the culture and perpetuated the religious faith, sometimes the language, of their patrons. Religious bodies were, therefore, in a position to oppose strongly any action which might curtail their control over their own schools and were able, in some instances, to set the pattern for all education.

The school district was also a factor, perhaps the strongest factor, in retarding the development of state supervision and control. The district, which, as has already been mentioned, had earlier superseded the town as the unit of school organization and administration in New England, spread in the early nineteenth century to New York and to the states of the new West, even making inroads into the South. The district came to be accepted as a splendid manifestation of an almost pure democracy. It fitted well into the philosophy, geography, and isolation of frontier communities. Its advantages no doubt were many, but the disadvantages arising from the decentralization for which it was responsible were greater. It became firmly fixed in the affections of the people, whose concern for local matters, often on an emotional basis alone, prevented them from seeing the education problem as a whole and as something involving the welfare of the entire state and nation. When the forces opposing centralization are reviewed, the accomplishments with respect to the establishment of state systems of education appear to be greater than might have been expected. They were, however, attained slowly and with many backward steps.

The districts became more powerful, as the states, either as a means of stimulating local effort or as a compromise measure designed to satisfy both those who favored and those who opposed the extension of public education, passed laws under which towns and other communities were permitted to organize as school districts, employ teachers, levy taxes, and administer the schools without more than a semblance of state control. As this process continued, it was clear that the districts would become even more powerful unless means were found by which they might be made more dependent upon the state. The control of funds raised for school purposes was a powerful means of persuasion. The legislatures generally adopted a policy of granting aid to districts which qualified by meeting certain conditions. Of course, the district might refuse to meet the requirements and reject the money offered, but the trend was toward acceptance. The demands made by the state were usually mild. Even when it required that school funds be raised locally, the state in some instances contributed twice the amount which the local district was obliged to raise. Other requirements — that attendance be reported, that the school term should be three or four months, perhaps that a properly certificated teacher be employed — did not immediately result in any large measure of control.

THE RISE OF THE STATE SUPERINTENDENCY

It was found, however, that not even the simplest laws administered themselves, and that the mere passage of a law did not always create the conditions aimed at by the legislators. The state, now with money to distribute, found that it needed an officer to receive the required reports, to compile statistics, to dispense the funds according to law, to see that the law was carried out, to keep the legislature informed, and to help create sentiment in favor of legislative provisions. To meet this need, state school officers were provided for by legislation in an increasing number of states.

New York, which had created the Board of Regents of the University of the State of New York in 1784 for the purpose of endowing and controlling secondary and higher education, extended its control of education in 1812 by providing for an officer, the superintendent of common schools, to represent the state in the work of establishing and maintaining schools and to dispense the income from the fund which had been accumulating for a number of years. At the same time the district system was adopted and a district tax for schools was permitted by law. Gideon Hawley, the first superintendent, worked vigorously to improve and establish schools, but the people's indifference (which had allowed the excellent state school law of 1795 to lapse without a serious effort being made toward its continuance) permitted the office to be abolished in 1821. From this date until the creation of the office of superintendent of public instruction in 1854, the secretary of state served ex officio as superintendent of common schools.

Other states, confronted with the same needs, followed the lead of New York. Maryland established the office in 1826, discontinued it in 1828, and re-created it in 1864. Michigan, the first state to establish an office to be continued without interruption to the present time, after several years of experience with a territorial superintendent of common schools created, in 1836, a constitutional officer, the superintendent of public instruction, whose title indicates a somewhat different concept of his function. In most of the states the chief school officer was elected, but other and better methods of selection were also practiced very early. In 1837 Massachusetts established a state board of education which selected a secretary as its executive officer. The other New England states followed the general pattern set by Massachusetts, but in most other states the laws provided either for ex officio superintendents or for elected regular officers, or, over a period of time, for both, sometimes in one order, sometimes in the other.

By 1850, sixteen of the thirty-one states had officers, nine of which were ex officio. A decade later twenty-eight states of the thirty-four had chief state school officers, with no more ex officio officers than at the earlier date. By the opening of the Civil War, additional supervision was provided in ten states by county superintendents and in twenty-six cities by city superintendents.[65]

[65] *Ibid.*, pp. 216–217.

LIMITING THE POWER OF THE DISTRICT

The chief state school officers, charged by the legislature with the establishment and improvement of schools but at the same time given, for the most part, only clerical duties and little authority, often considered themselves educational leaders dedicated to fighting all the forces which appeared to be retarding the development of state systems of schools. In this struggle they often found themselves opposed by the school districts and other local forces. When these latter were antagonized, the legislature in many instances refused to uphold the superintendent. In fact, no little part of the early legislation discontinuing the office after it had been established or changing it from a regular to an ex officio basis resulted from efforts of the legislature to placate local groups who resented the aggressive leadership of a person bent on fundamental reforms in the school system or on its extension to provide more fully for all the children of the state.

The district system had become firmly entrenched. Even the legislatures which provided for state systems in most instances adopted the district as a unit of school organization and increased its powers. By 1840, the system had spread from New England and New York to Ohio, Illinois, Indiana, Tennessee, Kentucky, North Carolina, and other states. By this time it had become a deeply rooted political institution, no less able than other institutions to resist attempts to modify it or to restrict its powers.

Although districts might provide schools of high quality if they could afford them and if they chose to do so, the fact remains that generally they provided poor schools and managed them badly. In some states teachers were allowed to teach without examination or certification; little concern was shown for keeping the textbooks uniform; some districts refused or neglected to tax themselves and to provide terms of even the minimum length; and some districts determined which subjects were to be taught. In one state, the extreme of decentralization was reached when parents were permitted to draw their shares of the school funds and to make their own contracts with teachers. The state legislatures which were unable or unwilling to take direct action were aided greatly in curbing the power of the districts by the judicious use of state school funds, which could, theoretically, be accepted or rejected by the districts. This fiction of a free choice made possible the stipulation of requirements that would not have been accepted otherwise. However, had not a large number of the early superintendents been educational statesmen of the first rank, and had not an occasional legislature shown a courage rare in such bodies, the development of systems with a measure of state control would have been long retarded.

Much of Mann's work, already described, was aimed at creating state supervision. His outspoken denouncements of the district system did not endear him to local politicians or, for that matter, to schoolmen generally. For a great part of his long term of office he was engaged in controversies which sprang from his efforts to extend state supervision — an action which wounded the sensibilities of many persons and operated against the selfish interests of many others. Similar activity on the part of Barnard led to his early departure from Connecticut, although, as will be remembered, he was later recalled to render great service in extending the influence of the state and in reducing the power of the districts. By the end of the period it was apparent that the state was reasserting its authority and that in most states the foundation had been laid for a system of schools under the general supervision of the state.

ELIMINATION OF SECTARIAN CONTROL

Local districts were not alone in their opposition to state regulation of education. Sectarian bodies, long accustomed to thinking of education in terms of religious aims and purposes and having in many places enjoyed a virtual monopoly of teaching the young, were extremely jealous of their authority and fearful of any movement which threatened to affect adversely the financing of church schools or to weaken the control which religious organizations exercised over education. For many years after the beginning of the national period, it was not unusual for church schools to receive land endowments, money grants, and other financial aid from the state. Because of increased immigration, the continued mobility of the American people, the growing diversity of religious denominations, and, perhaps, the spirit of the times, the practice gradually ceased. Even in Massachusetts, churches did not receive state support after 1833. Other changes indicated a decline of religious influence. The content of new textbooks clearly reflected a growing secularism. Mather's *Spiritual Milk for American Babes Drawn out of the Breasts of Both Testaments for Their Souls' Nourishment* had long since ceased to be required reading for children. The Woodstock edition of the *New England Primer,* published in 1823, dropped the old religious rhymes that through a hundred editions had taught children the alphabet. No longer were abecadarians confronted with couplets such as:

In Adam's Fall
We sinned all.

The rhymes substituted were, if nothing else, less religious, as is indicated by the rhyme which celebrated the Ape's mischief instead of Adam's sin.

> The Ape with mischief fraught
> Like children badly taught
> Will often play the fool
> As truants do from school.

Changes were made so slowly that many persons were hardly aware of them. A Massachusetts law of 1827 which prohibited the purchase with state money of sectarian books was largely a formal recognition of what had, in a great measure, already happened. The agitation caused by the appointment of a state board of education, however, served to call these changes to the attention of the public and the religious groups. Mann and the board were blamed by Episcopalians, Presbyterians, and other sectarian groups, who professed to believe that the schools should return to their old ways, but no one suggested a reasonable method by which this might be done. The religious forces, thoroughly awakened everywhere, zealously fought all attempts to eliminate sectarian books from the schools and to take away state subsidies, whether in the form of money grants or tuition paid out of relief funds for the education of pauper children, and they did their best to discredit the theorists who would disobey the Biblical injunction which prescribes use of the rod. In spite of all this rather largely disorganized opposition, secular influences were to prevail.[66] The attempts by religious forces to abolish the board of education in the Massachusetts Legislature of 1840 and 1841 failed. It appeared that, not only in Massachusetts but elsewhere, the strong trend toward the separation of religion and politics would carry with it the full secularization of education.

The immigration of large numbers of Catholics in the eighteen-thirties and forties, however, made the situation, which might otherwise have slowly disappeared, more acute, even though it perhaps did not prolong its duration. Catholics, insisting upon the right to educate their children in schools of their own faith, found both public schools and those operated

---

[66] The feeling engendered by the issue was intense, as is illustrated by the name-calling quarrel between Horace Mann and the Reverend M. Hale Smith. Smith preached a sermon, "The Ark of God on a New Cart," a bitter attack on Mann, the school board, normal schools, etc., which was published in the *Boston Recorder* and caused considerable comment. A little later Smith published the sermon in a pamphlet, *The Bible, the Rod, and Religion, in Common Schools,* which also contained the "Correspondence Between the Hon. Horace Mann and Rev. Matthew Hale Smith" and other items designed to discredit Mann. Mann quickly published his *Sequel to the So Called Correspondence Between the Rev. M. H. Smith and Horace Mann, Surreptitiously Published by Mr. Smith with the Reply Therein Promised.* Smith in his turn responded with his *Reply to the Sequel of Hon. Horace Mann, Being a Supplement to "The Bible, the Rod, and Religion, in Common Schools."* So far as the principals were concerned, Mann ended the argument with his pamphlet *Letter to the Rev. Matthew Hale Smith, in Answer to His "Reply" or "Supplement,"* but supporters on both sides continued to attack or defend Smith and Mann in newspapers and journals.

by non-sectarian school societies unacceptable. The public schools were likely to be under the control of an entirely Protestant board, and both kinds of schools, although non-sectarian, were almost certain to engage in certain religious activities, such as reading the King James Version of the Bible and others equally objectionable to the Catholic Church. In New York City, the demand of the Catholics for a share of the public funds with which to support their own educational enterprises precipitated a particularly heated controversy. In that city, it will be recalled, the Public School Society, a "non-denominational organization but with centralized Protestant control," had over a period of more than thirty years provided education for thousands of children who were not cared for in the religious schools of the city. Its schools constituted the nearest approach to a public school system in the city. New York City had been exempted from the operation of earlier state legislation which had established the district system upstate and had provided for public schools under local control. The demand of the Catholic group for a share of the funds was denied by the city council and was then carried to the state legislature. The legislature, pressed by the Catholics on the one hand and by an alliance of Protestant groups on the other, and urged by Governor Seward to extend the upstate system to New York, even though such action was likely to give control in some instances to the Catholics, deferred action for a year or two and then took action not entirely pleasing to either religious group and perhaps not altogether satisfactory to the Governor. It created a city board of education charged with the responsibility of establishing public schools, and at the same time it specified that in the future no public funds were to be given to any school in which sectarian doctrines were taught or inculcated. The legislature, in establishing the city system of publicly supported schools under the control of the local authority, did not prohibit the maintenance either of parochial or private schools or of those of the Public School Society. Religious bodies continued to support schools, but such action was taken with a growing realization that maintenance in the future was a matter of church rather than public concern. A decade later, the Public School Society, having outlived its usefulness, surrendered its buildings and property to the city board of education and disbanded.

The various attempts by religious groups to secure public support were no more successful in other states. The demand of the General Assembly of the Presbyterian Church for aid to denominational primary schools received little attention, as did the agitation of Catholics and Episcopalians for systems of parochial schools in Massachusetts to take the place of the non-sectarian state schools. The demands of the Catholics in several states for a division of the school funds was followed in Massachusetts by the adoption in 1855 of a constitutional amendment which provided that no religious sect should ever share in the state funds. In fact, no demands to divide the funds made after 1840 were successful anywhere. Between

1840 and the Civil War, six states amended their constitutions to forbid public support of religious schools and three new states made such provisions in their first constitutions.[67] That by the close of the period the trend was unmistakable is borne out by history.

Every state admitted to the Union since 1858, except West Virginia, has erected constitutional safeguards against possible attempts of religious groups to obtain a share of the public school funds.[68]

The agitation of the 1950's and early 1960's for increased federal aid has given rise to questioning on the part of some persons of the existing practices, and to fear, on the part of others, that some concessions may eventually be made to religious groups. Time may well bring different conceptions of what constitutes support of a religious body. The Supreme Court has upheld, in recent years, legislation providing for certain auxiliary services to children attending parochial schools; it has, for example, sustained the legality of paying the costs of transportation of pupils to parochial schools and of providing parochial-school pupils with free textbooks. Such expenditures are not regarded as aid to parochial schools but as aid to the children as recipients of the benefits of public-welfare legislation. The Catholic Church may be able, in view of changing circumstances, to move somewhat from its traditional position. In the nineteen-sixties both churchmen and educators are considering the proposal that Catholic children be permitted to attend public schools for instruction in mathematics, chemistry, physical education, and other subjects which have few if any religious overtones. It appears that some of the costs of education and welfare services for Catholic children may be shifted to the state. But it appears equally clear that such shifts will not be permitted to violate the traditional policy of separation of church and state.[69]

---

[67] Cubberley, *Public Education in the United States, op. cit.,* 238–239.

[68] For the provisions of the state constitutions, including those of Alaska and Hawaii (as they stood in 1961), see Richard A. Edwards (ed.), *Index Digest of State Constitutions,* Second Edition (New York: Oceana Publications, Inc. [for the Legislation Drafting Research Fund, Columbia University], 1959), pp. 363–419.

[69] In fact, in 1947 the Supreme Court of the United States handed down a decision (*Eversen* v. *Board of Education,* 330, U.S. 1) which makes it perfectly clear that direct federal aid to church schools is a violation of the First Amendment. The Court laid down the principle that the First Amendment, which was made applicable to the States by the Fourteenth Amendment, means separation of church and state, that it requires on the part of the state complete neutrality among all religions, and that no tax may be levied by either state or federal governments to support religious activities or institutions. In the words of the Court: "No tax in any amount, large or small, can be levied to support religious activities or institutions, whatever they may be called, or whatever form they may adopt to teach or practice religion. Neither a State nor the Federal Government can, openly or secretly, participate in the affairs of any religious organizations or groups, or vice versa. In the words of Jefferson, the clause against establishment of religion was intended to erect 'a wall of separation between Church and State.' The First Amendment has erected a wall of separation between Church and State. That wall must be kept high and impregnable. We could not approve the slightest breach,"

Questions and Problems for Study and Discussion

1. Describe the opportunities for education available to different regional and social groups at the opening of the period considered in this chapter.

2. What do you regard as the major factors that contributed to the development of public education during the period 1830–1860?

3. Evaluate the effect of the growth of urbanism on the development of the free public school.

4. Discuss the leadership of educational statesmen in the development of education. Evaluate the work and influence of Horace Mann, Henry Barnard, and Calvin Wiley. How do you account for the high quality of educational leadership in the different states?

5. Explain how the emergence of the democratic state affected the development of financial support of education during this period.

6. There is a trend today toward increased federal support of education. Do you favor it? Give your reasons. Do you think your reasons would have been more or less compelling in 1850 than they are today?

7. What contributions did this period make to the development of administrative control of education? Do you think that any of the remaining features of the patterns of control that were then developed have outlived their usefulness?

8. This period was marked by the rapid secularization of American education. What attempts have been made in recent years to check this trend? Do you think that the secularization of education has been carried too far?

Selected References for Further Reading

Bache, Alex. Dallas. *Report on Education in Europe, to the Trustees of the Girard College for Orphans.* Philadelphia: Lydia R. Bailey, 1839. Pp. xiv + 666.

Bode, Carl. *The American Lyceum: Town Meeting of the Mind.* New York: Oxford University Press, Inc., 1956. Pp. 275.

Brown, Samuel Windsor. *The Secularization of American Education as Shown by State Legislation, State Constitution Provisions and State Supreme Court Decisions,* Teachers College Contributions to Education, No. 49. New York: Teachers College, Columbia University, 1912. Pp. 160.

Carter, James G. *Essays upon Popular Education: Containing a Particular Examination of the Schools of Massachusetts and an Outline of an Institution for the Education of Teachers.* Boston: Bowles and Dearborn, 1826. Pp. iv + 60.

Carter, James G. *Letters to the Hon. William Prescott, LL.D., on the Free Schools of New England: With Remarks upon the Principles of Instruction.* Boston: Cummings, Hilliard & Co., 1824. Pp. iv + 124.

Cremin, Lawrence A. *The American Common School.* New York: Bureau of Publications, Teachers College, Columbia University, 1951. Pp. xvi + 248.

Cubberley, Ellwood P. *Public Education in the United States: A Study and Interpretation of American Educational History,* Revised and Enlarged Edition. Boston: Houghton Mifflin Company, 1934. Pp. xx + 782.

Cubberley, Ellwood P. *Readings in Public Education in the United States: A Collection of Sources and Readings to Illustrate the History of Educational Practice and Progress in the United States.* Boston: Houghton Mifflin Company, 1934. Pp. xviii + 534.

Culver, Raymond B. *Horace Mann and Religion in the Massachusetts Public Schools.* New Haven, Conn.: Yale University Press, 1929. Pp. xii + 302.

Curoe, Philip R. V. *Educational Attitudes and Policies of Organized Labor in the United States,* Teachers College Contributions to Education, No. 201. New York: Teachers College, Columbia University, 1926. Pp. viii + 202.

Curti, Merle. *The Social Ideas of American Educators, with a New Chapter on the Last Twenty-five Years.* New Jersey: Pageant Books, Inc., 1959. Pp. xliv + 613.

Davis, Sheldon Emmor. *Educational Periodicals During the Nineteenth Century,* United States Bureau of Education Bulletin 28. Washington, D.C.: Government Printing Office, 1919. Pp. 126.

Dowd, Jerome. *The Life of Braxton Craven: A Biographical Approach to Social Science.* Durham, N.C.: Duke University Press, 1939. Pp. xvi + 246.

Fish, Carl Russell. *The Rise of the Common Man, 1830–1850, VI: A History of American Life.* New York: The Macmillan Co., 1927. Pp. xx + 392.

Gobbel, Luther. *Church-State Relationships in Education in North Carolina Since 1776.* Durham, N.C.: Duke University Press, 1938. Pp. xvi + 252.

Hayes, Cecil B. *The American Lyceum: Its History and Contribution to Education,* United States Office of Education Bulletin 12. Washington, D.C.: Government Printing Office, 1932. Pp. xii + 72.

Hinsdale, B. A. *Horace Mann: And the Common School Revival in the United States.* New York: Charles Scribner's Sons, 1898. Pp. viii + 326.

Jackson, Sidney L. *America's Struggle for Free Schools: Social Tension and Education in New England and New York, 1827–42.* Washington, D.C.: American Council on Public Affairs, 1941. Pp. viii + 276.

Knight, Edgar W. (ed.). *A Documentary History of Education in the South Before 1860, III: The Rise of the State University.* Chapel Hill, N.C.: University of North Carolina Press, 1952. Pp. viii + 484.

Knight, Edgar W. *Public Education in the South.* Boston: Ginn & Company, 1922. Pp. xii + 482.

Mulhern, James. *A History of Secondary Education in Pennsylvania.* Philadelphia: published by the author, 1933. Pp. xvi + 714.

Noble, M. C. S. *A History of the Public Schools of North Carolina.* Chapel Hill, N.C.: University of North Carolina Press, 1930. Pp. xiv + 464.

Reisner, Edward H. *Nationalism and Education Since 1789: A Social and Political History of Modern Education.* New York: The Macmillan Co., 1929. Pp. xiv + 576.

Remarks upon Mr. Carter's Outline of an Institution for the Education of Teachers. Boston: Bowles and Dearborn, 1827. Pp. 26.

Swift, Fletcher Harper. *Federal and State Policies in Public School Finance.* Boston: Ginn & Company, 1931. Pp. xviii + 472.

Tharp, Louise Hall. *Until Victory: Horace Mann and Mary Peabody.* Boston: Little, Brown & Co., 1953. Pp. xii + 367.

Walz, John A. *German Influence in American Education and Culture.* Philadelphia: Carl Schurz Memorial Foundation, Inc., 1936. Pp. 80.

Wickersham, James Pyle. *A History of Education in Pennsylvania, Private and Public, Elementary and Higher; From the Time the Swedes Settled on the Delaware to the Present Day.* Lancaster, Pa.: published for the author by the Inquirer Publishing Co., 1885. Pp. xxii + 684.

Woodley, Thomas Frederick. *Thaddeus Stevens.* Harrisburg, Pa.: Telegraph Press, 1934. Pp. xvi + 664.

10

Education in the Emerging Democratic State: the Record of Educational Progress, 1828–1860

In the two preceding chapters we have examined the broad social forces that were transforming American commonwealths into democratic states and molding the three great competing sections into a single nation. We also noted that changing conditions had given rise to new attitudes and sentiments with respect to the role education should play in the life of the young republic. The present chapter will be devoted to a more detailed account of the educational gains made during the period beginning with the close of the first quarter of the nineteenth century and ending with the outbreak of the Civil War. It was, as has been noted, a remarkable period.

The educational needs of the emerging democratic state could not be satisfied merely by providing the barest elements for more children than had formerly received any education. Enrichment of the program, as well as the extension of opportunity to greater numbers, was also a pressing problem. As long as the religious purpose in education predominated, the efforts of the schools had been directed largely toward teaching children to read. Little else was necessary. At most, the ability to read, to write, and to figure accounts was sufficient to meet the needs of all except those few persons of position and wealth in whose hands economic power was concentrated and the control of government was vested.

The breaking of class rule in government was a corollary to the growing dignity of the common man who not only denied the doctrine of divine right as it applied to English kings but also was beginning to deny the theory of inherited differences among men. All things are good as they come from the hands of the Creator, said the philosopher, and the liberal political philosophy of the eighteenth century had stressed the duty of government to provide conditions under which the potentialities of each individual could be realized. Next to fluid institutions, education was looked upon as the most important means of achieving this end. Education would ennoble man by striking away the fetters of ignorance and of political and economic oppression. From this it should not be deduced that there was at any time a spontaneous uprising of the illiterate and unlearned demanding to be freed from the limitations which their ignorance imposed. At best, the masses came slowly to understand the implications of the liberal philosophy. The history of the educational legislation of the first fifty or more years of the national period provides ample evidence that the modest extensions and improvements of education were the result, to a considerable extent, of the constant pressure of a strong minority group which maintained a position far in advance of that which the great public had reached. All in all, however, the forces which for fifty years had been preparing the way for the democratic upsurge which eventuated in the election of Jackson were, when not the same, closely related to those which were to lead to the period of the so-called "public school revival." This was a period of marked acceleration in the growth of the conception of the function of education in a democratic state. There was unprecedented activity directed toward making education available to the masses, extending it beyond the rudiments, making its support an accepted responsibility of the state, and improving its general quality.

The Evolution of Elementary Education

At the beginning of the period, as has been indicated, although some progress had been made everywhere in the reorganization of elementary, secondary, and higher education, few of the states had established systems of public schools. Therefore, although all levels of education had felt the impact of new forces, it was not strange that the extension of opportunity for an elementary education and the modifications in its content necessary to meet the changed and changing social needs should be the first concern of the evolving democratic order.

The meagerness of the common-school program in the early nineteenth century is made evident by an examination of a *Code of Regulations* drawn up in 1799 by William Woodbridge, president of the Middlesex County (Connecticut) Association for the Improvement of Common Schools. This code, presented to the visitors and overseers of schools for their consideration, suggested the improvement of existing conditions by indicating what might be considered an adequate program. It is significant that the editor of the progressive *American Annals of Education and Instruction,* when recommending in 1837 the perusal of this code by the "friends of education," did not feel constrained to comment upon or even note the limited offerings recommended nearly forty years earlier. With respect to the school program, Woodbridge's code reads:

> In the morning, the Bible may be delivered to the head of each class, and by them to the scholars capable of reading decently or looking over. This reading with some short remarks, or questions, with the morning prayer, may occupy the *first half hour*. The second, may be employed in hearing the morning lessons, while the younger classes are preparing to spell and read. The third in attention to the writers. The fourth in hearing the under classes read and spell. The fifth in looking over and assisting the writers and cipherers. The sixth in hearing the under classes spell and read the second time; and receiving and depositing pens, writing and reading books. . . .
>
> In the afternoon one half hour may be employed in spelling together, repeating grammar, rules of arithmetic, and useful tables, with a clear, and full, but soft voice, while the instructor prepares pens, writing books, &c. The second and third half hours in hearing the under classes and assisting the writers and cypherers. The fourth in hearing the upper classes read. The fifth to hearing the under classes read, and spell the second time. The sixth in receiving and depositing the books, &c. as above.[1]

The recognition of the inadequacy of the colonial-type course of study, so narrow that it could be presented in a single volume, was only a first step in enlarging and enriching the curriculum. Each advance had to overcome the forces of inertia and poverty. The situation was also seriously aggravated by the tendency to divide and subdivide the units of school organization. The district schools, staffed by untrained and poorly educated teachers and handicapped by inadequate teaching materials and poor textbooks, were overwhelmed by the problems arising from the fact that pupils of all ages attended school — from those who formerly would have attended dame schools to those who for lack of other opportunity, either educational or recreational, came during the winter months far beyond the years of childhood.

Expansion of the curriculum and reorganization of instruction, no matter how sorely the need might be felt, could not take place rapidly. These reforms had to await not only recognition of their need, but also the growth of towns and cities, the development of union districts, and the appearance of textbooks adapted to the particular needs of the American people.

The Development of American Textbooks

In 1783 Noah Webster published a textbook in spelling, *The First Part of a Grammatical Institute of the English Language.* The last two volumes

[1] "Forty Years Ago," *American Annals of Education and Instruction,* VII (January, 1837), 18.

of the series (Second Part and Third Part) were devoted to reading and grammar. The Webster speller, on the general plan of Dilworth's earlier book, contained the alphabet, lists of words, the syllables, a number of fables, "Precepts concerning the Social Relations," and lessons of easy words designed to teach children to read. It made spelling a popular craze and gave it the dignity of a separate subject of instruction. About twenty-four million copies of the various editions of this book were sold before the death of the author in 1843. By that time its hold was weakening in the East, but it continued to be popular in the South until the Civil War and in the West to a much later date.

The tremendous sales of this and similar books indicate not only the growing popularity of spelling as a subject of instruction, but also that many books must have been purchased for children not enrolled in school and perhaps for adults as well. In this connection, a statement found in the preface of one of the most attractive of the spellers, Parsons' *Analytical Spelling Book,* published in 1836, may be noted: "Parents who have little skill in teaching can learn their children to read, where there are no schools, and adults with little assistance can learn by themselves."[2]

It may be noted also that spelling as a subject presented relatively few difficulties to the teacher, with regard to both knowledge of the content and the accepted method of instruction, and therefore it could be introduced relatively early, even in the overcrowded and understaffed schools of the countryside.

Arithmetic also began to find its way into the elementary-school curriculum before the close of the colonial period. It was made a required subject by the Massachusetts Legislature in 1789. When introduced into the common schools, only the four fundamental processes and perhaps a little of common fractions were taught. Those who progressed as far as simple proportion (the rule of three) were rated as mathematicians. In 1788, Nicholas Pike brought out his massive, encyclopedic work, which, endorsed by Washington and other notables, soon became a leader in the field, displacing the English works of Dilworth and Hodder. During the next half-century a hundred or more texts, most of them better adapted to the schoolroom than Pike's book, were published. One of these, Warren Colburn's *First Lessons in Arithmetic on the Plan of Pestalozzi,* published in 1821, helped decisively to place the subject, previously considered rather largely as belonging to the academy and the college, in the curriculum of the elementary school. The enthusiasm for Colburn's book, however, must have been more tempered than has often been reported. It was used in fewer towns in New York than Pike's book until 1835, and in 1838 was used in only 45 towns, while Daboll's was used in 358 or 359 towns, Adam's in 170, and Smith's in 87. However, a number of the

---

[2] As quoted in Clifton Johnson, *Old-Time Schools and School-Books* (New York: The Macmillan Co., 1904), p. 226.

new books which appeared during the second quarter of the nineteenth century were influenced by Colburn's ideas with respect to the content and method of arithmetic. As in the case of spelling, arithmetic did not, in the presence of adequate texts, tax unduly the poorly educated elementary school teacher.

Geography textbooks were introduced in the late eighteenth century. Morse's *American Universal Geography* (1784) and the *Elements of Geography* (1795), a shortened school edition of the earlier work, were almost entirely fact books. Dwight's competitive text, *A Short but Comprehensive System of the Geography of the World* (1795), was a question-and-answer treatment of world geography, with emphasis upon the United States. Treated in this fashion, geography could be taught almost entirely as a drill subject, in much the same way that arithmetic and spelling were taught. These early geography texts were followed by others, and, beginning about 1830, the number of texts multiplied rapidly. Among these, Woodbridge's *Rudiments of Geography* (1821), Goodrich's *Peter Parley's Method of Telling about Geography* (1830), Olney's *A Practical System of Modern Geography* (1831), and Goodrich's *Peter Parley's National Geography* (1845) developed considerable followings and helped make geography a valuable subject in those schools in which it was properly taught.

History was not accorded an important place in the elementary curriculum until well into the nineteenth century. Some little works giving dates of important events — e.g., the creation of the earth, the Flood, the fall of the walls of Jericho, the accession of certain kings, the last great fall of snow, and similar events — had appeared and had, no doubt, been used in some of the more progressive schools. Goodrich's *A History of the United States*, a Peter Parley book, published in 1822, was the first history text of note. It ran through many editions (forty-four by 1836) and sold some 150,000 copies during its first twelve years. Books by Webster, Hale, Taylor, Olney, and others, all very nationalistic in tone, also came into great demand in the schools during the period, and, perhaps to a considerable extent, became popular among older persons eager for reading materials.

Grammar, reduced largely to a study of rules, was early introduced into the schools. Webster's Second Part appeared in 1784 and Murray's and Bingham's grammars appeared some time later. It was not, however, until the second quarter of the nineteenth century that the subject was introduced on any large scale into the elementary schools.

The teaching and the content of reading, the oldest elementary-school subject, were both much improved. Few primers or readers for beginners appeared before 1825, but after that date they became numerous. Most of them contained easier material than that found in the spellers, and, although given to sticky moralizing over the adventures of Timothy

Trusty, Charles Mindful, Caroline Modesty, and other characters intended to be less attractive, they were generally better adapted than the earlier primers and readers to the needs and interests of younger children. Older children were also provided with secular reading materials. Beginning with Webster's Third Part, these texts reflected the efforts of their authors to adjust the curriculum to the child instead of the centuries-old procedure of making the child adjust to the curriculum. These books, one of the best of which was Bingham's *Columbian Orator,* stressed public speaking and helped make oratory an important aspect of the reading program. The effectiveness of the instruction in speaking is attested by the fact that probably no other period in American history produced so many skilled orators who could speak without the inhibitions which trained intelligence might have raised.[3]

Of all the readers, McGuffey's deservedly became by far the most popular. The first two readers of this remarkable graded set were published in Cincinnati in 1836. The third and fourth were published in 1837; the fifth was published in 1841. A few years later, they were made into six readers, and were revised several times in the years that followed. Throughout the remainder of the century these texts continued to be popular readers. It has been estimated that for more than a half-century fully one-half of the children attending school learned to read from them.[4] They were, in spite of shortcomings as measured by modern standards, remarkable for the nature of their content, for the excellence of their grading, and for the hold they had upon the public mind. In 1927 Henry Ford financed the reprinting of an edition of these greatly venerated readers, and until well into the twentieth century there were throughout the country numerous McGuffey clubs, the principal bond among the members of each being the high esteem in which they held the texts from which they had learned to read.

THE MULTIPLICITY OF TEXTBOOKS

Keen competition for the increasingly profitable textbook market resulted in the publishing of a greater number of books, continually improved in content, organization, attractiveness, and suitability for children of different ages and academic accomplishments. The multiplicity of textbooks, however, in some ways constituted a serious evil. Uncritical selection of well-advertised books resulted in considerable use of some of the poorer ones. Also, children within the same school were often permitted to use different texts, and within a single state so many books on the same subject might be used that a reasonable measure of uniformity

---

[3] *Ibid.,* pp. 265–300.

[4] Ellwood P. Cubberley, *Public Education in the United States,* Revised and Enlarged Edition (Boston: Houghton Mifflin Company, 1934), p. 294.

in the curriculums of the developing public schools was impossible. In 1837, the situation in Massachusetts was almost entirely out of hand.

> For the purpose of teaching reading and spelling, then, there are in use in the schools of Massachusetts no less than 100 different books; of Grammars, there are 28; of Histories, 24; of Arithmetics, 22; of Geographies, 20; of Dictionaries, 9; of Natural Philosophies, 4; of Astronomies, 4; of Chemistries, 3; of Geometries, 5; and of Composition, 2.[5]

In New York, the situation was little better. Table 3, compiled from data taken from the annual reports of the superintendent (ex officio) of common schools reveals something of this diversity, as well as the persistence of specific textbooks.

The variety in textbooks appears to have been greater at the elementary than at the more advanced levels. Nearly all the subjects which were to be taught during the remainder of the century were by 1840 represented by several, sometimes many, textbooks. Some of these subjects were first introduced in the academies and later shifted to the expanding and developing elementary schools. By 1830, United States history, civil government, physiology, music, and drawing were being added to the curriculums of the better schools, which had already been expanded to include arithmetic and then geography, spelling, and grammar. These subjects, along with reading and writing, constituted in the main the elementary-school curriculum until the Civil War.

Although the new content was available by the beginning of the period, most schools were unable to expand their curriculums rapidly. New studies were not always accepted without a struggle. Some of them were objected to on the ground that they would take attention from arithmetic and spelling. Some communities added the new subjects only when obliged to do so. Massachusetts made spelling, good behavior, arithmetic, English language, and grammar compulsory in 1789. Geography was added to this list more than a quarter century later, and United States history was added only shortly before the outbreak of the Civil War. The other New England states and the northern tier of western states followed in a general way the lead of Massachusetts. It must be remembered, however, that during the entire period a great majority of all of the nation's children attended rural, ungraded, one-room schools, and that such schools were obliged to be content, as a rule, with much less ambitious programs than were found in the less numerous but rapidly developing schools of the urban communities. However, it may be said that the period was less remarkable for the development of new subjects than for the introduction of the new studies to a widening circle of schools.

[5] "Schools in Massachusetts," *American Annals of Education and Instruction,* VII (March, 1837), 101.

TABLE 3. TEXTBOOKS IN ARITHMETIC AND SPELLING IN USE IN
THE TOWNS OF NEW YORK, 1827–1838*

Texts	Number of Towns Using Texts According to Annual Reports				
	1827	1830	1833	1836	1838
Arithmetic					
Daboll's	349	473	472	500	358
Adam's	91	96	91	119	170
Pike's	80	61	36	24	9
Ostrander's	16	45	48	48	41
Willet's	10	16	24	28	24
Colburn's	1	8	17	38	45
Root's	5	5	..	..	..
Starkweather's	..	1	1	..	..
Dilworth's	..	2	1	1	..
Alexander's	..	2	..	..	..
Parker's	..	1	2	1	..
Ruger's	..	..	14	22	36
Thompson's	..	1	3	4	5
Smith's	..	..	3	23	87
Baldwin's	..		1	1	1
Brandon's	..	..	1	..	..
Babcock's	..	..	..	..	1
Cobb's	..	..	..	3	11
Steven's	..	1	..	..	..
23 others used in these or intervening years	..	..	..	24	30
Spelling					
Webster's	302	417	433	332	265
Cobb's	59	209	235	242	270
Marshall's	60	85	61	39	27
Crandall's	55	62	62	42	38
Bentley's	16	41	36	36	35
Sear's	10	14	12	8	3
Picket's	10	19	16	4	6

* Compiled from New York State, *Annual Report of the Superintendent of Common Schools*, 1827–38.

GRADING INSTRUCTION AND CLASSIFYING PUPILS

The pressure of new subjects made desirable arrangements which would provide for economy of both the pupil's and the teacher's time. The new texts not only provided an enriched content but, as poorly graded as most of them were, also made possible some grouping of pupils of like attainments. "Classing" pupils was not without precedent. The Latin schools had followed the practice much earlier. The monitorial schools had stressed the idea of children being taught in groups, the members of each group being more or less equally advanced. The *Code of Regulations* recommended in 1799 for the Middlesex County (Connecticut) Schools, after listing the subjects to be taught, recommended the classification of pupils of equal attainments.[6] The course of study drawn up for the Providence schools of 1800 ordered that "Scholars shall be put into separate Classes, according to their several improvements, each Sex by themselves."[7]

The growth of population and increased democratization of elementary education led to greatly enlarged enrollments and a concentration of pupils, which in turn led to the multiplication of elementary schools, most of which continued to be of the ungraded type. The effect of the great variety of better texts, the introduction of new subjects, the gradual lengthening of the school terms, and the extension of the years of schooling were to make possible a new type of organization. The single elementary school, particularly in towns and cities, gave way to primary schools for the beginners and more advanced schools for the older pupils. When high schools were introduced, they were organized merely as upward extensions of these common schools to receive pupils who had passed through the succession of lower schools. In some cities there were only two divisions below the high school; in others, there was as many as five. Communities with the lesser number probably maintained independent infant schools or refused to admit children to the town schools until they had learned to read, while a city which had subprimary, primary, intermediate-primary, secondary, and grammar schools — all below the high school — probably permitted beginners to enroll in the public schools. Nearly all large cities and towns organized schools known as primary schools, some of them, as in the case of the Boston primary schools until 1854, under separate boards. The more advanced schools were given a bewildering variety of names. This differentiation into schools and divisions really amounted to grading the curriculum and classifying pupils into two to five grades. Children passed from one division to another — each with its curriculum, texts, and teachers.

---

6 "Forty Years Ago," *op. cit.*, 18.
7 As quoted in Cubberley, *op. cit.*, p. 301.

As Cubberley has pointed out, another important step toward the re-organization of elementary education was taken when the work within each school, whether it was a common school offering the entire elementary program or an intermediate or grammar school offering only two, three, or four years of such a program, was graded and the pupils were sorted according to their advancement. Duplicate schools within the same building were eliminated as their wastefulness became apparent and large school buildings with smaller classrooms were constructed. The first fully graded school is said to have been the Quincy Grammar School of Boston, reorganized in 1847 by Principal John D. Philbrick, who became superintendent of schools in Boston in 1856 and served in that capacity for more than twenty years. By 1860, the grading of elementary schools in the larger cities was well under way, but it should be remembered that at this date less than one-sixth of the population lived in cities. Most of the nation's children continued to be educated in primitive, ungraded, one-room rural schools.

The Democratization of Secondary Education

The three principal institutions that have provided secondary education to the American youth were all present during the period from 1828 to 1860. The Latin school was declining in importance, the academy reached the peak of its development, and the high school was in the process of taking form.

THE LATIN SCHOOL

The Latin grammar school, the oldest establishment of secondary education, continued to emphasize Latin and mathematics, and apparently served well its limited purpose of preparing boys for college. Unable to adjust to the changing conditions of American life, it responded but feebly to the growing demands for a broader curriculum. It continued to be, in the main, the traditional classical school of the past, admitting boys as young as nine years, provided they were able "to read correctly and with fluency" and "to write running hand," knew "all the stops, marks, and abbreviations," and had "sufficient knowledge of English Grammar to parse common sentences in prose."[8] There is some question as to the extent to which the pupils were held for the stated prerequisites. In Boston, in 1826 and perhaps much later, the boys were dismissed during the first two or three years of the five-year course for an hour each day in order

[8] "Public Latin School in Boston," *American Journal of Education*, I (May, 1826), 265.

that they might attend a writing school.[9] The Latin school continued to occupy an important place in secondary education; but step by step, as America repudiated the class system of society and government by the elite, the Latin school lost ground to the more democratic secondary schools, the academy and the high school.

THE ACADEMY

The academies, originating about the middle of the eighteenth century, increased rapidly in number. Between 1828 and 1860 they became so numerous that there were few communities which did not have access to one or more of them. Although it would be a mistake to think, as many writers have done, that the 6085 "academies and other schools" reported in the Census of 1850 were really secondary schools, the institutions that could probably be regarded as academies were plentiful enough to afford opportunity for advanced study to most children whose parents were able and willing to pay the tuition charges.

The academies reflected the growing democracy, the undisciplined individualism, and the unstabilized culture of the period. A few attempts were made at state organization, but for the most part the academies were independent and largely unsupervised institutions. The great majority were small, local, modest, and likely to be short-lived. Some, however, became firmly established and attained wide reputation and long-continued prestige. In 1838, for example, Daniel Webster presided over the exercises which were held to honor the venerable Dr. Benjamin Abbott on the occasion of his completion of fifty years of service to Phillips Exeter.

These schools appealed largely to the great middle class and provided preparation for the counting room, the sea, and the classroom as well as for college. Although the offerings varied from institution to institution, taken together they presented rather widespread training for any field, whether cultural, practical, classical, or purely vocational.[10] Although, as

---

[9] *Ibid.*, 266.

[10] Examples of varied activities of these schools are numerous. The Hartford Grammar School, an old Latin school, but incorporated in 1798, advertised in 1839 that "a class of 20 gentlemen who design to engage the coming winter in common school instruction in this state will be taught free by the kindness of a friend." Applicants were advised to attend promptly and were promised a position by Henry Barnard. *Connecticut Courant,* September 7, 1839, as cited in Vera M. Butler, *Education as Revealed by New England Newspapers Prior to 1850* (Doctor's thesis, Temple University, 1935), p. 169.

A few months later it was reported that twenty-three men, "nearly all of whom have had some experience as teachers, are now diligently attending the instruction and lectures." The courses offered by seven instructors were listed. Mr. Wright, among other activities, was explaining the "methods of School teaching and management"; the Rev. Mr. Gallaudet was explaining "the uses and best methods of teaching Composition" and promised soon to "take up the subjects of Spelling and School Government." It was further stated that Mr. Snow, Principal of the Centre District

a group, they met the widely varying needs of their constituencies, allowed almost free choice of subjects, experimented with new methods, provided for girls, and gave other evidence of democratic tendencies, these institutions, variously known as academies, institutes, seminaries, and colleges, were in one sense a denial of democracy. They were, in spite of the exemption from taxation which they generally enjoyed and the state grants and subsidies which they in some instances received, privately controlled tuition schools. For this reason, perhaps more than for any other, they were destined to be almost completely replaced during the second half of the nineteenth century by the publicly controlled and supported secondary school.

THE HIGH SCHOOL

The same factors which had led to the expansion and enrichment of public education at the lower levels operated to force its extension upward. The completion of the lengthened and improved elementary-school program by a greater number of children gave rise to an immediate and insistent demand for training, free of tuition charges, for intelligent and effective participation in the increasingly complex activities of the life of the period. Only through the upward extension of the tax-supported public school could such opportunity be provided to the numerous sons and daughters of the emerging middle class.

There is no evidence that the founders of the Boston English Classical School (renamed the English High School in 1824), generally credited as being the first American high school, had any awareness of the historical significance of their action. They saw the need for a school which would afford boys, "intending to become merchants and mechanics, better means

---

School, would "give every facility to the pupils to become acquainted with the methods of teaching and government pursued in his school." *Connecticut Courant,* October 19, 1839, as cited in Butler, *op. cit.,* pp. 169–170.

The prospectus of another variant of the academy, the Fellenberg School, which opened in Windsor, Connecticut, in 1824, noted that English, Latin, Greek, arithmetic, bookkeeping, geography, algebra, surveying, navigation, natural philosophy, history, rhetoric, logic, botany, chemistry, and mineralogy would be offered and went on to state:

"A farm is attached to the institution; and the students will have under their daily observation, the various operations of farming; and those, who are expecting to engage in agricultural pursuits, will receive a course of Lectures by which they will be made acquainted with the improvements which have been made, and are making, in the science and practice of Agriculture."

The facts that the tuition was $150 per year and that the students were promised that anything "having the appearance of drudgery, will be carefully avoided" may explain, in part, the failure of such schools to make a significant educational contribution or to attract a following. *Connecticut Courant,* May 18, 1824, and May 17, 1825, as cited in Butler, *op. cit.,* pp. 196–197.

of instruction than were provided at any of the public schools."[11] To meet this need, they established a school which, with respect to its offerings, resembled rather closely the better academies except that, since the town already maintained a Latin school to prepare boys for the university, the classical studies were omitted from its curriculum. In fact, the school committee which presented the plan for the English Classical School to the town meeting in January of 1821 thought of the school as an academy.[12] The members of the committee expressed concern that children in order to obtain an education for life outside the professions were under the necessity of attending a distant academy. The obvious step was to establish a publicly supported academy in Boston.[13] Other cities established high schools so soon after 1821, the date of the opening of the Boston English Classical School, that there must be some doubt with respect to claims that they were patterned after the Boston school or that their establishment was in any large way influenced by it. The movement to establish high schools, however, really got under way with the enactment of a law by the Massachusetts Legislature in 1827 which required the establishment of a high school in all cities, towns, or districts of five hundred or more families.[14] New Hampshire, Maine, and Vermont followed the example of Massachusetts. By the outbreak of the Civil War, high schools had been established not only in New England, where they were most numerous, but also in large cities elsewhere such as New York, Portland, Philadelphia, Baltimore, Chicago, Mobile, San Francisco, New Orleans, and Louisville. Some three hundred high schools were reported in the Census of 1860, but it is unlikely that all of these were tax-supported public secondary schools. On the other hand, it is likely that many schools commonly referred to as public grammar schools provided instruction above the elementary level and should have been reported as high

[11] *The System of Education pursued at the Free Schools in Boston,* 1823, as quoted in Ellwood P. Cubberley, *Readings in Public Education in the United States* (Boston: Houghton Mifflin Company, 1934), pp. 232–233.

[12] One of the proposals read: "To conduct this Academy there shall be one Principal Master at the salary of $1500, a Sub-Master at $1200, one Usher at $700 and one at $600." *Columbian Centinel,* January 17, 1821, as cited in Butler, *op. cit.,* p. 288.

[13] The similarity of the curriculum of this school to those of the English departments of the better academies is striking. Among the courses offered were "Intellectual and Written Arithmetic, Geography and the use of Globes, exercises in Grammar, General History, and History of the United States, Book-keeping by single entry, Elements of Some Arts and Sciences, Composition and Declamation. . . . Geometry, Algebra, Trigonometry and its applications, Book-keeping by double entry, various branches of Natural Philosophy, Natural History, Chemistry, Moral Philosophy and Natural Theology, Rhetoric, Evidences of Christianity, Intellectual Philosophy, Political Economy, and Logic." *The System of Education pursued at the Free Schools in Boston,* as quoted in Cubberley, *Readings in Public Education in the United States, op. cit.,* p. 233.

[14] *Laws of Massachusetts,* January Session, 1827, Chap. 143.

schools. For example, when the high school established for girls in Boston in 1826 was discontinued in 1828, it was ordered that girls be permitted to remain at the Girls' Grammar School an extra two years.[15] Other evidences of the close connection between grammar and high schools are not lacking. In 1831, the school committee of Salem planned to abolish the English High School of that city. The committee learned, however, that if the high school was abolished, they would, in order to meet state requirements, be obliged to provide its equivalent in the Grammar School and the plan was abandoned.[16] No doubt a number of cities met the state's requirements by adding the specified subjects which were not already taught to the courses of existing public schools.

Although established in response to a growing popular demand, high schools often were opposed by strong groups. For example, in 1831 a group objected to continuing the Salem English High School. They argued that it was proper to maintain grammar schools because "thus far all classes in the community must proceed together," but that beyond the grammar-school level schooling should not be public, because it "could be of advantage only to a few but was paid for by many." "That," stated the complaint, "is where public liberality should end and private expense begin."[17] As long as a considerable part of the people held such a view, the development of high schools could progress only slowly.

High schools for girls had to overcome not only the opposition of those who objected to providing secondary education at public expense but also that of those persons who continued to think that education above the rudiments was necessary or desirable only for boys — that overtaxing the weaker female intellect would lead to decay of the moral qualities. In 1826 there were fifteen public schools in Salem, including a "Grammar School to qualify boys for the University," but there was not a single public school for girls in the town.[18] The prosperity of the numerous private academies for girls was evidence, however, that many parents desired instruction for their daughters which the public schools did not provide. Furthermore, it was often a matter of public concern that money was drawn out of the town by academies and that "not a dollar comes in from out of town." These considerations, together with the conviction on the part of many that the education of all the children, including the future mothers and homemakers, was essential to the common welfare, led to the establishment of high schools for girls, although these schools were often inferior and not so highly regarded as those provided for boys. For example, although the Lancasterian system had been almost entirely re-

[15] *Boston Daily Advertiser*, February 12, 1836, as cited in Butler, *op. cit.*, p. 289.
[16] *Salem Gazette*, March 15, 29; April 5; May 20, 1831; as cited in Butler, *op. cit.*, pp. 295–296.
[17] *Loc. cit.*
[18] *Salem Gazette*, July 18, 1826, as cited *ibid*, pp. 294–295.

jected by Boston, its first high school for girls was organized on the monitorial plan. As with many halfhearted extensions of the educational program, the high school for girls was likely to be the first victim when retrenchment appeared desirable. The Boston school, opened in 1826, had been planned for 120 girls between the ages of eleven and fifteen. Nearly three hundred applied for admission and of these 133 of the age group, twelve to fifteen, were accepted. The following year none of the girls was ready to leave and 427 others were clamoring for admission. The enrollment was then limited to girls between fourteen and sixteen years of age. A few months later the committee temporarily solved its problem by discontinuing the school, but they were immediately confronted by new demands that later led to its re-establishment.

Separate high schools were not always provided for girls. Following the lead of the academies, high schools were organized increasingly with "female departments." This practice, adopted extensively in the East and almost exclusively in the West, was a step toward the reorganization of education on a coeducational basis.

By the close of the period the high school had taken form. Although in many respects it resembled the academies of the period, it was becoming increasingly differentiated from them. Of course, the fundamental difference between the two types of secondary schools related to their control and support. Both prepared for the varied life of the time and both prepared for college. In this connection, it would be a mistake to think that the exclusion of the college-preparatory function by the English Classical School of Boston established a precedent for the same practice elsewhere. The classical studies were not included in the curriculum of that school, but, most likely, this should be attributed to the fact that a highly regarded Latin school in Boston had been preparing boys, over a period of several generations, for the university. From the beginning the dual function of the high school was commonly recognized. The Massachusetts law of 1827 which established high schools in the larger towns and districts provided that when those towns or districts contained four thousand inhabitants, Latin and Greek were to be offered. In some cities, the standard classical course was made a part of the high school curriculum. Although high schools were distributed throughout all sections of the country and fitted well into the political and social philosophy of the time, few persons in 1860 would have predicted that this type of school would eventually almost entirely replace the academy.

Democratic Tendencies in Higher Education

At the beginning of the period, higher education was on the verge of a most remarkable expansion. Approximately three times as many colleges were founded during the two decades after 1840 as had been established in the sixty, in fact, in the two hundred, years which preceded that date.[19]

THE RELIGIOUS CHARACTER OF THE COLLEGES

All of the colonial colleges except one had grown out of religious and sectarian motives and, although denominational influences were weakening perceptibly under the impact of changing social, economic, and political forces, the new colleges generally reflected the religious motives and aspirations of the groups able and willing to promote their foundation and stand as sponsors for them. Complaints that a particular college was sectarian were met with the argument that colleges should be sectarian. For example, Harvard was attacked in 1831, not so much because it was sectarian but because, according to complaints, it had fallen into the hands of the Unitarians, who, it was said, claimed to have no creed and therefore could lay claim to no beliefs. Harvard, it was argued, had been established by the Puritan Fathers. If there must be a college for "no beliefs" the persons interested should establish one, but Harvard should be rescued from them by a state law which would restore it to the faith of its founders.[20]

ATTEMPTS BY THE STATE TO CONTROL HIGHER EDUCATION

A growing realization that the old educational foundations did not serve the varied interests and needs of the rapidly changing society led to the establishment of new institutions as well as attempts to change the character of those already established. As pointed out previously, many states sought to establish institutions whose policies would be subject to the control of the legislatures rather than of ecclesiastical bodies. The colleges generally were jealous of the rights which they claimed under their charters. They wanted grants and endowments from the state, but they resented any attempt on the part of the legislature to exercise a measure of control over them or to influence the nature of their curriculums. These

---

[19] The varying numbers of colleges reported for the same years and periods result, in part, from different definitions of a college. It is stated that more than five hundred colleges were established before 1861 in the sixteen eastern and midwestern states (both north and south), and that the rate of mortality was high. See Samuel Eliot Morison and Henry Steele Commager, *The Growth of the American Republic* (New York: Oxford University Press, Inc., 1950), I, pp. 513–516. The Census figures show an increase in the count from 173 colleges in 1840 to 467 in 1860. Cubberley, using a definition probably superior to that employed in the Census, reported that the number of colleges increased from 60 in 1830 to about 220 in 1860. See Cubberley, *Public Education in the United States, op. cit.,* p. 270.

[20] *Salem Gazette,* February 11, 15, 22, 1831; March 4, 11, 18, 1831; as cited in Butler, *op. cit.,* p. 32.

attempts to control chartered institutions precipitated a number of struggles. When the decision in the Dartmouth College Case settled the issue in favor of the colleges, religious denominations, having become numerous and strong, turned without fear of state interference to the founding of colleges. Every denomination wanted a college — in fact, it would be nearer the truth to state that every denomination wished to establish a college in each of the several states. The period has been described as one of great denominational effort.[21]

The desire of denominations to be widely represented and the pride that communities felt in having colleges located in them led to the rapid multiplication of these institutions. The increase in number, however, was far more remarkable than the growth of any single college. These colleges were largely supported by fees received from students, by gifts from the communities in which they were located, and by funds raised by the conferences of the various denominations.

THE RISE OF THE STATE UNIVERSITY

The state legislatures, thwarted in their attempts to seize control of chartered institutions, in some instances gained their ends by judicious use of grants. Harvard was urged on more than one occasion to free itself from such control as the state exercised over it.[22] Several states which had established colleges or universities earlier effected fundamental reorganizations. The University of North Carolina, opened in 1795, and the University of Georgia, opened in 1801, were subjected to a greater measure of state control. Virginia established her university in 1825 and in the western states, each of which had received grants of two townships for the endowment of a university, state schools were generally mandated by the constitutions. The fact remains, however, that at the outbreak of the Civil War there were only seventeen state institutions, although three or four private colleges had rather hazy state connections. The state institutions were supported by tuition fees, appropriations by legislatures, and land endowments.

MODEST BEGINNINGS

Most of the colleges and universities, state and private, were modest establishments with small faculties. They were generally poor and always in need of funds. The endowments of some appear today to have been absurdly inadequate; many colleges that have proved permanent began with

---

21 See Morison and Commager, *op. cit.,* pp. 513–514. It is reported that before 1861 Yale begat sixteen Congregational colleges and Princeton twenty-five Presbyterian ones.

22 *Springfield Republican,* June 1, 1850, as cited in Butler, *op. cit.,* p. 34.

less than ten thousand dollars in subscriptions.[23] Many institutions chartered as colleges were actually little more than secondary schools. This fact is partly responsible, no doubt, for the exaggerated contemporary reports with respect to the number and wide distribution of colleges, particularly in the South. One of the chief purposes of most of these colleges was the preservation of a learned ministry and the training of youth who would be kept true to the faith, and it is in this light that the curriculums of many of them should be viewed. Harvard, Yale, and other larger and more firmly established schools early fostered the development of a new curriculum by adding first one untraditional subject and then another, but neither they nor any of the other colleges attempted to organize the whole into any new educational scheme. The curriculum was slowly expanded; law, theology, and medicine were being removed from the regular curriculum and organized into professional departments and schools, but a great majority of the institutions continued to stress Latin and Greek. Instruction, whether in the newer sciences or in the classics, was still based on the old disciplinary idea.[24]

Perhaps the small denominational college which accepted as its first responsibility the training of a learned ministry should not be criticized for retaining a program that had successfully trained ministers for generations. The pattern of work in the small denominational college was set by the presence of students preparing for the ministry, although they formed a decreasing percentage of the student body. In 1826 the statement was made in a Connecticut newspaper: "In the ten colleges of New England there are 1400 students. Five hundred of these are hopefully pious and two hundred are preparing for the ministry in Massachusetts alone."[25]

The fact that most of the students not preparing for the ministry were looking forward to law, medicine, and other professions indicates that the professional aim was not absent in our colleges and universities, even from their early days.

EXPANDING THE CONTENT OF HIGHER EDUCATION

Although, in the main, college "courses remained grounded on Latin, Greek, and mathematics," the sciences, history, political economy, modern languages, particularly French, and other subjects were slowly being added to the college offerings. New inventions and scientific advances in industry, in the utilization of natural resources, in methods and means of

---

[23] Carl Russell Fish, *The Rise of the Common Man, 1830–1850* (New York: The Macmillan Co., 1927), p. 214.

[24] For an account of Emerson's attack on the existing collegiate curriculum, see *Salem Gazette*, February 9, 1844, as cited in Butler, *op. cit.*, p. 125.

[25] *Connecticut Journal*, September 26, 1826, as quoted in Butler, *op. cit.*, p. 124.

communication, in medicine, and in other fields fired the minds of many youth of the period, who were coming to believe in increasing numbers that science, rather than the culture of Greece and Rome, would be their guide to the necessary business of earning a livelihood in a rapidly changing world. Colleges increased their scientific and technological offerings as the demand for scientific training increased.[26] The founding of Rensselaer Polytechnic Institute in 1824 was followed by the establishment of other technical schools. The Sheffield Scientific School was established at Yale in 1846 and a year later the Lawrence Scientific School was founded at Harvard. Four years later (1851) the Chandler School of Science was founded at Dartmouth. Before the close of the period Michigan had established an agricultural and industrial college, and mining, engineering, and other branches of technology were being taught in an increasing number of technical institutions. A number of colleges now awarded the degree of bachelor of science, and already a resolution had been presented in Congress urging "a system of Industrial Universities liberally endowed, in each state in the Union, coöperating with each other, and with the Smithsonian Institution of Washington."[27]

Further reaction against the narrowness of traditional institutions led to the founding of additional schools of law and medicine and to the expansion of some of those already established. Several universities, with their enriched curriculums, their newly established scientific schools, and their older schools of theology, law, and medicine, began to take on a modern aspect.

The administration of the expanded curriculums necessitated fundamental reorganization in the colleges. On its opening in 1825, the University of Virginia offered a course of study divided into ten sections, from which the students were permitted to elect subjects.[28] Other institutions attempted in various ways to introduce a measure of election. For example, in 1841 Harvard instituted what was called a voluntary and elective system, which is explained in the following statement:

> A change in the course of study in the Institution has been proposed by the Corporation, consisting of the President and Fellows, and submitted to the Overseers for their consideration. This proposed change consists in the introduction of what is termed the Voluntary or Elective System; i.e., allowing the students, after the close of Freshman year, to take their choice of studies to be pursued for the remainder of their College courses.

[26] Elbert Vaughan Wills, *The Growth of American Higher Education: Liberal, Professional and Technical* (Philadelphia: Dorrance & Co., 1936), Chap. IV.

[27] Edgar W. Knight, *Education in the United States,* Revised Edition (Boston: Ginn & Company, 1934), p. 398. See also David L. Madsen, "History of an Idea: The University of the United States" (Doctor's thesis, University of Chicago, 1961).

[28] For a time law and medicine were two of these divisions, but later separate schools were organized for them.

It is intended, — and to be made a condition, on which the elective privilege depends — that the student shall, in his preparatory studies and by the close of his first Collegiate year, become acquainted, to a certain extent, with Latin, Greek, Mathematics, Natural and Civil History, and the French language. From this point as a foundation, he may pursue, at his option, any one or more of the branches taught in the College, till the close of his courses, according as he shall judge most useful in his future occupation in life. A committee of the Board of Overseers have had the subject under advisement, and in their report, recommended that the change proposed by the Corporation be approved by the Board, and that the Corporation be authorized to carry the same into effect.[29]

Faced with the fact that the greatly augmented curriculum, as it was administered, entailed superficial study of a large number of subjects, other colleges attempted to employ the elective system and other means by which they might better provide for the different needs of various groups. But the elective system as it is known today is a development of the second half of the nineteenth century.

THE QUALITY OF INSTRUCTION

From the testimony of men who seemed to have received fairly adequate training in the institutions of the period, it would appear that instruction was generally laborious and uninspired. Although it is probably true that the "instructional staffs were in many cases inferior in intellectual caliber to the average of their students, and not far above them in training," it is important to note that great teachers and administrators were beginning to appear. Jared Sparks, Harvard's great historian, succeeded Edward Everett at president in 1849. Benjamin Silliman of Yale was gaining a national reputation for his work in chemistry and geology. Mark Hopkins became president of Williams in 1826 and a year later Francis Wayland became president of Brown, a position which he held until 1855. Joseph Caldwell ended a long and useful career as president of the University of North Carolina in 1835. Francis Lieber was doing distinguished work in political science and law at the South Carolina College, from which he was later called to Columbia University. J. D. Dana, Asa Gray, Louis Agassiz, and others, mostly in the field of science, made notable contributions which added to the prestige of their institutions. Before the end of the period, colleges generally were becoming mindful of the value of men of wide reputation for scholarship and teaching.

Many individual instructors made attempts to vitalize instruction and occasionally a college would institute an ambitious program directed toward this end. As early as 1829 Rensselaer introduced a summer term

---

[29] *Salem Gazette*, February 23, 1841, as quoted in Butler, *op. cit.*, p. 33.

which Knight has likened to the much more recent "university afloat." The students were taken up the Hudson, through the Erie Canal, and on to Niagara Falls, being given "lectures and examinations in mineralogy, geology, botany, zoology, chemistry, philosophy, and practical mathematics" en route. They were to give their afternoons to collecting geological and botanical specimens.[30] At Rensselaer and elsewhere, some opportunities were afforded for independent work in close association with noted scholars. Activities outside the curriculum provided additional opportunities for learning and expression.

Fish thinks that it "was the development of extracurricular activities by the students themselves, assisted by the more alert of the professors and tutors," that "saved the colleges from dry-rot," and "caused them to appeal to the ambitious and train them for the work they had to do."[31] As in the preceding period, literary societies flourished and "the Greek-letter fraternity system" developed. Phi Beta Kappa, founded in 1776 at William and Mary, had been introduced into several colleges, but had no imitators until the third decade of the nineteenth century, when three similar societies were founded at Union College, giving that institution the repute of "mother of fraternities." These fraternities spread and others were established. In spite of "the Greek-letter designation, the activities of the fraternities did not, in this period, differ essentially from those of the pre-existing literary societies. In both cases, their substance was debates and orations on the current problems of the day, the declaiming of literary selections, and the production of plays, classic or original. It was, however, in the older literary societies that the men of the generation were trained."[32] Washington Gladden, in looking back upon his college days at Williams in the late fifties, stated:

> A large place in the life of the college was taken by the two rival literary societies — the Philologian and the Philotechnian — to the one or the other of which every student belonged. These societies had well-furnished rooms in one of the dormitories, with libraries of three or four thousand volumes each. Their weekly meetings were events of no little interest to the college community; the program generally included one or two original orations, a debate, sometimes a poem, an essay or two, and the report of the censor upon the performance of the previous meeting. The two societies were united in the Adelphic Union which gave three or four debates or exhibitions annually, in the chapel or the village church.[33]

The libraries of these societies were sometimes superior to the college library, the use of which, one author states, had not yet been discovered. It is stated that the college library at Dartmouth in 1817 "consisted of

[30] Knight, *op. cit.*, p. 396.   [31] Fish, *op. cit.*, p. 206.   [32] *Ibid.*, p. 207.
[33] Washington Gladden, *Recollections*, as quoted in Cubberley, *Readings in Public Education in the United States*, *op. cit.*, pp. 261–262.

about four thousand volumes, chiefly antiquarian." It was open for an hour each week and a fee was charged for each book withdrawn. By 1825 the volumes in the libraries of the Dartmouth societies numbered some six thousand. The libraries were open daily and circulated books freely, even for use during vacation.[34]

LIGHTER ASPECTS OF COLLEGE LIFE

From the numerous existing accounts of college life during the period, it appears that students did not spend all their time studying Latin, Greek, and the new subjects, nor did they find sufficient outlet for their surplus energy in debating and declaiming. The colleges reflected, perhaps in a mild sort of way, the individualism and impatience of restraint which characterized the period from 1828 to 1860. Nearly every college had its share of riots and other serious breaches of discipline. Some accounts leave the modern reader with the impression that student life was a continual "hell week," with the faculty occupying the position later taken over by freshmen and fraternity pledges.

A student riot at Harvard in 1834 was subdued by prosecution for damages. Serious fighting broke out between the freshmen and medical students at Dartmouth in 1846. In 1828 Yale students refused to eat the food provided; four ringleaders were expelled and a local paper applauded, "The Faculty have the right to rule."[35] In 1838 Bowdoin juniors and seniors refused to perform the public exhibitions. In 1837 a serious disturbance, resulting in the suspension of several Amherst students, was precipitated by the refusal on the part of a large number of them to accept degrees. On some occasions, as one writer has mildly put it, "exuberance bordered closely on license." At Harvard a bomb was exploded in 1842 under the chair of Professor Pierce, knocking the partitions out of three rooms. "A meeting was called but no ill feeling was apparent and no issue [was] made of it."[36] In 1843 a tutor at Yale died from three stab wounds received when he attempted to prevent the hazing of a freshman. The students drew up a resolution repudiating the murderer, who was punished. The resolution expressed no feeling with respect to the victim.[37] At Bowdoin the following outbreak occurred in 1827.

A group of students burned a tar barrel. A chain of powder was set under a Tutor's chair which went off during the class. The college bell valued at $200 was thrown into the river. A general good time seems to have been enjoyed by all except the three who were sent home.[38]

34 Fish, *op. cit.*, pp. 207–208.
35 *Connecticut Courant*, August 19, 1839, as cited in Butler, *op. cit.*, p. 74.
36 *Springfield Republican*, July 9, 1842, as cited in Butler, *op. cit.*, p. 32.
37 *Connecticut Courant*, October 28, 1843, as cited in Butler, *op. cit.*, p. 74.
38 Butler, *op. cit.*, p. 104.

Rioting broke out again in 1842 and Professor Godwin was injured by someone who threw sulphuric acid. The guilty sophomore confessed and was expelled.[39] In 1840 a professor was shot by a student at William and Mary in a political argument.[40] There was probably no connection between this last episode and the fact that the college advertised the following year for three professors, at salaries ranging from $3000 to $3900, a house to be included in each instance — salaries which, the *Connecticut Courant* stated, could not be had elsewhere.[41]

These are not isolated instances. The press was full of accounts of riots, disturbances, suspensions, and expulsions. Some were no doubt minor affairs, but others were extremely serious.

As time went on, the situation began to improve. At least, no student riot appeared to be so serious as one reported earlier at William and Mary, where, when two duelists were expelled, students rebelled and "completely wrecked the place, destroying books and equipment, and mobbing Judge Tucker, the Professor of Law. He resigned and the college was closed." The *Connecticut Courant* reported, perhaps with some feeling of satisfaction: "We hear the College of William and Mary at Williamsburg is completely broken up and the System of Education there discontinued. . . . This is all the foul effects of Jeffersonianism."[42] Although it is obviously unfair to characterize all the college students on the basis of reports of brawls in which some of them engaged, perhaps at rather wide intervals, such accounts may dispel some notions that are current concerning the nature of college youth during the period. Obviously the presence of many candidates for the ministry was not a particularly restraining influence.

THE HIGHER EDUCATION OF WOMEN

Before the establishment of the academies, women were afforded few advantages outside the home for education beyond the rudiments. Many of the academies developed to provide a finishing education for girls. By the end of the period a large number of seminaries and colleges for women had been established, although only one or two of these institutions were comparable to the better colleges for men. Emma Willard founded Troy Seminary in 1821. Mary Lyon established Mount Holyoke at South Hadley in 1837 and headed it until her death in 1849. Rockford College (Illinois) was opened as a seminary in 1849. Before 1860, sixty or more so-called women's colleges had been established. Thirty-two were founded in the South alone between 1850 and 1860. Some of these institutions for women, but not many, rose to full collegiate rank. For example,

39 *Salem Gazette,* April 22, 1842, as cited in Butler, *op. cit.,* p. 105.
40 *Connecticut Courant,* November 28, 1840, as cited in Butler, *op. cit.,* p. 142.
41 *Ibid.,* February 3, 1841.
42 *Connecticut Courant,* April 12, 1802, cited in Butler, *op. cit.,* pp. 140–141.

Mount Holyoke was chartered as a college in 1888, and Rockford became a college in 1892.

Authorization to grant degrees did not in itself make an institution a college. In March, 1838, it was reported that a female college in Mississippi giving instruction to sixty women had been given power to grant degrees. No one was misled as to the nature of the instruction given. Wesleyan Female Academy at Macon, Georgia, received favorable comment in the newspapers because it was authorized to grant degrees. The *Springfield Republican,* however, spoke with the voice of the age when it commented as follows:

> The Kentucky Legislative [*sic*] has conferred upon Messrs. Van Doren's Institution for Young Ladies in Lexington, the charter rights and standing of a College by the name of Van Doren's College for Young Ladies. A Diploma and honorary degrees of M.P.L. (Mistress of Polite Literature), M.M. (Mistress of Music), and M.I. (Mistress of Instruction) may be given.

The editor then suggested other possible degrees.

> M.P.M. (Mistress of Pudding Making), M.D.N. (Mistress of the Darning Needle), M.S.B. (Mistress of the Scrubbing Brush), M.C.S. (Mistress of Common Sense). The Professors should be chosen from farmer's wives and the Laboratory should be a kitchen. Honorary degrees might include H.W. (Happy Wife), H.H. (Happy Husband) and M.W.R.F. (Mother of a Well Regulated Family).[43]

Such displays of editorial wit were directed against better-conceived attempts to provide opportunities for women. A convention to promote women's rights which met in 1848 was ridiculed and condemned by press and pulpit. Higher education would make dissatisfied housewives.

Some time earlier (1833), however, Oberlin had opened its doors to men and women alike,[44] and in 1853 Antioch, under Horace Mann, began its great coeducational experiment.[45] Genesee College, later Syracuse University, was coeducational from its beginning in 1850, and in 1856 the University of Iowa opened as a coeducational institution. Michigan, opened in 1837, became coeducational in 1870; Indiana University first admitted women in 1868; Mississippi yielded in 1882; North Carolina in 1896; and some of the other state universities at

---

[43] *Springfield Republican,* March 14, 1835, as quoted in Butler, *op. cit.,* p. 147.

[44] Knight, *op. cit.,* p. 402. See also Thomas Woody, *A History of Women's Education in the United States* (New York: The Science Press, 1929), II, pp. 231–237.

[45] Edwin Grant Dexter, *A History of Education in the United States* (New York: The Macmillan Co., 1904), p. 446; see also Woody, *op. cit.,* pp. 237–238.

later dates.[46] Nearly all the state universities established since 1850 either have been coeducational from their beginning or became so within a decade or two after their opening. The older and better-established private institutions, however, were able to maintain themselves against the forces which were operating to make higher education for women socially desirable and respectable in quality, or at least equal to that provided for men.

The considerable activity of the period, the addition of new courses, and the innovations in method did not always improve the work of the college. More subjects were taught. Here and there some were well taught, but generally teaching was less thorough than during earlier periods. The disciplinary concept of education continued to prevail throughout the period, although it must be acknowledged that new aims were emerging. Summarizing the condition of higher education before 1860, Fish wrote:

> The changes which the people . . . desired to make for the benefit of their children were more of extension than of content. It was a part of the democratic movement of the time to provide for the education of the children of the common man, but the general satisfaction with things American and the absence of any effective critique of life prevented any systematic and general change in the character and aim of the education afforded. It was part of this condition that people were best satisfied with education at the top, and changes in the colleges were less important than those in the schools — nor did universities really develop in the period under review [1830–1850].[47]

It is perhaps the perspective which an understanding of much later developments provides that makes many of these activities appear more important to the student of education than they seemed to contemporaries or to later historians of the period.

Training Teachers for the Public Schools

The agitation for an adequate supply of better-trained teachers which eventuated in the normal-school movement was a part of the larger campaign to provide educational facilities for the children of all the people.[48]

---

46 Dexter, *op. cit.*, pp. 446–447.

47 Fish, *op. cit.*, p. 212. Used by permission of The Macmillan Co.

48 The necessity of providing adequately trained teachers was recognized and stressed by numerous advocates of the public school. The establishment of teacher-training institutions was regarded by them as a necessary part of the establishment of public school systems. Denison Olmsted stated before the American Institute of Instruction in 1839 that he "would have ten thousand dollars out of the one hundred thousand dollars, now distributed annually among the schools, set apart for the

INCREASED DEMANDS FOR TRAINED TEACHERS

Both the extension of schooling to greater numbers and the expansion of the curriculum made the problem of staffing the elementary schools acute. Recognition by the reformers of the importance of teacher training to the success of the public schools led them early to advocate teachers' seminaries as an integral part of the public school system.

The increased demands for teachers had resulted in the lowering of standards, which had never been high so far as elementary-school teachers were concerned.[49] At the beginning of the period, the only qualifications generally required of a teacher were that he profess Christianity, have some knowledge of the subject matter to be taught, and possess the ability to keep order. Since almost everyone could profess to be a Christian and since most communities lacked effective criteria for evaluating the teacher's knowledge, the chief requirement was most likely to be the strength to discipline unruly children, whose behavior reflected not only the crudeness and unbridled individualism of the time but also the tedium of the schools which they attended. This continued to be the qualification over which parents and school committees showed most concern as long as

---

establishing and supporting of a seminary for schoolmasters." — Denison Olmsted, "Observations on the School System of Connecticut," *The Lectures Delivered before the American Institute of Instruction, at Lowell (Mass.), August, 1838,* p. 108.

In an address before the same body a year earlier (1837), Charles Brooks quoted Cousin at length concerning the teachers' seminary as a part of the state school system. "The best plans of instruction cannot be executed except by the instrumentality of good teachers; and the state has done nothing for popular education, if it does not watch that those who devote themselves to teaching be well prepared. . . . In order to provide schools with masters, competent and conscientious, the care of their training must not be left to chance. The foundation of Teachers' Seminaries must be continued." — Quoted by Charles Brooks, "School Reform, or Teachers' Seminaries," *The Introductory Discourse and the Lectures Delivered before the American Institute of Instruction, at Worcester (Mass.), August, 1837,* p. 175.

Four years earlier (1833), Samuel R. Hall, in addressing this same organization, questioned the right of the government to lavish wealth upon high schools and academies and at the same time neglect to provide teachers' seminaries, upon which the success of the schools for seven-eighths of the population depended. — Samuel R. Hall, "On the Necessity of Educating Teachers," *The Introductory Discourse and the Lectures Delivered before the American Institute of Instruction, in Boston, August, 1833,* pp. 241–259.

[49] Speakers and writers painted a disheartening picture of the teaching profession. Instances were cited of teachers who carried a whiskey jug in one hand and a subscription list in the other; the teachers of entire communities were characterized as an ignorant, drunken, tobacco-chewing lot; half the teachers of Georgia would not be trusted, it was stated, with a pecuniary responsibility amounting to twenty dollars. The governor of South Carolina stated that, as a class, teachers in the free schools were "grossly incompetent, very ignorant," and possessed of an "easy morality," and that to be a teacher was regarded as *"prima facie* evidence of a want of qualification." See Samuel R. Hall, *op. cit.,* also Edgar W. Knight, *Public Education in the South* (Boston: Ginn & Company, 1922), p. 295; and Paul Monroe, *Founding of the American Public School System* (New York: The Macmillan Co., 1940), pp. 482–507.

teaching remained largely a matter of supervising drill and hearing the memorized responses of children, many of whom were bound to seek release from an almost stupefying boredom in activities not provided in the course of study.[50]

As early as the middle of the eighteenth century, some few persons showed concern over the lack of qualified teachers. The trustees of the academy promoted by Franklin stated one of the purposes as follows:

> That a number of the poorer Sort will be hereby qualified to act as Schoolmasters in the Country, to teach Children Reading, Writing, Arithmetic, and the Grammar of their Mother Tongue, and being of good morals and known character, may be recommended from the Academy to Country Schools for that purpose; The Country suffering at present very much for want of good Schoolmasters, and obliged frequently to employ in their Schools, vicious imported Servants, or concealed Papists, who by their bad Examples and Instructions often deprave the Morals or corrupt the Principles of the Children under their Care.[51]

It was not until the period beginning a half-century later, however, that educational thinkers began to draw up plans for institutions which would prepare young men especially for teaching, and it was even later before demands for better-trained teachers became insistent.

The Normal-School Movement

In 1820 James G. Carter published a pamphlet in which he urged the establishment of "an institution to train teachers." Later papers by Carter, Gallaudet, William Russell, James Caldwell, James L. Kingsley, and others pointed to the need for such schools and outlined plans for them.[52] By 1825 educational leaders had become acquainted with the Prussian system of teachers' seminaries. From about 1830 on, articles appeared in many parts of the country setting forth the advantages to be derived from such institutions and the establishment of teacher-training schools was urged by prominent persons and important organizations such

---

[50] For an excellent account of early teachers and teaching, see Paul Monroe, *op. cit.*

[51] *Petition by Trustees of the College, Academy, and Charitable School of Philadelphia for Aid from the City Treasury.* See Elmer Ellsworth Brown, *The Making of Our Middle Schools: An Account of the Development of Secondary Education in the United States* (New York: Longmans, Green & Co., 1902), p. 185.

[52] James G. Carter, "Outline of an Institution for the Education of Teachers," pp. 227–245. *The First State Normal School in America.* — Norton, the editor of this volume, states that the essays by Gallaudet, Carter, and Johnson were so strikingly similar in their recommendations as to suggest a common origin. All three plans were sufficiently like the Prussian "Teachers' Seminaries," as reorganized by the Prussian School of Law of 1819, to suggest that these institutions were known to the three writers. Johnson alone referred to them.

as the North Carolina Literary Society, the American Institute of Instruction,[53] and the numerous lyceums.

Except for the Lancasterian model schools, the first teacher-training school in America was established in 1823 by the Reverend Samuel R. Hall at Concord, Vermont. At this place and later at Andover, Massachusetts, and Plymouth, New Hampshire, he engaged until 1840 in the preparation of teachers for the common schools. In Hall's school, the elementary branches were reviewed and some secondary-school subjects were taught. Opportunity was provided for the observation of teaching, and during the third year, which was the final one, he introduced a subject called the Art of Teaching, the nature of which may be judged from his book, *Lectures on School-Keeping* (1829), the first professional book for teachers published in America. Like many of the early teacher-training institutions, his school was no further advanced than the typical academy, which it resembled except for the little professional instruction which was offered.[54]

Carter began what was probably the second school for the preparation of teachers at Lancaster, Massachusetts, in 1827. He tried to obtain financial support from the legislature but failed. His efforts to interest the state in providing facilities for the training of teachers were continued, however, until the state assumed responsibility for the work. The labors of Carter, the reports by Cousin[55] (published in America in 1835), Stowe[56] (1837), and others, the work of Charles Brooks, and the recommendations and petitions of organizations such as the American Institute of Instruction[57] bore fruit in Massachusetts in 1838. The state legislature accepted ten thousand dollars, donated by Edmund Dwight on the condition that the state provide an equal sum, and authorized the new State Board of Education to spend the money to qualify teachers for the common schools of Massachusetts.[58]

In making provision for the training of teachers, Massachusetts followed

[53] See "Memorial of the American Institute of Instruction to the Legislature of Massachusetts on Normal Schools," *The First State Normal School in America*, pp. 246–252. Also in Henry Barnard, *Normal Schools and Other Institutions, Agencies and Means Designed for the Professional Education of Teachers* (Hartford: Case, Tiffany & Co., 1851); Part I, pp. 85–91.

[54] See Cubberley, *Readings in Public Education in the United States, op. cit.,* pp. 323–324, and Henry Barnard (ed.), "Samuel Read Hall," *American Journal of Education,* V (1858), 371–388. The entire chapter, "The Beginnings of Teacher Training," *Readings in Public Education in the United States,* is excellent supplementary reading for this section.

[55] Victor Cousin, *Report on the State of Public Instruction in Prussia* (London, England: Effingham Wilson, 1834).

[56] Calvin E. Stowe, *Common Schools and Teachers' Seminaries* (Boston: Marsh, Capen, Lyon & Webb, 1839).

[57] For speeches before the Institute favoring the establishment of teachers' seminaries by Olmsted, Hall, Brooks, and others, see the early annual publications of the organization.

[58] For series of documents relating to the action of the state, see Cubberley, *Readings in Public Education in the United States, op. cit.,* pp. 335–337.

the pattern set by Germany and France of establishing special and separate institutions. A movement was under way in the United States, especially in the state of New York, to provide for the education of teachers in existing institutions, either public or private.[59] The New England leaders, however, chose to adopt European models and in time special institutions for the education of teachers were widely established. It should be noted that while American visitors to Prussia had been favorably impressed with the teachers' seminaries, they had failed to see that separate institutions for the training of teachers in that country reflected the class structure of society. Teachers in the *Volksschulen* in Prussia were recruited from the common people and the way was not open to them to attend either the regular secondary schools or the universities. Therefore in Prussia special institutions for the training of elementary teachers were essential to the maintenance of the class social structure. The influence of Prussia was a fundamental factor in the development in this country of teacher-education institutions separate and apart from the existing academies and colleges. These institutions, however, came to be known by the French name, normal schools.

The first state normal schools in America were opened in Massachusetts, the first in July, 1839, at Lexington, the second in the autumn of that year at Barre, and the third in 1840 at Bridgewater. New York established a short-lived normal school in 1844; Connecticut followed in 1849, Henry Barnard serving as the first principal; Michigan enacted a law providing for such schools in 1849; and by 1860 twelve normal schools had been established in nine states. In addition, six private normals had been founded and St. Louis had organized the first city normal school.

These schools were generally modest affairs. More often than not they were little better than secondary in level,[60] poorly attended, and never popular before the Civil War. The Massachusetts school at Lexington, restricted to girls, opened with one instructor and three students.[61] At the close of the first quarter the enrollment was only twelve,[62] at the end of the first year the students numbered only twenty-five,[63] and more than fifteen years later the enrollment was only thirty-five. The academies opposed

[59] There is no way of knowing how many of the academies offered a training course for teachers. Academies were prone to offer whatever was demanded. Notices and advertisements of academies indicate that many made some, if meager, provisions for prospective teachers, e.g., a "School for Teachers" at Northfield, Massachusetts, in 1832. The term was eleven weeks. "The tuition in the School Teaching Department for all English Studies is $4." *Massachusetts Spy,* June 13, 1832, as cited in Butler, *op. cit.,* p. 182.

[60] One criticism leveled at the normal schools was that they taught only elementary subjects. Their proponents replied that these studies "were taught only as a method," and that "the art of teaching cannot be taught abstractly but only through a review of studies to be taught." As quoted in Butler, *op. cit.,* pp. 300–301.

[61] *The First State Normal School in America, op. cit.,* p. 3.

[62] *Ibid.,* p. 9.   [63] *Ibid.,* p. 51.

the normal schools; teachers were suspicious of them or considered their establishment an unwarranted reflection upon the persons engaged in teaching; the opponents of public schools feared them for the contribution which they made to the success of the public school movement; and at least a strong minority in the legislatures were, for the foregoing or other reasons, unfriendly to them. In New York the opposition of selfish forces and the apathy of the people resulted in the abandonment of the normal school within four or five years of its founding, but all the attempts to abolish the normal schools in Massachusetts failed.[64] Although generally they were administered by able men and sponsored by the leading educational statesmen of the period, little was observable in the early normal schools to suggest that they would later occupy an important place in the American public school systems. If the basis for their later success in almost monopolizing teacher training were to be sought in the history of their early development, it would in all likelihood be found in their attempts at professional instruction and in the model schools which most of them maintained.

Teacher Training in Established Institutions

Classes to train teachers for the monitorial schools developed by the end of the first decade of the nineteenth century; private teachers' seminaries were introduced in the twenties; and state normal schools were established in 1839 and afterwards. Most of the teachers whose education extended beyond the elementary schools, however, received their training in the academies, which trained not only the greatest number of teachers during the period but also some of the best. Many graduates of the eastern academies followed the tide of immigrants to the West to find employment in the newly established and primitive schools of that region. Teaching was sometimes regarded as missionary effort.[65] Friends of public education subsidized the instruction of youth who promised to teach in the schools.[66] Private academies turned more and more to training teachers to meet the almost unlimited demand, and here and there states began to show an interest in subsidizing the efforts of the private schools.

In New York the Board of Regents declared, as early as 1821, that the academies must be looked to for teachers for the common schools. The legislature in the years that followed aided academies on the basis of

[64] For an account of the attack and defense of the normal schools in Massachusetts, see "Attack on Normal Schools in the Legislature of 1840," *The First State Normal School in America, op. cit.*, pp. 264–277.

[65] In 1848 a six-week course was offered in the Hartford Female Seminary to prepare "such as desired to go West to teach." Fifteen or twenty of Hartford's young ladies applied for the course. *Connecticut Courant*, February 26, 1848, as cited in Butler, *op. cit.*, pp. 395–396.

[66] *Connecticut Courant*, Sept. 7, 1839, as cited in Butler, *op. cit.*, p. 169.

work done in training teachers. In 1834 state aid was given to one academy in each of the eight judicial districts of the state to be used in qualifying teachers for the common schools under the regulation of the Board of Regents.[67] In 1844 New York established a normal school on the plan of Massachusetts, but when that institution closed, the state reverted in 1849 to its former practice of aiding academies engaged in teacher training. In other states, financial assistance to academies or seminaries which prepared teachers was urged, and in some instances the endowment of such institutions was advocated by the governors and others. In spite of all this activity and the remarkable progress made, the fact remains that most of the teachers of the period entered upon their duties without professional training of any kind and without having themselves advanced beyond the schools in which they taught.

Whether in normal schools or academies, the training was almost entirely academic in nature, though it sometimes included elementary courses in school management and the principles of teaching. The course varied in length. The normal-school program was generally three years, but students with a common-school education were usually admitted for much shorter terms, some for only a few weeks. Teacher training on a scale adequate to keep pace with the rapidly expanding public schools failed to develop during the period. The foundations had been laid, however, for systems of teacher education which, although never equal to the demands of public elementary education, were to become firmly established during the half-century after the close of the Civil War.

The Progress of Education, 1830–1860

The period 1830 to 1860 was one of marked educational advancement. As we have seen, it embraced what has been known as the Common School Revival, a movement to extend and improve facilities for popular education. In New England, under the leadership of Horace Mann, Henry Barnard, and others, the public school systems were revitalized and given an effectiveness they had not known before. Other sections registered material progress in establishing new schools and in maintaining old ones. Everywhere there was a definite tendency to shift from private to public support of education. Several normal schools were established to provide better-trained teachers for the common schools, the curriculum was expanded and enriched, steps were taken to improve administrative control, facilities for secondary and higher education were expanded, and educational institutions at all levels were receiving more liberal financial support. Exuberant democracies, urged on by educational

[67] For series of documents relating to the activity in New York, see Cubberley, *Readings in Public Education in the United States, op. cit.,* pp. 328–332.

leaders, publicists, and statesmen, were making legislative provisions for systems of education.

Great as the gains of this period were, they have commonly been exaggerated and in some respects misinterpreted. The laws were by no means always carried into effect and the recommendations of the reformers were, in most instances, received with great hesitancy. Early historians, overimpressed by what were fairly substantial gains, set a pattern of interpretation that has tended to persist to this day. Writers, particularly those in the field of education, have almost always exaggerated the development of certain aspects of the state school systems and generally have overemphasized the differences between states and sections. With respect to the South, unsupported generalizations have been made concerning the blighting influence of slavery and of an ideology inimical to the development of popular education. One statement that has been widely quoted, cited, and misinterpreted in works on education reads:

> By the close of the second quarter of the nineteenth century, certainly by 1860, we find the American public school system fully established, in principle at least, in all our Northern States. Much yet remained to be done to carry into full effect what had been established in principle, but everywhere democracy had won its fight, and the American public school, supported by general taxation, freed from the pauper-school taint, free and equally open to all, under the direction of representatives of the people, free from sectarian control, and complete from the primary school through the high school, and in the Western States through the university as well, may be considered as established permanently in American public policy.[68]

This statement, given the proper interpretation, may be true, but proper interpretation requires an understanding of the period obviously not possessed by many who have drawn upon the work of the author. The enactment of laws and the adoption of forward-looking programs may have served to establish educational systems in principle, but one must always keep in mind the difference between establishment in principle and accomplishment in fact. An entirely satisfactory index of the status of education must be based, in part, on measures of what was actually being accomplished in providing educational opportunity for children, not on what was being enacted in legislative halls or being said in educational conventions. An analysis of census data, not adequately used by most historians in their study of education, leads to the following generalizations:[69] (1) Practically all the states were making substantial progress in

[68] Cubberley, *Public Education in the United States, op. cit.,* p. 281.

[69] Herman G. Richey, "The Persistence of Educational Progress During the Decade of the Civil War. I," *Elementary School Journal,* XLII (January, 1942), 358–366; "The Persistence of Educational Progress During the Decade of the Civil War. II," *Elementary School Journal,* XLII (February, 1942), 456–463; and "Reappraisal of the State School Systems of the Pre-Civil-War Period," *Elementary School Journal,* XLI (October, 1940), 118–120.

the development of systems of public education. (2) But at the close of the period no single state can be said to have been providing any large percentage of its children and youth with schools well supported and well taught. (3) The facilities for secondary education were by no means so extensive as has commonly been reported. (4) The regional differences in educational development have been exaggerated; and (5) where sectional differences in school support and attendance did exist they appear to have been due more to differentials in urban and rural development than to differences in social attitudes and philosophies.[70] In view of the fact that educational development during the period has often been overemphasized and sometimes misinterpreted, a somewhat detailed presentation of statistical data in the pages that follow seems warranted.

THE ENROLLMENT IN THE SCHOOLS

Data pertaining to educational enrollment and income for 1850 and 1860 are presented in Tables 4 and 5 (pages 378–381).

Percentage of the population enrolled. It is not possible to ascertain the percentage of the children and youth of each age group attending school or college before 1860, but one can discover the percentage of the total population enrolled in some kind of educational institution. For the United States as a whole, 13.9 per cent, 18.2 per cent, and 19.9 per cent of the free population were enrolled in some type of school in 1840, 1850, and 1860 respectively. In 1840 Michigan and Ohio were the only states other than the New England and Middle Atlantic states to enroll as many as 8 per cent of their total population in schools.[71] In 1860 only three states enrolled less than 8 per cent of their total free population. For the states of the South the range was from 6.9 to 18.9 and for the northern states from 12.5 to 31.1 per cent. Only five of the northern states (the Pacific states excepted) enrolled less than 19.9 per cent of the total free population. The differences between the states decreased during the twenty-year period from 1840 to 1860. According to the census returns, all the New England states and the state of New York enrolled a smaller percentage of the population in 1860 than in 1840. This decrease in percentage of the population enrolled may have been due to the increasing number of children employed in industry. It is more probable that it is to be attributed to poor statistics.[72]

[70] These generalizations and the facts which will be presented to support them are based upon data taken from the United States Census and have been checked against available reports of state school officers.

[71] Note that the term "schools" as used here includes colleges, public schools, academies, and other schools.

[72] Many children in New England were obviously counted as enrolled in winter schools and again as enrolled in summer schools. Probably there were fewer duplicate enrollments, or at least fewer duplicate enrollments were counted, in 1860 than in 1840.

TABLE 4. EDUCATIONAL ENROLLMENT AND INCOME IN 1850, BY STATES*

State	Percentage of Free Population Enrolled		Percentage that Enrollment in All Schools Was of Total Free Population 5–15 Years of Age§	Percentage of Total Enrollment in Public Schools	Income of All Types of Schools		Public School Income Per Pupil Enrolled in Public Schools	Percentage that Public School Income from Taxes and Public Sources Was of Total Educational Income
	All Types of Schools†	Public Schools‡			Per Free Person	Per Pupil Enrolled		
Alabama	8.7	6.6	29.2	76.2	$1.22	$13.99	$11.12	11.0
Arkansas	6.8	5.2	22.3	76.9	.46	6.77	5.15	12.3
California	.2	.1	5.4	22.4	.19	81.60	73.47	0.0
Connecticut	21.3	19.2	101.4	90.2	1.16	5.45	3.24	45.1
Delaware	12.5	10.1	46.4	80.6	1.22	9.79	4.89	38.7
Florida	6.5	3.9	23.0	60.0	.74	11.34	11.92	.7
Georgia	8.3	6.2	27.5	75.5	.76	9.16	5.57	9.7
Illinois	15.3	14.8	53.4	96.5	.47	3.09	2.78	57.1
Indiana	17.1	16.3	58.4	95.7	.43	2.50	1.95	49.4
Iowa	16.0	15.4	54.6	96.3	.32	2.00	1.74	58.0
Kentucky	11.2	9.3	39.0	83.0	.77	6.93	2.97	14.7
Louisiana	11.3	9.2	47.0	81.2	2.27	20.07	13.96	46.6
Maine	34.3	33.1	136.6	96.5	.65	1.91	1.64	79.0
Maryland	9.1	6.8	36.3	74.0	1.14	12.56	6.62	27.3
Massachusetts	19.1	17.7	94.8	92.7	1.43	7.49	5.71	67.5

* From Herman G. Richey, "Reappraisal of the State School Systems of the Pre-Civil-War Period," Elementary School Journal, XLI (October, 1940), 120.
† Includes colleges, public schools, academies, and other schools.
‡ The term "public schools" used as in the Census reports.
§ Not the percentage of children 5–15 years of age enrolled, but the number enrolled divided by the number of children 5–15 years of age, ... more than 100 are caused by the enrollment of children over 15 and under 5 and, in some instances, by the fact that, in

State	Percentage of Free Population Enrolled		Percentage that Enrollment in All Schools Was of Total Free Population 5–15 Years of Age	Percentage of Total Enrollment in Public Schools	Income of All Types of Schools		Public School Income Per Pupil Enrolled in Public Schools	Percentage that Public School Income from Taxes and Public Sources Was of Total Educational Income
	All Types of Schools	Public Schools			Per Free Person	Per Pupil Enrolled		
Michigan	28.3	27.8	102.8	98.3	$.52	$1.84	$1.52	69.2
Minnesota								
Mississippi	8.9	6.3	29.4	71.5	1.25	14.11	13.56	17.9
Missouri	10.4	8.7	36.1	84.0	.64	6.23	3.11	20.3
New Hampshire	25.6	23.8	118.5	93.1	.70	2.72	2.21	70.5
New Jersey	18.0	16.0	72.4	88.6	1.07	5.93	2.77	27.0
New York	23.5	21.8	101.0	92.9	.78	3.34	2.18	54.3
North Carolina	19.4	17.9	69.6	92.6	.67	3.44	1.52	36.3
Ohio	25.4	24.4	92.1	96.3	.51	2.03	1.53	60.4
Oregon								
Pennsylvania	19.1	17.9	73.9	93.9	.94	4.91	3.42	63.0
Rhode Island	16.9	15.7	81.1	93.0	.93	5.50	4.34	68.6
South Carolina	9.2	6.3	32.4	68.5	1.80	19.63	11.25	7.3
Tennessee	15.0	13.6	50.6	90.3	.54	3.62	1.89	24.6
Texas	7.4	5.1	26.4	69.1	.55	7.37	5.55	0.0
Vermont	32.1	29.8	135.6	92.7	.79	2.45	1.88	60.3
Virginia	8.2	7.1	29.6	86.7	.75	9.11	4.67	14.7
Wisconsin	20.2	19.3	80.8	95.5	.45	2.21	1.92	79.6
United States including territories	18.2	16.8	69.8	92.1	$0.81	$4.44	$2.86	44.9

TABLE 5. EDUCATIONAL ENROLLMENT AND INCOME IN 1860, BY STATES*

State	Percentage of Free Population Enrolled		Percentage that Enrollment in All Schools Was of Total Free Population 5–15 Years of Age§	Percentage of Total Enrollment in Public Schools	Income of All Types of Schools		Public School Income Per Pupil Enrolled in Public Schools	Percentage that Public School Income from Taxes and Public Sources Was of Total Educational Income
	All Types of Schools†	Public Schools‡			Per Free Person	Per Pupil Enrolled		
Alabama	14.1	11.7	48.6	82.7	$1.58	$11.20	$7.93	31.5
Arkansas	7.4	5.9	24.4	80.6	.60	8.14	6.27	7.4
California	7.5	6.6	69.0	87.2	1.47	19.54	14.14	48.4
Connecticut	20.0	17.9	101.1	89.5	1.63	8.12	4.54	41.2
Delaware	12.5	10.6	49.3	85.1	1.13	9.01	5.78	49.2
Florida	8.3	2.6	29.3	31.2	1.21	14.65	9.89	3.3
Georgia	11.8	9.4	41.6	79.6	1.44	12.14	8.02	19.9
Illinois	26.2	25.3	104.1	96.4	1.47	5.61	5.05	81.5
Indiana	23.6	21.7	87.2	92.0	.65	2.77	2.34	72.8
Iowa	25.5	24.5	96.8	96.4	1.04	4.08	3.71	83.4
Kentucky	18.9	16.8	69.4	88.6	1.16	6.13	3.20	34.5
Louisiana	11.9	8.5	48.5	71.3	2.71	22.86	14.75	39.7
Maine	31.1	29.7	135.2	95.6	.88	2.84	2.43	76.0
Maryland	6.9	6.0	28.2	87.1	.85	12.28	6.71	37.2
Massachusetts	18.1	16.8	91.7	92.9	1.81	10.02	7.47	65.6

* From Herman G. Richey, "Reappraisal of the State School Systems of the Pre-Civil-War Period," *Elementary School Journal*, XLI (October, 1940), 121.
† Includes colleges, public schools, academies, and other schools.
‡ The term "public schools" used as in the Census reports.
§ Not the percentage of children 5–15 years of age enrolled, but the number enrolled divided by the number of children 5–15 years of age. Percentages of more than 100 are caused by the enrollment of children over 15 and under 5 and is some instance by the fact that in

TABLE 3 (continued)

State	Percentage of Free Population Enrolled		Percentage that Enrollment in All Schools Was of Total Free Population 5–15 Years of Age	Percentage of Total Enrollment in Public Schools	Income of All Types of Schools		Public School Income Per Pupil Enrolled in Public Schools	Percentage that Public School Income from Taxes and Public Sources Was of Total Educational Income
	All Types of Schools	Public Schools			Per Free Person	Per Pupil Enrolled		
Michigan	28.4	26.9	118.8	94.7	$1.09	$3.84	$3.24	70.6
Minnesota	19.2	18.1	85.8	94.0	.68	3.53	2.76	68.0
Mississippi	11.2	8.7	39.2	77.8	2.07	18.43	12.45	18.8
Missouri	18.8	16.5	70.9	87.8	1.18	6.29	4.57	44.7
New Hampshire	25.3	21.6	127.1	85.6	1.13	4.49	3.09	54.8
New Jersey	18.4	16.4	80.4	89.0	1.28	6.92	4.86	51.7
New York	20.3	18.0	91.4	88.6	1.30	6.43	4.79	61.6
North Carolina	18.1	15.9	67.1	87.7	1.15	6.33	2.56	31.6
Ohio	27.9	25.2	108.7	90.6	1.30	4.65	4.32	78.7
Oregon	19.6	15.5	81.8	79.5	1.39	7.12	6.04	39.7
Pennsylvania	20.7	19.5	83.2	93.9	1.16	5.61	4.41	71.9
Rhode Island	16.6	14.6	81.5	88.4	1.35	8.16	6.22	59.9
South Carolina	10.1	6.9	37.5	68.2	2.29	22.73	9.88	10.0
Tennessee	18.9	16.6	67.8	88.1	1.29	6.83	2.90	20.3
Texas	10.2	8.2	37.1	80.6	1.54	15.17	11.97	11.4
Vermont	28.2	25.7	128.6	91.0	.95	3.36	2.73	72.2
Virginia	9.2	7.7	34.4	84.2	1.17	12.71	5.84	13.7
Wisconsin	27.1	25.6	106.1	94.6	.98	3.62	3.00	75.4
United States including territories	19.9	18.0	81.0	90.5	$1.26	6.34	$4.55	54.6

There were remarkable gains in the states of the Northwest and smaller but substantial gains in the South. In the rural states of the Northwest and the South, with two or three exceptions, the percentage of the population enrolled in school doubled or tripled during the twenty-year period. The differences at the close of the period, however, were still large. The statements of writers concerning the backwardness of the South in establishing public schools free and open to all are fully warranted, but it should also be noted that on the basis of this one criterion — percentage of population enrolled in the schools — their statements should be broadened to include several northern states.[73]

If the percentage that the children enrolled represented of the total population is used as an index of the enrollment of children of school age, the same general trends may be observed in all parts of the nation.[74] The South, with relatively larger numbers of children, was failing to provide for a large share of them. In the North, by 1860, the number of enrollments in all schools was about nine-tenths as large as the number of the population between the ages of five and fifteen. Many enrollments, particularly in the western states, were for very short terms; attendance was poor; and facilities were extremely primitive.

Relatively more of the school children of the North were enrolled in public schools. In 1860 the states of the North (Oregon excepted) enrolled from 85.1 per cent to 96.4 per cent of their school children in public schools, and the southern states (Florida excepted) enrolled from 68.2 per cent to 88.6 per cent of their total enrollments in public schools. These facts, taken with those already presented, indicate that a number of states were far on their way toward the establishment of systems of public schools. The statistics must be interpreted, however, in the light of the meaning which the term "public school" conveyed during the period. It was used both in the census and in the reports of state school officers to denote some schools almost entirely supported by tuition. Many of the so-called "public schools" were public only because they were not privately owned and some measure of public control must have operated. In the North as well as in the South, these schools were not necessarily "free and open to all," nor were they all without the "pauper-school taint."

THE FINANCIAL SUPPORT OF EDUCATION

A study of the income for educational purposes reveals even more clearly than the statistics of enrollment the failure during the period to

[73] Richey, "Reappraisal of the State School Systems of the Pre-Civil-War Period," *op. cit.*, 122–123.

[74] The higher percentages enrolled in Vermont, Maine, New Hampshire, and perhaps two or three other northern states are probably due not only to the large enrollments in those states but also to the failure of the census to eliminate duplicate enrollments. Many children in New England were counted as enrolled in winter schools and again as enrolled in summer schools. This statement is borne out by comparisons of the census figures with those reported by chief state school officers.

make adequate educational facilities available. If the statistics for the urban population of the northern states are withdrawn from the compilations, the abject poverty and almost impossible conditions of the rural schools stand out even more clearly. School systems were developing, but, outside of a few eastern states and the towns and cities of the remainder of the United States, the schools were sorely inadequate to meet the requirements of an emerging democracy. They had little public money, and most of that little support was derived from land sales, rents, or other sources not involving taxation. In the South, thousands of children — a large percentage of the whole — were denied schooling of any kind, although more money was being spent for education per free person, or per pupil enrolled, than in the majority of northern states. Yet public systems of education were developing. It may be said, perhaps, that by the close of the period they had been established in principle, at least in the North. The facts with respect to school enrollments, school attendance, and educational income present an important aspect of the educational situation, however, that may be obscured if the history of the period is written in terms only of such factors as (1) the men who labored tirelessly and enthusiastically for the cause of education, (2) the theories developed, (3) the reforms demanded, and (4) the statutes enacted.

EDUCATION AT THE SECONDARY LEVEL

The decades from 1830 to 1860 were characterized by the rapid development of academies. The Latin grammar schools had almost disappeared, while outside the cities the public high schools had not made a great deal of headway. In ever increasing numbers youth, especially from the rising middle class, turned to the private and semi-public academies for a more advanced type of education than was afforded in the common schools. The academy has been properly called the people's college. For most it was a terminal school, offering instruction in a great many cultural and vocational subjects. At the same time, in most of the better academies, the pupil could, if he desired, prepare for entrance into college.

It is next to impossible to ascertain the exact number of academies in existence at any time before 1860, and it is equally difficult to determine how many of the institutions listed as academies were really of secondary grade and how many were in fact elementary schools masquerading under the more ambitious title. In 1840 the census returns show that there were in the United States 3242 academies and grammar schools, enrolling 164,159 pupils. The census data of 1850 relating to academies are difficult to interpret. The misrepresentation commonly given them is of enough importance to call for special comment.

Cubberley cites Inglis to the effect that by 1850, "when the wave of interest in their establishment reached its crest, there were, of all kinds [incorporated and unincorporated], 1007 academies in New England,

1636 in the Middle Atlantic States, 2640 in the Southern States, 753 in the Upper Mississippi Valley States, and a total reported for the entire United States of 6085, with 12,260 teachers employed and 263,096 pupils enrolled."[75] This statement is obviously based on data in the census of 1850, but the statement, which is followed by a clear implication that the schools enumerated were secondary schools, fails to take into account the fact that in the census educational institutions were classified in only three categories, (1) colleges and universities, (2) public schools, and (3) academies and other schools. More than six thousand "academies and other schools" were reported in the returns, but not all the institutions included in this category pretended to be academies and many were probably elementary rather than secondary schools. Under the head of "academies and other schools" returns were included for special schools for deaf-mutes, the blind, juvenile criminals, and orphans, as well as any private schools which were not classified as "public schools." The fact that many private elementary schools must have been included in the number may explain why the South according to the figures cited by Cubberley had more than 40 per cent of all the academies of the nation. In those areas where public education had not advanced very far, the census taker would find many "academies and other schools" to report. On the other hand, the relatively liberal support afforded "academies and other schools" leads one to suppose that perhaps a great majority of these institutions should have been classified as academies. The total income for the support of "academies and other schools" was somewhat more than $4,500,000, as compared with approximately $2,000,000 for colleges and something less than $10,000,000 for "public schools." The average income per pupil enrolled was about eighteen dollars, only 9 per cent of which was derived from endowments, public funds, and taxation. Other sources, largely tuition, accounted for more than 90 per cent of the total income of the "academies and other schools."

The development of public high schools, after the establishment of the first school of this type in Boston in 1821, was not very rapid. Most of the larger cities in time followed the example of Boston, but the number of high schools before 1860 was never large. The census reports did not record data on high schools as separate institutions, and it is, therefore, difficult to get precise information with respect to their number. In 1904 the United States Commissioner of Education compiled a table showing the number and distribution of high schools in 1860. His list includes 321 such schools, more than half of which (167) were located in Massachusetts, New York, and Ohio.[76] Since high schools in the early days

[75] Cubberley, *Public Education in the United States, op. cit.,* p. 247.

[76] *Report of the United States Commissioner of Education for the Year Ending June 30, 1904* (Washington, D.C.: Government Printing Office, 1906), pp. 1782–1989, as noted in Cubberley, *Public Education in the United States, op. cit.,* p. 252.

were primarily urban institutions, they were established in comparatively small numbers in the West and the South.

HIGHER EDUCATION

The number of institutions bearing the name of college or university and authorized to grant degrees multiplied rapidly during the three decades from 1830 to 1860. The Census of 1840 reported 173 colleges, in which were enrolled 16,233 students. Twenty years later the number of colleges was 467, with an enrollment of 56,120 students. The number of colleges about doubled between 1850 and 1860, and the number of students increased by slightly more than 100 per cent. The great majority of the colleges were the result of denominational effort, although state institutions existed in considerable numbers, especially in the South and the West. But even where state colleges or universities had been established, they received little support from taxation. Only six states employed this source of revenue and the total amount of taxes going to the support of higher education was $25,882. Of the three-million-dollar income which colleges received, about $134,000 was derived from public funds other than taxation.

College enrollment in relation to the total free population was materially higher in the South than in the other regions; and the same was true of the total revenue made available for higher education. With a free population constituting less than a third of that of the whole nation, the South provided in its own institutions nearly one-half of the total college enrollments and sent a considerable number of students to study in northern colleges. The slave states were spending on their colleges a sum almost exactly equal to that being spent for higher education in New England, the Middle Atlantic states, the West, and the Pacific states combined. South Carolina, with a free population only one-fourth that of Massachusetts, enrolled in her colleges 1384 students, as compared with 1733 in Massachusetts. The total income for higher education in South Carolina was $192,675, as compared with $195,110 in Massachusetts. Illinois, with a free population greater than that of North Carolina, South Carolina, and Georgia combined, enrolled less than one-half as many students in college as those three southern states and spent less than a fourth as much in support of colleges.[77] It is no doubt true that many

[77] The enrollment in Illinois was 2901 and the total income for colleges $97,412; the enrollment in North Carolina, South Carolina, and Georgia was 6226 and the total income for colleges $462,366.

Census reports exaggerate the number of colleges because the major criterion for inclusion in the census count appears to have been the right to grant degrees. Many schools found it much easier to acquire the degree-granting privilege than to institute a program of college-level education. The census definitions and figures are used in this and succeeding paragraphs because the cost, attendance, and other data used relate to the entire group classified as colleges by the Census.

of the colleges in the South, as elsewhere, were little better than academies or seminaries, but it is also true that a considerable number of the
southern institutions, such as the universities of Virginia, South Carolina,
North Carolina, Alabama, and Georgia, ranked relatively high among the
institutions of the day. At South Carolina College the scholarly Francis
Lieber was offering the most advanced work in political science to be
found anywhere in the country and Joseph Le Conte was carrying forward
pioneer investigations in science. "Even if in some respects the standards
of Southern colleges in 1860 can be criticized," says Professor Dodd, "it
remains true that they had made greater progress than similar institutions
in other parts of the country."[78] It must be kept in mind, however, that
progress in the development of higher education was not confined to the
South. In New England and the Middle Atlantic states enrollments were
increasing and the quality of instruction was improving. In the West
the number of denominational colleges was being multiplied and the
foundations were being laid for the development of great state universities.

Viewing the period as a whole, one may say that marked progress was
made in every section and at every level of education. In New England
and New York the main problem was to improve the educational systems
that had already been established and to secure additional support of
public as over against private schools. In the other Middle Atlantic states
the major problem was to establish systems of public schools to provide
more effective popular education than the parochial and private schools
had been able to afford. Definite progress was made toward this end.
In the West, the most democratic section of the nation, the prevailing
political and social philosophy required that at least some degree of education be provided to as large an element of the population as possible.
This attitude no doubt accounts for the fact that expenditure per pupil
enrolled in the public schools, in the academies, and in the colleges was
usually less in the West than in other sections. In the South, educational
policy reflected definitely the prevailing social philosophy — the ideal of a
Greek democracy. Colleges and academies were more numerous in relation to the free population and were more liberally supported than elsewhere. Even the public schools, though less numerous than in the other
sections, were usually provided with an income per pupil in excess of the
national average. The great problem of the South was to improve its
common schools, a goal which it had accepted as wholly compatible with
its ideal of a white aristocracy. In the matter of maintaining public schools
the South was more advanced than has commonly been supposed, and in
the rate of progress it was abreast with either the Northeast or the Northwest. It is clear, however, that despite great educational advances in all
sections, the battle for effective school systems had by no means been won.

[78] Dodd, *The Cotton Kingdom, op. cit.,* pp. 113–114.

Questions and Problems for Study and Discussion

1. How do you account for the fact that most of the educational leaders of this period put major emphasis on the development of the common (elementary) school? Was their decision to do so a wise one? How was the situation with which they were confronted different from those that exist today in the underdeveloped countries of the world?

2. What were the essential characteristics of the academy, and how did it affect the structure of the American educational system? The academy was extolled as a democratic institution and attacked as an aristocratic one. Evaluate the position of its champions and its detractors.

3. Do you think we have succeeded in making secondary education democratic? Defend your position.

4. Indicate the most significant developments in higher education during this period.

5. Why was the teacher-education function not incorporated in the regularly established colleges and universities? Do you think it would have been a better policy to do so? Why?

6. Account for the differences in the educational development of each of the major regions — Northeast, South, and West.

7. It has been said that by 1860 the American public school system was firmly established, in principle at least, in all the northern states. Evaluate this statement.

Selected References for Further Reading

Barnard, Henry. *Normal Schools and Other Institutions, Agencies, and Means Designed for the Professional Education of Teachers.* Hartford, Conn.: Case, Tiffany & Co., 1851. Pp. 436.

Brooks, Charles. "School Reform, or Teachers Seminaries," pp. 159–179, *The Introductory Discourse and the Lectures Delivered before the American Institute of Instruction, at Worcester (Mass.), August, 1837, Including the Journal of Proceedings, and A List of Officers.* Boston: James Monroe & Co., 1838. Pp. xxiv + 262.

Brown, Elmer Ellsworth. *The Making of Our Middle Schools: An Account of the Development of Secondary Education in the United States.* New York: Longmans, Green & Co., 1902. Pp. xii + 548.

Brubacher, John Seiler, and Rudy, Willis. *Higher Education in Transition: An American History, 1635–1956.* New York: Harper & Brothers, 1958. Pp. viii + 494.

Butler, Vera M. *Education as Revealed by New England Newspapers Prior to 1850.* Doctor's thesis, Temple University, 1935. Pp. x + 504.

Butts, R. Freeman. *The College Charts Its Course: Historical Conceptions and Current Proposals.* New York: McGraw-Hill Book Co., 1939. Pp. xvi + 464.

Cousin, Victor. *Report on the State of Public Instruction in Prussia; Addressed to the Count de Montalivet, Peer of France, Minister of Public Instruction, and Ecclesiastical Affairs.* Translated by Sarah Austin. London: Effingham Wilson, 1834. Pp. xxxviii + 334 + 36.

Dodd, William E. *The Cotton Kingdom: A Chronicle of the Old South,* The Chronicles of America Series, XXXVII. New Haven, Conn.: Yale University Press, 1919. Pp. x + 162.

The First State Normal School in America: The Journals of Cyrus Pierce and Mary Swift. With an Introduction by Arthur O. Norton. Cambridge, Mass.: Harvard University Press, 1926. Pp. lvi + 300.

Fish, Carl Russell. *The Rise of the Common Man, 1830–1850,* VI, *A History of American Life.* New York: The Macmillan Co., 1927. Pp. xx + 392.

Grizzell, Emit Duncan. *Origin and Development of the High School in New England Before 1865.* New York: The Macmillan Co., 1923. Pp. xvi + 428.

Hall, Samuel R., *Lectures on School-Keeping.* Boston: Richardson, Lord Holbrook, 1829. Pp. xii + 136.

Hall, Samuel R. "On the Necessity of Educating Teachers," pp. 241–259, *The Introductory Discourse and the Lectures Delivered before the American Institute of Instruction, in Boston, August, 1833, Including a List of Officers and Members.* Boston: Carter, Hendee & Co., 1834. Pp. xx + 317.

Johnson, Clifton. *Old-Time Schools and School-Books.* New York: The Macmillan Co., 194. Pp. vi + 382.

Knight, Edgar W. *Public Education in the South.* Boston: Ginn & Company, 1922. Pp. xii + 482.

Mangum, Vernon Lamar. *The American Normal School, Its Rise and Development in Massachusetts.* Baltimore, Md.: Warwick and York, 1928. Pp. xvi + 442.

Olmsted, Denison. "Observations on the School System of Connecticut," pp. 95–110, *The Lectures Delivered before the American Institute of Instruction, at Lowell (Mass.), August, 1838, Including the Journal of Proceedings, and a List of the Officers.* Boston: William D. Ticknor, 1839. Pp. xxiv + 187.

Page, David P. *Theory and Practice of Teaching: or the Motives and Methods of School-Keeping,* Seventh Edition. Syracuse, N.Y.: Hall and Dickson, Booksellers and Publishers, 1848. Pp. 349.

Richey, Herman G. "The Persistence of Educational Progress during the Decade of the Civil War," *Elementary School Journal,* XLII (January, February, 1942), 358–366, 456–463.

Richey, Herman G. "Reappraisal of the State School Systems of the Pre-Civil-War Period," *Elementary School Journal,* XLI (October, 1940), 118–129.

Stowe, Calvin E. *Common Schools and Teachers' Seminaries.* Boston: Marsh, Capen, Lyon & Webb, 1839. Pp. 126 + 16.

Taylor, J. Orville. *The District School.* New York: Harper & Brothers, 1834. Pp. xxiv + 25 + 336.

Tharp, Louise Hall. *Until Victory: Horace Mann and Mary Peabody.* Boston: Little, Brown & Co., 1953. Pp. xii + 367.

Wills, Elbert Vaughan. *The Growth of American Higher Education: Liberal, Professional and Technical.* Philadelphia: Dorrance & Co., 1936. Pp. 226.

PART THREE

The School in Modern Society —
the Past Century: Preview

The Civil War marked the end of a long struggle between the planter South and the rising capitalistic East to dominate the national state. The surrender of Lee at Appomattox represented also the triumph of industrial capitalism. The new occupants of the seats of power were not slow in putting into effect measures designed to promote the interests of business enterprise. With unbelievable swiftness America was transformed from a comparatively simple rural society into the most highly advanced industrial nation of the world; and although the farmer strove valiantly to maintain the relative economic and social dignity he had enjoyed during the earlier periods of our national life, each passing decade saw him forced to retreat further in the face of an ever advancing industrialism. Scientific advance and inventive genius were giving rise to a technological revolution that was to transform society to its very foundations. The impact of technology changed both the essential structure of the economy and the effectiveness of its operation. From the new economic order that now emerged stemmed much of the promise of American life; from it, too, stemmed many problems of grave importance. It is, perhaps, not too much to say that the technological revolution of the last century, and especially of the past few decades, has brought and is bringing about economic and social changes comparable to the transfer of society from a feudal to a capitalistic basis at an earlier day, or to the changes wrought by the Industrial Revolution of the eighteenth and nineteenth centuries.

No one can doubt that our generation is witnessing the closing of one age and the opening of a vastly different one. The main difference between the age that is closing and the one that is opening is a difference in concept with respect to the ways and means of adjusting to the processes of social change. However much in the past we could (or thought we could) rely on laissez faire — on automatic processes of adjustment — we now know that is no longer possible. Indeed, the central meaning of our time is the need of more conscious, deliberate, intelligent direction of human affairs, both at home and throughout the world.

The educational developments that have taken place in the United States during the past century can scarcely be understood unless viewed against this broad background of social change. More important still, if educational statesmen are to chart the future course of American education with integrity and wisdom, they must arrive at a fundamental understanding of the forces that are transforming our world. If education is to become a more positive instrument of social and political policy, as it must, it will have to cultivate in those who direct it, as well as in those who are nurtured by it, the knowledge, the understandings, and the motivations they will need to solve the problems they cannot avoid in working out cooperatively and experimentally the design of what we hope will be a better and more peaceful world. The movement of the United States into a position of leadership in the free world has made the task a more urgent, more important, and at the same time more difficult one. For these reasons considerable attention is devoted in Part Three of this volume to an analysis of social and economic developments before an examination in detail of the educational history of the period.

Chapter 11 is concerned with the change of the United States from an agrarian to an industrial civilization and appraises some of the more important social consequences of the impact of technology on American life. Chapter 12 presents an over-all view of the changes that have occurred in the structure of the economy. The problem of the relation of the government to the economy is discussed in Chapter 13. The remaining chapters of Part Three chronicle the educational adjustments that have been worked out to meet the demands of a changing social order and suggest lines along which future adaptations may take place.

11 🌿

Social and Technological Revolution — the Past Century

The changes in American life after 1860 were truly revolutionary. Many of these changes stemmed from the Civil War and the technological revolution that soon followed it. The Civil War has aptly been called the second American Revolution, for an appraisal of its effect on the economic, social, and political life of the nation justifies the conclusion that it was no less important than the first Revolution, which severed the political ties with England. Not many years were to pass after that war was over before America was caught in the grip of technological revolution which was to bring social changes fully as significant as those produced in Europe at an earlier date by the shift from a feudal to a capitalistic economy and by the Industrial Revolution of the late eighteenth and early nineteenth centuries. The change from a relatively simple rural economy to a complex industrial economy was amazingly swift. To those who looked upon the United States as still largely an agricultural country, it was perhaps a surprise to discover that in the early nineteen-thirties the farmers of the nation were the recipients of only about 8 or 9 per cent of the total national income and that the families living in four large cities — New York, Philadelphia, Detroit, and Chicago — were receiving as much of the national income as all the farm families combined.

The present chapter will be devoted to a consideration of some of the consequences of the Civil War, to the technological advances of the closing years of the nineteenth century and the first six decades of the twentieth century, and to some of the social effects of this technological change.

The Civil War and the Triumph of Industrial Capitalism

The Civil War has been interpreted by some as a war over slavery and by others as a struggle over states' rights. One contemporary historian has stressed the importance of sectional hatreds and emotional tensions in driving North and South into a clash of arms.[1] Certainly the issue of slavery was an important one. These and other factors need to be taken into consideration in explaining the conflict, but it was also a struggle between industrial capitalism and a landed aristocracy for control of the national state — a struggle dating as far back as the days of Hamilton and Jefferson. As Charles and Mary Beard point out, had the southern plantation owners been scattered throughout the nation, there would have been no war between sections, but there might have been a revolution, much like the French Revolution, to liquidate a landed aristocracy. One misses the real significance of the Civil War unless one views it, in some measure, as a bourgeois revolution, the liquidation of the landed aristocracy, the capture of the national government by financial and industrial interests. The surrender of Lee at Appomattox represented the victory of the eastern capitalists and their western farmer allies over the planter interests of the South and set the stage for the most spectacular industrial development the world had ever seen.

It is not necessary here to point out how the policy of Reconstruction of the South and the political strategy in dealing with the West were designed to keep the new masters of the national government in the seats of power. We might, however, examine the adoption of certain policies which greatly stimulated industrial development. During the Civil War tariff rates were materially advanced and in later years they were raised still higher. The American market, the greatest in the world, was amply protected against foreign competition. A new banking system and a monetary policy favorable to the financial and manufacturing interests were put into operation and maintained against the opposition of western farmers. The income tax which had been in operation during the war was repealed. The policy adopted for the disposition of the vast national domain made it easy for large financial and business interests to gain possession of rich mineral, forest, and grazing lands. The Homestead Act made it possible for persons twenty-one years of age and above to acquire one hundred and sixty acres of land by living on it five years and making improvements. At the same time immense grants of land were made to railroads — 158,000,000 acres between 1850 and 1873.[2] Grants of

[1] Avery Craven, *The Coming of the Civil War* (Chicago: University of Chicago Press, 1957).

[2] Louis M. Hacker, *The Triumph of American Capitalism.* (New York: Simon and Schuster, Inc., 1940). Also published by Columbia University Press (New York), 1947 and (Fourth Printing) 1959.

30,000 acres for each representative in Congress were made to the states for the promotion of agricultural colleges, and these lands could be purchased on fairly easy terms, even though they were mineral or timber lands of great value. The main point is that the program of disposing of the national domain — and the national domain embraced an area nearly as large as all the states in 1860[3] — made it possible for men of enterprise to acquire rapidly and on easy terms a large fraction of the natural resources of the nation.[4] Finally, the Fourteenth Amendment served to protect the business community from attacks on the part of state legislatures. Henceforth no state could deprive any person of life, liberty, or property without due process of law, and the terms "liberty," "property," and "due process of law" were left to the Supreme Court of the United States to define. In effect, the Court was in a position to declare unconstitutional practically any state police legislation of which it disapproved, and it exercised this power with due regard to financial and business interests.[5]

The capitalistic interests in America entertained a very different conception of the role of the political state from that which had been entertained by the planter South. The southern slaveholders had asked little of government; in fact, they had wished to control it in order to keep it inactive. The new possessors of political power were now making use of government to further the interests of business enterprise.

Other Factors Stimulating Rapid Industrialization

The conquest of the national state by eastern capitalistic interests was only one of the factors which stimulated the rapid industrialization of the United States. The abundance of natural resources, prevailing attitudes toward individualism and laissez faire, an availability of cheap labor from Europe, the progress of invention and technology, the new use now made of the corporation as a form of business organization — all these combined to make possible the extension of the industrial domain, the rise of cities, and the triumph of business enterprise.

The Abundance of Natural Resources

Fortunately, nature had been prodigal in bestowing on the territory embraced in the United States a large amount of the natural resources

---

[3] Charles A. Beard and Mary R. Beard, *The Rise of American Civilization* (New York: The Macmillan Co., 1927), II, p. 122.

[4] For a more detailed discussion, see *ibid.*, Chap. XX, and Hacker, *op. cit.*, Chaps. XXIV and XXV.

[5] Newton Edwards, *The Courts and the Public Schools*, Revised Edition (Chicago: University of Chicago Press, 1955), pp. 21–22.

essential for industrial development. Here were to be found in abundance timber, coal, iron, copper, lead, sulphur, and other minerals. The United States possessed about 40 per cent of the world's known mineral resources. Millions of acres of virgin forests were still untouched. In her energy resources — coal, oil, and water — America stood unrivaled.[6] Never before had business enterprise had such a golden opportunity.

THE INTELLECTUAL CLIMATE OF INDIVIDUALISM AND LAISSEZ FAIRE

The great natural resources of the American continent were to be developed within the framework of individualism and laissez faire. Most men firmly believed that the individual had the right to regulate his own economic affairs without governmental interference. To be sure, the principle of laissez faire was abandoned when the government was asked to supply favors in the form of protective tariffs or other subsidies, but, in general, government was not to impose regulatory measures. According to the prevailing economic theory, the law of supply and demand operating through the market mechanism would automatically regulate the myriad relationships involved in the process of production and consumption. Governmental interference with the "natural laws of economics" would court disaster. Freedom from political control of the economy was an important factor in influencing the course of industrial development.

CHEAP LABOR FROM EUROPE

American industry was able to draw heavily on Europe as a source of man power. Millions of European laborers stood ready to migrate to the United States and to help build railroads and man mines and factories at relatively low wages. In 1890 the foreign-born population in Chicago was about as large as its total population had been ten years earlier.[7] Other midwestern industrial centers were also drawing a flood of European emigrants; throughout the Middle West about one person in six was of foreign birth.[8] In 1890 persons born in other lands constituted a third of the population of Boston and a fourth of the population of Philadelphia. In Greater New York four out of every five persons were of foreign birth or foreign parentage.[9] By 1900, immigrants were coming at the rate of

[6] See C. K. Leith, *World Minerals and World Politics* (New York: McGraw-Hill Book Co., 1931); George S. Counts, *The Social Foundations of Education* (New York: Charles Scribner's Sons, 1934), Chap. II; C. K. Leith, J. W. Furness, and Cleona Lewis, *World Minerals and World Peace* (Washington, D.C.: The Brookings Institution, 1943).

[7] Arthur Meier Schlesinger, *The Rise of the City, 1878–1908* (New York: The Macmillan Co., 1933), p. 65.

[8] *Ibid.*, p. 64.　　　　　　　　[9] *Ibid.*, pp. 72–73.

about a million a year. This seemingly exhaustless supply of labor tended to keep wages low and to make it difficult for workingmen to organize. Laborers were told to vote for high tariffs to protect themselves from their less fortunate brethren in Europe, but no move was made to close the floodgates of immigration. At any rate, industrial leadership was able to profit as it would from a bountiful supply of relatively cheap labor.

THE PROGRESS OF INVENTION AND TECHNOLOGY

In the meantime, science and invention, translated into technology, were incredibly improving methods of production and increasing the output of industry. The number of patents issued is indicative of the technological advance, although it is not to be supposed that every patent resulted in some new mechanical device or industrial process. For the decade ending in 1870 there were 80,000 patents issued in the United States. The numbers for the decades ending in 1900 and 1930 were 221,000 and 421,000 respectively. In a single year, ending June 30, 1961, approximately 50,000 patents were issued.[10]

It is clear that with each passing year the United States was caught more firmly in the grip of a technological revolution. In a thousand ways and in every aspect of industrial life, technological innovations were making their influence felt. No matter where one turned — to the production of minerals, to transportation, to communication, to the generation of power, to the construction of buildings, or to office management — one found that industry had brought science and invention into its service.

THE LARGE CORPORATION AND THE SUPPLY OF CAPITAL

As industry expanded in the post-Civil-War period, it became increasingly necessary to have large aggregations of capital. It took money and a great deal of it to build huge factories, equip them with machines, buy raw materials, and employ a labor force. Individual capitalists or even partnerships were often unable to supply the necessary funds. The modern corporation as a form of business organization was the answer to this problem. The corporation was not a new idea, but it came more and more into use. It could sell its stocks and bonds to any number of purchasers and it was an instrument for raising funds sufficient to finance billion-

---

[10] United States Bureau of the Census, *Statistical Abstract of the United States, 1961* (Washington, D.C.: Government Printing Office, 1962), p. 540. See also *Recent Social Trends in the United States*, Report of the President's Research Committee in Social Trends, one-volume edition (New York: McGraw-Hill Book Co., 1933), pp. 125–126.

dollar enterprises. Moreover, the charter of the corporation could be and often was so drawn as to confer on the board of directors very large managerial powers. In time, as we shall see later, the large corporation came to dominate American economic life, and it was influential in changing the very structure and operation of the economy. The point to be stressed here is that the corporate form of business organization made it possible for industrial leaders to gather up the savings of a great number of people and thereby to finance business ventures of almost any proportions.

THE FAVORABLE ATTITUDE OF EDUCATION TOWARD BUSINESS ENTERPRISE

It is often the case that educational leaders, growing up in a particular social order, consciously or unconsciously come to accept its main features as desirable and good. Such is especially likely to be the case in a society that accepts laissez faire as a social theory and pins its faith on individualism. If the economic system can be trusted to right itself through the automatic operation of economic laws, there is little need for the cultivation of critical social analysis, in school or outside. Where the policy of social drift is widely accepted, few men are likely to concern themselves with the deeper forces that may be transforming the whole pattern of economic, social, and political arrangements. Minor ills may be diagnosed and corrected, but in general men float with the current of the stream in the expectation that it will flow through still greener valleys; their faith in the social order in which they have grown up and their ignorance of the moving forces of their day may silence the thundering sounds of the cataracts of economic collapse, depression, and war that lie ahead. Under such circumstances, education becomes a conservative and preservative force; it provides a sound emotional underpinning for the existing order.

An examination of the record discloses that from Lincoln to Wilson American educators, with few outstanding exceptions, insofar as they manifested any social theory at all, accepted the tenets of industrial capitalism. Most of them expressed loyalty to the democratic dogma; they labored valiantly to extend a richer educational opportunity to youth; they improved the processes of education by arduous scientific research; but they exhibited no great sensitivity to the forces that were transforming American life, and they failed to appraise correctly the social conflicts of their day. In the struggle between the farmers and the industrialists, they espoused the cause of the latter. When labor undertook to better its condition and to share more equitably in the national income, they took the side of capital. Even the social sciences were often so taught as to buttress the status quo. The planters of the South had found educators willing to give support to their particular social system; the industrialists of the North at a later day found educators little less willing to do the same. If southern educators had seen nothing ethically wrong with slavery, and if they had regarded the aristocratic slaveholders as the highest fruit of civilization, northern educators, with some notable exceptions, saw nothing wrong in the exploitation of natural and human resources in the interest of profits, and they held business leaders in no less regard than southern educators had held the masters of slaves.

Of the social philosophy and influence of W. T. Harris — Superintendent of Schools, St. Louis (1867–1880), United States Commissioner of Education (1889–1906), and outstanding educational philosopher and leader — Professor Curti says:

Harris not only defended capitalism against its critics, but explicitly pointed out how education might serve more effectively the established order. In greeting the National Education Association in 1894, when the country was in the throes of labor "disorders," he observed that the school provided the people with training in those habits of regularity, silence, and industry which would "preserve and save our civil order." In the public school, the center of discipline, the pupil learned "first of all to respect the rights of organized industry." In the kindergarten the child of the slum, the weakling of society, learned self-respect, moral ideals, industry, and perseverance. . . .

Who can say how far the reluctance of Americans to experiment seriously with social control, to abandon traditional *laissez-faire* individualism in spite of its patent contradiction by harsh facts, was related to the skill and plausibility with which Harris told two generations of Americans what they already believed, and what they wanted to believe? Who can estimate the influence of Harris in standardizing the school system, enveloping it with spiritual purposes, housing it in ivory towers, and excluding from its curriculum and its methods everything that did not confirm the existing economic and social structure?[11]

After a careful examination of the social ideas of American educators in this period, Curti concludes:

In furthering a more realistic analysis John Dewey was not altogether alone. But it was very unusual for educators to be thus in the vanguard. With few exceptions, they not only advanced social ideas thoroughly in keeping with the existing system of profit-making industrialism; they also aided it in its struggles with farmers and workers. Even within the frame-

[11] Merle Curti, *The Social Ideas of American Educators,* Report of the Commission on Social Studies (New York: Charles Scribner's Sons, 1935), Part IX, pp. 330–331, 347. Also published, with a chapter added, by Pageant Books (Paterson, N.J.: Pageant Books, Inc., 1959).

work of the capitalistic system, educators in this period between Lincoln and Wilson failed to deal in reforms for the remedying of obvious social disorders.[12]

The Sweep of Industrial Progress following the Civil War

During the post-Civil-War years conditions could scarcely have been more favorable for industrial development. As has already been pointed out, through the Civil War and the Reconstruction the forces of business enterprise had secured their hold on the political state. A virgin continent unbelievably rich in natural resources was at hand for development and exploitation. The widespread acceptance of individualism and laissez faire insured little social control or governmental interference. A constant stream of European immigrants provided an adequate supply of cheap labor. Science and invention made possible a tempo of technological advance hitherto undreamed of. The corporate form of business organization made possible the raising of capital sufficient for almost any enterprise. And organized education lent its support to the existing order and undertook to cultivate in youth the attitudes, values, and skills which that order demanded.

Nor did business enterprise fail to take advantage of all the opportunities afforded it. Soon there appeared on the scene a group of capitalists — many of them of petty bourgeois origin — who were capable, shrewd, hard-driving, and determined to build industrial empires and create immense fortunes. The Civil War was scarcely over before a new era of railroad-building was under way. In 1868 approximately 3000 miles of new lines were completed, and three years later new constructions amounted to 7379 miles.[13] Depression in the seventies temporarily slowed construction, but in a single year after recovery (1883), 11,569 miles of new track were laid down.[14] By the close of the century the United States had been tied together by a network of roads. The great railroad-builders, such as Jay Gould, William H. Vanderbilt, James J. Hill, and Edward H. Harriman, had accumulated fortunes beside which the fortunes of the old New England merchant princes or the southern slaveholders paled into insignificance.

Nor was progress any less striking in manufacturing, the extractive industries, and finance. In the following brief but vivid passage, the Beards recount the epic of industrial growth:

In four great provinces bound together by ever-constricting ties of federation — manufacturing, extractive industries, transportation, and finance — the leaders of business enterprise, sustained and assisted by a

[12] *Ibid.*, p. 259.   [13] Hacker, *op. cit.*, p. 403.   [14] *Ibid.*, p. 405.

host of liegemen, marched from victory to victory in the decades that followed the triumph of Grant at Appomattox. Statistics but dimly shadow their progress. In 1860, just a little more than a billion dollars was invested in manufacturing and only 1,500,000 industrial wage earners were employed in the United States. In less than fifty years the capital had risen to more than twelve billions and the number of wage earners to 5,500,000. During the same period, the value of manufactured products had leaped to fourteen billion dollars a year, fifteen times the total at the beginning of the epoch. The output of American iron and steel — that measure of modern power — was, in 1870, far below the tonnage of England or France; within twenty years the United States had outstripped them and was pouring from its forges more than one-third of the world's total annual supply. The iron crown, as Andrew Carnegie said, had been placed on the brow of Pennsylvania.

With a stride that astounded statisticians, the conquering hosts of business enterprise swept over the continent; twenty-five years after the death of Lincoln, America had become, in the quantity and value of her products, the first manufacturing nation of the world. What England had once accomplished in a hundred years, the United States had achieved in half the time.[15]

And the broad sweep of industrial progress was still to advance. Science and technology were to provide bigger and more efficient machines and great new industries were to be founded on new inventions. Each year the productivity of labor increased and the total output of industry mounted. Between 1899 and 1914 the total volume of manufactured goods in an extensive sample of industries increased 76 per cent, and between 1922 and 1929 the "aggregate output of movable goods . . . increased 34 per cent."[16]

As time passed, "big business" tended to pre-empt the field. By 1940, there were no fewer than thirty billion-dollar corporations, most of whose individual assets were greater than the total assessed valuation of many American states. In the early thirties, the American Telephone and Telegraph Company controlled more wealth than was "contained within the borders of twenty-one of the states in the country."[17] Clearly, the policies of Hamilton had triumphed over those of Jefferson. The old Northwest, which had helped to send Jackson to the White House to protect the interests of the pioneers and small farmers, had become, along with the Northeast, the heart of an industrial empire. And the old planter South and the Pacific Coast also were being drawn into the vortex of industry. No one could doubt that America had made the shift from a rural to an

[15] Beard and Beard, *op. cit.,* p. 176.

[16] Frederick C. Mills, *Economic Tendencies in the United States* (New York: National Bureau of Economic Research, 1932), p. 244.

[17] Adolf A. Berle, Jr., and Gardiner C. Means, *The Modern Corporation and Private Property* (New York: The Macmillan Co., 1932), p. 19.

industrial society. By 1930 less than a fourth of the population made their living tilling the land, and they received less than a tenth of the total national income. In 1950 the rural farm population constituted only 15.3 per cent of the total,[19] and agriculture provided employment to only 12.5 per cent of the employed civilian labor force.[20] By 1960 the per cent had declined to 8.6 (males, 10.3). And one may add, of course, that the sweep of industrial and urban progress, measured in terms of increased population and production, has continued down to the present.[21]

The Revolution in Agriculture

The decades following the enactment of the Homestead Act in 1862 and the closing of the Civil War witnessed a rapid peopling of the last great frontier. Veterans of the Union Army, joined later by many European immigrants, pushed across and filled up the plains of Iowa, Minnesota, Kansas, Nebraska, and the Dakotas. Between 1862 and 1914, about 147,146,000 acres of land were taken up under the Homestead Act alone.[22] Although the farm population was not increasing so rapidly as the non-farm population, between 1880 and 1910 the farmer showed an increase in absolute numbers of about five million.[23] And by the use of new types of farm machinery — the value of farm machinery rose from about a quarter of a billion dollars in 1860 to a billion and a quarter in 1910 — the farmer was able to increase vastly the volume of his production.[24] But with greater production the farmer faced rapidly falling prices.

Farmers in Distress

The Civil War, as we have seen, marked the transfer of the political allegiance of the western farmers from the planter South to the industrial East. According to the terms of the agreement, the East was to have its protective tariff and the West its free homesteads from the public domain.

[19] J. Frederick Dewhurst and Associates, *America's Needs and Resources: A New Survey* (New York: The Twentieth Century Fund, 1955), p. 72.

[20] United States Bureau of the Census, *Statistical Abstract of the United States, 1961* (Washington, D.C.: Government Printing Office, 1961), p. 203.

[21] Gerhard Colm and Theodore Geiger, *The Economy of the American People, Progress, Problems, Prospects,* National Planning Association Pamphlet No. 102 (Washington, D.C.: National Planning Association, 1958), p. 155.

[22] Avery Craven and Walter Johnson, *The United States: Experiment in Democracy* (Boston: Ginn and Company, 1947), p. 466.

[23] *Loc. cit.*

[24] *Ibid.,* p. 467.

As population pushed westward and new farms were opened up, it may have appeared that agriculture was advancing about as much as industry. As a matter of fact, however, rural America was constantly in retreat in the face of the ever advancing city. In the East, in the Middle West, and, to a lesser degree, in the South and the Far West, the city was a magnet, drawing youth from farms by the millions. The closing of the frontier about 1890 made the triumph of the city all the easier. As the nineteenth century drew to a close, it was clear that what Jefferson had feared had come to pass: The people were becoming concentrated in cities, a new social order was in the making, the old culture of rural America was giving place to the urban industrial order. The sons of the farmers who had joined in partnership on equal terms with the eastern industrialists in 1860 now found themselves junior partners in the concern; each decade they struggled with decreasing success to hold their own in the economic life of the nation. Again, to quote the Beards:

> An epoch had come to an end and the iron gates were locked. Industrial capitalists were organized to make their own prices; industrial workers were organized to fix wages; whereas farmers, with the exception of a few powerful groups, were still incorrigible individualists at the mercy of the market. Throughout wide areas, the independent, self-sufficient farm unit of Lincoln's era had become a specialized concern producing for profit, forced to employ large capital in the form of machinery and fertilizers, compelled to compete with European agriculture on more equal terms, and obliged to carry the weight of an increment in land values which had mounted with the years. With energetic members of the younger generation escaping to the cities to share in capitalistic enterprise, with new racial stocks occupying ancestral homesteads, with a remorseless competition determining prices of produce, with industrial capitalists and industrial workers compactly united to dictate terms on manufactured commodities, the economy and culture of historic American farming were crumbling into ruins.[25]

The farmer was in a disadvantageous position and his grievances were many. The price of the produce he had to sell dropped sharply — for example, the price of wheat dropped from $1.05 per bushel in 1866 to $.62 in 1900.[26] And so it was also with cattle, sheep, cotton, and corn. Many farmers had incurred heavy debts when money was depreciated, and now that mortgage rates had risen and the value of money had increased sharply, they found it difficult to pay their debts and to stave off mortgage foreclosures.[27] They felt that the railroads were charging exorbitant freight rates, that they were being exploited by the eastern financial in-

[25] Beard and Beard, *op. cit.*, p. 277. Used by permission of The Macmillan Co.
[26] Avery Craven, *Democracy in American Life* (Chicago: University of Chicago Press, 1941), p. 123.
[27] Craven and Johnson, *op. cit.*, pp. 470–471.

terests, that both capital and labor had conspired against them. Nor were the farmer's grievances wholly imaginary. His share of the national income had decreased from 24.1 per cent in 1870 to 15.8 per cent in 1890.[28]

But the farmer did not accept his status without a struggle. He entered the arena of political action and vigorously attempted to improve his position through the Greenback party, the Granger movement, and the Populist party. He was instrumental in the passage of the Interstate Commerce Act of 1887 and the Sherman Antitrust Act of 1890. But, even so, there was a general decline in agricultural prosperity from the Civil War to the coming of the New Deal under Roosevelt.

The technological breakthrough and the increase of production. The forces that produced a technological revolution in industry had a similar impact on agriculture. Following the Civil War, and well into the present century, many new machines and processes were applied in agricultural production. An even greater technological breakthrough in agriculture has occurred, however, since about 1940. During the past two decades technology has been applied to American agriculture at an unprecedented rate. The use of man and animal power has given place to the use of machines. The number of tractors employed on farms increased from 1,567,000 in 1940 to 4,700,000 in 1960. Comparable increases were registered in grain combines, corn pickers, milking machines, and other implements.[29] Technological advances were also registered in animal breeding, insect control, and soil science.

Technological advance has vastly increased agricultural production, with a corresponding decrease in man power employed (see Figure 1). In 1958 Halcrow wrote that since 1940 output per man-hour had about doubled. And although the number of those engaged in agriculture has decreased more than one-fourth, the production of crops has been about 25 per cent greater. Moreover, the output per man-hour in farming was expected to increase at least 35 per cent in the next ten years.[30]

The farmer's share of the national income. Agricultural production has increased faster than the total population. The result has been a serious imbalance between production and consumption. The market would not take the volume of farm products at a price satisfactory to farmers. Through federal legislation farmers have secured price support for a number of crops, such as wheat, cotton, and tobacco, and have thereby buttressed their income position; but, since farmers have long

[28] Leland DeWitt Baldwin, *Recent American History* (Rindge, N.H.: Richard R. Smith, Publisher, Inc., 1954), p. 568.

[29] Dewhurst and Associates, *op. cit.*, p. 801; *Statistical Abstract of the United States, 1961, op. cit.*, p. 639.

[30] Harold G. Halcrow, "Summary — Prospects and Proposals for Adjustments in Agriculture," Chap. XIX in Earl O. Heady *et al.* (eds.), *Agricultural Adjustment Problems in a Growing Economy* (Ames, Iowa.: Iowa State University Press, 1958).

Desolation in the South: "The Battle of Fredericksburg," by John Richards, ca. 1870, and "The Desolate Home," woodcut, 1867. The Civil War and its aftermath arrested the southern educational renaissance of the 1840's and 1850's.

Young workers leaving cotton mill. Photographed in the early 1900's.

Differences in American culture were reflected in the lives of children and youth.

"Family Group," by Eastman Johnson, 1871

The elimination of child labor was a necessary step in our quest for educational opportunity for all.

Tipple boy, West Virginia coal mine, 1908.

Oyster shuckers, Port Royal, South Carolina.

Girl and boy in textile mill, ca. 1909.

Purdue University: campus buildings, 1876; aerial view, 1960. Endowment of land-grant colleges from the public domain was authorized by Congress in 1862.

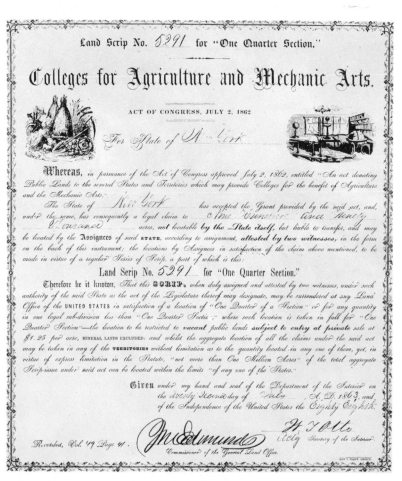

Land scrip granting public lands to the state of New York, July 2, 1862.

been a decreasing element in the national labor force, it is to be expected that their share in the total national income will show a marked decline (see Figure 2). The farmer's share of the national income decreased from 21.8 to 6.2 per cent between 1910 and the middle of the century. Even

FIGURE 1

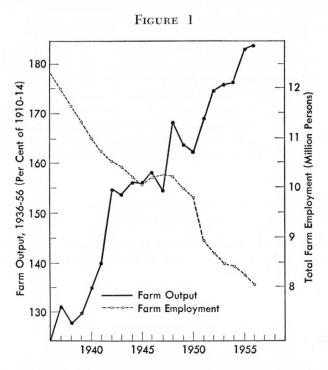

Index Numbers of Farm Output and Total Farm Employment, United States, 1936–56

Earl O. Heady, "Adjusting the Labor Force of Agriculture," Chap. IX in Earl O. Heady *et al.* (eds.), *Agricultural Adjustment Problems in a Growing Economy* (Ames, Iowa: Iowa State University Press, 1958), p. 147.

so, the real income per farm worker has doubled since 1910 (see Figure 3). Although the income position of the farm worker is materially stronger in the absolute sense, the advance of real income on the part of farmers has lagged very considerably behind that of non-farm workers. Between 1910 and 1955 the income per farm worker rose from about 20 to approximately 100 per cent of the 1947–49 average; for the same period the income of the non-farm worker increased from about 31 to nearly 136 per cent of that average.[31]

[31] Heady *et al., op. cit.,* p. 6.

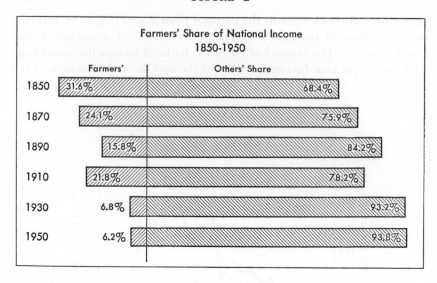

FIGURE 2

Farmers' Share of National Income
1850-1950

	Farmers'	Others' Share
1850	31.6%	68.4%
1870	24.1%	75.9%
1890	15.8%	84.2%
1910	21.8%	78.2%
1930	6.8%	93.2%
1950	6.2%	93.8%

*Farmer's Share of the National Income,
1850–1950*

Leland D. Baldwin, *Recent American History* (Rindge, N.H.: Richard
R. Smith, Publisher, Inc., 1954), p. 568. Used by permission of
American Book Company.

FIGURE 3

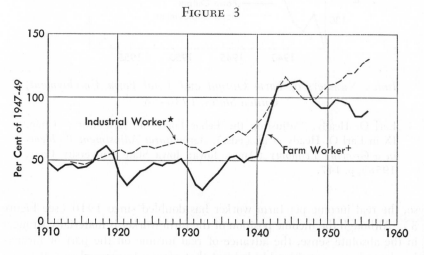

*Real Income of Farm and Industrial Workers,
1910–1956*

Sherman E. Johnson and Glen T. Barton, "Effects of Technological
Research and Education," Chap. III in Earl O. Heady *et al.* (eds.),
Agricultural Adjustment Problems in a Growing Economy (Ames,
Iowa: Iowa State University Press, 1958), p. 50.

The flight from the land. One of the most striking consequences of the impact of technology on American industry and agriculture has been the century-old decline in the number of people engaged in agriculture (see Figure 4). In 1850 the per cent of the total labor force working on farms was 64; by 1956 the percentage had dropped to 10, and it is estimated that it will drop to 6 by 1975. Technological advance has released vast numbers in the labor force from the task of supplying the food and fiber needs of the nation, and it has opened up in the cities job opportunities for a large part of the farm population. This movement from the land has been largely dominated by youth, especially southern youth. The necessity that so many farm youth have of seeking their fortunes off the land poses serious social and educational problems, which we shall consider later.

The reorientation of agriculture in the American economy. Few if any of our domestic problems are as significant or as difficult to solve as

FIGURE 4

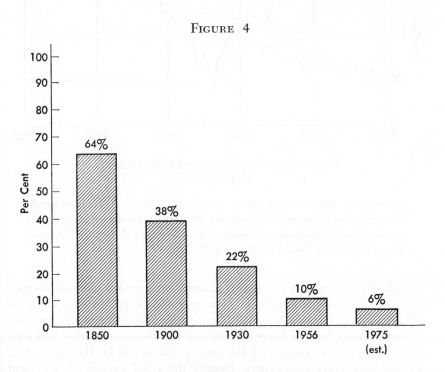

Per Cent of Labor Force Working on Farms,
1850–1975

Gerhard Colm and Theodore Geiger, *The Economy of the American People: Progress, Problems, Prospects,* National Planning Association Pamphlet No. 102 (Washington, D.C.: the Association, 1958), p. 25.

that of working out a satisfactory reorientation of agriculture in the American economy. The crux of the problem is, of course, the overproduction of farm products; since 1940 the increase in farm output has been materially greater than the increase in total population (see Figure 5). In some way an equilibrium must be established between farm production and market demand. Price support for farm products may be defensible

FIGURE 5

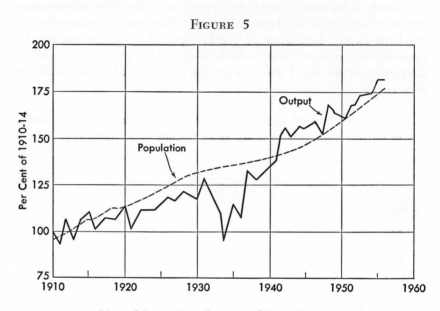

United States Population and Farm Output,
1910–1956

Sherman E. Johnson and Glenn T. Barton, "Effects of Technological Research and Education," Chap. III in Earl O. Heady *et al.* (eds.), *Agricultural Adjustment Problems in a Growing Economy* (Ames, Iowa: Iowa State University Press, 1958), p. 42.

as a short-run measure, but it can scarcely be regarded as a satisfactory long-run solution. Adjusting the resources and output in agriculture to the demands of the economy will require every possible effort to increase market demand, both at home and abroad, but the measure that will contribute most to the solution of the farm problem will be the removal of surplus labor from agriculture. Despite the rapid decline of the farm population, the blunt fact is that there are too many farmers. Measures need to be taken to expand industry so that it may absorb more of the farm population, to aid those seeking to transfer from farms to industry, and to guide effectively the many young people who seek to move from agriculture into urban employment. As Heady and Ackerman have well stated it, "To free labor from agriculture through technological progress, and then leave it stranded, is as inconsistent with economic growth as not having freed it in the first place."[32]

To assist many farm youth — and, indeed, many older farm workers — to move off the land and to find satisfactory urban employment is a major responsibility of American education. This responsibility education can meet by providing more effective programs of guidance; by making known the relative income opportunities in farming and other occupations; by contributing to a more efficient employment service, that will give information with respect to employment opportunities in various industries and in various sections of the country; and by offering adequate programs of vocational education. To quote Heady and Ackerman again:

> . . . Education to inform farm persons of the relative income opportunities in different occupations will, over the long run, be decidedly more effective than current farm programs in solving the basic farm problem. Proper education, with the research to support it, cannot alone effect the transfer of all surplus farm labor, but it can be the important catalyst in bringing about adjustments required in a rapidly growing and full-employment economy.[33]

The Growth of Cities and the Concentration of Job Opportunity

The growth of industry meant, of course, the urbanization of America. American culture had in large measure been the product of the frontier. Value patterns, traditions, habits of thought and action, emotional overtones — all these had been conditioned by forest and field. But now the city had become a new social force, and its cultural patterns, its values, its mode of life, its problems, and its solutions of those problems were often different from what the rural folk had known. By the closing years of the nineteenth century, the forces of urbanism had already triumphed in the North Atlantic states, and, to borrow a phrase from Professor Schlesinger, in the Middle West "rural America, like a stag at bay, was making its last stand."[34] By 1890 about three-fifths of the population in the North Atlantic states lived in towns and cities. The census of that year shows that "about two out of every three persons in New York and Connecticut were townsfolk, four out of every five in Massachusetts and nine out of every ten in Rhode Island."[35] So great was the exodus of

---

[32] Earl O. Heady and Joseph Ackerman, "The Income and Resource Problem," Chap. I in Earl O. Heady *et al.* (eds.), *op. cit.,* p. 15.
[33] *Loc. cit.*   [34] Schlesinger, *op. cit.,* p. 53.
[35] *Ibid.,* pp. 67–68.

farm youth to the city that many agricultural communities of the Middle Atlantic states and New England lost population and fell into decay. Between 1880 and 1890 there was a loss of population in about two-fifths of Pennsylvania, in five-sixths of New York State, and in 932 of the 1502 towns of New England.[36]

> Cellar holes choked with lilac and woodbine, tumble-down buildings, scrubby orchards, pastures bristling with new forest growths, perhaps a lone rosebush — these mute, pathetic memorials of once busy farming communities attested the reversal of a familiar historic process, with civilization retreating before the advancing wilderness.[37]

In the Middle West agriculture was also in retreat, but in 1890 only a third of the population lived in communities numbering as many as four thousand persons.[38] The twentieth century witnessed more rapid urbanization (see Table 6). The surplus farm population, the result in large

TABLE 6: POPULATION OF CONTINENTAL UNITED STATES, URBAN, RURAL NONFARM, AND RURAL FARM, 1920–1956*

Item	Number (Thousands)				
	1920	1930	1940	1950**	1960**
Total Population	105,711	122,775	131,669	150,697	179,323
Urban	54,158	68,955	74,424	88,927	113,056
Rural Nonfarm	20,159	23,633	27,029	38,722	66,267
Rural Farm	31,393	30,158	30,216	23,048	

	Percentage Distribution				
Total Population	100.0	100.0	100.0	100.0	100.0
Urban	51.2	56.2	56.5	59.0	63.0
Rural Nonfarm	19.1	19.3	20.5	25.7	37.0
Rural Farm	29.7	24.6	22.9	15.3	

* Adapted from Dewhurst and Associates, *op. cit.*, p. 72. J. Frederic Dewhurst and Associates, *America's Needs and Resources: A New Survey* (New York: The Twentieth Century Fund, 1955), p. 72. Figures for 1960 are from *Statistical Abstract of the United States, 1961*, p. 23.
** Previous urban definition, i.e., comparable to 1910–40.

part of a high birth rate on the farm, the mechanization of agriculture and increased production, and expanding job opportunities in the cities — all these were among the social forces that drew people from the land to urban communities. Between 1920 and 1945 the farm population suffered a net loss for every year except one, and during that quarter of a century the farms of America contributed a net total of nearly seventeen mil-

[36] *Ibid.*, pp. 68–69.   [37] *Ibid.*, pp. 69–70.   [38] *Ibid.*, p. 57.

lions to the growth of towns and cities.[39] The Depression years of the nineteen-thirties caused a marked decline in the rate of urban growth, but the lifting of the Depression and the prosperity following the end of World War II saw a marked increase of urban growth once again. By 1950 no less than 64 per cent of the population was living in urban territory (1950 definition of urban) and only slightly more than 15 per cent was living on farms,[40] and by 1960 69.9 per cent of the population was classified as urban.

Two aspects of this urban growth require special comment — the tendency of population to cluster in large metropolitan centers and the rapid growth of suburban communities. The Bureau of the Census defines a metropolitan area as a city of 50,000 or more, plus the county in which it is located and other territory linked to it economically. In 1960 there were 212 of these metropolitan areas, and they included about 90 per cent of the total urban population. And somewhat more than one-half of the people living in metropolitan areas lived in the twenty-three areas having a million or more people. Of the total population, one-third was living in cities of one million or more. It was, moreover, in these great metropolitan areas that population was gaining most rapidly. These areas (212) accounted for more than four-fifths of the total population increase between 1950 and 1960.[41] It was, however, in the suburbs of the central cities that population growth was most rapid. During the nineteen-fifties the rate of growth in the suburban areas was nearly 49 per cent, compared with 10.6 per cent in the central cities. During this decade more than three-fifths of the nation's population growth occurred in the suburbs (in metropolitan areas outside central cities.)[42]

The culture of the city has set its stamp on many aspects of American life; it is only in the most remote and isolated areas that one escapes the pervading influence of urban institutions and folkways. The city has not only transformed many of the physical aspects of living, it has done much to change old institutions and attitudes as well. The functions of the family are no longer the same. New attitudes develop toward marriage and divorce, the bearing of children, religion and morality, and the place of women in the economy. The city gives rise to new problems of housing, health, sanitation, recreation, education, and government. The typical city presents a picture of vivid contrasts: of riches and poverty; of palatial residential districts and of slums where crime and vice flourish; of places of high cultural advancement and of human degradation. But it has been in the city, with all its lights and shadows, that much of what

[39] Dewhurst and Associates, *op. cit.*, p. 71.

[40] *Ibid.*, p. 72; also *Statistical Abstract of the United States, 1961, op. cit.*, p. 23. These per cents are for urban, new definition. By previous definition they are 59 and 63 respectively.

[41] *Statistical Abstract of the United States, 1961, op. cit.*, pp. 14–20.

[42] *Loc. cit.*

men have called progress has taken place — in education, in art and literature, in science and invention, and in social betterment.

It was one of the most striking and significant facts in American life that, with the rise of great urban centers, the time had come when youth must turn increasingly to the city and not the farm in their attempt to pry open the doors of economic and cultural opportunity. Many youth, to be sure, could still find it possible to build their security on the land, but, for reasons we shall point out later, agriculture faced a long-time decline in employment opportunity. The time had come when only a fraction of the youth born on farms could be expected to find occupational opportunity in cultivation of the soil. In some way the city was required to provide employment, not only for its own youth, but for the incoming farm population as well. With the doors of opportunity for many youth opening, if they were to open at all, along the streets of the city rather than through the vistas of the forests or the sweep of the prairies, we had come to a reversal of a long-time historic trend.

For youth wishing employment in manufacturing establishments, employment opportunity had come to be highly concentrated in a comparatively few great industrial centers. In 1940 approximately 75 per cent

TABLE 7: REGIONAL PERCENTAGES OF
TOTAL WAGE JOBS IN
MANUFACTURING, 1899–1933*

Region	Wage Jobs			
	1899	1919	1929	1933
Northeast	55.65	49.33	44.24	45.18
Middle States	27.76	30.65	33.15	30.78
Northwest	2.08	2.20	1.94	1.83
Southeast	10.76	11.34	13.26	15.22
Southwest	1.06	1.66	2.05	2.00
Far West	2.69	4.82	5.36	4.99

* Adapted from United States National Resources Committee, *The Problems of a Changing Population*, Report of the Committee on Population Problems to the National Resources Committee, May, 1938 (Washington, D.C.: Government Printing Office, 1938), p. 68.

of all manufacturing activity was carried on in two hundred great industrial counties, most of which were located in the Northeast and Middle West.[43] A great manufacturing belt "extending from southern New England through the Middle Atlantic states and westward beyond the Great Lakes" in 1933 provided 70 per cent of all wage jobs in manufacturing.

43 United States National Resources Committee, *The Structure of the American Economy*, Part I: *Basic Characteristics* (Washington, D.C.: Government Printing Office, 1939–40), p. 36.

The Southeast provided 15 per cent of the jobs and the Far West 5 per cent.

Manufacturing, it will be noted, did not cross the Mississippi in any great volume, important industrial development in the West being confined to the Kansas City, Los Angeles, San Francisco-Oakland, and Seattle-Tacoma areas.[44] This high concentration of job opportunities in manufacturing took on importance in connection with the migration of rural youth. It was clear that many farm youth who might wish employment in industrial pursuits would have to seek it in some distant city.

Luckily, the situation has materially changed since the close of World War II. Employment opportunity is still highly concentrated in the great metropolitan areas, but, with industry spread more evenly throughout the nation, metropolitan areas have developed in very considerable number in the Southwest, on the Pacific Coast, and in the southeastern states. It is a highly significant fact, moreover, that many industries are establishing plants, often very large plants, in small communities, drawing a large percentage of their labor force from surrounding village and farm areas. Today a considerable percentage of the labor force lives in small villages or the countryside and commutes to places of employment.

The Impact of Technology on American Life

As the body of scientific knowledge enlarges, as new discoveries and inventions are made, it is possible to build machines which are increasingly effective in the production of goods. One must not, however, think of technology as limited to mechanical inventions; it includes as well non-mechanical processes which can be made to contribute to more efficient production. The assembly-line method; the standardization of parts; the selection of employees in terms of their capacity to do a particular job; the timing of work so as to prevent undue fatigue; the feedback principle, which enables one machine to control the work of another — all these are as much a part of technology as the invention of new machines for the rolling of steel, the milking of cows, or the picking of cotton.

No one attempting to appraise American society during the past half-century can fail to take into account the revolutionary effects of technological change. Invention is the great disturber of the ways of men. The influence of technology is all-pervasive; directly or indirectly, it affects every strand that goes to make up the warp and woof of the life of a people. Technology must be regarded as a revolutionary force which may be channeled in the direction of human welfare far beyond the goals dreamed of in the wildest Utopias; on the other hand, when improperly guided

[44] United States National Resources Committee, *The Problems of a Changing Population* (Washington, D.C.: Government Printing Office, 1938), p. 68.

and controlled it may be a force dangerously disruptive of economic and social arrangements. Already the impact of technology on American life has brought changes of the first magnitude. It has increased the productivity of labor and made possible such a vast increase in the production of goods and services that we have in fact an "affluent" society; it has wrought fundamental changes in the pattern of life of the industrial worker; it has contributed to the concentration of economic power in the hands of a few large corporations; it has altered income distribution; it has rendered obsolete, in large measure, the structure of local government and the system of taxation; it has modified the functions of the family and changed the status of women in society; it has influenced the birth rate and the growth of population; it has to a considerable degree erased the line which separated government from the economy; it has been a force in bringing about a unified culture in the United States; and it has acted as a solvent of world cultures and forced a reformulation of international policies. Nor is the end of technological change in sight; man, having discovered invention, it little likely to abandon his discovery. As the National Resources Committee has put it:

> The large number of inventions made every year shows no tendency to diminish. On the contrary, the trend is toward further increases. No cessation of social changes due to invention is to be expected. It is customary to speak of the present age as one of great change, as though it were a turbulent transition period between two plateaus of calm, but such a conclusion is illusory. Though the rate of change may vary in the future, there is no evidence whatever of a changeless peace ahead.[45]

Men are quick to adopt and use mechanical inventions, once they are made known; yet they are slow to change their social institutions and their modes of thought and feeling to conform to the changes in the physical environment. This cultural lag may be so great as to prove disastrous. It is certain that social technology is no less important than technology in the area of production; it is just as essential that man cultivate a spirit of invention and originality in the world of social relations as it is that he build new machines and develop new processes of production. The requirements of social inventiveness have laid a new and enlarged obligation on American education. To define the proper functions of government, to direct the economy in ways that will make it operate effectively and equitably, to meet the problems of a changing population, to help give direction to community and family life — in short, to formulate and put into operation a sound public and social policy — all this requires knowledge, broad and exact. Schools and colleges alike will need to cultivate in youth,

---

[45] United States National Resources Committee, *Technological Trends and National Policy* (Washington, D.C.: Government Printing Office, 1937), p. vii.

and in their elders as well, the knowledge, the attitudes, and the sensibilities required to adjust social institutions to the changes wrought in the physical environment by science and invention — by the ever broadening sweep of technology.

It will not be possible, of course, within the compass of this volume to deal at all adequately with many of the technological changes affecting American life. We have already noted some of the consequences of the impact of technology on agriculture. It seems desirable, now, to direct attention to those aspects of technological development which affect most crucially the operation of the non-agricultural economy, and which impinge most directly on the pattern of the worker's life.

THE EFFECTS OF TECHNOLOGY ON THE ECONOMY

We may now examine three aspects of technology which are of special importance: (1) the relation of technology to the concentration of economic power; (2) technology and the increased productivity of labor; (3) technology and unemployment.

The relation of technology to the concentration of economic power. As will be pointed out later in greater detail, one of the most striking features of American industry is the very great concentration of economic power. On this point, the President of the United States said in a message to Congress on April 20, 1938:

> Statistics of the Bureau of Internal Revenue reveal the following amazing figures for 1935:
>
> Ownership of corporate assets: Of all corporations reporting from every part of the Nation, one tenth of 1 per cent of them owned 52 per cent of the assets of all of them.
>
> And to clinch the point: Of all corporations reporting, less than 5 per cent of them owned 87 per cent of all the assets of all of them.
>
> Income and profits of corporations: Of all the corporations reporting from every part of the country, one tenth of 1 per cent of them earned 50 per cent of all the assets of all of them.
>
> And to clinch the point: Of all the manufacturing corporations reporting, less than 4 per cent of them earned 84 per cent of all the net profits of all of them.[46]

Technology is clearly one of the principal factors that have made possible such concentration of economic power in the hands of a compara-

[46] Seventy-fifth Congress, Third Session, Senate Document 173, *Strengthening and Enforcement of Antitrust Laws*, p. 2, as quoted in Temporary National Economic Committee, *Technology in Our Economy*, Investigation of Concentration of Economic Power, Monograph 22, Seventy-sixth Congress, Third Session, Senate Committee Print (Washington, D.C.: Government Printing Office, 1941), p. 195.

tively few large corporations. A close relationship exists between technological advance and the development of large units of production. It is not always true that large enterprises are characterized by greater operating efficiency than small ones, but the facts indicate that this is usually the case.[47] The use of large-scale equipment tends to result in maximum efficiency because, among other things, it makes possible (1) "smaller capital outlay per unit of capacity," (2) "greater mechanical efficiency," (3) "the use of a considerably smaller amount of fuel and also of labor per unit of capacity or of output," and (4) "the use of refinements and of auxiliary devices which result in improved efficiency of operation."[48] It is also true that large enterprises are generally able to employ a larger amount of electrical energy per man-hour. In this connection, it may be said that, "regardless of whether the establishment of a high degree of concentration has increased the power differential or whether an increase in the power differential has resulted in a greater concentration, it is evident that a primary causal factor of concentration is the existence of an advantage in operating efficiency of large plants over small plants."[49]

Large-scale industry is also at an advantage because of its greater ability to employ industrial research and to control patents. Industrial research is of itself a large enterprise, employing as far back as 1937 as many persons as were engaged "in the dyeing and finishing of cotton fabrics." If regarded as an industry, it would then have ranked among the forty-five industries providing the largest number of jobs.[50] Invention, by and large, has passed out of the realm of the individual inventor into organized groups working in the laboratories of large corporations. The General Motors Corporation, for example, in the nineteen-thirties was spending ten or twelve million dollars annually on research and engineering projects. The Temporary National Economic Committee reports:

> Industrial research is highly concentrated; there is probably no other basic function of general economic activity so dominated by a few enormous concerns. The National Research Project found that "13 companies with the largest research staffs, representing less than 1 per cent of

[47] See Temporary National Economic Committee, *op. cit.*, Part II, Chap. IV; William L. Crum, *Corporate Size and Earning Power* (Cambridge, Mass.: Harvard University Press, 1939); Temporary National Economic Committee, *Technology and Concentration of Economic Power*, Hearings, Part 30 (Washington, D.C.: Government Printing Office, 1940).

[48] David Weintraub, "Effects of Current and Prospective Technological Developments upon Capital Formation," in *Effects of Technological Developments upon Capital Formation* (Washington, D.C.: Works Progress Administration, National Research Project, 1939), p. 5.

[49] Temporary National Economic Committee, *Technology in Our Economy, op. cit.*, p. 208.

[50] *Loc. cit.*

all companies reporting in the National Research Council survey, employed in 1938 one third of all research workers, or as many as the 1538 companies with the smallest research staffs." Half of the country's industrial laboratory personnel was employed by only 45 large research laboratories, "all but 9 of which are owned or controlled by companies which are among the Nation's 200 leading nonfinancial corporations."

In individual industry groups the concentration was just as pronounced. In 1938 that quarter of the companies having the largest research staffs employed 59.3 per cent of all research workers in blast furnaces, steel works, and rolling mills; 82.2 per cent of all research workers employed in electrical machinery, apparatus, and supplies; 88.3 per cent in industrial chemicals; 89.0 per cent in motor vehicles, bodies, and parts; 85.0 per cent in petroleum; 82.8 per cent in radio apparatus and phonographs; 90.0 per cent in rubber products; 56.9 per cent in textiles and their products; and 78.5 per cent in utilities (gas, light, and power).[51]

And in recent years industrial research has vastly increased. Colm points out that "between 1945 and 1955, the number of professional scientists in industrial laboratories rose to almost two and one-half times, while the number of supporting technicians doubled."[52]

It is unnecessary to comment at length on the control of patents as a means of establishing dominance over an industry. The evidence, however, clearly indicates that "technological improvements protected by patents have been the means not only of securing a high degree of economic concentration but also the control of prices and marketing policies."[53]

When all the facts are brought into focus, it appears that in our society technology operates to the advantage of large-scale enterprise. Corporate earnings tend to increase with the size of the corporation (see Figure 6). "The larger the corporation," says Professor Crum, "the higher is the rate of return, on the average."[54] It is not possible to ascertain exactly the influence of technology on the concentration of economic power, but that it is an important factor seems unquestionable. Moreover, it appears that concentration of economic power operates to prevent our making full use of the technological knowledge which we already possess or might acquire.

Technology and the increased productivity of labor. Whatever else may be said of technology, one thing is clear: The productivity of labor, as measured by output per man-hour, has increased over a long period of years, and it has registered a particularly rapid increase since about 1910 (see Figure 7 and Table 8).

[51] *Ibid.*, pp. 211–212.
[52] Colm and Geiger, *op. cit.*, p. 53.
[53] Temporary National Economic Committee, *Technology in Our Economy, op. cit.*, p. 217.
[54] Crum, *op. cit.*, p. 32.

FIGURE 6

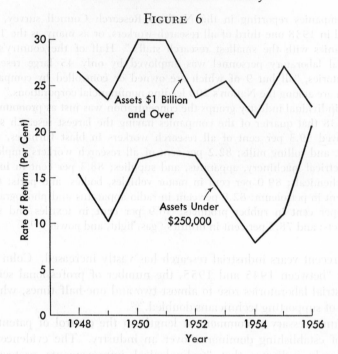

Average Annual Rate of Return before Taxes of
U.S. Manufacturing Corporations by Asset Size
(Profits as a Per Cent of Stockholders' Equity)

Gerhard Colm and Theodore Geiger, *The Economy of the American People: Progress, Problems, Prospects,* National Planning Association Pamphlet No. 102 (Washington, D.C.: the Association, 1958), p. 44.

We have already seen the importance of technology in bringing about increased output in agriculture. Productivity per man-hour in manufacturing increased about 3 per cent annually between 1909 and the outbreak of World War II.[55] Average weekly hours decreased from 60.2 in 1900 to 40 in 1950. Net output per man-hour increased from 60.2 cents in 1900 to 193.5 cents in 1950. And total national income at 1950 prices rose from 60 billion in 1900 to 217 billion in 1950, and to nearly 400 billion (in current dollars) in 1959.

Technology and unemployment. The rapid increase in the productivity of labor raises the question whether technology, in the course of years, results in lessened employment opportunity. The introduction of new

[55] A. J. Jaffee and Charles D. Stewart, *Manpower Resources and Utilization* (New York: John Wiley & Sons, Inc., 1951), p. 236.

FIGURE 7

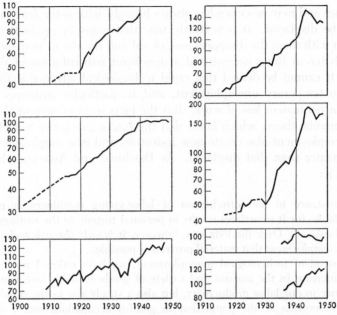

Selected Productivity Indexes for the United States
(1939 = 100)

A. J. Jaffe and Charles D. Stewart, *Manpower Resources and Utilization*
Principles of Working Force Analysis (New York: John Wiley & Sons,
Inc., 1951), p. 236.

TABLE 8: WEEKLY HOURS, OUTPUT PER MAN-HOUR,
NATIONAL INCOME, 1850–1960*

Year	Average Weekly Hours	National Income per Man-Hour in 1950 Prices (in cents)	National Income 1950 Prices (in billions of dollars)
1850	69.8	33.7	8.8
1860	68.0	40.6	14.1
1870	65.4	42.6	17.4
1880	64.0	44.4	23.8
1890	61.9	61.1	41.3
1900	60.2	75.5	60.0
1910	55.1	89.6	82.4
1920	49.7	93.2	88.6
1930	45.9	106.9	108.2
1940	44.0	131.5	130.3
1950	40.0	193.5	217.3
1960 (est.)	37.5	240.0	275.0

* Delbert C. Miller, "Influence of Technology on Industry," Chap. 11 in Francis
R. Allen *et al.*, *Technology and Social Change* (New York: Appleton-Century-
Crofts, Inc., 1957), p. 252, for which it was adapted from J. Frederick Dewhurst
and Associates, *America's Needs and Resources* (New York: Twentieth Century
Fund, 1955), p. 40. This table excludes governmental enterprises as well as
general governmental activities.

machines and new processes has always brought with it the fear that labor would be displaced. It is perfectly true that gains in productivity have brought with them the disappearance of old and the rise of new industries, and this has at times necessitated a significant redistribution of the labor force. It cannot be denied that rapid technological advance is the cause of some temporary unemployment, and in particular instances it may result in permanent loss of work. But the facts seem to support the orthodox economic theory which holds that the forces giving rise to technological unemployment also create new industries and new employment equal to or greater than that displaced. As Dewhurst and Associates have expressed it:

> Resistance to the introduction of labor-saving machinery is understandable, for it sometimes results in personal tragedy to the workers who are displaced. Over the long run, however, it is *only through technological disemployment* that material progress is possible. . . .
>
> Instead of technological unemployment, we have enjoyed not only a vast increase in the amount and variety of goods available and a marked advance in our labor productivity, but also a steady rise in the number of and proportion of the population in gainful occupations and a steady shortening of the work week. With some costly and painful interruptions, we have had our cake in the form of expanding employment, and eaten it in the form of increased leisure and an ever higher standard of living.[56]

The Impact of Technology on the Pattern of the Worker's Life

Technological progress, as we have seen, has affected the over-all economy in many ways; and its impact on the pattern of the worker's life has been no less significant. Technology has been an important factor in creating new occupations and industries; it often renders old skills useless and forces the worker into the ranks of the temporarily unemployed; it changes the quality and the quantity of the skills the worker must bring to his job; and it has reduced the hours of labor and increased leisure.

The changing pattern of work opportunity.   Within the past generation or two, amazing changes have taken place in the number and variety of occupations. Often within the span of a few years, old occupations decline in importance or disappear altogether and new ones rise to take their place. The bookkeeper, the wheelwright, and the glassblower give place to the automobile mechanic, the factory operative, the airplane pilot, the radar operator, the calculating-machine repairman, the engineer, and

---

[56] Dewhurst and Associates, *op. cit.,* pp. 909–910.

the scientist. The division of labor may create a score of jobs where one existed before, while science and invention may produce new industries, each opening wide the door to a hundred-odd new types of work. Today, as youth turn from school to work, they face a choice of many thousands of different occupations. Moreover, during their lifetime they will surely see employment opportunity greatly expand in some industries and contract equally sharply in others. Technological improvements, contraction and expansion of purchasing power, changes in consumption habits, and fluctuations in prices and wages — all these affect both the range and the quality of employment opportunity.

Changes in the pattern of work opportunity through the years are reflected in the percentage distribution of the labor force among the various occupations (see Table 9). The most striking feature of the changing

TABLE 9: PERCENTAGE DISTRIBUTION OF
THE LABOR FORCE, 1870–1950*

Classification	1870	1900	1920	1950
Agriculture, Forestry, Fishing	50.8	38.0	27.7	12.1
Mining	1.6	2.6	3.0	1.4
Construction	5.9	5.8	5.3	6.2
Manufacturing	17.6	22.1	26.4	25.8
Transportation, Communication, and Public Utilities	4.8	7.1	9.7	8.6
Trade	6.1	8.6	9.9	18.0
Finance, Insurance, Real Estate	0.3	1.1	1.9	3.2
Professional Service	1.6	2.5	3.6	6.3
Personal and Domestic Service	9.3	9.4	8.1	10.6
Government	2.0	2.8	4.5	7.9

* Merle Fainsod *et al., Government and the American Economy,* Third Edition, (New York: W. W. Norton & Company, Inc., 1959), p. 14.

occupational patterns has been the sharp decline in the percentage of the labor force employed in agriculture. As late as 1880 one-half of all gainful workers were engaged in agriculture, and as late as 1910 those employed in farming comprised the largest single group of the gainfully employed. Each decade since 1870, however, has registered a decline in the relative importance of agriculture as an occupation. In 1910 there began a decrease in the absolute numbers engaged in farming. By the middle of the twentieth century only 12 per cent of the labor force was employed in agriculture, and the percentage continued to decline throughout the nineteen-fifties. As we have already seen, the rapid mechanization of agriculture in recent years, together with other factors, makes it clear that farming faces an even further decline in employment opportunity.

The absolute number of those engaged in manufacturing has increased materially, but the percentage increase has not been especially striking since 1900. By 1950 the percentage of the labor force engaged in manufacturing was actually less than in 1920, the decline being from 26.4 per cent to 25.8 per cent. The decline in the number of those engaged in agriculture and the failure of manufacturing to acquire any marked increase in the percentage of those employed in it have released a large fraction of the labor force from physical production, making these people available for other work.

Employment opportunity has been markedly expanding in the distributive and service occupations. In recent years large numbers of our population have earned their living in jobs connected with the movement and distribution of goods from the factory to the consumer. The percentage of those engaged in trade has more than doubled since 1900, rising from 8.6 per cent in 1900 to 18.0 per cent in 1950. A striking increase has also occurred in the percentage of gainfully employed whose work falls in the service occupations. The professions, public service, and the clerical occupations have all absorbed a larger share of the gainfully employed. Those engaged in professional service increased from 2.5 per cent of the labor force in 1900 to 6.3 per cent in 1950. A sharp increase has also occurred in the number of those engaged in government service, the per cent rising from 2.8 in 1900 to 7.9 in 1950. These trends continued throughout the fifties, particularly with respect to the service occupations.

It is clear that for the past half-century and more our economy has been characterized by a rapidly shifting occupational pattern, by instability of job opportunity. The changes in the distribution of workers among the occupations "are a striking reflection of the transformation of our economic system from one organized around the exploitation of natural resources to one in which chief stress is on mechanical, managerial, professional and service functions."[57] Conditions in the future are so uncertain as to render predictions hazardous. One may be reasonably sure, however, that technological development will continue, and that the distribution of workers among the various occupations will exhibit constant change. It is, however, enormously important, both from the individual and from the social point of view, that the right persons with the requisite training be distributed among the various occupations. Herein lies one of the major social obligations of our educational system.

AUTOMATION — PROMISE AND THREAT

An adequate definition of *automation* would be very difficult, but a simple definition is that automation is the process by which one machine controls and directs the operation of another. Formerly, machines per-

[57] United States National Resources Committee, *The Problems of a Changing Population, op. cit.,* p. 441.

formed more or less separate or discrete functions; a good deal of human supervision was required to keep the machine doing its job and to co-ordinate and integrate the production process. The essential principle of automation is that through electric and electronic devices one machine controls and directs the operation of another, in such a way that hitherto separate and discrete functions of both men and machines are integrated into a single and continuous process requiring very little human direction. Pollock describes four features of a fully automatic plant as follows:

(i) Complete co-ordination of the various stages of the process of turning the raw material into the finished product — including pack-ing. . . .

(ii) Each separate stage in the manufacture of the product is linked with the preceding and following stages in such a way that the entire process proceeds smoothly and without the slightest interruption.

(iii) After every stage in the process of manufacture the product is automatically moved from one machine to the next.

(iv) The product is automatically checked after each step in the process of manufacture — and also at the end — so as to insure that the prescribed standards of workmanship have been maintained throughout. If the product does not reach this standard the necessary adjustment of the machine — or process — takes place automatically or, alternatively, the machine itself gives a warning so that it can be examined. Moreover, there are indicators on certain machine tools and special machines which warn the operator — before the breakdown occurs — that some part of the apparatus is wearing out.[58]

Automation is not something that the future may hold; it is a present reality. Already a good deal of progress has been made in introducing the principle of automation, wholly or in part, into the production of oil, paper, chemicals, food, and automobiles, and into the handling of records of many kinds.

To quote Pollock again:

There is a tyre factory in the United States in which the process of manufacture from raw material to finished product is entirely automatic. Here 300 tyres are made in an hour. Similar complete automatic proc-esses have been introduced in the production of glassware, the making of paper (continuous process from the cellulose pulp to finished article ready for delivery) and the manufacture of steel pipes for use in the oil-fields.

The armaments industry has made striking progress towards complete automation. It is reported that in the manufacture of rifle-grenades by automatic machinery only two workers are needed to produce 900 gre-

[58] Frederick Pollock, *The Economics and Social Consequences of Automation,* trans. W. O. Henderson and W. H. Challoner (Oxford: Basil Blackwell, 1957), pp. 7–8.

nades per hour whereas on the old conveyor-belt system 23 men were required to do the work. . . .

The best-known example of a completely automatic plant in the American armaments industry is the grenade factory at Rockford in Illinois. Only 140 men work on a shop floor 1,000,000 square feet in extent — including engineers and men responsible for handling and servicing the machinery. No human hand touches the product from the time when blocks of steel enter the manufacturing process to the time when the finished weapons have been packed. . . .

An example from civil industry of the automatic production of parts of a product is the manufacture of motor chassis in Ford's Cleveland plant. Here 26 machines carry out 532 operations to turn a six-cylinder steel block into an engine block. Only 41 men are required in such a plant. They include the job-setters who get the machines ready at the start of the process, the men who supervise the process, and the men who replace worn-out parts of the machinery when a control-device known as a "tool meter" gives the necessary signal. If the conveyor-belt system were used it would take 117 men four and a half hours to do the job. In the automatic plant 41 men can do this in three hours. . . .

Detailed information is available concerning the achievements of one of the largest American computers, which has been installed in a plant belonging to the General Electric Company. In two hours this machine calculates the wages of 12,000 workers. It provides information concerning net payments and the distribution of wage-costs over various accounts. All results are transcribed on to a magnetic band. In another four hours the computer prints the wages cheques for those employees who are not paid in cash; and wage sheets both for the pay-clerks and the accountant. This computer can perform in six seconds a task which formerly kept a large number of clerks occupied for a whole week. The machine has other functions as well. It supplies continuous information concerning stocks in hand and new materials required. It automatically co-ordinates requirements for all kinds of materials into a single production programme. The information is classified according to daily and weekly requirements. The machine shows what orders have to be completed every day. Moreover the computer is used to make preparations necessary to send out orders. It draws up the despatch plan. It plans the completion of a waggon-load of goods of different types made in different departments of the plant. It prepares invoices and accounts for customers. It keeps the records and accounts of the sales department. All the figures produced by these operations are automatically reproduced by the machine in statistical form for the accounts department and for those responsible for writing reports for the directors.[59]

The full economic and social consequences of automation cannot at present be clearly foreseen, and there is serious disagreement as to whether automation presents a threat or a promise. In 1955 an extensive

[59] *Ibid.,* pp. 24–25, 26–27.

investigation of the nature and possible consequences of automation was conducted under the auspices of the Congress of the United States. The members of the Committee making the investigation failed, however, to reach much agreement with respect to the economic and social implications of automation. But the Committee did agree that automation is something more than "an extension of mechanization." In its opinion:

. . . we are clearly on the threshold of an industrial age, the significance of which we cannot predict and with potentialities which we cannot fully appreciate . . . We have certainly not yet seen the full impact of these new technologies . . . We don't know what all this will add up to, but we might very well be wrong to think of it as simply "more of the same" technology which has always characterized American industry.[60]

There are some who fear that automation will create widespread and continued unemployment, that we are about to enter an era of factories without workers. There are those who fear, too, that the worker will be forced to surrender his intelligence and his skill to the machine and become its slave. Yet others share the optimism of Peter Drucker when he says:

There may actually be no workers on the production floor of tomorrow's push-button factory. There are practically none to-day in a power-generating station or an oil refinery. But at the same time incredibly large numbers of men will be required behind the scenes in new, highly skilled jobs as machine builders, machine installers, repairmen, controllers of the machinery and its performance, and as "programmers" to prepare and feed information into the machine. In addition, large numbers of highly educated men will be needed in new jobs as designers of machinery, draftsmen, system engineers, mathematicians, or logicians. Finally, large numbers will be needed for new managerial jobs requiring a high ability to think, to analyze, to make decisions, and to assume risks. And this increase both in number and in the demands made on them will be the largest of all the social impacts of automation. . . .

Mass production upgraded the unskilled laborer of yesterday into the semi-skilled machine operator of to-day — and in the process multiplied both his productivity and his income. In just the same way, automation will upgrade the semi-skilled operator of to-day into a highly skilled and knowledgeable technician — multiplying his income again.[61]

[60] *Automation and Technological Change: Hearings before the Subcommittee on Economic Stabilization of the Joint Committee of the Economic Report* (Congress of the United States: 84th Congress, First Session, Washington, 1955) and *Automation and Technological Change: Report of the Subcommittee on Economic Stabilization to the Joint Committee on the Economic Report* (Congress of the United States, Washington, 1955). Quoted *ibid.*, pp. 111–112.

[61] Peter F. Drucker, *America's Next Twenty Years* (New York: Harper & Brothers, 1957), pp, 26–27.

As we have already indicated, we are not yet in command of enough evidence to appraise with any great certainty the full impact of automation upon the economy or upon society generally. There are, however, certain conclusions that one may reasonably entertain.

(1) It appears that automation is something more than a mere acceleration of the kind of technological progress we have heretofore known; it represents, rather, a fundamental revolution, comparable to the first Industrial Revolution of the eighteenth and nineteenth centuries. Whatever may be the exact nature or dimensions of the changes automation may bring about, their impact on individual living, society, and education will be profound.

(2) The fear of widespread and long-sustained unemployment does not seem likely to be warranted. As in the case of technological advances in the past, automation may be expected, in the long run, to create as many new jobs and as much new work opportunity as it destroys. Nevertheless, the immediate impact of automation may be very disturbing. There may be, in the short run, a good deal of unemployment; certainly many workers — especially those engaged in office work — will have to shift to new jobs, and even new industries.

(3) Automation will require of business and management a higher level of intelligence, competence, and wisdom. This is so because automation involves far more than the use of electric and automatic devices and self-regulating machinery. It requires high-level planning. Management must correctly estimate and even create its market; it must provide the requisite automatic physical plant; it must ensure an ample and properly trained labor force; it must maintain the flow of the necessary raw materials; and — above all — it must schedule and integrate the flow of the entire productive process. Successful production is as dependent upon long-range integrated scheduling and planning as it is upon the integration of machine processes. And, finally, management has the high responsibility of formulating and carrying out policies that will be in the public interest.

(4) Automation may be expected to bring about a general upgrading of the labor force, a marked increase in the skill and intelligence the worker must bring to his work. It has been suggested that "automation's most important impact will not be on employment but on the qualifications and functions of employees." In the future the non-skilled and the uneducated will find themselves more and more barred from work opportunities. It is true that when automatic processes are introduced, many of the new jobs are such as not to require higher technical qualifications; but an increasing number of the new jobs do require a technical competence. We may expect a rising demand for scientists, engineers, technicians — men who can design, build, install, and repair the new machines. There will be a demand, too, for competent people who can feed

correct information into computing machines. Shortages of personnel to fill these more demanding jobs will prove to be one of the most serious manpower problems of the future.

(5) Automation will make new and enlarged demands for an intelligent and wise public policy. We can build automatic factories, but there is no automatic way by which society can adjust to the problems that automation will bring with it. A wise public policy to deal with the problems of automation will require patience, intelligence, and a high sense of social obligation on the part of all concerned — management, labor, government, and the general public.

(6) Finally, automation will require more and better education. It has been pointed out that automation can and will upgrade jobs, but that it cannot upgrade people. Herein lies the challenge to education. The demand for scientists, mathematicians, engineers, and technicians of many kinds will be great. To meet this demand schools, colleges, universities, and adult education agencies will need to re-examine and improve their programs of teaching and research. And in doing this it would be a great mistake to neglect the humanities and the social sciences. The insight, the breadth of view, and the perspective that come from a broad general education will be no less essential than technical competence.

The Upgrading of the Labor Force

Although the changing pattern of work opportunity is important, it is far more important to bring about an upgrading of the entire labor force. The ever increasing tempo of technological advance; the advent of automation; the world political crisis, which demands a constant strengthening of the economy — all these require a better-qualified labor force. And this need for greater competency is not confined to any particular segment or level of the labor force; it permeates the whole economy and affects all who work. The need for "creative man power" will be great in scientific research, in all the professions, in executive and managerial groups, and among all kinds of skilled workers. The demands on the labor force for intelligence, imagination, creativity, and skill may be expected to be such as to handicap severely the poorly educated and unskilled and to force them to remain on the periphery of employment opportunity.

An analysis of employment in the major occupations reveals a great deal with respect to the upgrading of the labor force (see Table 10).
In 1910, white-collar employees constituted 22.3 per cent of the labor force; by 1955 they constituted 38.7 per cent; and by 1975, it is estimated, they will constitute no less than 44 per cent. Since 1910 blue-collar employees have increased only 3 per cent and down to 1975 they are not expected to show any increase in percentage. The dramatic de-

TABLE 10: EMPLOYMENT IN THE MAJOR OCCUPATIONS OF THE UNITED STATES IN 1910 AND 1955 (ACTUAL AND IN 1965 AND 1975 PROJECTED)*

	Number (in Millions)				Per Cent			
	1910	1955	1965	1975	1910	1955	1965	1975
Total Employees	35.5	61.7	73.1	83.2	100.0	100.0	100.0	100.0
White-Collar Employees	7.9	23.8	30.5	36.6	22.3	38.7	41.6	44.0
Professional	1.6	5.7	7.8	10.0	4.6	9.2	10.6	12.0
Professional and Managerial	2.6	6.0	7.3	8.3	7.3	9.8	9.9	10.0
Clerical and Sales	3.7	12.1	15.4	18.3	10.4	19.7	21.1	22.0
Blue-Collar Employees	13.3	24.7	29.4	33.2	37.4	40.2	40.3	40.0
Craftsmen	4.2	8.2	10.2	12.0	11.8	13.4	14.0	14.5
Operatives	5.0	12.8	15.6	17.9	14.1	20.8	21.3	21.5
Laborers	4.1	3.7	3.6	3.3	11.5	6.0	5.0	4.0
Service Employees	3.4	7.2	8.1	9.2	9.6	11.3	11.1	11.0
Farmers and Farm Workers	10.9	6.0	5.1	4.2	30.7	9.8	7.0	5.0

*As compiled by Seymour L. Wolfbein, "The Creative Manpower Shortage in the United States," *School Review*, LXV (Spring, 1957), 31, from publications of the U.S. Bureau of the Census and the United States Department of Labor.

cline in the number and per cent of farmers and farm workers has already been noted. Commenting on expected changes in employment in the major occupations of the country, Wolfbein has the following to say:

1. One of the most impressive areas of growth is represented by the professional worker. If previous trends continue, professional personnel may hit close to the 8 million mark by 1965, accounting for a little over one out of every 10 workers — more than double the 1910 figure. There is real need for expansion in many of the important groups here. The one million workers in engineering and science, the one and a half million in teaching, and the million in medical services (doctors, dentists, nurses, etc.) will undoubtedly increase sharply and account for a major part of the expansion in professional employment over the next decade.

2. The two other groups comprising the white-collar occupations are also expected to increase — particularly clerical and sales people, who already account for one out of every five persons in the labor force today. Taken together, the white-collar occupations actually have reached a historic position. Our latest information shows that in 1956 they represented the single biggest group in the labor force, and they are expected to be further ahead by 1965 and 1975. A few years ago we reached a similar position in our industrial distribution: there were (and are) more people employed in industries producing services than those producing goods. Now the occupational distribution has reached the same stage: today we have more white-collar than blue-collar workers in the American labor force.

3. Another important group that is expected to expand, both numerically and percentage-wise, includes the industrial workers at the craftsman (skilled) and operative (semiskilled) levels. We expect increases particularly among the building trades; the metal trades, and the skilled mechanics, repairmen, and technicians.

4. On the other hand, reductions seem to be in prospect for both the farm segment of the economy and the less skilled laborers. If past trends and current technological developments, such as automation, are indicative, we may expect an actual decline in employment in these occupations in the face of an 11 million rise in the total number of jobs.

All this adds up to a continuing rise in the skill level of the American labor force: in the number and proportion of workers requiring extensive education, training, and skill developments; in the number of high-quality personnel we call "creative manpower"; in the need for the especially able or gifted in our population.[62]

This upgrading of the intelligence, imagination, and skill of the labor force obviously requires a corresponding upgrading of education at all levels. The intelligence and moral fiber of its youth is a people's most valuable resource. The requirements of our time call for a re-examination

[62] Seymour L. Wolfbein, "The Creative Manpower Shortage in the United States," *The School Review,* LXV (Spring, 1957), 31–32.

and a reformulation of our basic philosophy of education. School, college, and university alike will find it essential to re-examine and reconstruct their curriculums in order that they may better meet the needs of American life. The existing inequalities in educational opportunity must be removed in order that we may release in each child the full potentialities of self. It is especially important that superior talent be uncovered and developed to its fullest. If education is to meet its high obligations to the individual and to society, teachers in school, college, and university must combine high scholarly competence, an understanding of how individuals grow and develop, and the ability to teach. Nor is competent administrative leadership at all educational levels any less necessary. All of these things which are so sorely needed will require money and a great deal of it. But we must not lose sight of the fact that education is our most important capital investment, even more important than investment in productive plants.

Topics for Study and Discussion

1. During the decades following 1860, what were the forces or factors promoting rapid industrialization? Which of these factors or forces do you regard as the most important?
2. During the past half-century or so, what significant changes have taken place in American agriculture? Evaluate these changes in terms of their educational implications.
3. Evaluate the social, economic, and educational consequences of the impact of technology on American life.
4. In what ways does automation differ from the technology that has heretofore characterized American industry?
5. Explain how automation may be expected to make new demands upon the man power of the nation. What will probably be the educational implications of the new demands?
6. Do you agree that leisure is taking on a new meaning in our society, and that education for leisure poses a real problem? Discuss the issues involved.

Selected References for Further Reading

Allen, Francis R., *et al. Technology and Social Change.* New York: Appleton-Century-Crofts, 1957. Pp. xii + 529.

Anderson, H. Dewey, and Davidson, Percy E. *Occupational Trends in the United States.* Stanford, Cal.: Stanford University Press, 1940. Pp. x + 618.

Baldwin, Leland D. *Recent American History.* Rindge, N.H.: Richard R. Smith, Publisher, Inc., 1954. Pp. x + 812.

Bancroft, Gertrude. *The American Labor Force.* New York: John Wiley & Sons, Inc., 1958. Pp. xiv + 256.

Beard, Charles A., and Beard, Mary R. *The Rise of American Civilization, II: The Industrial Era.* New York: The Macmillan Co., 1927. Pp. 828.

Bloomberg, W. *The Age of Automation: Its Effects on Human Welfare.* New York: League for Industrial Democracy, 1955.

Cochran, Thomas C., and Miller, William. *The Age of Enterprise: A Social History of Industrial America.* New York: The Macmillan Co., 1942. Pp. x + 394. Also published in paperback (New York: Harper & Brothers [Torchbooks], 1961).

Colm, Gerhard, and Geiger, Theodore. *The Economy of the American People, Progress, Problems, Prospects,* Planning Pamphlet No. 102. Washington, D.C.: National Planning Association, 1938. Pp. viii + 167.

Counts, George S., *et al. The Social Foundations of Education,* Report of the Commission on the Social Studies, Part IX. New York: Charles Scribner's Sons, 1934. Pp. xiv + 580.

Crum, William Leonard. *Corporate Size and Earning Power.* Cambridge, Mass., Harvard University Press, 1939. Pp. 418.

Curti, Merle. *The Social Ideas of American Educators, with a New Chapter on the Last Twenty-five Years.* Paterson, N.J.: Pageant Books, Inc., 1959. Pp. xliv + 613.

Delger, Carl N. *Out of Our Past: The Forces that Shaped Modern America.* New York: Harper & Brothers, 1959. Pp. xvi + 484.

Dewhurst, J. Frederick, and Associates. *America's Needs and Resources: A New Survey.* New York: The Twentieth Century Fund, 1955. Pp. xxix + 1148.

Diebold, John. *Automation: The Advent of the Automatic Factory.* Princeton, N.J.: D. Van Nostrand Co., Inc., 1952. Pp. ix + 181.

Drucker, Peter F. *America's Next Twenty Years.* New York: Harper & Brothers, 1957. Pp. 114.

Drucker, Peter F. *Landmarks of Tomorrow.* New York: Harper & Brothers, 1959. Pp. xii + 270.

Educational Policies Commission. *Manpower and Education.* Washington, D.C.: National Education Association of the United States, 1956. Pp. vi + 228.

Edwards, Newton. *Equal Educational Opportunity for Youth: A National Responsibility,* A Report of the American Youth Commission. Washington, D.C.: American Council on Education, 1939. Pp. x + 190.

Fainsod, Merle, *et al. Government and the American Economy,* Third Edition. New York: W. W. Norton & Company, Inc., 1959. Pp. xv–xvi + 996.

Galbraith, John Kenneth. *The Affluent Society.* Boston: Houghton Mifflin Company, 1958. Pp. xii + 288.

Ginzberg, Eli. *Human Resources: The Wealth of a Nation.* New York: Simon and Schuster, Inc., 1958. Pp. viii + 183.

Hacker, Louis M. *American Capitalism: Its Promise and Accomplishment.* Princeton, N.J.: D. Van Nostrand Co., Inc. (Anvil Books), 1957. Pp. 192.

Hacker, Louis M. *The Triumph of American Capitalism: The Development of Forces in American History to the End of the Nineteenth Century.* New York: Simon and Schuster, Inc., 1940. Pp. x + 460.

Hasher, William, *et al. Manpower in the United States: Problems and Policies.* New York: Harper & Brothers, 1954. Pp. xi + 225.

Hays, Samuel P. *The Response to Industrialism, 1885–1914,* History of American Civilization Series. Chicago: University of Chicago Press, 1957. Pp. ix + 211.

Heady, Earl O., *et al. Agricultural Adjustment Problems in a Growing Economy.* Ames, Iowa: Iowa State College Press, 1958. Pp. xii + 316.

Hugh-Jones, E. M. (ed). *The Push-Button World: Automation Today.* Norman, Okla.: University of Oklahoma Press, 1956. Pp. ix + 158.

Jaffe, A. J., and Stewart, Charles P. *Manpower Resources and Utilization.* New York: John Wiley & Sons, Inc., 1951. Pp. xii + 532.

Lerner, Max. *America as a Civilization.* New York: Simon and Schuster, Inc., 1957. Pp. xiii + 1036. Also published in paperback, in two volumes (New York: Simon and Schuster, Inc., 1957).

Mighell, Ronald L. *American Agriculture.* New York: John Wiley & Sons, Inc., 1955. Pp. xii + 187.

Nevins, Allen. *The Emergence of Modern America, 1865–1878.* New York: The Macmillan Co., 1927. Pp. xix + 446.

Norton, T. L. *Public Education and Economic Trends.* Cambridge, Mass.: Harvard University, Graduate School of Education, 1939. Pp. 196.

Pollock, Frederick. *The Economic and Social Consequences of Automation.* Translated by W. O. Henderson and W. H. Challoner. Oxford: Basil Blackwell, 1957. Pp. viii + 276.

Recent Social Trends in the United States, Report of the President's Research Committee on Social Trends. New York: McGraw-Hill Book Co., 1933 (one-volume edition). Pp. xcvi + 1568.

Rosen, S. McKee, and Rosen, Laura. *Technology and Society: The Influence of Machines in the United States.* New York: The Macmillan Co., 1941. Pp. xiv + 474.

Schlesinger, Arthur Meier. *The Rise of the City, 1878–1898. A History of American Life,* X. New York: The Macmillan Co., 1933. Pp. xvi + 494.

Shister, Joseph. *Economics of the Labor Market.* Philadelphia: J. B. Lippincott Co., 1949. Pp. xxiii + 590.

Temporary National Economic Committee. *Technology and the Concentration of Economic Power,* Investigation of Concentration of Economic Power, Part 30, Hearings before the Temporary National Economic Committee, Seventy-sixth Congress, Third Session. Washington, D.C.: Government Printing Office, 1940. Pp. xxii + 16207–17600 + viii.

Temporary National Economic Committee. *Technology in Our Economy,* Investigation of Concentration of Economic Power, Monograph 22, Seventy-sixth Congress, Third Session, Senate Committee Print. Washington, D.C.: Government Printing Office, 1941. Pp. xvi + 314.

Thomas, Lawrence G. *The Occupational Structure and Education.* Englewood Cliffs, N.J.: Prentice-Hall, Inc., 1956. Pp. xiii + 502.

United States National Resources Committee. *Technological Trends and National Policy: Including the Social Implications of New Inventions,* Report of the Subcommittee on Technology of the National Resources Committee, June, 1937. Washington, D.C.: Government Printing Office, 1937. Pp. viii + 388.

Wolfbein, Seymour L. "Creative Manpower Shortage in the United States," *The School Review,* LXV (Spring, 1957), 27–34.

Wolfle, Dael. *America's Resources of Specialized Talent,* Report of the Commission on Human Resources and Advanced Training. New York: Harper & Brothers, 1954.

12 🌿

The Changing American Economy

The Importance of Relating Education to the Changes in the Modern Economy

The social and technological revolutions discussed in the preceding chapter were accompanied by, if they did not actually produce, a profound change in the structure and operation of the American economic system. These fundamental changes in the economic life of the nation affected the whole pattern of institutional arrangements; and the changes were especially important to education and its institutions at all levels. Conditions now required a vast expansion of the entire educational enterprise, extending from nursery schools through the universities and into the area of adult education. The shifting pattern of economic life was, moreover, the most important single force making it necessary to work out an educational program richer in content and extending over a longer period of years. It was no longer enough for the schools and colleges to concern themselves primarily with passing on the cultural heritage as it had been traditionally thought of; they now had the additional responsibility of preparing youth for and guiding them into vocational life, with its constantly increasing number of new occupations, its vast accumulations of new skills, and its instability of job opportunity. But education for efficient production was not the only new demand society was making on the schools: Education also had to prepare citizens for intelligent consumption and for a wholesome use of leisure time. More important still, because the new economy was giving rise to many and varied problems of social policy in community, state, and nation, education for effective citizenship now took on proportions unknown in the simple rural economy of former times. An expanded and enriched program of education, extended to include youth with the most varied backgrounds, capacities, and expectations, made it essential that provision be made for a more effective

432

teaching personnel. New institutional arrangements were developed for the education of teachers and the educational process in all its varied aspects was subjected to rigorous scientific study. As the functions of education changed to meet new conditions, it became necessary to reshape the structural organization of education — to develop new types of schools and to work out a closer articulation between them.

Changes in the structure and operational aspects of the American economy have still other important implications for educational policy and practice. When the economy fails to work efficiently and equitably, new problems arise in education and old problems take on added importance. Widespread unemployment among both young and older workers, a sharp reduction in the total national income, depression in agriculture, the development of geographical areas with large populations and meager economic resources, the movement of youth in large numbers from region to region in search of economic and social opportunity, a high concentration of income among the few with low income among the many — all these consequences of a defective economy are reflected in nearly every aspect of the educational program.

Finally, and most important, it appears that the over-all policy system with respect to the economy must be formulated and reformulated in a way that will ensure economic efficiency without loss of freedom. Decisions of the utmost importance have to be made regarding the economic organization of the future. To prepare youth for intelligent participation in these decisions in the years ahead has come to be one of the major responsibilities of institutionalized education.

An understanding of the development of American education during the past three-quarters of a century and of the problems of educational statesmanship in the future is so closely tied in with the changing pattern of economic life that the student of education stands in need of a clear picture of the structure and operational aspects of the modern economy. For this reason, the present chapter is devoted to an account of the changes that have occurred as we have moved steadily from a highly competitive and more or less self-regulating economy toward an economic order characterized by a high concentration of power and increasing dependence upon human decisions for its control and operation.

The Development and Essential Features of a Laissez Faire Economy

In the simplest terms, the economic system of a people may be thought of as the ways and means, the principles and practices, employed to produce and exchange the goods and services required and desired. During most of the colonial period and, indeed, well into the nineteenth century, most American families produced a large part of what they consumed and they consumed the greater part of what they produced. As the nineteenth century progressed, however, an advancing technology made possible an increased division of labor and the steady transfer of production from the family to the factory. In both England and America, where the economy was being transformed by the Industrial Revolution, the interrelationships involved in production, transportation, and exchange were becoming ever more complex. The Industrial Revolution had not developed very far in England before it appeared to be both desirable and necessary to formulate a theory which would explain how the new economic order could best operate to meet the needs of all concerned. Adam Smith, in his *Wealth of Nations,* published in 1776, gave classic expression to this theory, which came to be known as laissez faire. Smith's theoretical formulation of the principles and practices which he held should be operative in a free-enterprise economy found ready and widespread acceptance in America. The doctrine of laissez faire appealed to the political instincts of the builders of the new nation and it appeared to fit reasonably well the conditions of their economic life. They had an abiding fear of governmental regulation, born of long experience, and by and large they entertained a negative conception of the state. Individual initiative, free enterprise, private property, and profits were the cornerstones on which they were already erecting their economic structure. The conditions of economic life have nowhere ever conformed precisely to the theoretical formulations of laissez faire, but in this country during the first half of the nineteenth century the divergence between practice and theory was far less marked than it was to become in later years.

The theory of economy and government formulated by Adam Smith and his followers and incorporated in the American tradition was based upon a few fundamental principles or assumptions. The free-enterprise economy which they envisioned, and the theoretical operation of which they were trying to explain, was characterized by private property, the profit motive, free competition, flexible prices, and little or no governmental interference with business. The owners of numerous small business enterprises — farms, factories, and shops — would compete freely with one another to produce and exchange the goods and services required by people to meet their daily needs. The profit motive provided the driving force, the dynamics of the economy, and the open market served as the mechanism which ordered and coordinated the myriad of relationships involved in production and distribution. If numerous independent small producers competed with one another in the open market, the market mechanism would operate automatically to regulate prices. Under such a situation prices would be flexible; they would rise or fall according to supply and demand. If too many shoes, for example, were produced, the price would go down, incompetent producers would be eliminated, and capital and labor would be shifted to the production of some other commodity which could be marketed at a profit. Thus, the market mechanism would serve, without human intervention or judgment, to coordinate most of the activities that went to make up the economic life of the people. The market mechanism, if left free of governmental or other interference, would automatically operate to bring about full employment of both labor and capital. The profit motive would be an incentive to all to employ their labor and capital as energetically and efficiently as possible. Profits, however, would not be excessive because free competition among numerous small producers would tend to keep them down. If, for example, the producers of nails were making excessive profits, it would not be long before the producers of other, less profitable commodities would shift their capital and labor to the making of nails and profits would be brought into line. The profit motive, in fact, was a means of making sure that the goods and services required by society would be produced economically. Moreover, if each individual employed his capital and his labor to make the highest profit possible, he not only served his own best interests but those of society as well. Individual self-interest would add up to the social good. And, finally, since wages, profits, interest, and rent were the resultants of free competition in a free market, all the participants in the economy would receive a just reward for their several contributions. For the government to interfere with the operation of these "economic laws" would be to court disaster. In time, most Americans came to regard private property, private profits, individual initiative, free competition, flexible prices, and non-interference by government as the foundations of their economic life.[1]

LAISSEZ FAIRE IN ACTION

The American economic system never fully exemplified the principles of laissez faire. In actual practice, government rarely, if ever, occupied a neutral position; it fostered business enterprise with an indulgent hand, whether the privilege bestowed was in the form of high tariffs, bounties to railroads, patent rights, or the generous disposition of a rich national domain. And however much the economic system in practice may have departed from the theoretical formulation of a free-enterprise order, faith in the principles of such an order was in no degree weakened. This faith was grounded on the fundamental fact that the economy was on the whole operating satisfactorily. Many felt, to be sure, that they deserved more for

[1] For a more detailed discussion of the principles and practices of a laissez faire economy, see Caroline F. Ware and Gardiner C. Means, *The Modern Economy in Action* (New York: Harcourt, Brace & Co., 1936), Chap. I. For a statement of the historical development of control, see Harold Koontz and Richard W. Gable, *Public Control of Economic Enterprise* (New York: McGraw-Hill Book Co., Inc., 1956), pp. 5–19.

their labor and that others deserved less, but at any rate most of the time there was work for all, with an opportunity to earn a livelihood. Moreover, the level of economic well-being was more or less constantly on the upgrade, despite the temporary recessions of depression years (see Figure 8). The national income rose from $2,000,000,000 in 1850 to $81,-000,000,000 in 1929. The per capita income rose from $95 in 1850 to $668 in 1929.[2] With prices held constant as of 1926, the national

FIGURE 8

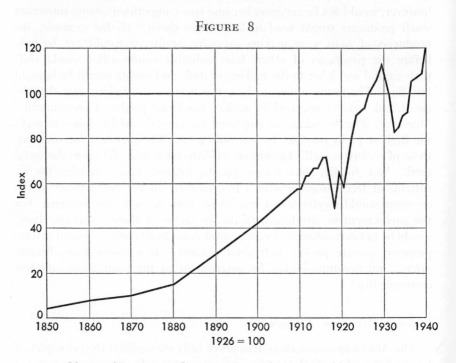

National Income in Constant Prices before World War II
(Income 1940 in 1926 Dollars)

Temporary National Economic Committee, *Economic Prologue: Investigation of Concentration of Economic Power,* Hearings before the Temporary National Economic Committee, Seventy-fifth Congress, Third Session (Washington, D.C.: Government Printing Office, 1940), Part I, p. 9.

[2] Temporary National Economic Committee, *Economic Prologue,* Investigation of Concentration of Economic Power, Hearing before the Temporary Economic Committee, Seventy-fifth Congress, Third Session (Washington, D.C.: Government Printing Office, 1940), I, p. 195. See also Simon Kuznets, *National Product Since 1869* (New York: National Bureau of Economic Research, 1946), and United States Bureau of the Census, *Statistical Abstract of the United States, 1961* (Washington, D.C.: Government Printing Office, 1961), pp. 300–326.

income grew from $4,700,000,000 in 1850 to $113,400,000,000 in 1929. Whatever may have been the wastes, inefficiencies, or injustices of the system, no one could deny that it worked to make the United States the greatest industrial nation in the world, with a per capita income higher than that to be found anywhere else.

The economic system of the nineteenth century operated within a framework of fact and circumstance that was most favorable. A virgin continent was at hand to be exploited and developed. No sooner was one frontier developed than another a little farther westward was calling for additional labor and new capital. Great cities were to be built and their inhabitants supplied with public utilities. The larger part of a continent was to be spanned with a network of railroads. Savings found a ready outlet for investment and the flow of money into capital goods expanded employment and increased the total national income. Great new industries, the product of technological advance, also stimulated economic growth. The building of railroads and the making of automobiles and radios, each in turn, provided opportunity for the investment of capital and the employment of labor. A factor of great importance in the extensive development of the American economy, and one that is sometimes overlooked, was the rapid growth of population. During the nineteenth century population increased more than fourteen-fold — from about 5,300,000 to something over 76,000,000. Each decade but one down to 1930 showed an increase greater than the one preceding it. From 1890 to 1930, "the net increment of increase from decade to decade" was greater than the total population in 1830.[3] An increasing population afforded an expanding market for goods and services. It has been estimated that from 50 to 60 per cent of the investment in capital goods during the latter half of the century went to meet the needs of a growing population. Men could afford to take risks in building new factories or opening new mines or other industries because the growing population afforded a constantly expanding market. And, finally, foreign markets in a world that was only partially industrialized afforded still other outlets for both capital and finished products.

It was difficult for most Americans to think in terms other than those of an expanding economy, and few were disposed to question the validity of the fundamental principles of laissez faire. In the nineteen-twenties a rising national income served to mask the fact that the economic system had developed fundamental defects and that the period of marked expansion was drawing to an end, at least for another decade. When the stock market broke in 1929 and the business outlook grew darker each day, many thought it was merely another passing depression and that the economy would soon right itself if left alone. Just before the crash,

[3] United States Bureau of the Census, *op. cit.*, p. 5; United States Bureau of the Census, *Historical Statistics of the United States, 1789–1945* (Washington, D.C.: Government Printing Office, 1949), p. 25.

President Hoover had publicly stated that "the fundamental business of the country" was "on a sound and prosperous basis," and as late as March, 1930, the President was quoted in the press as saying that "the worst effect of the crash upon unemployment will have passed during the next sixty days." At the beginning of 1930, Andrew W. Mellon, the Secretary of the Treasury, told the American people: "I see nothing in the present situation that is either menacing or warrants pessimism." And according to Arthur Brisbane " all the really important millionaires" were "planning to continue prosperity."[4]

But prosperity did not return. Year after year billions of dollars available for capital investment remained idle, fires in the furnaces of great manufacturing enterprises died out, and millions of workers remained unemployed. The government provided funds for the employment of some on public works programs, but at no time after 1936 did a program of this kind "provide work for more than a fourth of the employable un-employed."[5] The measures adopted by the government appear to have stimulated recovery to a degree, but for a full decade our economy was characterized by idle money, idle machines, and idle men. As late as September, 1939, the estimated number of the unemployed was 8,190,-000. By 1940 the total volume of industrial production was back to its 1929 peak, but "20 per cent fewer workers were employed."[6] And in this connection the fact cannot be overlooked that during the decade 1930 to 1940 the population of the nation had increased by some 8,894,000. Per capita income in 1938 was 17.9 per cent lower than in 1929. It took the exigencies of rearmament and war to dispel the semiparalysis that had fixed itself on the American economic system.[7]

The material and spiritual losses suffered by the American people through idleness of men and machines are not, of course, easy to estimate. Two estimates, however, have been made of the loss of income resulting from unemployment. One by Doctor Isador Lubin, Commissioner of Labor Statistics, Department of Labor, shows the loss suffered had the employable population of 1929 remained the same and had the level of employment remained unchanged. His estimates are "minimum estimates and assume that the total number of people available for work" remained exactly the same as in 1929.[8] As a matter of fact, as Doctor Lubin states,

[4] Stuart Chase, *The Road We are Traveling, 1914–1942: When the War Ends* (New York: Twentieth Century Fund, 1942), p. 37.

[5] Temporary National Economic Committee, *Taxation, Recovery, and Defense,* Investigation of Concentration of Economic Power, Monograph 20, Seventy-sixth Congress, Third Session, Senate Committee Print (Washington, D.C.: Government Printing Office, 1941), p. 14.

[6] *Ibid.,* p. 5.

[7] *Ibid.;* see also John Kenneth Galbraith, *The Great Crash, 1929* (Boston: Houghton Mifflin Company, 1955; also published in paperback, Sentry Editions, Boston: Houghton Mifflin Company, 1961).

[8] Temporary National Economic Committee, *Economic Prologue, op. cit.,* p. 12.

between 1929 and 1938 some six million people were added to the gainfully employable age group. The loss of income which would have been produced by this group is not included in the estimate. In the non-agricultural occupations the loss in man years between 1930 and 1938 was 43,435,000,[9] and the loss in salaries and wages was $119,000-000,000. Approximately $20,000,000,000 was lost in dividends paid out, assuming, of course, that the 1929 level of dividends paid out had been maintained. The gross farm income lost was approximately $38,-000,000,000. If all the losses are added together — those sustained by labor, agriculture, and investors — the grand total was $133,000,-000,000. This estimate eliminated the effect of price changes — in other words, it represents a loss of $133,000,000,000 at 1929 prices.

The National Resources Committee also made an estimate which takes into account the increased labor force between 1930 and 1937. Here an estimate is made "of what the real income would have been in the years after 1929 if there had been no depression following that year and economic activity had expanded to absorb the increased labor force which became available."[10] The loss of income due to idle men and machines was about $200,000,000,000, an amount which would have been sufficient to provide, at prewar prices, a new, if modest, house for every family in the United States. Nor could the loss be measured adequately in terms of income; unemployment and insecurity added up to personal frustration for a large fraction of the American people. And there was always the danger that personal frustration would build into social frustration of a kind that would be destructive to inherited political and economic institutions.[11]

Signs of Change in the Structure of the American Economy

As the Depression of the nineteen-thirties wore on and economists studied it more closely, both in its historical origins and its world setting, fundamental questions began to be raised with respect to the changes that had occurred in the structure of the American economy. A group of Harvard-Tufts economists came to the unqualified conclusion that the Depression represented something more than "a violent cyclical downswing"; that it represented "a basic change in trend," a significant modification of the economic life of the nation.[12] It was argued that the dis-

[9] *Ibid.*, p. 12.
[10] United States National Resources Committee, *The Structure of the American Economy*, Part I: *Basic Characteristics*, A Report Prepared by the Industrial Section under the Direction of Gardiner C. Means, June, 1939 (Washington, D.C.: Government Printing Office, 1939), p. 2.
[11] *Ibid.*, pp. 2–3.
[12] Richard V. Gilbert *et al.*, *An Economic Program for American Democracy* (New York: Vanguard Press, 1938), p. 22.

appearance of the frontier, the end of world expansion into new areas, and the declining rate of population growth had produced an alteration of "the whole structure of the economy." The period of *extensive* development was of necessity giving way to one "increasingly intensive in its character."[13]

Other economists also advanced the hypothesis or expressed the conviction that the century and a quarter ending in 1930 was a unique epoch, and that a fundamental change had taken place in the structure of the American economy — and, indeed, of the economy of the entire Western world.[14] Much of their thinking, too, was predicated upon an assumption of economic maturity somewhat similar to that expressed by the Harvard-Tufts economists.

The economists who entertained the view that the Depression was symptomatic of a fundamental change in the economy, not to be explained in terms of ordinary business-cycle analysis, stressed the development of conditions that made difficult the flow of savings into capital investment. Among these were not only the passing of the frontier, the decline of the rate of population growth, and decreased opportunity for foreign investment, but also the concentration of income in the hands of the few, resulting in savings too great to be absorbed. We were witnessing, it was said, a structural change in the economic order "no less basic and profound in character than the industrial revolution beginning 150 years ago and extending deep into the nineteenth century. . . ."[15]

It must not be supposed, however, that economists were agreed in their interpretation of events of the decades immediately preceding World War II. Some maintained unshaken faith in traditional principles and practices. Doctor Harold G. Moulton and some of his associates in the Brookings Institution challenged bluntly the conception of economic maturity. They discounted the effect of the disappearance of the frontier and the "apparent completion of the building of great industries"; they did not look upon the declining rate of population growth or the prospect of population decline as constituting any necessary check upon economic expansion; rather, they saw in the unfulfilled wants of the American peo-

[13] *Ibid.*, pp. 18–19.

[14] See the testimony of Professor Alvin H. Hansen before the Temporary National Economic Committee, *Savings and Investment,* Investigation of Concentration of Economic Power, Part 9, Hearings before the Temporary National Economic Committee, Seventy-sixth Congress, First Session (Washington, D.C.: Government Printing Office, 1940), pp. 3503–3545; Alvin H. Hansen, "Economic Progress and Declining Population Growth," *American Economic Review,* XXXIX (March, 1939), 1–15; Alvin H. Hansen, *Fiscal Policy and Business Cycles* (New York: W. W. Norton & Co., 1941); Alvin H. Hansen, *Full Recovery or Stagnation?* (New York: W. W. Norton & Co., 1938); Temporary National Economic Committee, *Taxation, Recovery, and Defense, op. cit.,* pp. 4–5.

[15] Temporary National Economic Committee, *Savings and Investment, op. cit.,* pp. 3503–3504. See also Galbraith, *op. cit.*

ple a new frontier calling for extensive investment in capital goods and a greatly expanded volume of production. Writing in 1940, they explained the phenomena of idle capital and unemployment largely in terms of governmental regulation of the economy and the consequent loss of confidence by the business community. They concluded an extensive investigation with the following statement:

> The re-establishment of the stable conditions which are so sorely needed in the United States at this critical period in world history largely depends upon the removal of unnecessary impediments to the flow of funds into constructive capital developments and the restoration of confidence in the future of private enterprise.[16]

It would appear from the vantage point of the sixties that the Depression of the thirties is not so neatly explained. But whatever interpretation one may give it, or whatever views one may entertain with respect to economic organization in the future, it is clear that during the past several decades fundamental changes have occurred in the structure and operation of the economic system.

The Passing of Laissez Faire

Loss of faith in the theoretical concepts of laissez faire. During the Depression of the nineteen-thirties, and in the years immediately following it, both the structure and the operation of the American economy were subjected to a series of detailed critical analyses.[17] One of the consequences of these investigations was a loss of faith in the theoretical concepts of laissez faire. As we have already seen, the classical economists had made free competition the central concept of the theoretical design which was intended to explain and describe the functioning of a laissez faire economy. Competition was the linchpin which held together the whole structure of ideas upon which the theory of laissez faire rested. If the economy were characterized by many small producers, no one of whom could produce enough to enable him to influence or control prices, if each

[16] Harold G. Moulton, George W. Edwards, James D. Magee, and Cleona Lewis, *Capital Expansion, Employment, and Economic Stability,* The Institute of Economics of the Brookings Institution, Publication 82 (Washington, D.C.: Brookings Institution, 1940), p. 336.

[17] See especially Adolph A. Berle and Gardiner C. Means, *The Modern Corporation and Private Property* (New York: The Macmillan Co., 1932); United States National Resources Committee, *op. cit.;* Arthur Robert Burns, *The Decline of Competition* (New York: published under the auspices of the Columbia University Council of Research in the Social Sciences by the McGraw-Hill Book Co., 1936); also the various volumes of the Temporary National Economic Committee, *Investigation of Concentration of Economic Power,* Senate Committee Print, Seventy-sixth Congress, Third Session (Washington, D.C.: Government Printing Office, 1940, 1941).

individual had to adjust to price changes growing out of free competition, the system would work. Free competition and flexible prices would permit the law of supply and demand to operate. Both capital and labor would automatically flow into those industries and types of production which consumers required. Moreover, neither the price of labor nor the price of commodities could be excessive; all involved in the economic process would receive their just rewards, and the whole economy would work efficiently. Under free competition there would be no problem of concentration of power, either on the part of private individuals or in government. Adequate competition would make undue concentration of economic power impossible to private individuals. And since there could be no undue concentration of economic power by private individuals, there would be no need for government to intervene in the conduct of the economy; for it to do so was both unnecessary and dangerous. Thus the market mechanism could be relied upon to regulate the economy automatically and efficiently.

The investigations of the functioning of the economy made following the Great Depression of the thirties made it clear that the character of competition had changed. Competition of the kind contemplated in the theoretical model built up by the classical economists simply did not exist. In large segments of the economy the many small producers who could not influence or control prices had been supplanted by a few large producers, who could and did influence and to a degree control prices. Outright monopoly was not common, but oligopoly was. As Professor Galbraith has observed:

> A vast distance separates oligopoly from the competition of the competitive model. Price-making in markets where there are a few sellers is not only measurably influenced by the actions of any individual firm but the individual must take into consideration the response of others to his initiative. If he correctly appraises what is advantageous for the industry as a whole, the others presumably will follow his lead. Otherwise they will not. When each seller considers the advantage of any action from the viewpoint of the profits of the industry as a whole he is obviously thinking much as would a monopolist. To assume that oligopoly was general in the economy was to assume that power akin to that of a monopolist was exercised in many, perhaps even a majority of, markets.[18]

And to quote Professor Galbraith further, "The important thing is that the doctrines of a monopolistic or imperfect competition paved the way for a destruction of the old assumption of competition on which the competitive model was erected."[19]

[18] John Kenneth Galbraith, *American Capitalism: The Concept of Countervailing Power* (Boston: Houghton Mifflin Company, 1956), p. 42.
[19] *Ibid.*, p. 43.

The Failure of Laissez Faire

Recognition of the existence of the concentration of economic power in the hands of a relatively few large producers and the control over prices implicit in oligopoly was not alone responsible for the loss of faith in laissez faire. Equally important was the obvious fact that the system had failed to work. According to classical economic theory, long-sustained periods of severe unemployment and depression were not possible. Competition, if sufficiently rigorous, would of itself keep such things from happening. And Say's Law of Markets strongly reinforced the concept that long-sustained unemployment and depression were impossible. According to this Law, as it was stated and widely believed, the very act of producing goods created the purchasing power, no more and no less, required to purchase the goods produced. Under this happy state of affairs demand would never fall below what was required to consume the goods produced, thus preventing unemployment and depression. By the same token, demand would never rise high enough to cause inflation.[20] But, as we have already seen, in the nineteen-thirties depression and unemployment struck with a terrific force.

It was now too clear for anyone to miss that the realities of economic life were far different from the conditions pictured in classical economic theory. With competition no longer, if it ever had been, of the kind to permit the market mechanism to regulate prices, and with depression and unemployment ever threatening, the foundations of faith in laissez faire were crumbling.[21]

The Growth of Corporate Enterprise

One of the most radical changes in the structure of the American economy has been the growth of corporate enterprise. During a large part of the nineteenth century, as has already been pointed out, most business enterprises in the United States were owned and operated by private individuals or a small group of partners. In the closing decades of the century, however, businessmen turned more and more to the corporation as a form of business organization. Even before the Civil War the corporate system was becoming important in the railroad industry, and in the postwar years it came to occupy a dominant position in many aspects of our economic life — in banking, insurance, public utilities, mining, and manufacturing. More recently the corporate system has become important in the mercantile field, construction, real estate, and even agriculture. It

[20] *Ibid.,* p. 21.
[21] For a fuller discussion of the loss of faith in laissez faire, see *ibid.,* pp. 10–23. That laissez faire has never been fully tried, see Koontz and Gable, *op. cit.,* p. 11.

is clear that the individual businessman is giving place to the corporation in all types of industry — that we are passing, or have already passed, from an individual to a corporate economy. By 1937 corporate activity had come to embrace the whole field of communication, as well as the production and distribution of electric light, power, and gas. No less than 92 per cent of all manufacturing was carried on by corporations (see Table 11) and the same was true of 89 per cent of the business done in the field of transportation. More important, perhaps, than the more or less inevitable growth of corporate enterprise has been the emergence of the relatively few corporate giants.

TABLE 11: IMPORTANCE OF CORPORATE ACTIVITY BY
BRANCHES OF INDUSTRY, 1937*

Industry	Per Cent of National Income	Per Cent of Business Done by Corporations in Each Industry
Agriculture	8.9	7
Mining	2.1	96
Electric light and power and manufactured gas	1.6	100
Manufacturing	24.0	92
Contract construction	2.1	36
Transportation	7.3	89
Communication	1.3	100
Trade	12.5	58
Finance	9.3	84
Government — including work relief wages	13.5	58
Service	11.9	30
Miscellaneous	4.2	33

* Bureau of Foreign and Domestic Commerce, as cited in Temporary National Economic Committee, *Economic Prologue,* Investigation of Concentration of Economic Power, Part I, Hearings before the Temporary National Economic Committee, Seventy-fifth Congress, Third Session (Washington, D.C.: Government Printing Office, 1940), p. 96.

The Growth of the Large Corporation and the Concentration of Economic Power

If corporations had remained small concerns, they would not have had a very profound effect upon the organization of American economic life. But some of them did not remain small. A few hundred of the largest corporations have come to occupy a dominant position in the American economy — a position so dominant, in fact, that many regard corporations as the major force in our society. Certainly the concentration of economic power in the hands of a few giant corporations has raised problems of the first magnitude, and certainly the American citizen who fails to understand the essential elements of those problems is living in an unreal world.

The dominant position that a few large corporations came to hold can be impressively indicated in a number of ways. First of all, one may compare the assets of these corporations with other assets in society, as, for example, the assets of all other corporations, total industrial wealth, and the total national wealth. In 1933, two hundred of the largest non-financial corporations controlled "approximately 19 to 21 per cent of the

TABLE 12: RELATION OF 200 LARGEST NON-FINANCIAL CORPORATIONS TO ALL NON-FINANCIAL CORPORATIONS, TO INDUSTRIAL WEALTH, AND TO NATIONAL WEALTH, 1933*

	Per Cent of Each Category Controlled by 200 Largest Corporations		
	All Non-Financial Corporations	Industrial Wealth	National Wealth
Total assets (involves some duplication)	57.0	..	..
Total assets less taxable securities (involves only minor duplication)	54.8	..	..
Total physical assets, land, buildings, equipment, and inventories (involves no duplication)	59.6	46–51	19–21
Total instruments of production, land, buildings, and equipment (involves no duplication)	64.2	..	..
Gross receipts from sales and services	29.9	..	..
Interest and dividends paid	64.0	..	..
Compiled net profits	..	..	..

* Adapted from United States National Resources Committee, *The Structure of the American Economy*, Part I: *Basic Characteristics*, A Report Prepared by the Industrial Section under the Direction of Gardiner C. Means, June, 1939 (Washington, D.C.: Government Printing Office, 1939), p. 106.

national wealth, between 46 and 51 per cent of the nation's industrial wealth, and approximately 60 per cent of the physical assets of all non-financial corporations."[22] These two hundred corporations controlled 64 per cent of the instruments of production under corporate control and they paid out 64 per cent of the interest and dividends issued by the many thousands of non-financial corporations (see Table 12). The degree of

22 United States National Resources Committee, *op. cit.*, p. 105.

concentration of assets in manufacturing, transportation, and two other industrial categories in 1933 is shown in Table 13. Among the fifty largest financial corporations — "thirty banks, seventeen life-insurance companies, and three investment trusts" — concentration was even more striking. The thirty large banks together held 34 per cent of all banking assets of the country outside the Federal Reserve banks, and the seventeen life insurance companies controlled about 81 per cent of the assets of all life insurance companies.[23]

Among the very large corporations — financial and non-financial — thirty controlled assets, in 1935, of a billion dollars or more each. In his final statement before the Temporary National Economic Committee, Senator Joseph C. O'Mahoney compared the assets of these thirty billion-dollar corporations with the assessed valuation of the several states.

TABLE 13: CONCENTRATION IN FOUR INDUSTRIAL CATEGORIES, 1933*

Proportion of Corporate Assets in Four Industrial Categories Controlled by Largest Corporations in These Categories	1933	
	Total Assets Less Taxable Investments, Less Depreciation	Land, Buildings, and Equipment, Less Depreciation
	Per Cent	Per Cent
75 largest manufacturing corporations	40.2	45.4
45 largest transportation corporations	91.7	91.6
40 largest public utility corporations . . . , . .	80.4	81.2
25 largest "other" non-financial corporations	14.8	17.4

* United States National Resources Committee, *The Structure of the American Economy,* Part I: *Basic Characteristics,* A Report Prepared by the Industrial Section under the Direction of Gardiner C. Means, June, 1939 (Washington, D.C.: Government Printing Office, 1939), p. 106.

It will be observed that there are only ten sovereign states which have within their respective borders property valued at more than the assets of either the Metropolitan Life Insurance Company or the American Telegraph and Telephone Company. Stated in another way, each of these two corporations is richer than any one of thirty-eight sovereign states. At the other end of the scale, there are eighteen states, the taxable wealth of each of which is less than the total assets of the smallest of the thirty "billion dollar" corporations.[24]

[23] *Ibid.,* p. 103.
[24] Temporary National Economic Committee, *Final Report and Recommendations of the Temporary National Economic Committee Transmitted to the Congress of the United States,* Seventy-seventh Congress, First Session, Senate Document 35 (Washington, D.C.: Government Printing Office, 1941), p. 677.

Five of the largest corporations in 1935 controlled assets greater than the assessed valuation of property contained in one-half of the American states in 1937. The assets of four great corporations exceeded the value of all the property, as measured by assessed valuation, of the eleven states that had made up the Southern Confederacy; and fifteen corporations controlled assets greater than all the taxable property located west of the Mississippi River.[25]

The importance of the large corporation in the manufacturing industries is indicated when size is measured by number of persons employed, by value added by manufacturing, and by value of products. The results of an investigation made in 1939 are summarized as follows:

> With size measured by employment:
> 100 companies employed 20.7 per cent of all the manpower engaged in manufacturing;
> With size measured by value added by manufacture:
> 100 companies contributed 24.7 per cent of all the value added in manufacturing activity;
> With size measured by value of product:
> 100 companies accounted for 32.4 per cent of the value of products reported by all manufacturing plants.[26]

It is clear that by the late nineteen-thirties there was a high degree of concentration in American manufacturing industries. The evidence indicates that during the past two decades there has been some further concentration, although the rate of increase has not been very great. As already pointed out, in 1933 Means found that 200 of the largest non-financial corporations had 57 per cent of the assets of all non-financial corporations. The Federal Trade Commission reported in 1947 that 113 of the largest manufacturing corporations, each with assets in excess of $100,000,000, owned 46 per cent of the capital assets (property, plant, and equipment) of all manufacturing, both corporate and non-corporate.[27] In the same year in 12 large manufacturing industries the 2 largest concerns owned 50 per cent or more of the capital assets of the industry and in 11 industries the 4 largest concerns owned 70 per cent or more of the assets of the entire industry. (See Table 14.)

A comparison of the total value of shipments for all manufacturing enterprises accounted for by the first 5, the first 50, the first 100, and

25 *Ibid.*, pp. 676–677.

26 United States National Resources Committee, *op. cit.*, p. 102.

27 Federal Trade Commission, *Report on the Concentration of Productive Facilities, 1947* (Washington, D.C.: Government Printing Office, 1949), p. 14. For a statement concerning the slower growth of big business during the last two decades, see Corwin D. Edwards, *Big Business and the Policy of Competition* (Cleveland, Ohio: The Press of Western Reserve University, 1956), pp. 13–15.

TABLE 14:
TWENTY-SIX SELECTED MANUFACTURING INDUSTRIES,
PROPORTION OF NET CAPITAL ASSETS OWNED BY
LEADING CONCERNS, 1947*

	Per Cent of Net Capital Assets Owned by —			
	One Company	Two Companies	Three Companies	Four Companies
1. Linoleum	57.9	80.8	92.1	96.6
2. Tin Cans and Other Tinware	55.2	92.1	95.3	96.4
3. Aluminum	55.0	85.0	100.0	
4. Copper Smelting and Refining	46.8	73.5	88.5	94.6
5. Biscuits, Crackers, and Pretzels	46.3	57.0	67.7	71.4
6. Agricultural Machinery	45.3	56.8	66.6	75.4
7. Office and Store Machines and Devices	42.0	56.3	69.5	74.3
8. Motor Vehicles	40.9	62.8	68.7	70.7
9. Cigarettes	36.6	64.4	77.6	87.8
10. Plumbing Equipment and Supplies	32.2	64.9	71.3	74.3
11. Distilled Liquors	29.0	53.3	72.4	84.6
12. Meat Products	28.8	54.7	64.0	69.3
13. Primary Steel	28.6	42.0	49.2	54.5
14. Rubber Tires and Tubes	27.8	49.9	70.3	88.3
15. Dairy Products	27.5	48.9	55.8	59.6
16. Glass and Glassware	24.9	49.1	57.4	62.2
17. Carpets and Rugs	24.1	36.8	48.9	57.9
18. Footwear (except Rubber)	23.6	39.6	43.4	46.8
19. Industrial Chemicals	21.5	36.5	45.5	51.8
20. Woolen and Worsted Goods	16.7	23.5	28.1	30.3
21. Electrical Machinery	15.8	28.8	41.7	47.5
22. Grain-Mill Products	15.6	23.5	30.2	36.3
23. Aircraft and Parts	13.6	25.4	35.2	44.0
24. Bread and Other Products (Excluding Biscuits and Crackers)	13.0	20.0	25.4	30.6
25. Canning and Preserving	10.7	21.4	32.0	39.4
26. Drugs and Medicines	8.4	16.6	23.5	30.0

* Federal Trade Commission, *Report on the Concentration of Productive Facilities, 1947* (Washington, D.C.: Government Printing Office, 1949), p. 21.

the first 200 in 1935 and 1950 reveals some percentage increase in each class of companies. In the case of the first 200 companies the per cent increase was 2.8.

TABLE 15:
PERCENTAGE OF TOTAL VALUE OF PRODUCT OF ALL MANUFACTURING INDUSTRIES ACCOUNTED FOR BY THE LARGEST MANUFACTURING CONCERNS, 1935 AND 1950*

Companies	1935 Per Cent	1950 Per Cent	Change (Percentage Points)
First 5 Companies	10.6	11.4	0.8
First 50 Companies	26.2	26.6	.4
First 100 Companies	32.4	33.3	.9
First 200 Companies	37.7	40.5	2.8

* Federal Trade Commission, *Report on Changes in Concentration in Manufacturing, 1935 to 1947 and 1950* (Washington, D.C.: Government Printing Office, 1954), p. 17.

In 1950 the 200 largest manufacturing companies accounted for 40.5 per cent of the value of product of all manufacturing enterprises. In 1952 there were 18 manufacturing concerns with assets above one billion dollars, 36 with assets exceeding one-half billion, and 94 with assets above one-quarter billion.[28] It will be noted that the increase in the concentration of industry has not increased greatly during the past thirty years and that the situation in the 1960's is far different from that projected in the 1930's on the basis of pre-Depression trends.

One of the factors contributing to economic concentration was the defense program of World War II and the manner of disposing of government-owned facilities at the end of the war. It was only natural, perhaps, that government contracts should have been let in proportionately large numbers to the larger corporations and that at the end of the war the large corporations should have found themselves in a favored position in the purchase of government-owned facilities. In any event, such was the case. Dimock has summarized the industrial concentration stimulated by the war and reconversion in the following words:

> To meet the requirements of the armed services during World War II for goods of every description, the government turned to the largest business corporations because they possessed advantages of capital, patents, and experience, and were also in a position to furnish wartime personnel to the government. By 1941, fifty-six firms — less than one half of 1 percent of all manufacturing firms in the nation — had been awarded 75 percent of all contracts and of these, six corporations held almost one third. Even during the Korean War, by 1951 General Motors alone had received 15 percent of all federal contracts up to that time. Thus the larger part of the government's war contracts was awarded to the big companies, which tended to become bigger, while

28 Edwards, *op. cit.*, p. 40.

the small companies, despite efforts through subcontracting arrangements and otherwise, lost ground.

Then under reconversion, in the two years between 1945 and 1947, the Federal government sold 70 percent of all publicly owned war plant to 250 large manufacturing firms already controlling more than 66 percent of all industrial facilities in the United States, while the remaining 30 percent of war plant was thinly spread out among some of the 262,000 smaller firms controlling only 33 percent of all facilities. One of these plants alone — the steel plant at Geneva, Utah — had cost the government $200 million and was sold to U.S. Steel, the colossus of the industry, for $45.5 million, making it the biggest producer of steel in the West as well as elsewhere. In 1955, twenty-four wartime synthetic rubber plants valued at some $400 million were sold for $285 million to the four biggest rubber companies in the nation, two combines of smaller concerns, and two major oil companies. As a result of such policies, by 1946 the 250 largest corporations in the United States held approximately two thirds of the nation's usable manufacturing facilities and either owned or were in a position to control facilities equivalent to those of all manufacturing corporations together in 1939. In addition, sixty-three manufacturing corporations "had sufficient liquid assets to buy all government-owned manufacturing facilities or to purchase the assets of some 70,000 smaller manufacturing corporations."[29]

The whole story of concentration of economic power is not told merely by setting down the assets of the large corporations and indicating the degree to which they dominate employment and production in their respective fields. The corporate community is bound together, in some instances rather tightly, by interlocking directorates (see Table 16). In 1935, four hundred persons held nearly a third of the 3544 directorships of the two hundred largest non-financial and the fifty largest financial corporations. Twenty-five corporations had no director in common with any other corporation on the list, but 151 companies, with assets about equal to three-fourths of the total represented by the whole group of 250, interlocked with three or more others. One corporation interlocked with thirty-five others.[30] The extent to which policy is coordinated through interlocking is difficult to say, but it is reasonable to suppose that in most instances individuals who hold more than one directorship carry over from one corporation to the other some of the deliberations on the affairs of each. Such was in fact found to be the case in a somewhat later investigation of interlocking directorates by the Federal Trade Commission. After an exhaustive study the Commission came to the conclusion:

> Among the largest companies there were in 1946 a substantial and significant variety of interlocking directorates, which, by virtue of the char-

[29] Marshall E. Dimock, *Business and Government,* Third Edition (New York: Henry Holt and Company, 1957), pp. 93–94.
[30] United States National Resources Committee, *op. cit.,* p. 158.

TABLE 16: NUMBER OF DIRECTORS AND THEIR HOLDINGS OF
DIRECTORSHIPS IN 200 LARGEST NON-FINANCIAL AND
50 LARGEST FINANCIAL CORPORATIONS, 1935*

Number of Director-ships Held by a Single Individual	Total Number of Directors	Total Number of Director-ships Held	Cumulative Number	
			Directors	Director-ships
9	1	9	1	9
8	3	24	4	33
7	6	42	10	75
6	6	36	16	111
5	19	95	35	206
4	48	192	83	398
3	102	306	185	704
2	303	606	488	1310
1	2234	2234	2722	3544
Total	2722	3544		

* United States National Resources Committee, *The Structure of the American Economy,* Part I: Basic Characteristics, a Report Prepared by the Industrial Section under the Direction of Gardiner C. Means, June, 1939 (Washington, D.C.: Government Printing Office, 1939), p. 158.

acter of the business of the companies, involved reasonable probabilities that competition would be reduced thereby.

In certain cases interlocking relationships involving several directors from the same company provided a broad base for the development of common policies and attitudes. In certain industries directors from various important companies sat together on particular boards which served as focal points of interlocking relationships. In certain other industries, though there were no focal points, there was such a multiplicity of interlocking relationships as to constitute a network in which it was evident that the effect of any one interlock was strengthened and supplemented by the existence of the others.[31]

The business community is further integrated and coordinated through formal organizations of one kind or another. These associations bring together certain economic-interest groupings on a national or interstate basis. In 1937 there were more than 2400 national and interstate trade associations. These organizations gather and disseminate information among their members, help to develop uniform policies within the industry involved, and in many instances bring pressure to bear to mold public opinion and to shape the policies of government. Some of the national associations are "to a significant extent dominated by" the larger corpora-

[31] Federal Trade Commission, *Report on Interlocking Directorates* (Washington, D.C.: Government Printing Office, 1951), p. 36.

tions and constitute avenues through which their influence may be extended.[32]

The United States Chamber of Commerce undertakes to speak for business as a whole, its primary function being "to obtain the matured judgment of business upon national questions, and to present and interpret those views to the agencies of government and to the public."[33] The Chamber of Commerce is able to bring its immense financial resources to bear in crystallizing and disseminating the opinion of its members. Writing in 1941, Donald C. Blaisdell said of this organization:

> . . . From its national headquarters across Lafayette Square from the White House emanate the opinions constituting the voice of the Nation's business. The desire of the Senator to know the thoughts of business would now be fully satisfied. Not only Congress, but also the President and his Cabinet, bureau chiefs, and heads of the independent agencies are thus informed of collective business opinion. Federated in the Chamber are 1500 commercial organizations and trade associations, including as members more than 7000 of the most important corporations, firms and individuals of the country. Representing such a constituency, and having under its direction in Washington a competent staff experienced in all phases of business activity, the Chamber is indeed in a strategic position to dispense its product — "service to American business."[34]

The National Association of Manufacturers has been no less important as an agency for crystallizing and expressing the view of American industry. The officers of this Association, and also the members of its important policy committees, are drawn to a considerable extent from large corporations. The La Follette Civil Liberties Committee, a subcommittee of the Senate Committee on Education and Labor, found in 1937 that the Association had been financed "by a small group of powerful corporations" and that a "clique of large corporations, not more than 60 in number," had "supplied it with active leadership."[35] The Association asserts that

[32] *Ibid.*, p. 163.

[33] Chamber of Commerce of the United States, *The Chamber of Commerce of the United States, Its Organizations, Functions, and Services* (Washington, D.C.: 1935), p. 4, as quoted in Temporary National Economic Committee, *Economic Power and Political Pressures*, Monograph 26, Seventy-sixth Congress, Third Session, Senate Committee Print (Washington, D.C.: Government Printing Office, 1940), p. 27.

[34] Temporary National Economic Committee, *Economic Power and Political Pressures, op. cit.*, p. 26.

[35] *Violations of Free Speech and Rights of Labor,* Report of the Committee on Education and Labor Pursuant to S. Res. 266 (74th Congress); *A Resolution to Investigate Violations of the Right of Free Speech and Assembly and Interference with the Right of Labor to Organize and Bargain Collectively,* Labor Policies of Employers' Associations, Part III, The National Association of Manufacturers, Senate Report No. 6, Part 6, 76th Congress, First Session (Washington, D.C.: Government Printing Office, 1939), pp. v + 335.

it is "the medium through which American industry is able to voice a united opinion on vital national questions," and it claims to be "the only organization exclusively representing the interests of American industry."[36] Certainly it has been extremely active in influencing public opinion.

The evidence clearly indicates that economic power in this country is highly concentrated in a relatively few big corporations. One hundred and thirty-five of them own 45 per cent of the industrial wealth of the United States — or almost one-fourth of the manufacturing assets of the entire world.[37] In something like 70 per cent of American industries a pattern of high concentration has emerged. In industry after industry a few large corporations dominate the field. As Berle has put it:

> Two or three, or at most five, corporations will have more than half the business, the remainder being divided among a greater or lesser number of smaller concerns who must necessarily live within the conditions made for them by the "Big Two" or the "Big Three" or "Big Five" as the case may be.[38]

The Ownership of Corporate Enterprise

Since the corporation plays such a dominant role in the American economy, it is important to know whether ownership is concentrated in the hands of a few large holders of stock or widely diffused among the people. In one sense, ownership of corporations in this country may be thought of as being highly dispersed. Many persons of moderate means have invested their savings in one or more corporations. But this wide dispersion of ownership should not be permitted, as has sometimes been the case, to mask the fact that the ownership of the major part of the stock in American corporations has been, at least until recently, concentrated in the hands of a relatively few persons. In 1937 about one-half of the stockholders owned stock valued at less than two thousand dollars, and the sum of their holdings was but a small fraction of the stock outstanding.[39] Fifty per cent of the stockholders received less than 5 per cent of the dividends paid by corporations to individuals, and 80 per cent of the stockholders accounted for not much more than 10 per cent of the divi-

---

[36] Chamber of Commerce of the United States, *op. cit.*, as quoted in United States National Resources Committee, *op. cit.*, p. 164.

[37] Adolph A. Berle, Jr., *The Twentieth-Century Capitalist Revolution* (New York: Harcourt, Brace and Company, 1954), p. 25.

[38] *Ibid.*, p. 26.

[39] Temporary National Economic Committee, *The Distribution of Ownership in the 200 Largest Non-Financial Corporations,* Investigation of Concentration of Economic Power, Monograph 29, Seventy-sixth Congress, Third Session, Senate Committee Print (Washington, D.C.: Government Printing Office, 1940), p. xvii.

dends paids to individuals. At the other end of the scale, a few large stockholders received the great bulk of the dividends.

The following summary statement with respect to the concentration of the ownership of corporations in 1937 is taken from a study made under the auspices of the Securities and Exchange Commission for the Temporary National Economic Committee:

> Thus the 10,000 persons with the highest dividend incomes, comprising not much over one-tenth of 1 percent of the total number of stockholders and about one-fiftieth of 1 percent of the total number of income recipients, received about 25 percent of all dividends paid to individuals and may, therefore, be estimated to have owned, directly or indirectly, about one-fourth of all stock of domestic corporations. Fewer than 75,000 persons, i.e., less than 1 percent of the number of stockholders and considerably less than one-fifth of 1 percent of the total number of income recipients, were necessary to account for one-half of all dividends received by individuals. This certainly represents an impressive degree of concentration of ownership.[40]

The data presented in the foregoing statement indicate that corporate ownership for all corporations in the aggregate has been highly concentrated. A similar story of concentration of ownership is revealed when individual corporations are considered. An analysis made in 1937 of the stockholding of the 1710 corporations listing their securities on a national securities exchange revealed that, in general, a relatively small number of shareholdings accounted for the majority of the stock outstanding. When individual corporations were considered, again it was discovered that dispersion of ownership was much more apparent than real. In 1937 it could be said: "Notwithstanding the large number of shareholdings in most large corporations, not much over 1 percent of the holders are required in most cases to account for the majority of the stock outstanding or for voting control."[41]

Analysis of the ownership of the 200 largest non-financial corporations (as they stood as of 1937) is also informative. These corporations had assets of nearly $70,000,000,000, or nearly 45 per cent of all non-financial corporations, and they accounted for nearly 45 per cent of the dividends paid by all non-financial corporations. They held a dominant position in most of the manufacturing industries of the country.[42] The ownership of these corporations provided "a significant clue to the ultimate center of economic power" in the United States.

The ownership of these corporations was highly concentrated. In general, a relatively few large shareholdings accounted for a large fraction of the stock outstanding.

[40] *Ibid.*, p. 13.   [41] *Ibid.*, p. 15.   [42] *Ibid.*, p. 4.

There were about 4,000,000 shareholdings with a value of $500 or less — out of a total of nearly 8,500,000 record shareholdings in the 200 corporations — but they comprised only 3 percent of the value of all shares of the 200 corporations. The 1,375,000 shareholdings worth $501 to $1000 apiece made up only another 3 percent. On the other hand, there were 415,000 shareholdings with a value of over $10,000 each which accounted for about 70 percent of the value of the total stock outstanding in the 200 corporations.[43]

The largest 3 per cent of the common shareholdings accounted for somewhat more than 50 per cent of the total value of shares outstanding. In the case of preferred stocks, it required only about 5 per cent of the largest shareholdings to account for 50 per cent of the total value of the issues.[44]

One of the striking features of the American corporate system has been the relatively slight degree of ownership vested in the officers and directors of the large corporation. Those who direct and manage the large corporations, as a rule, have owned only a small fraction of the outstanding stock. In 1937 the officers and directors of the 200 largest non-financial corporations held about 5.5 per cent of the outstanding stock of those corporations; the officers held 0.1 per cent of the outstanding stock, officer-directors held 1.9 per cent, and directors held 3.5 per cent.[45] This separation of ownership and management is of great significance and will be considered in greater detail in the following section. The reader should be cautioned here, however, that in some corporations, as, for example, those owned largely by a single family, this separation of ownership and management has not been carried very far and, indeed, may not exist at all.

It should be pointed out that with the widespread establishment of pension funds following World War II there began what has been called "an unprecedented democratization of business ownership."[46] Investment trusts, pension funds, and other fiduciary investors now own something like a third of marketable common stock. For example, the pension fund of Sears Roebuck owns about a fourth of that company's stock; the pension fund of General Motors has for investment annually nearly $100,-000,000; and the Massachusetts Investors Trust has assets of about a billion dollars.[47] Obviously, much of the capital required to maintain and expand the American economy is being supplied by the American middle and working classes.

[43] *Ibid.*, p. xvii.
[44] *Ibid.*, p. 40.
[45] *Ibid.*, p. 57.
[46] Peter F. Drucker, *America's Next Twenty Years* (New York: Harper & Brothers, 1957), p. 26.
[47] *Ibid.*, p. 37.

Control of the Large Corporation

The power of control of the large corporations is more highly centralized than is their ownership. In fact, one of the significant features of large-scale corporate enterprise in the United States is the separation of ownership and control. The great majority of stockholders, especially those who own stock in the large corporation along with many thousands of other stockholders, are not in a position to exercise much, if any, control in matters of fundamental policy. To be sure, the owners of a majority of the stock of a corporation have the legal right to elect the board of directors and through them to determine the major policies of the enterprise. As a rule, however, control is exercised by a small group who own materially less than one-half of the stock, or by management — the officers and directors of the corporation — who often own an inconsequential fraction of the stock. Not infrequently, the group which exercises control owns less than 10 per cent of the voting stock outstanding. Nor has the situation been materially changed by the development of investment trusts, pension funds, and other fiduciary investors to which attention has already been called. Those who invest these funds have commonly regarded themselves as investors and not as entrepreneurs; although they are the legal owners of large blocks of stock in various corporations, they commonly leave to the regular management of the corporations the business of policy-making and the day-to-day operation of the enterprise.

The separation of ownership and control came about in numerous ways. When the stockholders of a corporation were numbered by the tens of thousands, concerted action was extremely difficult. Few found it practicable to attend the annual meeting for the election of members of the board of directors. If one were to vote at all, one must vote by proxy. But individual stockholders were likely to know little or nothing of the merits of those who sought election to membership on the board of control. They were in no position to get at the facts with respect to the management of the corporation; they knew that dividends had been good or bad and that the price of stock had gone up or down, but they did not know why. They were citizens of a great industrial empire, but with an inadequate knowledge of its men and measures. As a rule, they either consigned to the wastebasket the request to designate proxies or signed on the dotted line. Under such circumstances, a small, compact group of shareholders was sometimes able to control a majority of the voting stock represented at the annual meeting of stockholders. More frequently, a small minority could gain a working control of the corporation, if it owned from 10 to 30 per cent of the stock, by gathering up proxies of scattered stockholders. As Dimock and Hyde point out:

Once in power a minority group is difficult to dislodge. It has, of course, picked a management which is congenial and cooperative. Then the proxy machinery, with expenses paid by the company, is commonly at its disposal. The proxy committee is in effect chosen by the control group and is used as a means of perpetuating itself. Naturally, the larger the corporation and the more dispersed the stock, the more difficult it is for a non-control faction to amass a sufficient number of proxy certificates to oust the control group and assume command.[48]

In those instances in which no single compact group owned a large percentage of the stock, as was the case in many of the large corporations, control was likely to rest with management. Since management was in control of the proxy machinery, its position was well-nigh impregnable. In the late nineteen-thirties most of the 200 largest corporations were controlled by the owners of a minority of the stock or by a management group which owned even less.

The virtual disfranchisement of the great majority of the stockholders in large corporations was also brought about by the adoption of certain legal devices. The most common of these was known as "pyramiding." A minority group would secure control of a corporation, which in turn owned the majority of the stock of another corporation. This process might be continued more or less indefinitely until a relatively small investment of the apex of the pyramid would give control of a whole network of corporations. By this device, an investment of only $20,000,000 was enough to give the Van Sweringen brothers working control over eight Class I railroads with assets of over $2,000,000,000.[49]

The issuance of non-voting stock was another device designed to legally concentrate control in the hands of a small minority group. Only certain classes of stock would carry the right to vote for directors. By disfranchising outright a majority of the stockholders and by buying up a majority of the voting stock, it was possible for a relatively small group to dominate a corporation. In one instance this device was so employed that the owners of voting stock valued at less than $2,250,000 were able to get control of a corporation having assets of more than $130,000,000.[50]

A third device was to issue stock with unusually great voting power. In one instance a million shares of preferred stock of a corporation were issued to a certain company, the value of the stock being one dollar a share. Each share carried one full vote, whereas the outstanding common stock carried only one-twentieth of a vote.

[48] Temporary National Economic Committee, *Bureaucracy and Trusteeship in Large Corporations,* Investigation of Concentration of Economic Power, Monograph 11, Seventy-sixth Congress, Third Session, Senate Committee Print (Washington, D.C.: Government Printing Office, 1940), p. 20.

[49] Adolf A. Berle, Jr., and Gardiner C. Means, *The Modern Corporation and Private Property* (New York: The Macmillan Co., 1932), p. 73.

[50] *Ibid.,* pp. 75–76.

In this way an investment of a million dollars was sufficient to give one company virtual control of a corporation with assets of approximately a billion dollars.[51]

The Role of Management in the Control of Large Corporations

One of the most significant aspects of the American economy has been the dominant role played by management — that is to say, the officers and directors of large corporations. The power and influence of management has not, as a rule, grown out of ownership of any appreciable amount of stock; it is, rather, the result of the diffusion of stock ownership and the use that was made of the proxy machinery. In 1937–39, nearly four-fifths of the large non-financial corporations were under minority ownership control. In such circumstances, and especially where the control group did not own a very large percentage of the stock, management could so employ the proxy machinery as to make its position almost invulnerable. On the importance of management in the control of corporations Dimock and Hyde comment as follows:

> The most common form of control among the large corporations may be termed management control. When stockholding is sufficiently diffuse the position of management becomes almost impregnable.
>
> Management does not need to own stock; the strategic advantages of its location are quite sufficient. A presumption of worth is in its favor, and more concretely, the proxy machinery is at its disposal. Management chooses the proxy committee and by making appointments from among the members of management assures its own continuance. The effectiveness of this machinery is too formidable for small stockholders to overcome. . . .
>
> Only the cataclysmic uprising of an indignant majority of the stockholders is sufficient to overthrow the management. . . .
>
> With the diffusion of ownership which we have noticed in a large sector of our economy, management is left with the responsibility for determining policies, including those affecting prices, production, and employment, within very broad limits and for all practical purposes without effective check from any source. When there is a degree of concentration of stockholdings, of course, the important stockholders may take part in determining broad policy, either through direct informal contact with the management (including the directors) or through choosing directors who will adopt the desired lines of action. Even here, however, the directors need not be responsive to the demands of those who elected them. Except in those relatively rare cases where the charter

[51] *Ibid.*, p. 76.

provides for removal, the directors are practically unfettered in making their decisions until re-election time comes. And in the large proportion of the corporate giants where management rules supreme, even election time is no cause for particular concern, for the means of returning themselves to office are securely in their own hands.[52]

The American economy has taken such form as to impose on the managers of corporate enterprise a whole complex of fiduciary relationships. Whether they know it or not, or whether they desire it or not, the men who form industrial policy have in fact assumed the responsibilities of trusteeship. They stand in a moral if not a legal fiduciary relationship (1) to the stockholders whose savings they manage, (2) to labor, whose opportunity to work depends in large measure upon their decisions, and (3) to the consuming public. More important still, theirs is the responsibility to shape policies that will result in efficient and equitable operation of the economy, that will prevent periodic economic collapse, that will release the productive energy still latent in science and invention, and that will pass on to the masses the gains that accrue from an advancing technology. The concentration of economic power has made trusteeship on the part of management no less important than constitutional restraint of the powers of government. Whether, without certain social restraints being imposed upon it, industrial leadership can be trusted to exercise the great power committed to its keeping is a political and economic problem that lies at the very heart of our democratic capitalistic society. Signs are not lacking that many business leaders are becoming aware of their new stewardship and that the people as a whole are beginning to see the necessity of working out a framework of governmental and business relationships that will prevent the development of either leviathan business or a leviathan state.

The Concentration of Production and the Regulation of Prices in Industry

The rise of large corporations to a dominant position in the economy has naturally resulted in the concentration of production of many commodities in the hands of a few large producers. In 1940 Crowder and Wimsatt made a detailed study of concentration of production in manufacturing. From the thousands of products listed in the "Census of Manufacturers" in 1937, they selected 1807 for analysis. This sample, which included almost one-half of the total census products, gave an over-all picture of the manufacturing industries in the United States. It

[52] Temporary National Economic Committee, *Bureaucracy and Trusteeship in Large Corporations, op. cit.,* pp. 21–23.

was found that for about three-fourths of the products analyzed, the leading four producers accounted for 50 per cent or more of the value output of each product; that for one-half of the products four leading producers accounted for 75 per cent or more of the output; and that for nearly one-third of the products the four leading producers accounted for about 85 per cent of the output.[53] In the case of 417 products, the four leading producers of each accounted for more than 90 per cent of the value of the produce,[54] and in the case of 291 products, the single largest producer manufactured from 50 to 75 per cent of the total output.[55]

In many of the most important industries the production of particular commodities is still concentrated in a few big companies. For example, in 1954 the four largest companies produced 100 per cent of the primary aluminum, 93 per cent of the electric lamps, 91 per cent of the aircraft propellers, 91 per cent of the locomotives and parts, 90 per cent of the gypsum products, 90 per cent of the safes and vaults, 89 per cent of the telephone and telegraph equipment, 88 per cent of the cereal breakfast foods, 87 per cent of the steam engines and turbines, 86 per cent of the chewing gum, 86 per cent of the salt, and 86 per cent of the soap and glycerin. In many other industries the four largest companies produced in excess of 50 per cent of a particular commodity (see Table 17).

Where a few manufacturers of a product dominate the trade, steps are almost sure to be taken to control or eliminate competition. Price leadership is a commonly accepted practice in many segments of the American economy. Small producers adopt and follow without much variation the prices announced by a large producer in the industry. When this is done, the large producers are able to prevent price-cutting and the smaller producers are in a position to profit by the higher prices set by the leader. In his volume *The Decline of Competition* Burns presents much of the evidence with respect to price leadership before 1936. Among the great corporations that had exercised leadership in their respective fields were the United States Steel Corporation, the Standard Oil Company of New Jersey and Standard Oil Companies in other parts of the country, the International Harvester Company, the Philadelphia and Reading Company (anthracite coal), the American Can Company, the Corn Products Company, the Virginia-Carolina Chemical Company, the United States Industrial Alcohol Company, and the National Biscuit Company.[56] A later study presented evidence of price leadership in the sale of steel,

[53] Temporary National Economic Committee, *The Structure of Industry*, Investigation of Concentration of Economic Power, Monograph 27, Seventy-sixth Congress, Third Session, Senate Committee Print (Washington, D.C.: Government Printing Office, 1941), p. 275.

[54] *Ibid.*, p. 276.   [55] *Ibid.*, p. 292.

[56] Arthur Robert Burns, *The Decline of Competition* (New York: published under the auspices of the Columbia University Council for Research in the Social Sciences by the McGraw-Hill Book Co., 1936), Chap. III.

TABLE 17:

SHARE OF PRODUCTION, BASED ON VALUE OF SHIPMENTS,
ACCOUNTED FOR BY THE FOUR LARGEST COMPANIES
IN SELECTED INDUSTRIES, 1954*

Industry	Per Cent of Shipments	Industry	Per Cent of Shipments
Primary Aluminum	100	Elevators and Escalators	66
Electric Lamps (Bulbs)	93	Blast Furnaces	65
Aircraft Propellers	91	Distilled Liquor	64
Gypsum Products	90	Electric Tubes	64
Safes and Vaults	90	Storage Batteries	64
Telephone and Telegraph Equipment	89	Railroad and Street Cars	64
		Glass Containers	63
Cereal Breakfast Foods	88	Photographic Equipment	63
Steam Engines and Turbines	87	Vacuum Cleaners	62
Chewing Gum	86	Aircraft Engines	62
Salt	86	Silverware and Plated Ware	61
Primary Copper	86	Chewing and Smoking Tobacco	58
Soap and Glycerin	85	Petroleum and Coal Products	58
Typewriters	83	Truck Trailers	57
Cigarettes	82	Pens and Mechanical Pencils	57
Sewing Machines	81	Concentrated Milk	55
Organs	81	Communication Equipment	55
Synthetic Fibers	80	Work Shirts	54
Tin Cans and Other Tinware	80	Furniture and Fixtures	54
Transformers	78	Steel Works and Rolling Mills	54
Motor Vehicles and Parts	75	Knitting Mills	53
Computing and Related Machinery	74	Synthetic Rubber	53
		Scientific Instruments	51
Matches	74	Household Furniture	50
Tractors	73	Industrial Trucks and Tractors	50
Biscuits and Crackers	71	Motors and Generators	50
Chocolate and Cocoa Products	70	Electrical Appliances	50
Cane-Sugar Refining	67	Motorcycles and Bicycles	50
Beet Sugar	66		

* *Concentration in American Industry,* Report of the Subcommittee on Antitrust and Monopoly to the Committee on the Judiciary, United States Senate, Eighty-fifth Congress, First Session (Washington, D.C.: Government Printing Office, 1957), pp. 243–250.

cement, agricultural implements, petroleum and gasoline, copper and lead, newspaper print, glass containers, and biscuits and crackers. Many, perhaps most, small manufacturing concerns get under the price umbrella raised by the larger companies; with respect to price policy, they have little initiative or freedom of their own.

Price leadership is only one of the many policies that have been adopted to control or limit price competition. Numerous trade associations have been formed for the primary purpose of helping producers limit competition and regulate prices.[57] Formal and informal agreements have been entered into among competitors to share markets and control prices. Frequently a few large concerns have adopted policies by which they would amicably share markets.[58] The net result is that in many segments of the American economy where a few large producers are able to dominate the market, price competition has largely been superseded by competition in packaging, in styling, and in advertising. A good deal of competition persists at the retail level; but even at that level, in a number of states, so-called fair-trade laws severely restrict competition.

The evidence indicates that in manufacturing production is so highly concentrated that it is possible for producers in many industries to determine prices through administrative decision. That is to say, in the case of many manufactured products, prices of goods to a major extent are formed on an administered basis rather than the basis of a free market.

The Limitation of Competition in the Labor Market

Concentration of production was accompanied by a decline of competition in the labor market; the picture of a society in which a large number of individual laborers bargained with a large number of employers in arriving at wages to be paid become more and more unreal. Wages, like the price of goods, were increasingly determined by administrative decision rather than by free competition in an open market. The individual laborer found that his bargaining power was severely restricted when only a few employers were interested in buying his particular skill and industry. In industries where labor was not organized, wages were administered to a considerable degree by employers. During the nineteen-thirties the position of organized labor was greatly strengthened by federal legislation. The percentage of the nation's labor force belonging to unions greatly increased. One of the main purposes of labor unions was to regulate wages through collective bargaining. Thus, labor rates tended more and more to be administered, either by employers or by labor organizations. Here again the old free-enterprise economy was giving place to an economy of administrative decision.

Price Regulation in Agriculture

The more price competition declined in industry and in the labor market — the more capital and labor were successful in putting a flooring under prices and wages — the worse the position of the farmer became.

[57] Simon H. Whitney, *Trade Associations and Industrial Control* (New York: Central Book Company, 1934), p. 38; Burns, *op. cit.*, Chap. II.

[58] Temporary National Economic Committee, *Competition and Monopoly in American Industry, op. cit.*, pp. 176 ff.

He had to buy in a market where prices were often rigidly controlled and he had to sell in one where prices were determined by competition. In the period immediately preceding World War I, farmers composed about one-third of the total population and received about 17 per cent of the national income; in the early thirties farmers made up approximately one-fourth of the population and their share of the total national income was around only 9 per cent.[59] It is not surprising that under these conditions farmers sought ways and means of limiting their output in order to raise farm prices. They turned to government for help and eventually received it. Industrialists, laborers, and farmers had now all abandoned, to a marked degree, the old free-enterprise economy and had all entered into a "groupistic regime." Each of these three major groups was now in a position, to a greater or lesser degree, to restrict production and to regulate the price of the goods or services it placed on the market.

The Economic Consequences of Administered Prices

The way prices are determined is of first importance in any economy. Where there are many small independent producers of goods and services competing with one another in the open market, prices are sufficiently competitive to permit the law of supply and demand to operate. In such a case, the economy can properly be regarded as a market-regulated economy. And a market-regulated economy is one that is more or less self-regulating; it requires a minimum of human decision and of governmental regulation and control. The case is vastly different when prices are brought under administrative control, either in industry, labor, or agriculture, and all the more so, as with us, when prices are brought under a measure of control in all three areas. As prices shift from a competitive to an administered basis, the whole nature of the economy is changed; a market-determined economy gives place to an administered economy.

The Recent Revolution in the Pattern of Economic Well-Being

One of the most striking changes in American economic life during the past few decades has been the rise in the general level of economic well-being. From 1929 to 1950 the aggregate family personal income in 1950 dollars rose from 118 to 217 billion, an increase of more than 80 per cent.[60] When allowance is made for the increase in the number of

---

[59] Henry C. Taylor, "The Farmer in the Groupistic Regime," *Journal of Land and Public Utility Economics*, XVI (August, 1940), 255.

[60] Selma Goldsmith, George Jaszi, Hyman Kaitz, and Maurice Liebenberg, "Size Distribution of Income Since the Mid-Thirties," *Review of Economics and Statistics*, XXXVI (February, 1954), 4.

consumer units, between 1935–36 and 1950 the average (mean) real income increased about 50 per cent.[61] Expressed in 1950 prices, per capita personal income rose from $990 in 1929 to $1590 in 1953, or by 73 per cent.[62]

More important, perhaps, than the increase in aggregate income has been the changed pattern of income distribution. Before 1929, and especially during the nineteen-twenties, there was a tendency for income to become more highly concentrated. That is to say, income was increasing most at the higher levels. In 1929 only one-tenth of 1 per cent of the families with the highest incomes were receiving as much of the total income as 42 per cent of the families at the bottom of the scale.[63] Since 1929 there has been a sharp reversal of this trend, so much so that we have had a veritable revolution in the pattern of income distribution. Greater productivity, higher wages, more members of families working, and progressive income taxes — all these have been contributing factors. The general shift in consumer units to higher income brackets is shown in Table 18.

In 1935–36, 77.7 per cent of consumer units received an income of less than $2000 in current dollars and 48.7 per cent received less than $2000 in 1950 dollars. (See Table 18.) From 1935–36 to 1950 those in the bracket receiving $3000 to $5000 (1950 dollars) increased from 19.6 per cent to 31.8 per cent, and those receiving $5000 or more increased from 11.5 per cent to 29.0 per cent.[64] Between 1950 and 1959, the percentage of consumer units receiving less than $2000 (current dollars) declined from about 23 to less than 14, and the percentage receiving $5000 or more rose to 54, nearly double the percentage for 1950.

Between 1941 and 1950 the purchasing power of the lowest quintile of consumer units increased 42 per cent and there was an increase, though less marked, in each ascending quintile. In contrast, the top highest 5 per cent suffered a slight loss. Between 1941 and 1959 the average income (before taxes) increased for each quintile, the largest increases being for the lowest and the next lowest quintiles (67 and 71 per cent respectively). The increase for the highest fifth amounted to 40 per cent and the percentage increase in average income for the top 5 per cent amounted to only 24.

It is clear that during the past few decades there has been a marked increase in the aggregate income of the American people and that the

[61] *Ibid.*

[62] J. Frederick Dewhurst and Associates, *America's Needs and Resources: A New Survey* (New York: The Twentieth Century Fund, 1955), p. 89.

[63] Maurice Level, Harold G. Moulton, and Clark Warburton, *America's Capacity to Consume*, The Institute of Economics of the Brookings Institution, Publication 56 (Washington, D.C.: Brookings Institution, 1934), pp. 55–56.

[64] Goldsmith *et al., op. cit.,* 4.

Table 18: Percentage Distribution of Families and Unattached Individuals, by Family Personal Income Levels, 1935–36, 1946, 1950, 1955, and 1959*

Family Personal Income Level (Before Taxes)	Current Dollars					1950 Dollars
	1935–36	1946	1950	1955	1959	1935–36
Under $1000	43.5	8.8	7.6	15.8	13.8	19.5
$1000–$1999	34.2	17.6	15.1			29.2
$2000–$2999	13.1	20.3	16.5	11.3	9.8	20.7
$3000–$3999	4.4	19.8	17.4	14.1	11.0	12.3
$4000–$4999	1.7	12.4	14.4	14.0	11.4	7.3
$5000–$7499	1.6	13.0	17.5	25.4	24.6	6.7
$7500–$9999	.6	4.0	5.9	10.0	13.8	1.8
$10,000 and over	.9	4.1	5.6	9.4	5.6	2.5

* Adapted from Selma Goldsmith, George Jaszi, Hyman Kaitz, and Maurice Liebenberg, "Size Distribution of Income Since the Mid-Thirties," *Review of Economics and Statistics*, XXXVI (February, 1954), 4 (Cambridge, Mass.: Harvard University Press, Copyright, 1954 by the President and Fellows of Harvard College) and from *Statistical Abstract of the United States*, 1961 (Washington, D.C.: Government Printing Office, 1962), p. 317. The 1950 percentages taken from Goldsmith *et al.* differ from more recent 1950 percentages by from .1 to .5 per cent.

TABLE 19: AVERAGE FAMILY PERSONAL INCOME RECEIVED BY EACH FIFTH AND TOP 5 PER CENT OF FAMILIES AND UNATTACHED INDIVIDUALS, 1941–1959

Rank by Size of Income	Average Family Income after Federal Income Tax Liability, in 1950 Dollars*			Average Family Personal Income before Taxes, 1950 Dollars**			
	1941	1950	Per Cent Increase in Purchasing Power, 1941–50	1941	1950	1959	Per Cent Increase in Average Income, 1941–50
Lowest Fifth	750	1060	42	746	1056	1243	67
Second Fifth	1730	2360	37	1731	2418	2966	71
Third Fifth	2790	3440	24	2809	3579	4443	58
Fourth Fifth	4030	4690	16	4085	4911	6204	52
Highest Fifth	8190	8880	8	8949	10,254	12,505	40
Top 5 Per Cent	15,040	14,740	–2	17,607	19,066	21,792	24

* Selma Goldsmith, George Jaszi, Hyman Kaitz, and Maurice Liebenberg, "Size Distribution of Income Since the Mid-Thirties," *Review of Economics and Statistics*, XXXVI (February, 1954), 26. (Cambridge, Mass.: Harvard University Press, Copyright 1954 by the President and Fellows of Harvard College.)

** United States Bureau of the Census, *Statistical Abstract of the United States, 1961* (Washington, D.C.: Government Printing Office, 1962), p. 316.

relative income has become more even. Planning and control, although they present problems that need to be resolved, have contributed to these social and economic gains. Taken together, increasing wealth and its more equitable distribution mean that not only has it been possible to spend mounting sums for education but, also, that the doors of educational opportunity have been opened wider for an increasing number of youth.

Implications of the Changing Economy for Social and Educational Policy

The summary overview presented in the preceding paragraphs should have served to make clear certain fundamental generalizations with respect to the changing character of the American economy. The concentration of economic power in the hands of a few large corporations is strikingly evident. In certain segments of the economy price competition still persists and prices are determined by supply and demand through the operation of the market mechanism. In many other segments of the economy, however, and in the more important segments, prices determined by free competition in the open market have been, to a marked degree, superseded by administered prices. In these segments of the economy competition tends to be expressed in advertising, packaging, design, and styling. The net result is that for some decades we have been moving away from an economy that operated more or less automatically to an economy that is more and more administered. A self-adjusting economy has been giving place to one that is being planned and controlled.

It is of the highest importance that in some manner the economy be given deliberate, conscious, intelligent direction and control. Decision-making with respect to economic policy must be placed high on the agenda of American democracy. And in a democracy decision-making in such an important area as the economy cannot be left entirely to the discretion of individual leaders in industry, labor, agriculture, and government. In the long run, the leaders' decisions must grow out of popular consensus and this consensus must be enlightened — it must rest upon an intelligent grasp of the issues involved. Herein lies one of the greatest challenges that face education today.

Questions and Problems for Study and Discussion

1. Compare and contrast the conditions of our economic life in 1890 and 1960. Show the influence of changing conditions on the transfer of educational functions from home and community to school and college. Do you think the transfer has been too great?

2. What relation do you see between the changing pattern of economic life and the problems of curriculum organization in American schools and colleges since 1865? Do you think the existing curriculums need to be modified to meet the changing conditions of our economic life?

3. Show how education for effective citizenship has been affected by the rise of the large corporation and the concentration of economic power; by the limitation of competition in the labor market; by price regulation in agriculture.

4. Show how the changing conditions of our economic life have affected the status of youth in our society. What educational changes have been made, and what changes do you think should be made in the future, to enable youth to adjust better to the changed status?

Selected References for Further Reading

Adams, Walter, and Gray, Horace M. *Monopoly in America.* New York: The Macmillan Co., 1955. Pp. xv + 221.

Adelman, M. H. "The Measurement of Industrial Concentration," *The Review of Economics and Statistics,* XXXIII (November, 1951), 269–296.

Allen, Frederick Lewis. *The Big Change.* New York: Harper & Brothers, 1952. Pp. xi + 308.

Arnold, Thurman W. *Democracy and Free Enterprise,* The Baxter Memorial Lecture Delivered at the University of Oklahoma. Norman, Okla.: University of Oklahoma Press, 1942. Pp. 81.

Beard, Charles A., and Beard, Mary R. "The Triumph of Business Enterprise, pp. 166–210 in *The Rise of American Civilization, II: The Industrial Era.* New York: The Macmillan Co., 1927. Pp. 828.

Becker, Carl L. *Modern Democracy.* New Haven, Conn.: Yale University Press, 1941. Pp. 100.

Berle, Adolph A., Jr. *The 20th Century Capitalistic Revolution.* New York: Harcourt, Brace and Company, 1954. Pp. 192 (also published in paperback: New York: Harcourt, Brace & Co. [Harvest Books], 1960).

Berle, Adolph A., Jr., and Means, Gardiner C. *The Modern Corporation and Private Property.* New York: The Macmillan Co., 1932. Pp. xiv + 396.

Bernheim, Alfred L. *Big Business: Its Growth and Place.* New York: Twentieth Century Fund, 1937. Pp. xvi + 102.

Burns, Arthur Robert. *The Decline of Competition: A Study of the Evolution of American Industry.* New York: published under the auspices of the Columbia University Council for Research in the Social Sciences by McGraw-Hill Book Co., 1936. Pp. xiv + 620.

Cochran, Thomas C., and Miller, William. *The Age of Enterprise: A Social History of Industrial America.* New York: The Macmillan Co., 1942. Pp. x + 394 (revision also published in paperback: New York: Harper & Brothers [Torchbooks], 1961).

Colm, Gerhard, and Geiger, Theodore. *The Economy of the American People.* Washington, D.C.: National Planning Association, 1958. Pp. xvii + 167.

Concentration in American Industry, Report of the Subcommittee on Antitrust and Monopoly to the United States Senate, Eighty-fifth Congress, First Session. Washington, D.C.: Government Printing Office, 1957. Pp. viii + 756.

Dewhurst, J. Frederick, and Associates. *America's Needs and Resources: A New Survey.* New York: The Twentieth Century Fund, 1955. Pp. xxix + 1148.

Dennison, H. S., and Galbraith, J. K. *Modern Competition and Business Policy.* New York: Oxford University Press, 1938. Pp. 120.

Dimock, Marshall E. *Business and Government,* Third Edition. New York: Henry Holt and Company, 1957. Pp. xiv + 559.

Drucker, Peter F. *America's Next Twenty Years.* New York: Harper & Brothers, 1957. Pp. 114.

Drucker, Peter F. *Landmarks of Tomorrow.* New York: Harper & Brothers, 1959. Pp. xii + 270.

Edwards, Corwin D. *Big Business and the Policy of Competition.* Cleveland, Ohio: The Press of Western Reserve University, 1956. Pp. x + 180.

Federal Trade Commission. *Report on Concentration of Productive Facilities, 1947.* Washington, D.C.: Government Printing Office, 1949. Pp. iv + 96.

Federal Trade Commission. *Report on Corporate Mergers and Acquisitions.* Washington, D.C.: Government Printing Office, 1955. Pp. vii + 210.

Federal Trade Commission. *Report on Interlocking Directorates.* Washington, D.C.: Government Printing Office, 1951. Pp. xiv + 496.

Galbraith, John Kenneth. *The Affluent Society.* Boston: Houghton Mifflin Company, 1958. Pp. xii + 288.

Galbraith, John Kenneth. *American Capitalism: The Concept of Countervailing Power,* Revised. Boston: Houghton Mifflin Company, 1956. Pp. xi + 208.

Goldsmith, Selma, *et al.* "Size Distribution of Income Since the Mid-Thirties," *The Review of Economics and Statistics,* XXXVI (February, 1954), 1–32.

Hoover, Glenn (ed.). *Twentieth Century Economic Thought.* New York: Philosophical Library, 1950. Pp. xviii + 819.

Houghton, Harrison F. "The Progress of Concentration in Industry: The Growth of Big Business," *The American Economic Review,* XXXVIII (May, 1948), 72–120.

Kaplan, A. D. H. *Big Enterprise in a Competitive System.* Washington, D.C.: The Brookings Institution, 1954. Pp. xii + 269.

Koontz, Harold, and Gable, Richard W. *Public Control of Economic Enterprise.* New York: McGraw-Hill Book Co., Inc., 1956. Pp. xii + 851.

Means, Gardiner C. *Industrial Prices and Their Relative Inflexibility,* Seventy-fourth Congress, First Session, Senate Document 13. Washington, D.C.: Government Printing Office, 1935. Pp. 38.

Moulton, Harold G. *Controlling Factors in Economic Development.* Washington, D.C.: Brookings Institution, 1949. Pp. xii + 397.

Nourse, Edwin G. *Price-Making in a Democracy.* Washington, D.C.: Brookings Institution, 1944. Pp. x + 542.

Stocking, George W., and Watkins, Myron W. *Monopoly and Free Enterprise.* New York: The Twentieth Century Fund, 1951. Pp. xv + 596.

Temporary National Economic Committee. *Competition and Monopoly in American Industry,* Investigation of Concentration of Economic Power, Monograph 21, Seventy-sixth Congress, Third Session, Senate Committee Print. Washington, D.C.: Government Printing Office, 1941. Pp. xii + 344.

Temporary National Economic Committee. *Final Report and Recommendations of the Temporary National Economic Committee Transmitted to the Congress of the United States,* Seventy-seventh Congress, First Session, Senate Document 35. Washington, D.C.: Government Printing Office, 1941. Pp. x + 784.

Temporary National Economic Committee. *The Structure of Industry,* Investigation of Concentration of Economic Power, Monograph 27, Seventy-sixth Congress, Third Session, Senate Committee Print. Washington, D.C.: Government Printing Office, 1941.

United States National Resources Committee. *The Structure of the American Economy,* Part I: *Basic Characteristics.* A Report Prepared by the Industrial Section under the Direction of Gardiner C. Means, June, 1939. Washington, D.C.: Government Printing Office, 1939. Pp. viii + 396.

13 🌿

The Relation of Government
to the Economy

The effectiveness with which the economy operates is an important factor in determining many of the conditions of American life. When full use is made of human and natural resources, the national income is at a relatively high level, the doors of occupational opportunity for youth swing open more widely and more easily, increased migration from farm to city relieves much of the pressure of population on the land, the farmer shares more equitably in the income, the support of an adequate program of education is easier, the stage is set for cultural-intellectual advance, human association is on a more fraternal basis, the ideal of social mobility is more nearly a reality, and the United States is in a position to exercise a more effective leadership in world affairs. When, in contrast, the economy falters and widespread unemployment develops and persists, a large fraction of the wage earners of the nation have to turn to the government for relief, the profits of business enterprise shrink or disappear altogether, past savings are wiped out in large volume, a youth problem emerges for which no amount of vocational education or guidance is a solution, the financial support of education and other public services is curtailed, personal frustration spreads, and the fear that personal frustration will add up to disastrous social frustration always lurks in the background. Moreover, should the economy be gravely disrupted, not only America's leadership of the free world but the existence of the free world would be threatened. Obviously, one of the main challenges of our generation is to work out a policy system with respect to the economic order which "will make us economically secure and keep us politically free." And perhaps the most complex problem involved in the development of such a policy system is to find an answer to the question, "What is the proper role of government in relation to the economy?"[1]

The working out of an over-all policy program through democratic processes will require much experimentation — and also understanding by the public of the proposed programs. Above all, fundamental decisions will have to be made with respect to the relation of government to the economy.[2]

It has been pointed out by Steiner and others that economic life has always been subject to some form of social control. However, in a simple rural economy like that of the United States a few generations ago, most men built their security on their own farms, shops, or small business concerns. As a rule, the means and tools of production were owned by those who used them. Under such conditions, the spirit of individual self-reliance was strong and the essential role of government was to maintain law and order.[3] Now, conditions are vastly different; most producers are employees, and such security as they have is based mainly on their jobs. It is not surprising, therefore, that, next to the problem of peace or war, unemployment has come to be the major problem of our time. Nor is it strange that the attitude of many has changed with respect to the relation of government to the economy, that many now regard government as the bedrock of their security, relying upon it to maintain the conditions that support full employment or to provide jobs when private industry fails to make them available.

The record discloses that during the closing decades of the nineteenth and the first six decades of the present century the increasing inter-relatedness and interdependence of human affairs created by techno-logical revolution fundamentally changed the role of government in Amer-ican life. Leviathan industry tended inescapably to produce the leviathan state. The old institutions of family, community, church, and state gov-ernment were unable to cope with problems that were no longer local but nation-wide in their sweep. Slowly at first, and later more swiftly, the federal government multiplied its functions and extended its controls. For fifty years before the outbreak of World War II, the expansion of the federal government, measured in terms of civilian employees, proceeded at a rate of about 50 per cent per decade.[4] Between 1939 and 1950 the number of civilian employees of government more than doubled, and, since mid-century the number has increased by some 10 per cent.[5]

The crises created first by the Depression and then by war forced the

[1] Harold Koontz and Richard W. Gable, *Public Control of the Economic Enter-prise* (New York: McGraw-Hill Book Co., Inc., 1956), p. 3.

[2] George E. Steiner, *Government's Role in Economic Life* (New York: McGraw-Hill Book Co., Inc., 1953), p. 386.

[3] *Ibid.*, p. 75.

[4] Harry C. Mansfield, "Government," *American Journal of Sociology*, XLVII (May, 1942), 960.

[5] United States Bureau of the Census, *Statistical Abstract of the United States,*

federal government to assume virtual control of the economic life of the nation. Stimulation and control of the economy were essential to the war effort, and since the end of World War II there has been little disposition to permit government to relinquish responsibility for expansion of the economy, improved standards of living, and a high level of employment. In fact, it is generally recognized that one of our major problems is to work out a configuration of policies that will insure reasonably full employment and at the same time define clearly the relation of the government to the economy.[6]

Few persons would advocate (and perhaps even fewer believe such a course of action possible) the government's ever again assuming the relatively passive role it occupied in the system of national policies inherited from the nineteenth century. The concentration of economic power appears to make this impracticable, if not impossible. The history of Western civilization seems to indicate that the state cannot for long tolerate in the society a power equal to or greater than its own. When the concentration of such power takes place in some other institution, be it church or industry, a struggle between that institution and the state seems certain to ensue. The nature of this struggle in our society was clearly foreseen by Professor Sumner Slichter of the Harvard Graduate School of Business Administration at the height of the prosperity of the nineteen-twenties. Writing in 1928 he said:

> Finally, and perhaps most important of all, large business units, more than any other feature of our economic arrangements, create the problem of the relationship between industry and the state. The history of government shows that whenever powerful extra-political organizations arise, the relationship which shall exist between them and the state becomes a major political issue. It was so in the Middle Ages when the power of the Papacy made the relationship between the church and the state perhaps the supreme political problem. Today the development of huge business enterprises has made the relationship between industry

1961 (Washington, D.C.: Government Printing Office, 1961), p. 396. See also J. Frederic Dewhurst and Associates, *America's Needs and Resources* (New York: The Twentieth Century Fund, 1955), p. 577. The number of federal civilian employees increased 9 per cent during the decade 1950–60. The large increases at all levels — federal, state, and local — are, in part, a function of population growth and are partly attributable to defense efforts. A large part, however, is the result of the expansion of government into new areas.

[6] Unparalleled expansion of national income during the fifties may obscure the fact that unemployment is still a major problem. In 1962 the Census Bureau estimated that 4,543,000 persons (one in eighteen of the total labor force) seeking work were unemployed during the week ending February 18. "In July, 1953, just before the 1953–54 recession, the unemployment rate was 2.6 per cent. Just before the 1957–58 recession the unemployment rate was 4.2 per cent. Just before the 1960–61 recession, the unemployment rate stood at 5.1 per cent." One out of six unskilled laborers was unemployed in February, 1962. (*The New York Times,* Sunday, April 1, 1961).

and the state *the* political issue of the age. It occupies much the same position in modern political life as did the problem of the church and the state in the Middle Ages.[7]

Few would deny that the relationship of the government to the economy is one of the central issues of our time, and all would agree that the relationship has been a changing one. Some regard it as the result of tinkering designed to maintain as nearly as possible the traditional relationship, regardless of the costs. Others point to the increased tempo of government control since the Depression, and, particularly, since World War II, and assert that a revolution has already taken place. Perhaps a vast majority of our citizens have no more than a vague impression of what has occurred. To weigh the possible consequences of alternatives that may present themselves in the future will make demands upon a kind of intelligence upon which we have placed too small a premium.

Education and Economic Policy

Changes in the structure and operational aspects of the economy, together with the new relation of government to the economic order, create for institutionalized education a new and enlarged responsibility. Decisions important for the future of the nation, and for the individuals composing it, will have to be made with respect to economic and social policy, and these decisions should be based upon an adequate knowledge of the issues involved.[8] Secondary schools and colleges, as well as the various agencies of adult education, will fail in their duty if they do not cultivate in the citizenry of the nation an understanding of both the structure and the operation of the economy. This understanding should be adequate to serve as a touchstone to proposed policies, whether they relate to the internal operation of the economy itself or to the relation of the government to the economic order. It is perhaps not an unfair criticism to say that most youth graduating from secondary schools and colleges today have been conditioned psychologically to accept an over-all policy system with respect to the economy that is in fact no longer operative. Many of them have not been made aware, in any real sense, of the choices they must make between conflicting policy systems, nor are they equipped with the understanding and insight required to make an intelligent choice. It is not a proper function of educational institutions to cultivate in youth the acceptance of specific formulas for the solution of economic and political problems or to develop in them allegiance to any

[7] Sumner H. Slichter, *Modern Economic Society* (New York: Henry Holt & Co., 1928), p. 147.

[8] See John Dewey, *The Public and Its Problems* (Chicago: Gateway Books, 1946).

particular over-all policy system. Secondary schools and colleges are places where critical inquiry should be cultivated, where youth should be trained to gather evidence, to balance arguments, and to reach their own conclusions. Certainly it is not too much to expect of our educational institutions that they prepare youth to pass intelligent judgment on important matters of public policy, whether in the area of government or of economy. The need for such judgment is a never-ending one.

The Choice of Policy Systems

As the nineteen-thirties drew to a close, it was clear that if acceptable social goals were to be realized in America, the relation of government to the business community would have to be defined in more consistent terms. Opportunism, *ad hoc* solutions of specific problems, were required to give place to an integrated and internally consistent system of political and economic policies. Leadership in government and business often worked at cross-purposes in the absence of some over-all policy system into which the solutions of specific problems could be meshed. The need of a system of policies was clear, but just what principles or elements should be incorporated in the system was far from clear. Lack of adequate knowledge of the structure and operation of the economy, inability to predict with certainty the outcomes of new policies or proposals, deep-seated prejudices and traditions, vested interests, the dangers involved in any fundamental change in social policy — all these made experimentation in working out a new policy system difficult. And yet experimentation, within the framework of democracy, appeared to offer the only hope of solution.

Although it may be expressed in different ways, one central problem is whether the system of policies that prevailed during the nineteenth century, during the period in which the United States was in the process of becoming the most powerful industrial nation in the world, is incompatible with modern economic life. Certainly only a fraction of the business community now entertains the view that there is no inherent incompatibility, that the old policy system is just as workable in the new as in the old economy. To some, change from the old principles has been the source of economic inefficiency and maladjustment, and if economic progress appears to follow departures from the old principles, it is being purchased at tremendous future costs; the acknowledged impossibility of returning completely to those policies from which we have departed is a warning against further departures. Others take the view that the old system of policies is inconsistent with the new economic structure. But here again there is a cleavage of opinion. Some hold that the structure of the economy should be so modified as to be consistent with older policies. Others are disposed to accept, in the main, the existing economic structure and to insist upon a modification of inherited policies to make them workable under new and changing conditions.[9] The opinion that both the old principles and the new economic structure are hopeless is not without its adherents. To some, at least, socialism is the only alternative. Each of these positions places a fundamentally different emphasis on the role of the political state in the economic life of the nation.

If one is to understand the basis of these differences of opinion, which go to the very heart of one of the most significant problems confronting the American people, one must keep in mind the essential elements of the system of policies inherited from the nineteenth century, as well as the changes that have occurred in the structure and operation of the national economy. As Gardiner Means points out, the three major functions of government in this system of inherited policies are:

(1) To establish conditions conducive to private enterprise by such actions as protecting property, enforcing contracts, and providing a safe money medium;

(2) to ensure reasonable prices by enforcing competition where the latter could be effective and by regulating or operating enterprise in those cases where competition was not regarded as a satisfactory regulatory device;

(3) to supply services which private enterprise could not effectively supply, such as police and fire protection, highways, postal service, and education.[10]

It was asserted that if government performed these functions reasonably well, "and if other matters were left to the initiative of individuals operating through free enterprise," the market mechanism would provide conditions for "reasonably full and effective use of resources."[11]

The major changes that have taken place in the economic system may be summarized, somewhat categorically to be sure, as follows. An economy of many small producers, no one of whom could produce enough to affect prices materially, has given place to an economy in which a few large corporations have come to occupy a dominant position. Diffusion of ownership of industrial enterprise has given place to a high degree of concentration of ownership. In the old economy, control of productive property was usually vested in the hands of those who owned it, but now control and ownership have, to a considerable degree, become separated.

---

[9] See United States National Resources Planning Board, "The Controversy over the Problem of Full Employment," *The Structure of the American Economy,* Part II: *Toward Full Use of Resources,* A symposium by Gardiner C. Means and others, June, 1940 (Washington, D.C.: Government Printing Office, 1940), pp. 9 ff.

[10] *Ibid.,* pp. 9–10.   [11] *Ibid.,* p. 10.

Relatively free competition has given place, in large segments of the economy, to monopolistic or regulated competition. Competitive, flexible prices in many industries, in much of the labor market, and, to a considerable extent, in agriculture, have given place to administered, inflexible prices. In short, what had been essentially a free-enterprise economy has become, to a remarkable degree, an administered economy. The market mechanism has been replaced by administrative decision throughout large segments of the economy.

Those who hold that the inherited system of policies is as workable in the new economy as in the old appear to underestimate, or to ignore, the essential changes that have occurred in the economic life of the nation. A far more realistic position is taken by those who still maintain that the inherited system of policies is workable in a technological society provided certain fundamental changes are made in the economic structure. Among the changes required, the most important is the restoration of free competition. This position implies "that every industry should be either effectively competitive or socialized; that government should plan definitely on socialization of . . . every . . . industry where competitive conditions cannot be preserved."[12] In other words, the state would take vigorous measures to break up many of the large corporations and to prevent associated action in any form which aimed at the restraint of trade. Apparently this position would also require withholding from labor organizations the right to maintain rigid wage scales as well as abandoning the policy of enacting legislation aimed at keeping farm prices at a noncompetitive level. If all the rigidities in the economic structure erected by industrialists, labor, and farmers to restrict competition were removed, the market mechanism could again be relied on to coordinate the myriad of relationships involved in the processes of production and distribution of goods and services.

Obviously, a decision to atomize American economic life to the point necessary to bring about free competition and a flexible price structure would require an exercise of governmental power far in excess of any that has ever been employed in times of peace. The state has so long neglected the positive exercise of the authority required to maintain free competition, and the concentration of economic power has become so great, that many despair of the possibility of carrying through "a positive program of laissez faire." The road to free competition in the American economy appears to lead through so much government restraint as to put in jeopardy the heritage of individual freedom. Moreover, many are fearful of the economic and social losses and dislocations which such a policy might well entail. To many it appears that a society of numerous

12 Henry C. Simons, *A Positive Program for Laissez Faire: Some Proposals for a Liberal Economic Policy*, Public Policy Pamphlet 15 (edited by Harry D. Gideonse) (Chicago: University of Chicago Press, 1934), p. 18.

small producers would find it impossible to make full use of technological gains. And finally, and perhaps most important, is the belief on the part of many that the old mechanisms relied on in a strictly free-enterprise economy would prove inadequate under the conditions of modern economic life. The question has been pointedly raised: "Is there sufficient sensitivity of goods, prices, wage rates, unit profits, and interest rates to allow the mechanisms underlying the inherited system of policies to work effectively?"[13] More specifically, as Gardiner Means puts it:

> Could the railroads be operated on a basis of quick readjustments in freight rates and wage rates whenever the traffic in one commodity or another fell off or when total traffic declined or expanded? Could the telephone system be operated on the basis of frequent short-run readjustments in rates with changes in the volume of messages being handled? Could automobile production be organized as efficiently as it is, if it were made so competitive that prices closely followed the fluctuation in orders, going down sharply whenever orders showed a tendency to fall off and rising sharply with rising demand? Could labor be sure of its share in total production, if in dealing with big corporate enterprise it was not able to resort to collective bargaining and fixed wage agreements, which in turn help to fix the labor costs of products for short periods of time? When two hundred corporations control approximately half of the industrial wealth of the country and nearly two-thirds of the land, buildings, and equipment that are owned by nonfinancial corporations, it is hardly reasonable to expect the type of competition which will produce that high degree of price sensitivity which is so typical of an agricultural economy such as characterized this country seventy-five or one hundred years ago.[14]

Of course, the answer to these queries on the part of those who insist on a positive program of laissez faire is that it is the duty of government to establish and maintain that degree of competition necessary to insure adequate price, wage, and interest-rate short-run sensitivity. But, as we have seen, to many such a policy appears impracticable because of political, technological, and economic considerations.

Economists and leaders in the business community who are disposed to accept the existing structure of the American economy and who feel the necessity of devising a new system of policies that will prove workable are divided roughly into two groups: (1) those who believe that the formulation and implementation of the new system of policies is the primary responsibility of the leaders of the business community; (2) those who look to government to play an important role in the development and execution of the new system of policies. Many members of the first group

[13] United States National Resources Planning Board, *op. cit.*, p. 14.
[14] *Ibid.*, p. 15.

are fearful of the future of private enterprise in America unless industrialists, labor leaders, and farm leaders are willing to abandon the policy of restricting production in the interest of their special groups and to place the general welfare above individual profit. But they are not without faith in both the ability and the inclination of persons in key positions in the economy to rise to a high level of economic statesmanship and to devise a system of policies that will work as satisfactorily as the old automatic mechanisms of an earlier day. The following quotations, one from a statement of an industrial leader and the other from a book by an economist, represent the point of view of those who look to the good will and the intelligence of the business community as the source of a new workable system of policies. Said the industrial leader:

> The financial and managerial components of our Free Enterprise System must prove, by deeds as well as by words, their full comprehension of their social responsibilities — their deep sense of public service — and their unmatched capacity to positively plan — to put into effect — and, if you will, to police by self-imposed rules, a constitution for industrial and commercial progress acceptable to the majority of our people — people whose economic security and destiny are vitally affected by the decisions of these controlling components of the system. And in the circumstances surrounding us today, who will doubt that this action must be prompt and positive, and of a character which will demonstrate, beyond the chance of successful challenge, that the public-spirited people administering private enterprise inherently and actually excel the people comprising political organizations — no matter how sincere the intentions of the latter may be — as instrumentalities for insuring an ever-increasing measure of economic freedom and security for all the people — save the indolent — all of the time?[15]

Doctor Edwin G. Nourse, in his *Price Making in a Democracy*, expressed much the same point of view:

> The executives of these corporate enterprises constitute a small class of economic administrative agents who accept — indeed seek — the responsibility of directing the private enterprise system. . . .
>
> They may interpret free enterprise in the aristocratic sense of maximum freedom for the strong, clever, or ruthless rather than the democratic sense of maximum assurance that each individual will have opportunity to express his personal enterprise as willingness to work according to his talents, however small. They may administer it in the aristocratic sense of progressive accumulation of ownership control in the hands of a

---

[15] Charles E. Wilson, Address before the American Institute of Electrical Engineers, January 29, 1941, as published in the *American Magazine* (November, 1941), and quoted in Edwin G. Nourse, *Price Making in a Democracy* (Washington, D.C.: Brookings Institution, 1944), p. 142.

functional group which tends to divert subsequent gains largely to itself. Modern industrialism builds up a class of professional managers — by no means identical with the ownership group — who may seek tenure of office by following unreservedly the dictates of the proprietary group. Or they may adopt policies designed to accelerate activity and maximize efficiency of the whole population. To do so implies that their own re-muneration shall be established in an open supply-and-demand market for managerial talent. It implies that capital shall find its return at the level which will just maintain plant in the volume which will be fully utilized and in the quality which will keep step with advancing techno-logical knowledge. Similarly, property values must find their level in conformity with the rate of capitalization and the earnings that result from full-scale use of labor. . . .

It is our belief that private enterprise thus organized and operated affords the most efficient scheme for carrying on the economic life of a free people. Opening the gates of production and exchange to assure product and letting valuation adjust itself freely to such activity would promote successful private capitalism. Withholding productive effort as a means of protecting predetermined valuations shrinks the total national dividend from which all must draw their shares, and thus in the end defeats the whole system.[16]

Others who are seeking a system of policies that will fit the conditions of modern economic life would assign to government a much larger role in policy formation. They accept the fact that a free-enterprise economy in the old sense has given place, in very large measure, to an adminis-tered economy; they still look to individual enterprise for the major part of actual production, but they regard it as a responsibility of government to determine, or at least to participate in determining, the general frame-work of policies within which private initiative is to operate.[17] In other words, both the public interest and the effective operation of the economy require that government play an important part in giving direction to the economic life of the nation. Since the old mechanisms of automatic adjustment have, in large measure, given place to administrative decision, it is essential that government take part in determining what the decisions should be. To quote Harvey C. Mansfield:

The administrative state is, in fact, the political response to the eco-nomic problems of a technological civilization. Interdependence means organization if social goals are to be attained, and a redefinition of free-dom if equality is still to be sought. In a policy of universal suffrage the equalitarian demand of common men that their basic material needs be provided for is irresistible; and democratic government consequently

[16] Nourse, *op. cit.*, pp. 141, 143–144.

[17] Marshall E. Dimock, *Free Enterprise and the Administrative State* (University, Ala.: University of Alabama Press, 1951), Chap. V.

cannot do else than turn increasingly to the regulation of economic affairs, blundering to competence as it goes and lucky if it manages to preserve the essential personal freedoms of thought and expression that dignify human life.[18]

Finally, socialism affords still another possible choice among policy systems. But socialism is commonly regarded as being foreign to the American way of life and its advocates have never been very numerous.

We face the problem of choosing from among a number of over-all policy systems within the framework of which our economy must be built. The various economic systems resulting from acceptance of one or another of these over-all policy systems may be described as follows:

(1) A free-enterprise economy in which the old automatic mechanisms could be relied upon to coordinate the relationships involved in economic activity. Government would adopt a laissez faire attitude with respect to the operations of economic life, but it would be forced to play a positive role in maintaining the conditions under which free enterprise could in fact operate.

(2) An economy in part free-enterprise and in part socialistic. The government would undertake to establish and maintain free competition in as many areas of economic life as possible but it would take over and operate all industries in which it proved impossible or impracticable to enforce free competition.

(3) An essentially administered economy, one in which the old automatic mechanisms would be largely replaced by human judgments, the judgments to be made in the main by corporation executives and others in key positions in the economic life of the nation, with a minimum of cooperation with, or "interference" by, government.

(4) An essentially administered economy, but with government playing an important role in policy formation.

(5) A socialistic economy, with government, of course, playing a dominant role.

It is important, in order to avoid too great confusion and working at cross-purposes, that the solution of specific problems be approached with some over-all policy system in mind. Opportunistic and *ad hoc* solutions can be relied on only as temporary expedients. National economic policy should have internal consistency and should conform to the actualities of economic life. If, as it appears, the old policy system is being, or has been, to a considerable degree abandoned, it is unwise to nurse the illusion that such is not the case. If a new policy is to be worked out, decisions

[18] Mansfield, *op. cit.*, p. 960. More recently, Koontz and Gable have pointed out that *whether* government should control the economy is an academic question, and that the questions to be faced by an intelligent citizenry today are: "In what areas, to what extent, and in what ways should government control the economic system?" (*op. cit.*, p. 19).

must be made with deliberation and full knowledge of the possible consequences. It is of special importance that the youth who will be called upon in their adult years to choose among policy systems be intellectually equipped for the task. Herein lies a major responsibility of the American school and college, and herein lies our hope for the future of democracy.

Questions and Problems for Study and Discussion

1. It has been stated by Koontz and Gable that since the beginning of recorded history it has been too late to ask *whether* government should exercise control over the economy. Give examples of government controls over aspects of the economic life in different periods of Western history — ancient Greece, Rome, the Middle Ages, etc.

2. In the United States, government has participated increasingly during the last three or four generations in the area of economic life. How do you account for this increase in government participation?

3. It has been stated that the defining of the role of government in the economy is and will continue to be a major problem of public policy in this country. Do you agree or disagree? Defend your position.

4. Make a clear statement of the functions of government in the economy of a laissez faire society and of a thoroughgoing socialistic state. What is the basis for the rejection by the American people of laissez faire? Of socialism?

5. Indicate the nature of the choices relating to the economy which the American people must make.

6. Define the kind of economic system you would advocate. Show how the acceptance of this kind of system by the people generally would affect the social studies curriculum in school and college.

Selected References for Further Reading

Arnold, Thurman W. *Democracy and Free Enterprise, The Baxter Memorial Lecture Delivered at the University of Oklahoma.* Norman, Okla.: University of Oklahoma Press, 1942. Pp. 81.

Arnold, Thurman W. *The Folklore of Capitalism.* New Haven, Conn.: Yale University Press, 1937. Pp. viii + 400. Also published in paperback (New Haven, Conn.: Yale University Press, 1959).

Clark, John M. *Social Control of Business,* Second Edition. New York: McGraw-Hill Book Co., 1939. Pp. xvi + 538.

Colm, Gerhard, and Geiger, Theodore, with the assistance of Manuel Helzner. *The Economy of the American People,* Planning Pamphlet 102. Washington, D.C.: National Planning Association, 1958. Pp. viii + 167.

Dimock, Marshall E. *Business and Government,* Third Edition. New York: Henry Holt and Company, 1957. Pp. xiv + 559.

Edwards, Corwin D. *Big Business and the Policy of Competition.* Cleveland, Ohio: The Press of Western Reserve University, 1956. Pp. x + 180.

Fabricant, Solomon, assisted by Robert E. Lipsey. *The Trend of Government Activity in the United States Since 1900.* New York: National Bureau of Economic Research, 1952. Pp. xix + 267.

Fainsod, Merle, Gordon, Lincoln, and Palamountain, Joseph C., Jr. *Government and the American Economy.* New York: W. W. Norton & Company, Inc., 1959. Pp. xv + 996.

Heilperin, Michael A. *Economic Policy and Democracy,* Public Policy Pamphlet 37. Chicago: University of Chicago Press, 1943. Pp. iv + 40.

Koontz, Harold, and Gable, Richard W. *Public Control of Economic Enterprise.* New York: McGraw-Hill Book Co., Inc., 1956. Pp. xii + 851.

Landauer, Carl. *Theory of National Economic Planning.* Berkeley and Los Angeles: University of California Press, 1944. Pp. 190.

Lippincott, Benjamin E. (ed.). *Government Control of the Economic Order: A Symposium.* Minneapolis, Minn.: University of Minnesota Press, 1935. Pp. viii + 119.

Lyon, Leverett S., *et al. Government and Economic Life: Development and Current Issues of American Public Policy.* 2 vols. Washington, D.C.: Brookings Institution, 1939.

Mansfield, Harry C. "Government," *American Journal of Sociology,* XLVII (May, 1942), 958–970.

Maurer, Herrymon. *Great Enterprise: Growth and Behavior of the Big Corporation.* New York: The Macmillan Co., 1955. Pp. 303.

Nourse, Edwin G. *Price-Making in a Democracy.* Washington, D.C.: Brookings Institution, 1944. Pp. x + 542.

Orton, William. *The Economic Role of the State.* Chicago: University of Chicago Press, 1950. Pp. x + 192.

Simons, Henry C. *A Positive Program of Laissez Faire: Some Proposals for a Liberal Economic Policy,* Public Policy Pamphlet 15. Chicago: University of Chicago Press, 1934. Pp. iv + 40.

Smithies, Arthur, *et al. Economics and Public Policy,* Brookings Lectures, 1954. Washington, D.C.: Brookings Institution, 1955. Pp. xii + 157.

Steiner, G. A. *Government's Role in Economic Life.* New York: McGraw-Hill Book Co., Inc., 1953.

Stocking, George W., and Watkins, Myron W. *Monopoly and Free Enterprise.* New York: The Twentieth Century Fund, 1951. Pp. xv + 596.

White, Leonard D. (ed.). "Future of Government in the United States," *Essays in Honor of Charles E. Merriam.* Chicago: University of Chicago Press, 1942. Pp. x + 274.

Wilcox, Clair. *Public Policies Towards Business.* Homewood, Ill.: Richard D. Irwin, Inc., 1955. Pp. 898.

14

The Expansion of the Educational Enterprise

The development of American educational institutions has been profoundly affected by social changes, some of the most important of which have been discussed in the preceding chapters. These changes have been responsible, at least in part, for the expansion of the educational enterprise to include within its services most children and youth, as well as large numbers of the adult population; for the enrichment of the curriculum; for the long-continued efforts to order the educational program so as to give it system and coordination; for the evolution of new types of structural organization; for the altered relations of government to education; and for the improvement of the quality of instruction through the systematic and scientific study of education and the more effective preparation of teachers. These aspects of the history of American education during the past century will be treated in this and the following chapters.

Social Forces and the Expansion of the Educational Enterprise

For a number of decades following the Civil War, home and community life outside the school continued to provide youth with the larger part of the experiences required to prepare them for competent citizenship. The Civil War had been a disturbing influence and had retarded educational development in both North and South. The closing decades of the nineteenth century, however, witnessed the beginnings of an educational expansion that was truly phenomenal. It is no exaggeration to say that no other nation in the world ever developed an educational system so extensive and so freely open to its youth as that which has taken form in the United States. Of the many forces other than the expansion of the population responsible for this remarkable development, special attention should be given to (1) the growth of an industrial economy, (2) the increase in the nation's ability to finance education, and (3) the growing sensitivity on the part of society to the needs of children and youth.

The Shift from an Agricultural to an Industrial Economy

In a little more than two generations America was transformed from a nation having a simple rural economy into one of the greatest industrial nations in the world. The urbanization of the population that accompanied the industrial growth and which serves as a rough index of it was traced in an earlier chapter.[1] From such analyses it may be deduced that the growth of towns and cities is not a new phenomenon.[2] However, gigantic increases in the urban population — e.g., 8,000,000 for each decennium, 1880–1900, with much smaller increments of rural population (less than 5,000,000 for each of the two decades) — were a phenomenon not observed until late in the nineteenth century.[3] During the century beginning in 1860, the urban population increased seventeen fold or more while the rural population (rural-farm and rural-nonfarm) increased less than two and one-half fold.[4] The growth of urban population and the increasing differentials in urban-rural growth have been among the most important factors in creating social and educational problems. But it was the cities, created or greatly enlarged by the growing industrialism, that were, in the main, to lead the way in remaking our educational program and in extending education to increasing numbers of children and youth.[5]

Although the urban dwellers of the nation did not outnumber the rural population until the period of World War I,[6] the change was foreshadowed during preceding decades by the tremendous increase in urban dwellers and the loss of rural population in many parts of the nation, notably in the North Atlantic states. By 1890 or even a decade earlier, thousands of abandoned farms and numerous deserted villages in New

[1] See Chapter 11; also J. Frederic Dewhurst and Associates, *America's Needs and Resources* (New York: Twentieth Century Fund, 1955), *passim*.

[2] See United States Bureau of the Census, *Historical Statistics of the United States, 1789–1945* (Washington, D.C.: Government Printing Office, 1949); United States Bureau of the Census, *Statistical Abstract of the United States, 1961* (Washington, D.C.: Government Printing Office, 1961).

[3] *Historical Statistics of the United States, 1789–1945, op. cit.,* p. 30.

[4] See *Ibid.,* p. 29; also *Statistical Abstract of the United States, 1961, op. cit.,* p. 23.

[5] See Arthur Meier Schlesinger, *The Rise of the City, 1878–1899* (New York: The Macmillan Co., 1933).

[6] *Statistical Abstract of the United States, 1961, op. cit.,* p. 23.

England were mute witnesses of the devastation wrought by the city's conquest. Cities and towns, not only in the East but in the Middle West and other areas as well, drew off large numbers of the rural population, which had been made excessive by changed patterns of farming, the inability of farm owners to compete with western stock raisers and grain growers, and the relatively high rate of natural increase which characterized the rural population.[7] Also, the industrial cities attracted and retained a vast majority of the millions of immigrants who poured into the United States during the last decade of the nineteenth century and the first decade of the twentieth.

Life in the developing industrial towns and cities was in many ways different from what it had been on the farms and in the rural villages. The urban community did not offer outside the school the educational experiences that the old rural community had afforded. In preindustrial America literacy was the main goal of the schools. In those days the typical American community was the semi-isolated village or town surrounded by its farms, rural schools, and churches. Most of the activities of life were comparatively simple and could be learned best by direct participation. In home, in field, in church, in village shops, and in political and other community meetings, children and youth were inducted into the ways of adult life. But with the development of urban industrial communities, the conditions surrounding children and youth were vastly changed. The old carriers of the most worthwhile educational experiences began to function poorly or not at all. Cities grew up and took form primarily to accommodate the demands of production and exchange, with little or no regard for the requirements of childhood. Inescapably, the responsibilities of institutionalized education were vastly expanded. More and more the school had to become the carrier of the experiences regarded as necessary for the socialization of youth, whether in the area of manners and morals, health, recreation, vocation, or civic behavior. Urbanization meant not only an increase of education through vicarious experiences but also a longer period of formal schooling.

In still other ways the shift from an agrarian to an industrial economy contributed to the expansion of institutionalized education. The successful operation of the economy now required mastery of an imposing volume of new knowledge and an array of new skills and techniques. Division of labor multiplied occupations by the thousands. Many new professions, and even more semiprofessions, developed. The pattern of life produced by industrialism was far more complex and at the same time more highly integrated than it had been in the old days, and it stimulated the opening up of new avenues of knowledge in the social as

[7] Schlesinger, *op. cit.*, pp. 68–70. Between 1880 and 1890 population declined in 62 per cent of New England's 1502 townships, in 59 per cent of Ohio's 1316 townships, and in 56 per cent of the 1424 townships of Illinois.

well as the natural sciences. Sociologists, economists, political scientists, psychologists, psychiatrists, and physicians all produced new knowledge with respect to human behavior that the educational program could not ignore. The problems of social policy became amazingly complex. The workings of social, economic, and political arrangements could no longer be comprehended by the simple processes of observation and participation. If they were to be comprehended at all, they had to be comprehended through some form of institutional study: thus the decline in the importance of home, community, and church as educational agencies, and the crowding into school and college of an increasing percentage of our young people.

The Increase in Ability to Finance Education

Two forces in industrial America, (1) the changing age structure of the population and (2) the increasing wealth of the nation, have operated to make it less difficult to support an expanding educational program. The trend toward a relatively smaller population of children and youth permitted succeeding generations to spend increasingly more for the education of each child without necessarily devoting to education a larger share of the social income.[8] Perhaps even more important, technological improvements continued throughout the entire period to result in a rapid increase in the productivity per worker and a substantial rise in real income of the nation. Between the onset of the Civil War and the beginning of World War II the ratio of youth to adults declined 50 per cent and the real income per worker nearly quadrupled.

After 1940 a tremendous upsurge in the birth rate reversed a trend that had existed, with only minor fluctuations, throughout the nation's history. Children, who in relation to the adult population had steadily declined

[8] The number of children and youth under eighteen years of age per thousand adults aged twenty to sixty-nine declined from approximately one thousand in 1860 to slightly under five hundred in 1940. See Newton Edwards, *Equal Educational Opportunity for Youth: A National Responsibility*, A Report to the American Youth Commission (Washington, D.C.: American Council on Education, 1939), pp. 16–17. In 1870, the group aged five to seventeen constituted 30.3 per cent of the total population. Corresponding per cents for 1930, 1940, 1950, and 1960 were 25.8, 23.0, 20.3, and 24.5 respectively. See United States Office of Education, "Statistics of State School Systems: 1957–58," p. 18 in *Biennial Survey of Education in the United States, 1956–58* (Washingon, D.C.: Government Printing Office, 1961); also, United States Office of Education, *Preliminary Statistics of State School Systems, 1959–60*, Circular No. 663, July, 1961 (Washington, D.C.: Government Printing Office, 1961), p. 5. The long decline in the birth rate of the American people was reflected in the decrease from 714 in 1860 to 342 in 1940 in the number of children under five years of age per thousand women aged sixteen to sixty-four. See Warren S. Thompson, *Population Problems*, Third Edition (New York: McGraw-Hill Book Co., 1942), p. 256.

in number, became increasingly a more important element of the population as heretofore unprecedented numbers were born annually. In 1940 there were about ten and one-half million children under five years of age; some fifteen years later, children in this age group numbered more than eighteen million. By the close of the 1950's, the number of children under five years of age approximated twenty million. As age groups approximating four million continued to reach school age down to the sixties and the number of births showed no decline, it became increasingly apparent that for many years to come the educational task would be of larger dimensions than had ever been experienced or previously anticipated.[9]

Accompanying the increase in the number of children born after 1940, there was an unprecedented rise in national income, which continued throughout the fifties, an increase from $81,634 million in 1940 to more than $400,000 million in 1960.[10]

So great has been the increase in national income that in spite of the tremendous growth in child population American society was not severely threatened in its capacity to provide expanded educational facilities, to extend the curriculum, and to improve the quality of instruction.

Growing Sensitivity to the Needs of Children and Youth

One of the most significant changes in our society during the past two or three generations has been the growing sense of social responsibility for children and youth. This increased sensitivity to the demands of childhood has been reflected in child-labor laws, and in a changing attitude toward childhood and youth as a period of growth and development.

In the early days of industrial development in New England, children made up a very large part of the labor force employed in factories.

[9] Between 1915 and 1940, the crude birth rate (corrected for underregistration) declined from 29.5 to 19.4. The rate increased to 24.1 in 1950. Throughout the fifties the rate approximated 25, declining or fluctuating to 23.6 in 1960. *Statistical Abstract of the United States, 1961, op. cit.,* p. 50.

[10] *Ibid.,* p. 303. The Council on State Governments estimated that the per capita income increased from $569 to $807 (both figures in 1939 dollars), or approximately 42 per cent, between 1940 and 1950. See *Washington Legislative Bulletin,* No. 105, June 17, 1952 (Chicago: The Council on State Governments).

Per capita personal income in both 1930 and 1940 was less than in 1920, but in 1950 per capita personal income before taxes was 50 per cent larger than in 1920 (1913 dollars). Per capita disposable personal income (after taxes) in comparable dollars increased 31 per cent between 1950 and 1958. See Research Division, N.E.A., *Economic Status of Teachers in 1958–59,* Research Report 1959–R3 (Washington, D.C.: N.E.A., May, 1959), p. 13; also United States Department of Health, Education, and Welfare, *Progress of Public Education in the United States of America, 1959–60* (Washington, D.C.: Government Printing Office, 1961), p. 17.

Throughout the nation the industrial expansion of the closing decades of the nineteenth century drew into gainful employment a considerable percentage of children between the ages of ten and fifteen. Children in this age group who were gainfully employed increased from approximately 13 per cent in 1870 to 18 per cent in 1890, from which level the percentage did not decline until after 1910.[11]

The employment of children in factories turned out to be something very different, insofar as the effect on the children themselves was concerned, from their working part-time on the family farm. It is not surprising, therefore, that during the closing decades of the last century a strong sentiment began to develop in favor of excluding children and youth from industry and in favor of providing for them expanded educational opportunities. This growing consciousness of the evils of child labor was reflected in legislation prohibiting children of certain ages from working in factories.

Many different conditions and motives stimulated the movement to exclude children from gainful employment. The humanitarian motive was perhaps the strongest. Organized labor commonly supported restrictions on the employment of children, in part because child labor competed with adult labor and in part because of genuine humanitarian interest. A social and economic structure was developing that made it more difficult to utilize the productive energy of young persons. As children and youth became relatively less numerous, the responsibility for carrying forward the productive work of the world was assumed more and more by the older elements of the population. The introduction of more complicated machinery into manufacturing operations tended to make the employment of children less desirable and in many instances positively disadvantageous. In some cases industrial management groups not only dispensed with child labor voluntarily, but even urged uniform legislation prohibiting the employment of children. The net result of the operation of all these forces was the rapid decline of child labor after about 1910. By 1930 the percentage of gainfully employed boys and girls ten to fifteen years old was only one-fourth as large as it had been two decades earlier, and agriculture was the only major occupation in which persons under sixteen years of age constituted more than 1 per cent of the gainfully employed.[12]

It was a significant fact, too, that even before the Depression of the nineteen-thirties the employment of youth at the upper age levels was declining. The proportion of the gainfully employed among those sixteen years of age declined from 40 per cent in 1920 to 25 per cent in 1930.

---

[11] Edwards, *op. cit.*, p. 9. Approximately one-fourth of the boys ten to fifteen years of age were in gainful occupations in 1890, 1900, and 1910. For the same census dates, the per cents of girls were 10.0, 10.2, and 11.9.

[12] *Ibid.*, p. 17.

During the same period, employment among the seventeen-year-olds de-creased from 50 to 39 per cent. At the onset of the Depression fewer than half of all youths sixteen to nineteen years of age were gainfully em-ployed.[13]

Although state legislation relating to child labor is uneven and the attempts to regulate it by amendment to the federal Constitution have been unsuccessful, the employment of young children, except for limited periods in some agricultural areas in which much seasonal and often transient labor is required, has become a relatively minor social problem.[14]

The general tendency to remove youth from occupational life was, of course, an important factor in expanding the educational enterprise. This exclusion of youth from the work of the world also made defective the existing program of education.

Legislation excluding children from gainful employment was accom-panied by statutory enactments requiring compulsory school attendance. In 1852 Massachusetts passed the first law to be enacted in this country requiring children to attend school. In time other states took similar action, and by 1918 all the states had some kind of compulsory attendance provisions in their statute books. Many of the early statutes were meager in their requirements and were poorly enforced, as indeed some of them still are. Nevertheless, the enactment of compulsory school-attendance legislation marked the modification of a long-established social policy, and it indicated significantly society's growing sense of responsibility for the welfare of youth. Meanwhile, a better understanding of the meaning of infancy made it clear that there are good biological reasons why human infants require a prolonged period of growth and development. Research also revealed something of the problems and processes involved in the in-duction of the individual into his culture. As the needs of childhood be-came better understood, society came to regard the proper education of its youth as one of its most sacred obligations. It came to be recognized, too, that many of the values stressed in an industrial society were unfavorable to the interests of children and that positive measures needed to be taken through formal education to make good the losses with which youth were threatened.

The Popularization of Education

In a previous chapter it was pointed out that during the decades pre-ceding the Civil War substantial progress was made in the development of state school systems. In the North and the West common schools for

---

13 *Ibid.*, pp. 8–9.

14 For an excellent statement concerning the adoption of child-labor and com-pulsory school-attendance legislation, see Edgar W. Knight, *Fifty Years of American Education: A Historical Review and Critical Appraisal* (New York: The Ronald Press Company, 1952), pp. 58–72.

the masses were emphasized and most children attended some kind of school for a longer or shorter period each year. In most rural communities and states in the North and the West, however, the support of education was so meager that maintenance of effective schools was impossible. In 1860 the expenditure per pupil enrolled for all types of education, elementary, secondary, and higher, was less than $5 in Ohio, Indiana, Iowa, Michigan, Minnesota, Maine, and New Hampshire and exceeded $10 in only one state of these sections, Massachusetts ($10.02). Most of the southern states were spending more money per free white person for educational purposes than the northern and western states. In fact, the South spent more per pupil enrolled at all educational levels — elementary, secondary, and higher. The South, as might have been expected from its aristocratic social structure, stressed the development of its colleges and academies to the partial neglect of its elementary schools. In 1860 in most southern states fewer than half the free children of school age were in attendance at any type of educational institution.[15] It is true, however, that the South during the decades preceding the Civil War was making marked progress in the development of its lower schools. In all sections of the country the educational efforts were strikingly similar. An appraisal of education based on measures of actual accomplishment in providing opportunity for the children reveals that, although differences existed in the adequacy of the provisions made by the various states and sections, the differences could be accounted for as easily in terms of the conditions that characterized rural society, both north and south, as in terms of geographical location or social organization.[16] It would be a mistake, however, to say that in any section effective systems of democratic education had been achieved. The battle for free public education may have been won in principle, but much still needed to be done to carry the principle into effective operation.

THE AFTERMATH OF CIVIL WAR AND RECONSTRUCTION, 1865–1890

The Civil War temporarily checked the extensive development of state school systems, but it does not appear to have arrested the expansion of educational opportunities to the extent that has sometimes been supposed. The number of school children five to fifteen enrolled in public schools decreased from 73.2 per cent of the total number of free children in 1860 to 64.8 in 1870. This is not surprising when it is remembered that many Negro children counted as free in 1870 had been slaves ten years

[15] Herman G. Richey, "Reappraisal of the State School Systems of the Pre-Civil-War Period," *Elementary School Journal*, XLI (October, 1940), 121.
[16] Herman G. Richey, "The Persistence of Educational Progress During the Decade of the Civil War. I," *Elementary School Journal*, XLII (January, 1942), 359.

earlier. The number of children (white and Negro) enrolled in all types of schools increased from 82.5 per cent of the total number of white children from five to fifteen years of age in 1860 to 87.0 per cent in 1870.[17] When the decade of the Civil War came to an end, a larger percentage of the nation's children was attending school than had been the case when the war began. Some progress was also made in the support of education. The income of all schools per pupil enrolled (elementary, secondary, and higher) increased from $6.34 in 1860 to $13.23 in 1870.[18] It must not be supposed, however, that many states, if any, had systems of education that were at all adequate. Support of schools was still often meager, teachers were seldom well prepared, and buildings and equipment were usually crude. Large enrollments cannot be taken as evidence of adequate programs of education in states in which expenditure per person enrolled was $5.38, as in Indiana, or $6.80, as in Maine.

The next two decades (1870 to 1890) registered considerable progress, although the social forces that were to bring about a phenomenal expansion of the whole educational enterprise had not yet come into full play (Table 20). The number of children attending public elementary

TABLE 20: INDEX OF EDUCATIONAL PROGRESS BASED UPON
STATISTICS OF SCHOOL ENROLLMENTS, ATTENDANCE,
AND EXPENDITURES, 1871–1890*

Year	1	2	3	4	5	6	7	8	9	10	Index
1871	36.94	48.70	132.10	.42	65.80	15.20	5.62	26.16	5.84	16.11	25.61
1880	40.78	53.10	130.30	.75	66.30	12.71	5.18	22.72	3.61	16.27	25.38
1890	43.97	59.20	134.70	2.49	73.44	17.23	7.58	32.18	5.97	21.03	29.57

1. Per cent of population, 5–17, attending school daily.
2. Average days attended by each child of school age (5–17 years).
3. Average number of days schools were kept open.
4. Per cent that high school attendance was of total attendance.
5. Per cent that boys were of girls in high school.
6. Average annual expenditure per child attending.
7. Average annual expenditure per child, 5–17 years of age.
8. Monthly expenditure (12 months) per teacher employed.
9. Expenditure per pupil in average daily attendance other than teachers' salaries.
10. Average monthly salary (12 months) of teachers.

* Adapted from Leonard P. Ayres, *An Index Number for State School Systems* (New York: Russell Sage Foundation, 1920).

schools increased from about 6,871,000 to 12,519,000, a rate of increase greater than that which characterized the child population of elementary-

[17] *Ibid.*, 365.
[18] Herman G. Richey, "The Persistence of Educational Progress During the Decade of the Civil War. II," *Elementary School Journal*, XLII (February, 1942), 161.

school age. Enrollments in public high schools increased from about 80,000 to 203,000. The percentage of children five to seventeen years of age enrolled in public schools increased from 57.0 to 68.6. In 1871, 37 per cent of the population five to seventeen years of age was attending school daily; in 1890, the corresponding percentage was 44. By 1881, nineteen states and territories, all in the North and the West, had passed compulsory-attendance legislation.[19] The support of the public schools when the nation as a whole is considered, however, showed very little or no improvement. For a full decade following 1877 the average annual expenditure per child attending school was lower than it had been in 1871. The monthly salary of teachers advanced only slightly, from $16 in 1871 to $21 in 1890.[20] The school term was only three days longer in 1890 than in 1871. The index number (based on the ten components in Table 20) for the nation's school system did, however, rise from 25.61 in 1871 to 29.57 in 1890. It should be observed, however, that the index number was no higher in 1881 than it had been in 1871 and that it was not until the late eighteen-eighties that much gain was registered. It is clear, too, that the major gain was in school attendance at both the elementary and high school level.

Educational progress during the period 1865 to 1890 was uneven among the states and sections of the country. The Civil War and Reconstruction created conditions unfavorable to educational development in the South. Before the war most of the southern states were improving their educational status even more rapidly than the western and eastern states, but for many years now the South fell far behind other sections in the rate of its educational progress. When Lee surrendered at Appomattox, the human resources of the South had already been greatly diminished and physical resources had been all but exhausted. A northern historian describes conditions in the South as follows:

> Now wreck, ruin, starvation were on every side. The ground over which the contending armies had fought in Virginia was a waste. . . . The rich Shenandoah Valley had been stripped. Both Federals and Confederates had swept it from end to end repeatedly, the final hand having been Sheridan's. He and his "barnburners" were to render the country such a waste that "a crow could not fly over it without carrying his rations with him." Barns, mills and other buildings were heaps of ashes. A garden had become a desert. The country lying between Washington and Richmond was in the same condition. The villages were represented by solitary chimneys standing over cellars filled with the wreckage of fire. Churches were down, timber had disappeared, farming land, untended, had returned to pasturage. . . . Richmond was a mass of blackened ruins. . . .

[19] Schlesinger, *op. cit.*, p. 161.
[20] Salaries figured on a twelve months' basis.

Sherman's army, on its way to the sea through Georgia and the Carolinas, had swept that part of the South so bare that it was almost without living reminders of human civilization. "You can have no idea of the desolation of this country," wrote a Northern visitor to South Carolina. The stores had been closed since 1861. The roads had known no recent attention and were unfit for teams. The railways had been torn up. The irons were twisted around trees and telegraph poles, and the sleepers had been burned. Everything edible had been eaten, and property had been stolen or destroyed from the Mississippi River to the seaboard. . . . The entire portion of Atlanta devoted to business, barring one block of buildings, had been laid in ruins. . . .

Charleston had been bombarded and burned. It was, said a visitor from the North in September, five months after the war ended, "a city of ruins, of desolation, of vacant houses, of widowed women, of rotting wharves, of deserted warehouses, of weed-wild gardens, of miles of grass-grown streets, of acres of pitiful and voiceless barrenness. . . ."

In Mobile the planks had been torn from the tops of the levees to be burned for firewood. The wharves were rotting in the rain and sun. Buzzards hovered over them in clouds. Half the warehouses and shops were closed. Torpor and decay reigned on every hand. . . .

A New York *Tribune* correspondent found Galveston "a city of dogs and desolation." He thought "no other city of its prominence so utterly insignificant and God-forsaken in appearance." Houses and stores had been sacked, and ruin was written over everything.

So it was on every hand. The serpent slipped through the brush, the owl and the bittern cried over fields in which valuable crops had once been gleaned. . . .

Everywhere the same pitiful story was heard. Carpets were in tatters, or had gone to make army blankets. Pianos, which had not been cut to pieces with axes in the hands of Sherman's "bummers," jangled; they had not been tuned in five years. Clocks had stopped; there were no clockmakers to keep them in repair. Furniture was broken and sat unsteadily on its legs. Windows were uncurtained; the stuffs had been taken down and converted into articles of clothing. Not a complete set of dishes could be seen. Pieces were missing from cups and plates; others were shabbily held together by cement. Many were eating from gourds. Hair and tooth brushes long ago had worn out and the use of them had been abandoned. Pins and needles were so scarce that they were lent about and returned. Few men any longer had pocket knives. Earthern mugs made out of local clays were seen instead of water glasses. When candles ceased to be procurable, light came from cups of pigs' grease with cloth wicks in them. Prongs were broken out of forks. In the hotels there were not enough chairs for the guests. They must sit down in turn. . . .

Everywhere plantations were offered for sale at preposterously low prices. . . . A hundred acres four miles from Macon were offered for fifty cents an acre, and any desired amount of land in that neighborhood could have been purchased for $2 an acre. . . . For the "richest estates" in North Carolina the owners asked from $1 to $10 an acre. . . . Virginia lands, worth $150 an acre before the war, could now be purchased for $2.[21]

The war had shattered the social and economic system of the South and had silenced its voice in the political councils of the nation. The task of shifting from slave to free labor and from a plantation to a small-farm economy was made more difficult by the lack of capital and by the plan of Reconstruction adopted by Congress. Confederate money was, of course, of no value and funds were not available to buy the needed seed, stock, and cattle, or to rebuild houses, barns, and fences. Scarcely anyone had enough to eat while planting and growing a new crop. Under these circumstances southern leaders turned to northern bankers for help, which could be had only at a high price. Southern bankers borrowed money from banks in Baltimore and New York at a high interest rate. They in turn lent money to small-town and village merchants throughout the South, exacting high interest rates in order to pay their northern creditors and to protect themselves against poor collections. The merchants in their turn extended credit to planters and farmers in the form of food, stock, and whatever was required to make a crop. The merchants took liens on the farmers' crops and usually required the farmers to devote most of their energy to the growing of cotton, the only crop for which there was a ready market. To protect themselves against crop failure and to pay the high interest rates exacted by the banks, the merchants charged extremely high prices for whatever they supplied the farmers. When autumn came and the cotton was sold, the merchant collected what was due him, leaving the farmer, more often than not, scarcely enough to live on until the planting season came around. Then the cycle started all over again. In this way the one-crop system was fastened more tightly on the South and the price of cotton dropped sharply as the result of overproduction. In the meantime tariff rates had been raised and southern farmers found themselves paying tribute to northern manufacturers as well as northern bankers. Slowly, however, the South was able to accumulate some capital and by the close of the century an industrial expansion had begun which, aided by northern capital, was to assume major proportions.

In the opinion of some writers the policies adopted by Congress for the Reconstruction of the South proved nearly as disastrous as the Civil War itself. Be that as it may, political life in the South was long characterized by uncertainty, bewilderment, and frustration. One of the main objects of Reconstruction policy was to insure that the southern representatives in Congress would favor a high tariff and other economic measures desired

[21] Ellis Paxson Oberholtzer, *A History of the United States since the Civil War* (New York: The Macmillan Co., 1926), I, pp. 56–62, 72. By permission of Winona McBride Oberholtzer (Mrs. E. P.).

by northern industrial and financial leaders. The Republican Party was to be established in the South and it was to draw its support from the newly enfranchised Negroes and from that part of the native white population which had long had a grievance against the slaveholding whites. The leaders of the Confederacy were disfranchised and the political power of Negroes, native whites (scalawags), and men from the North (carpetbaggers) was buttressed by military force. The new state governments established were commonly extravagant, and corruption and fraud on the part of officials were not infrequent. During the Reconstruction period, the southern state legislatures piled up a debt of more than $300,000,-000,[22] a sum which represented a very large fraction of the total wealth of the region. Unfortunately, most of this money was squandered and not used to rebuild the waste places of the South or to inject new life into the economic system. Irresponsible state legislatures levied taxes that were often confiscatory. In county after county a large fraction of the land was offered for sale to meet the demands of the tax collector.

The withdrawal of federal troops from the South in 1877 and the legal end of Reconstruction by no means restored political tranquillity. The conservative leaders of ante-bellum days, the masses of small farmers (white), and the Negroes all made their bid for political power. After much confusion and bitterness, the leadership of the old conservative elements was discarded, the Negro was virtually disfranchised, and political power came to rest for the first time in the hands of the great mass of white yeomanry.

In the meantime educational development in the South was far from satisfactory, but more progress was made than might have been supposed. Constitutional and statutory provisions were now more specific and mandatory with respect to the maintenance of schools. Perhaps the most notable advance was the increase in the number of children attending school. In North Carolina the number of children enrolled in public schools increased from 49,302 in 1871 to 225,606 in 1880. In South Carolina the increase for the same period was from 67,098 to 134,072; in Georgia, from 39,766 to 236,533; in Kentucky, from 160,446 to 265,581; in Mississippi, from 98,600 to 236,704. For the first time schools in any large number were open to Negro children. By 1890 more than a million Negro children were enrolled in the schools of ten southern states.[23] Available data indicate, however, that in most of the southern states the length of the school term was actually shorter in 1880 than in 1871, as, for example, North Carolina, South Carolina, Mississippi, and Louisiana. Some of the southern states during the decade reg-

[22] Edgar W. Knight, *Education in the United States,* New Edition (Boston: Ginn & Company, 1934), p. 468.
[23] Horace Mann Bond, *The Education of the Negro in the American Social Order* (New York: Prentice-Hall, Inc., 1934), p. 94.

istered material gains in the total expenditures for schools, although some, such as Alabama and Louisiana, were spending less than in 1871. The monthly salary of teachers declined generally throughout the South, as was the case in the nation as a whole.

The cause of public education in the South during the trying days of Reconstruction and later was materially advanced by the benevolence of George Peabody, a native of Massachusetts but at the time a resident of London. In 1867 he established a substantial fund to promote and encourage public education "in those portions of our beloved and common country which have suffered from the destructive ravages, and not less disastrous consequences, of civil war."[24] The fund, under wise leadership, became a powerful influence in the development of state school systems and its work in bringing about better facilities for the education of teachers was felt throughout the South. The period we are now considering (1865 to 1890), however, came to a close with the South lagging far behind the other great sections of the nation in the educational opportunities it was able to afford its children and youth.[25]

RAPID EXPANSION AND EXTENSION OF EDUCATION AFTER 1890

The social forces already described began to make themselves felt in an accelerated rate of educational expansion during the closing years of the nineteenth century. During the decades which followed, the percentage of the nation's children and youth attending school increased rapidly; the school term was lengthened and attendance made more regular; and education was given more adequate financial support.

Between 1890 and the beginning of the Depression decade (1930), public school enrollments (kindergarten through Grade 12) more than doubled, while the number of children aged five to seventeen years increased only about 70 per cent. The number of children in public schools per hundred of the school-age population (five to seventeen years) increased from 68.6 to 81.7, and the number attending public schools daily increased from 44.0 to 67.7 per cent of the number of children in the age group.[26] The school year was extended from 135 to 173 days; and in

24 Edgar W. Knight, *Twenty Centuries of Education* (Boston: Ginn & Company, 1940), p. 91.

25 Leonard P. Ayres, *An Index Number for State School Systems* (New York: Russell Sage Foundation, 1920), pp. 32–33.

26 It should be noted that, in this chapter, enrollment and other statistics are generally for public schools. They must be viewed as only part of the total. The percentage of the nation's children attending non-public schools has increased steadily since World War II. In 1940 the total non-public school enrollment was 2.6 million, or only about 9.3 per cent of the total enrollment. As late as 1958 the total non-public school enrollment was slightly more than 5.2 million, or about 13.5 per cent of the total. On April 14, 1960, the National Catholic Welfare Con-

unadjusted dollars the total expenditures, including capital outlay, per child aged five to seventeen years rose from $7.58 to $68.01 (see Table 21), and the average annual salary of teachers increased from $252 to $1420.[27]

Although the percentage of the school-age population enrolled in schools increased, the public school enrollment declined some 1,244,000 between 1930 and 1940 and an added 323,000 during the following decade. The increase of both school-age population and enrollment was extremely rapid after 1950. By 1960, the population five to seventeen years of age exceeded that of ten years earlier by almost 15,000,000 (up from 30,204,000 to 45,000,000), and public school enrollment (continental United States) had increased from some 25,000,000 to more than 36,000,000 during the same period.[28] It was predicted that the enrollment in public and private schools through Grade 12 (43,690,000 in 1960) would number more than 49,000,000 in 1965.[29] The increase in enrollments has been for years and must continue to be largely the result of an increase in child populations.[30] In spite of the tremendous increase in school enrollment the school year was approximately five days longer in 1960 than it had been in 1930 and the expenditures per child, aged five to seventeen, rose from $68 to about $376 during the thirty-year period.[31]

By 1930 more than 95 per cent of the children aged seven to thirteen years were enrolled in school. The elementary-school enrollments impressively reflected the declining birth rates, as, first, the absolute number of children entering school declined, and, later, the total enrollment dropped. Some 21,279,000 children were enrolled in public elementary schools (kindergarten through Grade 8) in 1930. This number was 2,446,000 in excess of the 1940 enrollment and 1,892,000 larger than that of 1950. Between 1950 and 1960 the (public) elementary-school

---

ference reported that the elementary- and high school enrollment in Catholic schools had reached 5,090,012. Other parochial schools enrolled some 400,000 students in 1959, and for that year public school enrollment was estimated to be a little under 42 million. It was estimated that in 1961 about one-seventh of the nation's school children were enrolled in non-public schools, as compared with about one-eleventh in 1940.

[27] "Statistics of State School Systems: 1957–58," *op. cit.*, p. 18.

[28] United States Office of Education, *Enrollment, Teachers, and School Housing,* Circular No. 634, Fall, 1960 (Washington, D.C.: Government Printing Office, 1960), pp. 1, 12.

[29] *Statistical Abstract of the United States, 1961, op. cit.*, p. 108.

[30] "Statistics of State School Systems: 1957–58," *op. cit.*, p. 18. The enrollment in public schools per hundred of the population, five to seventeen years of age, which increased from 81.7 in 1930 to 84.4 in 1940, did not increase thereafter.

[31] These expenditures are in unadjusted dollars and therefore exaggerate differences. In adjusted dollars, the differences for the thirty-year period would be reduced more than one-third. Also, the more recent expenditures include relatively large amounts for capital outlay.

The first public schoolhouse at Alton, Illinois, in 1866.

The Emerson School, ca. 1860.

Miss Blanche Lamont and school at Hecla, Montana, in 1893.

The nature of educational facilities varied in accordance with local aspirations and financial ability.

Schoolroom in New York's Lower East Side, ca. 1886. Educators were so hard pressed to meet the demands made of public education during the late nineteenth century that facilities, equipment, curricula, and the quality of teaching in many schools left much to be desired.

Brooklyn Public Library, ca. 1900. The interests of young readers were given little attention; children took whichever books the librarians offered them.

Immigrants landing at Castle Garden, New York, late nineteenth century.

Education for immigrants, ca. 1900.

Elmira College, chartered as the Elmira Female College in 1885. The course of study from the beginning was equivalent to those of the best colleges for men.

Higher education expanded remarkably in the 1900's. The ridicule of advocates of practical learning was biting but ineffective.

TABLE 21:
MEASURES OF EDUCATIONAL EXPANSION AND IMPROVEMENTS*

Year	Population 5 to 17 Years of Age		Public School Enrollment		Per Cent of Enrolled Pupils Attending Daily	Average Length of School Term (Days)	Total Expenditures for all Schools, Including Capital Outlay Per Child 5–17 (Unadjusted Dollars)
	Number (Thousands)	Per Cent of Total Population	Number (Thousands)	Per Cent of Number in Population, 5–17			
1889–90	18,543	29.5	12,723	68.6	64.1	134.7	7.58
1899–1900	21,573	28.4	15,503	71.9	68.6	144.3	9.97
1909–10	24,009	26.5	17,814	74.2	72.1	157.5	17.75
1919–20	27,556	26.4	21,578	78.3	74.8	161.9	37.60
1929–30	31,417	25.8	25,678	81.7	82.8	172.7	68.01
1939–40	30,150	23.0	25,434	84.4	86.7	175.0	77.75
1949–50	30,168	20.3	25,111	83.2	88.7	177.9	193.50**
1957–58	40,164	23.6	33,529	83.5	88.6	177.6	337.84**
1959–60	43,928	24.5	36,196	82.4	89.8	—	376.00**

* United States Office of Education, "Statistics of State School Systems: 1957–58," pp. 18–19, Chap. II, in *Biennial Survey of Education in the United States* (Washington, D.C.: Government Printing Office, 1961). See explanatory notes in source. See also *Preliminary Statistics of State School Systems, 1959–60*, United States Office of Education Circular No. 634.

** Relatively large capital outlay.

enrollment increased more than 6,400,000 (from 19,387,000 to 25,-814,000), and in 1960 it was conservatively estimated that the enrollment would approximate 36,000,000 by 1965.[32]

By the fifties, elementary-school enrollment had nearly reached the saturation point in most states. Except for moderate gains in the enrollment of five-year olds, future increases in elementary-school enrollment will be primarily a function of population increase. The elementary school has become the school for all young children.

The growth of the secondary school has been perhaps the most significant phenomenon of American education during the last sixty or seventy years. During the five decades ending in 1930 public secondary-school enrollment doubled five times (110,000 in 1880 to 4,399,000 in 1930). After 1930 the rate of increase declined rapidly. However, even the reduced rate of increase accounted for an absolute gain in enrollment of about 2,202,000 between 1930 and 1940. The large decline in the rate of increase was not, for the most part, the result of a drop in the percentage of youth enrolled. The period had been reached in which enrollment would of necessity be closely related to changes in the size of the school-age population.[33]

Between 1940 and 1950 enrollment in public high schools declined 876,000 (from 6,601,000 to 5,725,000), but as the higher birth rate of the forties made itself felt, enrollment increased about 1,259,000 by 1958. By 1960 the enrollment was more than 9,000,000; and it appears that by 1965 the enrollment will reach 12,000,000.[34]

The willingness on the part of the public to expand facilities to provide for the unprecedented numbers of children and the increase of high school enrollment to approximately five-sixths of the group aged fourteen to seventeen demonstrates that the American people have come to regard the secondary school as the school for all adolescents in much the same way as the elementary school is the school for all young children.

Although the nation as a whole saw rapid expansion of education, progress was uneven and the adequacy of educational facilities varied from state to state and from region to region. However, as the period progressed, the differences between states and regions became less striking than the differences between areas within many individual states. In 1890 the number of children five to seventeen years of age enrolled in public schools, per hundred of the population, ranged from 31.6 in Louisiana to 88.6 in Kansas. Generally the percentages of enrollment were higher in the North Atlantic, Great Lakes, and Plains states than in

[32] *Statistical Abstract of the United States, op. cit.,* p. 107.

[33] "Statistics of State School Systems: 1957–58," *op. cit.,* p. 18.

[34] *Statistical Abstract of the United States, 1959, op. cit.,* p. 107. Public and private school enrollments combined were 4,804,000 in 1930; 7,123,000 in 1940; 6,453,000 in 1950; and about 8,930,000 in 1958. See United States Department of Health, Education, and Welfare, *Progress of Public Education in the United States of America, 1959–60, op. cit.*

the states of the Southeast, the West, and the Southwest. By 1920 the differences among states with respect to enrollment were notably less. In 1961 the Office of Education reported statistics which showed that the percentage of enrollment in 1957–58 was highest in the West and the Southwest and that the median states of the Southeast enrolled 88.7 and 88.9 per cent of the population aged five to seventeen, as compared with 83.5 per cent for the continental United States.[35]

School attendance as well as school enrollment varied greatly from state to state, but the trend was more or less consistent toward greater uniformity among the states. In 1890 the percentage of the school-age population (five to seventeen years of age) attending school daily was highest in the North Atlantic states and lowest in the South and the West. In the North Atlantic states the per cents ranged from 45.3 in New Jersey to 67.2 in Massachusetts; in the South, the range was from 24.2 in Louisiana to 53.5 in Tennessee. In all the New England states, New York, and several southern states the per cents of school age children attending school were smaller in 1900 than in 1890. Even as late as World War I, New Hampshire, Rhode Island, Massachusetts, and Pennsylvania reported smaller per cents of attendance than were reported a generation earlier.[36] The smaller per cents may have resulted, in part, from more accurate reporting of attendance and some of the loss may be attributed to increased private-school enrollments, but non-attendance of upper-age immigrant children was most often noted to account for the decline in attendance, particularly for the decline in the North Atlantic states during a period when attendance was increasing generally throughout the nation. By 1930, greater uniformity in attendance in the various states was easily noted. Near the close of the 1950's, 88.6 per cent of the children enrolled in the public schools of the continental United States were attending school daily. The per cents for the different regions were not greatly different — 88.1 for the North Atlantic, Great Lakes, and Plains States, 87.2 for the Southeast, and 91.4 for the West and Southwest.[37]

Enrollment and attendance obviously have been responding to forces nation-wide in their influence. Everywhere, the percentages of children enrolled and attending have increased tremendously since the turn of the century. In most states, and increasingly within different areas of individual states, enrollment and attendance have approximated the practical maximum.

Not only expanding enrollments but also increasing financial support,

[35] "Statistics of State School Systems: 1957–58," *op. cit.*, pp. 62–63. The enrollment figures upon which the percentages are based are for public schools. A considerable portion (more than 13 per cent) of the nation's children five to seventeen years of age were enrolled in non-public schools in 1960. Non-public school enrollment is a much larger percentage of the total in some states than in others. Historically, it has been much smaller in the South.

[36] Ayres, *op. cit.*, pp. 31, 33, 35, 37.

[37] "Statistics of State School Systems, 1957–58," *op. cit.*, p. 41.

as measured by average expenditures per child of school age, per child enrolled, and per child attending, gave evidence of the progress and expansion of education in the several states and regions. With respect to support, progress was generally persistent after 1900.[38] Differences among states declined to a considerable extent, but it is a significant fact that the southern states were never able to support their educational systems at a level comparable with other sections.

The period which witnessed the rapid expansion of secondary education also witnessed a marked, if somewhat less spectacular, expansion of higher education. Even though college and university enrollments more than quadrupled between 1870 and 1900, fewer than 238,000 students were enrolled at the latter date. Between 1910 and 1940, enrollment again increased fourfold and in the following fifteen years it more than doubled.[39] In 1960 nearly 3,600,000 students were enrolled in higher institutions. Whereas in 1900 only 4 per cent of the youth of traditional college age (eighteen to twenty-one years) were attending colleges and universities, by 1960 the enrollment exceeded one-third of the number in the age group.[40]

Enrollment in higher institutions, which by 1960 had only begun to feel the impact of the increased birth rates of the nineteen-forties, will, barring catastrophic occurrences, rise at a rapid rate throughout the sixties.

College enrollment has during recent decades responded more to conditions created by major events than has that of the elementary and secondary schools. Although during the three decades after 1930 the enrollment in higher institutions nearly tripled and each decade registered large gains, the enrollment in 1933–34 was about 99,000 below that of the preceding year. Between 1939–40 and 1941–42, enrollment dropped nearly 339,000, and, owing to a number of causes, including the declining attendance of veterans and the Korean War, enrollment decreased some 357,000 between 1949–50 and 1951–52.[41]

For the years just preceding World War II, the number of students ad-

[38] In 1890 five states spent less than $5.00 annually per child attending and eight spent less than $2.50 per child of school age. In the same year, nine states spent more than $30 per child attending and twelve states spent more than $12 per child of school age. Seventy years later, current expenditures per child in average daily attendance were $376 for continental United States. Twelve states spent more than $425 and six spent less than $250 per child attending. See "Statistics of State School Systems: 1957–58," pp. 72–73; also "Preliminary Statistics of State School Systems, 1959–60," *op. cit.*

[39] United States Office of Education, "Statistics of Higher Education: 1955–56. Faculty, Students, and Degrees," Chap. 14, Sec. 1, pp. 6–7, in *Biennial Survey of Education in the United States, 1955–56* (Washington, D.C.: Government Printing Office, 1959).

[40] See *Statistical Abstract of the United States, 1961, op. cit.,* p. 108.

[41] *Ibid.,* p. 43. For the enrollment of degree-credit students in relation to population aged 18–21, 1939–60 and projected to 1970, see *Progress of Public Education in the United States, 1959–60, op. cit.,* p. 23.

mitted to college each year approximated 35 per cent of the number of high school graduates of the preceding year. By the early 1950's the number of entering college students each year was slightly less than one-half of the number of students graduating from high school the preceding year.[42]

The annual increase in the number of college graduates has hardly kept pace with the expansion of college enrollments. The number of Bachelor's (or first professional degrees) awarded annually increased from 15,539 in 1890 to 48,622 in 1920 and to 186,000 in 1940. The number graduating was depressed by the war, but returning veterans helped swell the total number of graduates to 433,734 in 1950.[43] After that year, the number of degrees awarded declined to 287,401 in 1954–55, after which the number increased sharply to about 400,000 in 1960.

The number of Master's degrees conferred rose from 1015 in 1890 to 26,731 in 1940, and after the war mounted to 75,700 in 1960. The number of persons receiving doctoral degrees increased from 382 in 1900 to 8903 in 1950 to about 9700 in 1959–60.[44] In 1940 there were 47,000 persons under seventy years of age who held doctoral degrees from American universities. By 1955 the number had doubled, and it is estimated that it will double again by 1970.[45]

The expansion of education — elementary, secondary, and higher — was not the only important educational development of the late nineteenth and the present century. However, it met the most obvious need, and the task that it imposed exhausted, in too many instances, available financial and intellectual resources. The expansion of education and educational facilities to make provision, if too often mediocre provision, for the growing and increasingly more heterogeneous clientele pushed into school by the developing democratic social climate was a necessary step in the direction of realizing the American ideal of equal educational opportunity for all children.

Inequalities of Educational Opportunity

The concept of equal educational opportunity has taken on new meaning within the last two or three generations, but the devotion of the

[42] *Ibid.*, p. 77.

[43] United States Office of Education, *Earned Degrees Conferred by Higher Educational Institutions, 1957–58,* Circular No. 570 (Washington, D.C.: Government Printing Office, 1959), p. 1; also *Progress of Public Education in the United States, 1959–60, op. cit.,* p. 19.

[44] *Earned Degrees Conferred by Higher Educational Institutions, 1957–58, op. cit.,* p. 89; *Progress of Public Education in the United States, 1959–60, op. cit.,* p. 19. The statistics are for continental United States.

[45] "Statistics of Higher Education, 1955–56," *op. cit.;* see also Dael Wolfe, *America's Resources of Specialized Talent,* The Report of the Commission on Human Resources and Advanced Training (New York: Harper & Brothers, 1954), pp. 24–29.

American people to the ideal of the equal chance is deeply rooted in distant past. More than a century ago Horace Mann voiced the abiding conviction of the common people of the United States when he asserted that education, above all other devices of human origin, is the great equalizer of the condition of men. No other institution has been so favorably regarded as a means for the achievement of social democracy. It must not be supposed that this emphasis on equality of educational opportunity grew wholly, or even mainly, out of a sensitive regard for the rights of the individual; it was grounded more fundamentally upon broad principles of public and social policy. Education was vested with a public as well as a private interest because it was felt that the very life of the democratic state was at stake in its program of education. The American people have put forth great effort to realize the ideal of equal access to educational opportunity. Certainly during the past half-century no other people in the world have done so much by way of providing educational facilities at the secondary and college level. And yet, despite all that has been accomplished, perhaps the most devastating criticism that can be justly leveled at the American educational system is its widespread failure to provide equality of opportunity. In a country of such vast extent, and of such differences in economic condition and cultural pattern, absolute equality of educational opportunity may not be expected. But the differences are not slight; they are of such magnitude as to create a challenge to social and educational statesmanship. Neither past progress nor the fact that the many remaining differences defy easy or quantitative description should obscure the fact of their existence. Society will fail to release its constructive forces in the measure that it fails to reduce these differences.

As has already been indicated, the progress of education has been unequal among the several states and sections; and it should also be noted that, regardless of latitude and longitude, the children of three large and somewhat overlapping elements of the American population — rural dwellers, low-income families, and minority groups, particularly the Negro — have had relatively meager educational opportunities.

Rural-Urban Differentials in Educational Opportunity

Historically, rural America has supplied the population reserves of the nation. During the century ending in 1950, rural population tripled while urban population increased twenty-five-fold (pre-1950 definitions of urban and rural). In 1936 it was estimated that people then living in cities had borne and reared only about one-half of the then-existing urban population.[46] The other half had been born in foreign countries or

[46] Harold F. Dorn and Frank Lorimer, "Migration, Reproduction, and Population Adjustment," *Annals of the American Academy of Political and Social Sciences,* CLXXXVII (November, 1936), 287.

in rural communities in America. In 1940 more than half of the population under twenty years of age were living in rural communities. The decline which followed in the percentage of urban population made up of the rural-born was not due to slowed migration of rural nonfarm or rural-farm population, but was the result of several forces, chiefly the relatively larger increase in the long-depressed urban birth rates, and the declining size of the rural population in relation to the total. In the early sixties it was evident that, barring unforeseen circumstances, the rural-farm population would continue to decline in actual numbers for many years and that, in relation to the total population, it would decline indefinitely.[47]

It is evident that migration from farms is related to the cycle of depression and prosperity. It is conceivable that, were a period of large-scale industrial expansion sustained long enough, excess farm population might be drawn off in such numbers that a balance might be struck between rural population and resources, and that country folk would not continue to be burdened by the care and education of the children of a marginal segment of the population. However, the relatively high birth rate among rural people will probably continue, and as late as 1962 the prospect continued to be that many children reared on farms and villages and educated in rural schools would become urban dwellers, poorly equipped, in too many instances, for life in an urban environment. The farm population has provided, and no doubt will continue to provide, not only the manpower needed by agriculture but also a considerable part of that required by an expanding industrialism.

Despite the vital role the farm and village have played in the life of the nation, their children and youth, as a class, have always been handicapped by unequal educational opportunities. For a half-century and more following the Civil War, the educational gains of the nation were regis-

---

[47] Between 1920 and 1930 the net loss of farm population by migration was 6,296,000, which, in spite of the large natural increase of the farm population, resulted in a decline of 1,445,000 in that population during the decade. The migration of rural folk was slowed by the Depression and the net migration for the decade 1930–40 was only 3,748,000, or slightly less than the natural increase. The rural exodus in response to increased demand for industrial workers mounted during the war years and thereafter. In 1956 the Department of Agriculture reported that "a net of 8.6 million persons alive at both the beginning and end of the decade migrated from farms between 1940 and 1950," and that the net migration rate for the period was 31 per cent, as "compared with 13 per cent for 1930–40, and 19 per cent for 1920–30." So large was the flight from the land during the decade 1940–50 that, although the population of the nation increased 14.5 per cent, the farm population declined 23.6 per cent. The decline in farm population continued throughout the fifties. The farm population declined from 25,000,-000 in 1950 to about 20,000,000 in 1960 (15,635,000 by new definition), or from 16.6 to 11.4 per cent (8.7 by new definition), of the total population. See U.S. Bureau of the Census, *Historical Statistics of the United States, 1789–1945, op. cit.,* p. 31; United States Department of Agriculture, *Farm Population; Net Migration from the Rural-Farm Population, 1940–1950,* p. 3; *Statistical Abstract of the United States, 1961, op. cit.,* p. 613.

tered primarily in urban communities, where both wealth and capacity for adaptation to new conditions were greatest. The conditions of frontier life had left an almost inerasable stamp upon the rural school. It was a significant, even a tragic, fact that for one generation after another the tides of progress swept over and around the rural school, leaving it almost unaffected. The little red schoolhouse was made of tough stuff; it yielded little to the forces that were transforming the conditions of American life. While the urban school was obtaining more adequate financial support, improving the material equipment with which it operated, drawing from the normal schools and colleges the best-trained teachers, developing a trained administrative and supervisory personnel, and enriching its instructional content, the rural school remained much as it had been for generations. The small district type of organization persisted; the financial support of education remained comparatively meager; schoolhouses were generally inadequate; rural teachers were poorly trained, immature, and poorly paid; the curriculum consisted, in the main, of a formal drill in the three R's; and supervision was practically unknown. The net result was that in many ways rural boys and girls were poorly prepared to compete, as they must, with their better-educated urban brothers and sisters.

The story of unequal opportunity between country and city could be documented almost without end.[48] It is recorded in the reports of the superintendent of public instruction of every state in the nation, in the comments on American education made by foreigners, in the reports and surveys of national committees, and in common observation. In 1869, for example, an official report on American education was made to the Canadian government by Doctor Adolphus Egerton Ryerson, Superintendent of Public Instruction of the Province of Ontario. He found urban schools superior to rural schools and remarked of rural schools as follows:

> Herein [that is, in the rural areas] most of the work of the States has begun to halt. There is no adequate provision to secure properly qualified teachers where schools are established. The result is that when you leave the cities and large towns and go into the rural parts of the State you will find our American neighbors are not so successful in their public-school economy and accomplish results far below and short of the

---

[48] In 1791 Robert Coram wrote: "The country schools, through most of the United States, whether we consider the buildings, the teachers, or the regulations, are in every respect despicable, wretched and contemptible." In the same treatise he added that "the country should have as good schools as seaport towns." Robert Coram, *Political Inquiries: To Which is Added a Plan for the General Establishment of Schools in the United States* (Wilmington: printed by Andrews and Brynberg, 1791), as cited in Allen Oscar Hansen, *Liberalism and American Education in the Eighteenth Century* (New York: The Macmillan Co., 1926). Preface and p. 96. See also the excellent volume by Kate V. Wofford, "An History of the Status and Training of Elementary Rural Teachers of the United States, 1860–1930" (Doctor's thesis, Faculty of Philosophy, Columbia University, June, 1934).

state appropriation for sound education of all the people. Such an imperfect state and deficiency of sound education could hardly be otherwise where the schools are kept open from four to six months in the year by boys and girls from sixteen to twenty years of age, themselves poorly educated. There cannot be a good school without a good teacher. In the neighboring states there is no state standard of teacher qualification, though in one instance there is a state board. There is no state program for the examination of teachers. The chief difficulties apparent in the American rural school are the deficiencies in the qualifications of teachers and the temporary employment of them.[49]

A commission of the French government sent to the United States to study the system of education in 1876 confirmed the impressions of rural education gained by the representative of the Canadian government during his visit a few years earlier. Said the commission in its report:

> We are trying . . . to do justice to this great country, but we must not conceal the fact that the schools in the rural districts are poor and badly managed. The salaries of the country teachers are so low that our French teachers have no reason to envy them. The characteristic trait of the country school is the absence of regular organization. There is no uniformity whatever.[50]

Reports from American sources confirmed the observations of foreign visitors. In 1880 the state superintendent of schools in New Jersey called attention to the fact that the local experience of teachers in urban schools was about three times that of teachers elsewhere in the state and the reports of other superintendents indicated that this condition was general throughout the country.[51] In the same year the United States Bureau of Education estimated that about one-fourth of the funds being spent on education was spent in seventy-one urban communities to provide schools for about one-sixth of the nation's children.[52] A careful study of some of the conditions of urban and rural schools in 1909–10 made by the United States Office of Education revealed that rural youth still stood in a disadvantageous position as far as opportunities for formal schooling were concerned (see Table 22). It is a striking fact that, although the rural areas provided 62.3 per cent of the total enrollment in elementary and secondary schools, urban teachers were receiving 54.5 per cent of the

[49] Rev. Adolphus Egerton Ryerson, *Special Report on Popular Education of Europe and the United States of America* (Toronto, 1869), p. 174, as quoted in Wofford, *op. cit.*, p. 11.

[50] *Report sur l'Instruction Primaire à l'Exposition Universelle de Philadelphia en 1876,* p. 120, as quoted in Wofford, *op. cit.*, p. 12.

[51] *New Jersey, Annual Report of the State Superintendent of Public Schools,* 1880, p. 58, as cited in Wofford, *op. cit.*, p. 9.

[52] *Report of the United States Commissioner of Education for 1880* (Washington, D.C.: Government Printing Office, 1882), p. lxxxi.

TABLE 22: COMPARISON OF URBAN AND
RURAL COMMON SCHOOLS, 1909–10*

Items	Per cent	
	Urban	Rural
Total Population	46.3	53.7
Enrollment	37.7	62.3
Average Daily Attendance	41.5	58.5
Aggregate Attendance	48.7	51.3
Teachers' Salaries	54.5	45.5

* Adapted from Harlan Updegraff and William R. Hood, *A Comparison of Urban and Rural Common-School Statistics,* United States Bureau of Education Bulletin 21, 1912 (Washington, D.C.: Government Printing Office, 1912), pp. 15, 16, 18.

amount spent for teachers' salaries. Throughout the nation the school term was markedly shorter in rural than in urban areas (see Table 23). The average number of days the schools were kept in session in urban and rural communities was 184 and 138 respectively. Differences in the length of school terms in town and country were especially great in the southern states. It is a fact of no little historical significance that the children of the rural South were long denied educational opportunities at all comparable with those afforded children living elsewhere in the nation.

TABLE 23: AVERAGE NUMBER OF DAYS SCHOOLS WERE KEPT
DURING THE YEAR 1909–10*

Geographical Area	Urban	Rural
United States	184.3	137.7
North Atlantic Division	188.5	159.7
South Atlantic Division	178.7	119.5
South Central Division	174.0	117.6
North Central Division	184.1	152.7
Western Division	180.7	145.0

* Adapted from Harlan Updegraff and William R. Hood, *A Comparison of Urban and Rural Common-School Statistics,* United States Bureau of Education Bulletin 21, 1912 (Washington, D.C.: Government Printing Office, 1912), p. 28.

Early in the present century educational leaders began to manifest a growing awareness of the fact that most of the educational gains in the nation had been made in the cities. It came to be recognized that the administrative organization of rural education was antiquated; that housing conditions were often pathetically inadequate; that the whole program of rural education was sorely in need of better financial support; that rural teachers, as a class, were young and poorly educated, poorly paid, and unstable of tenure; and that the curriculum of the rural school was commonly divorced from the realities of rural life.

For the last several decades rural education has shared increasingly in the educational gains of the nation. Progress has been made in bringing about more efficient types of administrative units.[53] Measures have been taken to bring into some of the rural schools at least a measure of supervisory service. An increasing volume of state support has strengthened the financial basis of rural education. The school term in villages and open country has been lengthened. Teacher-training institutions have become more aware of the needs of their rural constituency and have modified their curriculums to provide a greatly improved program for rural teachers. The rise of certification standards has more than offset the effects of the relaxation of those standards that occurred during the forties and fifties. In-service programs have become more professional in nature and have increasingly reflected the advance in the status of the teaching staff.[54] A higher type of educational leadership in rural education has led, in some communities at least, to a vitalization of the educational program. Increasingly, if still too infrequently, rural school programs are emerging which integrate school and community life, give attention to the personal and social problems of children and youth, and provide some facilities for occupational adjustment.

It must not be supposed from the foregoing statements that the problems of rural education have been solved. On many objective measures of effectiveness the rural schools still fall below schools maintained in the cities. Furthermore, the figures showing relatively larger rural gains in enrollment, attendance, and support, as significant as they are, fail to tell the entire story. Particularly at the secondary level, the obstacles to be overcome in providing, adequately and equitably, programs for all rural youth appear to be almost insurmountable. Conant's report[55] and numerous other studies have made clear that, in spite of past attainments, much more needs to be accomplished if the American people are ever to realize the ideal of reasonably equal access to education, particularly to secondary education.

Although the improvement of rural education, viewed as a whole, has been remarkable, it has been uneven between regions and states, and

[53] Between 1931–32 and 1959–60, the number of school districts in the United States decreased from 127,422 to 40,286 and the number of one-teacher schools decreased from 143,391 to 20,263. See "Statistics of State School Systems: 1957–58," *op. cit.*, pp. 23, 27; "Preliminary Statistics of State School Systems, 1959–60," *op. cit.*, p. 9. (The 1960 statistics are for fifty states.)

[54] Herman G. Richey, "Growth of the Modern Conception of In-service Education," pp. 35–66 in *In-service Education for Teachers, Supervisors, and Administrators,* Fifty-sixth Yearbook of the National Society for the Study of Education, Part I (Chicago: University of Chicago Press, 1957).

[55] James B. Conant, *The American High School Today: A First Report to Interested Citizens* (New York: McGraw-Hill Book Co., Inc., 1959).

differences among rural areas as well as urban-rural differentials point to
the need for further improvement. In too many states the structure of
rural education still stands in need of thoroughgoing reorganization. The
United States Office of Education reported that in 1960 there were
20,213 one-teacher schools in continental United States.[56] While some
of these exist in communities where conditions are such as to make one-
teacher schools appear necessary, many of them are to be found in communities where consolidation into larger units is both possible and desirable. More serious still, many of these one-teacher schools represent a
single administrative unit. As late as 1957–58, six of the eleven states
of the Great Lakes and Plains region maintained 10,526 districts, or 65
per cent of the total number of operating districts within those states,
for the sole purpose of operating a single elementary school. Ninety-one
per cent of such districts were located in the Middle States, with only
1102 being found in other states, for the most part in the West; and
several states, e.g., Kentucky and West Virginia, with relatively few districts had large numbers of one-teacher schools.[57] Even though a one-
teacher school may be defensible in many communities as an attendance
unit, the maintenance of a district administration unit for a school of this
type is highly questionable. It is certain that rural education will continue
to fail to achieve what it ought to accomplish unless its administrative
structure is modernized in many states, notably in the Middle West, to
enable it to meet social responsibilities that cannot be met by one-teacher
schools, and especially by such schools when they can draw only upon
the resources, financial and intellectual, of a single small community.

The rapid progress in the immediate past in reorganizing the structure
of rural education and in improving many aspects of it tends to obscure
the fact that place of birth continues to be an important factor in determining the quality of education that most children will receive. Our hope
for the future lies in the record of improvement in many, if not always the
most crucial, aspects of rural education.

In 1959, for the first time, the Office of Education added to its *Biennial Survey of Education in the United States* a periodical statistical survey
of rural county schools.[58] It noted that as late as the middle fifties over
100,000, or 75 per cent, of the nation's schools were located in centers
of less than 2500 population and that 45 per cent of the children attended these schools. In a detailed study of education in 1129 rural counties, or nearly one-half of the counties of the United States which did

[56] Two-thirds of these schools are in the Great Lakes and Plains region. See
"Statistics of State School Systems: 1957–58," *op. cit.,* p. 27; "Preliminary Statistics of State School Systems, 1959–60," *op. cit.,* p. 9.

[57] "Statistics of State School Systems: 1957–58," *op. cit.,* pp. 24, 27.

[58] United States Office of Education, "Statistics of Local School Systems: 1955–
56 (Rural Counties)," *Biennial Survey of Education in the United States — 1954–
1956* (Washington, D.C.: Government Printing Office, 1959), Chap. III, Sec. 4.

not have county-unit school systems, the Office presented evidence that indicated that ruralism was much less than formerly related to low holding power, high pupil-teacher ratios, the percentage of children enrolled who were attending daily, and other related factors. The report made clear, however, that rural communities must contend disproportionately with such problems as ungraded schools, limited offerings, crowded teaching schedules, inadequate instructional material, poorly paid and inadequately trained teachers, and lack of sufficient financial support in general.[59] However, the improvements in rural schools, which were large indeed, and the overlapping of rural and urban schools on many objective measures indicate that efforts are being made that may, in time, result in equitable provisions for the education of all children.

Educational Opportunity for
Low-Income Groups

It must not be supposed, from the emphasis in the preceding section on the inadequate facilities for rural children, that the doors of educational opportunity open wide for all young people living in towns and cities. Too often the assumption has been made that a high degree of educational opportunity is extended youth when good schools are maintained in a community and all who may wish have the privilege of attending. Neither the proximity of schools nor the existence of compulsory-attendance laws provides, in itself, assurance that equal opportunity for an education is enjoyed or is even actually available for all. Factors associated with persistence and success in school are numerous and interdependent, and the influence of any single factor cannot be measured. However, except for the aptitude of the pupil for the type of program offered, the occupation of the father and the family income are perhaps the best indexes of how far both urban and rural children will ascend the educational ladder.

During the nineteenth century and before, education above the rudiments was, of course, highly selective; but it was only a generation ago that the Maryland Youth Survey revealed that in Maryland seven out of

---

[59] The current expenditure per pupil in average daily attendance was $237 for the 1129 rural counties, as compared with $299 for the thirty-eight states within which the counties were located, $305 for small cities (population 25,000 to 99,999), and $333 for larger cities (population 100,000 or over). Expenditures per pupil for instruction averaged $160 in rural counties, as opposed to $199 in the thirty-eight states represented, $225 in the smaller cities, and $241 in the larger cities. The average salary of teachers in rural counties was $3137, as compared with $4155 for the thirty-eight states, $4750 for small cities, and $5392 for larger cities. See "Statistics of Local School Systems: 1955–1956," *op. cit.*, and more recent editions of the *Biennial Survey of Education in the United States*.

eight children whose fathers were farm laborers did not go beyond the eighth grade, while only one out of two whose fathers belonged to the "farm-owner-tenant" classification failed to enter some type of secondary school. Among the predominantly urban portion of the population, only one out of thirteen children whose fathers' occupations were classified as "professional-technical" did not attend school beyond the eighth-grade, while two out of three sons and daughters of the "unskilled" left school with an eighth-grade education or less.[60] On the basis of this investigation made during the late years of the Depression, the author commented as follows on the effect of the occupation of the father on the educational attainment of the child:

> Much has been said in the preceding pages about the profound effect that the occupation of the youth's father usually has upon his general social, economic, and educational status. In going through the data uncovered in all our areas of information, this reality, like a gloomy chorus in a Greek tragedy, has been an ever recurring theme.
>
> With a little professional license, one might consider the factors that influence grade attainment as a miniature deck of cards. However this deck is shuffled, one card — one fact — will be always on top: the strongest single factor in determining how far a youth goes in school is the occupation of his father.[61]

In 1942, Karpinos and Sommers concluded from data obtained from the National Health Survey (1935–36) that in the case of white urban youth the income of the family was an extremely important factor in determining, in all regions of the United States, the educational achievement of children. In the Northeast only 56.5 per cent of the male youth (ages 20 to 24) whose family income was less than $1000 had attained some high school education, as compared with 89.4 per cent of those whose family income was $3000 or more. The corresponding per cents for the other three major regions were: north-central states, 70.2 and 94.3; the South, 65.0 and 96.4; and the West, 84.9 and 97.9. For the nation as a whole, the percentages of children and youth who had attained specified educational levels above the primary grades increased as family income increased. Only about two-thirds of the white urban males 20 to 24 years of age of families with an annual income of less than $1000 had attended high school at all, as compared with 93 per cent of those of families having incomes of $3000 or more.[62]

---

[60] Howard M. Bell, *Youth Tell Their Story: A Study of the Conditions and Attitudes of Young People in Maryland between the Age of 16 and 24,* Conducted for the American Youth Commission (Washington, D.C.: American Council on Education, 1938), pp. 59–60.

[61] *Ibid.,* p. 63.

[62] Bernard D. Karpinos and Herbert J. Sommers, "Educational Attainment of Urban Youth in Various Income Classes," *Elementary School Journal,* XLII (May,

Other studies support the conclusion that equal educational opportunity is not assured merely by providing schools and making them free to all who may care to attend. In his study of the factors influencing high school attendance in Illinois, Richey found considerable correlation between the percentages of school children enrolled in high school and indexes of economic well-being such as living standards and assessed valuation.[63] Later, Edwards and Richey reported studies which related, for the more than 3000 counties of the United States, educational attainment to the level of living as indicated by per capita expendable income and several other indexes of either a cultural or an economic nature.[64] They noted the limitations of such studies but, nevertheless, concluded that the educational opportunity provided by the schools generally continued to be richest in communities in which cultural and other resources were greatest and poorest in communities in which cultural advantages were limited, the financial burden was relatively heavy, and the home had least to offer to the education of the child.

Studies made during the 1950's reflect the general rise in real income that followed World War II and also the fact that high school enrollments were, in many communities, approaching the saturation point. It was observed that elementary and high school enrollment or attendance was becoming a somewhat less discriminating measure of educational achievement of different groups of people than it had been. As early as 1950 the Bureau of the Census reported that about 84 per cent of all youth fourteen to seventeen years of age were in school. However, it was also pointed out that of the 2,016,635 pupils enrolled in Grade 5 of the public schools in 1943–44, only 1,849,990, or 91.7 per cent, were in Grade 7 in 1945–46, only 1,672,920, or 83.0 per cent, entered Grade 9 in 1947–48, and only 51.8 per cent completed high school four years later.[65] A number of studies of local situations made during the period indicated that family status, family income, and father's occupation — all highly related variables — continue to be factors that are closely related, not only to the years of schooling a child receives, but also, to some extent, to the degree in which the education received pertains to the student's

1942), 677–687; (June, 1942), 766–774. Income of family was defined "to include the combined salaries, wages, business profits, and net income from investments received by all members of the family during the year preceding the survey." Educational achievement was defined as the grade or type of school an individual had ever entered, regardless of whether he had completed it.

[63] Herman G. Richey, "Factors of High School Enrollment in Illinois," *School Review*, XLVIII (November, 1940), 567–576.

[64] Newton Edwards and Herman G. Richey, *The School in the American Social Order*, First Edition (Boston: Houghton Mifflin Company, 1947), Chapter 11, especially pp. 603, 611, 628, and 637.

[65] Walter H. Gaumnitz, *High School Retention by States*, United States Office of Education Circular No. 398, June, 1954 (Washington, D.C.: Government Printing Office, 1954), p. 16.

needs and aspirations. The pattern of precollegiate education is, no doubt, related to the intelligence of the child, the proximity of schools, the enforcement of compulsory-attendance laws, the attractiveness of the educational program, the educational status of the parents, and many other factors; but both the extent and the pattern of the child's schooling are, in a large measure, determined by the mere fact of his birth into a family of a particular social status, of which family income and the father's occupation are two of the major constants in a broad field of determinants.[66]

Today's boys and girls have a better chance of attending college than their grandparents had of entering high school. The ideal of equal opportunity has come increasingly to encompass post-secondary education for all who desire it and can profit from it. Yet the ideal is still far from being realized. The extension of education upward has been retarded by many factors, including the failure of higher institutions to develop meaningful programs for larger numbers of youth. It has also been limited by the lack of intellectual capacity on the part of many youth for the programs that have been available. However, at least in the past, the nature of the program and the lack of ability on the part of students or prospective students appear to have been less important factors operating to keep the doors of higher institutions closed to a large majority of high school graduates than socio-economic factors such as family income and social status.

To an even greater extent than at lower educational levels, family income has been an excellent if imperfect predictor of who among the high school graduates would or would not enter college.[67] One inescapable fact is that it costs money to go to college; and the importance of this fact is made evident by the investigations which have from time to time attempted to determine the percentage of families or family units having sufficient income to finance a college education for one or more of their members. The percentage of such families has increased rapidly since World War II, but, although estimates vary, perhaps fewer than one-third of the families in the United States had sufficient income during the high-income period of the nineteen-fifties and sixties to meet the costs of a college education without crippling sacrifices.

Among the variables not related to college attendance in the essential way that financial ability is related to it, but which are useful in predicting who will and who will not go to college, the occupation of the father, as might be surmised from earlier statements, has been consistently useful as

[66] For an excellent illustration of such studies, see James D. Davie, "Social Class Factors and School Attendance," *Harvard Educational Review*, XXIII, No. 3, 175–185.

[67] Dael Wolfle, *America's Resources of Specialized Talent: A Current Appraisal and a Look Ahead*, Report of the Commission on Human Resources and Advanced Training (New York: Harper & Brothers, 1954), pp. 140–141.   •

a predictor. On the basis of studies made by the Commission on Human Resources and Advanced Training and studies summarized by the Commission, including the extensive investigation of what happened to all the graduates of Minnesota high schools (1938 and 1950), Wolfle presented the following table of estimates:

TABLE 24:
THE RELATION BETWEEN FATHER'S OCCUPATION AND
PROBABILITY THAT A HIGH SCHOOL GRADUATE WILL ENTER COLLEGE
AND THAT A COLLEGE ENTRANT WILL GRADUATE[*]

Father's Occupation	Percentage of High School Graduates Who Enter College	Percentage of College Entrants Who Graduate from College	Percentage of High School Graduates Who Also Graduate From College
Professional and Semiprofessional	67	60	40
Managerial	50	55	28
White-Collar (Clerical, Sales, Service)	48	57	27
Farmer	24	44	11
Factory, Craftsmen, Unskilled, etc.	26	58	15

[*] Dael Wolfle, *America's Resources of Specialized Talent: A Current Appraisal and a Look Ahead,* Report of the Commission on Human Resources and Advanced Training (New York: Harper & Brothers, 1954), p. 160.

Wolfle also presented estimates of the percentage of the children of different occupational groups (fathers) which can be expected to continue in school to the end of college. These estimates indicate that only 6.5 per cent of all children and youth had professional and semiprofessional fathers but that 22 per cent of all college graduates came from this most favored group. Of the least favored groups, only 6 per cent of the sons and daughters of farmers and 8 per cent of the children of skilled and unskilled workers completed college, even though these two groups constituted respectively 16.2 and 48.7 per cent of all children and youth.[68]

Family status, variously described and representing a number of variables, has been even more closely associated with college than with elementary- or secondary-school attendance. Using Warner's five-class design, White found that in the Cleveland area 47.5 per cent of the college freshmen of the population studied came from the upper and upper middle classes, which together constituted only 24 per cent of his population.

[68] *Ibid.,* p. 162.

Slightly more than 50 per cent of the sample belonged to the two lowe:
(upper-lower and lower-lower) classes, and these supplied only 28 pe:
cent of the freshmen.[69]

In spite of the well-established facts that a considerable number o:
bright, well-prepared youth of financially able parents do not attend col
lege, that the differential in educational attainment of different socio
economic groups is less marked for children of superior ability, and othe:
data that point to the influence of many factors (sex, race, geography, anc
the like) in cutting short or prolonging the period of schooling, it appear
that economic and closely related factors play an important, perhaps th·
most important, role in determining which children will graduate from
high school and continue their education beyond that point.

The foregoing generalizations are supported by the record of highe:
education since World War II. Near the close of the war, the federa
government initiated a program of assistance to veterans who wished to
continue their education. For several years the enrollments of colleges anc
universities were swollen not only by students whose education had beer
temporarily deferred by military service but also by many students for
whom the program presented opportunities that previously had not beer
available to them. As federal aid to students diminished, higher institutions extended their efforts to aid needy students, and national foundations initiated or enlarged existing fellowship and scholarship programs
The federal government continued, directly and indirectly, to contribute
to the training of high-level talent in selected areas. The persistence of
a shortage of talent in many fields, the realization that our national resources were being wasted to the extent that competent youth were barrec
from higher education by their inability to pay for it, and public reaction to
several scientific and political events of world interest led the Congress
to pass the National Defense Education Act of 1958. This Act, although
poorly conceived in many of its details, did provide fellowships for many
students and funds to be lent on financially generous if otherwise unsatisfactory terms.[70] By the close of the 1950's assistance from many

---

[69] R. Clyde White, "The Potential and Probable Supply of College Students,"
College Admission (Princeton, N.J.: College Entrance Examination Board, 1954),
I, pp. 12–23.

[70] Three years after the passage of the National Defense Education Act, which
was designed primarily to strengthen instruction in mathematics, science, and foreign
languages, improve pupil guidance, and encourage able students to proceed to
higher education, the *New York Times* (June 18, 1961) summarized its accomplishments — 4000 fellowships awarded; approximately $130,000,000 granted in
student loans; about 3500 language laboratories provided (matching basis); 65
language centers set up in colleges subsidized up to 50 per cent of the cost; 5865
facilities (classrooms and laboratory units) for science, mathematics, and language remodeled; and the multiplication of state supervisors (matching basis) of
science, mathematics, and languages. Some provisions of the Act, however, are such
that, even with excellent administration, some of the listed accomplishments have
been more impressive as statistics than as acual improvements to our total educational program.

sources was adequate to provide for many students with high academic qualifications who needed and were seeking university education of several types at the graduate level. The undergraduate of exceptional ability can generally find a considerable measure of support. However, taking into account the college-age population as a whole, family income continues to be the most important factor in determining who will attend an institution of higher education.

Educational Opportunity for the Negro and Other Non-White Population

The freeing of the slaves brought many problems with which neither federal nor state governments were prepared to deal. The education of the Freedmen was not the least of these. Although the nature and scope of the task demanded more than philanthropy or the encouragement of philanthropic efforts, the federal government developed no sound long-range programs. The states in which most of the Negroes resided had suffered devastation in the war and, later, a disastrous period of Reconstruction. The bitterness growing out of the political strife in which race was made a major issue resulted, as much perhaps as poverty, in making the Negro's situation a poor one indeed. However, as the South recovered and prospered, and as new leadership developed, educational facilities for Negroes multiplied and Negro education generally became an approximation of that which was inadequately provided for whites.

We have failed over the many decades since the Civil War to establish equality of educational opportunity for the Negro. It must be pointed out, however, that progress toward that goal has been rapid since the turn of the century. Reports[71] published periodically by the United States Office of Education before the 1954 Supreme Court decision presented statistics not easily available since. These statistics showed an extremely rapid rate of progress as measured by common criteria and indexes. Also, the Bureau of the Census has presented figures which have shown for each decade since 1900 a significant gain in the proportion of Negro youth attending school. The per cent of the Negro population five to twenty years of age in attendance in some type of school increased from 31 to approximately 70 during the first half of the present century.[72] The 1950 Census revealed that 72.6 per cent of the Negroes sixteen years of

[71] *The Biennial Survey of Education* no longer contains some types of data relating to Negro education. For the period before 1954, see also such publications as U.S. Office of Education, *Statistics of Public Elementary and Secondary Education of Negroes in the Southern States, Circular* No. 444 (Washington, D.C.: Government Printing Office, 1955).

[72] United States Bureau of the Census, *Population — Special Reports,* Series P — 1943, No. 4; *Census of Population: 1950,* II, Part I, p. 206.

age were attending school.[73] Shortly after mid-century the United States Office of Education reported that the enrollment of Negro children in public elementary schools in seventeen states which maintained separate schools and in the District of Columbia amounted to more than 85 per cent of the number of children of school age, five to seventeen. The number of Negro pupils in this area enrolled in public high schools increased more than eleven-fold — from 33,341 to 372,362 between 1920 and 1952.[74]

Data presented by Pierce and his collaborators[75] reveal both the progress made in improving Negro education and the continuing inferiority of facilities and opportunities as they existed in thirteen southern states just prior to the Supreme Court decision of 1954. The facts represent what had been accomplished in states that continued to provide separate schools for Negroes. By 1940, Pierce notes, the percentage of children six to thirteen years of age enrolled in the schools of the southern states were substantially the same for both races. Older Negro children did not fare nearly so well. The enrollment of Negroes in high school, per hundred Negroes fourteen to seventeen years of age, was only 28.0 as compared with 63.9 for whites.[76] However, in 1950 the corresponding ratios were 44.6 and 65.1. Expenditures per pupil in average daily attendance continued to be larger for white than for Negro schools, but the differences had diminished rapidly during the preceding decade or two.[77] Salaries, still lower on the average for Negro than for white teachers, were, by the early fifties, much less widely separated than had been the case a decade earlier. In several states the salaries paid the two groups were approximately the same, and in two states the average salaries paid Negro teachers were higher than those paid white teachers — reflecting, no doubt, the longer preparation or experience, or both, of the Negro teachers.[78] The value of school property and equipment per pupil in average daily attendance was in 1952 still much higher for whites than for Negroes, but tremendous strides had been taken toward providing more adequately for the Negro.[79] In 1952 schools for the two races were kept

[73] *Census of Population: 1950,* II, Part I, *op. cit.,* p. 206.

[74] *Biennial Survey of Education in the United States, 1950–52, op. cit.,* Chap. II.

[75] Truman M. Pierce *et al., White and Negro Schools in the South: An Analysis of the Biracial Education* (Englewood Cliffs, N.J.: Prentice-Hall, Inc., 1955).

[76] *Ibid.,* p. 96.

[77] *Ibid.,* p. 165. In the nine states for which data were reported, the expenditures (for instruction) per white pupil (A.D.A.) ranged from $80.15 to $156.04, with an average of $132.38. The expenditure per Negro pupil (A.D.A.) ranged from $54.21 to $131.79. In North Carolina, the expenditure in average daily attendance was only 7 per cent higher for whites than for non-whites in 1951–52. This difference could be accounted for by unequal racial representation in rural and urban schools.

[78] *Ibid.,* pp. 107–108.

[79] *Ibid.,* pp. 219–220.

open about the same number of days, whereas in 1940 the average term of white schools was three weeks longer than that of Negro schools.[80]

The evidence, on the whole, supports the conclusion that the South, at least much of the South, was really accepting the "equal but separate" concept and was making tremendous if somewhat belated efforts to provide educational opportunities for Negro children comparable with those provided for white children (at least, as comparable as could be provided in segregated schools). However, as pointed out by Pierce *et al.,* equalization of opportunity was far from being realized and in some aspects and in some areas it was disappointingly slow. The 1950 census and other publications[81] revealed that the Negro population of all ages had completed, on the average, fewer years of schooling than whites of corresponding ages; that a smaller percentage of Negro than of white adults had reached any given level of education; that the differences varied from state to state and from region to region and were generally greater where Negroes constituted a considerable portion of the population; and that the educational status of the Negro was lower than that of the white in both the rural and urban areas of all states and regions.[82]

In spite of past progress, the fact remains that the Negro did not at mid-century, nor does he now, have opportunity equal to that enjoyed by members of the white race. The causes are many and deep-rooted, and the remedy involves more than the elimination of segregated schools by legislative enactment or court decision, although the Supreme Court made clear in 1954 its conviction that without the elimination of such schools, equality of opportunity could not exist. The decision of the Court declaring unconstitutional all provisions for segregated schools was handed down more than a century after segregation first became an issue in the courts. That judicial opinion over the years has undergone a great change is clear. In a very early case, the highest court in Massachusetts held that it was constitutional to segregate Negro pupils for purposes of school attendance, provided they were afforded substantially the same opportunities afforded white pupils.[83] Apparently this was the beginning of the separate-but-equal doctrine, which for many years served as precedent to state courts both north and south.

It made its appearance in the Supreme Court of the United States in the well-known case of *Plessey* v. *Ferguson.*[84] In that case the Supreme

---

[80] *Ibid.,* p. 235.

[81] Herman G. Richey, "Educational Status of Important Population Groups between the First and Second World Wars: Parts I and II," *School Review* (January, February, 1949), 16–27, 89–100.

[82] The number of school years attended do not reflect the educational situation in 1950, but represent, rather, the accumulated effect of a long period of unequal educational opportunity. The mid-century data exhibit a distinct pattern among adults of higher educational levels at successively younger ages for both whites and Negroes.

[83] *Roberts* v. *City of Boston,* 59 Massachusetts, 198.   [84] 163 U.S. 537.

Court sustained the doctrine as it applied to transportation facilities. With the passing of the years a number of cases came before the Supreme Court involving segregation in colleges and schools, but the Court was able to dispose of them without deciding whether or not segregation in schools is in and of itself unconstitutional. But in 1954 the issue came squarely before the court in the case of *Brown* v. *Board of Education*.[85] In that case the Court held unequivocally that segregation in the public schools because of race or color violates that clause of the Fourteenth Amendment which provides that no state may deny any person the equal protection of the laws. After considering at some length the social and personal consequences of segregation so far as Negro children are concerned, the Court stated:

> We conclude that in the field of public education the doctrine of "separate but equal" has no place. Separate educational facilities are inherently unequal. Therefore we hold that the plaintiffs and others similarly situated for whom the actions have been brought are, by reason of the segregation complained of, deprived of the equal protection of the laws guaranteed by the Fourteenth Amendment.

Public opinion concerning integration was not changed by the Court's decision. A number of states amended their constitutions[86] or adopted statutes which, it was hoped, would delay if not prevent integration. The federal courts, however, have stood firm, declaring much such legislation unconstitutional. Gradually most of the southern states have put integration into effect in some degree. It seems clear that segregation is on its way out, and that, under the law at least, all American children are entitled to equal educational opportunity.

However, as already noted, court decisions alone will not solve the basic problems of providing equal educational opportunity for all Negroes. This is true because school segregation and other discriminatory practices, whatever their effects have been, are not the entire cause of the educational backwardness of large classes of Negroes. The Negro, by and large, has long been a member of groups and segments of the population which, regardless of color or legal sanctions, have always been educationally disadvantaged. For example, Negroes have been largely rural dwellers, a group that has had relatively limited opportunity for education since the nation was founded; Negroes have lived predominantly in the South, which for generations has been unable to provide adequate programs of

---

85 347 U.S. 483.

86 For constitutional amendments providing for the disestablishment of public schools and other measures designed to circumvent or delay the implementation of the Court's decision, see Richard A. Edwards (ed.), *Index Digest of State Constitutions,* Second Edition (New York: published for the Legislative Drafting Research Fund of Columbia University by Oceana Publications, Inc., 1959).

education; and a disproportionate number of Negroes have been engaged in agriculture, an occupation characterized by a declining labor force and affording meager opportunity for economic advancement. But the Negro has been raising his educational level for generations; he has become increasingly mobile and tends more and more to seek out the better opportunities for work that are afforded in urban areas; he has raised his standard of living and his expectations for his children; he has become a force in politics; and he has witnessed the elimination of some of the types of discrimination that were most hateful to him. If equal opportunity is not yet his, he has for several decades been moving toward it at a rapid rate indeed.

Progress Toward the Ideal

When the educational enterprise is viewed as a whole, its expansion to meet the needs of all the people has been remarkable. It is safe to say that no nation has done so much. However, much still needs to be done to make real the American dream of equal and universal access to educational opportunity. The conditions of American life require further extensions of education upward and downward — upward to prepare for competent citizenship, for vocational efficiency and flexibility, and for creative and satisfying use of leisure time; downward to meet the needs of early childhood. Our ideal of an all-inclusive democracy has long supported, if not always with full effect, the proposition that every child, regardless of place of residence, financial status, level of ability, or color, should have opportunity to develop his fullest potentialities. With this ideal there can be no compromise.

Questions and Problems for Study and Discussion

1. During the past half-century the school has greatly expanded and has assumed new functions. Do present conditions make a still further expansion of our educational enterprise desirable? Defend your position, and, if your answer is yes, indicate the lines along which expansion should take place.
2. To what extent, in your opinion, is the financial support of education a responsibility of (a) the local community, (b) the state, (c) the federal government? Support your conclusion.
3. What percentage of the total cost of education is provided by the state government in your state? Do you think this is satisfactory?
4. Do you believe that the urban population of the United States should be taxed to help support education in rural areas? Defend your position.
5. What are the major forces that are working toward the realization of equal educational opportunity?

6. Within recent years some writers have argued that the continued expansion of higher education will lead to wasted years on the part of many youth and, perhaps, to a dangerous economic situation because there will be more college graduates than can find employment acceptable to them. How valid is this argument? What do proponents of this view propose to avoid the situation? Evaluate their arguments.

7. Compare with those presented in this chapter the most recent statistics available on size of school-age population aged 6 to 13, 14 to 17; enrollments in public elementary schools, public high schools, and private schools; college enrollment; and national income. Do any of these statistics suggest a change in trend?

Selected References for Further Reading

Allen, Hollis P. *The Federal Government and Education.* New York: McGraw-Hill Book Co., Inc., 1950. Pp. xvii + 333.

Bogue, Donald Joseph. *Population of the United States.* Glencoe, Ill.: Free Press, 1959. Pp. 873.

Bond, Horace Mann. *The Education of the Negro in the American Social Order.* New York: Prentice-Hall, Inc., 1934. Pp. xx + 502.

Chase, Francis, and Anderson, Harold A. (eds.). *The High School in a New Era.* Chicago: University of Chicago Press, 1958. Pp. xiv + 465.

Chase, Francis S., and Morphet, Edgar L. *The Forty-eight State School Systems.* Chicago: The Council of State Governments, 1949. Pp. x + 245.

Conant, James Bryant. *The American High School Today: A First Report to Interested Citizens.* New York: McGraw-Hill Book Co., Inc., 1959. Pp. xiii + 140.

Conant, James Bryant. *Education in the Junior High School Years.* Princeton, N.J.: Educational Testing Service, 1960. Pp. 133.

Edwards, Newton. *Equal Educational Opportunity for Youth: A National Responsibility,* A Report to the American Youth Commission. Washington, D.C.: American Council on Education, 1939. Pp. x + 190.

Frazier, E. Franklin. *The Negro in the United States.* New York: The Macmillan Co., 1957. Pp. xxviii + 770.

Judd, Charles H. *Problems of Education in the United States.* New York: McGraw-Hill Book Co., 1933. Pp. xii + 214.

Knight, Edgar W. *Fifty Years of American Education: A Historical Review and Critical Appraisal.* New York: The Ronald Press Company, 1952. Pp. 484.

Link, Arthur S. *A History of the United States Since the 1890's.* New York: Alfred A. Knopf, Inc., 1955. Pp. xxix + 724.

Miller, Herman P. *Income of the American People.* New York: John Wiley & Sons, Inc., 1955. Pp. xvi + 206.

National Education Association, Committee on Educational Finance. *Financing Education for Our Changing Population.* Washington, D.C.: the Association, 1961. Pp. 111.

Pierce, Truman M., *et al. White and Negro Schools in the South: An Analysis of the Biracial Education.* Englewood Cliffs, N.J.: Prentice-Hall, Inc., 1955. Pp. xii + 338.

Richey, Herman G. "The Persistence of Educational Progress during the Decade of the Civil War," *Elementary School Journal,* XLII (January, February, 1942), 358–366, 456–463.

Richey, Herman G. "Reappraisal of the State School Systems of the Pre-Civil-War Period," *Elementary School Journal,* XLI (October, 1940), 118–129.

Schlesinger, Arthur Meier. *The Rise of the City, 1878–1898: A History of American Life,* X. New York: The Macmillan Co., 1933. Pp. xviii + 494.

Social Factors Influencing American Education, Sixtieth Yearbook of the National Society for the Study of Education, Part II. Chicago: University of Chicago Press, 1961. Pp. x + 252.

Taeuber, Conrad, and Taeuber, Irene B. *The Changing Population of the United States.* New York: John Wiley & Sons, Inc., 1958. Pp. xv + 355.

United States Bureau of the Census. *Historical Statistics of the United States, 1789–1945.* Washington, D.C.: Government Printing Office, 1949. Pp. viii + 363.

United States Office of Education. *Biennial Survey of Education in the United States.* Washington, D.C.: Government Printing Office, 1961.

Updegraff, Harlan, and Hood, William R. *A Comparison of Urban and Rural Common-School Statistics,* United States Bureau of Education Bulletin 21, 1912. Washington, D.C.: Government Printing Office, 1912. Pp. 32.

Wofford, Kate V. *An History of the Status and Training of Elementary Rural Teachers of the United States, 1860–1930.* Doctor's dissertation, Faculty of Philosophy, Columbia University, June, 1934. Pp. vi + 170.

Wolfle, Dael. *Resources of Specialized Talent: A Current Appraisal and a Look Ahead,* Report of the Commission on Human Resources and Advanced Training. New York: Harper & Brothers, 1954. Pp. xviii + 332.

15

The Quest for
a Content of Education

The choice of the content of instruction has been a persistent and important problem of education since teaching and learning first became the business of a special institution, the school. It is not by accident that for more than two thousand years the leading thinkers of the Western world have concerned themselves with the problem of defining a valid curriculum for the schools of the society they knew or anticipated. The changing solutions to this problem that they and the society in general have worked out have always reflected their changing conceptions, beliefs, and values. Certainly the expansion and development of American education has been accompanied by ceaseless effort to meet the needs of American life as they changed and came to be better understood. About a century ago, the general acceptance of the ideal that education is the birthright of all stimulated new efforts to determine what the schools should teach. Herbert Spencer, one of the long line of philosophers to be concerned with the content of education, sought to define the proper curriculum as the answer to the query, "What knowledge is of most worth?" — a query which in later years took the form: What experience is of most value? The answers to these questions have been many and varied. They reveal strikingly the conflict of values and the confusion of purpose that have characterized the American educational system. But it could not have been otherwise in a democracy where decisions with respect to important matters of public policy were reached through free expression of opinion and unregulated experimentation. Fortunately, in the United States no central government has been in a position to control educational policy. Each community has been more or less free to formulate its own educational values and to implement them in such ways as it deemed best. This experimentation, however, has been carried forward within the framework of certain common ideals and has had as its common goal the discovery of a curriculum content — a body of experience — best suited to the changing conditions of American life. Conflict of values and confusion of purpose there have been, but much of this conflict and confusion must be regarded as the product of different ways of arriving experimentally at a common goal.

Factors Influencing the Development of the Curriculum

Many factors enter into the decisions of a people with respect to the experiences that are deemed suitable for an educational program. Such has been especially true of the United States during the past century. The ideal of equal educational opportunity; accumulations of new knowledge in many fields; new demands for vocational education growing out of technological change; the need for a better understanding of the workings of political, economic, and social arrangements; the findings of scientific inquiry in the field of education; new concepts with respect to the essential purposes of education and the experiences necessary to achieve those purposes — all these factors have had their influence on the development of the curriculum.

THE IDEAL OF EQUAL EDUCATIONAL OPPORTUNITY

The answer to the question, who shall be educated and in what degree, goes far in determining the instructional program in any educational system. If the education of the masses is to be confined to the rudiments plus a modicum of vocational training, and if secondary and higher institutions are designed for the cultivation of an intellectual elite to fill the professions and other positions of social importance, the curriculum will be one thing. It will be something very different where the people are trying to realize the ideal of equal opportunity for all, where each individual is guaranteed the right to achieve according to his capacity and effort and to participate freely in the common enterprise of improving the conditions under which men live.

For a century or more, the American people have been making steady progress toward realization of the ideal of equal educational opportunity. Yet as late as 1890 secondary education was highly selective; it was designed, in the main, to prepare a relatively few young people for entrance into colleges where most of them would pursue studies leading to one or another of the well-established professions — the ministry, law, medicine, teaching, or engineering. The problem of organizing a curriculum for this more or less homogeneous group of young people was relatively simple. They came, in the main, from upper- and middle-class homes; their intellectual capacity and ability to deal with abstractions was relatively high; and their occupational and social goals were not too diverse. By the turn of the century, however, a new situation was developing. Each decade now saw secondary-school enrollments double: The secondary school was becoming the school for all adolescents, in much the same sense as the elementary school was the school for all children. Youth were now entering the secondary school with the most diverse social and cultural backgrounds, with mental capacities ranging from the lowest to the highest, and with social and vocational destinations of the most varied kind. Some would go on to college, but the percentage doing so would be relatively small, and, for several decades, a declining one; most would leave high school to take their place in the life of the community.

The democratization of the secondary school tore it away from its old moorings and forced it to redefine its purposes and to modify its curriculum. Traditionally, the secondary school had fulfilled its mission by selecting and preparing youth for college. This responsibility it continued to meet, but each passing year the demands and needs of its new clientele were forcing it to take on more and more the character of a terminal institution. It was no easy task for the secondary school to sever the bonds that had for centuries bound it to the college and to develop a program of general education adequate to serve the needs of youth in a society being transformed by technological revolution.

Writing in 1925, Professor Leonard Koos described in the following significant passage the new conception of secondary education which had come to be entertained by leaders in the field:

> The profound nature of the differences between this older selective concept of the rôle of the American secondary school and present-day concepts at once becomes apparent when one attempts to summarize recent statements of the purposes which should dominate secondary education. The writer has essayed such a summary of the pronouncements of twenty-five leaders or groups of leaders . . . in materials appearing in print in recent years with interesting results. Over four-fifths of these statements propose training for social-civic responsibility, training for recreational and esthetic participation, training for physical efficiency, and training for occupational efficiency. That is to say, these leaders and groups of leaders are unanimous or well-nigh unanimous on the four large aims of an adequate education. Similar proportions urge a democratic secondary education which recognizes individual differences, while more than half propose a corollary purpose, affording opportunities for exploration and guidance. In striking contrast with these proportions are the small numbers contending that the secondary school should emphasize training for leadership and selection for higher education. Three

writers only definitely propose a continuation of the performance of these traditional purposes. Although fully two-thirds posit the necessity of affording the opportunities for college preparation, they tend to do so with the admonition that it should be accomplished for those only who should and can go on to higher levels of training or that it is to be only *one* of the functions of the American secondary school.[1]

The gist of the matter was that the secondary school had become, to a remarkable extent, not only a school for all American youth but also, for a large part of its clientele, a terminal institution. And to prepare youth for social-civic responsibility, for occupational efficiency, for healthful living, for recreation and creative use of leisure, and for homemaking called for a new program of studies. As the secondary school moved to meet its new responsibilities course offerings multiplied in great number. These course offerings were commonly organized into parallel curriculums designated as college preparatory, general, commercial, industrial arts, household arts, fine arts, agriculture, and the like. In numerous instances special vocational secondary schools were developed to prepare youth for entrance into agriculture, commerce, or industry. Moreover, the secondary school, in order to meet more effectively its responsibility to provide an adequate general education, began to extend its work vertically to include the first two years of college and the last two years of the elementary school. The challenge to secondary education was now threefold: (1) to develop integrated programs of general education that would meet the needs of all, regardless of social origins or occupational destinations; (2) to provide for those who would not go on to higher institutions special programs of vocational guidance and education; and (3) to give the youth who would go on to higher institutions the opportunity to supplement the work of their general education by such special studies as seemed appropriate. Thus the ideal of equal opportunity for all and the democratization of secondary education entailed by that ideal had gone far in changing the traditional curriculum.

The college curriculum was also affected by the general movement to democratize education. Beginning around 1890, the increase in college enrollments was little less spectacular than the increase of attendance in high schools.[2] Young people now appeared on college campuses with extremely diverse interests. Some were looking forward to entrance to one or another of the old-line professions; some intended to enter agriculture, industry, or commerce; some were primarily concerned with preparation

[1] Leonard V. Koos, *Trends in American Secondary Education* (Cambridge, Mass.: Harvard University Press, 1927), pp. 8–10.

[2] In 1890 the entire undergraduate enrollment was about 3 per cent of the number of persons in the traditional undergraduate age group, 18 to 21 years. Corresponding per cents were 4 for 1900, 5 for 1910, 8 for 1920, 12 for 1930, and 32 for 1956.

for homemaking; and some regarded a college education as a "natural sequence" to high school and exhibited no great concern about the more distant future. This influx of a new clientele was one factor influencing the rapid expansion of college curriculums. In fact, the offerings of most liberal-arts colleges became so numerous and so specialized that it was difficult for the student to get an integrated view of any large area of human experience, past or present. The situation was all the more aggravated by the widespread adoption of the elective system.

For a number of decades now, one of the major problems of higher education has been the development of a program of general education to replace the "splintered" curriculum which resulted from specialization and the elective system.

THE INCREASE OF KNOWLEDGE

Until the middle of the nineteenth century the ancient languages, mathematics, philosophy, and theology continued to hold their traditional place at the center of the educational stage. Some attention had been given to the sciences, to modern foreign languages, and to the social sciences, but none of these occupied a position in the curriculum of very great importance. After about 1865, however, the curriculum began to show the effect of an expanding volume of knowledge. As advances were made in the physical and biological sciences and new knowledge was translated into technology in both industry and agriculture, as medical research laid the basis for a more fundamental understanding of health and illness, as psychology and psychiatry opened the doors to a more adequate view of human behavior, and as the social sciences subjected man's history and the working of his contemporary institutions to a more searching analysis, new subjects began to force their way into the time-honored language-mathematics curriculum. Before the end of the nineteenth century, chemistry and physics, botany and zoology, physiology, physical geography, English language and literature, modern foreign languages, history, manual training, home economics, agricultural and business training, and art and music were all competing with the established subjects for a place in the curriculum.

The new additions to the college curriculums, reflecting both the expansion of new knowledge and the acceptance of its worth, made more obvious the basic defect of the elective system and more pressing the need of principles for selection of the basic content of a general education. The efforts to construct a proper curriculum have been continuous, and they will continue as long as knowledge expands and understanding grows of the nature of learning and the learner. Certainly, although each new generation may easily overestimate its own contribution to knowledge of both the world and man, the present generation has witnessed contributions of such magnitude, particularly in science, that the selection and reordering of curriculum elements is now perhaps a more formidable task than it has ever been.

EDUCATION FOR VOCATIONAL EFFICIENCY

Throughout the centuries, both in Europe and in the United States, secondary and higher education had had as one of its main purposes the preparation of a select group of young people for entrance to one or another of the professions. In this country, some provision had been made from colonial days for the vocational education of youth who were to enter commerce or industry, but for the most part proficiency in the trades, commerce, and agriculture was acquired through apprenticeship or on the job itself. Nor did the swift transformation of the United States into an industrial nation during the decades following the Civil War lead, as might have been expected, to a marked increase in vocational education. The enactment of federal legislation (the Morrill Act of 1862) whereby federal lands were donated to each of the states for the establishment and maintenance of a college of agricultural and mechanical arts stimulated the development of vocational education at both the college and secondary level. Here and there private commercial and industrial schools and a few public schools met in part the growing demand for vocational training, but it was not until the passage of the Smith-Hughes Law in 1917 that a widespread program of vocational education was developed. Thereafter, however, vocational education became increasingly important and the advocates of a liberal education, as it was traditionally defined, were forced to yield an important place in the curriculum to the newer vocational subjects and activities. Negative reaction to the trend has been strong at times, but the criticisms have not been directed so much toward the idea of vocational education as a function of the school as toward narrow and inadequate conceptions of the nature of the vocational preparation and of the academic underpinning required for it in the contemporary world.

THE NEED FOR MORE COMPREHENSIVE SOCIAL UNDERSTANDING

As long as the United States was essentially rural, the problems of social policy both in community and in nation were comparatively simple. Not only that, it was an age when men placed their reliance on laissez faire and in more or less automatic adjustment in the whole area of social relationships. But with the advance of technology and the transformation of America into a great industrial domain, the problems of social policy became increasingly complex. As the consequences of technologica change were woven into the whole fabric of social relationships, ol mores began to lose their sanctions and long-established institutions begai to exhibit the need of modification. Science and invention, translated int technology, had come to be the great disturbers of the ways of men. I was no longer possible to rely on the processes of automatic adjustment more and more, men were forced to cultivate ingenuity and experimenta tion in the whole area of social relations, whether of economy, government or ethics.

The need of social technology — the shift from faith in automati adjustment to reliance on social design — created for youth a vastly dil ferent world and for education a new center of interest. The concern and interests of youth were of necessity extended beyond the primary socia relationships of home, school, and community into the relationships of th great society. If youth were now to meet the demands made upon then by social technology, if they were to play their part in social experimenta tion, they would have to enter adult life with a far greater understandin; of the workings of economic, social, and political arrangements than thei elders had possessed. One of the most pressing needs of youth came to b the acquisition of that breadth and precision of knowledge which woul be required to participate intelligently in solving social problems. Thu one of the most important obligations of the school was to prepare youtl to pass sound judgment on fundamental matters of public and social policy Then, as America moved into a position of leadership in a world in whic] the scope of knowledge required for understanding of economic, social and political processes was expanding almost by the hour, new dimension were added to the schools' responsibility for inculcating social intelligenc in the nation's youth.

THE FINDINGS OF SCIENTIFIC INQUIRY

For three or four decades following 1865 the content of the curriculun was determined almost exclusively on the basis of personal judgment Lacking the benefit of scientific data, the leaders of each community in cluded in the educational program the content and the activities tha seemed to them desirable. By 1890 the curriculum of both the elementar and the secondary school had become so overcrowded with new subjects anc so disorganized that steps were taken by a number of national committee: (Committee of Ten on Secondary School Studies, 1891; Committee of Fifteen on Elementary Schools, 1893; Committee on College En trance Requirements, 1895) to introduce a degree of order and standard ization into the educational program at all levels. Although the conclu sions reached in the reports of these committees and the policies adopted as a result of their deliberations were not based upon scientific studies, the reports were extremely important in determining the content of the curriculum for decades to come and had the effect of making it difficult to apply the findings of scientific study to curriculum reorganization.

About 1890, however, the scientific study of education in this country began to get under way. G. Stanley Hall, a former student in the psychological laboratory of Wilhelm Wundt in Leipzig, had in 1884 established a center for the study of the mental development of children at Johns Hopkins University. Hall later became president of Clark University and made it a center of psychological study. Although the methods employed by Hall and his students were so unsystematic and so lacking in precision that no very significant body of scientific principles was uncovered, it can still be said that Hall and his followers called attention to the possibility of the scientific study of child development and that they succeeded at least in making the concept of adolescence a vital one in education.

During the closing decade of the nineteenth century and the first decades of the twentieth century, other leaders were subjecting the process of education to scientific analysis. J. M. Rice in 1897 initiated the testing movement by his investigation of spelling and it was not long before objective tests of many kinds began to appear. Soon after the turn of the century (1904), Edward L. Thorndike gave great impetus to the development of statistical methods in the area of education by the publication of his *Mental and Social Measurements*. In the years following, statistical methods were rapidly perfected and they afforded increasingly significant means of scientific inquiry. In educational psychology William James, Charles H. Judd, and Edward L. Thorndike were doing significant work. A large number of later investigators continued to increase the extent of knowledge about the nature of the learning process.

During the present century an immense volume of scientific research has been done in the field of education. In the area of the curriculum, investigations of handwriting, spelling, reading, and arithmetic have been especially fruitful, but practically all the school subjects have been intensively studied. Hypotheses relating to nearly all the curriculums of elementary, secondary, and higher education have been tested by continually improving techniques of scientific research. It is true, as the Commission on Social Studies pointed out, that scientific method "cannot in itself dictate purpose, policy, or program for either statecraft or education."[3] Value is essentially reaction to experience. But philosophies and value systems are themselves in large measure the product of experience

[3] *Conclusions and Recommendations of the Commission,* The Report of the Commission on Social Studies (New York: Charles Scribner's Sons, 1934), p. 3.

and they reflect the influence of science. Certainly the scientific study of education has affected the selection of the content of learning, the form of organization it has taken, and the methods employed in the educative process.

CHANGING CONCEPTS OF
THE PURPOSE AND CONTENT OF LEARNING

The curriculum is always influenced by the ends it is thought education should achieve and by the content of learning deemed most appropriate to attain those ends. Within the past century at least four major positions have been maintained by one group or another of educational leaders with respect to the essential functions of education. These four positions or concepts are not mutually exclusive, but each does have its own particular emphasis and its own special concern with respect to what constitutes the proper content of learning.

Adherents of the first position have regarded mental and moral discipline, or the training of the intellect, within the framework of universal and changeless values, as the essential goal of education. To some of the adherents of this position, universal values are the gift of revelation and to others they are the gift of metaphysics. In either case the eternal verities by which men live are the touchstone of education. Indeed, education becomes a kind of exegesis: It undertakes to explain the world of nature and of man in terms of first principles. All the adherents of this position agree on the necessity of reducing whatever human experience is employed in the process of education to some kind of systematic organization; they are at one in denying that the content of learning lies primarily in the experience of the individual as he proceeds to solve the problems arising in his daily life. This point of view with respect to the outcome of education was commonly held before 1860; it still prevails among many who feel that education should serve religious ends; and it has been revived in recent years by some who are seeking to erect an educational structure on a metaphysical basis. Proponents of the second and closely related position also have insisted that the chief end of education is mental discipline, or the training of the intellect. The purpose of education is to train the individual to think, to prepare him for all the adventures of the mind. The power to think, it is held, is not confined to any special kind of data but is of universal application. The individual who has cultivated the intellectual virtues, whose mind has been properly fashioned, can think precisely and correctly when confronted with any combination of physical or social data. This position was widely held during the second half of the nineteenth century. Those who have held to the doctrine of mental discipline have always found the major content of learning within the capital of human experience, within the systematic organization of the cultural heritage. Like those who adhere to the first position, the adherents of the doctrine of mental discipline have not accepted the view that the major content of learning is to be found within the experience of the individual learner. In fact, they have been the strongest advocates of traditional school subjects.

The third group of educational leaders has insisted that an integrated interpretation of those elements of human experience essential for living in contemporary society is the most important objective of education. According to this view, those who make the curriculum are always faced with the task of identifying the elements of human experience, through all its sweep and depth, that the individual must come to understand if he is to adjust most satisfactorily to the society of his own day. To be effective, the educational program must employ appropriate means of helping the individual understand and interpret those accumulations of ideas, knowledge, values, and skills that constitute the capital of human experience. The school fails to accomplish its fundamental goal unless the individual in the end has arrived at a systematic understanding and interpretation of the essential elements of race experience. The individual who has not attained a systematic understanding of the significant achievements of the race, who has confined his intellectual outlook to the contemporary and the local, or who has built his knowledge and his understandings around his personal needs and urges in the solution of his personal problems will never be able to participate effectively in many of life's activities. The individual who has selected and organized his experiences largely in terms of his own personality development, who has been permitted to select and organize his own cultural heritage, is likely to fail in reaching an understanding of the forces operating in the world about him. Lacking any fundamental understanding of the moving forces in human history, he will have little sense of social direction and will be unprepared to help formulate social policy. In short, the capital of human experience, it is said, is always the coin of the realm and to debase it is to bring about intellectual bankruptcy and ineffectual social action.

Here, as with the other groups previously mentioned, the content of learning falls chiefly in the broad area of organized human experience. Subject matter organized in advance is regarded as essential to the educative process. The existing subject matter employed at any given time may have been unwisely selected and ineffectively organized, but failure on these counts does not invalidate the need for selection and organization. The major task of the progressive realist in education is to help each new generation to select and reinterpret the essential elements of race experience.

Finally, the adherents of the fourth school of thought regard education as individual growth through self-direction and the continuing reconstruction of one's experience. Education is thought of as growth and the individual learner is always at the center of the process. Insofar as the curriculum takes any definite form, it crystallizes around the interests, felt needs, and problems of the individual learner. The growing individual as he organizes and reorganizes his experience to resolve his own concerns and problems is the measure of all things; the individual must identify and organize his own cultural heritage and fashion it to his own peculiar needs in a changing world in which tradition and authority and accepted values have little place. Some adherents of this point of view maintain that, although the content of learning falls mainly within individual experience, the individual will reorganize and reinterpret his experience until in the end it assumes a form approximately the same as that in which organized race experience, or subject matter, is presented to the mature person. Others, more radical, have appeared to be concerned chiefly with personality development, have looked with disdain upon the teaching of mere facts, and have regarded the organization of human experience into any kind of school subjects as contributing to the intellectual self-efface-ment of the learner.

These points of view with respect to the content and organization of the curriculum have not been mutually exclusive. All have insisted to some degree on the necessity of making use of the knowledge and values that have emerged from human experience; only the most radical have been willing to leave to immature children and youth complete responsi-bility for selecting the content of learning; the principle of organization has nowhere been completely abandoned; few, if any, have entirely lost sight of the goal of personal development; and all have more or less con-sciously oriented their educational program in terms of a system of core values. But the differences of emphasis indicated in the preceding para-graphs have been important in the development of the curriculum.

The Changing Program of the Elementary School

Historically, elementary education may be defined as that education which is deemed essential for every citizen, whatever may be his destina-tion. In simple societies the program of elementary education is cor-respondingly simple; in more complex societies the functions of the ele-mentary school are expanded and enlarged. In 1865 the elementary school in the United States aimed at three major objectives: (1) to de-velop in children some degree of competence in the use of the English language in spoken and written form, (2) to teach the rudiments of the number system, and (3) to socialize children and youth in terms of the prevailing mores and value system. A less important objective was to give pupils some understanding of the world of nature and of the society in which they lived. The first major objective was to be attained through emphasis on the traditional subjects of reading, spelling, writing, grammar, and declamation. The second purpose was to be accomplished, of course, through the study of arithmetic. A great deal of attention was given to "ciphering" and to mental arithmetic as well. The third purpose was accomplished to some degree through formal instruction in "manners" and proper modes of conduct, but more particularly through association between teacher and pupil. The whole atmosphere of the school was conducive to the acceptance on the part of the pupil of the existing pattern of economic, social, and political arrangements. The relatively slight attention to United States history, geography, and "object lessons" opened the door only a little way to a view of the world in which the pupil lived.

THE FURTHER DEVELOPMENT OF THE CONTENT SUBJECTS

Between 1865 and the close of the century, the elementary-school curriculum was materially enriched by the revision of old and the addition of new content subjects — subjects designed to give the pupil a better understanding of the physical world about him and of the world of social relations. The work of a number of earlier European educational theorists and reformers was influential in bringing about some of these changes. One of the most important of these theorists was the Swiss reformer Johann Heinrich Pestalozzi.

Through his writings and through the schools that he organized and conducted at Burgdorf and Yverdon, Pestalozzi attempted to define and demonstrate his educational principles. He was primarily concerned with freeing education from the deadly formalism that had long dominated it — from the teaching of facts and words that had little or no meaning for those who learned them. For the memorization of a body of formally organized content Pestalozzi would substitute the development of the instincts, capacities, and faculties of the growing child. He made sense impression the most important principle of instruction. He would have children observe, discuss, think; he would build up concepts and understandings by proceeding from the concrete to the abstract. He once said:

> If I look back and ask myself what I really have done toward the improvement of the methods of elementary instruction, I find that, in recognizing observation as the absolute basis of all knowledge, I have established the first and most important principle of instruction. . . .[4]

Elementary science and home geography. During the latter part of the nineteenth century Pestalozzi's influence was of great importance in the development of content subjects in the elementary school. Two sub-

[4] Henry Barnard, *Pestalozzi and His Educational System* (Syracuse, N.Y.: C. W. Bardeen, 1854), pp. 74–75.

jects especially, elementary science and home geography, reflected the influence of his ideas.

The followers of Pestalozzi in this country, notably Edward A. Sheldon in the Normal School at Oswego, New York, placed great stress upon object teaching. Children were put to observing and discussing a great variety of objects — paper, flowers, glass, lead, animals — with considerable emphasis upon the learning of scientific terms. Object teaching was hailed as a great step forward in getting away from formal *memoriter* work. Even object teaching, however, tended to become extremely formal, the pupil merely committing to memory the qualities and characteristics of objects described in the "object lesson." Moreover, the objects selected for study were not such as to develop any systematic pattern of thought or body of understandings. In time, especially after 1880, object lessons began to give place to a form of elementary science which stressed the learning of technical scientific classifications as the first step in scientific culture. The extreme emphasis on scientific classification proved to be inappropriate for young children, and after the turn of the century formal elementary science gave place to nature study, or "the simple observational study of common natural objects and processes for the sake of personal acquaintance with the things which appeal to human interest."[5] More recently, elementary science has come to stress the functional understanding of some of the principles and generalizations of science, with emphasis also upon the acquisition of a problem-solving attitude. Thus the science program in the modern elementary school has come to be far different from what Pestalozzi and his followers envisioned, but it stems from their emphasis on object teaching.

The influence of Pestalozzi on geography as a school subject was also important. During the earlier part of the nineteenth century geography was of the "dictionary-encyclopedia" type. Children were required to commit to memory many definitions and to memorize a large mass of unrelated facts about places, the customs of various peoples, and strange natural phenomena in the different parts of the world. Considerable space was devoted to political and commercial facts. Geography appeared to be a fit subject for the inclusion of any assortment of facts, and they were usually presented like pieces in a counterpane, as though they had no special relation to one another.

As might have been expected, Pestalozzi's emphasis on sense perception led to the introduction of home geography as a new subject. Pupils now began their study of geography by observing their immediate surroundings. Often after observing the type forms in their home community, they undertook to make maps in clay models. The changes in geography instruction initiated by Pestalozzi were carried forward by the great German geog-

[5] Samuel Chester Parker, *A Textbook in the History of Modern Elementary Education* (Boston: Ginn & Company, 1912), p. 339.

rapher Carl Ritter (1779–1859). It was the work of Ritter above all others that transformed geography from an unsystematic collection of facts into a science that formulated the general principles governing the relation of social development to physiographic conditions. A student of Ritter's, Arnold Guyot, came to the United States in 1848 and did much to introduce the ideas of Pestalozzi and Ritter with respect to the teaching of geography. Toward the end of the century (1889) Colonel F. W. Parker published his *How to Teach Geography,* a volume which applied the principles of Ritter and Guyot. Geography was now taking a place in the curriculum as an important content subject.

History and literature. By the close of the nineteenth century history and literature were also becoming important subjects in the elementary school. In 1860 only 1.35 per cent of the pupils in the common schools of Ohio, probably more or less typical of the country as a whole, were pursuing history as a subject of study.[6] By 1870, United States history had become generally accepted as a subject in the two upper grades of the elementary school, and here and there before 1900 history was moving down into the intermediate and primary grades. Soon after the turn of the century, history began to find wide acceptance as an elementary-school subject in the lower as well as the upper grades.

The followers of Johann Friedrich Herbart in this country were influential in bringing about a wider acceptance of history as a school subject. As early as 1831, Herbart, a professor at the University of Koenigsberg, Germany, began to lay the foundations of modern experimental psychology. He was also concerned with the application of psychology to teaching. It was not, however, until about a quarter of a century after Herbart's death that his principles of education gained much popularity in Germany. In 1865 Tuiskon Ziller, a professor at the University of Leipzig, began to popularize Herbart's teachings. Somewhat later, Professor William Rein established at the University of Jena an important center for the study and application of Herbartian principles. During the eighteen-eighties, a number of Americans, including Charles De Garmo and Charles and Frank McMurry, were students in Germany. They returned to this country extremely enthusiastic about Herbartian principles. In 1892 they were instrumental in the organization of the "National Herbart Society" (later the National Society for the Study of Education), which enrolled in its membership many prominent educators. Herbartian principles were introduced into many normal schools and became extremely popular in many parts of the nation, especially in the upper Mississippi Valley.

The chief end of education, as the Herbartians saw it, was the cultiva-

[6] Rolla M. Tryon, *The Social Sciences as School Subjects* (New York: Charles Scribner's Sons, 1935), p. 108.

tion of moral notions among children. Education should develop personal character and prepare the individual for social usefulness. Naturally enough, history was regarded as the most effective subject for the accomplishment of these ends. The Herbartians were influential in winning for history a place of importance in the elementary school. Moreover, the values they attached to history tended to free it from the narrow confines of mental discipline and to make it a tool for the cultivation of a real understanding of the development of human society and institutions.

It is easy to overemphasize the influence of the Herbartians in the development of history as a school subject. Other influences were also of great importance. The Committee of Ten of the National Education Association in its Report of 1893 recommended that history be taught as an important subject in the schools in each of at least eight years. The Committee of Fifteen — also a committee of the National Education Association — recognized in its Report of 1895 the importance of the study of history in the elementary school. From time to time other national committees, notably the Committee of Eight of the American Historical Association (1908), threw the weight of their influence behind the teaching of history.

After about 1900 literature also began to be given an important place in the elementary school. Theretofore reading had been confined almost exclusively to oral expression, with the result that the amount of material covered was discouragingly small. In 1890 President Charles W. Eliot of Harvard University published the results of an investigation that strikingly revealed the extremely limited acquaintance with literature which children in an average Massachusetts elementary school were getting during the last six years of their course. President Eliot reported as follows:

> I turned next to an examination of the quantity of work done in the grammar school under consideration — and, first, of the amount of reading. The amount of time given to reading and the study of the English language through the spelling-book and the little grammar which are used in that school, and through a variety of other aids to the learning of English, is thirty-seven per cent of all school-time during six years. But what is the amount of reading in this time? I procured two careful estimates of the time it would take a graduate of a high school to read aloud consecutively all the books which are read in this school during six years, including the history, the reading lessons in geography, and the book on manners. The estimates were made by two persons reading aloud at a moderate rate, and reading everything that the children in most of the rooms of that school have been supposed to read during their entire course of six years. The time occupied in doing this reading was forty-six hours.[7]

[7] Charles William Eliot, *Educational Reform* (New York: Century Co., 1909), p. 185.

Eliot and others, notably the Herbartians, who regarded literature next to history as an effective means for moral education, began to urge the use of whole literary classics instead of the selections found in the readers of the day. In time, complete poems like *The Vision of Sir Launfal* and prose literary masterpieces like *Gulliver's Travels* found their way into the curriculum and literature became firmly fixed as an elementary-school subject.

In recent years, it should be added, the tendency has been away from literary masterpieces, prose and poem, toward reading materials better suited to children's interests. A vast body of children's literature has been developed which is imaginative and entertaining and which at the same time serves to cultivate an understanding of the world of nature and the social relations surrounding children. In the meantime, too, the language arts have shifted from a formal study of grammar to functional expression. The aim is to teach children to talk and write easily and correctly in whatever situation they may find themselves, whether it be answering the telephone, meeting a caller at the door, introducing friends, writing letters, or preparing a formal report.

THE KINDERGARTEN INCORPORATED INTO THE PUBLIC SCHOOL SYSTEM

Fleeing the conservative reaction that followed the Revolution of 1848 in Germany, a number of German liberals sought refuge in the United States. Some of them were familiar with the ideas and practices of Friedrich Froebel, the originator of the kindergarten, and it was not long before institutions of this kind were being established throughout the country. It is said that by 1880 some four hundred kindergartens were in operation. For some years the kindergarten tended to be something of a special cult, more or less separate from the public school proper. In 1873, however, a kindergarten was opened as a part of the public school system in St. Louis and by 1898, according to the United States Commissioner of Education, public kindergartens were to be found in 189 cities.

Two basic ideas have governed the work carried forward in the kindergarten: (1) self-activity and (2) social participation. Froebel held that the process of education should be a natural unfolding of inner tendencies and drives, a continuing development of the inborn capacities of the child. He stressed motor activity and learning by doing. In his emphasis on child growth through more or less spontaneous activities, Froebel was reverting to principles advocated by Rousseau. Unlike Rousseau, however, Froebel insisted that the child grow up in a social environment and learn at an early age to participate in the processes of social cooperation. As Cubberley so aptly put it, the kindergarten had "individual development as its aim, motor expression as its method, and social co-operation as its means."[8] In more recent years, increased knowledge about the growth and development of children has led to modifications in kindergarten practices, but the basic principles of self-activity and socialization are still important.

THE ADDITION OF EXPRESSION SUBJECTS

Between the Civil War and the end of the century the elementary curriculum had been greatly expanded through the introduction or further development of content subjects — science, geography, history, civics, literature. At the same time the expression subjects — music, art, manual arts, domestic arts — were receiving attention in some of the more progressive city school systems. It was not until well after the turn of the century, however, that the expression subjects found widespread acceptance in the elementary schools and that a rich body of content was developed for them.

FREEING THE CURRICULUM FROM THE GRIP OF FORMALISM

During the forty years following the Civil War the American elementary school became a highly formalized institution. As the graded system became commonly accepted, it was necessary to classify pupils into their respective grades and to grade the subject matter appropriate for the work of each year or even half-year. Courses of study were developed which rigidly prescribed the subject matter to be mastered or the skills to be acquired. Textbooks were prepared, subject by subject, for each of the several grades, and it was the duty of the teacher to see that the pupils "covered" the prescribed pages within the alloted time. Much of the pupil's time was spent in memorization of textbook facts which for most pupils did not add up to general principles or significant configurations of meaning. Little attention was given to individual differences. At the end of each grade the pupil was tested, and if he could meet the minimum standard prescribed for all he was promoted; if not, he repeated the work the following year. The formal character of the elementary school of this period is vividly described in the following quotation from Professor Edward H. Reisner:

> The effect of all the factors surrounding the graded school of the generation following the Civil War was to develop a school machine. In contrast with the school conditions of a generation preceding there was a great deal more material included in the graded course of instruction, but

[8] Ellwood P. Cubberley, *Public Education in the United States*, Revised Edition (Boston: Houghton Mifflin Company, 1934), p. 459.

the quality of teaching and learning was improved hardly at all. From the lowest grade to the highest the pupils followed an endless succession of book assignments which they learned out of hand to reproduce on call. The chief end of pupils was to master skills and learn facts as directed by a teacher who in turn was under the automatic control of a printed course of study, a set of textbooks, and the necessity of preparing her class to pass certain examinations on the contents of a specific number of printed pages. From the standpoint of discipline the physical cruelties of the earlier day had to a large degree disappeared, but the control exercised over the pupils was at least negative. The business of the school being what it was, any movement, any conversation, any communication, were out of order. The spirit of control was military and repressive, not constructive and coöperative. Long rows of seats, military evolutions of classes, stated appearances for recitations, with the rest of the school time devoted to narrowly prescribed exercises, had for their moral equivalent being quiet, industrious at assigned tasks, and submissive to the rule of the drill-sergeant in skirts who unflinchingly governed her little kingdom of learn-by-heart-and-recite-by-rote.[9]

Numerous reform movements were directed at reducing the formal and institutional character of the traditional elementary school. Object teaching, sponsored by Doctor Edward A. Sheldon of the Oswego Normal School in the eighteen-sixties and seventies, was a definite attempt to substitute concrete experiences with common objects for the memorization of textbook content. The kindergarten movement, with its emphasis on self-activity, the value of individual experience, and respect for the personality of the child, was influential in changing practice in the elementary school, especially in the lower grades. The Herbartian movement of the eighteen-nineties also constituted an assault against the prevailing organization of subject matter as well as the method of teaching. The importance attached to interest in the learning process, the central position assigned to meaning in the organization of instructional materials, and the willingness to abandon traditional subjects in the interests of correlation all added up to an attack upon prevailing practice. Colonel Francis Wayland Parker, while he was superintendent of schools in Quincy, Massachusetts (1875–1880), and while he was principal of the Cook County Normal School in Chicago (1883 to 1899), led a movement to introduce the principles of Froebel into the elementary school. He was also a strong advocate of the concentration of instruction around a single core.

Toward the end of the century advances in educational psychology began to lay a basis for a scientific understanding of child nature and behavior. In time, the findings of experimental psychology opened up a wide field of new knowledge with respect both to individual dif-

[9] Edward H. Reisner, *The Evolution of the Common School* (New York: The Macmillan Co., 1930), pp. 427–428.

ferences among children and to the nature of the learning process. When
the findings of the scientific study of education on a wide front began to
receive application in practice, much of the most objectionable formalism
that had so long characterized the elementary school began to disappear.

PROGRESSIVE EDUCATION IN THE ELEMENTARY SCHOOL

The Progressive Education Association, formally organized in 1918,
sponsored a philosophy and a variety of educational practices originated
by a long line of educational theorists who had attacked the formalism of
the traditional school.[10] Many of the ideas of the Progressives could be
traced back to Rousseau, Pestalozzi, Herbart, and Froebel, but the leaders
in the movement looked to Professor John Dewey as the main source of
their inspiration. In a number of publications — *The School and Society*
(1899), *How We Think* (1909), *Democracy and Education* (1916),
Human Nature and Conduct (1922), *Experience and Education* (1938)
— Dewey laid the foundation for an educational philosophy which challenged sharply the practices of the traditional elementary school. The
following quotations will serve to indicate the nature of Dewey's criticism of the traditional school and will give some idea at least of the basic
principles of his own philosophy:

> The traditional scheme is, in essence, one of imposition from above
> and from outside. It imposes adult standards, subject matter, and methods
> upon those who are only growing slowly toward maturity. The gap is so
> great that the required subject matter, the methods of learning and of
> behaving are foreign to the existing capacities of the young. They are
> beyond the reach of the experience the young learners already possess.
> Consequently, they must be imposed; even though good teachers will use
> devices of art to cover up the imposition so as to relieve it of obviously
> brutal features.
>
> But the gulf between the mature or adult products and the experience
> and abilities of the young is so wide that the very situation forbids much
> active participation by pupils in the development of what is taught.
> Theirs is to do — and learn, as it was the part of the six hundred to do
> and die. Learning here means acquisition of what already is incorporated
> in books and in the heads of the elders. Moreover, that which is taught
> is thought of as essentially static. It is taught as a finished product, with
> little regard either to the ways in which it was originally built up or to
> changes that will surely occur in the future. It is to a large extent the
> cultural product of societies that assumed the future would be much

[10] For a scholarly treatment of Progressivism and Progressive education in the
total social setting, see Lawrence A. Cremin, *The Transformation of the School:
Progressivism in American Education, 1876–1957* (New York: Alfred A. Knopf,
Inc., 1961).

like the past, and yet it is used as education food in a society where change is the rule, not the exception.[11]

Dewey went on to formulate the essential principles of the philosophy of the Progressive schools, to which he himself had contributed.

If one attempts to formulate the philosophy of education implicit in the practices of the newer education, we may, I think, discover certain common principles amid the variety of progressive schools now existing. To imposition from above is opposed expression and cultivation of individuality; to external discipline is opposed free activity; to learning from texts and teachers, learning through experience; to acquisition of isolated skills and techniques by drill, is opposed acquisition of them as means of attaining ends which make direct vital appeal; to preparation for a more or less remote future is opposed making the most of the opportunities of present life; to static aims and materials is opposed acquaintance with a changing world.[12]

It is impossible, of course, in brief space to make an adequate analysis of Dewey's philosophy of education. Basic to his thinking, however, is the role of experience — or perhaps one should say *experiencing* — in the educative process. Education, he says, "is a development within, by, and for experience." Thus Dewey finds the content of learning within individual experience, rather than within the organized experience of the race. Appropriate subject matter, according to Dewey, does not consist of formally organized aspects of human experience; it is, rather, what the child learns in order to solve problems important and interesting to him.[13] The first step in the organization of subject matter, then, is to find the material for learning within the experience of the learner.

The next step is the progressive development of what is already experienced into a fuller and richer and also more organized form, *a form that gradually approximates that in which subject matter is presented to the skilled, mature person.*[14]

Dewey's insistence that the material for learning is to be found within the experience and interests of the learner logically led him to oppose the traditional organization of school subjects; to affirm that education is life, not preparation for life; and to advocate greater freedom for children in the schoolroom than was usually found in the "traditional school."

[11] John Dewey, *Experience and Education* (New York: The Macmillan Co., 1938), pp. 4–5. Used by permission of Kappa Delta Pi.
[12] *Ibid.,* pp. 5–6.
[13] John Dewey, *Democracy and Education* (New York: The Macmillan Co., 1916), Chap. XIV.
[14] *Ibid.,* p. 87. Italics ours.

The decline of Progressive education. Progressive education in the early years of its development was vigorously experimental, and the dramatic reforms which it sponsored attracted to its ranks many able and aggressive leaders. By the mid-thirties, Progressive ideas had to come to dominate teaching in many teachers colleges and schools of education, and they were implemented, too, in many schools — especially at the elementary level — throughout the country. But despite its early vigor and success, the Progressive movement had pretty well run its course by the mid-forties. The Progressive Education Association changed its name to the American Education Fellowship in 1944, readopted its original name in 1953, and disbanded in 1956. Its journal, *Progressive Education,* partially financed by the John Dewey Society in the later years of its thirty-five-year career, ceased publication in 1957.

It is not easy to explain how a movement as active and influential as the Progressive-education movement was in the mid-thirties came to lose its grip on most educational leaders and on the American public as well. One reason seems to be that Progressive education was never able to develop any distinctive philosophy of its own. As Professor Bode once put it: "The fact that the Progressive movement has never come across with an adequate philosophy of education warrants the presumption that it does not have any."[15]

Equally important, perhaps, the later leadership of the movement fell into the hands of extremists who overplayed their attack on traditional education and greatly exaggerated the merits of their own program. As Woodring has put it:

> It appeared to many that they stood in sharp opposition to academic scholarship, to intellectual discipline, to clear and consistent standards of achievement, to rationalism and intellectualism, and to civilized standards of behavior for children and adolescents. They overstressed their tenets until they became clichés, and because its adherents were uncritically tolerant of their own lunatic fringes, Progressivism came to be identified in the public mind with its own excesses.[16]

At any rate, the growing public criticism to which education was subjected in the forties and fifties was more often than not directed toward Progressive education, which had come to be equated in the public mind with an unrealistic conception of values and needs, planless and random improvisation, activity for its own sake, low academic standards, and lack of discipline.

Despite its weaknesses and excesses, Progressive education contributed

[15] Boyd Bode, *Progressive Education at the Crossroads* (New York: Newson and Company, 1938), pp. 85–86.
[16] Paul Woodring, *A Fourth of a Nation* (New York: McGraw-Hill Book Co., Inc., 1957), p. 16.

much that was lasting. It did much to free the school from the grip of formalism and to make it a more friendly, cooperative place for pupils and teachers to work. It helped to place the interests and needs of children in their proper perspective in the educational program. It made educators and teachers generally more aware of the importance of direct experience in the educational process. And, for better or for worse, its attacks on logically organized subject matter and its emphasis on projects developed around units of life experience have had a profound influence on the structural organization of the curriculum and on methods of teaching.

Professor Woodring has made what appears to be a fair and objective appraisal of the Progressive-education movement. Of it, he says:

> Progressivism was right in much that it emphasized, wrong in much that it rejected. In its earlier period it was right in emphasizing the importance of the individual child and the importance of interest, freedom, and activity in learning, for these things had been neglected in the preceding period. It was wrong in its attacks on scholarship, the academic disciplines, and the importance of factual knowledge. It was wrong in its refusal to establish a priority of goals — in its insistence that one goal could not be placed above another. It was wrong in its rejection of standards and in its demand that there should be no discipline except self-discipline; it was wrong in trying to make the schools responsible for all aspects of the child's development. And it was fatally wrong in refusing to listen to criticism from parents and other citizens. A reform movement can survive for a time on the basis of its opposition to prevailing trends, but a continuing philosophy of education must have a firmer base.
>
> Few informed people will deny that the Progressive movement contributed much of great and lasting value to American education. Still fewer will deny that it carried its principles to excess, distorted its own sound views, outlived its usefulness as a reform movement, and has now come to its logical end.[17]

THE ELEMENTARY SCHOOLS OF TODAY

The better — and, indeed, most — elementary schools of today differ in many significant ways from the elementary schools of a few decades ago. In the first place, the atmosphere in which learning experiences take the place is a more natural one.

New types of school furniture, television and other audio-visual aids, laboratory facilities of various kinds, extended and carefully selected libraries, and, here and there, "teaching machines" have contributed to the deformalization of the classroom and to the introduction of more flexible procedures than those of a generation or so ago. New knowledge

[17] *Ibid.,* p. 27.

and a broader understanding of the nature of the child and of the learning process, more satisfactory interpretations of group behavior, and new concepts regarding the role of the teacher have also contributed to the revamping of the classroom environment. Although change is uneven, the work of most schools is more meaningful and is conducted in a freer, friendlier, and more cooperative spirit than was the case except in the very exceptional schools of preceding generations.

Rigorous imposition of tasks by the teacher has given place to teacher-pupil planning of the activities to be carried forward. Individual differences are better understood and increasingly recognized, and the individualization of instruction has taken on a deeper meaning and purpose.[18] Efforts directed toward fitting the program to the needs and capacities of all children have led to changes in the internal organization of the school and have given rise to experimentation with multigrade and multiage grouping, non-graded schools,[19] and other arrangements and activities of various kinds.

The major substantive content of the many separate subjects — reading, writing, spelling, arithmetic, geography, history, civics, nature study, elementary science, hygiene, music, and drawing — that have found their way into the curriculum in the course of years is still taught. The number of subjects, however, has been reduced by more closely relating and integrating experiences of learning in such areas as language, the social studies, and the fine arts. In many elementary schools, the subject-type program of curriculum organization has been replaced by core-type or experience-type programs. That is to say, instead of studying logically organized subjects or subject areas, the pupils' learning experiences are organized within the framework of a "unit of life experience," a "center of interest," or an "area of living." The primary purpose of programs so organized is to provide all pupils with a common body of significant experiences and to develop in them habits and skills in problem-solving.

The Expansion and Organization of the Secondary-School Curriculum

From the close of the Civil War until about 1900, two significant changes were taking place in the instructional content of American secondary education. These were: (1) the increase in the number of subjects offered, and (2) the standardization of the work of the public high school.

[18] *Individualizing Instruction,* Sixty-first Yearbook of the National Society for the Study of Education, Part I (Chicago: University of Chicago Press, 1962).

[19] John I. Goodlad and Robert H. Anderson, *The Nongraded Elementary School* (New York: Harcourt, Brace & World, Inc., 1959).

THE INCREASE IN SUBJECTS, 1865–1900

The public high school which was now beginning to replace the academy as the dominant type of secondary school was especially responsive to those forces described in the opening sections of this chapter as influential in the development of the curriculum. The net result was a marked expansion in the number of subjects offered. It was now customary to retain the old subjects and to add such new ones as changing social conditions seemed to require. Among the new subjects the sciences led in numerical importance, although various subjects were added in the social sciences, the industrial and manual arts, homemaking, and occupational guidance. The extent to which new subjects were added during this period is illustrated to some extent by a comparison of Tables 25 and 26, which tabulate the frequency of appearance of subjects in twenty high schools for the period 1860–65 and in forty high schools for the period 1896–1900. It was often altogether impossible for a pupil to take all the subjects offered in a particular school and it became necessary to provide a number of courses from which the pupil might make his selection. An examination of the course offerings of sixty high schools for the period 1896–1900 revealed that twenty-five schools offered one course, twelve offered two, eight offered four, and one offered as many as seven. The courses were variously designated as Ancient Classical, Business and Commercial, College Preparatory, Shorter Commercial, Classical, English, English-Science, English-Latin, General, and Scientific. Altogether in these sixty schools no fewer than thirty-six different courses were offered.[20] As new subjects were added to the curriculum and new course organizations were worked out to meet the needs of an increasingly diverse high school population, the high school program tended to become chaotic and confused. The fact was that the emerging high school had no model to serve it in giving order and system to its work. Each community proceeded along lines that seemed best to it, some maintaining a high school with a four-year program and some providing for a course of two or three years. The entrance requirements of the college served to bring some degree of unity into high school programs, but the need continued to grow for a more highly standardized institution.

STANDARDIZING THE HIGH SCHOOL PROGRAM

The conditions described in the preceding paragraph led the National Education Association to appoint a Committee of Ten in 1892 to consider

[20] John Elbert Stout, *The Development of High-School Curricula in the North Central States from 1860 to 1918*, Supplementary Educational Monographs, Vol. III, No. 3, Whole No. 15, June, 1921 (Chicago: University of Chicago, 1921), pp. 49–50.

TABLE 25: FREQUENCY OF APPEARANCE OF SUBJECTS IN
TWENTY HIGH SCHOOLS, 1860–65*

Mathematics

Arithmetic, 17
Algebra, 18
Geometry, 19
Trigonometry, 12
Analytics, 2
Surveying, 8
Engineering, 3

Social Studies

Ancient History, 8
Medieval History, 3
Modern History, 6
United States History, 3
English History, 3
General History, 3
Universal History, 2
Science of Government, 3
United States
  Constitution, 8
Political Economy, 4
History, 2
History of Civilization, 1

English

Grammar, 12
English Analysis, 11
Word Analysis, 4
Reading, 6
Composition, 11
Rhetoric, 18
English Literature, 6
Literature, 1
Classics, 1
Elements of Criticism, 4
Elocution, 1
English, 1

Foreign Language

Latin, 16
Greek, 7
German, 7
French, 4

Commercial Subjects

Bookkeeping, 3
Business Forms, 1

Science

Physiology, 17
Physical Geography, 17
Natural Philosophy, 20
Physics, 1
Chemistry, 17
Geology, 14
Astronomy, 14
Botany, 14
Natural History, 5
Zoology, 4
Geography, 2

Miscellaneous Subjects

Mental Philosophy, 12
Moral Philosophy, 11
Logic, 5
Psychology, 2
Evidences of
  Christianity, 2
Ancient Geography, 2
Butler's *Analogy,* 1
Domestic Science, 2
Natural Theology, 2

* From John Elbert Stout, *The Development of High-School Curricula in the North Central States from 1860 to 1918,* Supplementary Educational Monographs, Vol. III, No. 3, Whole No. 15, June, 1921 (Chicago: University of Chicago, 1921), p. 60.

problems confronting secondary education. The Committee appointed nine subcommittees, or conferences, as they were called, to consider the following subject fields: Latin; Greek; English; other modern languages; mathematics, physics, astronomy, and chemistry; natural history (biology,

Mathematics

Arithmetic, 28
Algebra, 40
Geometry, 29
Plane Geometry, 12
Solid Geometry, 9
Trigonometry, 9

Social Studies

Ancient History, 15
Medieval History, 2
Modern History, 3
United States History, 18
English History, 20
French History, 4
General History, 26
Economic History, 1
History, 2
United States
  Constitution, 2
State Constitution, 1
Civil Government, 24
Civics, 10
American Politics, 1
Social Science, 1
Political Economy, 16

English

Grammar, 14
Analysis, 1
Word Analysis, 5
Reading, 4
Composition, 17
Rhetoric, 25
English Literature, 15
American Literature**
Literature, 14
Authors, 1
Classics, 5
History of English
  Literature, 2
Orthography, 2
First-Year English, 17
Second-Year English, 14
Third-Year English, 11
Fourth-Year English, 5

Foreign Language

Latin, 39
Greek, 10
German, 23
French, 4

Commercial Subjects

Bookkeeping, 29
Business Forms, 4
Commercial Arithmetic, 8
Commercial Law, 9
Commercial Geography, 3
Business Correspondence,
  1
Banking, 1
Stenography, 5
Typewriting, 5
Phonography, 1

Science

Physiology, 28
Physical Geography, 30
Natural Philosophy, 1
Physics, 37
Chemistry, 26
Geology, 9
Botany, 33
Zoology, 18
Biology, 4
Astronomy, 11
Natural History, 1
Geography, 2
Physiography, 1
Miscellaneous Subjects
Mental Philosophy, 1
Moral Philosophy, 1
Psychology, 9
Ethics, 2
Pedagogy, 6
Drawing, 6
Domestic Science, 1
Manual Training, 1

* From John Elbert Stout, *The Development of High-School Curricula in the North Central States from 1860 to 1918*, Supplementary Educational Monographs, Vol. III, No. 3, Whole No. 15, June, 1921 (Chicago: University of Chicago, 1921), pp. 67–68.
** Number not indicated.

including botany, zoology, and physiology); history, civil government, and political economy; and geography (physical geography, geology, and meteorology). Each conference was asked to consider matters such as: (1) the amount of time that should be devoted to the subject in the high school program, (2) the level at which work in the subject should be begun, (3) whether the subject should be accepted for admission to college, and (4) whether the subject should receive any different treatment for pupils going and not going to college.

Most of the conferences — all but those dealing with the classics, mathematics, and geography — recommended that more time be given to their subjects in the school program, and practically all of them outlined a four-year program for their subjects. Some of the conferences felt that their subjects should be begun in the upper grades of the elementary school and most of them recommended that work in their subjects be begun in the first year of the high school. On the last two issues there was complete agreement. All the conferences declared that "every subject which is taught at all in a secondary school should be taught in the same way and to the same extent to every pupil so long as he pursues it, no matter what the probable destination of the pupils may be, or at what point his education is to cease." Each conference recommended that its subject be accepted for college admission.

The Committee of Ten, acting on the recommendations of the several conferences, made the following statement with respect to subjects appropriate for the high schools:

> They are: 1. languages — Latin, Greek, English, German, and French (and locally Spanish); 2. mathematics — algebra, geometry, and trigonometry; 3. general history, and the intensive study of special epochs; 4. natural history — including descriptive astronomy, meteorology, botany, zoölogy, physiology, geology, and ethnology, most of which subjects may be conveniently grouped under the title of physical geography; and 5. physics and chemistry.

The Committee also advocated a policy of extensive study, on the part of any individual pupil, of a relatively small number of subjects. On this point its report read:

> Selection for the individual is necessary to thoroughness, and to the imparting of power as distinguished from information; for any large subject whatever, to yield its training value, must be pursued through several years and be studied from three to five times a week, and if each subject studied is thus to claim a considerable fraction of the pupil's school time, then clearly the individual pupil can give attention to only a moderate number of subjects.

The Committee found it necessary to make recommendations designed to resolve the problem of an overcrowded curriculum. If the pupil, as recommended, was to confine his attention to only a few subjects at a time and pursue each subject for a number of years, it would require far more than four years to complete the high school course. Three recommendations were made with respect to the secondary curriculum: (1) Organize a number of different curriculums, as, for example classical, English-modern-language, and scientific; (2) introduce the elective system; and (3) define a unit of instruction in terms of the number of hours of instruction given per week in the subject. On this last point the Committee suggested:

> A college might say — We will accept for admission any groups of studies taken from the secondary school programme, provided that the sum of the studies in each of the four years amounts to sixteen, or eighteen, or twenty periods a week — as may be thought best — and provided, further, that in each year at least four of the subjects presented shall have been pursued at least three periods a week, and that at least three of the subjects shall have been pursued three years or more.

Evidently, the Committee was suggesting to the high schools and colleges the adoption of a standard unit which would serve as a quantitative measure of secondary education. The adoption of such a standard unit that would serve as a national norm was further stimulated by the Report of the Committee on College Entrance Requirements (1899), which read:

> What is to be desired, and what the committee hopes may become true, is that the colleges will state their entrance requirements in terms of national units, or norms, and that the schools will build up their programs of studies out of the units furnished by these separate courses of study.[21]

Somewhat later, the Carnegie Foundation for the Advancement of Teaching adopted units of work done in high school as a standard by which it could classify higher institutions for the purpose of granting retirement allowances for professors. Institutions requiring fifteen units of high school work for entrance might be acceptable to the Foundation, a unit of work being defined as "a course of five periods a week throughout an academic year." This definition of a unit became widely accepted. In this way a national norm was developed for organizing high school instruction.

[21] "Report of the Committee on College Entrance Requirements," p. 672 in National Education Association, *Journal of Proceedings and Addresses of the Thirty-eighth Annual Meeting,* held in Los Angeles, Cal., July 11–14, 1899.

The report of the Committee of Ten and the development of a quantitative measure of high school work marked a turning point in the history of secondary education in the United States. The high school had now become a highly standardized institution. For at least four decades the subjects recognized by the Committee as appropriate for the high schools held a prominent if not a dominant position in the high school curriculum. The pattern of organization of the high school curriculum established by about 1900 also proved exceedingly difficult to change. As time passed, the adoption of a quantitative measure of secondary-school work tended in many quarters to establish the attitude that one subject was as good as another; after all, a unit of high school work was a unit. Thus, as Kandel has pointed out, the whole problem of value tended to lose its importance.

The Introduction of New Types of Subjects, 1900-World War II

In the early days of the present century the American high school confined its subject offerings, in the main, to those that had been regarded as appropriate by the Committee of Ten — English, ancient and modern foreign languages, mathematics, natural science, history, and geography. In 1905 approximately 98 per cent of the pupils in high school were enrolled in English; more than 87 per cent were enrolled in algebra, geometry, or trigonometry; some 50 per cent were enrolled in Latin, and something less than 50 per cent in modern languages; about 69 per cent were enrolled in history or government; and chemistry, physics, geology, physiology, physical geography, and astronomy, combined, accounted for more than 69 per cent of the pupils (Table 27). Students were generally enrolled in English for four years, in languages three to four years, in mathematics three to four years, in science two to four years, and in history and government from two to four years.

A number of statistical studies have been reported which show the rapid increase in course offerings in the high schools during the early decades of the present century. By making use of an earlier investigation, Van Dyke was able to compare the number of courses offered in thirty-five identical high schools in the north-central states at two periods — 1906–11 and 1929–30.[22] During this quarter-century, the total number of courses offered in these thirty-five schools increased from 53 to 306. The average number of courses increased from 23.7 to 48.1. There was a percentage increase in the number of subjects offered in all the subject groups, but the greatest increase was in the fine arts, industrial arts, physi-

[22] George E. Van Dyke, "Trends in the Development of the High-School Offering, II," *School Review*, XXXIX (December, 1931), 737–747.

TABLE 27: STUDENTS IN CERTAIN STUDIES IN
PUBLIC HIGH SCHOOLS, 1890–1934*

Subject	Percentage of Pupils Enrolled				
	1890	1905	1922	1928	1934
English	....	97.9	78.6	93.1	90.5
Latin	34.7	50.2	27.5	22.0	16.0
Modern languages	16.5	29.4	27.5	25.3	19.7
Algebra	45.4	57.5	40.2	35.2	30.4
Geometry	21.3	28.2	22.7	19.8	17.1
Arithmetic	....	....	10.5	2.4	2.3
Trigonometry	....	1.7	1.5	1.3	1.3
Astronomy	....	1.2	0.1	0.1	0.1
Physics	22.2	15.7	8.9	6.9	6.3
Chemistry	10.1	6.8	7.4	7.1	7.6
Physical geography	....	21.5	4.3	2.7	1.6
Zoology	....	....	1.5	0.8	0.6
Botany	....	....	3.8	1.6	0.9
Biology	....	....	8.8	13.6	14.6
Geology	....	2.3	0.2	0.1	0.1
Physiology	....	22.0	5.1	2.7	1.8
Hygiene and sanitation	....	....	6.1	7.8	6.5
General science	....	....	18.3	17.5	17.8
History	27.3	40.9	50.7	46.5	42.7
Government	....	18.0	19.3	20.0	16.3
Sociology	....	....	2.4	2.7	2.5
Economics	....	....	4.8	5.1	4.9
Problems of democracy	....	....	....	1.0	3.5
Agriculture	....	....	5.1	3.7	3.6
Home economics	....	....	14.3	16.5	16.7
Industrial subjects	....	....	11.3	13.3	14.0
Bookkeeping	....	....	12.6	10.7	9.9
Shorthand	....	....	8.9	8.7	9.0
Typewriting	....	....	13.1	15.2	16.7
Commercial arithmetic	....	....	1.5	7.0	4.9
Commercial law	....	....	0.9	2.6	3.2
Commercial geography	....	....	1.7	4.8	4.0
Commercial history	....	....	0.4	0.2	0.2
Penmanship	....	....	1.7	0.8	0.3
Office practice	....	....	0.4	1.4	1.6
Elementary business training	....	....	....	3.0	6.1
Drawing and art	....	....	14.8	18.6	15.3
Music	....	....	25.3	26.0	25.5
Physical education	....	....	5.7	15.0	50.7

* *Offerings and Registrations in High-School Subjects, 1933–34,* United States Office of Education Bulletin 6, 1938 (Washington, D.C.: Government Printing Office, 1938), pp. 28–29.

cal education, household arts, commercial studies, social studies, and English. The least expansion, as might be expected, took place in foreign languages, science, and mathematics. Other investigations describe similar trends to those revealed in Van Dyke's study. The other subjects which were introduced were confined chiefly to those designed to prepare youth to enter trade and commerce, and, because an increasing number of these and additional subjects were added, the high school curriculum rapidly lost much of its strictly academic character. The demands of a society that was becoming more highly industralized each passing year forced a significant change in the concept of the function of the secondary school.

By the close of the first quarter of the twentieth century, most educational leaders had become conscious of the fact that the high school was for most youth a terminal institution. It was essential, therefore, that the old concept of the high school as an institution primarily concerned with providing intellectual discipline and college preparation for a select body of youth be abandoned or fundamentally modified. The new goals of secondary education, necessitated by the impact of social change, were those stressed in the "Seven Cardinal Principles," which included such objectives as social-civic competency, healthful living, constructive use of leisure time, and occupational efficiency.[23] The general acceptance of these goals was reflected by the introduction of new and different types of subjects and by a decline in the percentage of high school students enrolled in the traditional ones. Table 27, derived from a study by the United States Office of Education, shows something of the extent of this development to 1934.[24] Between that date and the close of World War II additional new subjects were added but there was a growing tendency to question some of the elements of the expanding high school program. It was charged that the addition of courses had destroyed the effectiveness of these schemes of curriculum organization which had been developed in an attempt to reduce the chaos brought about by unrestricted expansion of the program. However, plans of curriculum organization and the development of numerous parallel curriculums did go far toward making the difficult situation tolerable.

The Organization of Curriculums, 1900-World War II

As it became increasingly necessary for secondary education to respond to the needs of new types of pupils in a school population which was becoming more and more heterogeneous, the total offerings of the school were organized into various types of curriculums, each of which was de-

[23] Commission on the Reorganization of Secondary Education, *Cardinal Principles of Secondary Education*, United States Office of Education Bulletin 35, 1918 (Washington, D.C.: Government Printing Office, 1918).

[24] *Offerings and Registrations in High-School Subjects, 1933–34*, United States Office of Education Bulletin 6, 1938 (Washington, D.C.: Government Printing Office, 1938), pp. 28–29. See also A. K. Loomis, Edwin S. Lide, and B. Lamar

signed to meet the needs of important subgroups found within the school.[25] As we have already seen, even before 1900 the expansion of offerings had made it impossible for any one pupil to take all the subjects taught. It was necessary to arrange varied programs, from which the pupil might make a choice. For a time some schools permitted free election of subjects by the pupil, but this practice did not long prevail. Four main schemes were developed for the organization of the program of studies. In some instances, all pupils were still required to take identical work throughout the four years. This is what Koos has called the "single-curriculum type."[26] In other cases, the pupils were permitted to select one curriculum from a number of curriculums, with all the subjects in each curriculum prescribed. This was designated as the "multiple-curriculum type" in its pure form. A third practice was to require all pupils to take certain prescribed subjects, the remainder of the work to be elected from a list of subjects available for each year's work. This curriculum was known as the "constants-with-variables type." Finally, provision was made for what was known as the "combination type" of program, which combined some of the features of the second and third types. This plan called for two or more curriculums, in each of which part of the work was prescribed and part elective. In these ways an effort was being made to adjust the work of the high school to the varied interests and needs of the individual pupil.

The desire to achieve this purpose is also evident in the number and types of curriculums developed as well as in the types of programs of studies adopted. Soon after 1900 an increase in the number of curriculums provided in high schools began to become apparent. An analysis of the programs of sixty high schools for the period 1906–11 revealed that the median number of curriculums offered was 2.5. In thirty-five of these same schools about a quarter of a century later the median number of curriculums being offered was 5.2[27] "By 1920," says Koos, "for high schools in cities with populations ranging from 25,000 to 100,000, the most common numbers of curricula were four, five, six, and seven, with some schools listing as many as twelve to fourteen."[28]

The types of curriculums also underwent a marked increase. When

---

Johnson, *The Program of Studies*, Monograph 19, and Leonard V. Koos and Staff, *Summary*, Monograph 1, *National Survey of Secondary Education*, United States Office of Education Bulletin 17, 1932 (Washington, D.C.: Government Printing Office, 1933).

[25] Leonard V. Koos, *The American Secondary School* (Boston: Ginn & Company, 1927), p. 516. By the term "curriculum" is meant the "arrangement of courses or subjects taken by a pupil or group of pupils during progress through a secondary school."

[26] *Ibid.*, p. 518.

[27] George E. Van Dyke, "Trends in the Development of the High-School Offering. I," *School Review* (November, 1931), 660.

[28] Leonard V. Koos, *Trends in American Secondary Education, op. cit.*, pp. 15–16.

curriculums first began to be differentiated, most of them were still academic. That is to say, most of the curriculums were designated as "the classic course," "the Latin-scientific course," "the scientific course," or "the college preparatory course." As the nonacademic subjects began to be given a place in the high school program, however, the following types of curriculums began to appear: commercial, industrial arts, household arts, and fine arts. An analysis of the programs of 150 schools located in communities ranging from 2500 to 100,000, and located throughout the nation, revealed that in 1925 as many as twenty-six different types of curriculums were being employed. The various kinds of curriculums in use and the frequency of their appearance in the schools of these cities may be seen by an examination of Table 28. These cur-

TABLE 28: FREQUENCY OF APPEARANCE OF CERTAIN KINDS OF CURRICULUMS IN A TOTAL OF 702 CURRICULUMS FOUND IN 150 PROGRAMS OF STUDIES*

Kind	Number	Kind	Number
1. College-preparatory	73	14. History or social science	6
2. Classical	40	15. Technical (preparatory)	23
3. Latin	13	16. Normal-preparatory	25
4. Academic	23	17. Nursing-preparatory	4
5. "Regular"	2	18. General	72
6. Foreign-language	6	19. English	12
7. French	2	20. Commercial	142
8. Spanish	1	21. Normal**	21
9. Modern-language	9	22. Industrial or manual arts	63
10. Latin-scientific	8	23. Household arts	55
11. English-scientific	3	24. Agriculture	16
12. Scientific	66	25. Fine arts	6
13. Mathematics	4	26. Music	7

* From Leonard V. Koos, *The American Secondary School* (Boston: Ginn & Company, 1927), p. 523.
** These curriculums are planned to prepare for rural-school teaching, whereas the "normal-preparatory" curriculums are mapped out to prepare for the normal school.

riculums, it should be noted, may be classified into three major groupings: (1) those designed primarily to prepare for college; (2) those designed to serve the needs of both college-going and non-college-going pupils; and (3) those organized around such special subjects as "commercial," "agriculture," "fine arts," and "music." According to Koos, who made the investigation here reported, "in the first group were found 43.9 per cent of all curricula; in the second, 12.0 per cent; in the third, 44.2 per cent."[29]

This long-time trend to organize the program of studies in the high

29 *Ibid.*, pp. 16–17.

school to make it serve more flexibly and effectively the individual needs of pupils is further confirmed by the following statement quoted from the summary monograph of the National Survey of Secondary Education published in 1934:

> We have been experiencing movement in the curriculum — movement in definitive directions. The curriculum is dynamic. . . . The trends have been toward the diversification of the offering, which increases the opportunities to ascertain and to recognize individual differences among the increasingly diverse secondary-school population. The same trends also make possible the recognition of many more aspects of complete living than were served by the older offering; the more recent offering is to a larger extent cast in terms of immediate values instead of the remoter and deferred values of college preparation and the presumedly pervasive mental discipline. Instances of this fact are found in the increased emphasis on training for participation in social and civic life, for maintenance of health, and for sharing in the aesthetic heritage represented in art and music.[30]

Here again, neither the situation described by Koos nor the direction of curriculum reorganization changed in any large degree during the decade that followed the publication of his investigation. Forces that were to lead to new emphases and, in some instances, to the threat of reversals in long-term trends of action were to have their origins not so much in considerations of the needs of an increasingly diverse secondary-school population as in the demands of a new postwar world of expanding technology, rapidly developing science, changing world relationships, and the cold war.

VOCATIONAL EDUCATION AND GUIDANCE IN HIGH SCHOOL AND JUNIOR COLLEGE

Despite the rapid development of the United States into a great industrial nation during the decades following the Civil War, comparatively little progress was made in providing vocational education for American youth. The reason for this lack of interest in a program of vocational education may be explained in part by the fact that many skilled workers were migrating to this country from Europe. Moreover, American manufacturers had not yet entered into the most vigorous kind of competition for world trade and were not fully conscious of the role a highly trained working class may play in such competition. And, finally, it was in the American tradition that occupational competency, below the level of the professions, could best be acquired through work on the job.

[30] Leonard V. Koos and Staff, *Summary,* National Survey of Secondary Education, Monograph 1, United States Office of Education Bulletin 17, 1934 (Washington, D.C.: Government Printing Office, 1934), pp. 172–173.

Between 1880 and 1917, however, when a national vocational education act was passed by Congress, some progress was made at the secondary level by way of providing agricultural, trade, and commercial training. The first publicly supported agricultural high school was established in connection with the University of Minnesota in 1888.[31] In some instances state or county agricultural high schools were established. Instruction in agriculture had been introduced into a considerable number of high schools by 1910. The number of high schools reported as affording instruction in agriculture increased from 19 in 1900 to 465 in 1910.[32] By 1900, too, a half-dozen or more trade schools had been established. In 1906, Massachusetts enacted a statute providing for a state system of vocational education. The act provided for the establishment and maintenance of schools for the teaching of the industrial, agricultural, and domestic arts. These schools were to be under the control of the State Commission of Industrial Education created by the act. Legislation enacted some years later authorized the state board of education to maintain a system of industrial schools. Wisconsin in 1907 initiated a policy of authorizing the cities of the state to maintain industrial schools separate from the regular school system. Other states during this period, notably New York, Michigan, New Jersey, Pennsylvania, and Virginia, adopted the policy of encouraging the regular local school authorities to provide instruction of an industrial nature.

In the meantime, many manufacturers and certain educational leaders began to urge the enactment of legislation that would provide federal support for vocational education. Manufacturers interested in world trade now began to fear competition from countries which had more advanced systems of vocational education and a large body of skilled workers.[33] The National Society for the Promotion of Industrial Education, organized in 1906, became active in urging upon Congress the enactment of bills providing for both agricultural and industrial education. Finally, Congress provided for a presidential commission to investigate the desirability of federal aid for vocational education. In its report, made in 1914, the commission contrasted the relatively slight provision for industrial education in this country with the provision made in certain other countries, notably Germany, and urged the establishment of an adequate national system of vocational education in the United States. In 1917 Congress passed a bill providing for federal aid for vocational education, popularly known as the Smith-Hughes Vocational Education Act. Federal funds were made available to the states accepting the Act to promote the teaching of agricultural subjects, the trades, home economics, and industrial subjects. The states were required to provide for vocational education

[31] Cubberley, *op. cit.*, p. 639.   [32] *Ibid.*, p. 640.
[33] See Lloyd E. Blauch, "Federal Co-operation in Vocational Education" (Doctor's thesis, Department of Education, University of Chicago, 1923).

a sum equal to that made available for this purpose by the federal government. The Smith-Hughes Act also created the Federal Board for Vocational Education, which, until its activities were transferred to the Office of Education in 1933, supervised and exercised a measure of control over the federally aided programs that were established in all the states as they accepted the provisions of the Act. The George-Reed Act, the Smith-Bankhead Act, and other legislation increased the federal appropriations, extended the benefits to Puerto Rico, the Virgin Islands, and the then territories of Hawaii and Alaska, and extended the activity of the federal government into the field of the vocational rehabilitation of persons disabled in industry. Enrollment in vocational subjects increased rapidly after the passage of the Smith-Hughes Act, and as state programs were expanded to include work in new fields. For example, when it became apparent that agriculture and industry were absorbing a declining percentage of the gainfully employed (see Chapter 11), and that job opportunities were expanding in such areas as transportation, trade, and clerical work, more adequate programs in those areas were made available through federal funds provided by the George-Deen Act of 1936, and many additional youth were enrolled in the federally aided courses.

There was a difference of opinion as to what constituted an appropriate institutional organization for vocational education. For a good many years some of the leaders in vocational education insisted upon a separate organization for vocational schools; they advanced arguments for the position that no genuine vocational education could be afforded in schools designed to provide general education. To support their contentions, they pointed to the quality and level of the industrial arts programs that had been developed as a part of the general education program of secondary schools. Experience indicated, however, that it was unsatisfactory to try to separate sharply general and vocational education at the secondary level. Where separate trade schools were established, it proved next to impossible to divorce general and technical education for any considerable period of time. Pupils and parents, convinced of the prestige value of an academic education, were so insistent on an opportunity for a broader training than that provided by purely technical subjects that even technical schools modified their curriculums in order to provide a place for general education — even in some instances providing a full academic course. It was clearly the opinion of the great majority of the American people that no youth of high school age should be segregated into trade or technical schools where they would or might be denied the opportunity for a general education. On the other hand, it was equally clear that the curriculum at the secondary level should not be wholly academic — as many opponents of vocational education advocated. In recent years, the principle appears to be more generally accepted that the secondary school must be a truly comprehensive school — that it must provide for the individual a curriculum that will insure a good general education as well as one that will make some provision for the cultivation of vocational and professional efficiency. To this end, James Bryant Conant, former president of Harvard, in his history-making study of the American high school, made the elimination of the small secondary school a top-priority task. This influential report may help to remove some of the stigma that the public, including schoolmen, have attached to vocational courses. Conant recommended without equivocation the provision within the public high schools of diversified programs for the development of marketable skills — in other words, that the high schools become comprehensive schools in fact. He stated:

> Programs should be available for girls interested in developing skills in typing, stenography, the use of clerical machines, home economics, or a specialized branch of home economics which through further work in college might lead to the profession of dietician. Distributive education should be available. . . . If the community is rural, vocational agriculture should be included. For boys, depending upon the type of community, trade and industrial programs should be available.
>
> . . . the students enrolled in programs which develop marketable skills should also be enrolled in English, social studies and other courses required for graduation.[34]

Conant would provide, in appropriate areas, the entire range of courses; for example, in mathematics, commercial arithmetic to calculus. And, in general, he supports Whitehead's dictum that the antithesis between a technical and liberal education is fallacious.

Another problem that developed in the area of vocational education had to do with the kind of training that was most appropriate. Should the schools provide training for specific jobs, or should they aim at training in basic skills and general knowledge useful in a great variety of situations? The following quotation illustrates the position of those who advocated a more general type of vocational education.

> The modern worker must be prepared to shift from job to job, from occupation to occupation, and even from industry to industry. . . .
> These shifts in the skills and technical training required of the workers, based on technological advance and changes in the relative importance of different industries, emphasize the necessity of adaptability on the part of the present-day worker, with corresponding implications for vocational guidance and training. Such training, whether carried on in the school or the factory, should seek to develop in the worker the essential quality of adjustability to the variety of situations which he is almost certain to meet.

[34] James Bryant Conant, *The American High School Today: A First Report to Interested Citizens* (New York: McGraw-Hill Book Co., Inc., 1959), pp. 51–52, 123–130.

In the face of these changes, it is a mistake for the schools to teach the separate trades to any large number of pupils or to insist upon a narrow specialization. Factory workers today need fundamentally not so much a training in the handling of a particular machine as a knowledge of the skills and operations basic to industry as a whole. Instead of training for specific jobs or even for specific occupations or industries, emphasis should be placed on those operations and processes common to a number of occupations and industries. . . . Jobs involved in the production of such different types of products as milk and cast iron often have common denominators. A realistic program of vocational education will seek out the common denominators of industrial operations and processes and concentrate attention upon them.[35]

Over against this position was that of those who insisted upon specific training for specific jobs. Within recent years we have apparently been moving in the direction of a compromise between these extreme positions, with the general tendency to recognize that it is idle to think that the schools can to any important extent relieve industry of its major responsibilities in the field of specific vocational training for particular jobs.

During the past four or five decades the changing conditions of American life and the new demands made upon secondary education have raised vocational guidance to a position of major importance in the secondary-school program. As America changed from a relatively simple rural to a complex industrial society, as new industries multiplied, as the division of labor segmented occupational life into an almost countless number of different jobs, each requiring different capacities and skills, youth found it increasingly difficult to arrive at a satisfactory occupational adjustment. If the secondary school was to meet its new responsibility for preparing youth for entrance into vocational life, it could not avoid the establishment of guidance programs.

Vocational guidance in the schools is, however, of relatively recent origin. Beginning in Boston about 1907, the movement gained momentum gradually. Three years later, some thirty-five cities had worked out programs of guidance or were attempting to do so. Within the past two decades the need for effective guidance programs has come to be generally recognized and in the schools of most large cities guidance service is provided. As late as 1937, however, the Advisory Committee on Education found that "in at least half of the cities in the United States of 10,000 or more population there are no vocational guidance programs in the public school."[36] It was found, too, that only in rare instances had rural high schools been able to provide adequate guidance services. Re-

[35] Newton Edwards, "Social Development and Education," in United States National Resources Committee, *The Problems of a Changing Population* (Washington, D.C.: Government Printing Office, 1938), p. 215.

[36] The Advisory Committee on Education, *Report of the Committee* (Washington, D.C.: Government Printing Office, 1938), p. 112.

markable progress has been made during the last two decades, but it is obvious that much still remains to be done before all youth in the secondary schools can be provided with the guidance services they so urgently need. Among other things, a much larger number of well-trained vocational guidance counselors is needed. It is imperative, too, that counselors have at their command more adequate information with respect to occupations and occupational trends. Recently the federal government has recognized the inadequacy of existing guidance services and has provided funds for their improvement. Conant in his 1958 report went so far as to urge the elimination of the thousands of small high schools, partly because they could not provide all the necessary services, an important one of which is counseling and guidance. Although Conant was thinking largely in terms of educational guidance, he emphasized the need for counselors who would be sympathetic to elective programs designed to develop "marketable skills." Furthermore, he noted that in a truly comprehensive high school, such as he advocated, a meaningful sequence of courses in the elective program of a majority of the students would be a series of courses leading to development of such skills.[37] He also stressed the importance of relating the student's program to the community's industrial, agricultural, service, and commercial activities. There is, actually, no fine line which separates vocational from educational counseling and guidance.

DEVELOPMENT OF GENERAL AND INDIVIDUALIZED PROGRAMS OF SECONDARY EDUCATION — THE POSTWAR PERIOD

As we have seen, the high school was long faced with two fundamental problems: (1) how to incorporate into the curriculum the rapidly expanding body of new knowledge, and (2) how to meet the needs of pupils with widely varying abilities, backgrounds, and future expectations. An attempt was made to meet the first problem by the multiplication of courses; it was hoped that the second problem could be solved by the use of varied kinds of curriculums. These solutions have not been entirely satisfactory. The multiplication of courses tended to splinter and fractionalize knowledge, and the offering of many varied types of curriculums contributed still further to the difficulty of the student's getting a well-rounded general education. With American society becoming ever more complex, and with a deepening need for cultural unity, this failure to provide an adequate body of common learnings could not long be ignored. Programs are now being developed that will equip youth with a wide community of ideas, values, and knowledge, and at the same time will provide for their individual needs.

Many schools continue to employ the multiple-curriculums type of or-

37 Conant, *op. cit.*, pp. 44–46.

Technology in agriculture created farmers without farms and the Depression produced idle men, but the expanding economy of the war and post-war years provided many new jobs.

The rural one-room school, once a useful and often wonderful institution, is now an obstacle to the realization of equal educational opportunity.

Third-grade Spanish.

Remedial reading.

For most children, schooling is becoming a more stimulating, interesting, and rewarding experience.

First-grade arithmetic.

Boy at teaching machine.

In well-supported mod schools, electronic aids c tribute to group and indi ual learning.

Tape recording in public speaking class.

ganization, but there is an observable trend toward a core of those common learnings which are essential for a good general education. And a good general education, it is further held, is essential both for effective citizenship and for individual development. A general education is essential for all, regardless of their occupational destination; it is just as necessary for those who are taking vocational courses as for those who are going on to college. In programs of this kind about one-half of the pupil's time would be devoted to the constants required of all students. The other half of the student's time would be taken up by electives chosen on the basis of individual counseling and guidance. Conant's excellent report, to which reference has already been made, makes the following recommendations with respect to the subjects that should be required of all students for graduation:

> Four years of English, three years of social studies — including two years of history (one of which should be American history) and a senior course in American problems or American government — one year of mathematics in the ninth grade (algebra or general mathematics) and at least one year of science in the ninth or tenth grade, which might be biology or general physical science. By a year, I mean that a course is given five periods a week throughout the academic year or an equivalent amount of time.[38]

The elective part of such a program would, of course, be designed to meet the needs of individual pupils. To quote Conant again:

> All students should be advised to have as the cultural core of their elective programs significant sequences of courses, either those leading to the development of a marketable skill or those of an academic nature.[39]

Although assignment to one of several tracks is still the common practice, there is clearly a tendency to move in the direction of individualized programs. It is significant that in seventeen of the twenty-four schools from which Conant obtained an academic inventory, students' programs had been organized on an individual basis. He makes the following recommendation with respect to individualized programs:

> It should be the policy of the school that every student has an individualized program; there would be no classification of students according to clearly defined and labeled programs or tracks such as "college-preparatory," "vocational," "commercial." In advising the student as to his elective program, the counselor will be guided by the minimum program recommended as a matter of school policy for the academically talented

---

[38] *Ibid.*, p. 47.
[39] *Ibid.*, p. 48.

or by recommended sequences leading to the development of skills market-able on graduation. It will turn out that many students of similar ability and vocational interests will have almost identical programs, but a student who has elected an academic sequence may shift to a vocational sequence and vice versa. Furthermore, with individualized programs, the students themselves do not feel that they are labeled according to the program they have chosen in the ninth or tenth grade. If flexibility is combined with a declaration of policy in regard to the programs for the academically talented, and if a good guidance service is available, the academic inventory should show results as satisfactory as the results in a school which has a clean-cut academic or college-preparatory track.[40]

The more or less permanent assignment of pupils to relatively stable tracks or programs against which Conant protests has been so strongly entrenched in American secondary education that the several notable attempts to provide an organization more conducive to the individualiza-tion of instruction have generally been of little more than local importance. However, since about 1955 many plans and procedures to provide fitting programs for all youth have been attempted or suggested. From experi-mentation with multigrade grouping, multiage grouping, non-graded schools, and the like, a more valid and effective organization of learning experiences may emerge.[41]

Recent Patterns of Curriculum Organization in Elementary and Secondary Schools

The entire outcome of an educational enterprise is profoundly con-ditioned by the particular pattern of curriculum organization that is em-ployed. The subject form of organization has long been the dominant form, but for a number of decades, and especially in the last few decades, it has been severely challenged. Over the years a considerable number of patterns of curriculum organization have emerged, but they can be reduced to three distinctive types: the subject curriculum, the core curriculum, and the activity curriculum.

The subject curriculum. Through the centuries mankind has accumu-lated a vast body of ideas, values, knowledge, skills, and techniques, all of which taken together constitute the capital of human experience. The

40 *Ibid.,* pp. 46–47.

41 *Individualizing Instruction, op. cit.;* J. Lloyd Trump and Dorsey Baynham, *Focus on Change: Guide to Better Schools,* Commission on the Experimental Study of the Utilization of the Staff in the Secondary School (Chicago: Rand McNally & Co., 1961); David Mallery, *New Approaches to Education: A Study of Experi-mental Programs in Independent Schools* (Boston: National Council of Independ-ent Schools, 1961).

elements of this experience which are logically related have been identified and organized into fields of knowledge. This logical organization of knowledge has made possible the development of civilization, and it has made possible, too, the further advancement of civilization.

School subjects represent an attempt to reduce the essential elements of human experience to a logical and sequential order for learning purposes. An understanding of this experience is designed to prepare youth for successful living in their own day and in their own society. To accomplish this end, school subjects can never be regarded as static. For two reasons they need constant revision and reorganization. In the first place, new knowledge has to be included and old knowledge that is no longer useful excluded. In the second place, and more important, each generation is faced with its own peculiar problems. In order to understand those problems and to solve them, a reinterpretation and reintegration of the record of human experience is essential. The process of reinterpretation and reintegration has long been employed. As was pointed out in one of the yearbooks of the American Association of School Administrators:

> Curriculum workers in the subject field have been unusually active over a long period of time. As a result, while retaining the advantages of logical systems of knowledge, these experts have also made innumerable studies of organization and content until today it is possible to teach subjects by psychologically sound methods and to use content that is defensible both in terms of social values and in terms of pupil maturity.[42]

As already indicated, the subject type of curriculum organization is the oldest and by far the most common type employed, especially in secondary schools. Many arguments have been advanced in its favor, but we shall confine ourselves to a few of the arguments that deal with its intrinsic features.

School subjects such as language, history, mathematics, and science are derived from the great scholarly disciplines, and they present an ordered, logical, and sequential organization of the essential elements in the capital of human experience. In other words, school subjects with their systematic organization constitute the most effective carriers of the culture; they may well be regarded as the distributing points of civilization. Schools, it is said, moreover, are places for the cultivation of the intellectual life. School subjects, representing as they do the systematic and logical organization of the great areas of human achievement, are most appropriate for the development of the intellectual powers of the pupil. Perhaps the strongest argument is that the subject type of curriculum organization is the most effective in providing youth with the systematic understandings of the

---

[42] American Association of School Administrators, *Thirty-first Yearbook* (Washington, D.C.: American Association of School Administrators, 1953), p. 59.

past and present that are essential for intelligent decision-making in an adaptive, democratic society.

The subject curriculum has come in for a good deal of adverse criticism. One of the most common criticisms is that it is fragmentary, that it splinters knowledge, which is by nature unitary and of a whole. Again, it is said that the subject type of curriculum fails to challenge the interests or meet the needs of the learner; it is divorced from the matters that concern him most and it affords little opportunity for him to solve experimentally his own personal problems. Teaching by subjects, it is said too, fails to develop powers of critical thinking; it stresses memory and emphasizes the acquisition of the thoughts of others. And, finally, it is said that subjects may not contain socially significant data.

In the subject curriculum each subject or subject field is taught more or less as an independent unit. In order to bring out more fully the interrelation of subjects a number of variations of the subject curriculum proper have been developed. These departures from the subject curriculum proper have been designated as correlation, fusion, integration, and broad fields. In correlation each subject keeps its essential unity, but the reciprocal relationships between two or more subjects are stressed. History and geography, for example, may thus be correlated. In fusion a number of separate subjects are combined to create essentially a new subject. A course in American Problems, by way of illustration, usually combines government, economics, and sociology. Biology presents a combination of biology, botany, and zoology. Physical sciences is a combination of a number of sciences. In integration the concept of fusion is carried a bit further, and, through the removal of subject boundaries, the subject matter of diverse fields is combined. The broad-fields approach abandons separate subjects, and combines much of the subject content of related subjects into a number of major areas. Typical broad-fields courses are: social studies, general science, general arts, general mathematics, and the language arts.

The core curriculum.   The core curriculum represents a violent reaction against the subject curriculum. Its essential characteristic is its commitment to what is regarded as the interests and needs of youth. The following statement by two of its strongest advocates clearly indicates what the core curriculum seeks to achieve:

1. It seeks to establish relationships among areas of living by the study of problems that challenge the pupil to explore and utilize the knowledge and skills of more than one subject.
2. It aims at larger objectives than would characterize any single subject area.
3. It involves the joint planning of those objectives, and the means of

achieving them, by both teachers and pupils. It is directly geared to the goal of increased skill in the processes of cooperative planning.

4. It requires a block of time longer than the traditional period.

5. It involves either a single teacher for two or more periods or a team of teachers who work together.

6. It is dedicated to improved guidance of individuals and groups of pupils.

7. Its basic emphasis in instructional planning is the present psycho-biological and social needs of the pupils themselves.[43]

The core-curriculum program seeks to develop in all youth the body of common knowledge which is essential for successful living in a democratic society. This end it seeks by abandoning school subjects and substituting for them "units of life experience," "centers of interest," "problem area studies," or "social living themes." There is no uniform pattern of area studies, but typical ones are these: Understanding My Body, Managing My Own Personal Affairs, Protecting Life and Health, Living in the Neighborhood, Earning a Living, Implications of Scientific Advancement, and the American Heritage.

The core-type of curriculum organization has had strong advocates and, perhaps, equally strong critics. Its advocates insist that the most effective curriculum is one organized around the problems of present-day life. The core curriculum challenges the pupil to identify socially significant content and to give it an orientation around significant problems of social living. In this way the pupil's interest is aroused, he becomes engaged in the study of problems that are of concern to himself, he learns to weigh and balance evidence, and he is prepared to cope with present-day problems.

The most common criticisms of the core pattern have been summarized as follows:

1. In actual practice content is exceedingly meager. Subjectmatter is not well selected in terms of problems. There is "a watering down" process. The coverage of important experience is inadequate.

2. Most schools do not have adequate instructional materials to conduct core classes. Some critics are doubtful that the materials exist at present.

3. Classroom teachers are not trained for core teaching. So much general knowledge is required of the core teacher that no one person can know enough to deal adequately with all the problems studied. Not enough teachers are well equipped to handle discussion, guidance, and reference activities.

4. Either there is not enough recognition of pupil interest, or there is too much recognition, depending upon the critic's point of view.

[43] Roland C. Faunce and Nelson L. Bossing, *Developing the Core Curriculum.* © 1951. Prentice-Hall, Inc., Englewood Cliffs, N.J. Reprinted by permission.

5. There is no adequate provision for sequential learning. Pupils do the same things year after year and grow toward maturity in a haphazard manner.[44]

The experience curriculum.   The experience type of curriculum organization has been given considerable theoretical discussion but actually it has been little employed at the elementary-school level and scarcely at all at the secondary level. Whereas the subject curriculum is organized around subjects and the core curriculum around problems of social living, the experience curriculum, or, as it is sometimes called, the activity curriculum, is organized around the "interests and purposes" of children. Child interest and needs constitute the sole organizing principle. Children are always active and they have their own particular interests and needs. It is the function of the teacher to discover these and to build the educational activities upon them.

By its very nature the experience curriculum precludes any previously formulated curriculum structure. But this does not mean that it is planless or that it neglects the use of subject matter. Teacher and pupils spend a good deal of time in uncovering pupil interest and purpose and when this is accomplished, subject matter is used in the fulfillment of the educational purpose. It has been said of the experience or activity curriculum:

> . . . subject matter is a means of fulfilling the purposes and aspirations of the individual or social group. It denies the traditional notion that the interests and purposes of children are merely aids in learning the subject matter that adults set out to be learned. In its view, subject matter is used in shaping and directing activities in response to the impulses and purposes of the individual. Knowledge thus originates in actions devoted to the realization of purposes. Children do not set out to acquire learning as such, but to do things. In the course of doing things, they have need of subject matter; and as a result of manipulating content and materials in doing these things, they learn.[45]

Within recent years, sharp conflicts in point of view have developed with respect to the organization of the curriculum. These differences stem from conflicting philosophies of education. The main issue is: Shall school subjects as such be retained, or shall they be abandoned in favor of the "common problems of youth," "centers of interest," and "problems of life"? Those who believe that subjects as such should be retained insist that progress is assured if subjects are made to represent a continuing reselection and reintegration of those elements of human experience which

[44] American Association of School Administrators, *Thirty-first Yearbook, op. cit.*, p. 66.

[45] B. Othanel Smith, William O. Stanley, and J. Harlan Shores, *Fundamentals of Curriculum Development,* Revised Edition (Yonkers-on-Hudson, N.Y.: World Book Company, 1957 [now published by Harcourt, Brace & World, Inc.], p. 272.

are essential for present-day living. Most of them are dissatisfied with both the selection and the organization of subject content as presented today, but all are unwilling to abandon subjects as tools of learning. Those who are in favor of abandoning subjects believe that the program which they would offer is more functional and establishes situations in which learning takes place most readily. Since the curriculum lies at the center of the educational enterprise, vigorous criticism of it and diverse experiments to improve it should be welcomed.

Higher Education

EXPANSION OF COURSE OFFERINGS

Higher education has been especially responsive to the dramatic changes that have occurred in American life since 1865. The rise of vast new industries, the gains made in technology, the division of labor and the multiplication of occupations, the development of new professions, the vigorous assertion of the spirit of individualism, the value placed upon material well-being, the discovery of new knowledge in many fields, the increase in the number of young people going to college — all these have had their influence on the college curriculum.

In the middle of the nineteenth century the three great subjects of the college curriculum were the ancient languages, mathematics, and philosophy. Other subjects, however, had begun to appear. By 1865 the proponents of modern foreign languages had secured for them what may be regarded as a regular, although not important, place in the curriculum. The study of English, long confined almost exclusively to rhetoric, had now come to embrace both literature and philology. Among the sciences, chemistry and geology had come to be the most important, although some attention was given also to physics, botany, zoology, and astronomy. The sciences, however, had not yet been accorded a position of high regard. The social sciences were even less well regarded. Chairs of history were to be found in relatively few colleges, and political science was almost wholly neglected.

During the closing third of the nineteenth century the subjects that had constituted the central core of the old curriculum began to decline in relative importance. The sciences were now making a vigorous bid for recognition and in the struggle that ensued between the classicists and the scientists the scientists won out. The increase of scientific knowledge, with its practical applications in industry and agriculture, made it possible for the advocates of the sciences to drive home their arguments with telling effect. Chemistry in its varied branches — physiological, physical, agricultural — physics, geology, botany, and zoology were by 1900 well-established subjects. At the same time, the social sciences and modern foreign languages were becoming not only respectable but important members of the academic community. History, political science, and economics had become well entrenched; psychology and sociology were on the point of making a determined bid for recognition. German and French had, by 1900, become relatively important subjects and English had further strengthened its already strong position.

Since 1900 the increase in the number of courses offered by colleges, whether independent institutions or organized as part of a university, has been phenomenal. Between 1900 and 1930 ten more or less representative independent colleges (Amherst, Carleton, Central, Colorado, Grinnell, Howard, Knox, Lafayette, Oberlin, and Pomona) increased the number of their course offerings from an average of about 100 to 290. Ten colleges connected with universities (Harvard, Princeton, Stanford, Chicago, Alabama, Colorado, Iowa, Virginia, Washington, and Wisconsin) increased, on the average, their offerings from 325 to 920 courses per school. One institution, organized on the quarter basis, offered nearly 1900 courses in 1930.[46]

After 1930 the record was mixed. Some institutions reduced the number of their offerings, but, although the trend toward reducing the number of choices open to any individual student continued, the trend toward more and more offerings, generally, was not reversed. In many colleges it would take a student several lifetimes to complete all the courses offered. Subjects have multiplied in the older fields of study and also in the new fields that have been added, such as education, social service, communications, and the like. This expansion of course offerings has taken place in response to society's demands that training be provided for the new professions and for almost any of the important activities of life. The old liberal arts college has become, with fewer and fewer exceptions, an all-purpose college.

Curriculum Organization in the College

Originally, the college provided a single program which was required of all. With the increase in the number of subjects offered, however, it became impossible for any single student to take all the courses provided. To meet this situation the elective system was developed. It had its origin under Jefferson's influence: The germ of the idea is in his plan for the reorganization of the College of William and Mary (1779), and its more extensive operation dates from the opening in 1825 of the University of Virginia, which he founded. By 1870 the elective principle had been

[46] *Recent Social Trends in the United States,* One-Volume Edition Report of the President's Research Committee in Social Trends (New York: McGraw-Hill Book Co., 1933), p. 338.

adopted to some extent in a number of institutions. It was, however, President Eliot of Harvard who gave the greatest impetus to the movement. In his inaugural address in 1869, he vigorously urged the acceptance of the elective principle, and in the years following prescribed work at Harvard was reduced to a minimum. The example of Harvard was widely followed by other institutions, most of which adopted the elective principle to a greater or lesser degree.

The elective system, when carried to an extreme, did not prove satisfactory. Immature students could scarcely be expected to choose from the several hundred courses offered the ones best suited to their needs and purposes. After about 1900, therefore, the general tendency was to plan the student's work more carefully and to return to some extent to the principle of prescription. Frequently the student was required to select some department as a field of major concentration and take from one-third to one-half of his work in that field. At the same time he would be required to select a second subject field for less intensive concentration, some time being left for free electives. Another plan was to require the student to distribute his work over a number of fields, such as the humanities, the social sciences, and the natural sciences. The tendency in recent years has been toward a greater prescription of the student's program.

For the past three decades or so the college curriculum has been the object of a great deal of criticism, much of which has been directed at its atomized and specialized character. It has been said that the multiplication of courses and specialization have gone so far that the organization of well-rounded programs of general education has become impossible in most institutions. What the student needs, it is urged, is a good general education acquired before he begins specialization, or, better still, while he is engaged in specialized study. The aim of such education is to give breadth and unity to the educational experience of the student; to give him an integrated view of the most essential fields of human knowledge and of the ideas and values that have been the moving forces in civilization.

It has proved extremely difficult to determine just what the content of a good general education should be and how that content ought to be organized. There have been a considerable number of approaches to the solution of this problem. One of these has been designated the "distributional plan." Under this plan the student is required to take a number of courses, in many instances specifically designated, in such fields as English composition, the humanities, the biological and physical sciences, and mathematics. These courses are often introductory courses of the various academic departments concerned. In other instances, the student is required to take two or more broad survey courses in major fields of learning. These courses are usually designated divisional courses. Another much-discussed approach is to abandon altogether the traditional subject-matter fields and to organize learning experiences along what are called "functional" lines. That is, the program of the student is organized around "problems of major import," both in the development of civilization and in present-day society. In still other instances the program is centered in the study of great books. These and numerous other patterns have been adopted by various institutions in an attempt to give breadth and unity to the student's program — to provide a general education.

Beginning in the early fifties, criticism of higher education mounted rapidly. Universities and colleges were not invulnerable to attack. In their efforts to provide for a rapidly expanding and increasingly diverse student population, too many of them had extended their curriculums to include learning experiences that required little intellectual effort, that were trivial in nature, and that represented a waste of instructional time. The result was particularly unfortunate in the case of youth who found it difficult or impossible to acquire, in the time available, the basic elements of a general education.

The Changing Curriculum

Progress in curriculum development at all levels, from the kindergarten to the university, has been a slow if persistent process throughout our history. Basically, the curriculum has been a reasonably valid expression of a people's philosophy, and the continuity of the development of this philosophy has only under exceptional circumstances been disturbed. Before further changes of any great import can be made in the curriculum, it will be necessary to define and evaluate new needs, ranging from a global outlook to a revised attitude toward the community, or, perhaps, the acquisition of marketable skills. New knowledge with respect to the way in which learning takes place must be incorporated with the best thought of preceding generations, particularly the immediately preceding one. In many instances, the traditions of a dead past must be overcome. Historically, new needs have not always been readily or clearly perceived; new knowledge has been slow to be widely understood and used; and tradition often has been uprooted only with great difficulty. Although curriculum development has been generally slow, the rate of change has been accelerated at times by great political, social, intellectual, economic, and religious upheavals. The second half of the twentieth century, it appears, will continue to be characterized by rapid change in all areas that affect mankind. Our past history gives rise to hope that sustained, intelligent use of the wide array of talent that is not fully utilized at present will contribute to the development of a curriculum that will, at any given time and place, more nearly harmonize with our values, our needs, and our aspirations.

Questions and Problems for Study and Discussion

1. Four major positions with respect to the nature of the curriculum were outlined in the preceding chapter. How would the proponents of each position define the term "curriculum"?
2. Formulate a statement indicating the nature and extent of the influence of the federal government upon what has been taught in schools and universities since 1862.
3. At what level of education have the greatest changes in the curriculum taken place during the last century? Why at that level?
4. In what further ways, if any, do you think the elementary- and secondary-school curriculums should be modified to serve better the needs of the individual student?
5. What evidence can you cite, if any, to support the criticism that the work of the school in most communities is not closely enough related to the life of the community?
6. Do you favor a curriculum that is organized around "subjects" or around the "felt needs and interests" of the pupils? If you object to the wording of the question, reformulate it before replying.
7. To what extent should the elective principle govern in the high school? What restrictions, if any, should be imposed upon the individual in the making of his program?
8. Do you think that in the future American secondary schools will give more or less attention to the development of marketable skills? Why?

Selected References for Further Reading

The Advisory Committee on Education. *Report of the Committee.* Washington, D.C.: Government Printing Office, 1938. Pp. viii + 244.

Aiken, Wilford M. *The Story of the Eight-Year Study: With Conclusion and Recommendations,* Adventure in American Education, I. New York: Harper & Brothers, 1942. Pp. x + 158.

The American Elementary School, Thirteenth Yearbook of the John Dewey Society. New York: Harper & Brothers, 1953. Pp. xi + 434.

Berelson, Bernard. *Graduate Education in the United States.* New York: McGraw-Hill Book Co., Inc., 1960. Pp. vi + 346.

Brubacher, John S., and Rudy, Willis. *Higher Education in Transition, 1636–1956.* New York: Harper & Brothers, 1958. Pp. vii + 496.

Butts, R. Freeman. *The College Charts Its Courses: Historical Conceptions and Current Proposals.* New York: McGraw-Hill Book Co., 1939. Pp. xvi + 464.

Carlin, Edward Augustine (ed.). *Curriculum Building in General Education.* Dubuque, Iowa: W. C. Brown Company, Publishers, 1960. Pp. 133.

Conant, James Bryant. *The American High School Today: A First Report to Interested Citizens.* New York: McGraw-Hill Book Co., Inc., 1959. Pp. xiii + 140.

Conant, James B. *Education in the Junior High School Years.* Princeton, N.J.: Educational Testing Service, 1960. Pp. 46.

Counts, George S. *Education and the Promise of America.* New York: The Macmillan Co., 1945. Pp. x + 158.

Cremin, Lawrence A. *The Transformation of the School: Progressivism in American Education, 1876–1951.* New York: Alfred A. Knopf, Inc., 1961. Pp. xiv + 387 + xxiv.

Dewey, John. *Experience and Education.* New York: The Macmillan Co., 1938. Pp. xiv + 116.

Douglass, Harl Roy. *Education for Life Adjustment: Its Meaning and Implementation.* New York: The Ronald Press Company, 1950. Pp. viii + 491.

Educational Policies Commission. *The Purposes of Education in American Democracy.* Washington, D.C.: National Educational Association of the United States and the American Association of School Administrators, 1938. Pp. x + 154.

Edwards, Newton. "Social Development and Education," pp. 193–221 in *The Problems of a Changing Population,* Report of the Committee on Population Problems to the National Resources Committee, May, 1938. Washington, D.C.: Government Printing Office, 1938. Pp. iv + 306.

Eliot, Charles W. "The New Education: Its Organization," pp. 29–46; "Shortening and Enriching the Grammar School Course," pp. 47–59; "Wherein Popular Education Has Failed," pp. 60–82; in *Charles W. Eliot and Popular Education,* ed. Edward A. Krug, Classics in Education No. 8. New York: Bureau of Publications, Teachers College, 1961. Pp. viii + 166.

Fliegler, Louis A. *Curriculum Planning for the Gifted.* Englewood Cliffs, N.J.: Prentice-Hall, Inc., 1961. Pp. 414.

Gwyn, John Minor. *Curriculum Principles and Social Trends,* Third Edition. New York: The Macmillan Co., 1960. Pp. 695.

Harvard University, Committee on the Objectives of a General Education in a Free Society. *General Education in a Free Society.* Cambridge, Mass. Harvard University Press, 1945. Pp. xix + 267.

Hawkins, Layton S., Prosser, Charles S., and Wright, John C. *Development of Vocational Education.* Chicago: American Technical Society, 1951. Pp. ix + 656.

Hutchins, Robert Maynard. *Education for Freedom.* Baton Rouge, La.: Louisiana State University Press, 1943. Pp. x + 108.

Hutchins, Robert Maynard. *The Higher Learning in America.* New Haven, Conn.: Yale University Press, 1936. Pp. 120.

Integration of Educational Experience, Fifty-seventh Yearbook of the National Society for the Study of Education, Part III. Chicago: University of Chicago Press, 1958. Pp. xi + 278.

Koos, Leonard V. *Trends in American Secondary Education,* The Inglis Lecture, 1925. Cambridge, Mass.: Harvard University Press, 1926. Pp. 56.

Koos, Leonard V., and Staff. *Summary,* National Survey of Secondary Education, Monograph I, United States Office of Education Bulletin 17, 1932. Washington, D.C.: Government Printing Office, 1934. Pp. x + 232.

Livingstone, Sir Richard. *On Education: Containing Two Books Previously*

Published Separately, *The Future of Education and Education for a World Adrift.* New York: The Macmillan Co., 1944. Pp. x + 158.

Loomis, A. K., Lide, Edwin S., and Johnson, B. Lamar. *The Program of Studies,* National Survey of Secondary Education, Monograph 19, United States Office of Education Bulletin 17, 1932. Washington, D.C.: Government Printing Office, 1933. Pp. x + 340.

Mallery, David. *New Approaches in Education: A Study of Experimental Programs in Independent Schools.* Boston: National Council of Independent Schools, 1961. Pp. xiii + 192.

National Education Association. *Report of the Committee of Ten on Secondary School Studies: With the Reports of the Conferences Arranged by the Committee.* New York: published for the National Education Association by the American Book Co., 1894. Pp. xii + 250.

Reisner, Edward H. *The Evolution of the Common School.* New York: The Macmillan Co., 1930. Pp. x + 590.

Rethinking Science Education, Fifty-ninth Yearbook of the National Society for the Study of Education, Part I. Chicago: University of Chicago Press, 1960. Pp. xviii + 344.

Smith, Payson, Wright, Frank W., and Associates. *Education in the Forty-eight States,* Staff Study I, Prepared for the Advisory Committee on Education. Washington, D.C.: Government Printing Office, 1939. Pp. xvi + 200.

Social Forces Influencing American Education, Sixtieth Yearbook of the National Society for the Study of Education, Part II. Chicago: University of Chicago Press, 1961. Pp. x + 252.

Spafford, Ivol, et al. *Building a Curriculum for General Education: A Description of the General College Program.* Minneapolis, Minn.: University of Minnesota Press, 1943. Pp. xvi + 354.

Stout, John Elbert. *The Development of High-School Curricula in the North Central States from 1860 to 1918,* Supplementary Educational Monographs, Vol. III, No. 3, Whole No. 15, June, 1921. Chicago: University of Chicago Press, 1921. Pp. xii + 322.

Thirty Schools Tell Their Story, Adventure in American Education, V. New York: Harper & Brothers, 1943. Pp. xxiv + 802.

Trump, J. Lloyd, and Baynham, Dorsey. *Focus on Change: Guide to Better Schools.* Chicago: Rand McNally & Co., 1961. Pp. 147.

Tryon, Rolla M. *The Social Sciences as School Subjects,* Report of the Commission on the Social Studies, Part XI. New York: Charles Scribner's Sons, 1935. Pp. xiv + 542.

Wahlquist, John Thomas. *The Philosophy of American Education.* New York: The Ronald Press Company, 1942. Pp. xiv + 408.

Whitehead, Alfred North. *Aims of Education and Other Essays,* New Edition. London: Williams and Norgate, 1950. Pp. vi + 248 (also published in paperback: New York: New American Library of World Literature, Inc. [Mentor Books], 1949; pp. 166).

Wills, Elbert Vaughan. *The Growth of American Higher Education: Liberal, Professional, and Technical.* Philadelphia: Dorrance & Co., 1936. Pp. 226.

16

Changing Patterns of Teacher Education

Teacher Education in 1860

A shortage of teachers is not a new phenomenon in American life, nor was it one a century ago. The modest expansion of the elementary-school curriculum, the increase in the size of the school-age population, and the extension of opportunity for education to increasingly larger percentages of the nation's children created, in the period preceding the Civil War, a greater demand not only for more teachers but also for teachers with higher intellectual attainments and more adequate professional training. Although the early private teachers' seminaries, training classes in academies, and few public normal schools were established in response to this demand, the importance of an adequate supply of trained teachers to the success of the expanding educational enterprise was not clearly sensed except by a relatively small group of educational statesmen and enthusiasts who were able only with great effort to prod a slowly yielding public into action.

The inertia of the general public is not difficult to explain. There had never been, except in isolated instances, serious questioning in America or England of the belief that the only necessary prerequisites of a good teacher were a knowledge of the subject matter to be taught and a will, backed up by physical strength and presence, to enforce rigorous discipline. In all educational endeavor imitation of accepted practices was the trusted method and experience the exalted teacher. Such was the case in all fields. In agriculture, no systematic instruction was provided. Schools neglected the new technology almost entirely. Engineering students were instructed in abstract theories and given formulas, and then were left to learn their profession through experience. In the United States there were some fifty medical schools, but they have been described as constituting a national and social disgrace. The comparatively few students attending these institutions were, in most instances, exposed to mediocre instruction which did not render them much more effective than the practitioners who obtained their entire training through a system of apprenticeship. It was truly an era of learning by doing, particularly at the higher levels of professional training. Unfortunately, although the system provided for the multiplication of practitioners, little was accomplished in the way of their improvement.

If important and highly specialized professions such as agriculture, engineering, and medicine could be pursued after such meager preparation as practice gave, it is obvious that teaching little children the rudiments of knowledge would not be looked upon as a task requiring any special preparation. Teaching school, it was agreed, was at best a lowly undertaking, which required little training, certainly no more than could be provided in the high schools and academies. The Committee on Education of the Massachusetts legislature, which in 1850 recommended the abolishment of the normal school, reported:

> Academies and high schools cost the Commonwealth nothing; and they are fully adequate to furnish a competent supply of teachers. . . . Considering that our district schools are kept, on an average, for only three or four months in the year, it is obviously impossible, and perhaps it is not desirable, that the business of keeping these schools should become a distinct and separate profession, which the establishment of Normal Schools seems to anticipate.[1]

Despite public apathy and other retarding factors, such as fear on the part of established teachers that their interests would be threatened, opposition by persons who were greatly concerned with costs, and the distrust with which some colleges and universities regarded any attempt to institutionalize the education of teachers, a little progress was made before 1860. A considerable number of academies had introduced one or more courses designed for the preparation of teachers, and state subsidies for such courses were not unknown. Also, by 1860 perhaps as many as two thousand youth were enrolled in public or private normal schools or somewhat similar institutions.

TEACHER-TRAINING SCHOOLS IN 1860

By 1860 twelve normal schools supported by state funds had been established in Massachusetts, New York, Connecticut, Rhode Island, New Jersey, Pennsylvania, Michigan, Illinois, and Minnesota. Several private

[1] As quoted in Charles A. Harper, *A Century of Public Teacher Education: The Story of the State Teachers Colleges as They Evolved from the Normal Schools* (Washington, D.C.: published by the Hugh Birch–Horace Mann Fund for the American Association of Teachers Colleges, National Education Association, 1939), pp. 35–36.

normals and a number of schools which had assumed the name without justification had been organized. The city normal supported by the municipality of St. Louis had begun its long and useful career. In several other cities schools not exclusively normal, such as the Girls' Normal School of Philadelphia and the Girls' High and Normal School in Charleston, South Carolina, had been opened. In the unpredictable West, a normal department had been established in the University of Iowa.[2] Except for meager and generally mediocre teachers' courses in the academies, the foregoing institutions represented the efforts of a generation of educators and statesmen in spreading the doctrine that teachers' education was intimately connected with public elementary education and that the success of the democratic experiment in government depended not only upon the maintenance of schools for all boys and girls at state expense, but also upon the extent to which an adequate teaching force was provided by the state.

Before 1860, and for several years thereafter, normal schools were, for the most part, unpretentious establishments designed primarily to prepare teachers for the elementary schools in which the children of the masses received their schooling. At best, teaching in such schools was regarded as a steppingstone to more respected positions, a stopgap to fill the interval between the end of schooling and marriage, a means of supplementing income through seasonal employment, or, in some instances, a missionary undertaking. At its worst, it was the refuge for incompetents. Neither prestige nor more negotiable rewards were attached to the lowly calling of the schoolteacher.

The students who entered the normal schools in order to prepare themselves for service in the public schools had been, in the main, prepared in the district schools. Few were denied admission. If the applicant met the minimum age requirement (usually sixteen to eighteen years), was in good health, and could provide a certificate of good moral character, only an examination in the common branches stood between him and matriculation. To lower further the level of the work of the normal school, the examinations served more to indicate deficiencies to be removed after admission than to screen out applicants of little ability or preparation.

The emphasis in instruction was on the branches of learning which the students expected to teach later. Seldom was the instruction above secondary level. The features which set the normal school apart from the academies of the day were the use of the model school, the attempt to approach the elementary subjects from the viewpoint of the teacher rather than that of the child, and the greater emphasis placed upon the prin-

[2] Andrew Phillip Hollis, *The Contribution of the Oswego Normal School to Educational Progress in the United States* (Boston: D. C. Heath & Co., 1898), pp. 11–12. See also Ellwood P. Cubberley, *Public Education in the United States: A Study and Interpretation of American Educational History,* Revised and Enlarged Edition (Boston: Houghton Mifflin Company, 1934), Chap. XI.

ciples of teaching, for the study of which several books were available, including Taylor's *The District School* (1834), Hall's *Lectures on School-keeping* (1829), Abbott's *The Teacher: Or Moral Influences Employed in the Instruction and Government of the Young* (1833), which had gone through twenty-five editions by 1860, and Page's *Theory and Practice of Teaching* (1847).

Ill-prepared students were admitted to these modest schools for short terms. Although the courses were normally one or two years in length, most students attended only a few months or even weeks. A graduate of the Bridgewater Normal (established in 1840) who entered the school in the early sixties later wrote that when he entered the institution it was twenty-three years old, but that he was in the sixty-first class.[3]

The faculties were small. In some instances the president also served as professor of pedagogy or didactics, supervisor of teacher training, and principal of the model school. Faculty members were sometimes college graduates, but more often they had no more formal training than that given in the schools in which they taught. As a saving grace, many had added to this meager preparation some years of experience as successful teachers or administrators. The normal schools, few in number, never aspiring to college rank, and enrolling poorly prepared students in short courses, were, in 1860, more important for what they were to become than for what they were.

The normal school, which before 1860 was attended by only a few of those who were to engage in teaching, became during the following three decades an integral part of the American school system — and a part deeply rooted in public esteem. The causes for their multiplication and for the great affection which the people came to have for them are to be found in the same conditions that gave rise to the expansion and extension of the common schools and to the enrichment of their programs. Closely related to this enrichment were a better understanding of the nature of the learning process and remarkable changes in the methodology of instruction. The acceptance of the normal school and its rapid growth in popularity must be attributed, at least in some measure, to the introduction of more vital principles of learning and teaching and to the development of a systematic methodology of instruction, both of which provided opportunity for greater usefulness on the part of teacher-training institutions. These new principles were derived largely from the theories and practices of Pestalozzi. As we shall note, the work of Pestalozzi was not entirely unknown in this country before 1860, but it was after that date that American education felt the full impact of his theories — and, also, of misinterpretations of them.

[3] For documents relating to the beginning of teacher training see Ellwood P. Cubberley, *Readings in Public Education in the United States* (Boston: Houghton Mifflin Company, 1934), Chap. XI.

PESTALOZZIAN THEORIES WHICH CONTRIBUTED TO TEACHER EDUCATION

Although Pestalozzi's theories concerning the aim and content of education had their greatest influence on the development of the curriculum, it was largely his insistence upon certain principles of method that resulted in the increased stress which came to be placed upon teacher preparation. Pestalozzi grounded his method upon three main principles: (1) the "reduction of all subjects to their unanalyzable elements . . . and the teaching of these subjects by carefully graded steps" (2) the "use of the object lesson," in which an attempt was made to appeal directly to sense experience rather than to verbalize about things unknown and unseen; and (3) the "oral teaching of all subjects."[4]

The results of the application of these principles were sometimes unfortunate. The unanalyzable elements did not always constitute the most satisfactory aspects of learning for beginners in such subjects as reading, art, and music. Fashioning pothooks was not the best first step in teaching children to write. The emphasis upon sense experience led to exclusion of books and unreserved acceptance of the value of objects. Pestalozzi's fear of words blinded him to the educational values of history and literature. Oral teaching, although it banished the textbook and formal exercises previously so important in education, did not always eliminate verbalism. The acceptance of Pestalozzian principles implied that teachers would be able to select and organize instructional materials into lesson units; that they would have not only sound knowledge of the subject matter and the ability to reduce it to teachable form, but also skill in questioning and in conducting drills and reviews. The teacher would be a person trained to stand alone, without the assistance of a textbook. The stress on teacher education which resulted from this redefinition of the proper activities of the teacher was one of the most significant results of the application of Pestalozzian theories.

PESTALOZZIAN INFLUENCE ON THE EDUCATION OF TEACHERS BEFORE 1860

The expansion of elementary education was perhaps the most important factor influencing the development of teacher education during the period 1820 to 1860. Before 1860 only a small part of the improvement can be attributed to Pestalozzi's influence. His ideas, which had transformed primary education in Prussia, and, to a lesser extent, in other German states, were not translated during this period into a system that could be applied in any large way to elementary instruction under

---

[4] Philip R. V. Curoe, *History of Education* (New York: Globe Book Co., 1921), pp. 150–151.

prevailing conditions. Pestalozzian ideas, however, were known to the thinking few early in the century, and, although never widely diffused, they exerted a small but increasing influence upon the curriculum and, less directly, upon teacher education.

Pestalozzianism reached America through a number of persons and agencies. Joseph Neef, formerly a co-worker of Pestalozzi in his school near Berne, in order to promote a private school which he was opening in Philadelphia, published a book in 1808 which outlined in some detail the ideas of his former master with respect to the teaching of speech, numbers, geometry, drawing, writing, reading, grammar, ethics, natural history, chemistry, natural philosophy, gymnastics, languages, music, poetry, geography, and lexicology.[5] In 1813 Neef brought out his *Method of Instructing Children Rationally in the Arts of Writing and Reading*. At the time, interest in education was at a low ebb. New England was more or less content to bask in the glory of the educational attainments of earlier generations, and the remainder of the country, without even a tradition of good schools, was in the first flush of excitement over the marching-club, mechanical, mass-production methods of the monitorial system. The influence of the two excellent treatises, however, was not entirely negligible.

Colburn's *First Lessons in Arithmetic on the Plan of Pestalozzi* (1821), a truly pioneering textbook, although it was neither so generally used nor so quickly adopted as has sometimes been stated, must have greatly influenced teaching in America and, indirectly, the nature of the preparation essential to the teacher of arithmetic. Pestalozzian ideas with respect to education, including teacher education, were introduced into this country by a number of persons who visited the Prussian Pestalozzian schools and who observed Pestalozzi at work. Among these, John Griscom spent the year of 1819–19 in Europe and on his return published an account of his experiences, including many observations on education and an excellent description of his visit to Pestalozzi.[6] William C. Woodbridge, who spent almost half of the third decade in Europe, published in the *American Annals of Education and Instruction* and other publications enthusiastic descriptions of the work of Pestalozzi and Fellenberg.[7] He published two texts in geography to demonstrate the new method. Some persons became acquainted with the new ideas through Stowe's report

[5] Joseph Neef, *Sketch of a Plan and Method of Education, Founded on an Analysis of the Human Faculties, and Natural Reason, Suitable for the Offspring of a Free People and for all Rational Beings* (Philadelphia: printed for the author, 1808).

[6] Selections from John Griscom, *A Year in Europe*, cited in Edgar W. Knight (ed.), *Reports on European Education; By John Griscom, Victor Cousin, Calvin E. Stowe* (New York: McGraw-Hill Book Co., 1930).

[7] See "Pestalozzi's Principles and Methods of Instruction," *American Journal of Education*, IV (March and April, 1829), 97–107. The *American Annals of Education and Instruction*, which succeeded the *Journal*, published during 1830 and 1831 a score or more of letters on Fellenberg and Pestalozzi.

on elementary education in Europe[8] and by the numerous articles and reports by Barnard, Julius, Bache, Brooks, Mann, and others.[9] Some of Pestalozzi's own writings were published in American journals and some found their way into print in book form during the period.[10] Educators urged reform and the adoption of methods in accord with Pestalozzian theories through the press and from the platform. The American Institute of Instruction, the lyceums, and the newly founded teachers' associations and institutes provided means for the informal dissemination of such innovations, at least among the more informed teachers and laymen.[11]

Object teaching on the plan of Pestalozzi was introduced into the state normal school at Westfield, Massachusetts, in 1848, but did not catch the fancy of schoolmen before it was abandoned. Its failure to become popular at this time has been attributed, in part at least, to the lack of competent instruction.[12] Pestalozzian principles, however, were not entirely abandoned or without some effect. Cubberley has pointed to the influence of Arthur Guyot, a Swiss who from 1848 to 1854 was an "Agent of the Massachusetts State Board of Education and State Institute Lecturer on the teaching of home and observational geography," and to that of Herman Krüsi, Jr., the son of one of Pestalozzi's teachers, who served in similar capacity for drawing and arithmetic between 1855 and 1857.[13]

In spite of the foregoing activities and attempts to acquaint America with Pestalozzian principles and practices, the fact remained that teaching and the training of teachers was little affected by them before 1860. Few teachers read the educational journals and perhaps fewer read or were able to understand the significance of the reports made by Stowe, Barnard, Mann, and others. Few of America's teachers were exposed to any professional literature at all, and those who did study the more popular works of the day on pedagogy, such as Hall's *Lectures on School-keeping*, Page's *Theory and Practice of Teaching*, Abbott's *The Teacher*, and other books dealing with the principles of teaching and school management, did not come in contact, even at second hand, with the ideas of the great

[8] Calvin E. Stowe, "Report on Elementary Public Instruction," *Common Schools and Teachers' Seminaries* (Boston: Marsh, Capen, Lyon, and Webb, 1839), pp. 1–81. This section is the "Report on Elementary Public Instruction" which was made to the General Assembly of Ohio in December, 1837. See also Calvin E. Stowe, *The Prussian System of Public Instruction, and Its Applicability to the United States* (Cincinnati, Ohio: Truman and Smith, 1836).

[9] Alex. Dallas Bache, *Report on Education in Europe, to the Trustees of the Girard College for Orphans* (Philadelphia: Lydia R. Bailey, 1839); Henry Barnard, *Pestalozzi and his Educational System* (Syracuse, N.Y.: C. W. Bardeen, 1881).

[10] Johann Heinrich Pestalozzi, *Letters of Pestalozzi on the Education of Infancy: Addressed to Mothers* (Boston: Carter and Hendee, 1830).

[11] See *The Introductory Discourse and Lectures Delivered before the American Institute of Instruction.* These lectures were published annually beginning with 1830 under slightly different titles.

[12] Hollis, *op. cit.*, p. 10.

[13] Cubberley, *Public Education in the United States, op. cit.*, p. 385.

educator. As Hollis has stated, Pestalozzian principles in America up to 1860 "remained largely a matter of lectures and books among the initiated few. To the rank and file of the teachers of the land, Pestalozzi was but a name or an eccentric personality."[14] Certainly neither teaching nor the training of teachers had been influenced in any large measure by Pestalozzian theory, although his own activities and the operation of the Prussian school system for a time at least provided the most outstanding example of a large-scale application of Pestalozzi's educational scheme.

Expansion and Extension of Teacher Education, 1860–1890

Normal schools, which in 1860 were few in number and insignificant in their contribution to the supply of teachers, became in the thirty years which followed firmly established and generally accepted as the most important agency for the training of teachers. The attainment of this well-defined place in the scheme of common-school education may be attributed not only to the enormously enlarged demand for trained teachers which resulted when the elementary curriculum was expanded and improved, but also to the development of a content and method of teacher education based upon a sound philosophy.

AMERICAN PESTALOZZIANISM

As already indicated, the new content and method of teacher education was drawn from the teachings of Pestalozzi. The great wave of educational theory which swept the country between 1860 and 1890 did not, however, stem directly from his teachings, but reached America only after being subjected to the formalizing influences of English pedants who had seized upon and given great emphasis to certain aspects of Pestalozzian principles. The English followers of Pestalozzi gave some of his theories an interpretation which in some ways missed almost entirely the spirit of the teachings of the great Swiss educator.

Elizabeth Mayo, in England, and the American reformers who followed her lead took as their beginning point the far from original assertion of Pestalozzi which reads:

> Observation is the absolute basis of all knowledge. The first object, then, in education, must be to lead a child to observe with accuracy; the second, to express with correctness the result of his observations.[15]

[14] Hollis, *op. cit.*, p. 6.
[15] As quoted in N. A. Calkins, *Primary Object Lessons for a Graduated Course of Development: A Manual for Teachers and Parents, with Lessons for the Proper Training of the Faculties of Children, and Programmes of the Grades and Steps,* Fifth Edition, Revised (New York: Harper & Brothers, 1862), p. iii.
Near the middle of the seventeenth century, Comenius wrote: "Instruction must

Oral teaching from objects was clearly implied in this statement of Pestalozzi's. The English and American educators acknowledged their great indebtedness to their master for having developed the principles of object teaching and set out to develop a system to implement those principles, a step which Pestalozzi himself had not taken, because, his disciples thought, he had lacked the practical sense required to translate his philosophy into practice.

Calkins, the author of the first important American book to be based upon the English conception of Pestalozzianism, paid tribute to the philosopher, but followed closely the work of his English contemporary and guide, Miss Mayo.[16] The book presents twenty lessons on developing the idea of forms such as pyramids, triangles, cubes, spheres, and cones; eighteen lessons on distinguishing and naming colors; eleven on developing ideas of number; eight on developing ideas of size; four on weight; four on sound; twenty on developing ideas of the human body; eight on ideas of place; three on moral ideas, such as the soul and "God as the kind Father"; and other sections on elementary reading and objects.

A typical object lesson, which was to lead the child to learn from experience the qualities and uses of water, follows.

WATER

Qualities — Liquid, transparent, colorless, tasteless, inodorous.

What is in this tumbler? "Water." I will now print the word on the blackboard — WATER. (The teacher pours a little of the water upon a piece of newspaper or cloth.) What has the water done to this paper? "Made it wet."

Now observe me. (The teacher pours the water out in drops.) Does the water hold together when I pour it out little by little? "No, it forms into drops."

Here is a little milk; observe it as I pour it out, and tell me whether it holds together or not. "It forms in drops, like water."

I will now tell you a name for anything that you can pour out so as to form it into drops, like water, milk, etc. It is called a *liquid*.

Now what may you call water and milk? "Liquids." Observe me as I print the word LIQUID, and name the letters as I form them.

Can you mention any other liquids? "Cider, beer, the juice of oranges and lemons."

Look into this cup of water; what do you see? "The bottom." Now what do you see? "A white button on the bottom."

What, then, may you say of water? "We can see through it; it is transparent."

---

begin with actual inspection, not with verbal descriptions of things. From such inspection it is that certain knowledge comes. What is actually seen remains faster in the memory than description or enumeration a hundred times as often repeated."

[16] Calkins, *op. cit.*

Here is a red wafer, a green leaf, a yellow flower, and a blue flower; which of these is like the color of water? "Neither of them."

I will put the yellow flower in the water; now what color is the flower? "It is yellow still."

You remember that I told you, when you could see through anything, and the objects at which you looked did not change their color, the object seen through had no color. Now what shall we say of water? "It has no color."

Very well; you may say water is *colorless,* which means that it has no color. (Print the word COLORLESS as before.)

Here is some fresh water in this tumbler; you may taste it, and tell me what you observe. "It is cold." What taste do you perceive? Has it any taste? "No." What, then, may you say of water? "It has no taste." It is *tasteless.* (Print the word TASTELESS.)

Smell of the water, and tell me what it smells like. "I cannot smell it." What, then, may you say of the smell of water? "Water has no smell."

We say anything that has a smell has an odor; if it has no smell, it is without odor, or *inodorous.* What, then, can you say of water? "It is inodorus." This is a long word, but I will print it on the blackboard for you. Name the letters as I make them — INODOROUS, inodorous.

What does inodorous mean? "Has no smell."

What use have you made of water today? "We have washed our hands and faces with it." Suppose the water was solid, like the stone of a slate, could you wash with it? Is a slate liquid? What quality must an object have to be used for washing? "It must be a liquid."

Milk is a liquid; would it be good for washing? "No, it would not make us clean."

Would not beer or cider answer for washing, since both are liquids? "No; they both have an odor and a color, and would not cleanse from dirt."

For what else do you use water? "For drinking." Yes, water is essential to every person, and God has kindly supplied it in great abundance.

Now let us see what has been learned about water.

"It is a *liquid;* it will wet; it is *transparent;* it is *colorless;* it is *tasteless;* it is *inodorous;* it is very useful for *washing* and for *drinking.*"[17]

This book, which went through five editions, including some revision in its first year, and through some forty editions before the object-lesson method lost its vitality, was the forerunner of a multitude of such efforts. It probably owed its long life, in part, to the influence of E. A. Sheldon, whose own book on object teaching first appeared in 1862. Both books were primarily for teachers and much of the discussion was addressed to them. For purpose of comparison, Sheldon's procedure for teaching that water is tasteless, a solvent, without smell or color, and reflective, and that it takes the shape of the enclosing vessel, exists in different states, is found in many places, and has many uses, is presented in full.

[17] *Ibid.,* pp. 312–314.

Sketch of a Lesson on Water
Points. — Qualities on which uses depend. Less obvious qualities.

MATTER	METHOD
1. Water is tasteless and refreshing, therefore useful to drink.	1. Children say why they like to drink water in summer. Whether there is anything they like better to drink. Whether they would like to drink cider or tea only whenever they were thirsty, and at every meal. (They would get tired of it.) Why they cannot get tired of water. Effect of drinking water when very thirsty.
2. Water is a solvent, without smell or color; therefore useful for washing, for fertilizing the ground, and for dissolving various substances.	2. *Experiment.* — Put a little sugar into water. Children say what the water does. Are told what water is. Find other things of which water is a solvent. Refer to water as nourishing plants, and explain that it does so by dissolving substances in the ground which are their food. Refer to use of water in washing. As beer is a solvent, lead children to find why it would not do to wash in that.
3. Water is reflective, which makes it a beautiful object in a landscape.	3. *Experiment.* — Water will serve as a mirror. Children find what does better than water, and why. Refer to the condition of people before mirrors were invented. Objects commonly mirrored in water. Effect of this reflection on the scene.
4. Water takes the shape of the vessel that holds it.	4. *Experiment* with — 1, plate; 2, basin; 3, vial. Children describe these as to extent — 1, wide and shallow; 2, not so wide, but deeper; 3, narrow across, but deeper. Fill each with water, and measure in different directions, showing how the extent of the water corresponds with that of the vessel. Children called on to say what will happen if the contents of the vessels be exchanged.

MATTER	METHOD
5. Water exists in different states — sometimes as a liquid, sometimes as a solid, and sometimes as a vapor.	5. *Experiment.* — Refer to the idea of liquid. Refer to a little girl who went for water on a very cold day. She found only ice. How this differed from liquid water. She put the solid ice into the kettle — put the kettle on the fire. Second change water underwent (vapor). Children to say where they expect to find much ice, and why the earth is often so dry in very hot countries.
6. Water is found in different places — in the clouds overhead, in the caves of the earth, underneath and on the surface of the ground.	6. By reference to the uses of water, and the sufferings caused by the scarcity of it, show the goodness of God in supplying it abundantly. Children say where it is to be found. Refer to where the vapor went, and tell them the clouds are made of this vapor. Thus some water is always floating in the air, whence it falls in rain. Some in hollow places in the earth, hence it gushes out in springs, and there is generally plenty on the surface of the ground, that we may get it easily.

As each point is worked out, let children form a sentence, which write on the board as found in "Matter."

For summary, read matter from the board, and rewrite from memory.

Students in training construct a sketch of a Lesson on "Mercury," or "Air," modelled after the "Lesson on Water."[18]

THE OSWEGO MOVEMENT

Sheldon was a remarkable man. In 1848 he established in Oswego, New York, a school for neglected children, much as Pestalozzi had done earlier in Switzerland. In 1851 he was elected superintendent of the schools of Syracuse, but in 1853 he returned to Oswego to be that city's first superintendent. He proceeded to grade the schools and to organize a course of study. He was, then, an experienced schoolman when in 1859

[18] E. A. Sheldon, assisted by M. E. M. Jones and H. Krüsi, *A Manual of Elementary Instruction, for the Use of Public and Private Schools and Normal Classes; Containing a Graduated Course of Object Lessons for Training the Senses and Developing the Faculties of Children* (New York: American Book Co., 1862), pp. 120–122.

he saw in Toronto a full set of the objects, models, "method-materials," and publications of the English Home and Colonial Infant Society. Much taken with these materials prepared for teaching according to the English version of Pestalozzianism, he set about reshaping the whole plan to fit American schools.

Sheldon imported books and apparatus and established a normal school in Oswego in 1861 to train teachers in the new method. Miss M. E. M. Jones, of the Society's Training College, was brought over from England and within a short time Herman Krüsi, Jr., the son of one of Pestalozzi's co-workers, joined the staff. For the next thirty years the Normal School at Oswego, under the direction of Sheldon, was the fountainhead of the new Pestalozzianism in America.

Sheldon provided not only principles of teaching but a methodology that could be taught to prospective teachers, who, by diligent application, could become skillful in selecting lesson materials and arranging them, and in framing questions and conducting the learning exercises. The subordination of textbooks and the greater emphasis placed upon perception, individual judgment, and generalization made necessary the development of a new type of teacher.

The rapid spread of the Oswego idea must be attributed in a large measure to the fact that numerous normal schools were being established, particularly in the western states. It was also facilitated by Sheldon's expertness as a publicizer. In December, 1861, the leading educators of the country were invited to visit the Oswego Normal School and to examine its program. The report of this group was very favorable to the plan. In 1863 Sheldon explained his system at the annual meeting of the National Education Association. It was discussed at the 1864 meeting and, after some adverse criticism of it had been made, a committee of the Association was appointed to make an appraisal of it. The report of the committee, made in 1865, was a complete vindication of Sheldon and his methods. In the words of the historian of the movement, Oswego soon became the Mecca of American education.[19] The school was almost from the outset a national institution in the scope of its influence. The second graduating class was made up of students from Massachusetts, Connecticut, Vermont, Michigan, and several sections of New York. It is stated that nineteen of the twenty-three members of this class taught outside Oswego — seventeen of them in other states, including Massachusetts, Connecticut, Maryland, West Virginia, Indiana, Illinois, Iowa, Michigan, Kansas, Georgia, Mississippi, and Ohio.

The Oswego school was made a state normal in 1866 and six additional normal schools were established in New York State, all on the Oswego plan. The new state, private, and city normal schools, particularly those established in the West, generally followed the pattern set by Oswego.

[19] Hollis, *op. cit.*

Graduates of Oswego were widely distributed throughout the country in the first quarter-century of the school's history (Table 29). Many of these held key positions. Some organzed and headed normal schools. It was a poor teacher-training institution indeed which did not number one or more Oswego graduates on its staff.[20]

THE IMPORTANCE OF THE NORMAL SCHOOL AS A TEACHER-TRAINING AGENCY

Between 1860 and 1890 the number of normal schools mounted rapidly. By the close of the period they had become recognized and established as the most important source of trained teachers for the elementary schools. It is, however, impossible to describe quantitatively the expansion of the normal school. The Commissioner of Education collected data and presented compilations of them in his annual reports, but lack of authority on his part to compel institutions to report resulted in incomplete statistics. Furthermore, the definition of a normal school varied from time to time and classifications were not consistent. For example, in 1886 the Commissioner reported only 36 private normal schools as against 132 in the report of the preceding year. The decrease in the number reported did not result from any great change in the facilities for teacher education, but from reclassifying as secondary schools many institutions previously reported as normal schools. Consistency in classification was impossible until the idea of what constituted a normal school crystallized. For example, during most of the period, city training schools, whether full-fledged teacher-training schools or nothing "more than a fifth year of high-school work, made up mostly of pedagogical courses, together with observation and practice-teaching in the grades," were listed as normal schools.[21] On the one hand, the teacher-training academies of New York, numbering ninety in 1889, were not listed. On the other hand, many private institutions were listed, some of which were certainly nothing more than "short cuts to the teaching profession." Of these latter institutions, Dexter wrote:

> Usually no prerequisites to admission are made, other than sufficient maturity; the courses are undefined and short, and the accomplishments are superficial. Not infrequently such schools are but subordinate departments of commercial schools. From the standpoint of the teaching profession, their only excuse as a class, for being, is that the facilities for the training of teachers are as yet inadequate, and that even the training that the poorest of them give, is better than none.[22]

[20] *Ibid.*, pp. 26–28, 80–111.
[21] Edwin Grant Dexter, *A History of Education in the United States* (New York: The Macmillan Co., 1904), p. 385.
[22] *Ibid.*, p. 384.

TABLE 29:　GEOGRAPHICAL DISTRIBUTION OF
OSWEGO GRADUATES, 1861–1897*

State	Number of Graduates Taught in State 1861–86	Number of Graduates, 1887–97, Teaching in State in 1897	State	Number of Graduates Taught in State 1861–86	Number of Graduates, 1887–97, Teaching in State in 1897
Massachusetts	32	20	Arizona	1	
Maine	10	1	Wyoming	4	
New Hampshire	5	2	Montana	1	
Vermont	35	16	Oregon	1	2
Connecticut	19		Washington	1	4
Rhode Island	3		Kentucky	9	2
New York	1276	505	Tennessee	4	2
Pennsylvania	70	14	North Carolina	8	1
New Jersey	72	55	South Carolina	6	1
Delaware	2		Georgia	8	2
Maryland	8	3	Alabama	7	1
Virginia	8	3	Florida	2	2
District of Columbia	5	1	Arkansas	4	
West Virginia	1		Mississippi		2
Ohio	60	10	Louisiana	7	1
Indiana	70**	5	Indian Territory	1	1
Illinois	94	10	Texas	1	1
Michigan	93	6	Foreign Country		
Wisconsin	17	2	Canada	4	2
Minnesota	66	12	Germany		3
Iowa	46	3	Mexico	1	
Missouri	24	2	South America	6	
Kansas	20		Japan	2	
Nebraska	36	11	Hawaii	3	4
Utah		5	India	1	
The Dakotas	3		Persia		1
South Dakota		5	China		1
California	20	4			
Colorado	10	2			

* Adapted from Andrew Phillip Hollis, *The Contribution of the Oswego Normal School to Educational Progress in the United States* (Boston: D. C. Heath & Company, 1898), pp. 153–154.

** Entry in Hollis is misprinted. This figure is from Ned Harland Dearborn, *The Oswego Movement in American Education,* Teachers College, Columbia University Contributions to Education, 183 (New York: Teachers College, Columbia University, 1925), p. 179.

But regardless of how the statistics may be interpreted, a remarkable expansion of teacher-training facilities during the period cannot be denied. From only 12 state and fewer private normal schools in 1860, the number increased to 22 state and a somewhat smaller number of private schools in 1865. In 1871 the Commissioner of Education reported the existence of 51 normal schools supported by 23 states with 251 teachers and 6334 pupils; 16 city normal schools with 112 teachers and 2002 pupils; 4 supported by counties with 83 pupils; and 43 others supported in various ways with 80 teachers and 2503 pupils; making a total of 114 schools, with 445 teachers and 10,922 students.[23] An examination of the list of schools, however, reveals that several of them were normal classes or departments in colleges or universities and others were institutions with very doubtful claims to normal-school status. In 1875, there were reported 73 state, 2 county, and 42 other (largely private) normal schools. Only 8 states, Deleware, Georgia, Kentucky, Louisiana, North Carolina, Ohio, Oregon, and Utah, of those then in the Union, were without such a school. By 1880 the number of public normal schools had increased to 84; by 1885, to 103; and by 1889, to 135. Enrollments and teaching staffs expanded accordingly. By 1895, it has been estimated, there were of all classes of teacher-training schools upward of 350, of which 155 were publicly controlled.

This rapid "growth went hand in hand with provisions for compulsory education of the nation's children, with organization of schools into graded systems, with the growth of state school funds and local taxation for schools, with the rapid growth of public high schools, and with the rise of supervision in states, counties, and cities."[24]

Normal schools increased in number and importance in response to insistent social demands, but the leadership of the normal-school movement and the sound view which it held with respect to the nature and function of teacher training were responsible, in part, at least, for the fact that by 1890 the normals had "established for themselves the right to be considered the chief agency for the education of teachers of the common schools."[25]

The Evolution of the Teachers College

During the half-century following 1890, the school for the preparation of teachers was transformed from one of secondary rank to one of full "collegiate rank, and, in some cases, to one of graduate standing."[26]

[23] United States Bureau of Education, *Report of the Commissioner of Education for the Year 1871* (Washington, D.C.: Government Printing Office, 1872), p. 53.

[24] Harper, *op. cit.*, p. 72.   [25] *Ibid.*, p. 96.

[26] Jessie M. Pangburn, *The Evolution of the American Teachers College*, Teachers College Contributions to Education, No. 500 (New York: Teachers College, Columbia University, 1932), p. 1.

In spite of the remarkable progress in teaching education made between 1860 and 1890, Pangburn, summarizing the situation as it existed at the latter date, wrote, after extensive and careful investigation, as follows:

> The institutions giving preparation for teaching in 1890 were normal schools, either state or private, certain high schools which maintained classes for teachers, departments of pedagogy, or normal departments in colleges and universities, and the New York College for the Training of Teachers. The normal schools admitted students of secondary rank and scaled their offerings to the ability of the students. They attempted to give command of elementary subject matter, academic secondary studies, and professional studies, including history of education, science of education, and methods in the elementary branches and mental science.
>
> The majority of city normal schools at that time admitted only high school graduates to a one-year course of narrowly technical nature.
>
> Provision for the training of teachers in colleges and universities was in many cases of preparatory rank, and did not excel the training given in the normal school.[27]

In spite of the enormous immediate demand for teachers to staff the expanding common schools, teacher-training schools were transformed into fully recognized degree-granting institutions requiring high school graduation as a condition of entrance and providing a course of four or five years. This development is evidence that strong social forces were operating to implement a new concept of education and a new attitude toward it.

Factors Promoting the Evolution of the Teachers College

The teachers college evolved as an adaptation to meet the changing conditions of American life. Pangburn has called attention to the fact that the teachers college, like the normal school before it, was "an outgrowth of public education" and had been subject to the same conditioning that had produced the public school system.[28]

Recognition of changes in the nature of education. With increasing recognition of the inadequacy of the old educational program to meet the needs of the rapidly evolving social order came, also, a growing recognition of the limitations of teachers whose cultural backgrounds were bounded by three, four, or five elementary-school disciplines and whose professional preparation was as meager as that provided in the short courses of the normal schools. The states, long in the process of centralizing administra-

[27] *Ibid.*, pp. 31–32.
[28] *Ibid.*, p. 1.

tive authority for the conduct of the schools, began to require graduation from high school as a condition for granting certain certificates. By 1911 one state had made high school graduation prerequisite for the lowest-grade certificate. Eleven states had this requirement by 1919, 33 by 1928; and during the next decade high school graduation became the minimum academic requirement for certification in all states. To maintain their position in the field of teacher education, normal schools were obliged to raise entrance requirements and to build their programs upon a base of secondary education. The increasing recognition by the states of professional training as a condition for issuing certificates strengthened the normal school in its struggle to maintain its position in the field of teacher education.[29]

The development of the high school. The influence of the development of the high school in the transformation of the normal school into the teachers college cannot be overestimated. Of this, Pangburn, in her scholarly study, wrote:

> Of all the changes in public education, the growth of the high school seems to have been most influential in bringing about the change of the normal schools into teachers colleges. In the typical community the high school was in reality merely an extension upward of the common school. This was especially true of the West, where in village after village, first the ninth grade, then the tenth, and finally the eleventh and twelfth grades were added to the elementary school. The increases in the numbers attending the high schools and in the number of teachers needed for them were so great that the insufficiency of the supply of teachers in that field was especially evident. Although college graduation was regarded as a minimum standard for the preparation of the high-school teacher, the annual output of the colleges was absorbed by the larger towns and cities, so that the graduate of the normal school was frequently the best teacher material the ambitious small community could secure for its embryonic high school. Recognizing this fact, the normal school modified its offerings to give the intending teacher the best preparation possible, in the limited time he could devote to training, for the work he would be called upon to do.[30]

The normal schools were generally confident of their ability to train high school teachers and, particularly in the West, insisted upon the right to do so. In the West, where the distinction between secondary and higher education had never been clearly drawn, normal schools, "colleges," and "universities" had long insisted that the level of the institution was to

[29] See *ibid.;* also Benjamin W. Frazier, *Teacher Training, 1926–1928,* United States Office of Education Bulletin 17, 1929 (Washington, D.C.: Government Printing Office, 1929).

[30] Pangburn, *op. cit.,* p. 11.

be judged in terms of the maturity of the students and the nature of the instruction rather than in terms of the content of courses. Having gained recognition as the chief agency for the preparation of teachers for the public schools, they were unwilling, when the common school was expanded to include the high school, to relinquish any of their rights.

The rise of accrediting associations.   It was soon evident, however, that training restricted largely to professional courses and to work in the branches to be taught, even when this work was taught from the standpoint of a mature person who was to teach, did not provide adequately the cultural background necessary for teachers of pupils who were, in increasing numbers, eventually to apply for admission to colleges and universities.

The threatened deluge of poorly prepared matriculants caused colleges and universities to take the lead in creating organizations of secondary and higher institutions. These associations set up standards for membership and the colleges agreed to accept the graduates of the member secondary schools. The premium which high schools came to place upon membership in one of these regional associations[31] gave higher institutions a large measure of control over secondary education, a part of which, at least, was wisely exercised. One result of the accrediting activities of these organizations was to raise secondary-school standards in many communities. Also, when, as in the case of the North Central Association of Colleges and Secondary Schools in 1902, one of these bodies provided that teachers of member high schools should be graduates of colleges or universities belonging to or recognized by it, normal schools of the region were placed under the necessity of being accredited if they were to continue to place their graduates in the better secondary schools. As stated by Pangburn, "this situation created a direct and powerful pressure upon the normal schools to raise their standards of scholastic preparation and to seek the degree-granting privileges."[32]

Normal-school leadership.   A number of motives and beliefs prompted presidents and other leaders of normal schools to seek full college status for. their institutions. Among these were the ambition to make normal schools academically respectable, the fear that the loss of the function of training secondary-school teachers would be the deathblow to the normal schools, and the conviction that this type of institution was superior to the liberal-arts college for the training of teachers at all levels. Several

[31] Association of Colleges and Secondary Schools of the Middle States and Maryland, organized as the College Association of Pennsylvania in 1887; New England Association of Colleges and Secondary Schools, 1884; Association of Colleges and Secondary Schools of the Southern States, 1895; North Central Association of Colleges and Secondary Schools, 1896; Northwest Association of Secondary and High Schools, 1918. See *ibid.,* p. 12.

[32] *Loc. cit.*

strong presidents, largely of western schools, were particularly aggressive in presenting the cause of the normal school. The influence of the Middle and Far West was, according to Harper, largely responsible for the action, on the part of the Department of Normal Schools of the National Education Association, of drawing up in 1908 a *Statement of Policy for the Normal Schools,* "which became a veritable platform for transforming normals into teachers colleges."[33] The report recommended:

1. That the state normal schools make high-school graduation, or equivalent, a basis for admission to the standard normal course;
2. That the normal schools prepare teachers for the entire public service — elementary and secondary;
3. That the preparation of the elementary teachers be two years, and of the secondary, four years;
4. That the normal schools establish well-organized departments of research work leading to the solution of problems affecting education and life;
5. That while the normal school is not the only agent for the training of teachers, it is the state's chief agent, and as such it should set up standards of teaching, determine ideals, and train men and women whose call is to educational leadership;
6. That the colleges and universities should not dominate the courses of study of the high schools to the end of making them preparatory schools, thereby preventing these schools from being the best expression of the whole people;
7. That the curriculum of the normal school should be broad enough in scope to touch all phases of special preparation demanded by the broadening curriculum of the public schools.[34]

The fact that the normal school had grown strong enough during a half-century of development to challenge the older institutions, but not so tradition-bound as to resist thorough reorganization, accounts in no small measure for its success in asserting its right to train teachers for the expanded and extended public schools.

STEPS IN THE EVOLUTION OF THE TEACHERS COLLEGE

To become teachers colleges, normal schools were obliged (1) to raise their entrance requirements, (2) to lengthen and enrich their curriculums, (3) to obtain the right to grant degrees, (4) to gain the recognition

---

[33] Harper, *op. cit.,* p. 138.

[34] National Education Association, "Report of Committee on Statement of Policy Regarding the Preparation and Qualification of Teachers of Elementary and High Schools," *Journal of Proceedings and Addresses of the Forty-sixth Annual Meeting,* held at Cleveland, Ohio, June 29–July 3, 1908 (Chicago: University of Chicago Press, 1908), p. 735.

of universities and colleges, and (5) to render a service not provided by the traditional liberal-arts college.

Raising entrance requirements.   Although many normal-school leaders voiced disapproval of fixing high school graduation as a requirement for admission, because, they argued, such a procedure would prevent many worthy rural youth from attending and would staff even the rural schools with city-bred girls, courses were increasingly restricted, particularly in city normals, to high school graduates. In 1890 the Albany Normal School made high school graduation a condition for entrance, a requirement which was to become general during the following two or three decades.

Curriculum changes.   The period of preparation was lengthened not only by demanding four years of secondary-school work as prerequisite for admission, but also by lengthening the curriculum of the teacher-training school to four years. By 1943, 29 of the 183 institutions recommended for membership in the American Association of Teachers Colleges by its Accrediting Committee were classified as Graduate Teachers Colleges, with, presumably, one or more curriculums leading to the Master's degree,[35] a situation which foreshadowed the rapid expansion during the next two decades of Master's or fifth-year pre-service programs, particularly in those states requiring five years of preparation for beginning high-school teachers.

The normal schools, more and more conscious of the necessity of extending the cultural background of prospective teachers and subjected to the pressure of accrediting agencies, added many liberal-arts subjects to their curriculums, which earlier had been largely professional and practical in nature. Also, a developing science of education and a new wave of educational theory were giving rise to professional literature in unprecedented volume. The American Herbartian movement, which swept the country during the last decade of the nineteenth century, made itself felt in every teacher-training institution in the land. Through the writings and teachings of Frank M. and Charles A. McMurry, Charles De Garmo, Elmer Brown, C. C. Van Liew, and others, and through their influence upon teacher education, professional work was expanded in the light of new concepts such as apperception, assimilation, correlation, concentration, culture epochs, the five formal steps, and the doctrine of interest. The university study of psychology was likewise making contributions to the professional curriculum.

The expansion of the curriculum to include both cultural subjects and

[35] American Association of Teachers Colleges, *Twenty-second Yearbook, 1943* (Washington, D.C.: American Association of Teachers Colleges, National Education Association, 1943), p. 124.

new professional materials resulted in its overcrowding, which even its lengthening did not entirely relieve. The problem was partially solved in differentiating and multiplying curriculums. Instead of being differentiated only with respect to their length, as was generally the case in the normal school, the new curriculums, nearly all four years in length, were differentiated on the basis of the type of preparation needed for particular positions in the schools — teaching the different subjects at various levels or supervising and administering the educational program.

Authorization to grant degrees. A bewildering variety of degrees, such as Bachelor of Elements, Bachelor of Elementary Didactics, Master of Pedagogics, and Licentiate of Instruction, were granted by normal schools of some states long before 1890, but none of them "represented the completion of a full four-year college course, and there seems to have been no intention that they should signify anything more than that a curriculum preparatory to teaching had been satisfactorily completed."[36] The first normal schools to confer degrees representing four years of college work were the Albany Normal College (Albany Normal School before 1890) and the Michigan State College at Ypsilanti. Albany was given authority to confer the Bachelor of Pedagogy and Master of Pedagogy degrees in 1890, but the curriculum at the time included only professional subjects; it was not until after a reorganization in 1905 that a four-year course leading to a Bachelor of Arts degree was established. In 1897 Michigan State Normal College was fully organized as a four-year college, requiring high school graduation for admission, but it did not grant a Bachelor of Arts degree until 1905. The state legislature of Illinois granted the four state normal schools the degree-granting privilege in 1907.[37] After 1915 the right to grant degrees was gained by school after school in rapid succession. The standard degrees have come to be Bachelor of Arts in Education, Bachelor of Science in Education, and Bachelor of Arts.

Gaining the recognition of universities and colleges. The vigorous, articulate, and sometimes overzealous normal-school leaders found the task of obtaining the degree-granting privilege much less difficult than that of becoming worthy of the privilege, or, if worthy, of overcoming the prejudice of the colleges and universities.

One of the greatest problems facing the teacher-training schools was the scholarship of their faculties. Ruediger in an investigation covering twenty-eight schools found that in 1895 only 37 per cent of the staff held degrees, the highest degrees held being the Bachelor of Arts degree (13 per cent of the teachers), the Master's degree (16 per cent), and the Doctor's degree (8 per cent). By 1905 the percentage holding degrees

[36] Pangburn, *op. cit.*, pp. 85–86.
[37] Harper, *op. cit.*, pp. 136–137.

had increased to 46. Seventeen per cent had only the Bachelor's degree, 18 per cent held the Master's, and 11 per cent had received the doctoral degree.[38] For a time improvement was slow, but during the thirties teachers colleges came, in many instances, to rival liberal-arts colleges with respect to the formal training of their faculty members.

As the normal schools raised their standards by improving the quality of the teaching staff, reducing the teaching load, providing more adequate facilities, and becoming teachers colleges, they slowly gained the recognition of accrediting associations and were, if perhaps grudgingly, accepted by the universities as of the same level as the traditional liberal-arts college. By 1920 many higher institutions accepted without qualification transfer students from teachers colleges, and graduates of teachers colleges were being admitted in increasing numbers to the graduate schools and departments of the universities.

The teachers college in its evolution from a normal school was obliged to change from a school of secondary rank, which did not articulate well either with the elementary school or with the college, to a liberal-arts college, the curriculum of which, in the opinion of many normal-school men, was yet too medieval in character to properly serve the teacher-training function. At the same time they had to continue to provide a unique service in order to justify their survival.

By the thirties the teachers colleges had solved many of the problems of transition. The staffs, buildings, and facilities of most of them compared favorably with those of typical liberal-arts colleges. They had organized their programs in terms of public school needs as those needs were generally envisaged. In spite of the rapid development of teacher training in the much more numerous liberal-arts colleges, teachers colleges provided considerably more than one-half of America's teachers. However, by 1960 it appeared that the teachers college is only a transitory institution, whose contribution in time will take its place with that of the normal school in marking a stage in the development of teacher education.

From Teachers Colleges to
Regional All-Purpose Colleges and Universities

Educational leaders who struggled to create an institution of full college status, devoted solely to the education of teachers, could hardly have anticipated that their creation — the teachers college — was soon to decline in number and importance, and was, perhaps, destined to disappear from the educational scene. But it was because their efforts to upgrade teacher training were so successful that teachers colleges could be easily trans-

[38] William C. Ruediger, "Recent Tendencies in the Normal Schools of the United States," *Educational Review*, XXXIII (March, 1907), 271–287.

formed into all-purpose colleges and, in some instances, into universities.

This transformation was hastened, no doubt, by the fact that it represented a means for providing college facilities to returning veterans and others who at the close of World War II sought to resume or initiate college work. But the transformation was also facilitated by a change of attitude on the part of many persons who had formerly believed that the teachers college served a unique function, one that could not, or at least would not, be performed by the older institutions. It was a matter of record that colleges and universities had increasingly organized successful teacher-education programs, and, accompanying this development, there was a growing conviction that strong liberal-arts departments, coordinated with professional departments rather than under the control of a professional school or college, would provide a better academic component for the teacher-education program.

For the foregoing reasons, and perhaps numerous other ones, "the collegiate institution devoted exclusively to the preparation of teachers had almost completely disappeared by the close of the sixth decade."[39] The United States Office of Education, in its directory of higher institutions published in 1959, listed only 122 institutions as "primarily teacher-preparatory."[40] It is true that the "teachers college" classification was retained in most reports of student enrollment in higher education, but for the most part, as Haskew has stated, "these designations had reference to historical origins rather than to current programs."[41]

The general acceptance of the teacher-education function by colleges and universities and the rapid transformation of teachers colleges into college-rank institutions were reflected in efforts to provide a program of accreditation. National accreditation of teacher education was first performed by the American Association of Teachers Colleges, beginning in 1923. This organization and two others involved in teacher education merged in 1948 to form the American Association of Colleges for Teacher Education. However, by 1951 only 246 institutions of the some 1200 engaged in teacher preparation were accredited by the AACTE, and it was recognized that its membership was too small, its influence not widely felt, and its standards and policies inadequate. The newly established and more broadly based National Council for the Accreditation of Teacher Education took over the accrediting function in 1954. After early opposition originating in colleges somewhat fearful of its structure, this organization has grown and has experienced a small measure of success

[39] Laurence D. Haskew, "Teacher Education — Organization and Administration," pp. 1454–1460 in Chester W. Harris (ed.), *Encyclopedia of Educational Research*, Third Edition (New York: The Macmillan Co., 1960).

[40] "Higher Education," Part III in United States Department of Health, Education, and Welfare, *Education Directory of the Office of Education, 1959–1960* (Washington, D.C.: Government Printing Office, 1959).

[41] Haskew, *op. cit.*, p. 1454.

in improving teacher education through "(a) the formulation of policies, standards, and procedures for the accreditation of institutional programs of teacher education, (b) the accreditation of institutional programs . . . , (c) the encouragement of constituent organizations and other groups in the performance of their respective roles in the improvement of teacher education."[42]

From the evidence at hand, it appears that by the close of the nineteen-fifties teachers colleges had made their great contribution, were rapidly losing their unique character, and were being absorbed into the mainstream of higher education. It has come to be generally accepted that the teacher-education function can be best served by institutions that combine the best features of the teachers college with those of institutions which provide a broad liberal education. In the following section, the steps will be briefly traced by which higher institutions moved from the position that education was unworthy of university study and that teacher education was not the function of colleges and universities to a ready acceptance of responsibility for the improvement of teachers and teaching.

Teacher Training in Colleges and Universities

The evolution of the normal school into the teachers college and the transformation of a large number of teachers colleges into all-purpose colleges, and, in some instances, universities, was accompanied by the development of university study of education — a development which was to make possible the formulation of an educational science and the advancement of teacher education from practical training to professional preparation. Although the movement is, to a marked degree, a twentieth-century phenomenon, its beginnings may be traced to an earlier period.

The first step toward making the study of education a matter of university concern was taken when colleges and universities began to make special arrangements for training public school teachers. The first efforts made by the universities for the preparation of teachers generally took place in the West. There were, to be sure, several isolated attempts to introduce teachers' courses in eastern colleges. New York University, for example, established a chair of the philosophy of education for "educating teachers of common schools" in 1832, but it was shortly discontinued. Another early attempt by an eastern institution was made by Brown University in 1850, when, on the recommendation of President Wayland, a normal department was established. In 1854 a state normal school was founded in Rhode Island. Since the purpose for which its normal department had been organized had been attained, Brown University suspended its pedagogical work and Samuel Stillman Greene, Professor of Didactics,

[42] *Ibid.*, p. 1455.

became Professor of Mathematics and Civil Engineering.[43] But in spite of these and other sporadic efforts to provide teacher-training courses, "it remained," says Judd, "for the state universities of the north-central states to effect a change in the whole situation."[44] Circumstances forced the West to modify old practices and to create new institutions.

In the East normal schools had been established to meet the demand for elementary-school teachers created by the expansion of the public schools in the thirties and forties. These public schools, generally providing inferior opportunities at the most elementary levels, were, in many sections, attended by few pupils intended for the university. Certainly the university felt no responsibility for the lowly public school, which was so far removed from it in "interests and constituency."[45] It was entirely satisfied to leave the training of teachers of these inferior schools to the normal school, which, in turn, aspired to nothing higher.

In the West normal schools had not as yet been established and the need for trained teachers subjected the western colleges to a pressure not felt by eastern institutions. Furthermore, the gap between higher and common-school education was often much narrower than was the case in the older states. It would be a mistake, however, to think that the western colleges and universities accepted the responsibility for training elementary teachers with any great show of enthusiasm. Generally the first efforts in the West "for the professional training of teachers did not take place in the universities . . . , but in their preparatory departments, or in separate normal attachments" under their supervision.[46]

Normal classes or departments were provided in or in connection with the University of Indiana (1852), the University of Iowa (1855), the University of Wisconsin (1856), the University of Missouri (1868), the University of Kansas (1876), the State Agricultural and Mechanical College of Kentucky (1881), and other institutions, including the state universities of Utah, North Dakota, South Dakota, and Wyoming.[47]

With the establishment of state normal schools and the rapid increase in the number of high schools, the universities discontinued their preparatory schools and normal departments.[48] Many universities would have retired from the field of preparing common-school teachers had not the rapid

---

[43] G. W. A. Luckey, "The Professional Training of Secondary Teachers in the United States" (Doctor's thesis, Faculty of Philosophy, Columbia University, 1903), pp. 63–64.

[44] Charles H. Judd, "The School of Education," in Raymond A. Kent (ed.), *Higher Education in America* (Boston: Ginn & Company, 1930), p. 160. By permission of Harvard University Press.

[45] *Ibid.,* p. 158.   [46] Luckey, *op. cit.,* p. 101.   [47] *Ibid.,* pp. 65–99.

[48] Indiana University closed its normal department in 1873, three years after the establishment of the Indiana State Normal School at Terre Haute; the normal department of the University of Wisconsin was discontinued in 1866. Also in 1866, the Board of Regents of the Normal School opened the first state normal school at Platteville, and two years later one at Whitewater. See *loc. cit.*

expansion of the common schools to include the high school created a demand for secondary-school teachers, the training of whom was everywhere considered a proper function of the university. With state normals insisting upon the right to train teachers for all grades of the common school, including the high school, and at the same time demonstrating that professional courses had value, the universities changed their normal departments to collegiate departments of pedagogics, or, if the old normal departments had been discontinued, created new arrangements for the professional preparation of teachers, such as departments of pedagogy, chairs of didactics, and departments of education.

The first state university to establish a chair of education having continuous existence to the present time was the University of Iowa, but Michigan provides the best example of the new development, the background of which may be traced far back into the educational history of the state.

Teacher training at the University of Michigan. The founders of the University of Michigan had conceived of their institution as the head of the state school system of lower schools, secondary schools, and branches of the university located in various sections of the state. Each of the branches was to have three departments, "one for the education of teachers for the primary schools, one for the higher branches of English education, and one for classical learning."[49] John D. Pierce, first superintendent of public instruction, in 1837 urged particularly the establishment of the department for the education of teachers:

> It is certainly of much consequence to the public interests that these branches be pushed forward with vigor, and be adequately sustained. They form the all-important connecting link between the primary schools and the University. They are especially intended to fit such young men for the regular classical course of the University as may wish to enter the institution; also, to prepare some for the profession of teaching, that the primary schools may be fully supplied with competent instructors; and to qualify others for those numerous employments of life which require a more extended education than is usually to be obtained at the district school. Unquestionably then, they are essential to the successful and harmonious action of the system. Without them every part of it must suffer and the department languish. Without teachers, thoroughly educated and bred to the profession, what essential benefit can rationally be expected to result from general establishment of primary schools? But where can we expect to find such teachers without furnishing them the necessary means to fit them for their work; and where can we better do it than in the contemplated branches of the University? Without these,

---

[49] Allen S. Whitney, *History of the Professional Training of Teachers; At the University of Michigan for the First-Half-Century, 1879 to 1929* (Ann Arbor, Mich.: George Wahr, 1931), p. 10.

where can we find young men prepared to enter the classic course of the parent-institution? It is indeed of the first importance to the great interests of education, in our own state, that these branches be well appointed and vigorously sustained. . . . What method so effectual for the support of schools throughout the state, as furnishing them with able teachers?

The proposed branches occupy the middle ground, being connected, on the one hand, with the primary schools, by the establishment of a department in each for the education of teachers; and on the other, with the University itself, by the establishment in each of them of a preparatory course, and being thus equally designed for the benefit of both the University and district schools. It seems no more than right that they should be supported from the funds of each.[50]

The efforts of Superintendent Pierce and his successors to provide professional training for teachers of the common schools through the university branches were not successful. Both regents and public were primarily interested in the branches as preparatory schools for the university and not as teacher-training agencies. Also, funds were not available to establish and maintain the branches as originally planned. However, as Judd points out:

The break between the University and the public-school system of the state never became complete in Michigan, in spite of the difficulties which prevented the complete realization of the hopes of the founders of the university.[51]

The failure of the House to concur in the action of the Senate, which adopted a bill in 1848 "to establish a branch at the University of Michigan as a state normal school," meant the loss of the teacher-training function as conceived by the founders. At the next session a bill was passed to establish a state normal school. This school was located in Ypsilanti and was opened for students in 1852.

Agitation continued at the University and President Tappan showed himself interested in the training of teachers. He knew well the Prussian school system and the Prussian program for the education of secondary-school teachers in universities. In 1858–59 the University catalogue announced a teachers' course in ancient languages. Doctor J. M. Gregory, superintendent of public instruction from 1858 to 1864, argued insistently that the universities and colleges should cooperate in providing a supply of competent teachers "by offering specific professional courses for all students planning to enter the work of teaching." He offered to teach a course on the organization, administration, and instruction of schools. President Tappan accepted the offer and the course of lectures

[50] As quoted *ibid.*, pp. 10–11.
[51] Judd, *op. cit.*, p. 161. By permission of Harvard University Press.

was given during the years 1861, 1862, and 1863. Whitney states that these lectures emphasized the following aspects of professional education:

1. The utilities of the course.
2. Educational philosophy.
3. The grades in education, or the proper organization and management of schools.
4. The teaching art, or methods of teaching appropriate to different branches of knowledge.[52]

Apparently the lectures ceased when Gregory relinquished office as state superintendent. But the issue of university education of teachers continued to be agitated. With respect to the course given by Gregory, Judd states that it marked the beginning of a new era of teacher training in this country.[53] President Angell in his annual report of 1874 recommended that instruction in pedagogics be provided and four years later renewed his recommendation. The Regents acted on his recommendation and in 1879 established a Chair of the Science and Art of Teaching and appointed William H. Payne to that chair. Their action was generally approved by faculty and students and was commented upon favorably by *Harper's Magazine* and other journals.

The University did not change by this one stroke the beliefs of reactionaries, who continued to belittle the "fifth wheel to the wagon," and "the substitution of method for academic attainment." It was also confronted with the opposition of the normal schools, which were seeking greater recognition and larger appropriations from the state legislature.[54] President Angell set forth his views with respect to these criticisms in his annual report for 1879:

> We desire it most clearly understood that we have no intention of invading the territory of our neighbors of the normal school. The line between their work and ours is very distinct. We wish simply to aid our undergraduates, who come here for collegiate study, to prepare themselves for the work of teaching, which they are certain to undertake, whether we have this new chair or not. If our effort to give specific instruction of this kind and of a high order is successful, it will tend to aid the normal school by strengthening in the minds of our graduates and of the public the conviction that there is indeed a philosophy, a science, of education, which we are aiming to teach to such of our students as intended to become teachers, while the normal school is also teaching it to every one of its hundreds of pupils in the manner most helpful to them. We earnestly hope to co-operate with and to aid in every proper way all

[52] J. M. Gregory, *Report of the Superintendent of Public Instruction, 1863*, pp. 6 ff., as quoted in Whitney, *op. cit.*, p. 19.
[53] Judd, *op. cit.*, p. 161.
[54] Whitney, *op. cit.*, p. 30.

the other educational institutions in the state. There is work enough and more than enough for us all to do. The prosperity of each conduces to the prosperity of all the rest.[55]

William H. Payne, the Professor of the Science and Art of Teaching, made it clear that there was no intention of encroaching upon the field which the University considered as belonging to the normal school. Stated Doctor Payne: "As at present constituted, the normal schools are not fitted to dispense the professional education needed by head masters, principals, superintendents, or even first assistants in high schools."[56]

The state normal school at Ypsilanti, which in 1878 had enlarged its curriculum and changed its practice of twenty-eight years to provide training for "assistants, principals, and superintendents in all classes of the public schools," probably disagreed, but Payne's statement represented the general view of the universities of the day.

Teacher training at other universities. Several universities were almost ready to establish chairs or departments of education at the time that the University of Michigan created its Chair of the Science and Art of Teaching. University chairs, departments, or schools of university grade were established at the University of Wisconsin in 1881; Johns Hopkins, Missouri, and North Carolina in 1884; Cornell and Indiana in 1886; Clark University in 1889; Stanford and Chicago in 1891; California in 1892; Illinois and Minnesota in 1893; Nebraska in 1895; Ohio and Texas in 1896; and Northwestern in 1898. Many of the early chairs of education, pedagogy, or didactics were created as a part of some established department, often philosophy, but a number of them were early made into independent units, such as teachers colleges, colleges of education, or schools of education. In this later movement the University of Michigan, which for a generation had been the leader in promoting university training for secondary-school teachers and the university study of education, failed to keep pace with many other institutions. A School of Pedagogy was organized by New York University in 1890 and a School of Education by the University of Chicago in 1901. Teachers College was founded in 1888 (chartered in 1889), became affiliated with Columbia University in 1893–94, and in 1898 became incorporated as an integral part of the University, exchanging its president for a dean but retaining a separate board of trustees.[57]

At a meeting of the National Education Association in 1890 it was

---

[55] *Proceedings of the Regents, 1879,* p. 415, as quoted *ibid.,* pp. 30–31.

[56] W. H. Payne, *Contribution to the Science of Education,* p. 307, as quoted in Luckey, *op. cit.,* p. 113.

[57] Walter L. Hervey, "Historical Sketch of Teachers College from its Foundation to 1897," *Teachers College Record,* I (January, 1900), 12–35; James E. Russell, "The Organization and Administration of Teachers College," *Teachers College Record,* I (January, 1900), 36–59.

reported that, out of the 361 colleges and universities in the land, only 21 had established a pedagogical chair and that many of these were only on paper.[58] This, of course, does not present a complete picture of all the teacher-training activities of the universities. By 1890, 114 of the colleges and universities reporting to the United States Commissioner of Education enrolled 3414 students in teacher-training courses. Most of these institutions were located in the Mississippi Valley. Many of them were obviously on the verge of establishing chairs or departments of education.[59] From this point on, growth was rapid. By 1891 professorships were reported in thirty-one institutions, chairs of pedagogics combined with another subject (usually philosophy) in forty-five more, and lectureships in education in seven universities.[60]

Many of the courses introduced were poor in quality and probably no more advanced than some found in normal schools. The courses, the chairs, and the instructors filling those chairs were generally looked upon as something which evil times had foisted upon the university. Faculties were inclined to keep the work in education as meager as outside pressure would permit and to keep the relationship of the department to the university as distant as possible. In 1892 De Garmo urged that departments be given organic connection with the university, likened professors of education to educational Robinson Crusoes, and spoke with some warmth of those who he felt were hindering the cause of education.

> Even the gentlemen who sneer at their own conception of what the study of pedagogy is good for, acknowledge by their attentive presence at these national conventions that there are important unsettled matters in education, worthy of this great annual gathering, quite deserving the long, thoughtful study of our best minds. Even President Eliot, himself, finds it worth while to rouse all New England by his proposals for strictly educational changes in the grammar-school curriculum.[61]

Eliot at Harvard was, however, in 1890–91 voicing his own and his faculty's distrust of pedagogics and urging the value of skillful teachers'

[58] Levi Seeley, "Pedagogical Training in Colleges Where There Is No Chair of Pedagogy," *Journal of Proceedings and Addresses of the National Education Association, Session of the Year 1890,* held in Saint Paul, Minn. (Topeka: Kansas Publishing House, Clifford C. Baker, 1880), p. 673.

[59] United States Bureau of Education, *Report of the Commissioner of Education for the Year 1889–90* (Washington, D.C.: Government Printing Office, 1893), II, p. 1020.

[60] *Report of the Commissioner of Education, 1891–92,* II, pp. 725–726, as cited in Pangburn, *op. cit.,* p. 21.

[61] Charles De Garmo, "Scope and Character of Pedagogical Work in Universities," *Journal of Proceedings and Addresses of the National Education Association, Session of the Year 1892,* held at Saratoga Springs, N.Y. (New York: J. J. Little & Co., 1893), p. 773.

teaching by example.[62]   Although Charles Kendall Adams, President Angell, and others, aware of the excellence of Prussian secondary schools and the contributions of the Prussian universities to educational development, urged the teaching of pedagogics in colleges and universities, Eliot spoke no doubt for a majority of the colleges.

First Steps in the Development of a Science of Education

As long as the main efforts had been directed toward the establishment of a system of elementary schools and the improvement of education at the lower levels, universities felt little responsibility for the training of teachers or for the study of their problems. Teacher education developed in Europe and in America, particularly in the East, as an extension of elementary education and almost entirely outside the university.

Even after American colleges and universities had in considerable numbers undertaken a measure of responsibility for the training of teachers of the expanding and rapidly multiplying high schools, they did little to improve the pattern or nature of instruction as it had been developed in the normal schools. Here and there halting efforts were made to expand the scope of teacher education and to place it on a more professional basis. These attempts were not very successful and, for the most part, they failed to convince most administrators or faculties of higher institution that the preparation of teachers involved professional work of really college caliber or that the problems of education were worthy of university study.

The reluctance on the part of the university to provide instruction and opportunities for research in education may be attributed, in part, to the fact that until the end of the nineteenth century the science of education had developed only a meager content. This is not to say that the contributions of American and European writers were unknown or that the influence of a developing educational journalism and the writings of a succession of educational statesmen and schoolmen were negligible. It is only that the effort to realize the ideal of free universal education absorbed the total energies of intellectual leaders. To provide the bare minimum demanded by the mounting numbers who sought the elements of an education severely strained the educational resources of the nation. The increasing magnitude of the educational enterprise, however, introduced new problems of instruction and administration and made more acute the problems which had already been recognized. Teachers and administrators, as the century progressed, were attempting to find the solution to their

[62] *Report of the United States Commissioner of Education, 1890–91*, p. 1076, as cited in Pangburn, *op. cit.*, pp. 22–23.

problems in the theories of philosophers and the methods of experts.

To meet the growing demand, educational literature increased throughout the entire period as the number of teachers and superintendents multiplied and their problems became more and more pressing. Newly founded journals made known to a steadily enlarging circle the educational achievements of the more advanced state and local systems, presented the views of educational leaders, and introduced many readers to the theories and practices of Pestalozzi, Fellenberg, Witherspoon, and numerous other writers. Barnard's *American Journal of Education* made know the works of many European scholars and described at great length the best of foreign practice. Several useful books appeared during the last years of the century, including some works on the philosophy of education, some treatises on method, a few descriptions of successful practices, a few accounts of the work of particular institutions, and a limited number of expositions on the management of schools. An examination of the material available at the close of the period, however, reveals that education was not yet a science to be studied or even, perhaps, an art to be practiced.

Nevertheless, the beginnings of an educational science had been made. Theories were being developed which threw new light upon the purposes and processes of education. Scientific methods developed in other disciplines were increasingly applied to the study of problems having profound implications for education. Scientifically trained scholars both in America and in Europe were seeking a better understanding of the human mind and the conditions for its operation.

THE HERBARTIAN MOVEMENT

The work of making the study of education attractive to university students, begun by Herbart in Germany, was continued by Rein at Jena, and the Herbartian ideas expounded there were becoming an inspiration to a number of Americans who had turned to Germany for advanced training. Among these were Charles De Garmo and Charles A. McMurry and Frank M. McMurry, whose books on methods became standard textbooks in teacher-training institutions and remained popular over a period of twenty years. In 1892, twenty-four years after the first establishment of a Herbartian Society in Germany, the National Herbart Society was organized in America. Although much in Herbartian theory and practice failed to withstand the onslaught of keen minds turned to applying new techniques to the study of educational problems, this professional organization and its successor, the National Society for the Scientific Study of Education (later, the National Society for the Study of Education), has continued, as the early Herbartians did, to play an important part in the development of a science of education. Its Yearbooks represent a rich source for the study of American educational theory and practice from the turn of the century to the present time.

The Child-Study Movement

Another development to make a contribution to educational science and to enrich the study of pedagogy was the child-study movement, initiated by G. Stanley Hall. After a broad training in theology, philosophy, neurology, psychology, and related studies at Williams, Union Theological, Harvard, Bonn, Berlin, and Leipzig, under famous teachers such as James, Wundt, and Trendelenburg, Hall in 1883 published his pioneering study, *The Contents of Children's Minds on Entering School.* As a teacher of psychology and pedagogy at Johns Hopkins (1882–88) and as president of Clark University (1889–1919), Hall and his disciples developed theories in education and psychology which helped to break the hold of traditional scholastic psychology. Clark University became the center for the study of genetic psychology and child study, the results of which were to survive and enrich the science of education even after Hall's assumptions, procedures, and doctrines had been outgrown and, to a considerable extent, discredited. Child-study programs instituted later at Yale, Iowa, Columbia (Teachers College), Chicago, and other centers were little influenced by Hall, and more recent treatises on child development have dismissed him with hardly more than a footnote. However, his work in arousing a scientific and experimental interest in children and in stimulating educational thought over a period of a generation should not be underrated.

Experimental Psychology

During the last quarter of the nineteenth century the techniques of the accepted sciences were applied to the study of human behavior. In 1879 Wundt established at Leipzig the first psychological laboratory and began a long series of experimental investigations of the psychological processes involved in reasoning, judgment, memory, and the senses of hearing, taste, smell, and vision. Students trained by Wundt were to develop further experimental methods to study the problems of education. Through Judd, one of his American students, the method of the laboratory was to receive emphasis over a period of forty years. Judd and Thorndike, both of whom accepted the pragmatic philosophy of James and Dewey, developed, adapted, and applied the new methods of investigation to make educational psychology the most influential branch of psychological study. Experimentation under scientifically controlled conditions has developed rapidly since 1900 and today all university departments and schools of education are equipped with laboratories for the study of educational problems.

THE DEVELOPMENT OF SCIENTIFIC MEASUREMENT

While the methods of the laboratory were being adapted to the study of human traits and educational problems, statistical principles were also developed for the measurement and interpretation of phenomena observed in the laboratory and elsewhere. Galton (1822–1911) in his studies on nature and nurture (*Hereditary Genius,* 1869, and *Natural Inheritance,* 1889) suggested the measurement of human traits and contributed to the development of mathematical techniques highly useful in such investigations. His pioneering work in statistical methods was extended by Karl Pearson in England and by Cattell, Thorndike, and others in America. Thorndike, more than any other person refined the techniques of measurement developed in biology and adapted them to education. In 1902 he offered at Columbia University the first course in educational statistics, and in 1904 he published a textbook on the measurement of mental traits which was to stimulate a large number of vigorous minds, then turning to the study of education, to investigate statistical methods. The development of procedures for the description of quantitative data was to advance so rapidly during the next six decades that the significant work of one decade was to appear elementary and unsophisticated in the next, and the development of electronic machines was to make possible the processing of data on a scale never envisaged by the pioneers workers in the field.

THE TESTING MOVEMENT

The development of mental tests. The application of statistical methods to the measurement of mental and other human traits, as defined in the laboratory of Wundt and other psychologists and by investigators such as Galton, was one of the most important advances in the development of a science of education. Cattell through his writings made known in America some of Galton's earlier work.[63] Thorndike refined the work of his predecessors in his aforementioned *An Introduction to the Theory of Mental and Social Measurements,* published in 1904.

The first attempts to measure mental traits were largely concerned with such things as sensory discrimination, reaction time, and memory. The first extensive and practical work in mental measurement must be attributed to two Frenchmen, Alfred Binet and Thomas Simon. The first scale appeared in 1905, and the better-standardized 1908 scale was re-

[63] J. McK. Cattell, "Mental Tests and Measurements," *Mind,* XV (1890), 373–380.

vised and published in 1911. Binet developed the concept of mental age — a concept that has been generally employed since.

The most important of the several translations and revisions of this scale was Terman's Stanford Revision, which, with subsequent refinement, has remained the best known and perhaps most widely used individual mental test.

Great impetus was given to the movement by the development of group tests, which were introduced into schools following their widespread use in the armed forces during the first World War. Numerous group tests have been constructed, some of a non-verbal type, in an attempt to measure not only intelligence, but also such traits as character and moral judgment. Although many of these have failed to accomplish satisfactorily the ends sought, new techniques have been formulated in their development and have generally contributed to a better understanding of the human mind and its working.

The development of achievement tests. In 1897 Doctor J. M. Rice reported in *The Forum* the development of a scale for measuring achievement in spelling. This was perhaps the first modern-type achievement test. There had been earlier attempts to improve the measurement of achievement, but they were insignificant and made little impression. In fact, little could be accomplished in this area before quantitative methods were developed and the idea that human behavior could be studied quantitatively had been accepted.

The publication in 1910 of Thorndike's Scale for the Measurement of Merit in Handwriting, based on the equal-differences theorem, may be taken as marking the real beginning of scientific measurement of the products of the educational program. After 1910 development was rapid. Many persons were engaged in constructing, validating, and standardizing tests. Practical schoolmen, however, were much slower to accept the ideas of measurement than were scholars such as Thorndike, Hanus, Ayres, and Courtis, but they too were, in time, won over. The Department of Superintendence of the National Education Association, which rejected measurement as a sound educational procedure by a small majority in 1912, adopted by a large majority a report favoring the movement in 1914. In 1918 the National Society for the Scientific Study of Education devoted its entire Yearbook to measurement. At that time, however, Judd remarked that teachers generally stood aloof from the movement.

In the years immediately following, the movement gathered momentum. Hundreds of tests were devised for the measurement of numerous types of learning and learning products. Schools and school systems established bureaus to make continuing studies of achievement. Techniques were refined and teacher-training institutions provided instruction in the proper use of tests.

More recently the emphasis has veered from testing achievement in school subjects to programs of evaluation involving the use of a wider range of measuring techniques, the measurement and description of a larger number of the results of learning and maturation, and the planning of educational programs on the basis of demonstrated progress toward the desired objectives.[64] The growth of the testing movement was to be reflected by the preparation of specialists, the development of public and private testing agencies, the establishment of specialized publishing companies, and the reliance placed upon test results by schools, colleges, business enterprises, and other organizations.

THE SCHOOL-SURVEY MOVEMENT

The school survey, it has been claimed, was a natural outcome of the testing movement. Intelligent efforts to improve administration of the schools no doubt also contributed to its development. Early schoolmen had made lengthy and searching analyses of the condition of education. Barnard in 1845 issued a report on the condition of education in Rhode Island based on a two-year study of the situation. Many superintendents' reports made during the nineteenth century went far beyond the presentation of statistics which constituted the bulk of a majority of such reports. The origin of the modern movement, however, commonly and perhaps correctly has been traced to the investigation of the Montclair, New Jersey schools made by Professor Hanus of Harvard in 1911. On the basis of his observations and expert knowledge, he wrote a report expressing his opinion concerning the educational situation which he had investigated.

Subsequent surveys — made by Cubberley, Brown, and Kendall (Baltimore, 1911); Cubberley (Portland, Oregon, 1913); Strayer (Butte, Montana, 1914); Ayres (Springfield, Illinois, 1914); and others — produced refined techniques and standardized procedures. In the Ayres survey of the Cleveland schools in 1915–16, extensive use was made of tests and statistical procedures. Surveys were definitely coming to be based upon scientific appraisals rather than upon expert opinion alone. The standardization of procedures for treating objective data quantitatively brought the survey into the curriculum of university departments and schools of education. Courses were organized in numerous institutions to provide training in the application of survey techniques and in the interpretation of survey results.

The movement spread rapidly. Many hundreds of surveys have been made. Some have been modest investigations of one or more aspects of the educational program; others have been large-scale comprehensive investigations. Some surveys of both types have been superficial; others have been

[64] Wilford M. Aiken, *The Story of the Eight-Year Study* (New York: Harper & Brothers, 1942).

of great significance, not only to the school systems surveyed, but also to the developing science of education. Universities have organized divisions to direct surveys and to provide the trained personnel needed to conduct them. Educational foundations have directed and financed surveys that otherwise could not have been made. The United States Office of Education, particularly during the twenties, carried on a number of investigations of state systems. This agency, as a part of its program to study education on a nation-wide scale, brought out during the first half of the thirties national surveys of the land-grant colleges and universities, secondary education, and the education of teachers.[65]

In the early forties new direction was given to the nation-wide study of aspects of the educational program. The Commission on Teacher Education, appointed by the American Council on Education and financed by the General Education Board, studied the "numerous and diversified problems in the education of teachers," drawing largely upon the experience and insight of institutions and associations already active in the field. Emphasis on implementation of existing knowledge, rather than on fact-finding, characterized the work of this organization.[66]

By the 1960's the survey movement had expanded to provide more and different types of service. The trend away from the "comprehension survey," toward the investigation and analysis of aspects or activities of school systems and of educational institutions and agencies, has continued. The improved quality of the leaders and staff of schools and school systems has been reflected by the increase in the number and improved quality of "self-surveys." However, universities and other agencies have continued to expand their survey services and the demand for such services has continued to increase.

SCHOOL ORGANIZATION AND ADMINISTRATION

The multitude of surveys helped reveal that during the nineteenth century the school had become a complex social institution. It was made apparent that the problems involved in efficient management of the educational program were becoming more and more complicated. The rapid expansion of the educational enterprise was perhaps the most important

[65] Arthur J. Klein, *Survey of Land-Grant Colleges and Universities,* United States Office of Education Bulletin 9, 1930 (2 vols.) (Washington, D.C.: Government Printing Office, 1930); Leonard V. Koos *et al., National Survey of Secondary Education,* United States Office of Education Bulletin 17, 1932 (28 monographs) (Washington, D.C.: Government Printing Office, 1933–34); E. S. Evenden *et al., National Survey of the Education of Teachers,* United States Office of Education Bulletin 10, 1933 (6 vols.) (Washington, D.C.: Government Printing Office, 1933–1935).

[66] *The Commission on Teacher Education. A Brief Statement of Its Origin and Scope* (Washington, D.C.: Commission on Teacher Education, American Council on Education, 1940); Maurice E. Troyer and C. Robert Pace, *Evaluation in Teacher Education* (Washington, D.C.: American Council on Education, 1944).

factor contributing to the acuteness of the situation. There was the fact, too, that not only were greater and greater numbers being drawn into the schools, but also that the function of the school was changing in such a way as to make management more difficult and expert management more necessary. The administrative problems involved in centralization demanded attention. The principles which had been worked out in business and government were examined, and Cubberley and others attempted to adapt those principles to procedures in staffing, supervising, and financing the schools. From all such activities, and from the whole survey movement, an extensive literature developed and the way was opened for the systematic training of educational administrators.

EDUCATION AND THE SOCIAL ORDER

As the school became more clearly recognized as an important social institution, a consciousness of the significance of its past developed. Earlier histories of education had dealt almost entirely with theory and were based largely upon the writings of educational philosophers. As education was viewed in a new manner, different aspects of its past took on a new significance and a new type of history began to appear. It was recognized that the history of education may be considered a part of social history and that understanding of an educational program requires a thorough knowledge of the social life of which the school is a part. Monroe and his students contributed a large amount of historical research to swell the growing body of scholarly educational literature. Later, Counts and others related the schools more definitely to the contemporary social order. Since World War II, the greatest expansion in the field has been, as might be expected, in the study of comparative education. There is at present every indication that the study of education in the future will focus as much upon the significance of social, economic, and political movements as it has focused upon psychological aspects during the past half-century.

EDUCATION AS A PROFESSION

From the typical teacher's course of the nineteenth century, which embodied a little history of educational theory, a meager philosophy, and an even less well-developed psychology along with some practical treatment of methods and classroom management, the curriculum in teacher education has been expanded to include new content in the areas of measurement, psychology, administration, supervision, and history. By 1920 a science of education had been well defined. In 1918 Judd wrote:

> The science of education aims to collect by all available methods full information with regard to the origin, development, and present form of

school practices and also full information with regard to social needs. It aims to subject present practices to rigid tests and comparisons and to analyze all procedure in the schools by experimental methods and by observation. It aims to secure complete and definite records of all that the school attempts and accomplishes. The results of school work are to be evaluated by rigid methods of comparison and analysis. To direct studies of the school the science of education must add full studies of the social life of which the school is a part and of the individual nature which is to be trained and molded through the educational processes. In the light of such studies the science of education is to suggest such enlargements and modifications of school practices as seem likely to promote the evolution of the educational system.[67]

In spite of college presidents and faculties who were distrustful of professional education for teachers and who held that neither the study of pedagogy nor the problems of education had any place in institutions of higher learning, teacher education and the development of a science of education were to become major activities of the early-twentieth-century colleges and universities. In 1890 there were in higher institutions only a few chairs of education or pedagogy and perhaps fewer than four thousand students in teacher courses, but by 1900 the study of education and professional programs were finding wide acceptance. By 1920 more than four hundred colleges and universities were providing some kind of program in education and, generally, the programs reflected the findings of the new science.

In the period that followed, the professionalization of the teaching staff proceeded at a rapid rate. University studies on the nature of the learner, the learning process, educational needs, and the techniques and materials of instruction were pointing to new skills and understandings that the teacher must acquire and to new roles that he must assume. The expansion of knowledge in many fields, particularly in science, and the need for greater social intelligence, on the part of teachers and the taught alike, added new dimensions to the teacher-education task. New programs of both in-service and pre-service education contributed to the immediate improvement of the quality of the teaching staff and also, in some measure, to the solution of problems of learning and teaching.

Higher institutions, through the study of education and the training of teachers, pointed the way to the professionalization of teaching, but other agencies too made contributions that universities alone could not have made. Pioneering school systems, educational statesmen, research bureaus with various affiliations, the National Education Association and other professional organizations, legislative bodies, and the great foundations — Carnegie, General Education Board, Kellogg, Ford, and many

[67] Charles H. Judd, *Introduction to the Scientific Study of Education* (Boston: Ginn & Company, 1918), pp. 305–306.

others — have contributed in their own way to the study of the basic problems of learning, teaching, and administration and to the closing of the gap between the discovery and the application of solutions.

By 1960 approximately three-fourths of the more than 1250 liberal-arts, technical, and professional institutions ("primarily teacher-preparatory" excluded) which offered academic or professional degrees, or both, were engaged in the preparation of teachers. Of the 171 institutions which offered a liberal-arts program and operated three or more professional schools, a large majority maintained schools of education.[68] Shortly after 1950 it was reported that approximately two hundred institutions offered advanced degrees in education, and that considerably more than half of them offered the doctorate.[69]

By 1961 scores of colleges and universities had introduced five- and six-year programs leading to degrees generally designated as the Master of Arts in Teaching.

The movement toward concern on the part of universities for the problems of teaching and learning has origins, it is true, that date far back, but it was not until the twentieth century that the study of education received support in any substantial way and that departments, faculties, and schools of education acquired standing equal to that of other professional divisions, colleges, and schools. The present concern for education and the support of research relating to it by universities and many other agencies promise much for the continued advancement of teaching as a profession and for the development of education as a science.

Questions and Problems for Study and Discussion

1. Explain why the normal school for the education of elementary-school teachers was established as an institution separate from colleges, universities, and other educational institutions. Under the conditions that existed, could this practice have been avoided? Why?
2. What were the forces that brought about the development of the teachers college from the nineteenth-century normal school?
3. What are the forces that have been influential in the development of teachers colleges into regional all-purpose colleges?
4. How extensive do you think the general education of teachers should be?
5. What is meant by the phrases "science of education" and "profession of education"? Can a profession of education be built except on the foundation of a science of education?
6. Show how the education of teachers has been affected, and should be further affected, by systematic, scientific study of the problems of education.

[68] "Higher Education," Part III in *Education Directory of the Office of Education, 1959–60, op. cit.*
[69] Haskew, *op. cit.,* p. 1458.

7. Select some problem in education — e.g., the nature of the learner, the nature of learning, the role of the teacher, the selection of curriculum materials, or some other problem of your own choice — and show how the scientific study of education has affected the solution presently accepted.

8. It has been stated that the education of teachers has centered too much around the concept of education as a psychological process and too little around the concept of education as a part of public and social policy. What is the basis for such a statement, and what is your reaction to it?

Selected References for Further Reading

Abbott, Jacob. *The Teacher: Or Moral Influences Employed in the Instruction and Government of the Young; Intended Chiefly to Assist Young Teachers in Organizing and Conducting Their Schools.* Boston: William Peirce, 1833. Pp. x + 286.

Armstrong, W. Earl, Hollis, Ernest V., and Davis, Helen E. *The College and Teacher Education,* Prepared for the Commission on Teacher Education. Washington, D.C.: American Council on Education, 1944. Pp. x + 312.

Bache, Alex. Dallas. *Report on Education in Europe, to the Trustees of the Girard College for Orphans.* Philadelphia: Lydia R. Bailey, 1839. Pp. xiv + 666.

Barnard, Henry. *Pestalozzi and his Educational System.* Syracuse: C. W. Bardeen, 1881. Pp. 852.

Barzun, Jacques. *Teacher in America.* Boston: Little, Brown & Co., 1945. Pp. vi + 321. Also published in paperback (New York: Doubleday & Company, Inc. [Anchor Books], 1954).

Calkins, N. A. *Primary Object Lessons for a Graduated Course of Development: A Manual for Teachers and Parents, with Lessons for the Proper Training of the Faculties of Children, and Programmes of the Grades and Steps,* Fifth Edition, Revised. New York: Harper & Brothers, 1862. Pp. x + 394 + 8.

Callahan, Raymond O. *An Introduction to Education in American Society,* Chaps. 17–19. New York: Alfred A. Knopf, Inc., 1956. Pp. xvii + 461 + iv.

Cubberley, Ellwood P. *Public Education in the United States: A Study and Interpretation of American Educational History.* Revised and Enlarged Edition. Boston: Houghton Mifflin Company, 1934. Pp. xviii + 782.

Education for the Professions, Sixty-first Yearbook of the National Society for the Study of Education, Part II. Chicago: distributed by the University of Chicago Press, 1962. Pp. xi + 312.

Elsbree, Willard S. *The American Teacher: Evolution of a Profession in a Democracy.* New York: American Book Co., 1939. Pp. x + 566.

Harper, Charles A. *A Century of Public Teacher Education: The Story of the State Teachers Colleges as They Evolved from the Normal Schools.* Washington, D.C.: published by the Hugh Birch-Horace Mann Fund for the American Association of Teachers Colleges, National Education Association, 1939. Pp. 176.

Herbart, John Frederick. *Outlines of Educational Doctrine.* Translated by Alexis F. Lange New York: The Macmillan Co., 1901. Pp. xi + 334.

Hollis, Andrew Phillip. *The Contribution of the Oswego Normal School to Educational Progress in the United States.* Boston: D. C. Heath & Co., 1898. Pp. viii + 160.

In-service Education for Teachers, Supervisors, and Administrators, Fifty-sixth Yearbook of the National Society for the Study of Education, Part I. Chicago: University of Chicago Press, 1957. Pp. xiv + 376.

Judd, Charles H. "The School of Education," pp. 157–191 in Raymond A. Kent (ed.), *Higher Education in America.* Boston: Ginn & Company, 1930. Pp. x + 690.

Knight, Edgar W., and Hall, Clifton C. *Readings in American Educational History.* New York: Appleton-Century-Crofts, Inc., 1951. Pp. xxiv + 799.

Krug, Edward A. (ed.). *Charles W. Eliot and Popular Education,* Classics in Education, No. 8. New York: Bureau of Publications, Teachers College, Columbia University, 1961. Pp. iv + 166.

Monroe, Walter S. *Teaching-Learning Theory and Teacher Education, 1890 to 1950.* Urbana, Ill.: University of Illinois Press, 1952. Pp. vii + 426.

Neef, Joseph. *Sketch of a Plan of Education Founded on an Analysis of the Human Faculties, and Natural Reason, Suitable for the Offspring of a Free People and for all Rational Beings.* Philadelphia: printed for the author, 1808. Pp. 168.

Page, David P. *Theory and Practice of Teaching: or, the Motives and Methods of Good School-keeping,* Seventh Edition. Syracuse: Hall and Dickson, Booksellers and Publishers, 1848. Pp. 349.

Pangburn, Jessie M. *The Evolution of the American Teachers College,* Teachers College Contributions to Education, No. 500. New York: Teachers College, Columbia University, 1932. Pp. vi + 140.

Pestalozzi, Johann Heinrich. *Letters of Pestalozzi on the Education of Infancy: Addressed to Mothers.* Boston: Carter and Hendee, 1830. Pp. viii + 52.

"Pestalozzi's Principles and Methods of Instruction," *American Journal of Education,* IV (March and April, 1829), 97–107.

Ruediger, William C. "Recent Tendencies in the Normal Schools of the United States," *Educational Review,* XXXIII (March, 1907), 271–287.

Sheldon, E. A., assisted by M. E. M. Jones and H. Krüsi. *A Manual of Elementary Instruction for the Use of Public and Private Schools and Normal Classes; Containing a Graduated Course of Object Lessons for Training the Senses and Developing the Faculties of Children.* New York: American Book Co., 1862. Pp. 472.

Stowe, Calvin E. *Common Schools and Teachers' Seminaries.* Boston: Marsh, Capen, Lyon and Webb, 1839. Pp. 126 + 16.

Stowe, Calvin E. *The Prussian System of Public Instruction, and Its Applicability to the United States.* Cincinnati: Truman and Smith, 1936. Pp. x + 112.

Taylor, J. Orville. *The District School.* New York: Harper & Brothers, 1834. Pp. xxiv + 336 + 24.

Teachers for Our Times. A Statement of Purposes by the Commission on Teacher Education. Commission on Teacher Education. Washington, D.C.: American Council on Education, 1944. Pp. xx + 178.

Troyer, Maurice E., and Pace, Robert C. *Evaluation in Teacher Education, Prepared for the Commission on Teacher Education.* Washington, D.C.: American Council on Education, 1944. Pp. xii + 368.

Whitney, Allen S. *History of the Professional Training of Teachers: At the University of Michigan for the First Half-Century, 1879 to 1929.* Ann Arbor, Mich.: George Wahr, 1931. Pp. x + 202.

Wofford, Kate V. *An History of the Status and Training of Elementary Rural Teachers of the United States, 1860–1930.* Doctor's thesis, Faculty of Philosophy, Columbia University, June, 1934. Pp. vi + 170.

Woodring, Paul. *New Directions in Teacher Education.* New York: The Fund for the Advancement of Education, 1957. Pp. ix + 142.

Woody, Thomas. *A History of Women's Education in the United States.* 2 vols. New York: Science Press, 1929.

17

Reshaping the Structural Organization of the Educational System

Although the structural organization of the school system of the United States evolved from origins inherited from Europe and continues, in some ways, to reflect these origins, it has become, in the progress of its development, uniquely American. It has reflected, at all stages of its evolution, the changes in American life, the changes in the aims and purposes of the school as conceived by succeeding generations, and the changes in point of view concerning the extent to which education should be made available for children and youth.

In general, the trend has been toward reorganization in harmony with the democratic ideal of equal educational opportunity. In the process, all levels of education have been affected. Both elementary and secondary education were redefined and extended, and, in order that the benefits deriving from their extension be more equitably distributed, attempts were made to standardize elementary and secondary education — to promote a reasonable measure of uniformity in the programs of schools of like grade. The college was so reorganized as to change it from an aristocratic, religiously oriented, language-focused, and highly selective institution into one for the education of an enlarged student body which was becoming increasingly heterogeneous in ability, educational background, cultural interests, and vocational aims.

Each unit — elementary, secondary, and higher — was so reorganized as to bring about greater uniformity throughout the country. Also, better articulation among the various units was produced. The trend was toward an arrangement of the several units into an articulated single whole which would provide a program extending unbroken from the kindergarten to the university.

The Disintegration of
the Inherited Educational Structure

A single articulated system could neither develop nor function in the class-structured society that had been transferred from Europe to America. Persons whose position in society was considered fixed, either by the unfathomable disposition of God or by circumstances over which the society could exercise little or no control, obviously needed education that would fit them for their proper station; therefore the aims and purposes, and consequently the programs, of education differed greatly from class to class. From the time of the Protestant Reformation there had existed, at least in theory, a basic theory of mass education, but only an occasional philosopher seriously contemplated anything more than the most rudimentary schools for the children of lower-class parents. On the other hand, the need of the directive classes for a more extensive education of a very different type was clearly and generally realized.

The earliest American educational institutions differed little from their European prototypes. The early colonial colleges and the transplanted secondary schools — the Latin grammar schools — were established largely for the purpose of training religious leaders. Historically, they had no connection with the common elementary schools originally established to provide very modest academic training for a class of children not represented in or aspiring to college. The relation of the college to the secondary school was not organic, but, since the Latin school directed its efforts, in the main, toward preparing boys for college study, a form of articulation and a basis for closer relationship did exist. Together these schools formed a single system and performed a well-defined function, but between them and the elementary schools, which performed a totally different function, there was no connecting link.

The development of a democratic system of education involved the uprooting of this aristocratic dual system, the expansion of curriculums, the creation of new and the modification of old administrative units, the development of standards, the establishment of a measure of uniformity throughout the land, and the articulation of the units at the various levels into a well-integrated whole. In the process various time-honored and well-defined institutions were replaced by new ones — generally ill-defined and more often than not of poor quality. The more or less uniform practices of the traditional system gave way to a multiplicity of practices, some good and some only expedient. It was in the confusion resulting from the breakup of the old class system of education that the integrated, uniform system of modern America had its beginning.

Factors Involved in
the Trend Toward a Democratic Structure

The trend toward a democratic structure of educational organization must, therefore, be described in terms of the redefinition of educational goals, the reorganization of institutions, the integration of new units, and the development of standards and uniform practices.

THE MOTIVATION TOWARD INTEGRATION

At first there appeared to be little in the situation that promised either to weld the two systems (the one for the masses, the other for the directive classes) into a single whole or to bring them into closer relationship. However, as indicated in earlier chapters, forces were operating from the beginning to reshape society and to modify its institutions. As certain features of the European social heritage failed to withstand the impact of the leveling forces released in the subjugation of a virgin continent, new political and social ideals emerged. The common man took on significance to accord with his importance in the new order. The same forces that were responsible for his rise thrust up more and more children through the lower schools and created a demand for the extension of their training to the point where all opportunities, including a college education, would be open to them. Improved articulation and greater uniformity resulted from continuing efforts to meet this growing demand.

Improved articulation was effected in several ways. For example, during the colonial period, when the Latin grammar schools raised their requirements for admission to include a higher level of competence in reading, writing, or computation, they were not only recognizing the fact that their students could obtain a larger share of their preparatory training in the town or other elementary schools; they were also taking a step in the direction of a greater measure of articulation between elementary and secondary education. As time went on, and more and more children destined for higher education were provided preliminary training in reading-and-writing schools, these schools were transformed into or replaced by district or other schools which, in many instances, provided both instruction in the elements and the subjects required for college admission. The attempt to serve in a single school the needs of children varying so greatly with respect to age, achievement, and educational aims resulted in the establishment of some relationship between the elementary and college-preparatory programs. The academy, the secondary school of the early national period, furthered the movement by accepting children from the elementary or ungraded schools and sending them on to college.[1]

With the development of the public high school, the relationship existing between the elementary and secondary levels became more nearly standardized. The articulation of the two was not perfect, but the fact that the high school had been created to extend further educational opportunities to children not aiming toward college was never entirely forgotten, even after the performance of this function came to be much neglected in favor of college-preparatory work.

The high school, financed by public funds and admitting youth of preparatory-school age, was bound to be drawn into a relationship, even if sometimes remote, with the rapidly developing colleges and state universities.[2] This was particularly true in the West, which was less bound by tradition and less adequately supplied with good private secondary schools.

The passage from a society based on classes to a democracy based on the principle of equal obligations and opportunities was long and difficult and, in fact, it has not yet been completed. The task of fashioning a democratic school system, free and open to all, extending from the first grade through the university, was no easier to achieve than were modifications in other fundamental social institutions and arrangements.

The Motivation Toward Standardization and Uniformity

As already indicated, the motivation toward redefinition and articulation of elementary, secondary, and higher education sprang from an upsurging democracy. The closely related main forces which encouraged standardization of the educational program and greater uniformity in educational institutions and practices throughout the country were the mobility of the people and the increasing integration of a rapidly developing industrial society.

As the individualism of the simple group life of pioneer days disappeared and local loyalties expanded to state loyalties, certain functions were transferred from the smaller to the larger group. In spite of the fact that the pioneer philosophy was constantly revitalized by the conditions of the expanding frontier, there was a transfer of functions and responsibilities from the local community to the state and, in a somewhat lesser degree, to the nation.

When the educational program was consciously made an instrument for promoting social integration, it was pointed toward civic rather than re-

[1] William A. Smith, *The Junior High School* (New York: The Macmillan Co., 1925), pp. 22–31.
[2] *Ibid.,* pp. 34–41.

ligious and purely individual ends. Education, thus, became the right and the obligation of every person — in short, a political necessity. The education of youth became during the nineteenth century a generally recognized responsibility of each of our states. At all levels, the state now felt compelled to participate in providing education in order to secure its own welfare. This increasing participation in education by the state led, particularly at the elementary and secondary levels, to the development and maintenance of standards with state-wide application. The transfer of educational responsibility to the state was under way in all the states before the Civil War.

The struggle over states' rights, which found its climactic expression in the Civil War, indicated that we were not ready for the federal government to share obligations and functions with the states. However, with growing complexity in social relations and with improved means of communication, it became clear that we were a single people, living together not as states but as a nation, and that greater uniformity in social arrangements — including those for education — was a necessity if the goals of an evolving democracy were to be attained. Many functions long regarded as belonging to the states were urged upon the federal government by an increasing number of persons and groups, but resistance to such transfer was strong, and it has been more or less successfully maintained. A federal Office of Education was created in 1868, but it has served largely as an advisory and service agency and source for the dissemination of information. Although the influence of the Office (termed Bureau until 1929) over the years has been considerable, the desirable uniformity which might have been secured through more active participation on the part of the federal government has been achieved, in a large measure, by other means — the development of a science of education which has imposed its authority upon practice, educational statesmanship of a high order, and the work of great voluntary educational associations.

The Organization of the 8-4-4 System

By 1880 the American educational system had taken form, and the organization and arrangements which had evolved were not to be greatly modified for many years. The emergence of the eight-year elementary school and the four-year high school and the expansion of opportunities for higher education, even though the colleges responded but slowly to the public will, provided the main outline for a complete system of education. In themselves the three institutions, however, did not insure the establishment of a unified and well-graded system. In fact, as the patterns of these institutions became more firmly fixed, new problems of articulation arose.

THE GRADED ELEMENTARY SCHOOL

The traditional elementary school was the school for the children of the lower classes, who were expected to be satisfied with the attainment of a low level of literacy, and who, for the most part, aimed no higher. Such a school might serve the needs of the underprivileged in an aristocratically organized society. It could not survive the passing of the class-structured social organization. It lost purpose and function when stripped of the social setting in which it had developed.

Long before the beginning of the national period, elementary education was in the process of being taken over by the district school, an ungraded school which accepted pupils of all ages — ranging from infancy to adulthood — and providing them instruction in the elements of learning and, in some instances, the higher branches. The nature of this school is revealed in a statement by Henry Barnard, who wrote:

> Our law does not enforce, or practically recognize, different degrees of instruction, by providing for schools and teachers of different grades. This omission, both in the law and in practice, is a radical defect, as it destroys anything like system in the arrangement and methods of each school, and affects injuriously, both the quantity and quality of the instruction actually given.
>
> The studies pursued are spelling, reading, writing, and arithmetic, in all of the schools, and the rudiments of geography, history and grammar, in nearly all. Bookkeeping, natural philosophy, astronomy, chemistry, algebra, geometry, surveying, and other branches, are pursued to some extent.[3]

This school was simply organized; it was democratic; it was subject to a large measure of local control. For a widely scattered rural population, the district school did not serve too badly. In the growing towns and cities, however, conditions developed that made it next to impossible for the ungraded district school to function at all adequately. In urban communities hundreds of children were often assembled in a single building. Insistent demand was made for the extension of educational opportunities to new elements of the population, and steps were being taken to introduce new curriculum materials. Under such conditions, the ungraded district school had to give way to some new type of organization. It was late in the nineteenth century, however, before it was entirely superseded, even in the cities, by a graded system.

Judd has presented a considerable body of evidence in support of the position that the district school was replaced by a graded school patterned

---

[3] "Second Annual Report of the Board of Commissioners of Common Schools in Connecticut together with the Second Annual Report of the Secretary of the Board," *Connecticut Common School Journal*, II (June, 1840), 207.

after the German *Volksschulen*. There can be no doubt that the men most active in promoting the grading of schools were familiar with the German, particularly the Prussian, system and had the greatest admiration for many features of it. It is likely that their thinking and efforts were influenced by their knowledge and understanding of German institutions and practices. On the other hand, the critics of Judd's position, who have argued that the similarities between the American and Prussian elementary schools were to a considerable extent superficial, have strongly supported the view that the American school is basically an indigenous institution.

Whether the graded elementary school of eight years was a German importation or a natural evolution is an interesting and significant problem; but in order to understand the relation of the school to the social order it is perhaps more important to trace the halting advance of the graded system and to examine the conditions which made possible, and desirable, substitution of the eight-year graded school for the district or ungraded school of more or less indeterminate length.

Recognition of the weaknesses of the ungraded school.   In spite of foreign example and American ingenuity, the district ungraded school persisted after its defects were widely recognized and after its failure to serve adequately the needs of an increasingly democratic and industrial society had been demonstrated.

Barnard,[4] Mann,[5] and others protested against the practice of assembling children of "ages from four and under to sixteen and upward" of both sexes, for all studies from the "alphabet of knowledge up to the higher branches of mathematics," in a single room to be taught by a single master.[6] In 1835 an article reprinted in the *American Annals of Education* emphatically condemned the most common feature of the district school.

> Such is the arrangement, that our schools are composed of all ages and of every trait of character. In fact, no regard whatever is paid to the ages of pupils, or their intellectual development. The district schools of New England, generally, are made up of pupils of every age, from the man of twenty-five, down to the infant that can hardly lisp the name of its parents. If this is not the true state of every school, it is not because the system does not admit of such things; for it is a well established fact, that every child *may,* in most places, attend a district school *as soon and as long,* as the parents think proper.[7]

[4] *Ibid.*
[5] *Second Annual Report of the Board of Education together with the Second Annual Report of the Secretary of the Board,* Commonwealth of Massachusetts, 1839, p. 29.
[6] "Second Annual Report of the Board of Commissioners of Common Schools in Connecticut," *op. cit.,* 207.
[7] "Classification of Pupils in Common Schools," *American Annals of Education and Instruction,* V (September, 1835), 401.

The editor, in commenting upon the article, restated the chief argument against the ungraded school. Said he:

> Here we have a just and forcible picture of the conditions of our district schools. . . . There is such a variety of ages, studies, progress, and moral character . . . it is almost impossible to introduce those important improvements in methods of instruction, which we could wish to see.[8]

Attempts were made to remedy the more serious defects, but fundamental changes or extended improvements were not to be accomplished within the framework of the existing structure.

Attempts to remedy the defects of the district school. Many suggestions for remedying the evils of the ungraded system were offered. Barnard declared that if these schools continued to neglect the primary branches in favor of the more advanced studies, "the variety of studies in any school, under a single teacher, should be limited by law."[9]

In many local communities, efforts were made to keep the size of the school within manageable limits. For example, in 1831 the School Committee of Gloucester, Massachusetts, ruled:

> No child under seven years of age will be admitted to a district school, kept by a master, between the last of November and the last of March. *Provided however,* that children five years old may attend such school, in a district not containing sixty scholars; in which case male children shall have the preference. Whenever there are in any such school, more than sixty pupils over seven years of age, the youngest shall be dismissed, until the number be reduced to sixty.
>
> No child under four years of age shall be admitted to a district school, kept by a mistress; nor under six years where the number of scholars exceed sixty; in which case female children shall have the preference.[10]

Even before the beginning of the nineteenth century, the classification of pupils in the district school was recommended. In 1799 a Code of Regulations drawn up by the president of the Association for the Improvement of Common Schools in Middlesex County, Connecticut, stated:

> Scholars equal in knowledge ought to be classed. Those whose progress merits advancement, should rise to a higher class, and those who decline by negligence should be degraded every month.[11]

8 *Ibid.,* 403.

9 "Second Annual Report of the Board of Commissioners of Common Schools in Connecticut," *op. cit.,* 207.

10 "Regulations of the School Committee of Gloucester, Mass.," *American Annals of Education and Instruction,* III (June 1, 1832), 289.

11 "Forty Years Ago," *American Annals of Education and Instruction,* VII (January, 1837), 17–20.

Other sections of these Connecticut regulations indicate that their author had in mind only two or three classes, each to be divided into sections. The recommended plan provided for much less grading and classification than was usual in the Latin grammar school, but the application of the plan to the district school was probably not too common. By 1831, however, when Northborough, Massachusetts, drew up a set of regulations providing for the organization of classes within the district school, the provision that each school should be divided into four classes and that, if the teacher found it expedient, the classes should be divided into sections, did not provoke comment from the editor of the *Annals* in which the Regulations were published. If the practice was not common, neither was it unique.[12]

The achievement of a measure of grading through the introduction of new units. The early attempts to group children with respect to age and intellectual attainment gave rise to much confusion. In the cities particularly the splintering of the district school resulted in the establishment of departments and schools designated by a bewildering variety of titles. Below the rapidly multiplying high schools, several units, each covering only a few years of the elementary-school period, were established. In cities in which high schools were not found, the upper units provided instruction in secondary subjects much as had been provided by the district ungraded schools. Many of the departments and schools which had been organized to replace the district schools persisted to the close of the nineteenth century. In the late sixties Barnard outlined the practices in a large number of cities. His findings with respect to a few of them may be summarized as follows.

In Columbus, Ohio, the schools were graded into primary, secondary, and intermediate schools, each two years in length; grammar schools including three grades; and a high school of four years.[13] In Dayton, there were district (ungraded) schools, a four-year high school, and other schools or classes designated as "senior, junior, first and second intermediate, first and second secondary, and first, second, and third primary."[14] Primary, intermediate, and high schools, each four years in length, were listed for Indianapolis.[15] In Madison, Wisconsin, the schools were classified as primary, intermediate, grammar, senior-grammar, and high, each school having a two-year program with each year divided into three terms.[16] In Kingston, New York, the terms primary, junior, and senior

[12] "Regulations for the Free Schools of the Town of Northborough (Mass.), Adopted November 4, 1831," *American Annals of Education and Instruction,* II (July 1, 1832), 384–386.

[13] "Public Schools in the District of Columbia," Special Report of the Commissioner of Education, pp. 13–144. [Barnard's] *American Journal of Education,* III (entire series, XIX, 1870), 89–90.

[14] *Ibid.,* p. 90.   [15] *Ibid.,* p. 96.   [16] *Ibid.,* p. 100.

were used to designate the three departments of the elementary division. The high school period was called the "academic."[17] In Oswego, New York, the schools were divided into four distinct grades, "primary, junior, senior, and high, each covering a period of three years."[18] The course of study in the primary and intermediate schools of Providence was "arranged for five years — two years and a half in each." The full course in the high school was four years in length, except in the classical department, in which pupils remained only three years.[19] The public schools of San Francisco were "known as ungraded, primary, grammar, and high schools."[20]

The situation found in Troy, Wheeling, Wilmington, St. Paul, Syracuse, Terre Haute, St. Louis, Rochester, New York, Philadelphia, New Orleans, Louisville, Detroit, Erie, Cleveland, Cincinnati, Chicago, and many other cities gives further evidence of the confusion which existed with respect to the organization of the school system, the names by which departments or schools were known, and the time allotted to the various units.

Although the situation appeared to be almost chaotic, order was developing. High schools in different communities were accepting children of about the same age and preparation, and the total period of elementary schooling tended to approximate eight years. A statement made in 1874 by the Superintendent of Public Instruction of Chicago is evidence that the confusion was being resolved and indicates one motive for the attempt to achieve greater uniformity.

> While in the matter of General Statistics we are able to compare our work with that of other cities, having a gradation somewhat similar to our own, it is found impossible to compare in detail, for the reason that our systems of gradation are as various as the cities themselves. At a meeting of City Superintendents held in Cleveland last Fall, it was determined to attempt a more uniform gradation, that we might better understand each other. It was ascertained that the requisites for admission to the High School were the same in the cities of Chicago, St. Louis, Cincinnati, Detroit and Cleveland; that the age for admission to the public schools was very nearly the same, and that the average age of those admitted to the High School varied but very little. It was also ascertained that the average time spent by pupils in the lower schools, from the lowest primary grade to the High School, is just about eight years. A division of our work into eight parts, each part representing one year in time, would therefore furnish a fair basis for detailed comparison. Whenever the time comes for a revision of our Course of Study, I would recommend such a change as will assign to each grade the work of one school year, and we shall thus reduce our own grades from ten to eight.[21]

[17] *Ibid.,* p. 97.   [18] *Ibid.,* pp. 112–113.   [19] *Ibid.,* p. 118.   [20] *Ibid.,* p. 119.
[21] *Twentieth Annual Report of the Board of Education* (for the year ending June 20, 1874), p. 36. Chicago, 1874.

By 1880, the primary, intermediate, grammar, and other schools which in cities had superseded the ungraded elementary school were being rapidly reorganized into graded schools of seven, eight, or nine years. The eight-year course was preferred in the northern and western sections of the country. In the South, a seven-year course was becoming popular and in parts of New England the preference was for the nine-year school. The schools of the different sections, however, were following somewhat the same pattern in their development. Separate schools of different levels were becoming departments and departments were losing their identities to become grades, leaving the terms by which they had been designated to indicate roughly the level of elementary education with which the original unit had been concerned.[22] Curriculums were taking on a semblance of uniformity; the period of elementary education was becoming fairly well defined; and instruction in the secondary subjects had been almost entirely moved out of those grammar schools in which it had been provided. Within these more or less uniform elementary schools, a high degree of articulation had been achieved.

A better-trained teaching staff, improved facilities, more satisfactory textbooks, longer terms, added years of schooling, improved attendance, and an integrated program greatly increased the possibilities of the elementary school. More and more children were being brought into it and were receiving a richer education than had been available at any earlier time. The expansion of the elementary school and the enrichment of its program resulted in greater numbers seeking the added opportunities which the high schools offered. Without the popularization and enrichment of elementary education, the remarkable development of the high school beginning a decade or two before the close of the nineteenth century could not have taken place.

THE PUBLIC HIGH SCHOOL

The high school, as earlier indicated, was not created to provide the middle rungs of an educational ladder whereby one could mount from the lowest grade of the elementary school to the most advanced courses of the university, but more as a people's college — an extension of the elementary school. If the common man had not continued to rise it might well have retained its terminal character. The organic connection between the elementary and high schools would have insured, no doubt, the development of a well-articulated total program had the function of the high school remained that of completing the education of elementary-school graduates. Public demand, however, was making the high school increasingly from its beginnings a connecting link between elementary and higher education.

[22] Frank Foster Bunker, *The Junior High School Movement, Its Beginnings* (Washington: W. F. Roberts Co., 1935), p. 120.

As early as 1874, Judge Thomas M. Cooley of Michigan succinctly stated the philosophy underlying the state's interest in secondary education. In a decision rendered on an action brought by a citizen seeking to prevent the school board from using public money to support education which was secondary in character (the famous Kalamazoo Case), Judge Cooley argued well the case for the public high school as a preparatory as well as a terminal institution.

> The instrument [the state constitution] submitted by the convention to the people and adopted by them provided for the establishment of free schools in every school district for at least three months in each year, and for the university. By the aid of these we have every reason to believe the people expected a complete collegiate education might be obtained. . . .
> The inference seems irresistible that the people expected the tendency towards the establishment of high schools in the primary-school districts would continue until every locality capable of supporting one was supplied. And this inference is strengthened by the fact that a considerable number of our union schools date their establishment from the year 1850 and the two or three years following. . . .
> If these facts do not demonstrate clearly and conclusively a general state policy, beginning in 1817 and continuing until after the adoption of the present constitution, in the direction of free schools in which education, and at their option the elements of classical education, might be brought within the reach of all the children of the state, then, as it seems to us, nothing can demonstrate it. We might follow the subject further and show that the subsequent legislation has all concurred with this policy, but it would be a waste of time and labor. We content ourselves with the statement that neither in our state policy, in our constitution, or in our laws, do we find the primary school districts restricted in the branches of knowledge which their officers may cause to be taught, or the grade of instruction that may be given, if their voters consent in regular form to bear the expense and raise the taxes for the purpose.[23]

The situation in Michigan from which Judge Cooley reached his decision was not typical throughout the other states of the nation and it would not be correct to conclude that the right of the high school to a place in the system of public education thenceforth went unchallenged or that there was general agreement that the high school should lead to the university. It became clear during the years that followed, however, that the high school was fast becoming a favored institution and a symbol of an evolving democracy — of a society which aimed to make the condition of the unfavored bearable and to find a way by which the worthy might rise to a position among the favored. The belief of Horace Mann and others of his generation in education as a means of elevating the individual and of curing social ills was becoming the faith of the people.

[23] *Stuart* v. *School District No. 1 of the Village of Kalamazoo*, 30 Mich. 69.

By 1880 the high school existed to give the older and more advanced children of the community a course of instruction appropriate to their age and needs, and was becoming, particularly in the West, the most important institution preparing for the university. The high school had taken over the preparatory function without extending its period, generally four years, and, although the college continued, as formerly, to offer in its program some work which logically belonged in the secondary school, it soon became apparent that the high school could not successfully provide a satisfactory preparation for college in the years allotted to it.[24] In the meantime, the more firmly established elementary school resisted changes in its curriculum and organization in the direction of introducing secondary work before the completion of the eighth grade.

DEMOCRATIZATION OF THE COLLEGE PROGRAM

The college, during the half-century preceding 1880, was not entirely unaffected by the increasing public demand that satisfactory means be found whereby the American ideal of giving every boy and girl a chance to rise to the top might be realized. However, the college was more successful in resisting change than either the elementary or the high school, both of which stood in a more direct relationship to the general public.

During the first half of the nineteenth century, and in fact until much later, the general practice was for the college to prescribe an almost uniform program for all students. Justification for this practice was found in the theory of mental discipline and the conviction that only the prescribed course contained the content which was essential to a thorough education.[25]

Articulation between the programs of the secondary school and the college was imperfect to the extent that admission to college, and the courses offered in college, presupposed a preparation often not provided in the lower school. Before the popularization of secondary education the problem was not a serious one. Then, most Latin school students, in the main a rather select group, found themselves at the completion of their course in a position to go on to higher studies. After the public high school program had been broadened to include many subjects not related to the college curriculum, the pupils who in increasing numbers selected the more "practical" subjects were unable to proceed to college without further preparation. For these young people the secondary school did not constitute a satisfactory connecting link in a program of complete education.

[24] Leonard V. Koos, *The American Secondary School* (Boston: Ginn & Company, 1927), p. 45.
[25] R. Freeman Butts, *The College Charts Its Course: Historical Conceptions and Current Proposals* (New York: McGraw-Hill Book Co., 1939), pp. 116–128.

Colleges could not entirely ignore the demands of a developing industrial society for subjects more valuable for making a living and the insistence of a growing democracy that all types of students be accepted. Attempts to provide for the needs of more youth by adding content to the single prescribed course largely failed to accomplish the end sought and resulted in only greater superficiality. The first fundamental change in the organization of the college curriculum in response to the growing demands of democracy was the introduction of the elective system. The idea had been put into practice to a limited degree before the middle of the century but it was not generally adopted until Eliot became president of Harvard in 1869.[26] He moved rapidly to extend the elective system. Seniors were freed from prescriptions in 1872; only themes were prescribed for juniors after 1879; and after 1882 sophomores were freed from all prescribed work except rhetoric and themes. After 1894 the only prescribed course in the University, for students who on admission had proved themselves proficient in both French and German, was a three-hour course in first-year English. However, Harvard was more liberal than most colleges and less fearful concerning the integrity of its degree. Furthermore, the phenomenal expansion of Harvard's staff made the introduction of a wide range of electives possible. Not all colleges could have followed Harvard's lead even had they been disposed to do so. Also, many were not unmindful of the defects of the elective system.[27]

Although colleges generally did not accept, to any considerable extent, the elective principle until late in the nineteenth century, greater freedom of choice was provided earlier by the introduction of professional and scientific courses paralleling the liberal-arts course and leading to new degrees, such as the bachelor of law, the bachelor of philosophy, and the bachelor of science. Each parallel course was largely prescribed, but the student was permitted to choose one of the two, three, or more courses offered.

The organization of these parallel courses within the framework of the traditional college was only one response to the demand for a more utilitarian education. New institutions approximating college grade and authorized to grant some kind of degree sprang up. Among the better technical and scientific schools of this class are Rensselaer Polytechnic Institute (1824), Brooklyn Polytechnic Institute (1854), Cooper Union (1859), Massachusetts Institute of Technology (1860), Worcester Polytechnic Institute (1865), Rose Polytechnic Institute (1874), and the Case School of Applied Science (1881). Scientific schools were also established in connection with the traditional colleges, as, for example, the Lawrence Scientific School at Harvard (1842), the Sheffield Scientific School at Yale (1847), and the Chandler School of Science and Arts at Dartmouth (1851).

[26] *Ibid.*, pp. 88–97.   [27] *Ibid.*, pp. 97–115.

As a general rule Latin and Greek were not required for admission either to the new courses or to the technical and scientific schools. Thus the doors of educational opportunity were opened to a greater number and, to a certain extent, a different type of youth. A number of newer high school courses — English, scientific, and others — as well as the classical course now prepared students for the advanced work of the college or other school of collegiate grade.

By 1880 the way had been opened from the first grade through the college for children of different educational backgrounds who were aspiring to widely varying educational and vocational ends. Much, however, remained to be done. Many areas within the United States were still almost untouched by the main currents of reform. The quality and level of instruction varied from section to section and from school to school. Standards for college work were as poorly established as were those for the high school. Improvement in the coordination of the educational program required standardization of the work, particularly at the secondary and higher levels.

The Development of Inspection and Standards

As the number of children completing high school mounted and more and more of them sought to continue their education, the requirements for admission to college became the prime determiners of what the high school should teach. The failure of the college curriculum to keep pace with the more rapidly expanding high school programs of study added to the difficulty of articulating the work of the two levels. In the absence of means for resolving their differences, the colleges criticized the offerings of the high schools and the quality of their product and the high schools resented the restrictions placed upon them by the varying requirements of the many colleges. With the exception of Stanford, established in 1891, and perhaps a few institutions of lesser note, admission requirements were generally inflexible until after the beginning of the twentieth century. Through examinations for admission the college dictated to a considerable degree the curriculum of the high school and also imposed, in no small measure, the methods of instruction employed in it.

The Beginning of State and University Accrediting of High Schools

Under President Angell, the University of Michigan in 1871 initiated a program of accrediting high schools. Graduates of the approved schools were permitted, on the recommendation of the principal, to enter the University without examination. Schools were admitted to the accredited

Well-equipped high schools, junior colleges, and colleges increasingly provide improved facilities for all types of work — from learning a language to shop experience.

Teachers survey the educational resources of the community and enlist the support of informed parents.

*Teaching English to foreigners: an important but
very small part of contemporary adult education.*

Modern public schools at all levels reflect America's continuing faith in education.

list after a committee of the faculty found them satisfactory with respect to organization, teaching staff, equipment, and quality of instruction.

In Indiana a system of accrediting was established in 1873, with the State Board of Education serving as the examining and accrediting agency. In the states of the Middle West and the West, the lead of Indiana and Michigan was generally followed.[28]

As Kandel states, the accrediting of high schools "removed some of the barriers between the high school and the college" and, at least to a limited extent, relieved the high schools of a measure of the domination exercised over them. Accrediting was successful also in standardizing the work of the high schools, but only, of course, within the separate states. Admission requirements and bases for accrediting differed from state to state and the high schools reflected these differences in their programs.

THE ORGANIZATION OF STANDARDIZING ASSOCIATIONS

As early as 1879 steps were taken in New England toward developing standards with more than state-wide application. The New England Association of Colleges and Preparatory (after 1914, Secondary) Schools was established in 1885. A year later there grew out of this organization the Commission of Colleges in New England on Entrance Examinations. In 1902 there was established the New England College Entrance Certificate Board, charged with the task of drawing up a list of schools whose graduates might be admitted to cooperating colleges without examination. The Board did not inspect high schools, but approved them on the basis of the college records of their graduates.[29]

Out of the Association of Colleges and Preparatory Schools of the Middle States and Maryland, established in 1892, there grew, near the beginning of the century, the College Entrance Examination Board, which soon became independent of the parent organization and extended its scope throughout the United States and even to foreign countries.

Regional associations. In the Middle West the North Central Association of Colleges and Secondary Schools was established, in 1894, on a somewhat broader base than concern over admission requirements. It was not indifferent to this consideration, but placed greater emphasis upon the development of closer relations between the college and the secondary school. It fixed the requirements for admission and, through its Commission on Accredited Schools, organized in 1901, defined the standards for approved programs of secondary education. It published a list of accredited schools in 1904. In the South, the Association of Colleges and

28 Koos, *op. cit.,* p. 36.
29 Kandel, *op. cit.,* p. 467.

Preparatory (changed in 1912 to Secondary) Schools was established in 1895; and in the Far West the Northwest Association of Secondary and Higher Schools was organized in 1918.[30]

Regional associations, on the whole, have played an important part in defining the program and developing the organization of secondary schools. Individually, they have contributed to the improvement of standards with respect to such matters as the quality of instruction, the length of the school year, the length of the class period, class size, pupil load, preparation of teachers, size of staff, salaries, and physical facilities. On some basic issues, such as the function of the secondary school and the content of secondary education, they were not in complete agreement. Only in limited fields did it appear that there was the prospect of cooperation among them.

Since the influence of regional associations and state departments was largely confined within geographical boundaries, and since the federal government exercised no direct control over education, the definition of education at the various levels and the development of standards with nation-wide acceptance was left to another agency. The task was assumed by the National Education Association.

THE STANDARDIZING INFLUENCES OF NATIONAL COMMITTEES

As a step toward resolving the confusion which extended to all levels of education, but chiefly to the secondary level, the National Education Association in 1891 appointed the Committee of Ten on Secondary School Studies.[31] The significance of the work of this Committee for the standardization of the curriculum has been discussed in a preceding chapter. The Committee clearly recognized the training-for-life function of the high school, but no differentiation of work was recommended in terms of the aims of preparatory and non-preparatory students. They stressed the importance of continuing the study of selected subjects over a considerable period. As far as the organization of the school system was concerned, however, the most important recommendation of the Committee was that such subjects as natural science, algebra, geometry, and foreign languages be introduced earlier, or, as an alternative, that the high school period be lengthened to six years by adding to it the last two years of the elementary-school period.

[30] *Ibid.*, pp. 469–470. For a detailed account of the growth and development of one of these regional associations, see Calvin O. Davis, *History of the North Central Association* (Ann Arbor, Mich.: the North Central Association of Colleges and Secondary Schools, 1945)

[31] *Report of the Committee of Ten on Secondary School Studies. With Reports of the Conferences Arranged by the Committee* (Washington, D.C.: Government Printing Office, 1893).

Further definition of the high school program and improvement of the articulation of the work of the secondary school and the college were the special tasks of the Committee on College Entrance Requirements, appointed in 1895 by the National Education Association. Its final report, presented in 1899, recommended adoption of a six-year high school course, higher standards for secondary schools, and recognition by colleges of the wide range of electives offered by high schools. Although the principle of election was recognized, the Committee urged that a large part of the high school program be made up of a common core of courses.[32]

The Committee's presentation of an over-all course of study from which different curriculums and programs might be fashioned, the importance that it attached to requiring a goodly number of constants, and its workable definition of a unit of work went far to establish a measure of uniformity on a national scale. The hope of the Committee that requirements would be stated in terms of national units and that secondary schools would build their programs out of the recommended courses of study was to be realized within a few years.

The Report of the Committee on College Entrance Requirements, although somewhat conservative, contributed to the establishment of more harmonious relations between the high school and the college. Together with the *Report of the Committee of Ten*, it fixed, perhaps too firmly, the character of secondary education. The weight of these pronouncements was so great that in time they became real obstacles to further adjustment. Although the conclusions of these Committees served a splendid purpose in the contemporary scene, they proved an inadequate guide for the development of future high school programs as new social and economic arrangements displaced the old.

The Reorganization of the 8-4-4 System

By 1890, the efforts to weld the three units of the educational system into a single whole were partially successful, but it was becoming clear that the widely accepted 8-4-4 plan of organization was an obstacle to the improvement of articulation and to fundamental revision of the curriculum. It had become, in short, an important factor in the failure of the school to discharge the added obligations which social change was placing upon it.

It is true that no unbridgeable chasms cut the educational highway, but there were obstructions which slowed the progress of all and proved

---

[32] National Education Association, "Report of the Committee on College Entrance Requirements," *Journal of Proceedings and Addresses of the Thirty-eighth Annual Meeting,* held at Los Angeles, Calif., January 11–14, 1899 (Chicago: University of Chicago Press, 1899), pp. 656–668.

impassable barriers to many. Articulation, particularly within the lower school, had been greatly improved, but defective coordination of the elementary and secondary programs and of the work of the high school and the college continued to be especially important causes of the inefficiency and waste in the educational system. It is also true that the curriculum had been expanded and was in the process of being revised. The 8-4-4 system of organization, however, was a hindrance to the early introduction of differentiated courses and placed definite limitations upon curriculum revision, particularly at the elementary and secondary levels.

The social conditions in which the accepted system had evolved had changed. Rapid industrialization, particularly after 1890, led to increased wealth and concentration of population. Increased utilization of machinery lessened the need for child labor. With the chances of youth to find employment greatly reduced, the realization of the democratic ideal of equal educational opportunity became more possible. As already indicated, high school enrollments expanded so enormously that children continuing beyond the lower grades became more heterogeneous with respect to academic ability, educational aims, and cultural background. Less marked but similar trends were found in the enrollments of higher institutions and in the character of their student bodies. Even the elementary-school population was changing. More children were attending school for longer periods, and the greater number, denied firsthand contact with the educational activities of farm, shop, and a self-contained home life, increased the need for a modified elementary program.

The schools were slow to change. The results of their failure to adjust to changing social conditions or to make full use of the developing educational science were noted with growing concern. It was pointed out that too many children left school on or before the completion of the elementary program; that many failed to make normal progress; and that many were denied the opportunity to develop their special abilities or to realize fully their potentialities for growth. These considerations led to demands that the entire system be re-examined and reorganized in the light of emerging concepts of democracy and in harmony with the new knowledge concerning the nature and methods of the learning process, human variability, and the social, mental, and physical development of the child. Following these insistent demands for reform, efforts were made to provide enriched and differentiated curriculums, to improve instruction, to eliminate failures, and to make provision for individual differences by introducing greater flexibility into the promotion procedures, by sectioning classes on the basis of mental ability, by providing for coaching classes and remedial work, and by other means. A few of the many programs that had their origin in such efforts and that attracted attention for a greater or lesser time have been the Gary platoon, or work-study-play plan; the Winnetka plan of individual instruction; the Pueblo plan; the cooperative group plan; the New Cambridge plan of parallel elementary-school courses; the child-centered school; and the Baltimore differentiated-course plan.

As admirable as most of these innovations were, their contributions, as a rule, would have been much less important had there not been under way a supporting movement toward the redistribution of the time allotted to elementary and secondary education. This movement, as has already been indicated, was not new. During the nineties it was repeatedly argued that waste of time in the elementary school and lack of adequate time in the high school were largely responsible for the inferiority of the secondary-school product. Attention was called to the fact that although the elementary-school program had been expanded over the years, the concept of the eight-year school as a terminal institution had not been fundamentally altered. The schools had added subjects which bore little relation to the interests or needs of the children. To fill in time, teachers had resorted to reviewing in the seventh and eighth grades the work of earlier years. Little had been accomplished in the way of introducing secondary subjects before the ninth grade. This delay had resulted in the misuse of time, harmful both to those who went on to high school and to those who did not. It was urged, therefore, that the elementary-school curriculum be purged of irrelevant materials and enriched with vital content — largely in the natural sciences, mathematics, and foreign languages — or that it be shortened to permit the extension of the secondary school to include the years that should be devoted primarily to secondary work.

THE JUNIOR HIGH SCHOOL

Some twenty years after the first urgings of Eliot, and after continued recommendations by the Committee of Ten (1895), the Committee on College Entrance Requirements (1899), the Committee of Five (1907, 1908, 1909), and other committees of the National Education Association, several cities which had become convinced of the validity of the general indictment of the 8-4 arrangement began to reorganize their school systems.[33]

There was general agreement that the period of elementary schooling was too long, that the period of secondary education was too short, and that, consequently, college-bound students spent too much time in acquiring inadequate preparation. However, at first there was no clear idea as to the scope of the instruction or the grades which should be included in the different units of the reorganized systems. In some cities, the units of the system continued to comprise the same grades as formerly, with the

[33] Francis T. Spaulding, O. L. Frederick, and Leonard V. Koos, *The Reorganization of Secondary Education*, National Survey of Secondary Education, Monograph 5, United States Office of Education Bulletin 17, 1932 (Washington, D.C.: Government Printing Office, 1935), pp. 27–28.

repetitious reviews and other non-essential content of the seventh- and eighth-grade curriculums replaced by secondary courses. In other cities, the attempts to redistribute the time allotted to elementary and secondary education resulted in a variety of plans of revised organization, such as the 6-6, 7-5, 7-4, 6-2-4, and 6-3-3 plans. In general, the trend was toward an equal distribution of time between the two levels, and the most common arrangement of reorganized systems came to be a six-year elementary school, a high school reduced to the three highest grades, and an intermediate school — the junior high school — made up of the seventh and eighth grades of the traditional elementary school and the ninth grade of the four-year high school.[34]

Conflicting claims regarding the date and place of the origin of the junior high school reflect different definitions of what constituted such a school. Richmond, Indiana, organized its schools on a 6-2-4 basis as early as 1896 and during the following decade the organization of the schools was, more or less, modified in several other cities. In 1910, Superintendent Bunker, in the reorganization of the program of the Berkeley schools, established a 6-3-3 system.[35] Most writers have not regarded the earlier modification of the 8-4 organization as junior high schools, and have generally referred to the middle unit of Berkeley's 6-3-3 system as the first one. Grand Rapids, Los Angeles, and a number of other cities soon followed Berkeley's lead.

Although opposed by strong forces, the movement for reorganization gained rapidly after 1910. By 1917, 272 towns and cities claimed to have junior high schools. By 1922, 11.1 per cent of all public high schools reported to the United States Bureau (later Office) of Education were classified as reorganized schools — junior high, junior-senior and undivided, and senior high schools. Shortly after 1950 the corresponding per cent was 57.2.[36] During the same thirty-year period, the per cent of pupils in the last four high school years enrolled in reorganized schools increased from 13.5 (1922) to 65.9.[37] The Office of Education has not published statistics on the extent of reorganization since 1952, but less comprehensive data indicate that reorganization proceeded at a rapid rate throughout the fifties.

[34] *Ibid.*, pp. 28–29, 38–44.

[35] Bunker, *op. cit.*

[36] The Office of Education, at irregular intervals, reported corresponding per cents as follows: 1930, 26.0 per cent; 1938, 38.7 per cent; 1946, 43.1 per cent; 1952, 57.2 per cent. See United States Office of Education, "Statistics of Public High Schools, 1945–46," Chapter V in *Biennial Survey of Education in the United States* (Washington, D.C.: Government Printing Office, 1949); Walter H. Gaumnitz *et al.*, *Junior High School Facts, a Graphic Analysis*, United States Office of Education Miscellaneous Bulletin 21, November, 1954 (Washington, D.C.: Government Printing Office, 1954).

[37] Leonard V. Koos, *Junior High School Trends* (New York: Harper & Brothers, 1955).

Although statistics clearly indicate the growth of the movement for reorganization, they do not reveal the influence that reorganized schools have had upon the programs and policies of schools which continue to maintain the traditional units of eight and four years.

On the whole, reorganization has contributed fundamentally to the improvement of the educational program and to the democratization of education. It has led to increased retention of pupils and has attempted, with marked success, to serve each pupil as fully as possible, regardless of ability or educational aims — a responsibility of the school early recognized in the reports of several committees of the Commission on the Reorganization of Secondary Education (appointed 1913) and in the many reports of other influential committees and commissions of more recent times. Although reorganization, particularly at the junior high school level, has resulted in improved programs for all types of students, and although further extension of the 6-3-3-2 or other similar plan of organization would, no doubt, increase school enrollments, particularly in senior high schools and junior colleges, enrollment in these institutions appears to be more closely related to social economic status than to the type of educational organization.

THE JUNIOR COLLEGE

Long before there was any considerable agitation for the downward extension of the secondary school, suggestions were made that it be extended upward by transferring to the high school that part of the work of the college which was secondary in character. The advisability of such a transfer was suggested by President Henry P. Tappan of the University of Michigan in 1852.[38] In 1869 President W. W. Folwell of the University of Minnesota spoke in favor of transferring the first two years of college work to the high schools.[39] Others expressed an interest in "lopping off the bottom" in order to promote "growth at the top," but these early pronouncements seem to have had no permanent effect.

Near the end of the century President Harper sponsored the reorganization of the college of the University of Chicago into two units, the lower one embracing the freshman and sophomore years. This unit, first christened "academic college," was later renamed junior college. Harper enthusiastically urged the establishment of such colleges, not only in connection with universities, but also as independent organizations.

The arguments advanced by Harper for the organization of the junior college as a unit of the American educational system were many: that

[38] Walter Crosby Eells (ed.), *American Junior Colleges* (Washington, D.C.: American Council on Education, 1940), p. 11.

[39] William Watts Folwell, *University Addresses* (Minneapolis, Minn.: The N. W. Wilson Co., 1909), pp. 37–38.

many students whose best interests would be served by leaving college at the end of the two-year program would do so; that many would undertake the shorter course who could not afford the longer one; that many persons who enrolled for the two-year course would remain to complete the longer one; that high schools and academies would be improved through the acceptance and discharge of the added function; that the possibility of remaining at home during the first two years of college would lead to greatly increased enrollments for these years; and that many colleges poor in resources could become good junior colleges.[40]

Many educational leaders, notably David Starr Jordan, President of Leland Stanford University, and Professor A. F. Lange of the University of California, convinced that the first half of the college program was concerned with secondary rather than higher education, vigorously urged the junior-college idea. Several junior colleges, all privately controlled, were established before 1900. The first public junior college to survive was organized, fittingly enough, through the influence of Harper, in Joliet, Illinois, in 1902.[41]

Before 1910 development was slow, but by 1920 the movement had gained considerable momentum. Conditions obtaining in California, Texas, and Missouri led to more rapid growth in those states than elsewhere, but in 1919 junior colleges were located in twenty-three states.[42] The increase in the number and enrollment of junior colleges has continued, somewhat unevenly but without cessation, for more than a half-century.

Legislation permitting junior-college organization was passed by California in 1907. By 1960 slightly more than one-half of the states had enacted general legislation pertaining to junior colleges, and more than half of the remaining states had enacted special legislation which related to them. In 1961 they existed without express legal authority in all other states, save one.

Public junior colleges have outnumbered private ones since about 1950, and they have enrolled a larger number of students since the twenties. Of the 74 junior colleges listed by Eells for 1915, 55 were private and 19, or 26 per cent, were public institutions.[43] In 1939, 258 junior colleges in 32 states and the Canal Zone, with an enrollment of approximately 140,000, were publicly controlled; 317 in 42 states and the

[40] *The Report of the President of the University of Chicago, July 1898–July 1899* (Chicago: University of Chicago Press, 1900), pp. xx–xxi.

[41] Ellwood P. Cubberley, *Public Education in the United States: A Study and Interpretation of American Educational History,* Revised and Enlarged Edition (Boston: Houghton Mifflin Company, 1934), p. 557; Tyrus Hillway, *The American Two-Year College* (New York: Harper & Brothers, 1958), pp. 36–39.

[42] F. M. McDowell, *The Junior College,* United States Bureau of Education Bulletin No. 35, 1919 (Washington, D.C.: Government Printing Office, 1919).

[43] Eells, *op. cit.,* p. 18.

TABLE 30: NUMBER OF JUNIOR COLLEGES
AND ENROLLMENTS, 1900–1960*

School Year	Number of Colleges	Enrollment
1900–1901	8	100
1915–1916	74	2363
1921–1922	207	16,031
1925–1926	325	35,630
1930–1931	469	97,631
1935–1936	528	129,106
1940–1941	627	267,406
1945–1946	648	295,475
1950–1951	597	579,475
1955–1956	635	765,551
1957–1958	667	892,642
1958–1959	677	905,062
1959–1960	663	816,071**

* *1961 Junior College Directory, Data for June 1, 1959 to May 31, 1960*, Edmund J. Gleazer, Jr. (ed.), Washington, D.C.: American Association of Junior Colleges, 1961), pp. 39–40.

** "The apparent decrease from 677 to 663 junior colleges is largely a result of changes of programs in a number of university extension centers which leave them no longer essentially two-year colleges." *Ibid.*, p. 40. The decrease in the number of students can be largely attributed to the same cause.

District of Columbia, with an enrollment of some 56,000, were privately controlled.[44] In 1945, 261 (45 per cent) of the 584 junior colleges listed in the "Junior College Directory" were under public control.[45] In 1960, 390, or 58.8 per cent, of the 663 junior colleges listed, enrolling 712,-224, or 87.3 per cent, of all junior-college students, were publicly controlled.[46] Although the average enrollment of both private and public junior colleges has increased, it has been largely the growth of the public institutions — in size as well as in number — that has accounted for the rapid increase in the total junior-college enrollment.

Historically, junior colleges have offered programs to prepare students for the first years of a baccalaureate program, to provide terminal education, or, more often, to serve both functions. In the late fifties only about 5 per cent of these institutions provided only terminal programs and fewer than 15 per cent offered transfer programs exclusively. Four-fifths of the junior colleges were providing both academic programs and programs which prepared for more immediate entry into the vocational world.

[44] *Ibid.*, p. 27.

[45] "Junior College Directory, 1945" (compiled by Walter Crosley Eells), *Junior College Journal*, XV (January, 1945), 17–39.

[46] *1961 Junior College Directory, Data for June 1, 1959 to May 31, 1960*, Edmund J. Gleazer, Jr. (ed.), (Washington, D.C.: American Association of Junior Colleges, 1961).

Vocational education has been expanded materially, particularly in junior colleges under public control, to meet new demands for better-trained personnel in industry and commerce and in semiprofessional and service positions. During the decade beginning in 1948, the number of vocational curriculums reported increased from 47 to 76, an increase of 60 per cent.[47] Although these vocational curriculums have been and are being offered, in the main, by junior colleges offering both general and preparatory programs, there has been some development within recent years of the technical-institute type of school, which, although it may provide a non-technical general-education program, does not offer preparatory work leading to the baccalaureate degree. It appears that the increase in the number of vocational programs and in the number of junior colleges offering them is related, in some measure, to the increase in the number of persons enrolling in adult-education programs. Technological advance and social change have been creating the need for refresher courses and training for increased job competence on the part of workers, as well as for more and improved initial vocational training for persons about to enter the labor force.[48] It is to be noted, however, that the increase in the number of participants in the adult-education programs of junior colleges has been less rapid than the increase in the number of college-status students. In 1950 about 55 per cent of the total enrollment was made up of special and adult students; a decade later, college-status students constituted 55 per cent of all persons enrolled in junior colleges.[49]

Thus it may be observed that junior colleges, in their development, have served several functions, have been organized in different ways, and have been established and controlled by various agencies. They have developed under the auspices of religious and other private bodies. They have been established and supported by local school districts, junior-college districts generally embracing several local districts, and states. The first two years of four-year colleges have been made into distinct units; the high school program has been extended upward to include two years of college work; and two-year schools of collegiate rank have been established independent of either traditional college or high schools. Some junior colleges have stressed only the terminal function, and others — a larger number — have served almost entirely to provide the first two years of the baccalaureate program; but most of them, by far, have served both functions. Some of those aiming to serve the terminal function have placed

---

[47] James E. Reynolds, "Junior Colleges," in Chester W. Harris (ed.), *Educational Research*, Third Edition (New York: The Macmillan Co., 1960), p. 741.

[48] *Loc. cit.*

[49] *Junior College Directory 1952, Data for June 1, 1950 to May 31, 1951*, C. C. Colvert and H. F. Bright (eds.) (Washington, D.C.: American Association of Junior Colleges, n.d.); *1959 Junior College Directory, Data for June 1, 1957 to May 31, 1958*, Edmund J. Gleazer, Jr. (ed.), (Washington, D.C.: American Association of Junior Colleges, n.d.).

major emphasis upon general education, others have leaned heavily toward the vocational. Although there are these differences in organization, control, function, and curriculum, nearly all junior colleges have been two-year institutions designed, in the main, to advance the education of secondary-school graduates. A few variants have attracted widespread attention but only local or limited response.

Among the junior colleges deviating from the general structural pattern, those designed to provide four-year programs (Grades 11 to 14) have been most widely discussed and longest championed. For many years leading educators and policy-forming agencies pointed to the superiority of the 6-4-4 over the 6-3-3-2 and other plans of organization. It was argued that the first two years of college were devoted to secondary-school work, and that secondary education (Grades 7 to 14) should be divided into two equal units, one a four-year high school embracing Grades 7–10, and the other a "college" of equal length, made up of Grades 11–14.[50] In spite of the urgings of national bodies, and of Koos and other scholars and investigators, the plan was rarely adopted and, if once adopted, not always continued. Pasadena reorganized its schools on the 6-4-4 plan in 1929, but by the advent of World War II only ten widely scattered systems had adopted the plan. A small gain and subsequent decline in the number of such systems left only some twenty in existence in 1960. The reorganization of the "College" of the University of Chicago to provide a program for the youth normally found in Grades 11 and 12 of the high school and in the first two years of the traditional college was perhaps the most widely publicized of all the efforts to affect a thorough reorganization of the program for the final years of general education. This attempt had little influence on the structural organization of American education. It was faced not only with the obstacles that had prevented a wider adoption of the 6-4-4 plan in tuitionless public school systems, but also with considerations of cost, doubts concerning the wisdom of moving eleventh-graders from home and community, and divided opinion regarding the validity of the philosophy underlying its curriculum. After a decade of persistent and zealously directed efforts to define a curriculum and to obtain a wider acceptance of the College, the University was obliged, early in the fifties, to reshape its structure to conform more nearly to traditional lines and to revise its curriculum to the extent that the modified structure required.

Another significant development in American education at the junior-college level was the organization of the "General College" at the University of Minnesota, a college paralleling the first two years of regular college. This institution was designed for persons with capacities, interests, and vocational aims quite different from those of the students enrolled in the freshman and sophomore classes of the University of Minne-

[50] Spaulding, Frederick, and Koos, *op. cit.*, pp. 391–415.

sota College of Science, Literature, and Arts.[51] The General College grew out of the conviction of a state that its welfare would depend upon the cultivation of social, practical, and economic intelligence in all its citizens; that the educational responsibility of the state extends to persons not included among the intellectual elite. Moreover, the General College would not necessarily be a terminal institution for students demonstrating a capacity to profit from further work in the regular College and University.

Opposition to the junior colleges, at times, has been strong. This opposition has stemmed from several sources. The junior-college movement has been fought by all groups traditionally opposed to the extension of popular education. It has been opposed also by those who feared that the breakup of the traditional four-year college would mark the end of opportunity for many of the splendid experiences that this institution has provided. Although many universities have supported the movement, many others have opposed it on the grounds of low scholarship or incompetent faculties — a charge not entirely unfounded in earlier years. As already noted, some higher institutions welcomed relief from the heavy load of first- and second-year students, but many others have opposed junior colleges because they threatened to reduce the enrollments of the established four-year institutions.

REORGANIZATION AT THE LEVEL OF HIGHER EDUCATION

The efforts of colleges and universities to define general education and to provide programs at the junior-college level constitute only one evidence of their concern for the improvement of education. The continuing internal ferment within higher education, exemplified in recent decades by developments at Harvard, Chicago, Princeton, Columbia, Minnesota, St. John's, Bennington, Sarah Lawrence, Florida, Michigan State, and numerous other institutions, has indicated areas of concern and dissatisfaction, and has led, in some instances, to changes that have had a measure of influence upon higher education throughout the nation. Some of these changes, such as those aimed at the improvement of methods of selecting students, the organization of programs for orienting freshmen, and the improvement of teaching, do not necessarily involve modifications in structural organization. On the other hand, attempts to integrate the curriculum better and to expand provisions for especially gifted students and for the increasing numbers possessing more limited or, at least, a different type of talent have led to organizational changes.

In the United States, higher institutions, including those financed by

[51] Ivol Spafford *et al., Building a Curriculum for General Education: A Description of the General College Program* (Minneapolis, Minn.: University of Minnesota Press, 1943), pp. 1–9.

the states, have possessed an autonomy which permitted them, in a large measure, to define their goals and functions and consequently to organize their curriculums, and, to a lesser degree, to determine their internal structure. This has resulted in the great diversity that has characterized the development of higher education and that has contributed to it, even though, as some critics have charged, development was too often unplanned and fortuitous. Public higher institutions have failed, it is also charged, to define their proper roles and to harmonize accepted functions with their structural organization. They have not always been primarily concerned with the public interests. They have, in too many instances, unnecessarily duplicated expensive programs; they have expanded their functions to gain prestige rather than to serve the educational interests of the state; and they have competed with one another for faculty, students, legislative esteem, and public funds. The remedy for such ills has been sought in centralization of planning and coordination of all programs of higher education provided by the state and by private colleges and universities. By the nineteen-sixties some twenty states had established either governing boards or coordinating boards as state agencies. The former were established to govern all public institutions of higher learning within the state; the latter, much more numerous, were formed to control and coordinate selected activities of such institutions but not to exercise general governing or administrative powers. Critics of such boards argue that they stifle initiative and lead to overstandardization and stagnation. Function and organization tend to become frozen. Proponents point to the advantages of coordination and centralization, and find little evidence to show that state agencies have in any way impeded fundamental adaptations or changes with respect to the aims, functions, curriculum, or general structure of higher education.[52]

It has been noted that the autonomy which appears to be threatened in a small way may be used to resist needed change as well as to initiate it. Higher education, it is true, has been the most reluctant of the three levels to change its purposes, modify its content and methods, and alter its structural organization. But American universities and colleges, historically viewed, have been fluid in their development. They have never allowed themselves to become disassociated from society. Admittedly, the needs of modern civilization require scientific and social understandings to be not only more fully developed but also more widely diffused than ever before; but if higher institutions remain as adaptable as they have been in the past, there appears to be no need to set up rival leadership in the task of solving the problems faced by the American people and in performing the other functions required in a new and uncharted age.

[52] For an excellent discussion, see Lyman A. Glenny, *Autonomy of Public Colleges: the Challenge of Coordination* (New York: McGraw-Hill Book Co., Inc., 1959).

The Changing Structure of Education

Structure and function in human institutions are always closely related. Such has been the case with respect to school, college, and university in the United States. As the purpose of education has moved in the direction of cultural democracy, and as attempts have been made to frame programs to meet the changing and varied needs of the people, the structural organization has been repeatedly, if sometimes reluctantly, modified in the hope that each unit in the system would more adequately perform its own peculiar function and that a closer articulation and coordination of the total program would be achieved.

The structural organization is and has been characterized by great diversity. This has made it incomprehensible to persons not familiar with the history of its development. To the charge by such persons that the structure is chaotic and that it reflects chaos in education generally, the answer is, as suggested by Conant, that it has served in a fairly satisfactory manner and that it has fitted reasonably well into the plans of Americans for the realization of their aspirations.

Questions and Problems for Study and Discussion

1. It is often said, with some truth, that form follows function, that the structure of an institution is always affected by the functions its performs. Show how the changing functions of school and colleges in America have affected the structural organization of our educational system.
2. Is it also possible for structure to affect function? Did the adoption of the graded system affect the curriculum? If so, how?
3. Indicate the arguments advanced for the expansion of the secondary school downward to include the seventh and eighth grades and upward to include the thirteenth and fourteenth. Evaluate each argument with respect to its validity.
4. What are the major differences, if any, between the junior college and the community college?
5. Indicate the major objectives that you would advocate for the junior-college program.
6. Do you favor the establishment of free public junior colleges that would be easily accessible to all youth? If so, describe the kind of school you have in mind.
7. If junior colleges were to be made accessible to all, indicate some of the major problems involved, e.g., school-district reorganization.
8. Indicate the type of structural organization of American education that you think would best serve during the next two decades.

Selected References for Further Reading

American Education in the Postwar Period, Fourty-fourth Yearbook of the National Society for the Study of Education, Part II: *Structural Reorganization.* Chicago: University of Chicago Press, 1945. Pp. x + 324.

Brubacher, John Seiler, and Rudy, Willis. *Higher Education in Transition: An American History, 1636–1956.* New York: Harper & Brothers, 1958. Pp. viii + 494.

Bunker, Frank Forest. *The Junior High School Movement — Its Beginnings.* Washington: W. F. Roberts Co. 1935. Pp. xiv + 427.

Butts, R. Freeman. *The College Charts Its Course: Historical Conceptions and Current Proposals.* New York: McGraw-Hill Book Co., 1939. Pp. xvi + 464.

Changing Conceptions of Educational Administration, Forty-fifth Yearbook of the National Society for the Study of Education, Part II. Chicago: University of Chicago Press, 1946. Pp. ix + 186.

Chase, Francis S., and Anderson, Harold A. (eds.). *The High School in a New Era.* Chicago: University of Chicago Press, 1958. Pp. xiv + 465.

Conant, James Bryant. *The American High School Today: A First Report to Interested Citizens.* New York: McGraw-Hill Book Co., Inc., 1959. Pp. xiii + 140.

Conant, James Bryant. *Education in the Junior High School Years.* Princeton, N.J.: Educational Testing Service, 1960. Pp. 133.

Davis, Calvin O. *The History of the North Central Association.* Ann Arbor, Mich.: The North Central Association of Colleges and Secondary Schools, 1945. Pp. xvii + 286.

Glenny, Lyman A. *Autonomy of Public Colleges: The Challenge of Coordination.* New York: McGraw-Hill Book Co., Inc., 1959. Pp. 325.

Harris, Chester W. (ed.). *Encyclopedia of Educational Research,* A Project of the American Educational Research Association. New York: The Macmillan Co., 1960. Pp. xxix + 1564.

Individualizing Instruction, Sixty-first Yearbook of the National Society for the Study of Education, Part I. Chicago: University of Chicago Press, 1962. Pp. xiii + 337 + vi.

Judd, Charles H. *Education and Social Progress.* New York: Harcourt, Brace & Co., 1934. Pp. xii + 286.

Kandel, I. L. *History of Secondary Education: A Study in the Development of Liberal Education.* Boston: Houghton Mifflin Company, 1930. Pp. xviii + 578.

Koos, Leonard V. *The American Secondary School.* Boston: Ginn & Company, 1927. Pp. xii + 756.

The Public Junior College, Fifty-fifth Yearbook of the National Society for the Study of Education, Part I. Chicago: University of Chicago Press, 1956. Pp. xi + 338.

Reisner, Edward H. *The Evolution of the Common School.* New York: The Macmillan Co., 1930. Pp. xii + 590.

"Report of the Committee on College Entrance Requirements," pp. 656–668 in *Journal of Proceedings and Addresses of the Thirty-eighth Annual Meeting of the National Education Association.* Chicago: University of Chicago Press. Pp. 1258.

Report of the Committee of Ten on Secondary School Studies Appointed at the Meeting of the National Educational Association, July 9, 1892, with the Reports of the Conferences Arranged by the Committee and Held December 28–30, 1892. Washington, D.C.: Government Printing Office, 1893.

Smith, William A. *The Junior High School.* New York: The Macmillan Co., 1925. Pp. xvi + 478.

Spafford, Ivol, *et al. Building a Curriculum for General Education: A Description of the General College Program.* Minneapolis, Minn.: University of Minnesota Press, 1943. Pp. xvi + 354.

Spaulding, Francis T., Frederick, O. L., and Koos, Leonard V. *The Reorganization of Secondary Education,* National Survey of Secondary Education, Monograph 5, United States Office of Education Bulletin 17, 1932. Washington, D.C.: Government Printing Office, 1933. Pp. xii + 424.

Structural Reorganization, Forty-fourth Yearbook of the National Society for the Study of Education, Part II: *American Education in the Postwar Period.* Chicago: University of Chicago Press, 1945. Pp. x + 324 + xl.

The Structure and Administration of Education in American Democracy. Washington, D.C.: National Education Association of the United States, 1938. Pp. vi + 128.

Trump, J. Lloyd, and Baynham, Dorsey. *Focus on Change: Guide to Better Schools.* Chicago: Rand McNally & Co., 1961. Pp. 147.

18 🌿

Charting the Future Course

The preceding chapters of this volume have presented a partial documentation of the thesis that institutionalized education is always anchored in the civilization of which it is a part. The history of education in the United States reveals a ceaseless flow and counterflow of consequence between society and school. The location of political and economic power, the extent to which the state has been regarded as an instrument of power, the arrangement of social classes, the dignity and worth accorded the individual, aesthetic standards and moral commitments — all these have had their influence on the structure and purpose of American education. The counterflow of consequence from school to society has been no less significant. Our achievements and failures as a civilization have been profoundly conditioned by what did or did not go on in the classrooms of our lower schools and higher institutions.

It must not be supposed, however, that education is always caught in the iron grip of the present, that it has no obligation to the future. Quite the contrary is true. In any civilization that has a sense of direction, that has moral commitments, the school will play an important role in the processes of social transition. Certainly, in an age such as ours, when the economic, political, and ethical foundations of society are undergoing profound changes, teachers have a responsibility for the shape of things to come which they cannot in good conscience evade. They need to know where they are going and why, and they need a set of values that will give them a sense of direction at all stages of the journey.

We must give thought to the future. It is not possible, of course, to order the more distant future according to some present plan, but it is possible for a people, through intelligence and determination, to build into their civilization the essential elements of their value system and realize the way of life they deem good. The educator of today, if he is to rise above mere improvisation and *ad hoc* solutions, must have a vision of tomorrow's world. It is this vision that gives a sense of direction and serves as a touchstone to both policy and program. The challenge to the teachers of our generation is to catch the vision of a society in which the highest hopes and aspirations in the American tradition will be realized in the lives of men, and to plan and carry into effect the kind of educational program that will contribute most to the realization of this more humane world.

The Prospect of Tomorrow's World

If education is to find its sense of direction in the kind of civilization we hope to build, we must, of course, reach some agreement upon the core values that will serve as the touchstone of human behavior. Moreover, those values need to be defined in fairly concrete terms; we do not get very far by giving allegiance to such abstractions as the true, the beautiful, and the good. We shall have to aim toward something more definite than the contemplation of the attributes of wisdom and virtue. It is equally important that we be willing to perform the ardous task of arriving at an understanding of the conflicting social forces of our day and that we have the moral courage to undertake to channel those forces experimentally into the institutional forms best suited to the realization of accepted values.

Toward a More Perfect Democracy

The unique contribution of American civilization is not to be found in the relatively high level of material well-being we have attained or in the forms of political institutions we have developed, or yet in our aesthetic or intellectual accomplishments. It lies, rather, in our conception of the nature and destiny of man, in our high regard for individual personality. Peopled in the main by common men from other nations and far removed during its early history from the aristocratic traditions of the Old World, America has afforded a unique opportunity for an experiment in democratic living. Attempts to establish a stratified social structure have been made, and they have not been wholly without success, but the American people have achieved a conception of democracy which at its best combines the highest idealism of the Greco-Roman world and of the Hebraic-Christian ethic. No one would deny that accomplishment has fallen far short of purpose, that America is full of sharp contradictions, that profession of faith and overt act are often far apart. But it may be said to our credit that we have not renounced the faith, that we are not shameless in our violations of it, that we still believe that as a nation we have set our feet along the path that leads to an all-inclusive cultural democracy.

If we are to strive for a more perfect democracy, if we are to make democratic ideals the touchstone of social policy, the measure of men and institutions, we shall have to understand clearly what the basic assumptions of democracy are. Some of the major assumptions on the validity of which democracy stands or falls may be formulated as follows:[1]

(1) Men may be accorded political freedom; they are capable of governing themseves, of managing their own affairs; they may be trusted to achieve their own destiny. Democratic government must rest upon the assumption that citizens will be informed with respect to matters of public policy and that they will have enough good will toward one another and enough loyalty to the commonweal to compromise their differences without resort to force. The sense of justice, tolerance, and fair dealing among men is such that they may be relied upon to employ the instruments of conference and deliberation, debate and compromise, to build the political state upon the solid rock of common consent.

(2) Men must be accorded intellectual freedom in the interests both of the individual and of society. Tyranny over the mind of man is tyranny at its worst; democracy is an idle dream if "Forbidden" signs are to be erected along any of the highways and byways that lead through the depth and breadth of human experience. The quest for truth must be untrammeled and men must be free to speak the truth as they see it. And a corollary of freedom of intellect is tolerance of spirit. Men cannot be intellectually free in any real sense unless they are tolerant of one another's sentiments and opinions. The right to seek the truth where he will; to form his own convictions and to convey them to whom he will; to formulate his own value system so long as it does not conflict with the rights of others; to petition, protest, and debate; and to be accorded a tolerant hearing by his peers — these are rights of the citizen in the democratic state.

(3) Men must be afforded the opportunity for complete self-realization. The ideal of the equal chance lies at the base of the American democratic tradition; it is the core of American idealism. As our forefathers pushed ever deeper into the shadows of the wilderness and subdued a raw continent to their needs, they became more sensitive to individual human worth, and they came to entertain a concept of equality that was something new in the world. And when they established a new nation, they dedicated it to the proposition that men are born equal and that they are endowed with certain inalienable rights. They were perfectly aware, of course, that men will always differ greatly in ability, in accomplishments, in worldly goods, in contribution to community and nation, and in social esteem. But however great these and other differences may be, all should be afforded equal opportunity to release the potentialities of self, to achieve according to their talent and effort. Equal educational

[1] See in this connection Charles E. Merriam, *What is Democracy?* (Chicago: University of Chicago Press, 1941); Avery Craven, *Democracy in American Life* (Chicago: University of Chicago Press, 1941); Carl L. Becker, *Modern Democracy* (New Haven, Conn.: Yale University Press, 1940).

opportunity, equality before the law, equal opportunity to participate in the political and economic life of the nation, equal chance to realize one's God-given talents — these are the meanings of equality in the American tradition and in the way of life we still seek to achieve.

(4) Men have the capacity of association on a fraternal basis. Democracy is far more than a form of political organization; it is a great faith, a faith in the humanity of man. It is an assumption of democracy that man is not by nature depraved; that he is in fact capable of achieving a humaneness, a dignity, and a worth which all should respect.

(5) Citizens will submit to moral and legal restraint in the interests of the common good. Liberty and rights inescapably have their counterpart in self-restraint and obligation; always, "the price of freedom is its responsible exercise." Irresponsible self-interest is incompatible with freedom; only those are really free who in the innermost recesses of soul have come to hold a high regard for the common good. A democratic society will not long endure if men insist on pursuing their selfish ends in clear opposition to the public interest. It is a fundamental assumption of democracy that citizens will have a genuine devotion to the public welfare, that they will subordinate self-interest to it, that they will temper freedom with mutual concern for the good society. It is also an assumption of democracy that citizens, when the public interest requires, will unite in restricting freedom of action by legal enactment. Government is an instrument of social power, and its authority must be commensurate with the responsibility which the people, by common consent, see fit to place upon it. The citizen's birthright of freedom can be secure no other way than through responsible social behavior.

(6) The gains of civilization will be mass gains. During the long centuries of man's past, the greater gains of civilized life have accrued to a small directive class, to those able to control the state and other instruments of power to exploit the labor of their fellow men. It is an assumption of democracy that this condition will not persist, that men will share their common heritage, each according to his effort and capacity. Class monopoly — of the conquests of mind, of educational opportunity, of the benefits of technological advance — has no place in a democratic society.

(7) American democracy accords high priority to the right to be different. Within the broad framework of common loyalty to the values and ideals that lie at the base of our way of life there is ample room for individual and creative genius. The intellectual frontier is open to all. New ideas, new proposals of public and social policy, new patterns of human relations — all these are afforded a tolerant hearing. This right to be different is rooted in a deep respect for individual personality and in the recognition of an essential characteristic of human beings. This unique characteristic is the sovereignty of self. However much the individual may share the ideals of others and work with them in the attainment of

common ends, he should never wholly surrender himself to the group, he should never become a mere cell in a social organism. It is for these reasons that we have upheld a free market of ideas, refused to tolerate intolerance, insisted on the right of dissent, welcomed erratic genius, and been patient with the less gifted. The particular talent of America has been its ability to maintain unity of purpose without resort to narrow conformity.

(8) Men may look to the long future with hope for the perfectibility of human personality and institutions. Democracy presupposes faith in the nature and capacity of man. Progress is attainable because man, through reason, can explore and release his potentialities and perfect the institutions required to improve the quality of human living.

These assumptions lie at the base of the American conception of life. In trying to weave them into the fabric of our civilization, we have had many failures, but we have also had inspiring success. The challenge of the future is clear: We have set our hand to the plow and we can do nothing less than follow the furrow to the end.

TOWARD SECURITY AND EQUALITY

During the long past most men have been haunted by the fear or stung by the reality of insecurity. Through the centuries one basic fact persisted and men could not escape its all-pervasive influence, no matter where they might take up their abode. This basic fact was an economy of scarcity; men had not learned how to produce enough goods and services to go around. Poverty, hunger, and insecurity have not been conducive of good will among men; they have been the source of selfishness and brutality, of inhumanity and oppression. If one has to snatch the bone from his neighbor's hand in order to survive, one usually snatches the bone. Not only that, one is likely to justify his act by arguing that, after all, his neighbor was an inferior fellow, not worthy of too much consideration. Since men have been unequal in capacity and ruthlessness, some have been able to force others into slavery and serfdom. Caste and class originated in an economy of scarcity and have been sustained by a monopoly of opportunity and wealth.

But the future holds a brighter prospect. It appears that we are only in the beginning stages of a technological revolution that is sweeping us into a different world. Technology is making possible an economy of relative plenty. It is clear that we have the capacity to produce enough to go around, at least to the point of providing reasonable security and a comparatively high level of living for all. Technology inescapably means mass production and mass production can have no other basis than mass consumption. Fortunately, an economy characterized by a high degree of technology has to operate fairly equitably or it will bog down in depression. Over any long period of time, the gains that accrue from technological advance have to be mass gains or the whole economy is disrupted.

An economy of plenty may be expected to change fundamentally the pattern of human association. As Merriam aptly puts it, "It is easier to be good neighbors when there is enough to go around."[2] An economy of plenty would mean much more than a general improvement in living standards; it would go far to destroy the foundations of caste and class; it would hasten the day when men will associate with one another on a more fraternal basis. A class-structured society stems in part from the differences in the innate capacities of men, but it is more largely the product of a monopoly of possessions and opportunity. When most men are able to acquire economic goods adequate to their needs and when the avenues leading to cultural and intellectual advance are barred only by lack of ability or effort, snobbishness and exclusiveness are less common. This is not to say that there will be no differences in the status of men; it is to say, rather, that distinctions will be based more on personal merit and attainment.

Technological gains in and of themselves, however, insure nothing but greater capacity to produce; they do not insure more security or greater equality of possessions or opportunity. The forces unleashed by technology may be mobilized for abundance; or they may be so channeled as to disrupt the economy and defeat the ends of democracy. In a technological society, with its concentration of economic power, it turns out that absolute economic freedom is incompatible with equality and security. Freedom to regulate one's economic life has long been regarded as essential in a democracy, but absolute economic freedom may, and usually does, mean wealth, security, and opportunity for a few, and poverty, insecurity, and lack of opportunity for the many. Some degree of governmental regulation of the economy — that is, some surrender to the state of individual freedom in private enterprise — appears to be necessary if technological gains are to be translated into a more abundant life for all. But if men even partly surrender their economic freedom to gain security and greater equality, will they not in the end completely lose their political and intellectual freedom? Here is a problem which must be resolved or else democracy perishes. The masses of men are fully aware of the benefits that would accrue to themselves if the gains of technology were translated into mass gains, and they will be content with nothing less. As Carl Becker has forcefully put it:

> The very technology which gives peculiar form and pressure to the oppression of common men in our time has freed common men from the necessity of submitting to it. The time has gone by when common men could be persuaded to believe that destitution is in accord with God's

[2] Merriam, *op. cit.*, p. 56.

will, or to rely upon the virtues of *noblesse oblige* to ease their necessities. Through education and the schools, through the press and the radio, common men are made aware of their rights, aware of the man-made frustration of their hopes, aware of their power to organize for the defense of their interests. Any civilization of our time, however brilliant or agreeable it may appear to its beneficiaries or to posterity, which fails to satisfy the desires of common men for decent living will be wrecked by the power of common men to destroy what seems to them no longer worth preserving. The ultimate task of democracy may be to establish a brilliant civilization; but its immediate task is the less exalted one of surviving in any form, and the condition of its survival is that it shall, even at the sacrifice of some of the freedoms and amenities of civilization as we have known it, provide for the essential material need of common men.[3]

To resolve this conflict between freedom in the area of economic life and equality, and to resolve it through democratic processes, constitutes one of the most difficult problems democratic leaders must solve. The solution lies in the direction of moral restraint rather than legal compulsion. If men do not have a genuine devotion to the public welfare and if they are unwilling to subordinate selfish interest to it, if they refuse to temper freedom with mutual concern, if they fail to recognize their common stake in the good society, they will eventually drive themselves to the extremity of the totalitarian state. We are determined that this shall not happen in America. It is our task, through conference and discussion, through experiment and compromise, through moral restraint and necessary government action, to develop an economic order in which common men will be more secure and participate on more equal terms in the common affairs of life.

Toward Higher Ethical and Aesthetic Standards

Man does not live by bread alone; material well-being, important though it is, is not the goal of life. We may achieve an economy of plenty, we may live with security in ease and comfort, we may bring it about that the doors of opportunity open with more or less the same ease to all, but the quality of individual living, and of our whole civilization, may still be extremely poor. Contemporary American civilization has been excoriated, not without some justice, for its crass materialism, its worship of money, its sometimes excessive regard for the gadgets that contribute to the comfort and ease of life. Ours has been described as an "Age without Standards," moral, intellectual, or æsthetic. We are, it is said, in the midst of "a spiritual revolution — the weakening or dissolution of the traditions and

---

[3] Becker, *op. cit.*, pp. 85–86.

beliefs which for many centuries have ruled Western civilization and held it together."[4] In short, it is said, we are in a world adrift, without compass and without goal; such character as we possess is rooted in habit rather than in any fundamental philosophy of life.

No civilization is without its defects. The criticisms voiced of our own are not wholly without justification. However, they present only a partial view. The fact that we are given less to philosophical speculation and more to scientific inquiry, that we rely less on the "eternal verities" and more on the accumulated capital of human experience, that we are bound less by the traditions and beliefs of the past and concerned more with the reality of the present and the hope of the future, should not be taken to mean that we are without character or purpose. It cannot be denied that our generation is giving the ideals of democracy a more positive content, in both individual and social behavior. Those who labor long and hard to increase our knowledge of the world of nature and of man, to devise and carry out programs of social action designed to free common men from insecurity, poverty, and fear, and to give them equal participation in the cultural accumulations of the race are not to be told that they are utterly confused, devoid of a value system, and acting without purpose.

All this is not to say that we can remain content with our value system. The measure of a civilization is its moral commitment, its sense of good and evil. From the record of human experience through the ages and from the findings of scientific investigation, it will be within our power to define and redefine a system of values that will enable men to release the potentialities of personality and to live together with greater justice and good will. This we shall propose to do.

A great civilization is one that respects human sensibilities, that acknowledges the importance of proper behavior and the amenities of life, that stresses grace of style, refinement of taste, and beauty of form and expression. In the past, culture in its more restricted sense has been almost exclusively the possession of the few with the leisure and wealth to acquire it. Now we are faced with the important fact that as democracy becomes more of a reality the æsthetic standards of common men assume an increased importance. In the future, the task will be to bring æsthetics from the museum and art gallery to the home and market place, from creative artists and scholars to the man in the street.

In the industrial age that lies ahead we can build a civilization with its values rooted only in materialism and in the satisfactions of the moment, or we can endow it with the tested values of human experience — the wisdom, goodness, and beauty that man has found essential for the enrichment of life.

[4] Sir Richard Livingstone, *Education for a World Adrift* (Cambridge: the University Press, 1943), p. 15.

GIVING THOUGHT TO TOMORROW

One of the essential differences between the age that appears to be drawing to a close and the one that is opening is the difference of concept with respect to the ways and means of human progress. The idea of progress, formulated shortly before the middle of the eighteenth century, de-developed in a society in which an emerging capitalist class was struggling to free itself from the regulations and restraints of mercantilism. Eager to conduct his business as he would, the capitalist championed most of the freedoms associated with democratic liberalism; he sought freedom of restraint, whether in the area of government, economy, or conscience. The spirit of individualism and laissez faire which dominated the capitalistic culture gave the concept of progress much of its essential content. If man could contrive through scientific research to bring Nature into his service, if the individual were left free to pursue his economic interests as he would, and if the government pursued a hands-off policy in relation to the economy except when the capitalist himself sought a favor, there would be satisfactory progress. The over-all policy system of the capitalistic societies of the nineteenth century gave little place, therefore, to plan and design; it relied on the processes of automatic adjustment.

But reliance upon individual initiative and upon more or less automatic adjustment in the broad area of societal relationships did not work out satisfactorily. In a society and a world becoming increasingly more complex and interrelated, a policy of drift and automatic adjustment had to be abandoned for one of plan and design. As events turned out, the lack of design — refusal to plan a world order — repeatedly ended in armed conflict. Nor did failure to plan, to try to shape the course of events, work much better in the area of internal national affairs. The fact is that the effects of technology have so modified the material aspects of our culture that institutional reorganization is imperative. Change in the physical environment has forced all the great social institutions — family, community, religion, economy, and government — to modify their functions and in some instances to change their structure. Experience now makes it clear that in the future we shall have to cultivate the spirit of invention in the whole area of social relations. We shall have to recognize the imperative of social technology, the requirements of a positive social policy, the necessity of constructing and reconstructing our social institutions according to experimental designs. We shall have to give thought to tomorrow.

The Reorientation of Educational Values

No other age has ever laid at the door of educational statesmanship a greater challenge. If educational statesmanship is to rise to the occasion, if schools and higher institutions are to meet their social obligations, it will be necessary to redefine and to reorient educational values. No generation of educators has needed more urgently than ours to see clearly the task of education and to see it whole. But no other generation has been more given to the exploitation of the partial view. In the face of a situation which calls for unity of purpose and community of action, we have permitted ourselves to become divided into opposing schools of thought, and each in his own camp has magnified unduly the values of his particular philosophy. The result is that American education is now characterized by confusion and conflict, and this is true in the area of fundamental purpose as well as in the area of ways and means. We need a set of educational values in which the part will not be mistaken for the whole and in which the whole will contain all the essential parts.

IMPROVEMENT OF THE QUALITY OF EDUCATION

The American people may be justly proud of their educational record. Throughout our history we have been more deeply committed to the ideal of universal education than any other nation, and more than any other we have afforded opportunities to the great masses of our youth. Our schools and colleges have inculcated the spirit of democracy and made possible the successful operation of our democratic political institutions; they have stimulated scientific inquiry and contributed much to the accumulation of a vast store of knowledge; they have improved human resources, and in this way have contributed vastly to the increased productive capacity of the economy; they have made it possible for us to absorb millions of newcomers from other lands and at the same time maintain national unity; and, by the enrichment of the human personality, they have contributed greatly to the quality of individual living.

Our record of educational progress is one of which we may be proud; but it is not one with which we can rest content. The new era we are entering in our national life and in the world order is creating educational obligations and responsibilities that are new in human history. It will be necessary to take steps to implement more fully the ideal of universal education. As we have already pointed out, the advance of technology, especially the advent of automation, is wiping out unskilled jobs and making new demands on intelligence and technical skill in every area of occupational life. In the future the unskilled and the poorly educated will find little or no opportunity for gainful employment. The future development of the economy calls for a drastic upgrading of education. Nor will the demands upon intelligent citizenship be any less. Problems of social and public policy are becoming more difficult and complex, and if our citizens are to make informed and responsible decisions the general level of education will have to be raised. And, finally, if we are to enrich the quality of individual living on the part of the masses of our people, it will be necessary to enrich the quality of the education they receive.

No greater problem faces American education than that of raising the quality of performance. Our effort to popularize education has been praiseworthy, but unfortunately it has resulted in a leveling downward of standards. Far too often the brighter students have gone unchallenged, and we have been content with mediocrity. Too many of us at times seem to have forgotten that education is intrinsically and essentially intellectual and that the way to cultivate intellect is through the disciplined acquisitions of ordered knowledge. The time has come when we must set out in earnest to make schools and colleges "places for study and learning." Our talented youth are our greatest resource; and if the United States is to move ahead and meet its responsibility of leadership in the free world, we shall have to devise educational arrangements that meet their interests and inspire them to the highest possible achievement. It is important that standards be raised for the more able pupils; and it is also important that the quality of the education afforded the less gifted be enriched. All pupils, whether they expect to go to college or not, whether they are fast or slow learners, will have to meet the responsibilities of citizenship and build for themselves as human and humane a life as they can. All should have the opportunity, through the pursuit of general education, to acquire as much of the cultural accumulations of the race as their abilities will permit. This they can do through the study of history, literature, the sciences, and all the other subjects that make up a liberal curriculum. Far too often those who do not expect to go to college, or who are regarded as slow learners, are advised — if not directed — to take vocational courses, to the serious neglect of their general education. This is not to deny the great value of vocational education; it is to insist that there are educational values that are essential for all. It will be necessary, to be sure, to devise a variety of means for the general education of pupils with wide differences in background and ability, but, difficult as the task is, it must be faced. And at the college level, too, it is imperative that provision be made for the general education of a larger percentage of youth. Colleges and universities will properly be concerned with raising standards, especially for the more able student. The evidence indicates, however, that something like one-half of the nation's youth have the ability to acquire at least the basic elements of a liberal education; and our society cannot refuse them the opportunity to do so, even though the task may necessitate special administrative arrangements at the college level.

INDIVIDUAL GROWTH AND
CULTURAL ADJUSTMENT

Any set of values will certainly assign a place of large importance to the needs of the growing, maturing individual. Some of these needs grow out of his nature as a human being. In guiding the child through all the intricate processes of development that lead to physical and emotional maturity and excellence, the school must draw upon all pertinent knowledge with respect to human growth, whether found in psychology, psychiatry, medicine, biology, or other sciences. Knowledge from these sources indicates, however, that the "inherent" needs of the individual are materially less than formerly supposed. As Sherman puts it:

> Many educators have also proposed programs of education on the basis of inherent needs. A careful evaluation of the nature of these supposed needs has shown, however, that they are mainly reformulations of the instincts which the nineteenth-century psychologists believed were inherited. . . . We must regard with doubt and suspicion, therefore, the statements of some educators that a child develops in a "natural" way, and that the function of the educational process is merely to enhance this "naturalness."[5]

This is not to say, of course, that inheritance is an unimportant factor in human development; but it does mean that personality as an end product owes less to inheritance than to formal or informal training.

In guiding the development of the individual, then, the school has to gives special consideration to the demands of the environment, to the culture into which the child is born and in which he develops. Personality does not develop and does not operate apart from a social context; self does not exist apart from society. At birth the child begins his transformation from a biological individual into a social person; he begins the long and arduous task of adjusting himself to his culture — to the intricate and often baffling patterns of human relationships, to the mores and values of his own particular family, to the institutions basic to civilized life generally, and to the institutional forms and arrangements of the society. It is the task of the school to develop the intelligence of the child; it is also its task to incorporate the core values of the culture into the structure of his personality. Experiences must be provided that will develop in the individual the motivation, the desires, the attitudes, the sensibilities, the initiative, and the creative interests that will best enable him to adjust to his world of social reality. The school of the future will be called upon to give more attention to the development of the individual who will possess emotional stability even in the face of novel and difficult situations and who will have initiative and versatility. This can be done, in part at least, by equipping him with a body of generalized experience which will help him to meet new conditions and enable him in some degree to subordinate emotion to reason.

[5] Mandel Sherman, "Education and the Process of Individual Adjustment," in Newton Edwards (ed.), *Education in a Democracy* (Chicago: University of Chicago Press, 1941), pp. 65–66.

This emphasis on personality development, on the importance of inducting the individual into his culture in such ways as to avert destructive anxieties and conflicts, is really what is meant when it is said that the teacher should teach children and not subjects. In far too many schools today little attention is given to the problems of individual growth and cultural adjustment. On the other hand, in some quarters it is held that "the harmonious development of personality" should be the almost exclusive goal of all educative endeavor. Those who take either of these extreme views are mistaking an essential part for the whole. The development of personality is an important responsibility of the schools; but it is by no means the whole responsibility.

THE SCHOOL'S OBLIGATION TO PASS ON AND IMPROVE THE CAPITAL OF HUMAN EXPERIENCE

As mankind has traveled the long and devious road from barbarism to civilization it has accumulated a body of ideas, knowledge, values, and skills which constitutes the capital of human experience. Decisions with respect to the use that will be made in the educational program of this accumulation of experience are of prime importance. Three important issues are involved: (1) To what extent is racial experience to be drawn upon? (2) How shall the essential elements in this experience be identified? (3) What organization shall these elements be given?

Within recent years the very term "cultural heritage" has fallen into disrepute in many quarters; there has been a definite tendency to discount the intellectual content of education. Dissatisfied with the choice of the elements in human experience that have gone so largely to make up the curriculum in the past, and rebellious against the kind of organization those elements have been given in the traditional school subjects, many of our contemporaries have come to discount the value of organized past experience for the youth of today. Instead of facing the hard intellectual job of making a more satisfactory identification and of working out a more effective organization, many have preferred to orient education wholly around the interests and needs of children and youth as they arise in the problems of daily living. However appealing the arguments for the latter kind of program may be, it must be evaluated mainly in terms of its effectiveness in leading to an understanding of the accomplishments of civilization. Although emphasis upon the immediate and the contemporary is always essential, and especially so when the contemporary is full of crises, education is chiefly concerned with enduring values. Man cannot escape his past; civilization is a continuum; no new generation can start *de novo* without relapse into barbarism and savagery. The accumulated capital of human experience cannot be written off. In one way or another, it must be made an essential part of any successful program of education.

Men will always disagree with respect to those elements of human experience which have greatest meaning for the present, but in our own day the differences of opinion have been especially marked. Some consider the classical and religious traditions the carriers of the most essential values and knowledge; others find in the metaphysics of great books the ideas and values which they think may give life meaning and direction; still others assign a higher worth to the generalized experiences of mankind and to the findings of scientific investigation. None of these points of view is without merit, but it appears to many that the last affords the greatest hope for an effective educational program. The whole of Western culture is not embraced within the religious and classical heritage, as some seem to suppose.[6] Nor will the study of metaphysics alone give one an adequate knowledge of human experience. Moreover, the cultural heritage which is of value to each succeeding generation is not rigid and fixed. Each generation adds to it and reinterprets and reintegrates it in terms of its own needs. What is required is a body of values, of generalized experience garnered from the whole of human experience, and a knowledge of the success and failure of the institutional arrangements mankind has employed to carry value systems into practical operation.

The problem of how to organize race experience most effectively is also one that besets us today. The logical organization of knowledge according to traditional subjects is under attack. The classification of knowledge into such subjects as English, history, science, or mathematics is, it is said, no longer defensible, at least for teaching purposes. But those who would cast the traditional subjects aside are not wholly agreed among themselves with respect to what should be substituted in their place. Some insist on what they call a "functional" rather than a logical organization of knowledge. They contend that subjects as we have known them tend to destroy the unity of experience. The problems of human living through the ages have been much the same and it is around those problems that knowledge should be oriented. History, mathematics, science, and the rest, according to this view, should give place to a curriculum organized around the major functions of social life, such as "protection and conservation of life, property, and natural resources," "production of goods and services and distribution of the returns of production," and "expression of æsthetic impulses."

Others would discard all subjects, buth old and new, because they insist upon an "experience curriculum"; the important thing in education is not the mastery of any body of content previously organized, but the experiencing of the individual as he struggles to solve his problems. Education is through and for experience, and the experience involved is that of the individual learner rather than any systematic presentation of the

[6] See Walter Lippman, "Education vs. Western Civilization," *American Scholar,* X (Spring, 1941), 184–193.

experience of the race. As the individual proceeds to solve his problems by the use of whatever subject matter may serve his purpose, he will, it is thought, build up patterns of generalized experience — fundamental generalizations — that will enable him to function as a competent person and an informed citizen. Just what subject matter will be drawn upon to help the individual solve his problems after "subjects" have been discarded and forgotten is not made clear. What will happen to human experience when it is no longer reduced to some kind of systematic organization is a fair question.

Not even the most ardent champion of the traditional organization of knowledge can defend the way knowledge has been fractionalized and splintered by the multiplication of subjects and courses. All are agreed on the need for greater integration, for larger configurations of meaning, for seeing more clearly the interrelationship among various existing classifications of knowledge. It is not impossible that the historic classifications of knowledge are outmoded as the most effective carriers of human experience. And yet, if school subjects are to be abandoned and departmental lines in colleges and universities effaced, some centers of orientation must be devised to take their place. Certainly the student cannot be expected to attack the whole continent of knowledge simultaneously on all fronts and subdue it in one grand effort. We should not permit the reaction against overspecialization to throw us into confusion. It is a fair question to ask: Just what are those about who propose the abandonment rather than the reorganization of subjects and departments? What new orientations do they propose: the problems of children and youth, the metaphysics of great books, the major functions of social life?

School subjects, it must be remembered, are designed to make the achievements of civilization available to the individual in a systematic and economical way. The arrangement of the subjects may be defective, the elements included in them may have been unwisely selected, and the organization of their content may not be defensible. Though we grant that many subjects taught in school and college today suffer from these defects, the question still remains: Shall we attempt to remedy these defects, or shall we seek new orientations of the kind already suggested? No categorical answer can be given to this question, but we can encourage experimentation with new types of orientation, and guide our future policy by the results.

The School as the Carrier of Core Values and Common Knowledge

Every society is held together by the acceptance on the part of its members of a body of core values. A society is possible only because the individuals that form it have a common sense of reality and are bound together by common loyalties and common traits. Systems of social relationships attain the status of institutions only when they are accepted as being in conformity with the essential value premises of the society.

In every culture, as Linton has observed, there is a common core of universally accepted traits. Surrounding this common core is a zone in which traits are shared by certain individuals but not accepted by all. The common core may be regarded as the area of the Universals and the surrounding zone as the area of Alternates. The common core gives the culture form and stability; the outer zone makes possible social experimentation and change. If the common core becomes too small, the members of the society cannot cooperate through institutional forms and the society disintegrates into a mere aggregation. Says Linton:

> Actually, all cultures consist of two parts, a solid, well integrated, and fairly stable core . . . and a fluid, largely unintegrated, and constantly changing zone of Alternatives which surround this core. It is the core which gives a culture its form and basic patterns at each point in its history, while the presence of the fluid zone gives it its capacity for growth and adaptation. If we study any culture continuum we will be able to detect a constant process of give-and-take between these two parts, with traits moving from one to the other. New traits, beginning as Individual Peculiarities, gain adherents, rise to the status of Alternatives, and finally pass into the core as they achieve general recognition. Old ones, as soon as they are brought into competition with new ones, are drawn into the zone of Alternatives and, if they are inferior, finally drop out of the culture. . . .
>
> The proportion which each of these two parts of a culture bears to its total content may vary greatly at different points in its history. In general, the more rapid the contemporary rate of change, the higher the proportion of Alternatives. . . . When a culture is changing very rapidly, as our own is at present, the Alternatives may become so numerous that they quite overshadow the Universals. . . . Each new trait, as soon as it is accepted by any part of the society, draws certain traits which were formerly Universals . . . out of the core of the culture into the fluid zone. As the content of the core is reduced, the culture increasingly loses pattern and coherence.
>
> Such a fluid, disorganized condition within culture has inevitable repercussions upon the society which bears it. It is the common adherence of a society's members to the elements which form the core of their culture which makes it possible for them to function as a society. Without a wide community of ideas and habits the members of the group will not react to particular stimuli as a unit, nor will they be able to co-operate effectively. . . . When there are very few elements of culture in which all the members of a society participate, i.e., when the proportional size of the culture core has been greatly reduced, the group tends to revert to the condition of an aggregate. The society is no longer able to feel or act as a unit. Its members may continue to live together, but many forms of social inter-

course will be hampered by the impossibility of predicting the behavior of individuals on any basis other than that of their known personalities. Even economic co-operation will be seriously interfered with, due to the lack of fixed standards of integrity and fair dealing. It is obvious that this condition puts the society at a marked disadvantage, and it is probable that there is a point below which participation cannot fall without a resulting collapse of both the society and the culture. . . .

In modern civilizations, therefore, the core of culture is being progressively reduced. Our own civilization, as it presents itself to the individual, is mainly an assortment of Alternatives between which he may or frequently must choose. We are rapidly approaching the point where there will no longer be enough items on which all members of the society agree to provide the culture with form and pattern.[7]

The acceptance of common value premises and the existence of common loyalties, important as they are, are not enough to insure a high degree of social integration. It is perhaps of no less importance that the members of a society share a body of common experience and knowledge. The individuals composing a society may accept its core values and work toward the same general goals, but, lacking common experience and knowledge, they may differ violently with respect to the policies required to arrive at their common ends. Wise decisions in a democracy with respect to matters of public and social policy usually require a common knowledge of essential facts.

It is an important function of institutionalized education to bring youth to the acceptance of the core values of the culture. These values, which with us are the values implicit in the democratic way of life, dictate the spirit in which men meet and work together, serve as a touchstone to statecraft, and can be made the criteria for passing judgment on proposals. The schools and colleges of this country have no more important responsibility than that of providing experiences that will develop in children and youth a deep loyalty to the principles of democratic liberalism. But values and principles, to be of much consequence, must find expression in social institutions: in the government, with all its facets of policy and actions; in the economy, with its intricate processes of production and distribution of goods and services; in the community, in the church, and in the home, with all their problems of human association and cooperation. The fundamental premises of democracy are little affected by time and circumstance, but the social institutions through which democracy is made a reality must change as conditions require. If citizens are to cooperate effectively in the shaping and reshaping of their social institutions as carriers of values and policy, they must share a body of common knowledge and experience. It is a function of school and college in America to create an

[7] From *The Study of Man,* by Ralph Linton, pp. 282–284. Copyright, 1936, D. Appleton-Century Co., Inc. By permission of Appleton-Century-Crofts, Inc.

environment in which young people will receive an integrated view of their culture, come to accept the basic assumptions of democratic behavior, and acquire a body of common knowledge essential for effective citizenship.

Education for Decision-Making

If anything is clear in our uncertain world today, it is that ours has become an adaptive civilization. Capacity for adjustment and adaptation has come to be the price of survival for individuals and for nations as well. One fundamental difference between the age that has closed and the one that is opening is a difference of concept with respect to ways and means of dealing with new social forces. In the past, we could, or thought we could, rely on the operation of more or less automatic processes as a means of social evolution. An unseen hand gave direction to the whole economy, and the spirit of laissez faire had its way in practically every area of human life. God was in his heaven and all was right with the world, and somehow good would finally prevail. We in the United States, and, indeed, in the whole Western world, long deluded ourselves into believing that we could substitute *ad hoc* decisions and improvisations for over-all policy and long-range programs. It is clear that many of the social crises of our times are the direct results of this flight from decision. It is equally clear that in the future we shall have to chart a different course. The forces that are transforming the modern world, whether in economy, government, or international relations, are forces that require channeling and direction. The need for wisdom and knowledge on the part of the citizenry to bring about more conscious, deliberate, and intelligent direction of human affairs has become crucial in our time. In the years ahead we, as a people, will be making decisions fateful to ourselves and all mankind.

As we shift the basis of historic liberalism — as it seems we must — from more or less irresponsible self-interest and drift to responsible action and more conscious direction of human affairs, it will be necessary to give education a new orientation, a new center of interest. In the future, schools and colleges alike will need to give more attention to the education of the citizen, to the cultivation of that breadth and precision of knowledge of the workings of our political, economic, and social arrangements essential for informed and responsible decisions with respect to matters of public policy. In the not very remote past, life was highly individualistic; decision-making was confined, in the main, to face-to-face relationships in home and community; and no great attention had to be given to broad and positive programs of civic action. The future presents a different prospect. The individual will, of course, always be the basic unit in a democratic society, and the local community will remain the focal point of decision-making, and of vast importance for its members; but the welfare of both individuals and communities is coming to be affected more and more by policy decisions at the national and international levels. The larger society of nation and world confronts the citizen with more complicated problems than those he will ever encounter in his local community. In agriculture, in industry, in labor, in practically every phase of the operation of the economy, in social welfare, in the proper functions of government — in these and other areas of our national life there are, and will be, problems of policy of vast significance. Even more fateful are the problems of international order. Many of the peoples of the world today are in a restless movement in search of a way of life that will have less poverty and insecurity. Old colonial systems are crumbling and new political forms are emerging. So-called backward countries are striving to reorganize their economic systems and to reorient them in the world economy. And they look to us for help, if not leadership. To bring about understanding and cooperation among nations, to help safeguard human freedom, and to make possible extension of the benefits of science and technology to the masses of mankind — these are responsibilities the American citizen cannot avoid.

The need of a new emphasis on education for decision-making — for effective citizenship — grows in part out of the fact that we have tended to neglect it. Partly in the effort to preserve our humanistic and religious traditions and our economic and social theory, we have let education in America be too individual-centered; its fruits have been more private and personal than public and social. Almost the sole concern of our educational system has been to bring the individual to intellectual, emotional, and physical maturity and excellence and to make him occupationally proficient. Even the scientific study of education has been oriented around the concept of education as psychological process rather than around the concept of education as public and social policy. No one, to be sure, would quarrel with individual development as the primary objective. Individual excellence is, of course, essential in any great civilization. But in the kind of adaptive civilization ours has come to be, it is not enough. For children and youth in school today, the quality of individual living in the years ahead will be determined quite as much by the kind of world they are living in as by the personal qualities they bring to building a life. The conditions of our time require that education become a more positive instrument of social policy, a means of providing youth with learning experiences that will enable them to comprehend, as fully as possible, the moving forces of their day and to meet with fidelity their high duty as informed citizens.

The history of education in the United States, when viewed in relation to the social forces that have influenced it, reflects the importance the American people have attached to their educational institutions as a means of realizing the way of life they have deemed best. Through school, college, and university some reality has been given to the ideal of the equal chance. Free education, it has been thought, would contribute much to the achievement of social mobility in a society unrestricted by sharp class distinctions. On a raw continent, where the hardships of daily life threatened to snuff out the light of learning, school and college in the early days managed to keep alive much of the idealism and humanism of the Western tradition. Men have never lost sight of the obligation that education bears to the public weal. The ideal of free inquiry and free expression, though not always fully realized, has been cherished as a priceless heritage. It must be confessed that ideals have not always, if ever, been realized, and that accomplishment has fallen far short of purpose, but even so as a people we have refused to accept defeat or to renounce faith in honest resolve and trained intelligence as means of solving the problems of human living.

The history of education in the United States is a record from which those who undertake to chart the future course may draw wisdom, inspiration, and hope. To those who have the privilege and opportunity to carry on the work begun, the challenge of the future is to provide a freer and more universal access to education and to build a program that will make adequate use of the accumulated capital of human experience, give intelligent guidance and direction to the individual as he attempts to adjust to his culture, cultivate the acceptance of a body of core values, and develop in both youth and adults an understanding of the society in which they live — an understanding that is adequate for participation in the making of public policy. Above all, the challenge to those who teach will be to develop in men the moral courage, the strength of will, and the social insight required to solve the conflicts of their day and to work out cooperatively the design of a more just and humane society.

Questions and Problems for Study and Discussion

1. In what ways, if any, are the changing conditions of our time such as to make it desirable, and even necessary, that we reconsider the functions and purposes of education?

2. What assumptions are involved in the proposition that American education should find its sense of direction in the kind of civilization we hope to build? To what extent has education been consciously guided by this consideration in the past?

3. If we accept the point of view that education should find its sense of direction in the kind of social order we desire to establish, what are the core values we shall seek to build into our civilization?

4. If you agree that there is a need for a reorientation of educational values in the United States, indicate what you consider the essential educational values to be.

5. If we assume that the curriculum should be broadly functional, to what extent should it (1) consist of logically organized race experience, (2) be organized around the major functions of social life, (3) find its orientation in the problems of children and youth?

6. Do you think that the school should seek to develop the acceptance of core values? If so, indicate what you think those values are. How can the acceptance of such values be developed without resorting to "indoctrination" in the sense that the word is generally used?

7. Indicate to what extent you think it is the proper function of the school (1) to maintain the social order as it exists, (2) to accept the existing social order as a starting point and appraise its functioning critically with the view of helping to shape its future course, (3) to plan an essentially new social order and develop in youth an acceptance of it?

Selected References for Further Reading

American Association of School Administrators. "The Ideals We Live By," pp. 51–66 of *Education for American Citizenship,* Thirty-second Yearbook of the Association. Washington, D.C.: the Association, 1954.

Becker, Carl L. *Freedom and Responsibility in the American Way of Life.* New York: Alfred A. Knopf, 1945. Pp. xii + 122. Also published in paperback (New York: Random House [Vintage Books], 1955).

Becker, Carl L. *Modern Democracy.* New Haven, Conn.: Yale University Press, 1941. Pp. 100.

Chase, Francis, and Anderson, Harold A. (eds.). *The High School in a New Era.* Chicago: University of Chicago Press, 1958. Pp. xiv + 465.

Clark, Burton R. *Educating the Expert Society.* San Francisco: Chandler Publishing Co., 1962. Pp. xiv + 301.

Clark, John M. *Alternative to Serfdom.* New York: Alfred A. Knopf, 1948. Pp. xii + 140. Also published in paperback (New York: Random House [Vintage Books], 1960).

Conant, James Bryant. *The American High School Today.* New York: McGraw-Hill Book Co., Inc., 1959. Pp. xiii + 140.

Conant, James Bryant. *Education in a Divided World.* Cambridge, Mass.: Harvard University Press, 1948. Pp. x + 249.

Conant, James Bryant. *Education and Liberty.* Cambridge, Mass.: Harvard University Press, 1953. Pp. xii + 168.

Counts, George S. *Education and American Civilization.* New York: Teachers College, Columbia University, 1952. Pp. vii + 491.

Craven, Avery. *Democracy in American Life: A Historical Review.* Chicago: University of Chicago Press, 1941. Pp. xi + 150.

Drucker, Peter F. *America's Next Twenty Years.* New York: Harper & Brothers, 1957. Pp. 114.

French, William, and Associates. *Behavioral Goals of General Education in High School.* New York: Russell Sage Foundation, 1957. Pp. 247.

Hook, Sidney. *Education for Modern Man.* New York: The Dial Press, 1946. Pp. xiv + 237.

Hutchins, Robert M. *The Conflict in Education.* New York: Harper & Brothers, 1953. Pp. 112.

Hutchins, Robert M. *Education and Freedom.* Baton Rouge: Louisiana University Press, 1943. Pp. x + 108.

Lieberman, Myron. *The Future of Public Education.* Chicago: University of Chicago Press, 1960. Pp. 294.

Livingstone, Sir Richard. *Education for a World Adrift.* Cambridge: the University Press, 1943. Pp. xvi + 158.

Manpower and Education. Washington, D.C.: Educational Policies Commission of the National Education Association and the American Association of School Administrators, 1956. Pp. 127.

Maritain, Jacques. *Education at the Crossroads.* New Haven, Conn.: Yale University Press, 1943. Pp. xvi + 158. Also published in paperback (New Haven, Conn.: Yale Books, 1960).

Merriam, Charles E. *What is Democracy?.* Chicago: University of Chicago Press, 1941. Pp. xii + 116.

Ponds, Ralph L., and Bryner, James B. *The School in American Society.* New York: The Macmillan Co., 1959. Pp. xxi + 518.

Shindler, G. D. "Education in a Transforming American Culture," *Harvard Educational Review* (Summer, 1955), 145–153.

Stevenson, Adlai E. *The New America.* New York: Harper & Brothers, 1959.

Thayer, V. T. *The Role of the School in American Society.* New York: Dodd, Mead, & Co., 1960. Pp. xii + 530.

Ulich, Robert. *Crisis and Hope in American Education.* Boston: Beacon Press, 1951. Pp. xiv + 235.

Woodring, Paul. *A Fourth of a Nation.* New York: McGraw-Hill Book Co., Inc., 1957. Pp. vii + 255.

Illustration Credits

INSERT FOUR

Page 1. All, The Bettmann Archive.

Page 2. Above, The Bettmann Archive; below, Monkmeyer.

Page 3. Above, *Gleason's Pictorial,* December 29, 1855; below, The Bettmann Archive.

Page 4. Above, Culver Pictures, Inc.; below, The Bettmann Archive.

INSERT FIVE

Page 1. Above, F.S.A. photo, Library of Congress; middle, Library of Congress; below, Ford News Bureau, Dearborn, Michigan.

Page 2. Above, Strickler from Monkmeyer; below, Anderson from Devaney.

Page 3. Upper left, Merrim from Monkmeyer; upper right, Hays from Monkmeyer; below, Merrim from Monkmeyer.

Page 4. Above, courtesy of Dr. B. F. Skinner; below, Devaney.

INSERT SIX

Page 1. Both, Devaney.

Page 2. Both, Shelton from Monkmeyer.

Page 3. Wolf from Black Star.

Page 4. Above, Devaney; below, Schnall from F.P.G.

Index

675

schools, 315, 317, 369–375; Pestalozzian influence on, 580–587; in regional all-purpose institutions, 598–
600; and the science of education,
607–616
Teachers, certification of, 141, 335,
593; in colonial America, 103–104,
140, 141, 142, 225–226; great, 364;
need of training for, 243, 308, 592–
593; and pupils, planning by, 546;
and rising middle class, 245; salaries
of, 293, 493, 498, 507–508, 511*n*,
518; unqualified, 292, 315, 347,
370–371; *see also* Teacher education
Teachers College, Columbia University,
605, 609
Teachers colleges, 591–598
Teaching methods, 102–103, 311; *see
also* Object teaching
Technical education, 253, 295, 363,
633–634; and general education,
559–560
Technology, 389, 395, 399, 434, 655,
660; in agriculture, 400, 402, 405;
government and, 472; impact of, on
American life, 411–425; social, 412–
413, 529–530, 659
Tenant farmers, 47, 158
Tennessee, 232, 233, 282, 283; educa-
tional organizations in, 302; school
attendance in, 501; school districts
in, 337
Terman's Stanford Revision of Binet-
Simon test, 611
Testing movement, 531, 610–612
Tewksbury, Donald G., 231
Texas, 216, 258, 264; junior college in,
642; University of, 605
Textbooks, 225, 249, 347–352, 608
Theocracy, 39, 40; decline of, 42–43,
86, 97
Theology schools. *See* Divinity schools
Theory and Practice of Teaching (Page),
579, 582
Thompson, Benjamin, 60
Thorndike, Edward L., 531, 609, 610,
611
Thornwell, John H., 269
Tobacco, 119–120, 123, 260, 264, 272,
287
Torry, Samuel, quoted, 43
Tory party, 194, 229
Town meeting, 41, 83, 98
Town schools, 55–58, 63, 90–92, 101,
107, 108, 111, 209, 245
Trade associations, 461–462
Trade schools, 558, 559
Transcendentalists, 259, 278

Transylvania University, 253
Troy Seminary, 367
Tuition schools, 137, 139, 291, 246,
356, 382; *see also* Private schools
Tupper, Silas, 103
Turner, Frederick J., 283; quoted, 321
Tutors, 140, 144, 156, 160, 293
Tyler, Lyon G., 142

Unemployment, 416–418, 424, 438,
443, 472, 473*n*,
Ungraded schools, 353
Uniformity, Act of, 11
Union College, 248, 365
Union districts, 333
Unions. *See* Labor, organization of
Unitarianism, 105, 259, 278, 312, 360
United States Bank, 285–286
United States Chamber of Commerce,
452
United States history, as a subject, 537
United States Industrial Alcohol Com-
pany, 460
United States Military Academy, 253
United States Office of Education, 613,
624
United States Steel Corporation, 460
Urbanization, 296–298, 401, 407–411,
485–486, 504
Utah, state university of, 601

Value system, 532, 657–658; educa-
tional, 659–668; school's obligation to
pass on, 665–668
Vanderbilt, William H., 398
Van Dyke, George E., 552, 554
Van Liew, C. C., 596
Van Sweringen brothers, 457
Van Tyne, Claude H., quoted, 196
Vaux, Roberts, 242
Vermont, 58, 198, 220, 223; high
schools in, 294, 357; permanent
school fund in, 326; University of,
232–233, 248
Vernacular elementary schools, 21, 63
Vesalius, 24, 25
Veterans, education for, 599
Vieta, 24
Virginia, 117, 119, 125, 126, 127, 129,
141, 152, 194, 235, 283, 558; ap-
prenticeships in, 132–134, 135; Col-
lege of William and Mary in, *see*
William and Mary; free schools in,
135, 236, 332; Jefferson's plan for
education in, 217–220, 227; Literary
Fund in, 222, 223; permanent school
fund in, 326; plantations in, 120,
121–122; slavery in, 122, 260, 261;